Global Issues

Global Issues

Selections from *The CQ Researcher*

CQ PRESS

A Division of Congressional Quarterly Inc.
Washington, D.C.

CQ Press
A Division of Congressional Quarterly Inc.
1414 22nd Street, N.W.
Washington, D.C. 20037

(202) 822-1475; (800) 638-1710

www.cqpress.com

Printed and bound in the United States of America

04 03 02 01 00   5 4 3 2 1

⊗ The paper used in this publication meets the minimum requirements of the American National Standard for Information Sciences—Permanence of Paper for Printed Library Materials, ANSI Z39.48-1992.

A CQ Press College Division Publication

Director	Brenda Carter
Acquisitions editor	Charisse Kiino
Managing editor	Ann Davies
Composition	Paul Cederborg
Cover designer	Dennis Anderson
Indexer	Joyce Teague
Print buyer	Liza Sanchez
Sales	James Headley

Library of Congress Cataloging-in-Publication Data

Global issues : selections from The CQ researcher.
        p. cm.
    Includes bibliographical references and index.
    ISBN 1-56802-622-6 (alk. paper)
     1. Globalization. 2. International economic relations. I. Congressional Quarterly, inc.

JZ1318 .G558 2000
327—dc21

                                                            00-048630

Contents

ENVIRONMENT

HUMAN RIGHTS AND DEMOCRATIZATION

Annotated Table of Contents

The 16 *CQ Researcher* articles reprinted in this book have been reproduced essentially as they appeared when first published. In a few cases in which important new developments have occurred since an article came out, these developments are described in the following overviews, which highlight the principal issues that are examined.

SECURITY

Chemical and Biological Weapons

The United States ratified a global treaty banning the production, stockpiling and deployment of lethal agents; this treaty required the U.S. to destroy its stockpile of chemical weapons by 2007. Recent events are adding new elements to the debate over ways to curb chemical and biological weapons. Studies of Gulf War Syndrome are examining whether these weapons cause disabling chronic illnesses as well as death. And the release of deadly sarin nerve gas in the Tokyo subway by members of a religious cult demonstrates the devastating impact these easily produced weapons of mass destruction can have on civilian targets as well.

Banning Land Mines

Anti-personnel mines kill and maim long after wars and civil strife end. More than 100 million active mines lie hidden in more than 80 countries, claiming 26,000 victims—mostly civilians—each year. Mines are cheap to produce and costly to remove, and 20 new mines are planted annually for every one cleared. A worldwide movement to ban the production and use of land mines has drawn support from more than 100 countries that signed the Ottawa Landmine Treaty in December 1997. While it endorses an eventual ban on anti-personnel mines, the U.S. has supported a treaty that would allow it to continue using some of its mines until alternative weapons are developed. One of the exemptions the U.S. seeks is for "smart" mines, which self-destruct after a few hours or days.

Defense Priorities

A decade after the Soviet Union's demise, questions persist about the adequacy of U.S. defense capabilities. Without the Soviet threat, the rationale for a large, standing army and a vast, nuclear arsenal seemed to evaporate. Instead, the per-ceived threat to American security fragmented into a number of hostile regional powers. NATO's bombing campaign in Yugoslavia was the latest overseas operation involving American military forces since the end of the Cold War. Like the Gulf War and the interventions in Somalia and Haiti, the operation was far more limited in scope than wars fought by American soldiers in the last century. Meanwhile, military experts continue to question the defense strategy, weapons-procurement practices and readiness of U.S. forces in this new global environment.

INTERNATIONAL POLITICAL ECONOMY

European Monetary Union

On Jan. 1, 1999, 11 of the 15 members of the European Union took a giant stride toward economic integration by adopting a single currency, the euro. Initially, it will be used for non-cash transactions such as stock purchases, but in three years the nations in the new monetary union will begin using euros for all transactions. Supporters of European integration hope that the demise of the mark, the franc and other venerable European currencies will remove a major obstacle to economic unification. Achieving economic integration brings uncertainties and risks, however. The countries involved must cede sovereignty over monetary policy to the new European Central Bank, while the United States must confront a new competitor in the world trade arena.

International Monetary Fund

In 1997, an economic crisis that started in Thailand quickly spread to Asia and Russia. It soon threatened Brazil and the rest of Latin America. In trying to stabilize the global economy, the International Monetary Fund (IMF) prescribed some painful fiscal medicine. In exchange for the loans it provided to member countries to help them ward off financial crises, the agency required governments to adopt austerity measures, including spending cuts to reduce government deficits and debt as well as higher interest rates to shore up weak currencies. Many critics say the IMF's "cure" has been worse than the disease, causing essentially healthy Asian economies to become weak. Some say the time has come for fundamental reform of the 53-year-old system of oversight provided by the IMF.

World Trade

World trade has emerged as a critical issue among Americans concerned about how opening new markets affects people's lives in the U.S. and abroad. The debate spilled onto the streets of Seattle and Washington, D.C., in demonstrations that rivaled the antiwar protests of the 1960s. It re-emerged before the House vote in May 2000 to normalize trade with China. Critics charge that globalization benefits only corporations that relocate factories to countries with cheap labor and weak environmental laws, worsening working conditions abroad, polluting the environment and threatening American jobs. But proponents say that free trade is the key to improving living and working conditions in developing countries, creating high-paying jobs in the U.S. and protecting the global environment.

Oil Production in the 21st Century

Twenty-five years ago the Organization of Petroleum Exporting Countries struck at the heart of the American economy with an embargo on oil exports to the United States. The resulting rise in energy prices sparked a round of inflation and stagnant economic growth that lasted more than a decade. A quarter-century later, OPEC has once again driven up oil prices by curtailing output, but this time the cartel's stranglehold is much weaker than before. Non-OPEC producers supply much of the oil, and major new deposits in the Caspian Sea region promise to keep the oil spigot open for the foreseeable future. But the good times for consumers will not last forever. In a matter of time the world's oil will run out, and it's far from certain that there will be sufficient alternative energy sources.

China Today

China is becoming a more powerful nation—and more willing to spar with the United States over a range of issues. But nothing has the potential to bring the two countries into conflict like Taiwan. Although the U.S. officially supports the island's reunification with the mainland, it has warned China not to threaten a takeover if Taiwan seeks independence. Moreover, some American policymakers urge the United States to adopt a tougher line against Beijing and to abandon its "one China" policy in favor of a policy backing Taiwan's right to self-determination. Meanwhile, despite continuing controversy, China's admission to the World Trade Organization in 2001 appears inevitable. While many say WTO membership will turn China into a more open society, others say it could lead to greater political repression.

ENVIRONMENT

Population and the Environment

At the dawn of the 20th century, there were 1.6 billion people on Earth. At the beginning of the 21st century, there are nearly 6 billion. The phenomenal population growth has renewed a longstanding debate about how many people Earth can support. Thomas Malthus launched the debate 200 years ago, predicting that the increasing global population would eventually overwhelm food supplies. Technological advances thus far have enabled agricultural productivity to outpace population growth. But the rekindled debate over human survival is about more than food supplies: Population growth causes environmental problems ranging from water shortages to global climate change.

Saving the Rain Forests

Jolted by widespread tropical fires, growing concern about global warming and warnings of a nearly unprecedented wave of plant and animal extinction, officials across the globe are stepping up efforts to save the world's remaining rain forests. The World Bank is studying the best way to make limited use of the forests without destroying them; Brazil, the Philippines and other nations are trying to restrict logging and other destructive activities. For fiscal 2000, the U.S. Congress appropriated $13 million to forgive debts owed to the United States by developing nations in an attempt to encourage them to spare their forests. But unless population growth and worldwide poverty can be addressed, most of the rain forests likely will be gone by the middle of the next century.

HUMAN RIGHTS AND DEMOCRATIZATION

Democracy in Asia

Democracy has not fared well in Asia throughout history or in recent times. Today, most Asians live under communist governments, military regimes or virtual one-party states. But Asia also includes two big, long-established democracies: India and Japan. And with the recent fall of Indonesia's autocratic, longtime president, Suharto, the world's fourth most populous country could be joining the ranks of democratic nations. First, however, the country's current president, B. J. Habibie, must deal with economic recovery and some reformers doubt his commitment to political change. In addition, some Asians continue to debate whether democracy conflicts with Asian values, and U.S. policymakers are often at odds with interest groups on how best to promote democracy in Asia.

Human Rights

In 1998, human rights advocates marked the 50th anniversary of the United Nations' Universal Declaration of Human Rights, the first comprehensive charter of individual freedoms. More than 50 years later, most of the world's countries have ratified a series of binding treaties committing them to respect key civil, political, social and economic rights. Human rights advocates say that conditions have improved since 1948 and that the U.N.'s human rights machinery has been strengthened. But they also say that flagrant abuses continue to occur in countries throughout the world. The United States has been criticized for failing to ratify many human rights treaties and for opposing a new proposal to create an International Criminal Court for serious human rights violations.

Women and Human Rights

Ethnic and religious conflict throughout the world has sparked horrific violence against women and girls in recent years. From Bosnia to Rwanda, combatants use rape, mutilation and enslavement to terrorize civilian populations. Islamic militants in Afghanistan subject women to severe punishment for minor offenses. In the absence of conflict, women still face violence— from wife-burning in India to "honor killings" of rape victims in the Middle East to forced prostitution in Asia. An international women's rights movement is gathering strength, with strong support from the United Nations, but the U.S. Senate has yet to ratify a key U.N. convention designed to protect women.

Islamic Fundamentalism

The February 2000 election of reform candidates to Iran's parliament dealt a blow to the nation's strict Islamic government. Despite Iran's generally free elections, many Westerners say that democracy is inherently impossible in countries run by Islamic fundamentalists. Since the ruling clerics believe God inspires their policies, it is argued, there is little room for the kind of public debate that is vital to a democracy. In addition, fundamentalist states such as Iran, Sudan and Afghanistan are seen as supportive of terrorism and generally hostile to the West. Other experts on the Middle East say the threat posed by fundamentalist states has been exaggerated, largely by the media. They also contend that Iran's elections are proof that Islamic fundamentalism and democracy can coexist.

IMMIGRATION

Assisting Refugees

The refugee crisis in Zaire and Rwanda focused world attention on displaced people. Affecting more than 5 million people, the crisis forced refugee-aid groups, governments and others to reassess the way aid to refugees is rendered. For the U.N. High Commission for Refugees and other humanitarian relief organizations, the situation raises fundamental questions about aiding refugees: Can efforts to help make matters worse? How can tragedies like the one in Central Africa be prevented or at least mitigated in the future? For the United States and other developed nations, the crisis has reopened the debate over whether using soldiers to assist humanitarian relief efforts is appropriate, and whether dramatic media coverage of crises can lead to bad policy decisions.

Global Refugee Crisis

After a NATO bombing campaign that lasted more than two months in 1999, the United States and its NATO allies forced Yugoslav President Slobodan Milosevic to stop driving ethnic Albanians from Kosovo. Although the "ethnic cleansing" has stopped, it has produced Europe's worst refugee crisis since World War II. Military intervention was the latest in a series of efforts to stem a rising tide of refugees fleeing ethnic conflicts and civil wars that erupted all over the world in the 1990s. Critics of U.S. military involvement say the bombing only made the refugees' situation worse. But supporters of military action call it an unqualified success. Other critics say that resettling the refugees in the United States makes it unlikely that they will ever return home.

Preface

Instructors are always in search of material that will spark intelligent and lively debate in the classroom. We believe *The CQ Researcher,* a weekly policy brief that brings into focus the often complicated and controversial issues on the world stage, presents students with an array of questions guaranteed to get them thinking. Are labor standards the best means of improving the lot of workers in poor countries? Has the United Nations been effective in promoting international human rights? Does the IMF handle monetary crises effectively? In today's world, products, services and ideas are exchanged so rapidly that the influence of domestic events often has far-reaching consequences internationally. Instructors can help prepare their students for an increasingly global world through exposure to such issues.

As scholars continue to theorize about the impact of globalization, the readings in *Global Issues* aim to add color and depth to our understanding of this complex process by introducing students to the range of opinion on a number of salient topics making headlines worldwide. Balanced accounts of trade and economic relations, the protection of human rights, the preservation of the environment and the security of a country's people and resources allow instructors to explore these tough questions in a thorough manner, challenging students to enter into the dialogue and form their own views.

This reader is a compilation of 16 recent articles from *The CQ Researcher.* Offering in-depth, objective and forward-looking reporting on a specific topic, each article chronicles and analyzes past action as well as current and possible future political maneuvering. *Global Issues* is designed to encourage discussion, to help readers think critically and actively about these vital issues and to facilitate further research. It provides clear, real-world examples that add substantive detail to college courses while showing students how the policy debate affects their lives and their futures.

The collection is organized into five subject areas that span a range of important international policy concerns: security, international political economy, environment, human rights and democratization, and immigration. It is an attractive supplement for courses on world affairs in political science, geography, economics and sociology. We also believe interested citizens, journalists and business and government leaders will turn to *Global Issues* to familiarize themselves with key issues, actors and policy positions.

The CQ Researcher

The CQ Researcher was founded in 1923 under a different moniker: *Editorial Research Reports.* ERR was sold primarily to newspapers, which used it as a research tool. The magazine was given its current name and a design overhaul in 1991. Today, *The CQ Researcher* is still sold to many newspapers, some of which reprint all or part of each issue. But the audience for the magazine has shifted significantly over the years, and today many more libraries subscribe. Students, not journalists, are now the primary audience for *The CQ Researcher.*

People who write *Researchers* often compare the experience to that of drafting a college term paper. Indeed, there are many similarities. Each article is as long as many term papers—running about 11,000 words—and is written by one person, without any significant outside help.

Like students, staff writers begin the creative process by choosing a topic. Working with the publication's editors, the writer tries to come up with a subject that has policy implications and for which at least some controversy exists. After a topic is set, the writer embarks on a week or two of intense research. Articles are clipped, books ordered and information gathered from a variety of sources, including interest groups, universities and the government. Once a writer feels well informed about the subject, he or she begins a series of interviews with experts—academics, officials, lobbyists and people working in the field. Each piece usually requires a minimum of ten to fifteen interviews. Some particularly complicated subjects call for more. After much reading and interviewing, the writer begins to put the article together.

Chapter Format

Each issue of the *Researcher,* and therefore each selection in this book, is structured in the same way, beginning with an introductory overview of the topic. This first section briefly touches on the areas that will be explored in greater detail in the rest of the chapter.

Following the introduction is a section that chronicles the important debates currently going on in the field. The section is structured around a number of questions, known as "Issue Questions," such as, "Can people profit from rain forests without destroying them?" or "Can monetary union work without greater fiscal and political integration?" This section is the core of each chapter: the questions raised are often highly controversial and usually are the object of much argument among those who work in and think about the field. Hence, the answers provided by the writer are never conclusive. Instead, each answer details a range of opinion.

Following these questions and answers is the "Background" section, which provides a history of the issue being examined. This look back includes important events and actions as well as insight into how current policy has evolved. An examination of existing policy follows the background section. Each "Current Situation" provides an overview of important developments that were occurring when the article was originally published. Each selection ends with an "Outlook" section that looks to the near future.

All selections contain other regular features to augment the main text. Each selection includes two or three sidebars that examine issues related to the topic. An "At Issue" page, from two outside experts, provides opposing answers to a relevant question. This yes-no feature is an effective starting point for class discussion. Also included are a chronology, which cites important dates and events, and an annotated bibliography, which details some of the sources used by the writer of the article.

Acknowledgments

We wish to thank many people for helping make this collection a reality. First is Tom Colin, editor of *The CQ Researcher,* who gave us his enthusiastic support and cooperation as we developed this collection. He and his talented staff of editors and writers have amassed a first-class library of *Researcher* articles, and we are privileged to have access to that rich cache. We also thankfully acknowledge the advice and feedback from the scholars who commented on our plans for the volume. In particular, we thank Dan Cox, University of Nebraska, Kearney; Thomas Dolan, Columbus State University; Joseph Hewitt, University of Missouri; Cynthia Hody, University of Maryland, Baltimore County; Mark Peceny, University of New Mexico; and John Tures, formerly at the University of Delaware.

Some readers of this collection may be learning about *The CQ Researcher* for the first time. We expect that many readers will want regular access to this excellent weekly research tool. Anyone interested in subscription information or a no-obligation free trial of the *Researcher* can contact Congressional Quarterly at www.cq.com; at (800) 432-2250, ext. 279; or at (202) 887-6279.

We hope that you are as pleased with *Global Issues* as we are. We welcome your feedback and suggestions for future editions. Please direct comments to Charisse Kiino, CQ Press, 1414 22nd Street, N.W., Washington, D.C. 20037, or by e-mail at ckiino@cq.com.

—*The Editors of CQ Press*

1 Chemical and Biological Weapons

MARY H. COOPER

In the heady days following the allied victory over Iraq in the Persian Gulf War in 1991, Brian Martin received the kind of order that combat engineers relish. Martin and his unit from the 37th Engineer Battalion had stumbled onto a vast ammunition depot, abandoned by fleeing Iraqi soldiers. Blow it up, they were ordered.

"Witnessing these awesome explosions was a remarkable sight," the 27-year-old Martin told a House panel recently. "The explosions blew straight into the air, and then would spread at the top. Many of us joked that this would be the closest thing to a nuclear mushroom cloud that we would . . . ever hope to see."[1]

The awe turned to horror, however, when missiles from the exploding bunkers and warehouses in Kamisiyah began raining down on Martin's unit. "Men were running everywhere for cover," he said. "Hiding behind our vehicles for safety, we felt all hell had broken loose."

The battalion retreated to a safer location, but for Martin's unit, the nightmare had just begun.

Actually, Martin told lawmakers, he had been suffering a variety of symptoms even before the ammo dump explosion. "Since just before those days at Kamisiyah, I have suffered from symptoms and ailments that have altered everything about me and my family's lives," he said. "It started in early 1991 with blood in [my] vomit and stools, blurred vision, shaking and trembling like I was on a caffeine high." Martin was diagnosed with multiple chemical sensitivity, inflammatory bowel disease, brain damage and other ailments and was discharged in December 1991 with permanent and total disability.

About 80,000 of the 697,000 Ameri-

U.S. Army/Arms Control Association

can men and women who served in the Persian Gulf during Operations Desert Shield and Desert Storm say they suffer from the broad range of ailments known collectively as Gulf War Syndrome. The most common symptoms include joint pain, fatigue, headache and memory loss.

From the first deployment of U.S. troops in the region in August 1990 until their pullout in June 1991, the operation was initially hailed as a resounding victory, a "clean" war that had achieved its objective at a relatively low cost of 293 American deaths and 467 wounded.

But returning servicemen soon started complaining of sickness. Iraq was known to have stockpiled chemical and biological weapons. But because the Defense Department initially denied that personnel had been exposed to such agents, the symptoms were attributed to unknown causes or to post-traumatic shock, a mental disorder caused by stress.

Amid growing criticism of the government's response to the veterans' complaints, the Pentagon last June revealed that the Kamisiyah ammuni-

tion facility had indeed contained chemical weapons. But the official government position continued to be that the exposure to chemical agents had been insufficient to cause physical symptoms. (See story, p. 6)

At the White House on Jan. 7, a presidential advisory committee presented its 16-month study of Gulf War Syndrome. The 13-member panel said it found no conclusive evidence that the reported symptoms were caused by chemical or biological weapons and recommended further research.

The panel also offered scathing criticism of the government's handling of its investigations and its treatment of sick veterans. "Investigatory efforts have been slow and superficial, and no credible attempts to communicate with the public on these investigations have been made," they concluded. "Our most severe criticisms are reserved for this issue. Regrettably, [the Defense Department] did not act in good faith in this regard."[2]

Many gulf war veterans were frustrated by the panel's failure to link their illnesses to chemical weapons. Some senators, meanwhile, have been reluctant to act on a treaty to outlaw the very chemical agents that the veterans say cause Gulf War Syndrome. Indeed, the Chemical Weapons Convention failed to even reach the Senate floor for debate.

The Chemical Weapons Convention, the result of a draft treaty drawn up by the administration of Ronald Reagan in 1984 and signed by President George Bush in 1993, would ban the production of chemical weapons, as well as their use. Building on the 1925 Geneva Protocol for the Prohibition of the Use in War of Asphyxiating, Poisonous or Other Gases, and of Bacteriological Methods of Warfare, which only bans the actual use of chemical weapons, the new treaty also contains exhaustive provisions for verifying compliance. Signed by more

From *The CQ Researcher*, January 31, 1997.

The Deadliest Chemical and Biological Agents

The Chemical Weapons Convention (CWC) that goes into effect April 29 lists three categories of chemicals that would be banned or regulated. The deadliest 25 chemicals, grouped in Schedule 1, are banned altogether and cannot be produced, sold or stored. Thirty other chemicals, mostly materials that have commercial use but could be transformed into weapons, are in schedules 2 and 3 and come under the treaty's monitoring regime, which allows for inspections of plants and storage facilities. These chemicals include:

Mustard gas: First used by Germany in World War I, mustard gas causes blistering over the entire body, including the eyes and lungs, blinding victims and often causing death by respiratory failure. Easy to produce and long-lasting, mustard and other so-called blistering agents make ideal chemical weapons because they force targeted soldiers to wear cumbersome protective gear. Blistering agents are all banned by the CWC and include nitrogen mustard and Lewisite.

Phosgene gas: Also used in World War I, phosgene is a choking agent, damaging the respiratory system and causing the lungs to fill with water and choke the victim. Because they dissipate quickly in the wind, choking agents, which also include chlorine gas, are less useful as weapons than blistering agents. Because they have broad commercial use, these agents either fall into Schedule 3, the least restrictive CWC category, or are unlisted.

Cyanogen chloride: When this Schedule 3 blood agent is inhaled, it destroys tissues by interrupting the supply of oxygen to the cells. Like choking agents, it dissipates quickly in the atmosphere.

Sarin: Developed in the 1930s, Sarin is one of several so-called G-series nerve agents that quickly paralyze and kill victims after minuscule amounts come in contact with the skin or lungs. Death is caused by respiratory paralysis. Similar nerve gases include soman, tabun and GF. All nerve agents are banned under the CWC.

VX: Developed in the 1950s, VX belongs to a class of chemicals called V-series nerve agents, which act by inhibiting a nervous system enzyme. Others are VE, VG, VM and VS.

Biological Agents and Toxins

The 1925 Geneva Protocol and the 1972 Biological and Toxin Weapons Convention ban the production, stockpiling and use of any biological agents as weapons. The most common agents used in weapons are anthrax, botulinum toxin and ricin. Other pathogens that are potential ingredients include emerging infectious agents, as well as a virtually endless range of microorganisms that may be produced through bioengineering. The broad range of potentially deadly pathogens includes:

Anthrax: Produced by a fermentation process similar to that used to make beer, anthrax, or the spores of the bacterium *Bacillus anthracis,* will kill if even minute quantities are inhaled or ingested. Death typically comes within five days of exposure if penicillin is not administered before the onset of symptoms. Death results from pneumonia, general infection and organ failure. One gram of anthrax would be enough to kill more than a third of the U.S. population.

Botulinum toxin: Produced by the common bacterium *Botulinum clostridium,* this toxin blocks the transmission of nerve impulses, causing paralysis and death, usually within two days, unless antitoxin is administered. One form of the toxin requires only one microgram to kill a person.

Ricin: This toxin, easily made from castor beans, is lethal when inhaled, usually within two hours. It attacks the circulatory system, causing fluid buildup in the lungs.

Q fever: This is one of several microorganisms known as rickettsiae, or intracellular parasites, that are similar in structure to bacteria. Others that are suitable for weapons include typhus and Rocky Mountain spotted fever.

Plague: A well-known but rare bacterial disease caused by contact with *Yersinia pestis,* plague was widespread in medieval Europe. A highly contagious form, pneumonic plague, broke out in India in 1994. The theory, later discounted, was that it was caused by a biological attack. Plague usually kills within five days unless antibiotics are administered.

Ebola virus: One of a number of "emerging" viruses unknown until recent outbreaks, Ebola has no known cure. It has killed about 90 percent of the infected people in natural outbreaks, usually within days. Death occurs as a result of "bleed-out," when organ systems break down. Because they cannot be controlled, emerging viruses are considered to be relatively poor candidates for weapons production.

Sources: Central Intelligence Agency, Business Executives for National Security

than 160 countries and already ratified by 67, the convention will enter into force on April 29, whether the United States ratifies it or not. Although the convention is strongly supported by the Clinton administration, its passage is uncertain.

The new treaty was prompted by the proliferation of chemical-weapons use in recent years. The Germans used deadly mustard gas on allied soldiers in World War I, but chemical weapons weren't used again in combat until Iraq turned them against Iran during their 1980-1988 war, as well as against dissident Kurdish communities in Iraq itself.

Today, the number of countries believed to have chemical weapons programs has grown from about a dozen in 1980 to about 20. [3]

Concern over chemical weapons mounted in March 1995, when members of Aum Shinrikyo, a fanatical Japanese religious cult, released deadly sarin gas in the Tokyo subway system, killing 12 people and injuring more than 5,000. This first known use of chemical weapons by a terrorist group raised the specter of further terrorism using lethal chemicals, which are relatively easy to obtain and fashion into weapons of mass destruction.

"We have learned from the study of terrorism in the past that when a highly publicized incident occurs, it is more likely to be repeated," says Brian M. Jenkins, a terrorism expert and deputy chairman of Kroll Associates, an international investigative and consulting firm in Los Angeles. "I don't believe that chemical, Tokyo-type attacks are going to become the truck bombs of the second half of the 1990s. But I would assert that an event like the Tokyo attack is more probable than it was before March 1995."

Biological weapons could cause even more widespread devastation than chemical weapons. Lethal pathogens like anthrax bacilli and botulinum toxin are even easier to produce and conceal than deadly chemicals because they exist freely in nature. (*See story, p. 2.*) And unlike the Tokyo sarin attack, which affected the victims immediately, some biological weapons could kill long after they come into contact with people.

"Because of incubation periods, diseases take a while to develop after exposure," says James M. Hughes, director of the National Center for Infectious Diseases, a branch of the Centers for Disease Control and Prevention (CDC) in Atlanta. "That's what makes this type of weapon particularly insidious. It allows for the geographic dissemination of infected

people, and some of these agents, such as pneumonic plague, are transmissible from person to person."

The 1972 Biological Weapons Convention bans the production, stockpiling and use of biological agents. The United States, a signatory, says it stopped all production of biological weapons in 1969, though it continues to conduct research on lethal pathogens. Amid evidence that the Soviet Union and as many as 14 other countries were continuing or establishing biological-weapons programs, the parties to the treaty have tried

Reuters

Japanese army chemical warfare specialists decontaminate a Tokyo subway car after the March 20, 1995, sarin gas attack that killed 12 and injured more than 5,000.

to strengthen its verification provisions, but to little avail. [4] The most recent conference on the treaty, held last November, yielded no significant progress.

For now, however, the Tokyo attack and uncertainties surrounding Gulf War Syndrome have focused the arms control debate on chemical weapons. Critics of the current treaty charge that for all its provisions to ensure compliance, the Chemical Weapons Convention is no improvement over the existing ban on the use of such weapons established by the Geneva Protocol.

"It would be very nice to rid the world of chemical weapons if we

could," says Frank J. Gaffney Jr., director of the Center for Security Policy. Gaffney, formerly deputy assistant Defense secretary for arms control during the Reagan administration, stresses that chemical weapons are much easier to make and conceal than nuclear arms, the target of most existing arms-control initiatives. "But as a practical matter," Gaffney says, "that cannot be done, considering that any high school student can whip up a chemical agent if he wants to. Therefore, we should concentrate on what's practical, and what's practical here is ensuring that nobody uses the stuff and stipulating what we will do to them if they do."

Proponents of the Chemical Weapons Convention agree that production and even deployment of chemical agents are hard to monitor. "The worst part about all this is that the methods for making sarin gas and other nerve gases have been in the open scientific literature since the 1950s," says Leonard Cole, a political science professor at Rutgers University and an expert on biological and chemical agents. "The ultimate question is, 'What can we do to stop this?' I say you can't do much more than you can to prevent somebody from throwing a grenade or spraying somebody with gunshots."

But Cole and other proponents of the treaty insist it has value as a statement by the world community that chemical weapons will not be tolerated. "Verification is not going to be foolproof, but I think it will create a substantial disincentive," Cole says. "More than that, though, the treaty is a renewal of an old, international contract that chemical weapons are wrong and that we ought to get them off the table."

The Clinton administration has placed ratification of the convention near the top of its foreign policy agenda. "As we continue to investigate gulf war illnesses," the president said in accepting the panel's report on Jan. 7, "let me again take this opportunity to urge the Congress to ratify the Chemical Weapons Convention, which would make it harder for rogue states to acquire chemical weapons in the future and protect the soldiers of the United States and our allies in the future."

As the debate unfolds over the treaty's implications for U.S. defense against weapons of mass destruction, these are some of the issues under consideration:

Will the Chemical Weapons Convention slow the spread of chemical weapons?

Chemical weapons are one of three categories of so-called weapons of mass destruction. The other two, nuclear and biological weapons, are regulated by separate multilateral treaties, both signed by the United States. The 1968 Nuclear Non-Proliferation Treaty prohibits the transfer or manufacture of nuclear weapons outside the five recognized nuclear powers and ensures that all 168 signatory countries have access to civilian nuclear technology. [5] The 1972 Biological Weapons Convention bans the production, possession and use of biological weapons.

Until this year, the only constraint on chemical weapons was the ban on their use in combat under the 1925 Geneva Protocol. Efforts to ban their production and deployment as well began in the 1960s but were held up by disagreements among negotiating countries over verification.

Iraq's use of chemical weapons in its eight-year war against Iran lent new urgency to the task of drawing up a tougher chemical weapons ban. The momentum picked up after the 1991 gulf war, during

which civilians and soldiers alike often donned gas masks in fear of chemical attacks by Iraq. When United Nations Secretary General Boutros Boutros-Ghali presented the Chemical Weapons Convention for signature in January 1993, 131 countries signed, including the United States.

Unlike nuclear weapons, whose production and deployment can be monitored by spy satellites, chemical weapons are relatively easy to hide. For this reason, the convention includes extensive inspection measures and limits on trade in commercially used chemicals — known as dual-use chemicals — that can be transformed into weapons.

In order to be ratified by the United States, the Chemical Weapons Convention must be approved by two-thirds of the Senate. Treaty opponents, who derailed efforts to bring the agreement to a vote in September, cite two main reasons for their stance — the "ineffectiveness" of its verification provisions and its potential cost to American businesses.

Although most of the 186-page treaty is devoted to verification measures — chiefly inspections of suspected chemical weapons facilities on short notice — opponents say it can't begin to stop production of chemical arms.

"As the proponents are wont to say, this has got to be the most intrusive, complex and comprehensive verification regime of any arms control treaty ever drafted," Gaffney says. "The problem is that it still won't work. At the end of the day, you can have an enormously complex, intrusive and comprehensive verification regime, and if it does not materially increase the chances that you'll be able to detect — let alone ensure enforcement in instances of non-compliance — it isn't worth a hill of beans."

Senate Foreign Relations Chairman Jesse Helms, R-N.C., a leading congressional opponent to the treaty, agrees. "The thing that bothers me most, I suppose, about the way this

convention is being presented is the psychology of it, where people are assuming things are going to be all right just so we ratify this treaty," Helms said. "And I think we all know that's not so." [6]

Helms points to evidence that many of the 14 countries believed to have chemical weapons programs have not ratified the treaty. * "Russia, the country that possesses the largest and most sophisticated chemical weaponry in the world," Helms said, "has signaled that it has no intention of abiding by our bilateral agreement to get rid of the chemical weapons stockpile. To the contrary, over the past six years Russia consistently has refused to come clean about the true size of its chemical weapon stockpile and about the status of its binary chemical weapons program."

Proponents of the convention agree that it will be hard or even impossible to prevent the development of chemical weapons. But they claim that the treaty will allow for the early detection of violations by governments and terrorist groups alike. "The CWC would make it more difficult and more costly for terrorists to acquire or use chemical weapons," wrote Sen. Richard G. Lugar, R-Ind., a senior member of the Senate Foreign Relations and Intelligence committees, in a Sept. 11, 1996, letter to Senate colleagues. "The CWC will provide access to international declaration and inspection information and will strengthen the intelligence links between the United States and the international community that will help us detect and prevent chemical attacks."

Treaty supporters also warn that the Senate's failure to ratify would deny the United States any say in the treaty's enforcement. "It's far better . . . that we have some of our people in the inspec-

---

* The U.S. government does not provide an officially acknowledged list of states with chemical weapons. Helms mentioned Libya, Syria, Iraq, Egypt, Taiwan, North Korea, Russia, China, Iran and India.

tion teams to conduct these inspections in various countries than we have no participation at all," Defense Secretary William Cohen said Jan. 26 on ABC's "This Week." The former Republican senator from Maine became the new Pentagon chief on Jan. 24.

Chemical weapons often are made of substances commonly used in commercial manufacturing. For example, thiodoglycol, a chemical used as a solvent in ball-point pen ink, is a key ingredient of mustard gas. To ensure that these dual-use chemicals are not diverted to make weapons, the treaty requires manufacturers to document their production and, if necessary, to open their facilities to international inspection.

Though these requirements would increase the cost of producing chemicals, the Chemical Manufacturers Association and the Synthetic Organic Chemical Manufacturers Association, representing the bulk of U.S. producers, both have endorsed the treaty. They say failure to ratify the treaty would be costlier than not ratifying it because it bars signatory countries, including some of the United States' biggest trading partners, from importing many dual-use chemicals from non-signatory countries. The chemical industry estimates that the cost of that provision to its members would be as much as $600 million a year in lost sales — the value of current imports and exports of these items.

But treaty critics say the bulk of the cost will fall on other U.S. manufacturers, including firms with valuable proprietary information that would be easy targets, under the treaty's inspection provision, for economic espionage by foreign competitors. "While the chemical manufacturers are quite satisfied that the costs to them are manageable," Gaffney says, "there are costs to everybody else in the country who is going to be subjected to this, whether they use chemicals, whether they happen to produce chemicals as part of their production process, or

Iraqi rockets filled with sarin nerve agents are readied for destruction by members of a United Nations team in Kamisiyah, Iraq, in March 1991.

whether they just happen to be on the target list of French intelligence or anybody else who can use the inspection provision as an opportunity to get in and find out what they're doing."

Gaffney also charges that the chemical manufacturers stand to actually gain business if the United States ratifies the treaty. That's because of a little-noticed provision in the treaty that requires industrialized signatory countries to provide signatory countries in the developing world with advanced technology to produce chemicals for commercial use. Modeled on the Atoms for Peace provision of the Nuclear Non-Proliferation Treaty, this provision — dubbed "poi-

sons for peace" by treaty opponents — serves as an inducement to join the chemical weapons ban. But unlike nuclear technology, chemical technology can be put to offensive use with little know-how or obvious warning. "If I sell you a fertilizer plant, you can at the flip of a switch change it over from making phosphates for fertilizer to making deadly phosgene gas," Gaffney says.

Chemical manufacturers strongly reject Gaffney's contention that they have a financial stake in selling chemicals to potential weapons proliferators. "It is not true that we're going to gain financially because of the Chemical Weapons Convention," says Michael Walls, senior assistant general counsel for the Chemical Manufacturers Association. "In fact, if the United States stays out of this convention, we stand to lose." He says the clause in the treaty that calls for providing technological assistance to signatory countries in no way erodes existing U.S. export controls barring the sale of dual-use chemicals and equipment that could be used to make weapons.

"The so-called debate on the Chemical Weapons Convention has been nothing but a string of distortions from opponents like Mr. Gaffney about what the convention's impact will be on the commercial sector," Walls says. "The chemical industry has supported this treaty because it's the right thing to do. We don't want to see our legitimate products diverted to illegal uses. That's the principal motivation here."

Treaty supporters also insist that ratification by the world's strongest military

The Pentagon's Handling of Gulf War Syndrome

Two fundamental questions have been raised by the 80,000 chronically ill gulf war veterans: Were they exposed to chemical and/or biological weapons during the 1991 conflict? And did that exposure sicken them? To many observers, an equally troubling question is whether the Pentagon held back information on Iraq's use of chemical weapons. The following chronology was culled from a wide range of media, government and think tank sources.

Jan. 16, 1991
The 39-day air war against Iraq begins. Most chemical-weapons factories and storage depots are destroyed.

Feb. 24, 1991
The four-day ground war begins.

March 4-15, 1991
U.S. blows up ammunition facility in Kamisiyah, Iraq, which contained chemical weapons.

August 1992
Veterans Affairs Department (VA) sets up Persian Gulf Registry to provide medical examinations to all veterans.

May 1993
CIA reports that Iraq did not use chemical agents during the war and had removed chemical weapons from the war zone before the fighting.

September 1993
Senate Banking Committee report contains testimony from veterans describing exposure to chemicals.

June 13, 1991
The last U.S. ground troops return home.

Fall 1991
Gulf veterans begin seeking treatment for combat-related illnesses.

May 26, 1995
President Clinton establishes a panel of independent experts to assess the government's response to veterans' health complaints.

June 21, 1996
Pentagon announces that it now has evidence that 300-400 U.S. troops near Kamisiyah may have been exposed to chemicals.

Oct. 8, 1996
Pentagon discloses log books on biological and chemical warfare compiled during the war for Gen. H. Norman Schwarzkopf, the allied commander, which show no entries for the period when the Kamisiyah facility was destroyed.

June 7, 1994
Pentagon sets up Comprehensive Clinical Evaluation Program to evaluate care for gulf veterans.

Dec. 19, 1996
Defense Secretary William J. Perry calls perceptions of a Pentagon cover-up of evidence linking veterans' illnesses to chemical weapons "dead wrong."

Jan. 7, 1997
Presidential Advisory Committee on Gulf War Veterans' Illnesses reports no conclusive evidence linking illnesses to chemical or biological weapons, but that the Pentagon "did not act in good faith" in its investigation of Gulf War Syndrome.

Dec. 10, 1996
British Defense Ministry launches study of possible link between chemicals and chronically ill British veterans.

Oct. 22, 1996
A new Pentagon estimate says that up to 20,000 troops were near the Kamisiyah depot when it was destroyed.

Jan. 9, 1997
Senate Veterans' Affairs Committee wins permission to examine Gen. Schwarzkopf's personal notes. Secretary Perry again denies knowledge of a Pentagon cover-up.

Jan. 21, 1997
VA study suggests a direct link between severe joint pain, a symptom of Gulf War Syndrome, and chemical weapons released at Kamisiyah. This is the first official acknowledgment by a federal agency of such a link.

Jan. 29, 1997
Gen. Schwarzkopf tells Veterans' Affairs Committee he never received information about Iraqi use of chemical weapons "before, during or after hostilities."

Sarah M. Magner

power would constitute a persuasive deterrent to anyone contemplating the use of chemical weapons. Military leaders who support the treaty cite the gulf war to bolster this argument. Although Iraq was known to have a chemical arsenal, it refrained from using it against U.S. troops after then-Defense Secretary Dick Cheney repeatedly vowed to retaliate against any chemical attack with "absolutely overwhelming" and "devastating" force.

Even in the absence of such an immediate threat of retaliation, supporters say the treaty is likely to reduce the risk of further chemical weapons proliferation because it allows for the use of sanctions and even force to stop it — even against countries that are not parties to the agreement. "No one is claiming that this treaty will be foolproof or that it will guarantee 100 percent that no country will cheat," Cole says. "But most everybody who has an interest in the issue recognizes that it will lower the chance that anybody is going to cheat."

In the end, treaty proponents say, the United States would be better off with the Chemical Weapons Convention than without it. "If we refuse to ratify, some governments will use our refusal as an excuse to keep their chemical weapons," writes retired Adm. Elmo R. Zumwalt Jr., who served as chief of naval operations from 1970-1974. "At the bottom line, our failure to ratify will substantially increase the risk of a chemical attack against American service personnel." [7]

Is it feasible to protect Americans from the threat of biological or chemical attack?

Because biological and chemical weapons are easy to produce and

conceal, civilians have few defenses against potential attackers. All it took for the Aum Shinrikyo terrorists to turn the Tokyo subway system into a deadly gas chamber were holes poked in a few plastic bags of strategically placed sarin. Closer to home, the truck containing the bomb that devastated

Members of a U.N. chemical weapons team monitor air contamination in Kamisiyah, Iraq, after destroying hundreds of Iraqi rockets filled with sarin nerve agents.

U.N. photo 159097/H. Arvidsson/Arms Control Association

the World Trade Center in 1993 was later found to have contained sodium cyanide. Had the device containing the cyanide not malfunctioned, it would have released a cloud of deadly cyanide vapor into the skyscraper, causing many more casualties. [8]

Although biological and chemical weapons have been readily available

for many years, there are few defenses in place to protect civilians against an attack. In 1995, an Ohio man, Larry Harris, a former member of the white supremacist group Aryan Nations, had no trouble ordering by mail three vials of *Yersinia pestis,* the bacterium that causes bubonic plague, from a laboratory supply house. However, a company employee became suspicious about the order and alerted the Federal Bureau of Investigation. Harris was apprehended before he could carry out his alleged plan to make a biological weapon out of the material. But because there were no laws prohibiting the distribution of *Yersinia pestis* and other potentially lethal pathogens, Harris was released after serving a brief sentence for mail fraud for providing false information on the order form. [9]

"When we called in the authorities on the plague incident, CDC's response was that there was nothing they could do about it because Mr. Harris had done nothing illegal by having it in his possession or using it," says Kaye Breen, a vice president of American Type Culture Collection, the Rockville, Md., firm that provided the pathogen. "All of our requirements to have detailed information in writing are voluntary."

Later this year, however, tough, new regulations that were included in anti-terrorism legislation passed last April will go into effect, limiting the availability of many pathogens. The regulations impose penalties for the illegal possession and distribution of dangerous biological agents. But Breen says the new rules may do little to deter a terrorist or madman bent on conducting biological mayhem. "Even if you took all the 450 major [pathogen] culture collections around the world, they still collectively represent about 20 percent of the distribution of biologicals," Breen says. "The bulk of it is from researcher to researcher, and anyway, every single one of these biologicals is available in nature. If you're a true terrorist, why go where you have to leave a paper trail?"

Given the limits of effective defense, some experts say important steps are being taken to protect civilians against biochemical attack. "We're working on it," says Hughes of the National Center for Infectious Diseases. He offers as a model a detailed plan of action drawn up by various agencies to intervene quickly in case of an infectious-disease outbreak, whether by natural causes or as the result of a biological attack.

During last summer's Olympic Games in Atlanta, he says, "We set up a special infectious-disease surveillance system in which hospitals, emergency rooms and outpatient centers reported daily on disease encounters. The key to surveillance is the alert clinician or health-care worker who recognizes and reports."

Biological attacks, unlike those using chemicals, can be indistinguishable from spontaneous outbreaks if no one claims responsibility for the act. "Otherwise, it is going to present exactly like any other infectious-disease epidemic," Hughes says. "That's the reason we argue that we need, first and foremost, to strengthen surveillance and response capacity at the local, state, federal and

even global levels so that these incidents can be detected early and a response can be rapidly mounted."

The CDC has drawn up a strategy for dealing with outbreaks that follows these suggestions. But even Hughes acknowledges the limits of civilian defenses against bioterrorism. "Another aspect to this issue is the availability of agents to treat these things should they occur on large

Security police at the U.S. air station in Sola, Norway, participate in chemical warfare exercises.

Arms Control Association

numbers of people," he says. "You could easily overwhelm the health-care delivery system and exhaust available supplies of antibiotics or antisera that aren't used very often. They're adequate to deal with things that you could anticipate occurring in a natural setting.

"But if somebody should put botulinum toxin in the New York City water supply, there's not enough botulinum antitoxin in the world to treat the people who would be exposed."

Did exposure to chemical weapons cause Gulf War Syndrome?

For more than five years, the Defense Department denied that — with

one small exception — U.S. military personnel serving in the gulf war had come into contact with any Iraqi chemical or biological weapons. The only officially recognized case of exposure involved an Army sergeant who received superficial mustard burns on his arms while he was near an Iraqi bunker. [10]

Last June, the Pentagon acknowledged that 150 soldiers might have been exposed to low-level amounts of chemicals that were released into the air when American troops blew up the Iraqi ammunition storage facility at Kamisiyah shortly after the war's end. With mounting evidence that winds may have carried the resulting poison cloud farther south toward the bulk of U.S. troops, the official count of potentially exposed personnel grew. By October, the Pentagon had raised the official estimate of troops who were exposed to as many as 20,000.

While acknowledging the possibility that U.S. service personnel were exposed to chemical weapons at Kamisiyah, however, the Pentagon holds firm to its position that the exposure cannot be positively linked to Gulf War Syndrome. "The current orthodox, scientific view is that with exposure to a chemical agent, if you do not get enough exposure to become ill at the time, you will not have chronic symptoms or symptoms down the road," said Stephen P. Joseph, assistant secretary of Defense for health affairs. "There really is no basis at the present time, beyond cocktail chatter, to say that a low-level exposure at Kamisiyah below the level that would give acute symptoms, is responsible for a whole series of symptoms that we're seeing now [several] years later." Following repeated accusations by veterans and some lawmakers that it had ignored veterans' reports linking chemical exposure to their illnesses, however, the Pentagon announced in November that it was expanding its investigation into the issue. [11]

The official Pentagon view is supported by many experts in the field, including the Presidential Advisory Committee on Gulf War Veterans' Illnesses. Though it is known that allied air strikes in January and February 1991 damaged two Iraqi storage facilities containing sarin and mustard gas, the panel concluded: "The best evidence available indicates theaterwide contamination with chemical warfare agent fallout from the air war is highly unlikely." [12]

The committee based its conclusion on the fact that chemical agents known as organophosphates, such as sarin, when delivered in doses suitable for weapons, immediately cause convulsions, neuromuscular blockage, airway obstruction and ultimately death from respiratory paralysis — all within one to two minutes of exposure. Mustard agents can take a couple of hours to work, but a victim of a mustard-gas attack has unmistakable symptoms: severe blistering of the eyes, skin, lungs and digestive tract. Neither sarin nor mustard are known to have long-term health effects at low concentrations, such as those the gulf veterans probably experienced. [13]

Numerous gulf veterans, health professionals and other researchers dispute these findings. "Chemical agents had clearly been detected — repeatedly — by U.S., U.K., French and Czech forces during and after the war," said Patrick G. Eddington, a former CIA analyst who began investigating the government's handling of veterans' claims two years ago. "There were credible reports of a sublethal chemical and/or biological agent attack against coalition units at the Saudi

port of Al Jubayl in the early morning hours of Jan. 19, 1991.

"Additionally, eyewitness accounts of several Iraqi SCUD [missile] attacks on American units in Saudi Arabia described symptoms consistent with low-dose chemical or biological agent exposure during or immediately after those attacks." Eddington claims that "tens of thousands of Desert Storm veterans" may suffer the ill effects of chemical or biological weapons exposure. [14]

The most recently published non-governmental studies leave open the possibility that at least some sufferers of Gulf War Syndrome were indeed injured by chemical weapons. [15] A small group of gulf war veterans who complained of confusion and impaired balance were found to have abnormalities in nerve and brain function that the researchers said may have been caused by exposure to harmful chemicals, such as pesticides and possibly poison gas. This same group included soldiers who reported they were exposed to a cloud of nerve gas that blew over northeastern Saudi Arabia early in the war.

At least one expert claims that some of the veterans' symptoms may be the result of exposure to biological weapons, which Iraq is suspected of having deployed since before the war. Biochemist Garth Nicholson, director of the Institute for Molecular Medicine in Irvine, Calif., says he successfully treated some of his gulf war patients with antibiotics and suspects that the culprit in those cases may be a genetically altered form of a disease-causing bacterium, *Mycoplasma fermentans*.

Other infectious-disease experts are skeptical, however. Hughes, whose CDC institute has helped investigate this hypothesis, says Nicholson's findings have not been replicated elsewhere. "Obviously, the Gulf War Syndrome is a complicated thing, and I don't know how it will play out," Hughes says. "But I'm not persuaded that there's any significant evidence for the role of biological agents in this syndrome."

The Pentagon, the Department of Veterans Affairs and non-governmental researchers will continue to study the possibility of long-term effects of exposure to chemical and biological warfare agents. But widespread skepticism surrounding the Pentagon's investigations to date prompted President Clinton to extend the presidential panel's term, which would have expired in December, at least through the end of fiscal 1997, ending Sept. 30. ∎

BACKGROUND

Early Horrors

Poison has been used to assassinate enemies and wipe out communities — often by contaminating well water — since the beginning of recorded history. But modern biochemical warfare dates to April 22, 1915, when German troops entrenched at Ypres, Belgium, opened 6,000 chlorine cylinders, releasing a cloud of deadly gas into the wind blowing toward their French adversaries. Thousands perished in this first large-scale use of chemical warfare.

Two years later, Germany introduced another deadly chemical to the battlefield as well: mustard gas. By the war's end, chemical weapons had inflicted 1.3 million casualties, including almost 100,000 deaths. [16] Germany also introduced biological agents during the conflict, reportedly using anthrax to kill the allied forces' horses and mules. [17]

The horrifying images of soldiers dying blistered and gagging on the battlefield led to the 1925 Geneva Protocol. The United States was among the signatories, though it did not ratify the agreement until 1975 because of senators' concerns that it might constrain the use of non-lethal chemical herbicides and tear gas. The Senate ratified the treaty on Jan. 22, 1975, after President Gerald Ford affirmed that the United States would renounce the first use of herbicides in war except for uses "applicable to their domestic use" and the first use of tear gas except for riot-control use in "defensive military modes to save lives."

Because the agreement did not prohibit the development of biological or chemical arsenals, it lacked verification or enforcement provisions. The agreement served rather as a statement that it is morally contemptible to use these weapons in combat.

By World War II, nonetheless, all the major combatants — Germany, Japan, the United States, Britain, Canada and the Soviet Union — had developed biochemical arsenals. Violations of the Geneva Protocol occurred throughout the war: Soviet soldiers reportedly spread typhus and typhoid fever in eastern Germany, Italy used chemical weapons against Ethiopia and Japan dropped bombs carrying plague germs as well as chemical agents over China, raising concern that U.S. forces in the Pacific might also come under biochemical attack.

The United States began its biological and chemical weapons programs during World War II on the premise that they would be used to retaliate in kind against an enemy attack. Such attacks never occurred. During the 1950s and '60s, the programs were expanded and revised. Up until the late 1950s, the Army even tested its biological and chemical readiness by releasing supposedly harmless agents over populated areas of the United States to see how widely they dispersed. [18]

At the height of the biochemical warfare programs in the 1960s, the United States developed chemical herbicides as well as munitions armed with organisms that cause Q fever and tularemia. A product of this research was Agent Orange, the controversial defoliant used to expose enemy hideouts during the Vietnam War that later was linked to cancer and other serious illnesses among Vietnam veterans. [19]

Arms Control Efforts

The development of a U.S. biochemical arsenal drew much of its urgency from the Cold War-era arms race with the Soviet Union, which also was building up its own supplies. But President Richard M. Nixon, arguing that it was not necessary to retaliate in kind against a biological or chemical attack, ended that policy in November 1969 when he unilaterally dismantled the U.S. biological weapons program. In February 1970, he also suspended development of weapons made with toxins produced from living organisms, such as staphylococcal enterotoxin.

By 1973, all U.S. stocks of bacteriological weapons and anti-crop substances had been destroyed, according to the Pentagon. All that was left of the U.S. biological weapons program were military and civilian laboratories used for research and the development of substances and systems for use in defensive measures. These include decontamination agents and vaccines and antibiotics against specific pathogens, as well as detection systems, gas masks and protective clothing designed for battlefield use.

During this period, the United States signed the 1972 Biological and Toxin Weapons Convention. By prohibiting the "development, production, stockpiling, acquisition or retention" of biological weapons, and not just their use, the new treaty went far beyond the Geneva Protocol. The Senate ratified the treaty on Dec. 16, 1974, and President Ford signed the ratification on Jan. 22, 1975.

Biological weapons are very hard to detect, and the Biological Weapons Convention contained no provisions to ensure compliance. This weakness became clear in the wake of an anthrax outbreak in Sverdlovsk, Russia, in April 1979. Though the Soviet government at the time claimed the outbreak was caused by contaminated meat, there was widespread suspicion that it stemmed from an accidental leak at a munitions complex. That was recently confirmed by Russian President Boris N. Yeltsin, who in April 1992 announced he was discontinuing biological programs being operated by Russia in violation of the treaty.

The anthrax outbreak prompted signatory countries to the Biological Weapons Convention to hold a series of review conferences to try to strengthen the treaty. Most changes have involved so-called confidence-building measures, notably agreements to exchange information on national programs to defend against biological attack and immediately notify the World Health Organization of any infectious-disease outbreaks.

Iran Offensive Prompts Chemical Weapons Treaty

Throughout the Cold War, international control of chemical weapons remained limited to the Geneva Protocol's ban on their use. Until the 1980s, the treaty appeared to have been successful in deterring poison gas attacks. In 1983, however, Iraq began launching chemical attacks against Iran that continued until the war between the two nations ended in 1988. During the 1980s, the Iraqi government also used poison gas to kill Kurdish civilians in northern Iraq. The United States and its NATO allies knew about Iraq's repeated violations of the Geneva Protocol — including the genocide of its own countrymen — but failed to strongly denounce the breaches. They had been reluctant to take sides in a war between two countries that had been hostile to the West during the oil embargoes of the 1970s and to Israel, the United States' main ally in the Middle East,

Confronted by the Geneva Protocol's loss of deterrent value, the United States

Chronology

1910s-1920s
The first use of chemical and biological weapons in combat leads to efforts to ban their use.

April 22, 1915
The first use of chemical weapons in combat occurs in World War I when Germany releases chlorine gas onto the battlefield near Ypres, Belgium. Two years later, Germany launches mustard gas attacks as well. By the war's end, the death toll from chemical weapons approaches 100,000 people.

1925
The Geneva Protocol prohibits the use of biological and chemical weapons in war. The United States signs, but fails to ratify, the treaty.

———— • ————

1950s-1970s
As the United States and the Soviet Union build arsenals of biological and chemical weapons, international pressure mounts to draw up new treaties to curb such weapons.

Nov. 25, 1969
President Richard M. Nixon unilaterally renounces the use of biological weapons in war by the United States and restricts research to immunization and safety efforts. Three months later, he extends the ban to include toxins.

1972
The Biological and Toxin Weapons Convention enters into force, banning the production and stockpiling of these weapons.

Jan. 22, 1975
The United States ratifies the Biological and Toxin Weapons Convention as well as the 1925 Geneva Protocol.

April 1979
An outbreak of anthrax occurs in Sverdlovsk, Russia. The incident, initially described as a natural outbreak, is later found to be the result of a leak from a Soviet biological-weapons facility.

———— • ————

1980s
Arms control initiatives fail to curb biological and chemical weapons proliferation.

1980-88
Iraq uses chemical weapons in its eight-year war against Iran as well as against dissident Kurdish communities in Iraq — the first use of chemical agents in combat since World War I.

1984
The Reagan administration presents a draft treaty to ban the production and storage of chemical weapons to the Conference on Disarmament in Geneva.

———— • ————

1990s
Concern over exposure to chemical and biological weapons during the Persian Gulf War increases support for international treaties.

May 13, 1991
Shortly after the allied victory against Iraq, President George Bush announces that the United States will renounce the use of chemical weapons for any reason once an international treaty banning them takes effect.

April 1992
Russian President Boris N. Yeltsin declares that Russia's biological weapons programs is being discontinued.

January 1993
President Bush signs the Chemical Weapons Convention banning the production and use of chemical weapons.

March 20, 1995
In the first terrorist attack using chemical weapons, members of Aum Shinrikyo, a Japanese religious cult, release sarin nerve gas in the Tokyo subway, killing 12 people and injuring more than 5,000.

1995
Larry Harris, a white supremacist from Ohio, obtains three vials of deadly plague bacteria by mail order from a laboratory supply house. Alleged white supremacist Thomas Lewis Lavy is apprehended while trying to smuggle the toxin ricin across the Canadian border.

Jan. 7, 1997
The Presidential Advisory Committee on Gulf War Veterans' Illnesses finds no conclusive evidence linking Gulf War Syndrome to exposure to chemical or biological weapons.

April 15, 1997
New regulations aimed at limiting access to chemicals and pathogens that could be made into weapons go into effect under the 1996 Antiterrorism and Effective Death Penalty Act.

April 29, 1997
The Chemical Weapons Convention goes into effect. As of late January, it had more than 160 signatories and 65 ratifications.

and other Western countries pressed for a stronger chemical weapons treaty. On May 13, 1991, shortly after the gulf war against Iraq ended, President Bush announced that the United States would renounce the use of chemical weapons for any reason once such a treaty took effect. The Army has already begun destroying its stockpiles of sarin and other chemicals used in weapons.

In January 1993, the Chemical Weapons Convention was presented for signature at the United Nations. Unlike the treaty banning biological weapons, the chemical convention contains extensive provisions for monitoring compliance with the ban, including intrusive inspection rights and allowance for sanctions and the use of force against violators.

Arsenals Proliferate

Efforts to rid the world of biological and chemical weapons have thus far failed to halt the global demand for their lethal ingredients. In the absence of aggressive verification measures, it is impossible to say exactly how many governments — or terrorist groups, religious fanatics and otherwise deranged individuals — actually possess workable chemical arsenals. But all estimates suggest a significant proliferation over the past two decades. Since 1980, the number of countries known or suspected to possess biological weapons has grown from one — the Soviet Union — to 17. [20] Chemical arsenals are even more widespread, numbering about 20, up from about a dozen in 1980. Many of the governments that have these weapons are hostile to Western interests — in particular the United States. [21]

Iraq — said to be the most blatant offender of existing biochemical accords — has maintained and openly used both types of weapons since before the gulf war. The Iraqi arsenal was long believed to include anthrax, botulinum, mustard and sarin, as well as VX, one of the most lethal forms of nerve gas. [22] The United Nations Special Commission on Iraq (UNSCOM), set up after the gulf war to conduct on-site inspections of Iraq's weapons of mass destruction, has confirmed their existence.

Since the gulf war, evidence of chemical weapons proliferation has mounted. Yugoslavia, Bosnia and Croatia had access to, and may have used, chlorine-filled shells during fighting in the region in the early 1990s. [23] And Russia, which inherited the vast chemical and biological arsenals built up by the Soviet Union, has recently weakened its commitment to disarm. Last fall, Prime Minister Viktor S. Chernomyrdin suggested that his government may no longer abide by a bilateral agreement with the United States to destroy existing arsenals.

Japanese Cult Raises Specter of Terrorism

Arms control treaties, of course, primarily serve to restrict governments' deployment of biological or chemical weapons. They do little, however, to curb access of groups or individuals to the lethal agents of which they are made. This reality became abundantly clear on March 20, 1995, when members of the Aum Shinrikyo cult released sarin gas in the Tokyo subway system at the height of the morning rush hour. Police investigating the incident discovered that the cult had bought air-filtration equipment, lasers and other sophisticated equipment in the United States to make its weapons. Members even bought a sheep station in Australia where they tested nerve gas. They also used chemicals to assassinate several people in Japan and sent representatives to Zaire during the 1992 outbreak of Ebola virus in search of samples of the deadly pathogen to use in future attacks. [24]

To date, no other group is known to have developed as lethal a biochemical capability as Aum Shinrikyo. But several incidents in the United States demonstrate this country's vulnerability to similar attacks. They include the mail-order sale of bubonic plague virus to white supremacist Harris in May 1995 and, later that year, the arrest of Thomas Lewis Lavy, another alleged white supremacist with ties to survivalist groups, who was apprehended as he tried to smuggle 130 grams of the deadly toxin ricin — enough to kill thousands of people — across the Canadian border. [25] ∎

CURRENT SITUATION

Gulf War Studies

The health effects of most poisons used in biological or chemical weapons have long been known. Chemical weapons act immediately or within hours. Nerve gases, for example, kill almost as soon as they are inhaled. Most biological weapons act more slowly. Deadly viruses have incubation periods as long as several weeks. But the potential for longer-term effects of these agents on human health is only beginning to be investigated in earnest, largely in response to the complaints of chronic health problems by thousands of gulf war veterans.

More than 100 studies of Gulf War Syndrome have been carried out or are currently in progress. Even more investigations are expected to begin as a result of the Pentagon's recent decision to expand its own research into the problem. On Nov. 12, Pentagon spokesman Kenneth Bacon announced that the Defense Department would spend $27 million in fiscal 1997 on research into the effects of low-level exposures to chemical weapons and other potential causes of the syndrome, doubling the 1996 budget for this research.

The most recent non-governmental studies, released Jan. 8 by a team of researchers at Southwestern Medical Center at the University of Texas in Dallas, suggest that the main cause of the syndrome in at least some veterans is damage to the nervous system due to exposure to one or more of a class of toxic chemicals called organophosphates, such as sarin and mustard. These chemicals were also present in the war zone as pesticides contained in flea collars many soldiers wore around their ankles to ward off insects or sprayed around their encampments. [26]

The Presidential Advisory Committee on Gulf War Veterans' Illnesses concluded its 16-month study with disappointing news for veterans eager for confirmation that their illnesses were the direct result of exposure to chemical or biological weapons. The panel also failed to link the syndrome to the wide range of other toxins present in the war zone, including pesticides, vaccines, pyridostigmine bromide (an antidote to nerve gas distributed to soldiers), infectious diseases, depleted uranium, smoke from oil-well fires and petroleum products.

But the panel's scientists were careful not to dismiss the veterans' claims and stressed the need for more research. "Prudence requires further investigation of some areas of uncertainty," the panel concluded, "such as the long-term effects of low-level exposure to chemical warfare agents

and the synergistic effects of exposure to pyridostigmine bromide and other risk factors." [27]

In addition to extending the life of the panel, President Clinton has announced that he supports making disability aid available to more sick gulf war veterans. Current rules require veterans who claim their "undiagnosed" illnesses can be traced to military service to prove the symptoms began

Officer candidates wearing gas masks prepare for a mock assault at the Marine Corps training facility at Quantico, Va.

within two years of leaving the gulf area. Many veterans who say they did not fall ill until several years after Desert Storm have been denied disability benefits by the Department of Veterans Affairs. VA Secretary Jesse Brown is expected to issue new time limits for these cases in March. [28]

Defense Strategies

The now-recognized fact that at least some U.S. military personnel were indeed exposed to Iraqi chemical weapons has raised concern over

the United States' preparedness for attacks using these as well as biological agents. Some critics of the Chemical Weapons Convention even question the wisdom of abandoning the U.S. chemical capability, citing its deterrent value. "We've got to try to make the use of chemical weapons as unattractive an option as possible," says Gaffney, who calls for more evaluation of the question. "Historically, it has been the case that the threat of retaliation in kind is a powerful disincentive. Hitler is widely believed to have refrained from using large quantities of chemical weapons that he had at his disposal because he feared retaliation in kind. It is also the case that most, if not all, uses of chemical weapons have been against people who didn't have the means to retaliate in kind."

But reestablishing a chemical, much less a biological, capability seems highly unlikely. Shortly after the gulf war, President Bush announced that the United States was formally forswearing the use of chemical weapons for any reason — including retaliation against a chemical attack — as soon as the treaty enters into force. Indeed, Gen. John M. Shalikashvili, chairman of the Joint Chiefs of Staff, said the gulf war showed that eliminating chemical weapons from the U.S. arsenal in no way made the United States more vulnerable to chemical attack. "Desert Storm proved that retaliation in kind is not required to deter the use of chemical weapons," he said. [29]

Meanwhile, Congress has acted to strengthen U.S. defenses, especially against biological weapons, in the

U.S. Marine Corps/Arms Control Association

CHEMICAL AND BIOLOGICAL WEAPONS

wake of incidents such as the 1995 mail order sale of plague bacteria. The 1996 Antiterrorism and Effective Death Penalty Act, passed last April, includes new regulations aimed at limiting access to chemicals and pathogens that could be made into offensive weapons. Under the new rules, which will take effect April 15, the Health and Human Services Department will regulate the transfer of 36 lethal viruses, toxins and other biological agents by mail.

Improving Global Surveillance

But the main emphasis of new defensive efforts against biological weapons has been on improving global surveillance of and response to infectious disease outbreaks. Ironically, the scientific community's success in combating infectious diseases in recent decades has eroded its ability to deal with outbreaks. When plague broke out in two cities in India in 1994, for example, there was only one World Health Organization lab with the ability to respond to the disease. According to Hughes of the NCID, the CDC's plague branch had been reduced from 16 researchers to just one. "Because of all this complacency that's developed over the years," he says, "the number of experts who work with these agents is relatively limited. So there is a vulnerability. There's no doubt about that."

Recognizing that most U.S. cities are within 36 hours by commercial airliners of any area of the world, President Clinton issued a new policy directive on June 12 that would strengthen federal, state and local health agencies' ability to identify and combat disease outbreaks. The new policy covers all outbreaks, whether they arise from a biological weapons attack or natural causes, such as the recent outbreaks of Ebola in Zaire and hantavirus in the Southwestern United States. [30]

The new policy also would enhance U.S. cooperation with other countries to quell outbreaks wherever they may occur. "Emerging infectious diseases present one of the most significant health and security challenges facing the global community," said Vice President Al Gore in announcing the policy. "Through President Clinton's leadership, we now have the first national policy to deal with this serious international problem." [31]

There are limits, however, to what the U.S. government, or any government, can do to prevent a biological or chemical attack from taking place once a country, group or individual has decided to launch one. "Certainly, the government is paying more attention to this issue than before," says terrorism expert Jenkins. "This in part is a result of fears raised during the gulf war, which I think have been exacerbated by the events in Tokyo. Having said that, one has to recognize the difficulty in this area of prevention. This is not a problem that can be as easily addressed as airplane hijackings or keeping bombs and guns off airplanes." ∎

OUTLOOK

Treaty Debate

Opponents of the Chemical Weapons Convention surprised most observers last September when they garnered enough support to force the treaty's backers to postpone the scheduled Senate discussion and vote on its ratification. The new 105th Senate is expected to take up the treaty once again early this year. A vote is expected before April 29, when the agreement will go into effect — with or without the United States as a party — and backers are urging its prompt approval.

"I urge my colleagues to support ratification of this treaty, which establishes an important international orga-

nization to suppress the threat of chemical warfare and terrorism," Sen. Lugar said in response to the Jan. 7 statement of support for the treaty by the Clinton administration. "The CWC would require other countries to destroy their chemical weapons, as the U.S. is already doing. Unless the U.S. ratifies the treaty by April 29, we will have no input in its rules and administration."

According to some experts, the Senate's action on the convention will also affect the United States' ability to curb the threat from biological weapons. "I think that chemical and biological agents — the way they're perceived and in some ways the way they behave — are similar enough that if one of the conventions isn't successful, it will drag the other treaty down, and if one is successful it will pull the other up," Cole says.

The detailed verification measures included in the chemical weapons treaty offer a model for monitoring lethal biological agents that could be added to the Biological Weapons Convention, Cole says. "But even without verification measures, these treaties have value as a kind of moral statement, and I see these two weapons systems as sufficiently linked that as one goes, so will the other."

Even in the absence of stronger international controls, some experts offer hope that the threat of biological or chemical weapons may be less immediate than the widely publicized incidents of the past few years may suggest. "Outside a few criminal extortionists and incidents involving fanatical cults such as Aum Shinrikyo, there is little evidence that other types of terrorists have done anything more than express a modest interest in chemical or biological agents," Jenkins says. Because of their objectives, he says, terrorists are unlikely to unleash a wave of mass killings using these weapons. "Terrorism is not about killing people," he says. "It is aimed at the people watching, and at creating psychological reactions." To avoid undermining all sym-

At Issue:

Does exposure to chemical weapons explain Gulf War Syndrome?

MAJ. RANDY LEE HEBERT
United States Marine Corps

FROM TESTIMONY BEFORE THE GOVERNMENT REFORM AND OVERSIGHT SUBCOMMITTEE ON HUMAN RESOURCES AND INTERGOVERNMENTAL RELATIONS, DEC. 10, 1996.

*i*n December 1990 I was assigned to the 2nd Combat Engineer Battalion, 2nd Marine Division, in Saudi Arabia.... On 23 February 1991, the eve prior to our ground attack, we moved into our attack position approximately ... three miles from the border of Kuwait. ... On G-day, 24 February 1991, we were to link up with a section of tanks; this never happened. ... I decided to halt my men south of the berm dividing Saudi Arabia and Kuwait. I proceeded ... to a traffic control point.

As we approached, we received the hand and arm signal for chemical attack. We put on our masks and gloves. In doing so, I recall my right hand feeling cool and tingling. I was mad because we were just starting and already receiving the sign for chemicals. I jumped from the vehicle and asked the Marine MP in strong Marine Corps language who had told him to go to (MOPP) Level 4. ...

We drove back and radioed to my Marines to get to MOPP Level 4. When we arrived, some were, others were not. The driver and I jumped from the vehicle giving the sign for chemicals. I approached the MP controlling traffic to ask why he wasn't in MOPP Level 4. He told me the alarm was false. I was angry and removed my mask. I now feel that was a mistake. I radioed to Battalion Three and told him, "We are rolling and we have not made contact with the tanks." He said, "OK." Within a minute of rolling he called back saying that, "Your lane is dirty, chemical mine has gone off, go to MOPP 4...."

Around the 22nd of February, I started taking pyrostigmine bromide pills for anti-nerve agent protection. I believe I took the pills for 11-14 days. Once we returned to Saudi Arabia in early April, I began to have some difficulty with sleep. This continued upon my return home on 15 May 1995 until early July, at which time I have having difficulty reading and remembering what I had read. I was extremely aggressive, moody and excitable. I had headaches, vomiting and diarrhea. I was also diagnosed with moderate depression. ...

In October 1995 I was diagnosed with ALS (amyotrophic lateral sclerosis, also known as Lou Gehrig's Disease). I believe the medical problems I have discussed are due to low-level chemical exposure over an extended period.

I learned after the war that the chemical mine detonated in Lane Red One was confirmed for the nerve agent sarin and also the agent Lewisite mustard gas by a FOX vehicle in the lane. It has been brought to my attention that there have been at least seven other cases of ALS in service members who served in the gulf. To me, this is more than mere chance or coincidence.

PRESIDENTIAL ADVISORY COMMITTEE ON GULF WAR VETERANS' ILLNESSES
FROM "FINAL REPORT," DECEMBER 1996.

*i*raq successfully used chemical weapons in its war with Iran, with massive casualties not seen in the gulf war.

A Department of Defense (DOD) review of U.S. Army hospital admissions records identified no admissions for chemical warfare (CW) agent exposures during the gulf war. The U.S. Army officer responsible for chemical-biological warfare (CBW) agent medical surveillance during the war has testified to the committee that only one accidental casualty was treated. Additionally, UNSCOM * reported to us that Iraqi officials have denied to them any use of chemical weapons during the war. Lastly, veterans groups testifying before this committee concede there were no widespread chemical attacks. Based on the information compiled to date, there is no persuasive evidence of intentional Iraqi use of CW agents during the war. ...

During the gulf war, Coalition forces conducted air attacks on suspected Iraqi CW agent manufacturing and storage facilities. Some veterans and independent researchers have suggested that fallout from Coalition bombing of these sites led to large-scale nerve agent contamination in [the Kuwait theater of operations]. The committee looked at evidence of the effects of Coalition airstrikes on Iraqi chemical munitions storage sites to examine this hypothesis. In late January and February 1991, Coalition forces conducted aerial bombings that damaged chemical munitions stored at two sites in central Iraq: Muhammadiyat and Al Muthanna. Subsequent UNSCOM investigations indicate these are the only sites (among 11 known storage sites) where Coalition airstrikes actually damaged or destroyed chemical agents. ...

To assess possible hazards to U.S. forces from CW agent releases at Muhammidiyat and Al Muthanna, atmospheric modeling was conducted for the [Central Intelligence Agency] for all possible bombing dates at each site. This modeling indicates that on the bombing date ... Muhammadiyat releases, at worst, would have resulted in downwind contamination for up to 300 kilometers (km) at general population exposure levels established by DOD. This modeling also indicates that on the bombing date when southerly winds were most pronounced, Al Muthanna releases, at worst, would have resulted in downwind contamination for up to 160 km.... During the air war, the nearest U.S. personnel were in Rafha, Saudia Arabia — more than 400 km from Muhammadiyat and Al Muthanna. ...

The best evidence available indicates theaterwide contamination with CW agent fallout from the air war is highly unlikely.

* UNSCOM, the United Nations Special Commission on Iraq, carries out on-site inspections of Iraqi biological, chemical and missile capabilities.

FOR MORE INFORMATION

AMERICAN LEGION, 1608 K St. N.W., Washington, D.C. 20006; (202) 861-2700, www.legion.org. The legion's Persian Gulf Task Force is among the most vocal critics of the Pentagon's treatment of U.S. servicemen who say they suffer from Gulf War Syndrome.

ARMS CONTROL AND DISARMAMENT AGENCY, 320 21st St. N.W., Washington, D.C. 20451; (202) 647-4800. The ACDA advises the president and secretary of State on arms control policy and develops verification procedures for arms control agreements, such as the Chemical and Biological Weapons conventions.

CENTER FOR SECURITY POLICY, 1920 L. St., N.W., Suite 210, Washington, D.C. 20036; (202) 835-9077, www.security-policy.org. This defense and foreign-policy research organization opposes ratification of the Chemical Weapons Convention.

CHEMICAL AND BIOLOGICAL ARMS CONTROL INSTITUTE, 2111 Eisenhower Ave., Suite 302, Alexandria, Va. 22314; (703) 739-1538, www.cbaci.org. The institute promotes arms control and the elimination of chemical and biological weapons.

pathy for their political agendas, Jenkins expects most terrorists to continue exercising a certain degree of restraint. "Terrorists have always had the capacity to kill more people than they have actually killed. Moreover, if you want to kill a lot of people, exotic weaponry is not required." ∎

Notes

[1] Martin testified Sept. 19, 1996, before the House Government Reform and Oversight Subcommittee on Human Resources and Intergovernmental Affairs.

[2] Presidential Advisory Committee on Gulf War Veterans' Illnesses, *Final Report,* December 1996, p. 7.

[3] U.S. Arms Control and Disarmament Agency, "The Chemical Weapons Convention, Fact Sheet," Dec. 17, 1996. See also Leonard A. Cole, *The Eleventh Plague* (1997), pp. 4-5. See "War Crimes," *The CQ Researcher,* July 7, 1995, pp. 585-608.

[4] Office of Technology Assessment, *Proliferation of Weapons of Mass Destruction,* August 1993, p. 82.

[5] For background, see "Non-Proliferation Treaty at 25," *The CQ Researcher,* Jan. 27, 1995, pp. 73-96. The five nuclear powers are the United States, China, France, Russia and Great Britain.

[6] Helms spoke March 28, 1996, at Senate Foreign Relations Committee hearings on chemical and biological defense capabilities.

[7] E.R. Zumwalt Jr., "A Needless Risk for U.S. Troops," *The Washington Post,* Jan. 6, 1997.

[8] See Laurie Mylroie, "WTC Bombing — The Case of 'Secret' Cyanide," *The Wall Street Journal,* July 26, 1996.

[9] See Robert Ruth, "Judge Who Nixed Deal in Plague Case May Step Down," *The Columbus Dispatch,* Nov. 20, 1996.

[10] Presidential Advisory Committee, *op. cit.,* p. 96.

[11] Joseph spoke Nov. 12, 1996, at a Pentagon news briefing.

[12] Presidential Advisory Committee, *op. cit.,* pp. 40-41.

[13] *Ibid.,* p. 107.

[14] Eddington, who is writing a book about Gulf War Syndrome, testified Dec. 10, 1996, before the House Government Reform and Oversight Subcommittee on Human Resources and Intergovernmental Relations. See also Patrick G. Eddington and Mark S. Zaid, "The True Costs of the Gulf War Syndrome," *The Washington Post,* Jan. 1, 1997.

[15] Robert W. Haley, "Is There a Gulf War Syndrome: Searching for Syndromes by Factor Analysis of Symptoms," *Journal of the American Medical Association,* Jan. 15, 1997, pp. 215-222.

[16] See Cole, *op. cit.,* pp. 1-2. Unless otherwise noted, information in this section is based on Cole's book.

[17] See W. Seth Carus, "The Proliferation of Biological Weapons," in Brad Roberts, ed., *Biological Weapons: Weapons of the Future?* (1993), p. 20.

[18] See Cole, *op. cit.,* pp. 17-41.

[19] See Thomas Dashiell, "A Review of U.S. Biological Warfare Policies," in Roberts, *op. cit.,* p. 3.

[20] See Leonard A. Cole, "The Specter of Biological Weapons," *Scientific American,* December 1996, p. 62. The 17 countries cited by Cole are Iran, Iraq, Libya, Syria, North Korea, Taiwan, Israel, Egypt, Vietnam, Laos, Cuba, Bulgaria, India, South Korea, South Africa, China and Russia.

[21] The Arms Control and Disarmament Agency does not identify chemical weapons states, but says it suspects "some 20 countries have or may be developing chemical weapons." See ACDA, *Fact Sheet: The Chemical Weapons Convention,* Dec. 17, 1996. Countries most often cited are Israel, Libya, Iraq, Egypt, Iran, Syria, Taiwan, North Korea, Vietnam, Myanmar, China, Pakistan, South Korea, India and Ethiopia. See Office of Technology Assessment, *Proliferation of Weapons of Mass Destruction: Assessing the Risks,* 1993, p. 80.

[22] See John F. Sopko, "The Changing Proliferation Threat," *Foreign Policy,* winter 1996-97, p. 4.

[23] See "Bosnia Produced Chemical Arms, Report Says," *The New York Times,* Dec. 4, 1996.

[24] Cole, "The Specter of Biological Weapons," *op. cit.,* p. 60.

[25] Sopko, *op. cit.,* p. 6.

[26] See David Brown, "New Studies Indicate 6 Patterns of Gulf 'Syndrome'," *The Washington Post,* Jan. 9, 1997.

[27] Presidential Advisory Committee, *op. cit.,* p. 125.

[28] See David Brown, "Liberalized Rules Weighed for Gulf Disability Aid," *The Washington Post,* Jan. 8, 1997.

[29] Cited by Arms Control and Disarmament Agency, *op. cit.*

[30] For background, see "Combating Infectious Diseases," *The CQ Researcher,* June 9, 1996, pp. 489-512.

[31] Gore spoke on June 12, 1996, before the National Council for International Health in Crystal City, Va.

Bibliography

Selected Sources Used

Books

Cole, Leonard A., *The Eleventh Plague: The Politics of Biological and Chemical Warfare,* **W. H. Freeman, 1997.**

The author, a Rutgers University professor of science and public policy, outlines the history and potential dangers of biological and chemical weapons proliferation. He argues that arms control agreements can provide an imperfect but necessary protection against these weapons.

Roberts, Brad, ed., *Biological Weapons: Weapons of the Future?,* **The Center for Strategic and International Studies, 1993.**

A strong defense in nuclear and conventional weapons and strengthening of the Biological Weapons Convention are needed to counter the growing danger of biological weapons attack, concludes the editor of this collection of essays on biological warfare.

Weinberger, Caspar, and Peter Schweizer, *The Next War,* **Regnery, 1996.**

Weinberger, Defense secretary during the Reagan administration, and Schweizer, an analyst at the conservative Hoover Institution, offer several hypothetical war-game scenarios to illustrate their contention that defense spending cuts have left the United States vulnerable to biological, chemical and nuclear attack.

Articles

Newman, Richard J., Mike Tharp and Timothy M. Ito, "Gulf War Mysteries," *U.S. News & World Report,* **Nov. 25, 1996, pp. 36-38.**

Recent congressional testimony suggests that Iraqi chemical weapons may be responsible for many gulf war veterans' health complaints, but the link may never be fully established.

Sopko, John F., "The Changing Proliferation Threat," *Foreign Policy,* **winter 1996-97, pp. 3-20.**

According to Sopko, a counsel for Sen. Sam Nunn, D-Ga., before the senator's recent retirement, the United States is dangerously unprepared to counter attacks using biological, chemical or nuclear weapons by rogue states or terrorists.

Thompson, Mark, "The Silent Treatment," *Time,* **Dec. 23, 1996, pp. 33-34.**

The author reviews investigations into Gulf War Syndrome, which thus far have failed to satisfy veterans' claims that they were sickened by exposure to chemical or biological weapons.

Reports and Studies

Business Executives for National Security, *Twelve Myths about the Chemical Weapons Convention,* **January 1997.**

A group of business leaders concerned about U.S. defense policy rebuts the main arguments presented by critics who oppose Senate ratification of the 1993 treaty aimed at curbing chemical-weapons proliferation.

Central Intelligence Agency, *The Chemical and Biological Warfare Threat,* **undated.**

This primer includes a review of the technology, proliferation and arms control efforts involving biological and chemical weapons, as well as a description of the main substances and microorganisms used to produce them.

National Science and Technology Council, Committee on International Science, Engineering, and Technology Working Group on Emerging and Re-emerging Infectious Diseases, *Infectious Disease — A Global Health Threat,* **September 1995.**

The NSTC, a Cabinet-level council charged with coordinating federal science policies, identifies the microorganisms involved in recent infectious disease outbreaks and offers a plan for responding more effectively to them, whether they result from natural causes or from deliberate use of biological weapons.

Presidential Advisory Committee on Gulf War Veterans' Illnesses, *Final Report,* **December 1996.**

This 13-member panel of experts commissioned in 1995 by President Clinton finds no conclusive evidence that Gulf War Syndrome is linked to exposure to chemical or biological weapons during the 1991 conflict.

Rodrigues, Leslie A., "The Emerging Threat of Chembio Terrorism: Is the United States Prepared?" *The Arena,* **Chemical and Biological Arms Control Institute, November 1996.**

The 1995 release of sarin gas by terrorists in the Tokyo subway system raises questions about vulnerability to similar attacks in the United States, according to this report by a group that supports tighter arms control in the area of chemical and biological weapons.

Selden, Zachary, *Assessing the Biological Weapons Threat,* **Business Executives for National Security, January 1997.**

This study analyzes the technology of biological warfare, proliferation of these weapons and recent efforts to strengthen the 1972 Biological Weapons Convention.

U.S. Arms Control and Disarmament Agency, *Convention on the Prohibition of the Development, Production, Stockpiling and Use of Chemical Weapons and on Their Destruction,* **October 1993.**

The federal agency that advises the president on arms control analyzes in detail the Chemical Weapons Convention, due to go into effect April 29.

2 Banning Land Mines

MARY H. COOPER

I t's not surprising that 11-year-old Elsa Armindo Chela triggered the land mine. There are, after all, more than 100 million land mines planted around the world — one for every 60 human beings on Earth. And Angola, where civil war raged for years, is a virtual minefield.

Elsa was picking mangoes in her village, Kuito, when she stepped on the mine. She lost a leg and an eye. Two and a half years later, she suffers bouts of depression and shies away from other children.

"Angola should buy tractors and seeds, not land mines," said Elsa's father, who worries her injuries will prevent her from completing school and finding a husband. "I appeal to the international community not to sell us any more of those weapons."[1]

Elsa is one of the 26,000 people around the world who are killed or maimed each year by anti-personnel mines. Each month, according to the American Red Cross, land mines kill 800 people and maim 1,200 — a victim every 20 minutes. The vast majority are civilians — farmers tilling fields, women collecting firewood or children playing. Most of the mines were left behind by combatants of conflicts that ended years earlier; many were used to terrorize local populations and deliberately targeted at children and other civilians.

Used for over a century, anti-personnel mines are small explosive devices, some no bigger than a can of shoe polish, originally designed to keep enemy soldiers from infiltrating vital areas or tampering with larger and less sensitive anti-tank mines. Because they explode on contact, anti-personnel mines also free up

From *The CQ Researcher*, August 8, 1997.

Landmine Survivors Network/J. Rodsted

soldiers for other operations.

"To shoot somebody with a gun, you've got to point it, to fire artillery you've got to set it, to drop bombs out of a plane you've got to use a release mechanism," explains Robert O. Muller, president of the Vietnam Veterans of America Foundation. "Anti-personnel mines are totally indiscriminate, in that it is the victim of the weapon, as opposed to a command decision, that triggers the weapon."

Easy to use, hard to detect and resistant to the elements, land mines laid during the regional conflicts that raged for most of the post-World War II era have become a peacetime scourge. Long after combatants sign an armistice and the conflict fades from memory, the land mines they left behind continue to wage their indiscriminate war. Up to 120 million of these forgotten weapons lie hidden in more than 80 countries.[2] (*See map, p. 20.*)

In addition to the personal tragedy borne by victims such as Elsa, the devastating legacy of land mines afflicts entire societies. Land mines are concentrated among the poorest

countries in the world, where the cost of treating and rehabilitating victims far exceeds the capacity of health-care systems, and the cost of demining is equally daunting. Post-war economic recovery is often hampered as refugees and former combatants alike are prevented by uncleared mines from returning to their homes and fields. Large areas of mine-infested agricultural land lie fallow, forcing farmers onto fragile, marginal sites where farming causes environmental damage. Industrial development is crippled in some countries where mines block access to power plants, bridges and other infrastructure.

"The problem with land mines is that wars end, peace treaties are signed, armies march away, the guns grow silent — but the land mines stay," said Sen. Patrick J. Leahy, D-Vt., a leader in the fight to ban land mines. "To the child who steps on a mine on the way to school a year after the peace agreement is signed, that peace agreement is no protection. To the farmer who cannot raise crops to feed his or her children because the fields are strewn with land mines, that peace agreement is worth nothing. To the medical personnel and humanitarian workers who cannot get polio vaccine to a village where it is needed because of the land mines, that peace agreement is useless."[3]

If current trends continue, the humanitarian crisis sparked by land mines can only get worse. Land mines are cheap, ranging from $3-$30 each. But it costs at least $300 to detect and remove a planted mine. Each year, about 100,000 land mines are cleared, but 2 million more are planted. And the supply is vast. In addition to the tens of millions of mines in the ground, there are an estimated 200 million more stockpiled around the world. At current removal rates, the

A Victim Every 20 Minutes

Up to 120 million land mines in more than 80 countries around the world kill or maim 26,000 people a year — one every 20 minutes. Most of the victims are civilians, typically agricultural workers, villagers gathering firewood and children. Each year, demining activities remove about 100,000 land mines, but some 2 million new mines are planted.

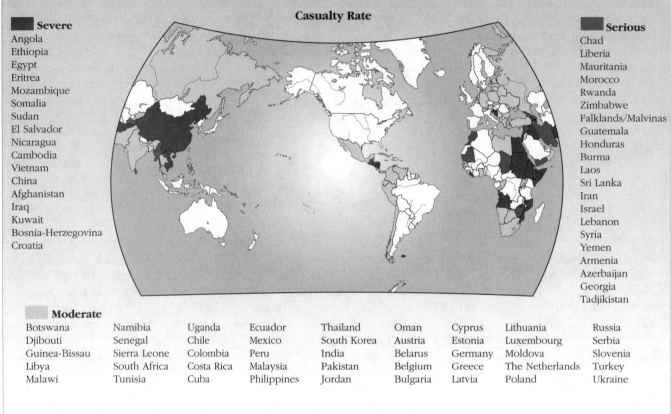

Casualty Rate

■ Severe

Angola
Ethiopia
Egypt
Eritrea
Mozambique
Somalia
Sudan
El Salvador
Nicaragua
Cambodia
Vietnam
China
Afghanistan
Iraq
Kuwait
Bosnia-Herzegovina
Croatia

■ Serious

Chad
Liberia
Mauritania
Morocco
Rwanda
Zimbabwe
Falklands/Malvinas
Guatemala
Honduras
Burma
Laos
Sri Lanka
Iran
Israel
Lebanon
Syria
Yemen
Armenia
Azerbaijan
Georgia
Tadjikistan

■ Moderate

Botswana	Namibia	Uganda	Ecuador	Thailand	Oman	Cyprus	Lithuania	Russia
Djibouti	Senegal	Chile	Mexico	South Korea	Austria	Estonia	Luxembourg	Serbia
Guinea-Bissau	Sierra Leone	Colombia	Peru	India	Belarus	Germany	Moldova	Slovenia
Libya	South Africa	Costa Rica	Malaysia	Pakistan	Belgium	Greece	The Netherlands	Turkey
Malawi	Tunisia	Cuba	Philippines	Jordan	Bulgaria	Latvia	Poland	Ukraine

Sources: Vietnam Veterans of America Foundation, U.S. State Department, United Nations

American Red Cross estimates it would take 1,100 years to rid the world of land mines, even if no more were deployed.

Despite the havoc wreaked by land mines for decades, efforts to respond to Elsa's father's plea have only recently gained momentum. "They've been killing people for quite a while," says a senior Defense Department official. "But with the Cold War and other things that were going on around the world, land mines just did not get the attention they deserved."

The world began to pay more attention to land mines in the early 1990s, as relief workers struggled with the ter- rible legacy of regional wars in Afghani- stan, Angola and other countries where Cold War superpowers had supported opposite sides in civil conflicts.

"Land mines were the Saturday night specials of Cold War arma- ments," says Andrew Cooper, a re- search assistant for the Human Rights Watch Arms Project. "The land mine issue surfaced when the United Na- tions first went into Afghanistan to implement the Soviet withdrawal and introduce relief mechanisms there. In such countries, even if they stop the fighting it's actually impossible for them to demilitarize their warring sides when they can't get back to their farms because they're mined. Now public awareness is very high."

Non-governmental organizations (NGOs) such as the Red Cross, Medico International and the Vietnam Veterans of America Foundation have been re- sponding to land mine victims for years by setting up clinics to treat victims and provide them with prosthetic devices. They also launched a movement to ban land mines that has grown in just a few years from a handful of relief workers to a global coalition of more than 1,000 organizations — including some 250 in the United States.

The International Campaign to Ban Land Mines has spearheaded an initiative that is expected to produce by year's end an international treaty in Ottawa, Canada, to halt forever the production, transfer, stockpiling and use of these weapons. A number of major powers, however, including the United States, China and Russia, are not currently planning to sign the Ottawa treaty. Instead, the United States is attempting to launch negotiations on land mines at the Conference on Disarmament in Geneva, Switzerland (*see page 35*).

Although the U.S. has been a major producer of land mines for many years — and has about 11 million mines stockpiled — it took an early lead in promoting a global ban. Leahy has led the effort in Congress, sponsoring a bill in 1992 that would have halted the export of U.S. anti-personnel mines. In a 1994 speech to the United Nations General Assembly, President Clinton called for the elimination of land mines. In January, the president announced he was imposing a permanent ban on U.S. sales of anti-personnel mines to other countries and promised to destroy most of the nation's inventory of so-called "dumb" mines, which do not self-destruct.

Despite these moves, some critics say President Clinton has adopted a policy that undermines American leadership in the effort to ban land mines. On May 16, 1996, the president announced that he would pursue a land mine treaty with two controversial exceptions for the United States. The first would allow the U.S. to continue deploying "smart" mines, which self-destruct after a few hours or days, until an international ban takes effect or alternative weapons are developed. Because they become harmless shortly after they are deployed, American-made smart mines are not responsible for the humanitarian crisis caused by land mines, the administration says.

The president also insisted that a treaty had to contain an exception

for some 1 million "dumb" U.S. mines planted near the demilitarized zone (DMZ) that separates North and South Korea. These mines are out of the reach of civilians, the administration argues, and would provide an essential defense for American soldiers stationed in South Korea if North Korea attacked.

Fearing that land mine talks in Geneva would never get off the ground, Canadian Foreign Minister Lloyd Axworthy last fall launched an open invitation to all countries to draw up and sign a treaty in Ottawa in December 1997 that would completely ban anti-personnel mines. Arguing that the world's biggest producers of land mines — Russia and China — would never agree to such a treaty, Clinton announced in January that the United States instead would seek a separate land mine treaty at the ongoing U.N. Conference on Disarmament in Geneva. The 61-nation conference, which recently produced the Chemical Weapons Convention, includes both Russia and China.

Unlike the Ottawa negotiations, the Geneva process requires consensus, which in effect grants veto power to opponents of a ban. And the likelihood that a total ban won't come out of the Geneva talks, critics say, is the real reason behind U.S. participation there.

"This is a stalling tactic" by the administration says Jody Williams, coordinator of the International Campaign to Ban Landmines, a leading promoter of the Ottawa process and a nominee for the 1997 Nobel Peace Prize. "They say the Conference on Disarmament is a universal forum, but only 61 countries are members. That's not exactly universal."

By contrast, a June meeting in Brussels, Belgium, of countries participating in negotiations leading up to the Ottawa treaty drew 115 countries. "The Ottawa process negotiations are open to everyone," Will-

iams says. "We have 115, and you have 61 in this closed club? This is not exactly logical."

Supporters of a total ban have brought renewed pressure on the White House this summer. On June 12, Sens. Leahy and Chuck Hagel, R-Neb., introduced the Land Mine Elimination Act, which would ban U.S. deployment of all anti-personnel mines beginning in the year 2000. The measure drew 59 cosponsors. The same day, more than 160 House members signed a letter to the president drafted by Reps. Jack Quinn, R-N.Y., and Lane Evans, D-Ill., urging him to join the Ottawa process. Five days later, Lady Diana, Princess of Wales, joined American Red Cross President Elizabeth H. Dole in Washington in calling for a total land mine ban.

So far, however, the administration has stood by the policy it laid out more than a year ago to seek through the Geneva process a land mine treaty that contains the two exceptions for Korea and smart mines. "This initiative," the administration declares, "sets out a clear path to a global ban on [anti-personnel land mines] but ensures that as the United States pursues a ban, essential U.S. military requirements and commitments to our allies will be protected." [4]

Some critics say President Clinton's stance on land mines stems from a dogged reluctance to take on the military. "The Pentagon is institutionally incapable of giving up a weapon because of the nature of its responsibilities," says Robert Gard, a retired Army lieutenant general and one of 15 senior retired officers who have urged the president to forgo all land mines and join the Ottawa process. (*See "At Issue," p. 33.*) "But our Constitution does not provide for military considerations to be overriding; it provides for a civilian commander in chief in the office of the president. In this case, however, the president does not feel confident enough to risk a breach with the Joint Chiefs of Staff."

Since the end of the most recent Conference on Disarmament session, in June, the Clinton administration says it has been re-evaluating its policy on land mines.

As the debate over a total ban continues, these are some of the questions being asked:

Do anti-personnel land mines play a vital role in U.S. military strategy?

The U.S. has used anti-personnel mines since the Civil War, and the Pentagon claims that they continue to play a vital role in military strategy. In an extraordinary letter to Senate Armed Services Committee Chairman Strom Thurmond, R-S.C., 16 four-star generals and admirals, including Gen. John M. Shalikashvili, chairman of the Joint Chiefs, recently defended continued reliance on anti-personnel mines as vital "to ensure maximum protection for our soldiers and Marines who carry out national security policy at grave personal risk." [5]

According to the "64 stars letter," as it has been dubbed, land mines have become even more important as a "combat multiplier" in the wake of the post-Cold War drawdown of U.S. military forces around the world. With fewer soldiers available to protect units' flanks, the Pentagon brass told Thurmond, anti-personnel mines can free manpower for other operations. They also can protect small contingents sent into contested territory to secure vital resources, such as landing strips or seaports, before backup units arrive.

"Until the United States has a capable replacement for self-destructing [anti-personnel land mines], maxi-

mum flexibility and war-fighting capability for American combat commanders must be preserved," the officers wrote. "The lives of our sons and daughters should be given the highest priority when deciding whether or not to ban unilaterally the use of self-destructing anti-personnel land mines."

While all the services are united in the effort to continue current U.S. use of land mines, the Army and the

Former Gen. Norman H. Schwarzkopf, commander of Allied forces in the gulf war, supports a total ban on anti-personnel mines. Gen. John M. Shalikashvili, chairman of the Joint Chiefs of Staff, supports U.S. use of anti-personnel land mines.

Marine Corps are especially reluctant to give them up. The Army is responsible for defending South Korea, while securing vital assets in the early stages of battle usually falls to Army airborne units or the Marine Corps.

"It's only natural that the Army and the Marine Corps would be the most concerned [about a ban] because they are the two services that have the most to worry about," the senior Defense Department official says. While both services have begun to change their strategies to accommodate an eventual phaseout of the weapons, "both of these services are concerned that if we suddenly went

without land mines tomorrow, that would put their people at risk because we're still several years away from having an alternative." A preliminary study by the Pentagon of alternatives to land mines is expected to be completed by early fall.

Critics of the Pentagon's stance, including many combat veterans, say the military is vastly overstating the tactical advantages of land mines. In a widely circulated open letter to President Clinton, 15 retired generals, including David C. Jones, former chairman of the Joint Chiefs, and Norman H. Schwartzkopf, commander of Allied forces during the 1991 Persian Gulf War — asserted that forsaking anti-personnel mines "would not undermine the military effectiveness or safety of our forces, nor those of other nations." Banning these weapons, the officers wrote, would be "not only humane, but also militarily responsible." [6]

The Clinton administration down-plays its differences with the supporters of an immediate and total ban. "We absolutely share the goal of a ban," says Robert L. Cowles, director of Humanitarian Demining and Anti-personnel Landmine Policy at the Pentagon. "Where we disagree is over strategy, tactics and timing. And the big reason we disagree is that we have to be very careful about risking the lives of American soldiers."

The Pentagon's claim that land mines protect American soldiers was recently challenged in a study based on Army documents by the Human Rights Watch Arms Project and the Vietnam Veterans of America Foundation. During the Korean and Vietnam wars, the study concluded, most mines used against U.S. troops came from captured U.S. stockpiles, creating a "blow-back effect" in which American soldiers were injured or killed by American weapons. [7] More recently, 34 percent of Americans killed in the gulf war were felled by land mines, while all five casualties among Americans serving with U.N. peacekeeping forces in Bosnia to date have been from land mines.

"Land mines took a devastating toll on our troops in Vietnam," says Muller, a former Marine lieutenant who was paralyzed from combat injuries in 1969. "I'm sitting in a wheelchair because I got shot, but before I got shot I got blown up by a land mine. In 90 percent of the cases where we had Americans getting blown up by these land mines, they were either our mines or were constructed with our components. Parts would regularly get recycled, or we'd lose track of where we'd put the damned things down and end up walking on our own minefields."

In Muller's view, Pentagon officials are ignoring battlefield realities in their defense of land mines' military value.

"With all due respect, Shalikashvili has never heard a shot fired in anger, and he'll be the first to admit that he's not a combat veteran," Muller says. "What we've got here is a classic situation where you've got guys that are in situation rooms theorizing about conflict. Then you've got schmucks like me out there walking around in

this stuff getting blown up, because this is an indiscriminate weapon; it doesn't differentiate between the bad guys out there and us."

In response to the Human Rights Watch report, the DOD said in a statement Aug. 1, 1997, that the report "fails to mention how we solved" the land mine problem. "Over 20 years ago, we developed self-destructing/self-deactivating mines that do not contribute to the humanitarian prob-

In the United States, leaders in the fight to ban land mines include Robert O. Muller, president of the Vietnam Veterans of America Foundation, center, Sen. Chuck Hagel, R-Neb., right, also a wounded combat veteran, and Sen. Patrick J. Leahy, D-Vt.

lem and save the lives of U.S. soldiers by eliminating the problems outlined in the study ... We appreciate their concern for the lives of U.S. soldiers, but unfortunately their efforts will ban the very system we developed to solve these problems."

If anti-personnel land mines have proved less than effective in protecting American soldiers in past conflicts, what about the future? The Clinton administration insists on keeping its minefield along the DMZ in Korea as an essential defense of American and

South Korean troops stationed there to defend South Korea from invasion by a million North Korean infantry soldiers poised just 30 miles away.

"There's significant risk of aggression in Korea," said the senior Defense Department official. "And the way that the opposition forces are postured, it gives a very small response time for us to react." He described the 1 million dumb mines currently deployed there as "essential in order to defend the peninsula." [8]

Some veterans of the 1950-53 Korean War say land mines would do little to deter a North Korean invasion. "Our experience has been that people like the North Koreans and the Chinese just move right through minefields," says Gard, who served in both the Korean and Vietnam wars. "So they take a few casualties on the way. They aren't going to stop because we've got anti-personnel land mines out there." A more effective strategy, he argues, would be to strengthen other weapons systems in the south. "My guess would be that the South Koreans could probably afford some more rocket launcher battalions and some field artillery battalions to compensate" for a land mine ban.

In any case, Gard says, the Pentagon's argument for the Korean exception in any land mine treaty is specious. "No one is proposing that they have to run in and dig up the mines that are in the DMZ," he says. "The proposals are for no new deployments. People are still getting blown up by mines that were planted

Durable, Deadly and Hard to Detect

Hundreds of versions of anti-personnel mines are produced by scores of countries around the world, including the United States. Most mines fit into one of a few basic designs. Because they are durable and hard to detect, the following mines are typical of the weapons responsible for the humanitarian land mine crisis today.

PMN
Manufacturing countries: Former Soviet Union, China, Iraq
Using countries: Afghanistan, Cambodia, China, Egypt, former East Germany, Iraq, Laos, Libya, Nicaragua, former Soviet Union, Vietnam, Namibia, Mozambique, Zambia, Angola, Somalia, South Africa, Eritrea, Ethiopia
The PMN has a spring-loaded firing device encased in a waterproof plastic body. Used extensively by the former Soviet Union and its allies, the PMN is possibly the most widely used anti-personnel mine in the world. Designed to be tamper-proof, the PMN killed or injured many deminers as they cleared Iraqi minefields in Kuwait after the 1991 Persian Gulf War.

PFM-1
Manufacturing country: Former Soviet Union
Using countries: Former Soviet Union, Afghanistan, former East Germany
The Soviet armed services first deployed this small, plastic, scatterable mine after they invaded Afghanistan. Known as a butterfly mine for the way it seems to flutter through the air, it consists of a pressure-fuzed liquid explosive in a green or sand-brown plastic case and has been used extensively to interdict trails and resupply routes in Afghanistan. The PFM-1 mine is a copy of the original butterfly mine, the U.S.-designed BLU-43 used in Southeast Asia, and is extremely effective in causing casualties. When stepped on, the mine typically blows off the victim's foot.

M16
Manufacturing country: United States
Using countries: United States, Angola, Eritrea, Ethiopia, Mozambique, Zambia
The M16, also known as a "bouncing Betty," is a bounding fragmentation mine and is designed to operate in two phases in order to inflict the greatest possible injury. When the fuze goes off, triggered by pressure or a tripwire, a black powder charge propels the mine into the air. When it's about waist-high, the main charge ignites, expelling cast-iron fragments in all directions.

SB-33
Manufacturing countries: Italy, Greece, Spain
Using countries: Italy, Afghanistan, Argentina, Greece, Iraq, Portugal, Spain
The Italian-designed SB-33 is a scatterable, blast-resistant, plastic-encased mine with low metallic content, making it hard to find with metal detectors. Its unique irregular shape is also designed to impede visual detection. The mine can be planted by hand or scattered. The pressure fuze is designed to resist explosive countermeasures. An electronic version incorporates an anti-handling device to deter mine clearance.

in World War II. So if, in fact, the mines that we planted near the DMZ in Korea are as good as the ones that we used in World War II, they ought to last a long time."

Should "smart" mines be exempted from a treaty banning land mines?

In addition to the exception for the mines in Korea, the Clinton adminis-

tration wants to deploy self-destructing "smart" mines whenever commanders deem them necessary. Because of the shift toward more flexible, mobile forces, the Pentagon's

Cowles says, "we made a decision about 20 years ago to go to a different type of land mine that would work more efficiently with our other systems. Because we often have to maneuver through the same areas ourselves, we didn't want a land mine that stays active forever. We wanted a land mine that turns itself off."

According to the Pentagon, the military has already destroyed about 1.3 million of its stockpiled, older, dumb mines. Except for a million dumb mines kept for use in Korea and for training purposes, Cowles says, 10 million smart mines account for the entire U.S. stockpile. There are three versions of U.S. smart mines. About 5 percent of them remain active for 15 days, Cowles says, while another small percentage lasts for 48 hours. Most, he says, stay active for only four hours.

Smart mines either self-destruct by blowing up or self-deactivate by turning off after the allotted period. As a safeguard, smart mines are equipped with 90-day batteries to run the fuzing mechanisms. "So if everything else fails, the battery runs out in 90 days, and the mine becomes a piece of junk," Cowles says. "It can't explode."

Some types of smart mines have proved faulty in tests, and at least 1,700 U.S. smart mines reportedly failed to self-destruct during the Persian Gulf War.[9] But Cowles says that flaws observed in the sensors of some early versions of smart mines have been overcome.

"We have tested 32,000 smart land mines, and we've had exactly one failure, and that one was an hour late turning itself off," he says. "And you can be sure that we've never built a battery that doesn't die. So we're comfortable with these mines' reliability. Remember, we designed these mines so that we could go through those areas ourselves, so we have to have a pretty high rate of confidence in them."

But even if smart mines were 100

After the Cold War began, users of land mines began targeting civilians as well as military targets.

percent reliable, critics say they still pose risks to civilians. "When aircraft are dumping tens of thousands of land mines into areas where refugee columns are passing close to where there is fighting, civilians are going to be trapped," Cooper says. "In perfect laboratory test conditions, maybe you can see the land mine on the ground, but if you're in a jungle or a paddy field or a desert, the mines are going to be hidden. You can imagine what would happen if you had a column of refugees in an unmarked smart minefield. Self-destructing mines would suddenly start exploding around them, and they would be literally trapped."

Critics say the U.S. insistence on a treaty exemption for smart mines will undercut negotiations for a total ban on land mines. "The United States is the only one really out there with smart mines," says Muller, who notes that the United States and Britain failed to convince other mine-producing countries, many of which lack the technology to make smart mines, to accept an exemption for these weapons in 1994.

"Country after country said, 'Are you crazy? Do you think we're going to make the world safe for U.S.-produced mines? Just because you have a high-tech version of this weapon, we're all supposed to come to you and buy your mine systems and [get rid of] ours?'"

"When the United States says our smart mines are not the problem out there because our smart mines self-destruct, that's fine and great," Muller says. "But if we don't give up our mines, they're not going to give up their mines. And the name of the game is to get rid of the mines. And the mines that we're going to run into out there are their mines."

Would a treaty banning anti-personnel mines be effective?

Typically, arms-control treaties provide for verification measures to ensure compliance. Signatories often have the right to conduct on-site inspections of each others' arms-production and storage facilities if they suspect violations of the treaty's terms. These provisions have built confidence among signatories that treaties such as the Strategic Arms Limitation Treaties (SALT I and II) are enforceable.

But intrusive inspections and strict enforceability are realistic goals primarily for nuclear weapons, which must be produced in large, easily identifiable plants and also require specialized vehicles and launchers to move and deploy. And no country can conceal a test nuclear explosion. A treaty banning land mines, on the other hand, would be all but impossible to enforce through on-site inspection or even satellite surveillance.

Supporters of a ban on all types of anti-personnel mines argue that strict verification measures are unnecessary to make such a treaty work. They point to the Convention on Chemical Weapons and other treaties to ban unacceptable weapons that are easy to hide. [10]

"Chemical weapons can effectively be made in someone's garage," Muller says. Like anti-personnel mines, he says, "They are cheap, easy to manufacture and available to anybody. But we now have an across-the-board ban on chemical weapons."

Treaties that ban weapons deemed inhumane by most societies rely more on moral suasion by establishing an international norm of acceptable behavior. "The power of a ban is the stigmatizing of this weapon, so that you wind up being labeled an outlaw if you use it," Muller says. "In the world community today, the game is economic development. And if you're not deemed an acceptable player, you can win your war but lose anyway because you won't be allowed at the table for the purpose of being integrated into the world market."

But the senior Defense Department official argues that it is unreasonable to expect the United States, whose smart mines are designed to avoid civilian casualties, to sign a treaty whose effectiveness relies on moral suasion. "Our systems don't contribute to the problem — neither the smart land mines nor the mines in Korea, which are behind a number of fences," he says. "They're asking that we give up these systems that don't contribute to the problem in order to set an example for the bad guys. We're supposed to risk the lives of American soldiers — men and women — in the hope that the bad guys who cause this problem will be inspired by that example to do the right thing. When has this ever happened? We're committed to a land mine ban, but our concern is that we don't risk soldiers while we're getting it."

The Clinton administration's main justification for pursuing a land mine treaty at the Conference on Disarmament, instead of in Ottawa, is that the Geneva negotiations would include the world's main producers of dumb land mines — Russia and China. And the administration contends that their participation would be essential to the effectiveness of any treaty.

But supporters of the Ottawa process say the effectiveness of a land mine ban depends more on the participation of mine users than producers. "Our view is that the most important nations to have on board are the ones that have used the damned weapons, such as Angola, Mozambique, Afghanistan and Cambodia — not China and Russia," says Williams of the international campaign. "If all the rest of the world is part of a ban treaty that does not permit them to use, stockpile, produce or transfer the weapons, where are China and Russia going to sell their mines anyway?" ■

BACKGROUND

Use in World Wars

The more than 100 million anti-personnel mines scattered around the world are the legacy, in a sense, of a form of static warfare that predates the invention of explosives. For millennia, armies have known that they could collapse an enemy's fortifications by digging under them rather than facing the risk of an armed assault. [11] Later, when stoked with gunpowder, tunnels became far more destructive, and were used extensively to destroy fixed targets in the Civil War and World War I.

World War I also saw the first widespread use of mines to impede the movement of troops and tanks, which could withstand much existing conventional artillery. The 1918 Armistice Agreement launched the first major counter-mine operation, requiring Germany to hand over maps and other documents identifying unexploded minefields. Counter-mine operations were slowed, however, by the lack of technology to detect and safely remove mines, forcing deminers to painstakingly probe and lift them from the ground one-by-one.

By the outbreak of World War II, land mines had been incorporated as integral parts of the arsenals and battlefield tactics of all parties to the conflict. They were especially valued as anti-tank weapons. Anti-personnel land mines were initially devised as booby traps to prevent enemy soldiers from removing anti-tank mines. In offensive maneuvers, anti-personnel mines also were used as "force multipliers" or "silent soldiers," laid along unprotected flanks of advancing troops to deter enemy attack and release soldiers for combat. Most land

Chronology

1980s More than a century after their introduction in warfare, anti-personnel mines are restricted by international treaty.

1980
The Conventional Weapons Convention limits the use of anti-personnel mines.

1989
Sen. Patrick J. Leahy, D-Vt., sponsors legislation that establishes a $5 million annual program to aid war victims, including land mine survivors.

———— • ————

1990s Support builds for a global ban on land mines.

1991
The Vietnam Veterans of America Foundation and Medico International, a German relief organization, establish the International Campaign to Ban Landmines.

Oct. 23, 1992
President George Bush signs a one-year moratorium, sponsored by Sen. Leahy and Rep. Lane Evans, D-Ill., on exports of U.S. anti-personnel mines.

1993
President Clinton signs a three-year extension of the land mine export moratorium.

1994
President Clinton calls for the "eventual elimination" of anti-personnel mines in a speech before the United Nations General Assembly, which en-dorses his goal. The Clinton administration announces a policy promoting the limited use of land mines and the development of "viable and humane alternatives" to anti-personnel mines. The U.S. and Britain fail to convince other countries to accept an exemption for "smart" mines in a land mine ban.

Aug. 4, 1995
The Senate approves a Leahy-sponsored amendment to the fiscal 1996 defense authorization bill imposing a one-year moratorium on the use of anti-personnel mines, except along international borders and demilitarized zones, beginning in February 1999. The amendment is later dropped in conference committee.

March 1996
The Pentagon announces a review of its policy on land mines. Then-U.N. Representative Madeleine K. Albright writes the president that land mines cannot be eliminated "in our lifetimes" unless current U.S. policy is changed.

April 3, 1996
Fifteen retired senior U.S. military officers call on President Clinton to ban anti-personnel mines.

May 1996
A review conference of the Conventional Weapons Convention in Geneva adopts a provision prohibiting non-detectable anti-personnel mines and requiring that some mines contain self-destruct devices by 2006. On May 16, President Clinton declares that the United States will "aggressively pursue" an international agreement to ban anti-personnel mines but will continue to use dumb mines in Korea and smart mines elsewhere until agreement is reached.

Oct. 5, 1996
Canada announces plans to negotiate a treaty banning land mines, to be completed in Ottawa in December 1997.

Jan. 17, 1997
The Clinton administration announces that it will seek to negotiate a treaty banning land mines at the U.N. Conference on Disarmament in Geneva. Clinton also permanently bans the sale of U.S. anti-personnel mines to other countries and promises to destroy all U.S. "dumb" mines.

June 12, 1997
Sen. Leahy and 59 cosponsors introduce the Landmine Elimination Act banning new U.S. deployments of anti-personnel mines, except in Korea, beginning in 2000. More than 160 members of the House call on Clinton to join the Ottawa initiative.

June 27, 1997
Ninety-seven countries meet in Brussels to draw up the Ottawa treaty supporting a total ban on land mines without the exceptions sought by the Clinton administration.

Sept. 1, 1997
Formal negotiations on the Ottawa treaty are scheduled to begin in Oslo, Norway.

Dec. 2-4, 1997
The signing ceremony for the land mine treaty is to be held in Ottawa.

Clearing Minefields Takes Time and Money

It would take 1,100 years to find and remove the more than 100 million mines scattered around the globe, according to the American Red Cross.

"Counter-mine activities — the things you do to breach an enemy's minefield for military purposes — involve the use of big equipment designed to get the military through a minefield in combat," says Robert L. Cowles, director of Humanitarian Demining and Antipersonnel Landmine Policy at the Defense Department. "They go through at high speed, under fire, in all weather. They can afford to take casualties, and they can miss some mines. When you're doing humanitarian demining, the standard is different. Children are going to play here, and you can't miss a mine. So we have to go much slower."

The United States has spent $137 million since 1993 on humanitarian demining operations. The Pentagon received $15 million in fiscal 1997 for its program, in which 276 U.S. military personnel are training indigenous people — 1,200 to date — in 14 countries to detect and clear mines. [1] American soldiers do not participate in the demining effort itself.

Demining techniques have changed little in decades. Typically, deminers mark off a small area where land mines are suspected and then painstakingly search the ground using metal detectors or fiberglass probes before moving to the next marked area. Dogs often are used to detect mines because they can smell the explosives from as far away as 10 meters. "They're more reliable than other detectors," Cowles says. "The only problem with the dog is that it can get tired on you very quickly, and the dog can't tell you he's tired. So you need a very experienced handler working with the dog."

The Pentagon is currently studying new technologies to speed demining operations, such as ground-penetrating radar. But critics say that effort is unlikely to improve the job of demining anytime soon.

"For the purpose of demining, the idea that there is any sort of silver bullet on the horizon is just crazy," says Robert O. Muller, president of the Vietnam Veterans of America Foundation. "What they need is a dependable, hand-held system that some dodo-brain out there who's getting hired for $50 a month is going to be able to use. The technology that will solve this problem is absolutely not there."

Some new systems, such as heavily armored threshers or bulldozers that can safely blow up mines, are useless in many settings where mines are concentrated. "You can't drive a bulldozer through the jungle," Muller says.

Once they find a mine, deminers in the Pentagon's program blow it up on the spot. "We don't teach defuzing and dearming mines because then they can be reused," Cowles says. "The problem with blowing them up, however, is that it scatters the vapor around. If you're using dogs, it makes the dogs less effective. It also creates environmental and other problems. So we're looking at a number of technologies to destroy the mines better."

Despite the technical obstacles to clearing existing minefields, Cowles says that the four-year-old demining program has already made a significant difference, contributing to a 94 percent drop in the death rate from mine injuries in Namibia and a 50 percent drop in some provinces of Cambodia.

To spread its mine-awareness message, the Pentagon distributes instructive comic books to children, posts signs near known minefields and gives out bandages stamped with graphic descriptions of ways to reduce blood loss for various types of mine injuries. The program also provides free information on the Internet to help deminers identify mines and find out how best to destroy them.

Critics say the Pentagon's demining effort has a lot of room for improvement. "The Pentagon will tell you they have doubled the amount of money spent on demining, or they have gone from serving 12 to 14 countries," says Robert G. Gard, a retired Army lieutenant general who supports a total and immediate ban on land mines. "The resources that have been allocated for that purpose have been relatively quite small, and you have to remember the mines are in 70 countries. Also, I think it is unfortunate that Americans are precluded from demining operations. That gives new meaning to the notion of leading by example."

Trained dogs are highly effective in detecting land mines, but most demining must be done by individual deminers.

Landmine Survivors Network/J. Rodsted

---

[1] The United States runs demining programs in Afghanistan, Angola, Bosnia, Cambodia, Costa Rica, Eritrea, Ethiopia, Honduras, Jordan, Laos, Mozambique, Namibia, Nicaragua and Rwanda. The National Security Council acts as coordinator for the Defense Department and the five other U.S. government agencies that participate in demining operations, among them the State Department and Agency for International Development. They plan to spend $54.7 million for demining and $20 million for research in fiscal 1998.

mines of both types were made according to a simple design — encased explosives equipped with firing devices, or fuzes, that could be set off either by the user from a remote position or by the target upon contact with one.

Land mines played a vital role in World War II, beginning in the North African campaigns, where mine warfare was successfully blended into highly mobile operations. Mines laid along the Egyptian-Libyan border helped the British stave off an Italian advance into Egypt in 1940. During the same conflict, Italian forces introduced the first scatterable mines, so-called "thermos bombs," which were dropped from the air over British positions. Both German and British forces laid vast quantities of mines in the operations that culminated in the 1942 halt of German Field Marshall Erwin "The Desert Fox" Rommel's offensive across the Sahara at El Alamein.

Mine warfare was even more vital in the outcome of hostilities on the Eastern front, where the Soviet military developed elaborate systems of mine deployment against the German advance, including radio-controlled mines, mines with delayed charges and a vast network of anti-tank ditches and minefields around Moscow. The Soviet Union deployed an estimated 222 million mines during World War II, making it the greatest practitioner of mine warfare in history. Soviet forces supplemented their highly effective wooden-box mine with vast quantities of captured German mines.

Advances in military demining tech-

nology improved counter-mine operations during the hostilities. Electronic mine detectors facilitated detection, and heavily armored tanks equipped with chain flails were sent through minefields to explode mines along a path wide enough for troops and vehicles. But at the July 1943 battle of Kursk, Soviet forces overwhelmed German counter-mine measures by blanketing the area with so many anti-tank and anti-personnel mines that they were able to repel the 3,000-tank German offensive.

A Moldovan soldier probes for mines last year during a training exercise on mine awareness at Camp Lejeune, N.C.

Aside from their exposure to German mines in North Africa, U.S. forces did not encounter heavy mine warfare in World War II until 1944. During the battle for Cassino, Italy, German mines caused 13 percent of American casualties. On D-Day, June 6, 1944, the U.S. and Allied landing in Normandy was slowed by about 6 million anti-tank and anti-personnel mines planted by Rommel's forces. Allied forces encountered even heavier minefields along the Siegfried Line before breaking through to the German heartland.

Overall, mines accounted for about 20 percent of all tank losses and 2.5 percent of battlefield deaths in the

European theater. Because the Japanese military did not rely heavily on land mines, mine warfare had little impact in the Pacific theater.

Korea and Vietnam

The outbreak of the Cold War was accompanied by a shift in land mine use in Europe from a battlefield weapon to a defensive barrier weapon that was deployed extensively along both sides of the Iron Curtain separating Eastern and Western Europe. But land mines also figured prominently in the regional wars that erupted throughout the nearly 50-year East-West standoff.

Mine warfare in the Korean War differed little in technology or doctrine from World War II. But because of the Korean peninsula's mountainous terrain, tanks were forced to travel along established roadways, enabling both sides in the conflict to effectively sabotage enemy advances. The United States was the main source of land mines in the conflict, but North Korean troops were able to capture large numbers of the U.S. weapons and use them against the U.S.-led U.N. force defending South Korea. According to the State Department, land mines accounted for about 4 percent of American casualties during the Korean War. North Korean forces and their Chinese allies suffered far

Savage Injuries to the Poorest of the Poor

The savage injuries that land mines cause kill most victims — 59 percent in Afghanistan, for example, according to Doctors Without Borders, a French volunteer organization. [1] Those who make it alive to the hospital typically suffer from one or more of three types of debilitating injuries: loss of the foot or leg from stepping on a blast mine; multiple fragment injuries of the legs and often the head, neck, chest and abdomen from triggering a fragmentation mine; or hand, arm, face and eye injuries from handling a mine of any type.

Survivors of mine blasts face an excruciating course of treatment. Blasts often drive dirt and shrapnel into the groin, causing abdominal infection. Where limbs have been blown off, bone infection also is common. Bones are often cut to the wrong length, or sharp pieces of bone may be left, aggravating stump tissues and making it hard to fit prostheses once the wounds have healed. Successive operations may be needed to drain postoperative infections. Within about two weeks of amputation, patients must begin physical therapy and walk with crutches to prevent muscle contracture and maintain upper-body strength.

Amputees whose postoperative conditions allow for fitting with artificial limbs can hope to resume a life of limited mobility. But for children, the most vulnerable of land mine victims, the initial fitting for prostheses marks only the beginning of a lifetime of painful therapies.

"A young child will need several different fittings as he or she grows older," said Lady Diana, Princess of Wales, who visited with land mine victims in Angola last January, "because the bones, although shattered, continue to grow through the stump." [2]

In addition to the physical distress, mine victims face often insurmountable obstacles to treatment. The International Committee of the Red Cross (ICRC), which has declared 1997 as the year of assistance for mine victims, places the cost of lifetime surgical and prosthetic treatment for each surviving land mine victim at $3,000-$5,000.

"This is an intolerable load for a handicapped person in a poor country," said Diana, who is campaigning for a land mine ban on behalf of the British Red Cross. "It is something to which the world should urgently turn its conscience."

To help poor countries defray the costs of treating victims,

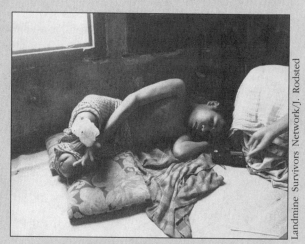

Cambodia has the highest concentration of land mines in the world; one of every 246 Cambodians has lost an eye or a limb to a land mine.

Landmine Survivors Network/J. Rodsted

the ICRC operates programs in 10 countries that provide rehabilitation and prosthetic devices for land mine victims. It has provided some 100,000 prosthetic devices for 68,000 amputees in 22 countries. The American Red Cross, an ICRC affiliate, is principally involved in the program in Cambodia, where it has provided prostheses for more than 2,400 people and nearly 1,000 wheelchairs each year since its program began in 1991. "That's a lot of new beginnings and new hope for Cambodian land mine survivors," said American Red Cross President Elizabeth H. Dole. [3]

The Vietnam Veterans of America Foundation operates prosthetics clinics in Vietnam, Cambodia, El Salvador and Angola — all countries where land mines are an enduring legacy of conflicts in which the United States played a significant, if not direct, part.

"I'm a little bit embarrassed to admit it, but when I was an infantry officer with the Marines, land mines never distinguished themselves as really a category of weapon," says Robert O. Muller, the foundation's president. "I went back to Asia some 20 years later and realized that, goddammit, these things are still out there, they never got put away in the armory, and they continue to take their toll. And the people we've wound up fighting are civilians, people trying to work the land or gather firewood. Then we realized that it was the poorest of the poor, those least able to deal with the disability, that were the ones who got blown up."

In 1991, Muller, who uses a wheelchair because of injuries he received in combat, and several other disabled Vietnam veterans started the prosthetics program in Cambodia.

"We didn't have a real history of being a rehabilitation organization, but it's something we'd lived through," Muller recalls. "A couple of our guys are multiple amputees from the Vietnam War. So we know a little bit about how much it can benefit you to gain mobility, that it's clearly doable. You can recover from these disabilities."

---

[1] Material in this section is from Doctors Without Borders/Médecins sans Frontières, *Living in a Minefield: An MSF Report on the Mine Problem in Afghanistan*, May 1997.

[2] Speaking at a June 17 press conference held by the American Red Cross in Washington, D.C.

[3] Speaking at the June 17 press conference in Washington, D.C.

more casualties because they employed the "human sea" tactic of clearing minefields by sending waves of troops ahead to be sacrificed. [12] Since the armistice in 1953, U.S. and South Korean forces have maintained a minefield along the DMZ separating North and South Korea.

Land mines were a major weapons system during the Vietnam War. The Viet Cong used mines against civilian and military targets in their campaign against South Vietnam leading up to the Vietnam War, while South Vietnamese forces used mines to protect bases and villages. Once U.S. troops were deployed in force in 1965, they used anti-personnel mines as perimeter defenses around airfields and other facilities. They also used both anti-personnel and anti-tank mines to deter infiltration along trails and as a defensive barrier along the DMZ.

As the war spread to Cambodia and Laos in the late 1960s and early '70s, the United States began deploying new, self-deactivating land mines that were scattered from aircraft or fired from artillery. Many of the newer mines were made primarily of plastic, making them harder to detect and clear. Another U.S. innovation during the Vietnam War was the Claymore mine, which is not included among the land mines to be banned by treaty because it is detonated on command instead of by random contact with a person or a vehicle.

As in Korea, Vietnamese forces relied heavily on appropriated enemy land mines, especially the Clay-

more and other U.S. ordnance. The chaotic conditions of jungle warfare also made it hard to accurately map defensive minefields. Because of these conditions and the extensive use of land mines, U.S. forces often fell victim to their own arsenals. As

To teach the children of Bosnia-Herzegovina to avoid the land mines that dot the landscape, DC Comics published "Superman: Deadly Legacy" in cooperation with UNICEF and the U.S. State Department. The comic is distributed through the Mine Action Center in Sarajevo.

many as 30 percent of the 41,840 American ground soldiers killed in battle in Vietnam were land mine victims. Moreover, about 90 percent of the mines that killed U.S. soldiers were American-made or contained U.S. components.

Land Mine Producers

An estimated 55 countries have produced anti-personnel land mines for decades; 35 of them have also exported the weapons. [13] As the world's largest arms exporter, the United States long played a major role in land mine production and export. [14] From 1985-1996, according to the United States Campaign to Ban Landmines, the United States produced more than 10 million new mines. The United States also supplied other countries, exporting 4.4 million anti-personnel land mines from 1969-1992. [15]

In 1992, the United States became the first major producer to stop exporting anti-personnel land mines, following the Oct. 23 enactment of a one-year moratorium on mine exports introduced by Sen. Leahy and Rep. Evans. The moratorium was later extended, and on Jan. 17, 1997, made permanent by President Clinton. Meanwhile, as of June 23, 59 countries had announced either a ban or a moratorium on land mine exports, and six others had declared that they were not currently exporting the weapons. Only five countries known to have exported mines in the past — Bosnia, Iran, Iraq, Serbia and Vietnam — had failed to stop mine sales. [16]

Despite the near-universal halt to the open trade in land mines, production of these weapons remains widespread. An estimated 35 countries continue to make them, ostensibly for domestic use. The major producers that are suspected of supplying land mines today are China, which claims that it does not export them currently, and Russia, which has declared a limited moratorium on exporting them. [17]

According to the Human Rights Watch Arms Project, land mines have not been produced in the United States since the end of last year, when the Pentagon completed its restoration of U.S. stockpiles drawn down during the Persian Gulf War. In January, President Clinton announced a cap on the U.S. inventory of land mines, which was later set at 11 million. According to a Pentagon document, there is no planned production of anti-personnel mines in the United States at least through fiscal 2004. [18]

The Arms Project has identified 47 U.S. companies that have been involved in the manufacture of anti-personnel land mines. Following the group's investigation of the matter, 17 companies agreed to renounce all future production. Motorola Corp., whose trademark was clearly visible in a Chinese land mine shown in a television documentary on the humanitarian crisis in Cambodia, was the first American company to publicly renounce its involvement in land mine production. Although the company's contribution was limited to electronic chips that also are commonly used in a number of consumer goods, Motorola agreed to take steps to ensure that companies it supplies also are not involved in land mine production.

Other companies that have announced they would no longer make mines or their components include Hughes Aircraft and AVX Corp. Seventeen companies, including such familiar manufacturers as General Electric Co., Lockheed Martin Corp. and Raytheon, have declined to renounce future involvement in land mine production, saying the decision on ending land mine use is up to the government. [19]

Human Rights Watch has launched a "stigmatization campaign" against the 30 U.S. mine producers that have either refused to renounce future

mine production or failed to respond to its query. Most of the targeted companies have only produced components for land mines, and company spokesmen have denounced allegations of their involvement in mine production. [20] One company, however — Alliant Techsystems, Inc. of Hopkins, Minn., has manufactured almost finished anti-personnel land mines, which are shipped to military facilities for final assembly. ■

CURRENT SITUATION

Targeting Civilians

Since the turn of the twentieth century, some 100,000 Americans have died in anti-personnel mine explosions. The vast majority of these casualties occurred in war. But today the overwhelming majority of the world's land mine victims are civilians who stumble onto these hidden weapons.

Some are relics of long-forgotten wars. "Some of the older mines were put in by forces many years ago," Cowles says. "If they kept records of where they placed the mines, they've long since disappeared." He tells of a 10-year-old Egyptian girl who was killed earlier this year and her brother, who was blinded, when they triggered a land mine planted by Rommel's forces during the Africa campaign in 1942.

But land mine use and the people who use them have changed in recent years, Cowles says. "Almost every one of the countries where mines are a major problem right now

are, or were, involved in internal conflicts," he says. "Most of the land mines going in now are not used by disciplined military forces, who use them in a patterned, regular way. They are using them indiscriminately, putting them anywhere and in some cases even targeting civilians. The change is that land mines have become a weapon of terror as much as a military weapon."

Countries where land mines are a leading cause of death illustrate the scope of the problem:

• **Cambodia:** More than two decades of war have left Cambodia with the highest concentration of active land mines in the world. One Cambodian in every 236 has lost an eye or a limb to a land mine. "In Cambodia, land mines were not as much a militarily significant factor for conventional warfare purposes, where you've got troops that have set up defensive positions, as weapons of terror," Muller says. "They're put under shade trees, where people go on hot days, they put them in water wells, around power lines, in pagodas. They're designed to intimidate and terrorize the population." More than 300 Cambodians are killed or maimed by mines each month.

• **Angola:** Some 15 million mines — more than the African nation's 10 million population — are deployed throughout the country. They were deployed most heavily over a 34-year period that included the 1976-1994 civil war between the pro-Soviet government and Jonas Savimbi's U.S.-supported UNITA rebels. Impoverished by the war's economic upheaval, civilians have been forced to search for food in mine-infested areas. "What is so cruel about these wounds is that they are almost invariably suffered where medical resources are scarce," said Princess Diana, who has become a highly visible supporter of a land mine ban since visiting Angolan mine victims

At Issue:

Would a total ban on anti-personnel mines undermine U.S. military strategy?

GEN. JOHN M. SHALIKASHVILI
Chairman of the Joint Chiefs of Staff, the Joint Chiefs and the 10 regional and functional commanders in chief (CINCs)

FROM A LETTER TO SENATE ARMED SERVICES COMMITTEE CHAIRMAN STROM THURMOND, R-S.C., JULY 10, 1997

We are seriously concerned about the new legislative proposal to permanently restrict the use of funds for new deployment of anti-personnel land mines (APL) commencing Jan. 1, 2000. Passing this bill into law will unnecessarily endanger U.S. military forces and significantly restrict the ability to conduct combat operations successfully. As the FY 1998 Defense Authorization bill and other related legislation are considered, your support is needed for the service members whose lives may depend on the force protection afforded by such land mines.

We share the world's concern about the growing humanitarian problem related to the indiscriminate and irresponsible use of a lawful weapon, non-self-destructing APL. In fact, we have banned non-self-destructing ("dumb") APL, except for Korea. We support the president's APL policy, which has started us on the road to ending our reliance on any anti-personnel land mines. Having taken a great step toward the elimination of APL, we must, at this time, retain the use of self-destructing APL in order to minimize the risk to U.S. soldiers and Marines in combat. However, we are ready to ban all APL when the major producers and suppliers ban theirs or when an alternative is available.

Land mines are a "combat multiplier" for U.S. land forces, especially since the dramatic reduction of the force structure. Self-destructing land mines greatly enhance the ability to shape the battlefield, protect unit flanks and maximize the effects of other weapons systems. Self-destructing land mines are particularly important to the protection of early entry and light forces, which must be prepared to fight outnumbered during the initial stages of a deployment.

This legislation, in its current form, does not differentiate between non-self-destructing and self-destructing APL. Banning new deployments of APL will prevent use of most modern U.S. remotely delivered land mine systems to protect U.S. forces. This includes prohibiting use of most anti-tank land mine systems because they have APL embedded during production. Self-destructing APL are essential to prevent rapid breaching of anti-tank mines by the enemy. . . .

Until the United States has a capable replacement for self-destructing APL, maximum flexibility and war-fighting capability for American combat commanders must be preserved. The lives of our sons and daughters should be given the highest priority when deciding whether or not to ban unilaterally the use of self-destructing APL.

GEN. DAVID C. JONES
Former chairman of the Joint Chiefs of Staff, and 14 other retired senior military officers

FROM AN OPEN LETTER TO PRESIDENT CLINTON, THE NEW YORK TIMES, APRIL 3, 1996

We understand that you have announced a United States goal of the eventual elimination of anti-personnel land mines. We take this to mean that you support a permanent and total international ban on the production, stockpiling, sale and use of this weapon.

We view such a ban as not only humane but also militarily responsible.

The rationale for opposing anti-personnel land mines is that they are in a category similar to poison gas; they are hard to control and often have unintended harmful consequences (sometimes even for those who employ them). In addition, they are insidious in that their indiscriminate effects persist long after hostilities have ceased, continuing to cause casualties among innocent people, especially farmers and children.

We understand that there are 100 million land mines deployed in the world. Their presence makes normal life impossible in scores of nations. It will take decades of slow, dangerous and painstaking work to remove these mines. The cost in dollars and human lives will be immense. Seventy people will be killed or maimed today, 500 this week, more than 2,000 this month and more than 26,000 this year, because of land mines.

Given the wide range of weaponry available to military forces today, anti-personnel land mines are not essential. Thus, banning them would not undermine the military effectiveness or safety of our forces, nor those of other nations.

The proposed ban on anti-personnel land mines does not affect anti-tank mines, nor does it ban such normally command-detonated weapons as Claymore "mines," leaving unimpaired the use of those undeniably militarily useful weapons.

Nor is the ban on anti-personnel land mines a slippery slope that would open the way to efforts to ban additional categories of weapons, since these mines are unique in their indiscriminate, harmful residual potential.

We agree with and endorse these views, and conclude that you as Commander-in-Chief could responsibly take the lead in efforts to achieve a total and permanent international ban on the production, stockpiling, sale and use of anti-personnel land mines. We strongly urge that you do.

in January. "For those whose living is the land, loss of an arm or leg is an overwhelming handicap which lasts for life." [21]

• **Afghanistan:** Until it withdrew in defeat in 1989, the Soviet army scattered at least 10 million anti-personnel land mines in its 10-year attempt to quash a civil war against the Soviet-backed government. Although both sides in the conflict used mines, the Soviet minefields around cities and military posts are the source of most civilian casualties. Among the most pernicious remnants of that conflict are Russian "butterfly" mines, small plastic devices that are designed to blow a victim's foot off. Scattered by the millions, these mines have taken an especially heavy toll among curious children who see them as playthings. "Children found they could pick it up and throw it several times and it wouldn't go off because it takes a slow pressure to set it off," Cowles says. "But they don't know how many times it's been thrown before, so one of these things can suddenly blow up in a child's hand."

• **Bosnia-Herzegovina and Croatia:** The civil war that broke out in 1991 in the former Yugoslavia has set a new standard for the use of land mines as weapons of terror. Some 3 million mines have been placed by all parties to the conflict not only on roads but in apartment houses, agricultural areas and churches. "In Bosnia they even mine cemeteries," Cowles says. "It's perfectly logical, if you want to target the families of a particular ethnic group, what better way to do it? You get exactly the people you're targeting. It's horrible,

but that's the sort of thing they do. This is not warfare as we know it."

The bright spot in this picture is the apparent decline of land mine placements in recent years. "Fewer land mines are going in now because there are no major organized mine-laying efforts by states," says the Defense Department official. "The biggest single factor in this trend

An American Red Cross outreach program provides prosthetic devices and wheelchairs for land mine victims in Cambodia.

probably is the work of the NGOs and the movement to ban land mines. It's far too soon to declare a victory, but the consciousness of people around the world has been elevated to the point where we are not seeing land mines going in the ground in the numbers we were."

Movement Grows

In countries plagued by land mine injuries, NGOs have almost single-handedly brought the land mine crisis to the world's attention. The International Campaign to Ban Landmines was launched in fall 1991 by

the Vietnam Veterans of America Foundation and Medico International, a German relief organization. "Both organizations were doing prosthetic work, and 99 percent of the victims are land mine victims," says Williams, who was tapped to coordinate the campaign for her experience in human rights activities in Central America. "Since then, the campaign has grown from just two to 1,000 non-governmental organizations in 55 countries. Like anything else, success breeds success, and because we have been so successful, people want to be part of it. This is the most fascinating work I've ever done."

The campaign is credited with a significant shift in public opinion about land mines. Its grass-roots effort to build support for an international ban on land mines has paid off with the suspension of exports and production by many of the world's mine producers. "The non-governmental organizations around the world have just done a tremendous job in highlighting what a terrible problem this is," Cowles says. "I think this is the first time we've seen such a broad-based, international partnership among non-governmental organizations, private voluntary organizations and so many national governments around a common goal."

On the diplomatic front, the first major avenue pursued toward a land mine ban was the 1994-96 round of negotiations to strengthen the land mine protocol of the 1980 Conventional Weapons Convention, which bars the use of inhumane weapons. Because the talks included China, Russia and other opponents of a ban, however, the new protocol, adopted in May 1996, fell short of expectations. It requires that all anti-personnel land mines be detectable and that certain of them be equipped with self-destruct devices. Land mine producers have nine years to comply with these standards.

Frustrated by the new protocol's limitations, Canadian Foreign Minister Axworthy launched a different strategy: fast-track negotiations for a treaty banning land mines altogether. At a meeting of 74 governments and numerous NGOs held in Ottawa last October, he invited all countries to join Canada in negotiating the ban and sign a treaty to that effect by the end of 1997.

U.S. Policy

The United States took an early lead in the effort to ban anti-personnel land mines, which has been championed for the past eight years by Sen. Leahy and the cosponsors of his legislation establishing a moratorium on U.S. exports. "This human disaster was described to me by a Cambodian I had in my office on a snowy winter afternoon at Christmastime in Vermont, one of the most beautiful times of year in our state," Leahy explained. "It became far less beautiful as he said, 'We clear our land mines in Cambodia an arm and a leg at a time.'" [22]

After introducing legislation in 1989 that established a $5 million a year fund to provide artificial limbs for land mine survivors, Leahy in 1992, along with Rep. Evans, sponsored a bill that imposed a one-year moratorium on anti-personnel mine exports. It was

later extended and then made permanent by President Clinton. On June 12, Leahy introduced legislation to ban new deployments of anti-personnel mines by the United States, except in Korea, beginning in 2000. Among the 59 cosponsors of the 1997 Landmine Elimination Act are all six Vietnam combat veterans in the Senate, including Sen. Hagel. *

"There is no U.S. senator in this body who supports more strongly the U.S. military," said Hagel, who was wounded in Vietnam by a land mine, as was his brother. "But we do not need indiscriminate killing machines like anti-personnel mines in order to defend [our] liberties." [23]

President Clinton was also an early leader of the effort to get rid of land mines. In a 1994 speech before the U.N., he called for the "eventual elimination" of anti-personnel mines. "Ridding the world of those often hidden weapons will help save the lives of tens of thousands of men and women and innocent children in the years to come," he declared.

But with his announcement last year that the United States would continue to use dumb mines in Korea and smart mines elsewhere, Clinton heeded the advice of his top military advisers and took a more cautious

stance. Muller recalls a White House dinner last year when he, together with former Gen. Jones and Gard confronted the president on the issue.

"I said, 'Mr. President, for God's sake, we've got Bob Dole cosponsoring everything Sen. Leahy's ever put out of the Senate, we've got Bob Dole's wife Elizabeth openly testifying before Congress as head of the American Red Cross to ban the weapon. We have America's retired military elite telling you this is the militarily responsible thing to do. We don't have a single member of Congress that's standing up and saying we need this weapon. What more can we do?'

"He said, 'I can't afford a breach with the Joint Chiefs.' The only thing Clinton cared about was his relationship with the Joint Chiefs. You can get into the psychology of that as easily as I can, but this is not what you want a commander in chief's posture to be. The fact that we have to move heaven and earth to get rid of this stupid piece of garbage is nuts."

Clinton's Jan. 17 announcement that the United States would pursue a land mine treaty in Geneva, however, has failed to undermine support for the Ottawa process among American proponents of a total ban.

"We already have a coalition of more than 225 non-governmental organizations just in the U.S. alone," says Mary Wareham, coordinator of the United States Campaign to Ban

---

* The other Senate Vietnam combat vets are: John Kerry, D-Mass., John McCain, R-Ariz., Charles S. Robb, D-Va., and Max Cleland, D-Ga.

Landmines, founded in the early 1990s to pursue the issue in the U.S. "It includes all of the major religious denominations in the country, all of the major humanitarian relief and development organizations — such as Save the Children and CARE — women's groups, children's groups, environmental groups such as Greenpeace, large grass-roots organizations like Peace Action, as well as the research-oriented groups like Human Rights Watch and the United Nations Association." ■

OUTLOOK

Moving Toward Ottawa

Supporters of a total and immediate ban on anti-personnel land mines are confident that the Canadian initiative will produce a treaty ready for signature in time for the scheduled Dec. 2-4 signing ceremony in Ottawa. After their most recent negotiations, conducted June 24-27 in Brussels, representatives of 97 countries signed a declaration supporting an Austrian draft treaty that would ban land mines without the exceptions sought by the Clinton administration.

"There will be a treaty signed in December, no question," Williams says. "Canada has put so much diplomatic effort into it, it's now obviously unstoppable."

The Clinton administration promised supporters of the Ottawa process that it would re-evaluate its position at the conclusion of the

Conference on Disarmament's most recent session on June 27. Aside from appointing Australian Ambassador John Campbell as special coordinator to establish a mandate for future negotiations on land mines, participants at the Geneva talks failed to make significant progress toward formulating a land mine ban agreement of their own.

Meeting in mid-July, Clinton's advisers on land mine policy were unable to reach a final decision on whether or not to join the Ottawa process. But the administration will have to decide before Sept. 1, when final negotiations on the treaty's provisions begin in Oslo, Norway. The effort to reach a policy on participation in Ottawa includes the National Security Council, DOD and State Department.

"I would hope that the United States will be there," Williams says. "But if they are not going to Ottawa in good faith to negotiate a simple, comprehensive ban with no exceptions, no reservations and no loopholes, I want them to stay away. I don't believe that the United States is so damned important that the rest of the world cannot establish a norm without it." ■

Notes

[1] From the Vietnam Veterans of America Foundation's Internet Web site, www.vvaf.org/land mine/elsa.htm.
[2] The International Campaign to Ban Landmines estimates there are 100 million active, deployed land mines. The American Red Cross puts the number at 120 million.
[3] From a Senate speech on June 17, 1997.
[4] From a White House statement, May 16, 1997.

[5] From a July 10, 1997, letter to Sen. Thurmond.
[6] From an open letter to President Clinton, The New York Times, April 3, 1996.
[7] Andrew Cooper, In Its Own Words: The U.S. Army and Antipersonnel Mines in the Korean and Vietnam Wars, Human Rights Watch Arms Project and Vietnam Veterans of America Foundation, July 1997.
[8] The official spoke July 3, 1997, at a Defense Department background briefing on anti-personnel mines. He agreed to be quoted, but not by name.
[9] From "Self-Destruct Mines," an undated information sheet distributed by the Vietnam Veterans of America Foundation. See also Cooper, op. cit., pp. 10-11.
[10] For background, see "Chemical and Biological Weapons," The CQ Researcher, Jan. 31, 1997, pp. 73-96.
[11] Material in this section is based on U.S. Department of State, Hidden Killers: The Global Landmine Crisis (December 1994), pp. 3-7.
[12] See Cooper, op. cit., p. 4.
[13] See Shawn Roberts and Jody Williams, After the Guns Fall Silent: The Enduring Legacy of Land Mines (1995).
[14] For background on the U.S. arms industry, see "Arms Sales," The CQ Researcher, Dec. 9, 1994, pp. 1081-1104.
[15] See the campaign's Web site at www.vvaf.org/land mine/uscbl-resource. htm.
[16] From a press release distributed on the Vietnam Veterans of America Foundation's Web site at www.vvaf.org/land mine/1997/brussels3.htm.
[17] Ibid.
[18] See Andrew Cooper, Exposing the Source: U.S. Companies and the Production of Antipersonnel Mines, Human Rights Watch Arms Project, April 1997, pp. 9-10.
[19] Ibid.
[20] See Philip Shenon, "Rights Group Presses Drive on U.S. Makers of Land-Mine Parts," The New York Times, April 18, 1997.
[21] Princess Diana, representing the British Red Cross, spoke in Washington at a June 17 press conference held by the American Red Cross, and appeared at a dinner to raise funds for land mine victims..
[22] From a Senate speech on June 17, 1997.
[23] From a Senate speech on June 17, 1997.

Bibliography

Selected Sources Used

Articles

Beardsley, Tim, "War Without End?," *Scientific American,* **June 1997, pp. 20-22.**

The introduction of sophisticated sensors to detect land mines is helping reduce the incidence of injury to deminers in some countries. But as long as these weapons continue to be deployed, high technology alone will not significantly increase the rate of mine removal.

Burkhalter, Holly, "Phantom Pain: Banning Landmines," *World Policy Journal,* **summer 1997, pp. 30-34.**

The advocacy director of Physicians for Human Rights, an advocacy group in Washington, D.C., describes the growing domestic pressure for a global ban on land mines and calls on the United States to join the "Ottawa process" that is expected to produce a ban treaty this December.

Pasternak, Douglas, "Wonder Weapons," *U.S. News & World Report,* **July 7, 1997, pp. 38-46.**

Pentagon research into exotic weapons using laser, ultrasound, microwave and other technologies may eventually yield non-lethal arms to replace anti-personnel mines if a global ban takes effect.

Will, George, "Parchment and Pacification," *Newsweek,* **July 21, 1997, p. 80.**

Even if the United States is allowed to continue using "dumb" mines in Korea and "smart" ones elsewhere, Will writes, a treaty banning land mines is against U.S. interests because the weapons are essential elements of the U.S. arsenal and military doctrine.

Reports and Studies

Cooper, Andrew, *Exposing the Source: U.S. Companies and the Production of Antipersonnel Mines,* **Human Rights Watch Arms Project, April 1997.**

According to this research group, 47 U.S. companies have been involved in the production of land mines, their components or delivery systems. Seventeen companies have agreed to the group's appeal to cease future production of these weapons.

Department of Defense, *Report to the Secretary of Defense on the Status of DoD's Implementation of the U.S. Policy on Anti-Personnel Landmines,* **May 1997.**

Issued a year after President Clinton issued his new land mine policy, this report to Congress states that non-self-destructing anti-personnel mines have been elimi-nated from war plans except for the Korean demilitarized zone.

Doctors Without Borders/Médecins Sans Frontières (MSF), *Living in a Minefield: An MSF Report on the Mine Problem in Afghanistan,* **May 1997.**

The French nonprofit group that provides emergency medical care in developing countries describes its efforts to treat land mine victims in Afghanistan. It advocates a ban on the weapons and calls for increased funding of demining and rehabilitation programs around the world.

In Its Own Words: The U.S. Army and Antipersonnel Mines in the Korean and Vietnam Wars, **Human Rights Watch Arms Project and Vietnam Veterans of America Foundation, July 1997.**

U.S. forces in the Korean and Vietnam wars suffered a deadly "blow-back effect" from their own land mines, as troops stumbled onto their own mines and enemy forces used captured American mines against U.S. troops.

Interagency Working Group on Humanitarian Demining, **U.S. Government Interagency Humanitarian Demining Strategic Plan, Department of Defense and Department of State, undated.**

Since 1993, when it was created by President Clinton, the seven-agency working group has set up programs to detect and clear land mines from more than a dozen countries.

Office of International Security and Peacekeeping Operations, Department of State, Hidden Killers: *The Global Landmine Crisis,* **December 1994.**

This report analyzes the presence of hidden land mines by region. It also assesses the status of demining programs by the United States and other countries.

Roberts, Shawn, and Jody Williams, *After the Guns Fall Silent: The Enduring Legacy of Landmines,* **Vietnam Veterans of America Foundation, 1995.**

Almost one-third of the more than 100 million active land mines that lie hidden in scores of countries around the world are in six countries — Afghanistan, Angola, Cambodia, Mozambique, Croatia and Bosnia-Herzegovina. This report assesses the scope of the problem in these countries.

Vietnam Veterans of America Foundation, *Banning Landmines: A Chronology,* **September 1995-July 1996.**

Compiled by the organization that spearheaded the international movement to ban land mines, this collection of newspaper and magazine articles as well as official documents and transcripts traces the movement's spread and its impact on U.S. military policy.

3   Defense Priorities

American pilots dropped some 23,000 bombs and missiles over Yugoslavia this spring. [1] Only about a dozen seriously missed their marks. Moreover, not a single U.S. serviceman died in combat during the 78-day mission, which succeeded in driving Serb forces out of Kosovo.

The statistics mean different things to different people. "The number of errant bombs that really missed and did damage was minuscule," says Air Force Col. Phil Meilinger, a leading expert on air power who teaches strategy and policy at the Naval War College in Newport, R.I. "In addition, we fought for two and a half months and suffered no deaths. That's just astonishing."

Seen from another perspective, however, the campaign was a disaster. "Unfortunately, we started so slowly and so late that the intervention didn't preclude the ethnic cleansing," says Don Snider, a retired Army officer who teaches political science at the United States Military Academy at West Point, N.Y. "So what did we accomplish? We beat up on a poor, little country and in the process alienated a significant number of our own allies and diminished our standing as a great power."

The jury is still out on the final outcome of NATO's campaign to halt Yugoslav President Slobodan Milosevic's persecution of ethnic Albanians in Kosovo. Serb forces have retreated, the refugees are going home and NATO peacekeepers are stationed in the beleaguered province. [2] But Milosevic remains in power, ethnic tensions continue to erupt and Kosovo's political future is far from certain. As military experts analyze NATO's mission in Kosovo, there is little con-

From The CQ Researcher, July 30, 1999.

sensus on its implications for future U.S. military operations.

Indeed, the continuing controversy over U.S. involvement in the Balkans is only the most recent chapter in an ongoing debate over the role of U.S. military power since the Soviet Union's collapse ended the Cold War nearly a decade ago. That single event changed the focus of American military strategy almost overnight, as the perceived threat to American security fragmented into a number of potentially hostile regional powers.

In response, the Pentagon has undertaken extensive reviews of military doctrine, modernized its arsenal and restructured its forces into a leaner, more mobile military capable of responding quickly to a number of crises in different parts of the world. The blueprint has evolved slightly as each conflict involving U.S. military forces since 1990 has left its imprint — including the 1991 Persian Gulf War against Iraq, the 1994 intervention to restore democracy in Haiti and the growing number of peacekeeping operations involving American soldiers around the world.

The recent campaign in Yugoslavia is likely to add its own stamp to the evolving blueprint for U.S. military strategy and doctrine. Virtually all aspects of U.S. defense are being re-evaluated: How many and what types of weapons are needed? How many personnel from which services

are required to carry out future military operations? And, of course, how much money will be needed to pay for it all?

"Kosovo shows why, even in the face of pressing current needs, we must set aside substantial sums for the future," said Defense Secretary William S. Cohen at a May hearing on President Clinton's fiscal 2000 defense budget request. "We must modernize our weapons, electronics and other critical systems because they need to be exceedingly accurate, fast, reliable and capable of giving U.S. forces an overwhelming advantage." [3]

The defense debate began heating up even before NATO intervened in Kosovo. Early this year, Clinton responded to warnings from the Pentagon of dangerously short supplies of military equipment and low troop morale by proposing the biggest defense-spending increase since President Ronald Reagan's military buildup of the 1980s. Clinton requested $264.9 billion in budget authority for defense in fiscal 2000, $14.4 billion more than Congress appropriated for defense last year. The Senate has approved $264.7 billion in defense spending, the House $268.7 billion; a conference committee will iron out the differences later this summer. They also provided $11 billion in additional funding for the Kosovo campaign, almost twice the administration's request.

Recent estimates of a higher than expected federal budget surplus in coming years may keep the funding spigot open for defense spending. But money alone will not ensure that the U.S. military is ready to face future threats to national security. Critics say the Pentagon has been slow to adjust its procurement practices to develop weapons and troop structures that are suited to the rapidly changing global environment.

Defense Priorities   39

America's Downsized Defenses: 1989 vs. 1999

U.S. defense capabilities in 1989 reflected the nearly 50-year Cold War arms race with the Soviet Union and its Warsaw Pact allies in Eastern Europe. After the collapse of the U.S.S.R. in 1991 eliminated the dominant threat to the United States, the U.S. military underwent a massive downsizing. The number of troops on active duty, for example, fell by more than one-third.

	1989	1999
Active-duty military personnel	2.2 million	1.4 million
Military bases	495	398
Strategic nuclear warheads	10,563*	7,958
ARMY:		
Main battle tanks	15,600	7,836
Armored personnel carriers	27,400	17,800
NAVY:		
Strategic submarines	36	18
Tactical submarines	99	66
AIR FORCE:		
Tactical fighter squadrons**	41	52
Long-range combat aircraft	393	206

* September 1990
** Squadrons contain from 12-24 aircraft.

Sources: Defense Department, Arms Control Association, International Institute for Strategic Studies (The Military Balance 1988/89 and 1998/99).

U.S. Air Force and U.S. Navy Photos

"All other things being equal, how much you spend on defense is not as important as how you spend it," says Richard N. Haass, director of foreign policy studies at the Brookings Institution, a Washington think tank. While most of the spending increases have been earmarked for new weapons, Haass says, not all are necessarily relevant. At the same time, closing underutilized bases around the country could save money. "Although there has been a problem of a lack of resources, there's also been a problem that people have not been willing to make some of the necessary decisions," he says.

Defense officials agree that base closings have not proceeded as quickly as they should have. "Since 1988 there has been a 37 percent cut in active-duty military personnel, but only a 22 percent cut in the number of major military installations," says Glenn Flood, a Pentagon spokesman. "So base closures haven't kept pace. Why pay for something we don't need, especially when weapons modernization and improved quality of life for our military men and women are a high priority?" But many lawmakers are reluctant to start another round of base closings, citing allegations that President Clinton in-

tervened during the last round in 1995 to save jobs at bases in vote-rich Texas and California. In May the Senate rejected a round of base closings proposed for 2001. [4]

Another aspect of the defense policy debate to intensify in recent months involves U.S. preparedness to defend both the United States and its overseas allies from weapons of mass destruction — nuclear, biological or chemical. Evidence of China's theft of information on U.S. missile technology from Energy Department research labs has raised concern about China's intentions not only toward Japan, Taiwan and other

American allies in East Asia but toward the United States itself. North Korea's successful test of a long-range missile in August 1998 only added to such concerns.

These developments, coupled with missile proliferation in Iraq, Libya and other so-called "rogue" states, have renewed support in Washington for the creation of a national missile-defense system to defend the United States from missile attack. [5] Congress this spring endorsed such a program, as has President Clinton, who long opposed the concept as a violation of the 1972 Anti-Ballistic Missile (ABM) Treaty with the Soviet Union. That agreement barred deployment of a broad-based missile-defense system in hope of slowing the U.S.-Soviet nuclear arms race.

First proposed by Reagan in 1983, the Strategic Defense Initiative (SDI) was quickly dubbed "Star Wars" by critics. They warned that a national missile-defense system was technologically unfeasible and politically dangerous because it had the potential to fuel another round in the arms race. Today, despite the broadening consensus for such a system, the controversy remains alive.

The intervention in Yugoslavia has added yet another element to the ongoing debate over defense policy. Most military experts agree that the air war demonstrated the superiority of U.S. precision armaments, not only over Yugoslav defenses but also over those of America's NATO allies, who were reduced to a support role for U.S. pilots, who manned most of the bombing missions.

But the very success of U.S. precision weapons over Yugoslavia may pose a dilemma for future military involvement by establishing a precedent for zero U.S. casualties and minimal "collateral damage," the military's term for civilian casualties.

"There is now a tendency in this country to not want to hurt anybody,

which is, of course, impossible in war," says Meilinger of the Naval War College. "Like a good cop, we're just supposed to disarm the bad guy and lead him away for trial."

As the world's sole, remaining superpower continues to define its military posture in the post-Cold War era, these are some of the questions about U.S. defense policy being asked:

Is the United States prepared for today's most likely military threats?

As the Soviet Union moved toward its final collapse in 1991, eliminating the dominant threat to the United States, the U.S. military underwent a massive downsizing. Nearly a hundred bases have been closed, and the number of troops on active duty has fallen by more than a third, from 2.1 million men and women in the late 1980s to 1.4 million today. Defense spending also has fallen, from $349 billion in 1991 to $265 billion in 1998, in constant 1998 dollars.

To deal with the post-Cold War security environment, Pentagon analysts devised a new doctrine calling for the pared-down U.S. military to be ready to wage two regional wars simultaneously. Under this scenario, the gravest threats were posed by relatively small, hostile countries with powerful military forces, such as North Korea and Iraq.

Just how well the United States has adjusted to the new security environment is a source of ongoing debate, especially on Capitol Hill, where the issue is a central consideration in the defense appropriations process. Many lawmakers say defense spending has fallen too far to ensure military readiness.

"Immediately after the collapse of the Soviet Union, there was no doubt that the United States could defend its interests in any situation," said Sen. Pete V. Domenici, R-N.M., chairman of the Senate Budget Commit-

tee. "We have squandered that moment and missed many opportunities to capitalize on our success. In fact, out of complacency and misplaced perceptions of the post-Cold War world, our defense capacity today is insufficient to match the threats to our national interests." [6]

The Clinton administration has accepted this argument, and this year proposed an increase in defense spending by $112 billion over six years. Republican lawmakers called for $25 billion more than the president requested. But some Democrats worry that the Republicans' additional increase would require offsetting decreases in other government programs, such as environmental protection, health care and crime-fighting. In a letter to more than 300 social-advocacy groups, 27 Democratic lawmakers warned on March 25 that the increases "go far beyond what is needed for our national security" and "will come at the expense of every other function of the federal government."

"If these groups don't join us in opposing giving the military a much bigger piece of a fixed budget," said Rep. Barney Frank, D-Mass., "then every group that seeks federal funding to deal with domestic problems other than education will be in the position of competing with, and trying to reduce funding for, other worthy programs." [7]

Some military experts say that, at least from a technological standpoint, the military is ready for any potential adversary. "I'm not sure I would have said this several years ago, but it's hard to argue with success," says Meilinger, who points to the versatility of aircraft such as the B-1 and B-2 bombers and the F-15 and F-16 fighters. "What has astounded me is the flexibility of the various platforms that we have. They can fight a nuclear war, a major conventional war against [Iraqi President] Saddam Hussein or

North Korea if they have to and still work against Milosevic and do them all reasonably effectively."

Others are somewhat more skeptical of the American arsenal's capabilities. "Readiness is a subjective judgment, because you always have to ask yourself, 'Readiness for what?'" says Haass. In his view, military planners have failed to fully prepare the United States to defend against the most likely threats. "We seem to be a little bit too focused on the more traditional scenarios that envision large set battles, say in the Persian Gulf or Northeast Asia," he says. "We don't seem sufficiently prepared for dealing with the smaller, Kosovo-like scenarios, where we find ourselves involved with increasing frequency."

During the Kosovo fighting, military leaders warned that they were running short on air-launched cruise missiles and other equipment. "We have a lot of personnel and traditional aircraft and tanks," Haass says, "but we seem to lack some pieces of the puzzle. Had there been another crisis, say, in the gulf, we would have found ourselves having to make some hard choices about where to deploy our JSTARS [surveillance and battle-management systems], AWACS [surveillance aircraft] and advanced munitions or smart bombs."

Other experts say the United States is not fully prepared to deal with an attack by nuclear, biological or chemical weapons. A bipartisan commission headed by former CIA Director John M. Deutch, for example, recently concluded that efforts to trace the proliferation of weapons of mass destruction overseas are disorganized and thus unable to provide the necessary degree of protection from at-

tack. [8] That report came on the heels of recent allegations of Chinese nuclear spying at the weapons labs run by the Energy Department.

Readiness also involves manpower, and some experts say the downsizing of the early 1990s has left the services with too few personnel to carry out their mandate. "Except for the Air Force, which is always in favor of buying more technology, the services have bigger manpower problems now than they have technology problems," says West Point's Snider, who says the Army will fall short of its recruitment goal in 1999 by 7,000

The F-15 tactical fighter jet has been in service for 20 years, but now the Air Force wants to replace it with a newer model.

servicemen for the second year in a row. Indeed, he says, only the Marine Corps is likely to meet its goal this year. "When all is said and done, you can have the best technology in the world, but it's useless if you don't have soldiers, sailors and airmen to use it."

Snider says the problem has arisen in just the past couple of years. He blames the booming economy, which is enabling young people to find other sources of college tuition than the grants they can receive to attend college after spending four years in the service.

"Young Americans are increasingly

deciding that somebody else can serve," he says. "They have plenty of jobs to select from, and they have so many more options today about how to get money to go to college. In any case, those grants have not kept up with the cost of education."

Is intervention in foreign civil wars an appropriate use of the U.S. military?

Even as the services have shrunk, U.S. military forces have been involved in a growing number of so-called "military operations other than war," including peacekeeping and relief missions. American troops are currently serving as peacekeepers in such far-flung places as Haiti, the Sinai Peninsula, Bosnia and now Kosovo. American pilots have been enforcing no-fly zones over Iraq since 1991, while other service personnel in Central America are providing relief in the aftermath of Hurricane Mitch and trying to halt the flow of illegal drugs to the United States.

In the view of some experts, the United States has acted too hastily in committing its military forces to noncombat roles over the past decade. The 1994 intervention in Haiti and the U.S.-led U.N. peacekeeping mission to Somalia in 1992 are often cited as examples where American intervention was ineffective or inappropriate. Haass adds to the list the recent campaign in Yugoslavia. "I don't think the problems in Kosovo were sufficiently bad in February or March to warrant our intervention," he says. "To put it bluntly, not every repression is a genocide, and I think we've got to be willing to draw distinctions or we will exhaust ourselves."

Haass adds that the decision to

U.S. Defense Spending

President Clinton's proposed $264.9 billion fiscal 2000 defense budget request represents the biggest defense-spending increase since President Ronald Reagan's military buildup of the 1980s. The increase reflects Pentagon warnings of inadequate supplies of military equipment and low troop morale. Republican lawmakers approved even bigger increases. Critics say that the possible benefits of defense-spending increases have been offset by the Pentagon's failure to develop weapons and troop structures suited to the rapidly changing global environment.

(In $ billions)

'75 '76 '77 '78 '79 '80 '81 '82 '83 '84 '85 '86 '87 '88 '89 '90 '91 '92 '93 '94 '95 '96 '97 '98 '99 '00* '01* '02* '03* '04* '05*

U.S. Air Force Photo

Note: All amounts are in fiscal 2000 dollars.

* Department of Defense budget request

Source: Department of Defense, March 1999

refrain from intervening in especially brutal wars, such as the civil war in Rwanda that killed a half-million people in 1994, may also be inappropriate. "We will want to intervene on some occasions, but not others," he says. "I just think we need to be more careful. I'm more worried about the temptation to intervene too often than too little."

Some lawmakers agree. "As a superpower, the United States should be shaping events, not reacting to them," writes Sen. Kay Bailey Hutchison, R-Texas. "Isn't America capable of drawing distinctions

among humanitarian emergencies, political realignments, civil wars and real dangers to U.S. national security? Not doing so is draining our own resources." [9]

Many military experts say the non-combat duties inherent in peacekeeping are causing serious morale problems among American servicemen. "Intervening where it's only marginally successful is wearing awfully thin with the military services," says Snider, who says this practice is contributing to the armed forces' difficulties in meeting their recruiting goals. "What really has changed in Haiti,

Somalia or Bosnia?" he asks. "Little has changed in any of those situations in any long-term sense. Young people are willing to serve for patriotic causes, and these small wars and interventions are simply of marginal interest to the public. We're not threatened in America by what's going on in the Balkans. We're morally indignant about it, but that doesn't translate into a propensity to enlist in the military service."

The one mission over the past decade that Snider says was an appropriate use of U.S. military might was the gulf war, where American forces led a military coalition that repelled the Iraqi invasion of Kuwait and ensured the uninterrupted supply of oil from the region. In that case, he says, U.S. energy security was clearly at stake. "As crude as it sounds, we're a greedy nation," he says. "We know we use two-thirds of the world's consumption of oil, but we enjoy it."

But the aftermath of the allied victory against Iraq is taking a toll on American servicemen, particularly Air Force pilots who enforce the no-fly zones over Iraq. "Day after day, they're out there flying 'orbits,'" says Meilinger. "For the past eight or nine years, they've just been drilling holes in the sky. Pilots get no training out of it, and they hate that. I've been in the Air Force for 29 years, and we've always been willing to pay a very heavy price to do what we feel is important for the nation, but when you're doing something that seems unnecessary you begin asking yourself, why am I doing this?"

Meilinger attributes the shortage of pilots in the Air Force to the "operations tempo," the pace of deployments in Iraq and other locations where U.S. forces are required to carry out noncombat operations. "The operations tempo now is very high, and as a consequence people are voting with their feet," he says. "If you're sitting there as a pilot living in a tent in the desert and you're gone six months out of the year and missing your daughter's birthday or graduation, you think to yourself, I could go to Delta Airlines, where I'd make twice as much money, work half

as long and see my family once in a while."

President Clinton continues to defend the use of military forces for peacekeeping and humanitarian purposes. Indeed, he recently appeared to advocate a further expansion of those roles for the military. "There will be some days you wish you were somewhere else," the president told American soldiers assigned to peacekeeping duties in Kosovo. "But never forget, if we can do this here, we can then say to the people of the world, whether you live in Africa or Central

The Army's Theater High Altitude Area Defense (THAAD) system, built to seek out and destroy incoming missiles, failed to destroy test missiles in its first six tests.

Lockheed Martin Corp.

Europe or any other place, if somebody comes after innocent civilians and tries to kill them en masse because of their race, their ethnic background or their religion, and it's within our power to stop it, we will stop it." [10]

Should the United States develop a national missile defense system?

Many scientists dismissed President Reagan's 1983 Strategic Defense Ini-

tiative, geared to an all-out nuclear attack by the Soviet Union, as technologically unfeasible. At the end of the 1980s, as the Cold War was coming to an end, Sen. Sam Nunn, D-Ga., then chairman of the Senate Armed Services Committee, and other lawmakers proposed developing a less ambitious, technologically more feasible system aimed at defending against an accidental or unauthorized Soviet missile launch. President George Bush supported such a system, to be expanded as the technology evolved. Now, with the threat of a nuclear attack by Russia less likely, the focus of a national missile-defense system has broadened to include a number of countries that are rapidly developing missile capabilities of their own, including Iran, Iraq, Libya and North Korea.

The Clinton administration, initially skeptical of the project, has become more supportive of a national missile defense since North Korea successfully tested a long-range missile in August 1998; it reportedly plans another test this summer. [11] Adding to those concerns, a panel of lawmakers investigating apparent Chinese thefts of U.S. nuclear technology, led by Rep. Christopher Cox, R-Calif., recently concluded that China will have the capability to threaten the United States with nuclear missiles as early as 2002. [12]

Clinton announced in his State of the Union address in January that the United States would pursue a national missile-defense system. The administration said it would decide what type of system to develop by June

2000. But Congress tried to speed up the timetable, passing legislation this spring calling for deployment of a limited missile-defense system "as soon as technologically possible." Clinton, who vetoed a similar measure in 1995, signed this year's version. But a heated debate continues to rage over the technological feasibility and political advisability of developing such a defense system. (*See "At Issue," p. 53*.)

Although defense technology has advanced considerably since SDI was first proposed, critics say it cannot provide the kind of "nuclear umbrella" over the United States that Reagan envisioned, in part because it is generally easier to overcome defensive systems of any kind than it is to make them impregnable.

John Pike, director of space policy at the Federation of American Scientists, points to NATO's victory over Yugoslavia to illustrate this principle. "Serbian air defenses were about as good as they get," he says. "But their air defenses were ineffective, not because they didn't work at all, but because NATO's countermeasures were more effective. Obviously there's a difference between the sort of countermeasures you'd use for air defense and those you'd use for missile defense, but both have the same set of problems — find the target and hit it."

Those problems have plagued the missile defense program since its inception. Interceptors built to seek out and destroy incoming missiles have failed repeatedly to hit their mark. One interceptor under development, at a cost of $4 billion to date, the Army's Theater High Altitude Area Defense (THAAD) system, failed to destroy test missiles in its first six tests.

But supporters of missile defense took heart from a test launch on June 10, when a THAAD missile finally intercepted and destroyed a ballistic missile. "Today's successful intercept is the one that we have been waiting for," said Rep. Curt Weldon, R-Pa., chairman of the House Armed Services Research and Development Subcommittee. [13]

But critics like Pike remain skeptical. "The problem we've got right now is that we've got interceptors that have been known to work on occasion, but certainly have not been demonstrated to work under ideal conditions with any degree of predictability," he says.

Another issue in the debate over missile defense is the status of the 1972 ABM Treaty between the United States and the former Soviet Union. The treaty allows deployment of up to 100 ground-based interceptor missiles at a single site, but prohibits mobile, ground-based interceptor missiles as well as sea-, air- or space-based interceptors.

The Clinton administration says that preserving the ABM Treaty is important to U.S. security and that any changes to the treaty needed to accommodate a future U.S. national missile defense should be negotiated with Russia. [14] At their June 20 summit in Cologne, Germany, Clinton and Russian President Boris N. Yeltsin agreed to try to negotiate changes to the treaty that would enable both countries to mount a limited missile defense.

Supporters of the original SDI approach tend to dismiss the ABM Treaty as an outdated relic of the Cold War. "The ABM Treaty was crafted at a time when nobody but the Soviet Union had missiles," says Frank J. Gaffney Jr., director of the Center for Security Policy in Washington and former Defense Department official who led the Reagan administration's push for developing SDI.

"It's daft to think that deterrence of the kind that we knew and relied upon during the Cold War can work in a world where the mullahs of Iraq think the shortcut to paradise is killing infidels and where the lunatic regime of North Korea is destroying millions of people by famine as it pursues efforts to build up missile and nuclear weapons capability," Gaffney says. "It is the height of irresponsibility to think that an ABM Treaty with a country that no longer exists is of any value in protecting the people of the United States against these kinds of threats."

Indeed, Gaffney says, the Clinton administration's reluctance to abandon the ABM Treaty is a major cause of one of the missile-defense program's biggest technological obstacles — the decision to base it on land, specifically at an existing missile installation at Grand Forks, N.D. "Anybody who has the most elementary understanding of the task of defending the country against missile attack understands that the optimal way to do this is from space," Gaffney says. "The next best and the fastest way to do it is from the seas. The least effective and most costly way is from the ground. And the idea of defending the country from North Dakota is frankly absurd." Such an installation would be unable to stop a short-range missile attack against Alaska, Hawaii or much of the continental United States, he says.

Gaffney says a faster, cheaper and more effective alternative is already under development in the Navy's 22-ship Aegis fleet, a theater missile-defense system designed to protect overseas U.S. forces and allies against missile attacks of limited scale. "Thanks to the investment the country has made over the past 29 years, the Aegis fleet air-defense system, the infrastructure for a global missile defense has already been bought, paid for and deployed," he says. "It does need to be modified, but the modifications are trivial compared to the costs of building a system from scratch, which is what you would have to do under any of the alternative approaches."

Missile-defense critics say that diplomacy is still the best defense against missile attack, given the technological limitations. "Will the thing ever work well enough that we could get into a nuclear war with, say, North Korea, and operate under the assumption that there would be no way that they could attack us with their long-range missiles?" Pike asks. "No. The only thing that's going to prevent North Korea from attacking us is the fact that they know that if they attack us we will blow them up, and they don't want to get blown up."

But missile-defense supporters say such logic may not deter such hostile leaders as North Korea's Kim Jong Il, Libya's Muammar el-Qaddafi or Iraq's Saddam Hussein. "It's hard to put yourself in the head of a madman," says Gaffney. "But I think you cannot rule out the possibility that a lunatic like Kim Jung Il may decide to launch a missile attack against the United States as a final spasm of hatefulness and revenge as his own team is going down." ∎

BACKGROUND

Cold War Strategy

T he military strategy that prevailed throughout the nearly 50-year Cold War focused primarily on "containment," or preventing Soviet expansion beyond the borders of the Soviet Union and its Warsaw Pact allies in Eastern Europe. To apply this policy, the U.S. military deployed large numbers of soldiers, airmen, heavy artillery and tanks, notably in West Germany and other countries

of the U.S.-led NATO alliance. Navy carriers and warships were also stationed in the Mediterranean, western Pacific and Indian Ocean to protect U.S. allies such as Japan, southern Europe and major oil-producing countries of the Middle East. Long-range Air Force bombers and fighters were stationed in the United States and at a number of overseas bases.

A distinguishing characteristic of the Cold War was the development of nuclear weapons on both sides, sparking a nuclear-arms race that was only slowed by the negotiation of the U.S.-Soviet Strategic Arms Limitation Treaties (SALT) and Strategic Arms Reduction Treaties (START) of the 1960s-80s. [15] While it consumed billions of dollars, the arms race is thought to have helped deter the outbreak of hostilities between the two superpowers. Under the principle of "mutual assured destruction," each side understood that a direct attack by one would likely unleash a punishing counterattack by the other, ending in a rain of nuclear missiles with possibly catastrophic results for the planet.

The Soviet Union's collapse in 1991 largely eliminated the rationale for the United States' postwar military strategy. The former Warsaw Pact allies cast aside their communist governments and adopted Western democratic systems. Some applied for membership in the NATO alliance and gained admittance (Poland, Hungary and the Czech Republic). [16] Russia, the Soviet Union's successor, was in economic disarray and by itself lacked the resources to maintain its once formidable military forces. As a result, the United States almost overnight found itself the world's sole superpower.

Having "won" the Cold War and facing no major adversary, the United States was poised to reap a "peace dividend" in the form of lower defense spending. The number of ac-

tive-duty military personnel was reduced. Bases were closed. Major defense contractors were forced to merge with their competitors to cope with the sudden fall in orders for weapons and other equipment. In 1994, for example, Lockheed Corp., the second-largest weapons producer, merged with Martin Marietta Corp., the third-largest contractor, to become Lockheed Martin Corp. By 1999, the defense budget of $270 billion was down $100 billion from the 1980s average when inflation is taken into account. [17]

Gulf War Lessons

F or all the euphoria that greeted the Cold War's end, the peace dividend was not as big as many had initially anticipated. As the sharp division between the superpowers' spheres of influence fell away, regional powers emerged to try to fill the vacuum. After Saddam Hussein invaded neighboring Kuwait in August 1990, the United States led a United Nations-endorsed coalition of forces to expel the Iraqis. In that first major conflict of the post-Cold War era, air, land and sea forces were called into play just as in World War II, the Korean War and the Vietnam War.

But the gulf war marked the first combat test of the most recent U.S. military technology, notably precision-guided "smart" bombs able to hit targets at greater distances than ever before, thus providing unprecedented margins of safety for U.S. forces. The Iraqi army, the fourth largest in the world at the time, was routed in a matter of days with few allied casualties. Of about 700,000 American troops deployed to the region, 148 soldiers were killed by hostile fire.

Chronology

1970s *The Cold War enters its third decade and continues to dominate U.S. defense policy.*

1972
The United States and the Soviet Union sign the Anti-Ballistic Missile (ABM) Treaty.

1977
A protocol to the 1949 Geneva Convention, which the United States does not ratify, prohibits "indiscriminate" methods of combat or attacks that cannot be "limited" to military objectives.

——— • ———

1980s *Responding to calls for higher defense spending, President Reagan launches the "rearming of America."*

1983
With his Strategic Defense Initiative (SDI), Reagan calls for the development of a space-based missile-defense system to defend the United States from a Soviet nuclear attack. Critics dub the project "Star Wars."

——— • ———

1990s *The Cold War's end prompts a sweeping review of U.S. defense policy.*

1991
President George Bush's National Security Strategy calls for force reductions, cuts in defense spending and the creation of a "minimum essential military force — the Base Force."

Jan. 16-March 6, 1991
A U.S.-led United Nations force expels Iraqi forces from Kuwait.

Dec. 25, 1991
Mikhail S. Gorbachev gives up the presidency of the U.S.S.R., marking the official demise of the Soviet Union.

Sept. 1, 1993
The Clinton administration calls on the U.S. military to prepare to fight two regional powers simultaneously.

1994
In one of many mergers of defense contractors sparked by the fall in weapons procurement, Lockheed Corp. and Martin Marietta Corp., merge to form Lockheed Martin.

March 25, 1994
U.S. forces withdraw from Somalia after a failed peace-keeping mission.

Sept. 19, 1994
U.S. forces occupy Haiti to restore to power the island nation's democratically elected president, Jean-Bertrand Aristide.

1995
Citing the ABM Treaty's restrictions, President Clinton vetoes a measure calling for the development of a national missile-defense system.

1996
Lawmakers try to accelerate the pace of military reforms with the National Defense Authorization Act, requiring the Pentagon to conduct a "complete re-examination of the defense strategy."

May 1997
The Quadrennial Defense Review (QDR) calls for further cuts in U.S. forces, which by 2002 are expected to total about two-thirds of their Cold War levels. The review also reiterates the call for planning to fight two overlapping regional wars.

December 1997
Clinton shifts U.S. nuclear strategy by ordering the Pentagon to adopt a more flexible stance for its air-, land- and submarine-launched nuclear weapons and use them to deter smaller powers from deploying weapons of mass destruction.

Aug. 31, 1998
North Korea successfully tests a long-range missile capable of carrying weapons of mass destruction as far as the U.S.

1999
The defense budget amounts to $270 billion, down $100 billion, after inflation, from the average in the 1980s.

January 1999
Clinton announces in his State of the Union address that the United States will pursue a national missile-defense system.

May 20, 1999
The House passes legislation, identical to a Senate-approved measure, calling for deployment of a limited missile-defense system "as soon as technologically possible."

June 11, 1999
U.S. and other NATO forces enter Kosovo as part of a peace-keeping mission after an 11-week air war against Yugoslavia.

"At the time the war started, everybody felt that the Iraqis were really tough, but they never had a chance," says Meilinger of the Naval War College. As a result, he says, the gulf war forced potential adversaries of the United States to alter their military strategy. "What that victory did was deter war," he says. "From that point on, everyone who thinks about fighting the United States with conventional weapons knows they don't have a chance if they use traditional, heavy armies consisting of lots of tanks, heavy artillery and vehicles put together in large formations."

At the same time, political and ethnic tensions erupted into open hostilities in a number of countries, such as Rwanda and Yugoslavia. As these hostilities intensified and threatened to destabilize entire regions, the United States increasingly intervened both diplomatically and militarily, with U.S. forces often serving as peacekeepers to oversee U.S.-brokered agreements.

Evolving Strategy

With a series of sweeping reviews, the Pentagon revised its strategy and restructured U.S. military forces to adjust to the changing world environment. In place of a force designed to face a single rival superpower, military planners have pared down the size of U.S. forces, closed military bases both at home and abroad and reduced procurement of weapons. But the focus of the force realignment has evolved over the decade.

The first review came in 1991, when President Bush's National Security Strategy called for the creation of a "minimum essential military force — the Base Force." This strategy emphasized the continued deployment of a "forward presence" of U.S. troops

and equipment close to potentially unstable regions. The main innovation of the new plan was its call for force reductions and cuts in defense spending. But because it was based on a perceived need to contain regional threats, including a conventional invasion of Europe, the Base Force strategy was criticized as outdated and excessively reliant on Cold War logic. [18]

A slightly different scenario

A U.S. soldier searches a Kosovo Liberation Army member in Urosevac, Kosovo, on June 20, 1999. KLA members cannot carry weapons under the NATO cease-fire with Yugoslav President Slobodan Milosevic.

Reuters/Radu Sigheti

emerged from the Pentagon's Bottom-Up Review, released on Sept. 1, 1993, during Clinton's first year in office. Taking their cue from the recent war against Iraq, then-Defense Secretary Les Aspin and his advisers decided the most likely worst-case scenario for the U.S. military would be to face two such adversaries simultaneously.

To deal with each of the two "major regional contingencies" envisioned by the review, the experts proposed a force comprised of four

or five Army divisions, a similar number of Marine brigades, four or five Navy carrier battle groups, 10 Air Force fighter wings, as many as 100 bombers, and special forces troops. Each of the two forces would be about the same size as the one that had prevailed in the gulf war.

But lawmakers, dissatisfied with what they considered the slow pace of military reforms, sought to accelerate the process with the 1996 National Defense Authorization Act. It required the Pentagon to conduct a "complete re-examination of the defense strategy, force structure, force modernization plans, budget plans, infrastructure and other elements of the defense program and policies with a view toward determining and expressing the defense strategy of the United States, and establishing a national defense program, as we enter the 21st century." [19]

The Quadrennial Defense Review (QDR) was completed in May 1997. Like earlier strategy reviews, it called for further cuts in U.S. forces, which by 2002 are expected to total about two-thirds of their Cold War levels. The review also reiterated the call for planning to fight two overlapping regional wars, specifically to repel invasions of South Korea and a Persian Gulf ally. Under this scenario, rapid-deployment forces would be immediately mobilized to shore up allied defenses while air- and ground-based long-range weapons would be used to weaken the invading army. After about three months, U.S. ground reinforcements would be ready to launch a major counteroffensive,

The Pentagon's Weapons Dilemma: Upgrade or Replace?

The changing nature of military threats over the past decade has forced defense planners to take a hard look at the U.S. arsenal. During the previous half-century, the Pentagon acquired weapons — heavy battle tanks, nuclear submarines, long-range bombers — suited for conducting a major, conventional land war in Europe or a nuclear exchange with the Soviet Union.

With the disintegration of the U.S.S.R. in 1991, however, "rogue" states such as Iraq, Libya and North Korea have emerged as the main threats to U.S. security. Already well-armed, they have stepped up their procurement of modern weaponry and development of nuclear and biological weapons of mass destruction.

To counter these new threats, the Pentagon is mothballing or upgrading outmoded weapons and developing new ones from scratch. But the decision to upgrade or replace a weapons system is often hotly debated. Billions of dollars and thousands of jobs are often at stake, not to mention the political careers of lawmakers whose constituents include large defense contractors.

The debate was renewed most recently when the House voted on July 22 to cancel funding for the Air Force's biggest procurement priority, the F-22 Raptor, a new fighter jet slated to replace the aging F-15. Defense officials argued that the new plane — faster, more agile and equipped with stealth technology to evade enemy radar — is essential to achieving U.S. dominance in the air and ideal for the kinds of rapid-response intervention that has become the norm in the post-Cold War era.

But Rep. Jerry Lewis, R-Calif., chairman of the Defense Appropriations Subcommittee, persuaded fellow lawmakers that the new plane is not only too expensive but also redundant because the Pentagon is also developing two other fighter jets, the F/A-18E/F for the Navy and the Joint Strike Fighter for the Navy, Air Force and Marines. In place of the F-22, critics say the Air Force should make do with modifications to the F-15 and F-16, both more than 20 years old.

The House vote against the F-22 caught Defense officials off guard. Never had Congress canceled a weapons system that was so close to production and with so much money — $20 billion — already invested in it. The first six F-22s — out of 336 envisioned by the Pentagon — were scheduled to roll off the assembly line in 2005.

"Critics of the F-22 make much of its cost," writes the Air Force's historian, Richard P. Hallion, "but that cost . . . buys capabilities that ensure the survival of those who have volunteered to put themselves at risk in their nation's service."[1]

Lewis and other F-22 critics insisted that cancellation was not intended to eliminate the plane altogether but to give lawmakers time to study the alternatives. Pentagon officials will now focus their lobbying efforts on the Senate, which earlier approved the full $1.8 billion requested by the administration to buy the first six F-22s in its version of the defense-spending bill. With 27,000 potential jobs at stake in 46 states, the F-22 program has many supporters. The final decision will come with a conference committee that will iron out the differences between the two bills later this summer.

Defense planners and lawmakers face a similar dilemma in deciding whether to upgrade other weapons or scrap them for new models.[2] Several major weapons systems are under scrutiny including the:

❑ **M-1 tank and Bradley armored troop carrier** — The 70-ton M-1 and the 30-ton Bradley are vestiges of Cold War combat scenarios, such as a Soviet land attack in Europe. But they are too heavy to be quickly transported in large numbers to far-flung areas of conflict today. They also are ill-suited for steep terrain, as in Yugoslavia. The Army is upgrading both vehicles with night-vision gear and digital-communications equipment to enable troops to better coordinate their movements and monitor those of the enemy. But it also is collaborating with the Pentagon's Defense Advanced Research Projects Agency to develop lighter, more versatile combat vehicles.

❑ **Apache helicopter** — Congress has approved funding to equip the much-vaunted assault helicopter, which carries anti-tank missiles, with radar to find ground targets in bad weather and upgrade its electronic gear. The Pentagon is also developing a smaller, armed helicopter, the Comanche, that will incorporate radar-evading "stealth" technology to make it less vulnerable to missile attack than the Apache.

❑ **B-2 stealth bomber** — Designed to carry nuclear bombs from the United States to the Soviet Union, the B-2 was used this spring to drop conventional, precision-guided bombs on targets in Yugoslavia. Congress has approved upgrades in the bomber's communications gear to improve its ability to locate targets.

❑ **Crusader mobile cannon** — The Army plans to deploy this new vehicle in 2005, but lawmakers have objected, saying it is no lighter than the weapon it would replace. But they relented after officials convinced them that new communication links in the Crusader will make it more effective on the battlefield.

---

[1] Richard P. Hallion, "Why We Need the F-22," *The Washington Post*, July 22, 1999.

[2] See Pat Towell, "Lawmakers Urge Armed Forces to Focus on High-Tech Future," *CQ Weekly*, June 26, 1999, pp. 1564-1566.

repel the invasion and possibly invade enemy territory to destroy the aggressors. [20]

Nuclear strategy also has shifted. Instead of aiming missiles at Russia and other former Soviet republics, as it did during the Cold War, the United States has adopted a more flexible stance for its air-, land- and submarine-launched nuclear weapons. In December 1997, Clinton ordered the Pentagon to plan for using its nuclear arsenal to deter smaller powers from using weapons of mass destruction. [21] ∎

CURRENT SITUATION

Lessons From Kosovo

As in the gulf war eight years before, the allies owed their victory in large part to the superiority of U.S. weaponry. Despite widely publicized mistakes, such as bombing the Chinese Embassy in Belgrade, B-2 bombers and satellite-guided bombs hit targets with unprecedented accuracy.

But critics say the Kosovo operation revealed serious flaws in military planning. Just a few weeks into the conflict, U.S. forces ran short of cruise missiles and precision-guided bombs and were forced to divert planes and supplies to the region from other installations.

"Clearly, we've got some shortfalls in advanced munitions, light armor, the sorts of command-and-control aircraft you need for advanced warfare and in sea and air-lift assets," says Haass. "Had there been another crisis, say in the gulf, we would have found ourselves having to make some

hard choices about where to put JSTARS or AWACS, as well as smart bombs. We just lack enough of the real force multipliers," or critical weaponry.

Some military experts say the victory will profoundly affect the way future wars involving the United States are fought. "I think Kosovo is fairly typical of the kinds of conflicts we're going to see," says Meilinger of the Naval War College. "I also think our response to it, even if it's not necessarily something I would prefer, is going to be fairly standard. Wars are going to continue, but if anyone thinks that the United States

The Air Force's highest procurement priority is the F-22 Raptor, a new, high-performance fighter jet slated to replace the aging F-15. The House voted on July 22 to cancel funding for the plane.

is going to get involved again they're going to try to do what Milosevic did because it was reasonably successful for a long time."

To evade U.S. bombs, for example, Serb commanders broke their troops into small units and ordered them to travel at night or under heavy camouflage and avoid major roads. "If I were an adversary looking at the United States, I would do what Milosevic did, in addition to using more Scud and cruise missiles and more biological and chemical weapons to use as

threats," Meilinger says. "I also would try not to be so stupid and nasty as to pit the entire world against me."

Some experts worry that the very success of the Kosovo intervention may bode ill for future U.S. military operations by creating the unrealistic expectation that the United States can win wars without sacrificing servicemen. Clinton promised early in the conflict that he would not send American ground troops into Kosovo, a move that many critics say prolonged the war by assuring Milosevic that his troops could operate unimpeded on the ground.

"I'm not sure that Americans have become casualty-intolerant," Meilinger says. "But it's indisputable that American politicians think they are casualty-intolerant and that they're basing their plans and their strategies on that assumption."

Other experts dispute that notion. "In my judgment this is just a big myth," says Snider of West Point. "Americans are not casualty-averse as long as they are convinced that a mission will be successful and in their interests." The problem with the operations in Kosovo and Bosnia, he says, is that most people did not identify those conflicts as ones in which U.S. national interests were clearly at stake.

Snider fears that Kosovo has set a different precedent, one that flies in the face of longstanding U.S. military tradition. "Traditionally, we fight wars by fighting armies," he says. "The Kosovo exercise demonstrated that we are without peer in the world in precision bombing. The question is

Troubling Behavior by the Russian Military

It was a scene reminiscent of postwar Germany, when the Red Army surprised its wartime allies — the United States, France and Britain — by advancing into Berlin and occupying eastern Germany. The Iron Curtain was to divide East and West Germany for nearly 50 years and serve as the Cold War's main symbol until the Soviet Union's demise in 1991 swept it away.

In June 1999 Russian troops staged a mini-replay of that critical maneuver when they sped across the Yugoslav border into the disputed province of Kosovo and occupied the airport outside Pristina, the provincial capital. Even the players were the same, except this time Germany was among the allies. Once again, the element of surprise was key to the Russians' success.

The sudden move may have been sparked by Russia's uncertainty about the role it would play in Kosovo. Its counterparts in the negotiations that ended NATO's 11-week bombardment of Yugoslavia had not yet settled on Russia's military presence in the peacekeeping mission to Kosovo. When the British contingent of NATO peacekeeping troops, known as KFOR, arrived the next day as scheduled, they were presented with a fait accompli. As if to drive home the point, Russian armored vehicles raced noisily up and down the air strip as the British commander tried to speak with reporters.

Russia, which had protested NATO's invasion to halt the persecution of ethnic Albanians by Yugoslav President Slobodan Milosevic, was clearly frustrated by its own inability to mount a stronger defense of its Serb allies. Did the sudden incursion of Russian troops mean the Russians were preparing to stage a counteroffensive on Milosevic's behalf? After avoiding a hot war with the Soviet Union for a half-century, was the West about to actually face a military offensive by Moscow?

The explanations from Moscow were far from reassuring. At first, Russian Foreign Minister Igor Ivanov said the whole offensive was an "unfortunate" mistake, suggesting that the military had acted without even consulting the civilian government of President Boris N. Yeltsin. He later retracted that statement and said it had been authorized by no other than Yeltsin himself. Prime Minister Sergei Stepashin did little to clear up the matter, telling a reporter recently, "I believe the episode can be explained by a lack of coordination between our military and NATO." [1]

Barely two weeks after the incursion into Kosovo, Russian strategic bombers flew over Norway and Iceland, coming within striking distance of the United States. Norwegian and U.S. aircraft scrambled to intercept the Russian aircraft and escort them out of NATO air space. Though U.S. officials said the flights were part of extensive exercises by Russian armed forces, it was the first time that Russian bombers had infringed on NATO air space since the end of the Cold War nearly a decade ago.

Some experts worry that these latest actions may reveal Russian military leaders' frustration with Yeltsin's apparent inability to counter NATO's expansion and willingness to intervene outside its territory.

Once again, the official Russian explanation shed little light on Moscow's reasoning. In the words of Col. Gen. Anatoly Kornukov, commander of the Russian Air Force, the incursion was part of planned exercises — "nothing more, nothing less." "It is time we gauged the real state of affairs in the army and navy and their combat and mobilization capacities," he said.

"Russians of all persuasions are thrilled that their military officers have managed to create such a fuss with so few chessmen on the board," writes Marshall I. Goldman, associate director of Harvard University's Russian studies program. "The endgame may not be clear, but Russian troops have certainly demonstrated to NATO and the West that Moscow cannot be taken for granted." [2]

---

[1] Quoted in Lally Weymouth, "Partners . . . Should Respect Each Other," *The Washington Post*, July 25, 1999.

[2] Marshall I. Goldman, "Power Plays: Russia's Mixed-Up Moves Reveal Its Dangerous Divide," *The Washington Post*, June 20, 1999.

---

to what end and with what morality. It simply is not in America's historical character to fight wars by beating up on little countries by taking out their social infrastructure and leaving their ill-begotten leader still in power. We are now the bully on the block. Once we study this in detail, we may decide that this is not how America wants to be known and behave in the world."

Indeed, Human Rights Watch, a non-governmental humanitarian organization, condemned NATO's use of cluster bombs against Yugoslavia as a violation of internationally accepted rules of warfare. A 1977 protocol to the 1949 Geneva Convention, which the United States has not ratified, prohibits "indiscriminate" methods of combat or attacks that cannot be "limited" to military objectives. [22]

Allocating Resources

Many experts say that Kosovo demonstrated the need for further changes in defense planning. While the military is about a third smaller than its peak size in the mid-1980s, it is more active, as troops are carrying out peacekeeping and relief roles in addition to doing combat duty in such civil wars as the recent conflict in Yugoslavia. As a result of these increased operations in combination with reduced spending, critics say, defense resources are being spread too thin.

"We have overdone it again in our efforts to cash in on an illusory peace dividend," says Gaffney. "We have again hollowed out the military, and we have to again put a lot more money back into it to reconstitute a ready, capable combat force for today and to give the forces of tomorrow the equipment that they're going to require."

One of the most hotly contested weapons programs is the proposed national missile defense system. Critics say the program is a waste of resources because it is technologically unfeasible, analogous to trying to hit a bullet with a bullet. They cite the repeated failures of the THAAD missile to make their point.

But even some critics of missile defense say THAAD's failures — aside from its successful launch in June — are to be expected in a military space program. "Space is a grotesquely risky business," says Pike of the Federation of American Scientists. "It's simply an actuarial fact of life that every 10 or 20 times you launch a rocket it's going to blow up." THAAD has been plagued by more than its fair share of problems, Pike concedes. "But military space overall has been intensely boring for the last five years or so because they pretty much seem to be doing the right things, and the things they're doing pretty much seem to be working."

Pike says that may change under current spending plans for the military space program, especially for the next generation of imagery-intelligence satellites, which are expected

to start orbiting Earth in five years. "It's an iron law of the space business that you always wind up spending too much money on the satellite relative to the amount of money you spend on processing the data from the satellite," he says. In this case, Pike says, there is a mismatch in funding between the National Reconnaissance Office, which is building new satellites, and the National Imagery and Mapping Agency, which is responsible for analyzing the images.

"The number of pictures that our spy satellites are producing today are probably 10 times the number that

Iraqi tanks destroyed by U.S. forces during the 1991 Persian Gulf War to oust Iraq from Kuwait waste away outside Kuwait City.

were being produced when Reagan was president, but the number of people we have who are looking at the pictures now has remained about the same," he says. "So the new satellites' capacity to take pictures is on the verge of totally overwhelming the ability of imagery interpreters to look at them."

Changing the way the Pentagon plans for future defense needs will not come easily, however. "It is a familiar feature of organizations that they tend to be slow to adapt," says Haass. "There are all sorts of vested interests that feel threatened by

change."

Another obstacle to change is the lack of strong leadership in the procurement process, Haass says. Congressional committees, the services, the office of the Defense secretary, the commanders in chief and the Office of Management and Budget all have a say. "There are an awful lot of people involved in defense procurement, but there's no one clearly in charge," he says.

Another obstacle to efficient use of defense funds is the inclination of lawmakers to tack on additional funds to defense spending bills to help influential constituents back home. "I have asked rhetorically on the floor of the Senate many times when we are going to stop this destructive and irresponsible practice of adding projects to the defense budget primarily for parochial reasons," said Sen. John McCain, R-Ariz., a leading supporter of defense-spending reform. He estimates that lawmakers added almost $6 billion in unrequested projects to the fiscal 2000 defense and military construction appropriations bills. That included $220 million for four F-15 fighters not requested by the Air Force — "one of the more disgraceful acts I've witnessed since, well, since we went through the same exercise last year." [23]

Interservice rivalry, long an obstacle to procurement reform, also continues to hamper efforts to reallocate defense resources efficiently, experts say. "We've got plenty of money for defense, but the problem is how the money is being divided among the services," says Meilinger.

Although a balanced approach

At Issue:

Should the United States deploy a national missile-defense system?

SEN. JESSE HELMS, R-N.C.
Chairman, Senate Foreign Relations Committee

FROM A SENATE FLOOR SPEECH, MARCH 15, 1999.

i have long regarded as beyond belief that the Clinton administration still refuses to commit to the immediate deployment of a national missile defense. I wonder, given the fact that North Korea now has a three-stage intercontinental ballistic missile capable of dropping anthrax on U.S. cities in Alaska and perhaps Hawaii, how much indifference could so dictate such a perilous do-nothing attitude by the president and his advisers. . . .

I trust I am very clear on this point: It is an absolute, irrefutable fact that a hostile tyrant today possesses missiles capable of exterminating American cities. . . .

Indeed, China, North Korea and Iran can today hold the American people hostage to missile attack because of the do-nothing attitude of the president of the United States, who . . . has consistently refused to build, or even consider building, the strategic missile defenses necessary to protect the American people from such an attack.

For years, liberals have tut-tutted that no long-range missile threat existed to necessitate a missile defense. But now, in the wake of the Rumsfeld Commission's report and North Korea's missile launch, even the most zealous arms control advocates have been forced to admit that their critical lapse of judgment and foresight has put our nation at heightened risk.

Though these people now admit the existence of a serious threat, just the same, they cannot bring themselves to agree to the deployment of a shield against missile attack. . . .

I'll tell you why. It is because of an incredible and dumb devotion to an antiquated arms control theory. Critics of the National Missile Defense Act of 1999 claim that Henny Penny's sky will fall because even the most limited effort to defend the American people will scuttle strategic nuclear reductions. . . .

The truth is that arms control agreements are not controlling force levels. Fiscal and strategic realities are. Why is Russia allowing its forces to fall to historically low levels? I will tell you. For the same reason as is the United States. We no longer live in a Cold War world in which huge nuclear arsenals are our top spending priority. The notion that limited ballistic missile defenses will somehow set off a new arms race — or forestall further reductions — is absurd. . . .

[A]ny further delay in the development by the United States of a flexible, cost-effective national missile defense is unconscionable.

SEN. BYRON L. DORGAN, D-N.D.

FROM A SENATE FLOOR SPEECH, MARCH 16, 1999.

t wenty-four years ago our country built an antiballistic missile system in my home state. It is the only ABM, or antiballistic missile, system anywhere in the free world. That ABM — or what we would now call national missile defense — system cost over $20 billion in today's dollars.

On Oct. 1, 1975, the antiballistic missile system was declared operational. On Oct. 2, one day later, Congress voted to mothball it. We spent a great deal of money. I encourage those who are interested in seeing what that money purchased to get on an airplane and fly over that sparsely populated northeastern portion of North Dakota. You will see a concrete monument to the ABM system. It was abandoned a day after it was declared operational.

Did that system make us safer? Did taking the taxpayers' dollars and building that ABM system improve national security in this country? The judgment was it was not worth the money after all. Yet here we are, nearly a quarter of a century later, debating a bill that would require the deployment of a national missile-defense system, another ballistic missile defense system, as soon as technologically feasible. . . .

It is technologically feasible for my 11-year-old son to drive my car. I wouldn't suggest that someone who meets him on the road would consider it very safe or appropriate . . . but it is technologically feasible. . . .

If we deploy a national missile-defense system before it is ready — not just technologically possible, but tested and ready — then what are we getting for our money? What does the taxpayer get for the requirement to deploy a new weapons program, albeit defensive, before it is ready to be deployed? Detecting, tracking, discriminating and hitting a trashcan-sized target traveling 20 times the speed of sound, landing in 20 or 30 minutes anywhere in the world after it is launched — intercepting that with another bullet that we send up into the skies? To put it mildly, that is problematic. Our efforts to date under highly controlled test environments, come nowhere close to meeting the requirements a ballistic missile system would need to satisfy and justify deployment. . . .

[And] if we deploy this system before we have renegotiated with Russia the Anti-Ballistic Missile Treaty, we are sure to jeopardize the enormous gains we have already made in arms reduction efforts.

Arms Control Treaties Still in Force

During the early years of the Cold War, the United States and the Soviet Union engaged in an arms race that left both sides with enough nuclear warheads to annihilate each other — and probably the rest of the world — several times over. In an effort to slow the arms race, the two superpowers began in the late 1950s to devote considerable effort to negotiating treaties to limit or reduce their respective nuclear arsenals.

Early treaties included the 1959 Antarctic Treaty banning all military activity on that continent; the 1963 Limited Nuclear Test Ban Treaty banning weapons testing under water, in the atmosphere and in outer space; the 1966 Peaceful Uses of Outer Space Treaty banning all nuclear weapons from space; and the 1968 Nuclear Non-Proliferation Treaty banning the transfer of nuclear weapons to countries that did not possess them.

Negotiations to cap production of nuclear warheads began in 1970 with the Strategic Arms Limitation Talks (SALT). Signed by then-President Richard M. Nixon and Soviet leader Leonid I. Brezhnev and ratified by the Senate in 1972, SALT I froze the number of land- and submarine-launched ballistic missiles. SALT I also included the Anti-Ballistic Missile (ABM) Treaty, which strictly limited the development of defensive systems to protect against nuclear attack.

In 1974, Brezhnev and President Gerald R. Ford agreed to negotiate further limits to their nuclear arsenals. These talks produced SALT II, signed by Brezhnev and President Jimmy Carter in 1979, which limited the number of nuclear-delivery vehicles and banned any increase in the number of allowed warheads as well as testing of several types of missiles. In protest over the Soviet invasion of Afghanistan in December 1979, however, Carter asked the Senate in January 1980 to delay consideration of SALT II.

In 1982, President Ronald Reagan called for new arms negotiations. Under his Strategic Arms Reduction Talks (START) proposal, Reagan called for both sides to reduce the number of nuclear warheads and ballistic missiles. The talks soon broke down over intermediate-range missiles based in Europe.

Citing the impasse in arms control negotiations, Reagan in 1983 presented his controversial Strategic Defense Initiative (SDI), a plan to build a space-based defensive system to protect the United States from a Soviet nuclear attack. Critics dismissed the plan, which they dubbed Star Wars, as technologically unfeasible and inherently destabilizing because it would violate the ABM Treaty.

In 1987, Soviet and U.S. negotiators finally overcame their differences regarding missiles based in Europe with the Intermediate-range Nuclear Forces (INF) Treaty, signed by Reagan and Soviet leader Mikhail Gorbachev. START talks resumed and resulted in a treaty that set the maximum number of deployed warheads at 6,000. Further reductions were agreed to under START II but have not taken effect because the Russian Duma (parliament) has blocked the treaty's ratification since January 1993.

While continuing to observe the ABM Treaty's ban on developing a broad-based missile defense, the United States has been developing a theater missile-defense system designed to protect overseas U.S. forces and allies.

But concerns over missile development by North Korea and other potential adversaries have increased support for the development of a national missile defense as well. In his January State of the Union address, President Clinton lent his support for such a system over the objections of arms control advocates and promised to decide by June 2000 what form it would take.

Meanwhile, at their June 20 summit in Cologne, Germany, Clinton and Russian President Boris N. Yeltsin agreed to try to negotiate changes to the ABM Treaty that would enable both countries to mount limited missile defenses.

may seem fair from the services' point of view, it may not help the U.S. military as a whole prepare for the kinds of future contingencies outlined by the Pentagon's own planners in the Quadrennial Defense Review and other studies.

"If they told us we needed two more Army divisions but not two more fighter wings for the Air Force, for example, it would be too tough to make that tradeoff," he says. "It's much easier to just cut all three services by 5 percent so that everybody could maintain their existing force structure."

■

OUTLOOK

Budget Debate

A wild card in the debate over defense spending appeared in early July, when the Congressional Budget Office predicted that the federal budget surplus would reach about $1 trillion over the coming decade. [24] Earlier projections had placed the cumulative surplus at about $800 billion by 2009. [25] A partisan debate immediately broke out over what to do with the fiscal windfall. Republican lawmakers want to return the bulk of the surplus to taxpayers and are calling for a $800 billion tax cut over 10 years. The Clinton administration and Democrats in Congress want to limit the tax cut to $300 billion and use the rest to shore up Social Security and Medicare, as well as national defense.

The Pentagon is lobbying intensely against deep tax cuts, which they fear will drain money from defense modernization plans. Republicans contend that there is enough money for both the tax cut and increased defense spending. But defense officials warn that the Republican tax-cut proposal would wipe out the administration's plan to invest $127 billion of the projected surplus through 2009 in new weapons and other military equipment, as well as benefits for servicemen, in an effort to replenish the U.S. arsenal and boost troop morale.

The defense-spending increase would be the first since Reagan's military buildup of the early 1980s. Without the funds, officials said, the Pentagon would have to either reduce troop levels significantly or cancel plans to procure new fighter jets and ships. [26] The wish list includes three new types of fighter jets, lighter, more maneuverable armored vehicles, better-equipped attack helicopters, more precision-guided bombs and missiles, a new helicopter carrier and a new class of surface warship.

Those worries grew on July 12, when the House Appropriations Committee endorsed a proposal by Rep. Jerry Lewis, R-Calif., to reject the administration's proposal to produce the new F-22 fighter plane, a top Air Force priority. Clinton had requested $1.8 billion to buy the first six F-22s, designed to replace the 20-year-old F-15. The full House rejected the funding proposal on July 22. Because the Senate version of the defense appropriations bill funds the new plane, the final decision will come in conference.

"We have taken the $1.8 billion that would be spent on those planes and put it into desperately needed programs to retain our pilots, improve our weapons and surveillance programs, and upgrade our already superior fleet of aircraft," Lewis said. [27]

"We are very concerned that with-

U.S. soldiers from the 101st Airborne Division serving as peacekeepers patrol a street in Port-au-Prince, Haiti, in 1996.

AP Photo/Daniel Morel

out the F-22 we will mortgage the future of our air-dominance capability," said Air Force Lt. Gen. Gregory Martin, deputy Air Force secretary for acquisition. "The F-22 is the right airplane for today's modernization priority." Without the F-22, he said, the United States will risk incurring more casualties in future wars. "I don't think we're going to lose [a] war in 2010," he said. "I just think we're going to see more people come home in body bags." [28]

Supporters of a national missile defense are guardedly optimistic that a budget surplus will improve the prospects for accelerated development of the program. "The fact that there is now this huge surplus makes the argument for doing it easier because there's clearly going to be more money going into defense in general," says Gaffney. "I guarantee you that we will have a missile defense in this country, and I guarantee you that it will be a sea-based missile defense first. The only question that really remains is whether we have it in place before we need it or after we needed it, at which point — let's be honest — there's not going to be any further discussion about whether it's compatible with our commitments under the ABM Treaty."

Barring a missile attack against the United States in the near future, however, deployment of a missile defense system may be stymied by the Clinton administration's belated support of the program.

"This administration just didn't think the threat was a big deal, and they didn't want to move fast on it," Snider says. "But the threat is proceeding much faster than we thought, and I think that in the next administration you'll see a larger political consensus for action." ■

Notes

[1] See Jim Hoagland, "Kosovo: What the Bearhugs Can't Hide," *The Washington Post*, July 11, 1999.

[2] For background, see Mary H. Cooper, "Global Refugee Crisis," *The CQ Researcher*, July 9, 1999, pp. 569-592.

[3] Cohen spoke on May 11, 1999, before the Senate Defense Appropriations Subcommittee.

[4] See "Senate Blocks Base Closings," *The Washington Post*, May 27, 1999.

[5] See Adriel Bettelheim, "New Challenges in Space," *The CQ Researcher*, July 23, 1999, pp. 617-640.

[6] From an address to the New Mexico Veterans of Foreign Wars convention in Farmington, N.M., on June 21, 1999.

[7] From a statement of March 25, 1999.

[8] See Walter Pincus, "U.S. Preparedness Faulted," *The Washington Post*, July 9, 1999.

[9] Kay Bailey Hutchison, "A Foreign Policy Vision for the Next American Century," Heritage Lectures, Heritage Foundation, July 9, 1999.

[10] Clinton addressed United Nations troops in Skopje, Macedonia, on June 22, 1999.

[11] See Elizabeth Becker, "U.S. Says Photos Show North Korea Preparing for Missile," *The New York Times*, June 18, 1999.

[12] The report of the Select Committee on U.S. National Security and Military/Commercial Concerns with the People's Republic of China was released on May 25, 1999.

[13] Quoted in Bradley Graham, "Missile Defense Test is Successful," *The Washington Post*, June 11, 1999.

[14] See Stephen Daggett, "National Missile Defense: Status of the Debate," CRS Report for Congress, May 29, 1998.

[15] For background, see David Masci, "U.S.-Russian Relations," *The CQ Researcher*, May 22, 1998, p. 470, and Mary H. Cooper, "Arms Control Negotiations," *Editorial Research Reports*, Feb. 22, 1985, pp. 145-168.

[16] For background, see Mary H. Cooper, "Expanding NATO," *The CQ Researcher*, May 16, 1997, pp. 433-456.

[17] See Michael O'Hanlon, "Defense and Foreign Policy," *Brookings Review*, winter 1999, pp. 22-25.

[18] See David Isenberg, "The Quadrennial Defense Review: Reiterating the Tired Status Quo," Policy Analysis, Cato Institute, Sept. 17, 1998.

[19] Isenberg, *op. cit.*

[20] O'Hanlon, *op. cit.*

[21] See Steven Lee Myers, "U.S. Shifts A-Bomb Readiness to Smaller Wars," *The New York Times*, Dec. 7, 1997.

[22] See "Ticking Time Bombs: NATO's Use of Cluster Munitions in Yugoslavia," June 1999, posted at www.hrw.org, and Michael Dobbs, "A War-Torn Reporter Reflects," *The Washington Post*, July 11, 1999

[23] McCain addressed the Senate on June 17, 1999.

[24] Congressional Budget Office, "The Economic and Budget Outlook: An Update," July 1, 1999.

[25] Congressional Budget Office, "An Analysis of the President's Budgetary Proposals for Fiscal Year 2000," April 1999.

[26] See Bradley Graham and Eric Pianin, "Proposed Tax Cuts Worry Pentagon," *The Washington Post*, July 10, 1999.

[27] From a statement issued July 12, 1999.

[28] Martin spoke at a Pentagon briefing on July 15.

FOR MORE INFORMATION

Brookings Institution, 1775 Massachusetts Ave. N.W., Washington, D.C. 20036-2188; (202) 797-6000; www.brook.edu. This think tank conducts studies on foreign policy, national security and international energy, economics and trade issues.

Cato Institute, 1000 Massachusetts Ave. N.W., Washington, D.C. 20001-5403; (202) 842-0200; www.cato.org. This public policy research organization discourages U.S. military intervention in foreign conflicts and supports development of a national missile-defense system. It generally advocates limited government and reduced spending.

Center for Defense Information, 1779 Massachusetts Ave. N.W., Suite 615, Washington, D.C. 20036; (202) 332-0600; www.cdi.org. This educational organization advocates a strong defense while opposing excessive expenditures for weapons and policies that increase the risk of war.

Center for Security Policy, 1920 L St. N.W., Suite 210, Washington, D.C. 20036; (202) 835-9077; www.security-policy.org. This educational institution advocates the development of a national missile-defense system.

Department of Defense, The Pentagon, Washington, D.C. 20301-1000; (703) 697-5737; www.defenselink.mil. The Pentagon develops national security policy and has overall responsibility for administering national defense. It also provides information to the public about national defense matters.

Federation of American Scientists, 307 Massachusetts Ave. N.E., Washington, D.C. 20002; (202) 546-3300; www.fas.org. The federation monitors legislation on U.S. nuclear arms policy, including the Strategic Defense Initiative, and provides information on compliance with arms control agreements.

Bibliography

Selected Sources Used

Books

International Institute for Strategic Studies, *The Military Balance 1998/99*, Oxford University Press, 1998.
The latest annual report by the IISS, a military-research institute, describes in detail the military force structure and defense spending of 168 countries, including the United States.

Perry, William James, and Ashton B. Carter, *Preventive Defense: A New Security Strategy for America*, Brookings Institution, March 1999.
Former Defense Secretary Perry and Carter, assistant secretary for international security policy, argue that proliferation of nuclear, chemical and biological weapons from the states of the former Soviet Union poses the biggest threat to U.S. national security.

Articles

"The Koreas," *The Economist*, July 10, 1999, Survey pp. 1-16.
South Korea's reluctance to adopt sweeping economic and political reforms is undermining its ability to face an inevitable crisis with North Korea, which is heavily armed, suffering famine and on the verge of collapse.

Cohen, Eliot, "Calling Mr. X," *The New Republic*, Jan. 19, 1999, pp. 17-19.
After nearly a decade of force reductions and an unrealistic reliance on its two-war strategy, the U.S. military needs an infusion of new funding to stem falling morale among the troops and a dangerous depletion of essential weaponry.

Glennon, Michael J., "The New Interventionism: The Search for a Just International Law," *Foreign Affairs*, May/June 1999, pp. 2-7.
With the recent war with Yugoslavia, the United States and NATO have abandoned the restrictions on intervention in local conflicts defined in the United Nations Charter but have failed to spell out new rules to replace them.

Greider, William, "Fortress America: The New Economics of the Military-Industrial Complex," *Rolling Stone*, November 1997, pp. 38-46, 117-120.
One of three articles on U.S. defenses, this survey of the American defense industry describes how it has survived the downsizing of the 1990s and stayed profitable by convincing lawmakers to continue funding unnecessary weapons programs.

Hartung, William D., "Ready for What?: The New Politics of Pentagon Spending," *World Policy Journal*, spring 1999, pp. 19-24.
The U.S. military does not need the increase in funding called for by President Clinton, writes this defense analyst, but better planning focused on terrorism, weapons proliferation and the spread of ethnic conflicts.

Hillen, John, "Defense's Death Spiral: The Increasing Irrelevance of More Spending," *Foreign Affairs*, July/August 1999, pp. 2-7.
The military services continue to organize and equip their forces according to separate and often incompatible visions. If the United States is to maintain a viable military, the budget process needs to be changed so that the right weapons are procured for a changing world-security environment.

Newman, Richard J., "Tougher Than Hell," *U.S. News & World Report*, Nov. 3, 1997, pp. 42-49.
U.S. special forces are undergoing a grueling training regime to prepare them for hostage rescues, refugee evacuations and other non-traditional military operations as the United States expands the role of American military forces.

O'Hanlon, Michael, "Defense and Foreign Policy: The Budget Cuts Are Going Too Far," *Brookings Review*, winter 1999, pp. 22-25.
The current two-war strategy is unrealistic and costly, writes O'Hanlon. By reducing the size of the U.S. military a little more, the Pentagon could save $5 billion a year and invest the savings in new weapons that are needed to keep the force safe and reliable.

Szamuely, George, "Globocop: When Uncle Sam Becomes Dirty Harry," *American Outlook*, spring 1998, pp. 8-14.
With little debate, the United States has taken on the role of global policeman. But it lacks both the military force and clear purpose required to make good on so sweeping a commitment.

Reports and Studies

Peña, Charles V., "Theater Missile Defense: A Limited Capability Is Needed," Policy Analysis, Cato Institute, June 22, 1998.
Rather than developing theater missile defenses to protect allies and U.S. forces deployed overseas, the United States should limit foreign military interventions and focus on developing missile defenses for U.S. territory.

4 European Monetary Union

MARY H. COOPER

A round the world, the count-down to the new millennium has begun. But in Brussels, Belgium, the huge digital clock in front of European Union (EU) headquarters is ticking off the hours until another momentous event.

On Jan. 1, 1999, a new economic powerhouse will debut on the world stage. Eleven of the EU's 15 member states will start using a new common currency — the euro.

Moreover, Germany, France, Spain and the eight other charter members of the Economic and Monetary Union (EMU) — dubbed Euroland —will hand over considerable policy-making control to a new European Central Bank.* If all goes according to plan, the euro will foster a new era of prosperity in Europe and a formidable new challenge to U.S. dominance of global trade and finance.

"Eleven European states, joining 290 million inhabitants, will share the same currency for the first time since the fall of the Roman Empire," said Yves-Thibault de Silguy, a member of the European Commission, the EU's executive branch. "This is undeniably a historic event. It is also a sweeping economic and monetary event: The euro zone will be the world's leading trading power, and it will carry an economic weight comparable to that of the United States." [1]

All 15 members of the EU were invited to apply for membership in the EMU. But Greece failed to meet the criteria for membership, and the United Kingdom, Denmark and Sweden chose not to join, at least initially. (See map, p. 60.)

Even without the other EU members, Euroland will be a major player in the

*The 11 nations are Austria, Belgium, Finland, France, Germany, Italy, Ireland, Luxembourg, the Netherlands, Spain and Portugal.

From *The CQ Researcher*, November 27, 1998.

global economy. Its members account for 20 percent of global trade, even more than the United States (16 percent). Exports from the 11 members are 25 percent greater than those of the United States and twice those of Japan, the world's second-largest exporter. Euroland's combined gross domestic product (GDP) is 80 percent that of the United States but half again greater than Japan's. [2] (See table, p. 61.)

At first, the new currency will be used only for non-cash transactions, such as purchases of stocks and bonds, government accounting and some business invoicing. But on Jan. 1, 2002, ordinary citizens will start using euro notes and coins for all exchanges. And six mounths later, in July 2002, national currencies such as the German mark, French franc and Italian lira will disappear altogether, marking the demise of powerful symbols of national identity.

Monetary union came to fruition so quickly that it caught many Europeans by surprise, but the idea is hardly new. Europeans had wrangled for decades as they tried to create what British Prime Minister Winston Churchill envisioned as a United States of Europe as early as 1946. Until recently, however, progress was blocked by bickering over agricultural subsidies, trade barriers and other issues, as well as the Continent's sluggish economy and high inflation and unemployment.

But the end of the Cold War and subsequent economic growth jumpstarted consolidation. In December 1991, even as former Soviet-bloc nations in Eastern Europe were clamoring to join the EU, its member nations were meeting in a small city in the Netherlands to create the common currency. The resulting Maastricht Treaty set strict economic standards that all participating countries would have to meet before joining the EMU and adopting the euro. Mainly, applicants had to reduce inflation and budget deficits and stabilize their exchange and interest rates (see p. 70).

Efforts to meet Maastricht's strict criteria have paid off. "Europessimism" has given way to "Euro-optimism" as Italy, Spain and other nations with lackluster economies have made unprecedented strides toward reining in inflation and government spending.

In fact, the continent's overall economy has grown so strong in the past few years that Europe is being touted as the most economically stable region in the world, a safe haven for investors burned by the Asian financial crisis and the roller-coaster ride stock prices have taken in the United States.

Monetary union offers a number of potential benefits to member countries. Adoption of a single currency is designed to help stabilize prices, the main objective of EMU and the European Central Bank's foremost obligation under its charter. A single currency will eliminate trading against swings in currency values, reducing a major cost of trade both within Europe and with non-European importers and exporters. A single currency also will make it harder for companies to charge more for their products in one country than another, thus making it easier for consumers to pay fair prices.

Prices also should fall as inefficient European companies, long protected from outside competition, are forced either to become competitive

A New Alliance in Europe

The 11 charter members of the new Economic and Monetary Union (EMU) form a powerful trading alliance that will begin using the new euro currency in 1999; all are members of the European Union.* Four EU members are not in the monetary union: Greece sought membership but was rejected, and the United Kingdom, Denmark and Sweden chose not to join. Six other nations seek to join the EU and may then seek membership in the monetary union.**

*The 11 members are Austria, Belgium, Finland, France, Germany, Italy, Ireland, Luxembourg, the Netherlands, Spain and Portugal.
** The six are the Czech Republic, Estonia, Hungary, Poland, Slovenia and Cyprus (not shown).

Source: European Union

in the larger European market or fail. Both consumers and businesses are expected to enjoy lower borrowing costs. And tourists traveling in Euroland will no longer have to trade currencies at every border crossing.

Many American analysts predict that the euro will also benefit the United States. U.S. exports to the European Union totaled more than $140 billion in 1997, accounting for a fifth of U.S. exports. Although European firms are rapidly becoming more efficient by entering into cross-border mergers and shedding government ownership through privatization, American companies retain a competitive edge in Europe.

"Most U.S. companies have already gone through the hard decisions on bringing costs under control," says Charles Ludolph, deputy assistant secretary for Europe at the Commerce Department's International Trade Administration. "In the aftermath of the 1980s, anybody still standing had brought costs under control, and this was reflected in the prices of their products. In Europe, they haven't gone through that at all."

If there is a downside to euro membership, it is the budget cuts and higher taxes that Italians, Spaniards and other Europeans endured to join Euroland and will have to endure in the future, lest inflation return and force governments to pay steep penalties.

The call for lower public spending also challenges a deep-rooted culture throughout most of Europe that looks to the government for generous unemployment compensation and pensions and other social-welfare programs. Unemployment, which remains a key concern for many Europeans and is thought to have helped unseat German Chancellor Helmut Kohl, may remain high for some time to come.

And there is another downside to monetary union. By adopting the single currency, Euroland governments will lose control over a vital instrument for managing a national economy — the power to mint money and influence its value by adjusting interest rates. If a euro nation's economy goes into recession, its government can no longer lower interest rates to spur borrowing and thus help boost production and employment. It will have to await action from the European Central

European Economies at a Glance

In meeting strict economic criteria for membership in the new Economic and Monetary Union (EMU), members instituted austerity measures that had the unwanted effect in many cases of increasing unemployment.

EU Countries	Population (in millions)	GDP (in $ billions)	Inflation Rate	Unemployment Rate	Deficit (% of GDP)	Debt (% of GDP)
Germany	82.1	1,452	0.6	9.5	-2.7	61.3
France	58.6	1,200	0.5	11.9	-3	58
*United Kingdom	57.6	1,190	1.5	6.5 (est.)	-1.9	53.4
Italy	56.8	1,080	2.1	12.0 (est.)	-2.7	121.6
Spain	39.1	593	1.6	18.5	-2.6	68.8
Netherlands	15.6	302	1.3	4.4 (est.)	-1.4	72.1
Belgium	10.2	197	0.8	8.8	-2.1	122.2
*Sweden	8.9	184	-0.1	7.7	-0.8	76.6
Austria	8.0	152	0.6	4.5	-2.5	66.1
Portugal	9.9	116	2.2	4.6	-2.5	62
*Denmark	5.3	113	1.1	4.3	0.7	65.1
*Greece	10.6	102	5.0	9.2 (est.)	-4	108.7
Finland	5.1	92	1.4	11.2	-0.9	55.8
Ireland	3.6	55	2.8	8.8	0.9	66.3
Luxembourg	0.4	10	0.7	2.2	1.7	6.7

Sources: *European Union, The New York Times 1998 Almanac*
*Not members of the Economic and Monetary Union
Note: Population and GDP figures are from 1997; all other data are from 1998.

Bank in Frankfurt, and there is no guarantee that the bank will lower rates if the recession is localized. Without the power to lower interest rates or devalue its currency, the country in recession would face rising unemployment. The loss of sovereignty is an especially sensitive issue in Britain, whose currency, the sterling, was the dominant currency in world trade before the dollar superseded it after World War I.

There are signs of discord in Euroland as well. While the political leaders of all 11 member countries express enthusiastic support of the new currency, not all citizens of Euroland are convinced. The euro enjoys wide support in Italy and in the smaller countries involved, such as Luxembourg, the Netherlands and Belgium. But ironically, support for the euro is weak in Germany and France, the two countries whose leaders have led the push toward European unification. Kohl, who was succeeded by Gerhard Schroeder in the Sept. 27 election, counted monetary union as one of the crowning achievements of his 16-year tenure. "The previous government and, to a somewhat lesser degree, the new government are formally very much for the euro," says Meinhard Miegel, director of the Bonn Institute for Economic and Social Research. "But this very optimistic approach to the new currency somehow has not convinced the majority of the population. Germans are still very hesitant when it comes to this change."

Signs of conflict are evident even at the official level. On May 2, when European heads of state announced the admission of the 11 members to the euro club, a crack in the veneer of official accord suddenly developed over the leadership of the European Central Bank. Although it was agreed that Wim Duisenberg, a former central banker from the Netherlands, would become the bank's first president, as expected, France suddenly blocked the appointment. A compromise was reached with an informal agreement that Duisenberg would resign halfway through his eight-year

Expansion of the European Union . . .

As the European Union becomes stronger, many countries now outside the EU see membership as a ticket to security and prosperity. Eleven countries are seeking admission to the exclusive club of Europe's wealthiest countries. Admission to the EU would be a first step tward membership in the new Economic and Monetary Union (EMU).

Expansion has always been central to the EU's ultimate vision of creating a continental federation, a kind of United States of Europe. From its founding membership of six countries in 1958, the EU has expanded to 15 countries. Turkey has been trying to join since 1963, and the disintegration of the Soviet bloc after 1989 freed Central and Eastern European countries to apply for membership as the surest way to embrace the Western economic and political model, and Western military protection.

Not everyone covets EU membership. Switzerland has stayed away to preserve its traditional neutrality. And Norwegian voters chose not to join when the Scandinavian countries put EU membership to a referendum in 1997. Together with Iceland and Liechtenstein, they belong to a free-trade area of their own called the European Free Trade Association (EFTA). Talks now under way to include Canada in the EFTA may soon result in the first transatlantic trade agreement.

But most non-member countries are eager to join the EU. At a summit on enlargement held last December in Luxembourg, the EU invited six countries to become candidates for EU membership. Five others — Bulgaria, Latvia, Lithuania, Romania and Slovakia — were encouraged to improve conditions with an eye to gaining EU admission at a later date. On March 31, negotiations began with the six — the Czech Republic, Cyprus, Estonia, Hungary, Poland and Slovenia — which were picked for early admission on the basis of their economic, political and social conditions.

"These negotiations will take time," cautioned European Commission member Yves-Thibault de Silguy of France. "It's a matter of integrating more than 100 million people whose average income is far below the EU average." [1]

Even after they gain admission to the EU, unlikely to occur before 2003, the new members will have to meet a new set of criteria to join the EMU and adopt its new currency, the euro.

There are several obstacles to EU expansion, the most obvious concerning the euro itself. For monetary union to work, participating countries must have relatively sound economies. The criteria for adopting the euro include low interest rates, low inflation and little government red ink. Even among the relatively wealthy members of the EU, meeting the criteria has proved difficult. Greece failed to satisfy the criteria in time to join Jan. 1, and it will be even harder for less advanced economies, especially those that are still struggling to shift from Soviet-style state ownership to a system based on private enterprise.

The Czech Republic, one of the six candidates for early admission to the EU, has greatly reduced its budget deficit, but at the cost of worsening unemployment. And the Czechs have made little progress in privatizing companies

---

term to make way for French central banker Jean-Claude Trichet.

Indeed, some economists say support for greater European union is eroding, even as the Jan. 1 start-up date approaches. "Increasing numbers of people in Europe are beginning to be Euroskeptics, not just on the currency itself, but on the entire European concept," says Bruce Alan Johnson, a senior fellow at the Hudson Institute, a public policy research organization in Indianapolis. "The currency is scaring them because it's so close to home. This is an issue that's beginning to feel like a barbed arrow piercing their hides."

But many other economists say the willingness of Italy, Spain and some other faltering European economies to lower inflation and reduce government spending bodes well for the new arrangement. "I'm not a Eurofanatic in any sense," says Richard Portes, an economics professor at the London Business School, "but I've become increasingly convinced over time, as we've seen the adjustments that have been made, that this is going to work."

Another source of optimism for the euro has been Europe's ability thus far to weather the financial crises in Asia and Russia, though there are signs that the crises have begun to cut into European exports. "For now, at least, we have withstood a trial by fire over the past few months," says Angelo Cicogna, financial attaché at the Italian Embassy in Washington. "The financial markets in Europe have shown no sign of concern about the prospects of monetary union. The fact that things have gone so well in such a difficult situation is very encouraging."

As the euro's introduction fast approaches, these are some of the issues that economists and policymakers are considering:

Is Europe ready for monetary union?

The Maastricht Treaty, ratified in 1992, set five strict "convergence criteria" for EMU membership:

• Inflation within 1.5 percentage points of the three best-performing EU countries;

• annual budget deficits of no more than 3 percent of gross domestic product (GDP);

• exchange-rate stability for two years;

... Is Key to Federation

and financial markets and passing laws necessary to meet the EU's labor and environmental standards.

Another obstacle to expansion lies in the EU's institutions and programs. For example, EU decision-making relies on unanimous approval, and if membership expanded beyond the current 15 members, the EU's policy-making apparatus could become paralyzed.

In addition, expensive EU programs such as agricultural subsidies and development assistance to economically depressed countries could be swamped when poor, rural countries are admitted. Poland's overwhelmingly agricultural economy is based on roughly 2 million small, family-owned farms that are ill-equipped to compete with the EU's advanced agribusinesses. Absent a wrenching consolidation of the farming sector, Poland's admission would overwhelm the EU's agricultural program. [2] The EU already plans to spend $80 billion to help the new applicants make necessary reforms, and there are calls to greatly reduce the subsidy programs before they join.

There are also political complications involved in admitting new members. Opposition to expansion runs high in Germany, the main contributor to the EU's budget, where expansion is seen as a further drag on the economy. Germans are especially worried that the early admission of neighboring Poland, Hungary and the Czech Republic would encourage immigration from these countries, worsening unemployment.

Another divisive issue involves Turkey, whose application for EU membership dates back to 1963. Turkey was again rebuffed last year, ostensibly because of its poor record on human rights and its ongoing dispute with Greece over the status of Cyprus. Many Turks see their continued exclusion from the EU as nothing more than an act of European racism against a Muslim country. Indeed, opposition to Turkey's membership runs high in Germany, where the presence of millions of Turkish migrant workers is already a controversial political issue.

Many critics of the latest enlargement decision view Turkey's admission to the EU as a vital way to tie Turkey, a key NATO ally, more solidly to Europe. "Few things could be more important for our security than that Turkey should remain democratic and well-disposed toward the West," writes Michael Portillo, who served in former British Prime Minister John Major's Cabinet. "It is very difficult for the Turkish government to sell to its people the merits of being a good member of NATO, and it is difficult for us to persuade Turkey to be reasonable over the Cyprus problem, when it is offered so little and treated so brusquely by the EU." [3]

---

[1] Speaking at a Sept. 25 meeting of the European Commission in Vienna, Austria.

[2] See Peter Finn, "Poland's Family Farms Face Being Plowed Under," *The Washington Post*, Oct. 20, 1998.

[3] Michael Portillo, "Europe on the Brink," *The National Interest*, spring 1998, p. 36.

• long-term interest rates within 2 percentage points of rates in countries with the lowest interest rates; and

• government debt of no more than 60 percent of GDP.

With less than seven years to meet the criteria, countries with large budget deficits and high inflation and interest rates adopted painful austerity measures. In Italy and Spain, for example, qualifying for the euro meant imposing tough budget cuts and tax increases, which have been especially painful at a time of persistently high unemployment.

By the May 1998 deadline, all but one of the 12 countries that had sought admission to the EMU had met the standards. Greece, whose budget deficit remained too high for admission in the first wave of applications, will try to qualify again by 2001.

The quest to meet the Maastricht criteria has given Europe's financial health a big boost over the past few years. While the Asian financial crisis sent U.S. stocks into a nose dive last summer, and Russia defaulted on its loans, international investors poured money into European stocks and bonds. Though Europe's stock markets also took a hit in late summer, projected growth for the EU in 1999 stands at around 2 percent, down only slightly from last year's 2.5 percent growth rate.

The rosy economic picture, combined with the unprecedented convergence of economic and financial conditions in most of the EU, leads many economists to agree with Europe's political leaders that the time is ripe for monetary union. "There's very little doubt in my mind that they are ready," says Portes of the London Business School. "They have satisfied the formal criteria, which I always believed to be excessively precise and have relatively little economic justification."

But other experts are concerned that several countries are less prepared for monetary union than the statistics would suggest. They say that only a few countries actually met the criteria but that the numbers were fudged to enable Italy and some other countries into the union to bolster confidence in the euro.

"If they had been going by the letter of the Maastricht Treaty, they

German farmers at European Union headquarters in Brussels, Belgium, last March protest plans to expand the EU, known as Agenda 2000. To help pay for expansion, tariff protection and price supports for EU farmers would be eliminated or reduced. The placard reads "Agenda, not that way."

government debt below 60 percent of GDP. The rest — including such economic giants as Germany — slipped in through a loophole in the Maastricht Treaty that exempted countries where debt ratios are falling "at a satisfactory pace." [3]

"Clearly, not all the euro participants are ready," says Miegel of the Bonn Institute for Economic and Social Research. "The weak man in the whole thing is Italy. Everybody knew that, but when the final meeting came about, the heads of state and government decided to take Italy in."

A clear sign of Italy's inability to live by the Maastricht agreement, Miegel says, was the Oct. 9 collapse of Prime Minister Romano Prodi's government, which introduced the policies that enabled Italy to qualify for the EMU. "The communists were not willing to support his stringent budgetary policies, and that is why he had to leave," Miegel says. "The majority of the Italian parliament said they were not willing to fulfill the Maastricht agreement's requirements."

Prodi's successor, Massimo D'Alema, has promised to continue Prodi's program. However, D'Alema's role as leader of the Democratic Party of the Left, which succeeded the defunct Italian Communist Party, would suggest support for more government spending, not less.

Miegel questions D'Alema's ability to keep Italy on track with the EMU requirements. "If he wants to get a majority in parliament, he will have to be rather lenient in regard to his policies," Miegel says, "and that is not a good omen for the euro."

Italian officials reject these criticisms out of hand, citing a halving of inflation and a cut in the budget deficit from 7 percent of GDP to 3 percent over the past three years. "Italy's readiness on the economic-front is apparent from the statistics," says Cicogna at the Italian Embassy. "Italy fully satisfied all the economic convergence criteria for public fi-

would have gone for about six countries, not 11," says John Grahl, an economist at the University of North London Business School. "The others haven't met the required fiscal con-

straints, and their inclusion was a political override."

The European Commission itself acknowledged that only three of the applicant states managed to reduce nance, inflation, interest rates and exchange rates.

"If it were true that the numbers were just an aberration, that would have become apparent later, but the economic trends continue to be strongly positive. Inflation remains very low and fell even lower recently, interest rates are completely in line with those of other European countries, and the exchange rate is very stable, as it was throughout this summer's turmoil."

While governments have been tightening their belts, European companies have also been gearing up for the increased competition that is expected to result from monetary union. Many of Europe's biggest companies are state-owned and have been sheltered from the competition that forced American companies to shed unprofitable divisions in the 1980s. But in preparation for the EMU, governments have been privatizing some of their biggest concerns, including telecommunications giants Deutsche Telekom AG and France Telecom and Italian oil and gas producer ENI SpA.

While the privatizations are still under way, other companies are seeking to capture market share by cutting costs and merging with partners in other Euroland countries. Some of the biggest are extending their reach beyond the region, notably Germany's Daimler-Benz, which bought Chrysler Corp. this year. Largely as a result of the merger activity, 38 of the world's largest 100 companies are European, up from 27 only a year ago. [4]

Can monetary union work without greater fiscal and political integration?

Viewed strictly from the American experience, the answer may well be no. After all, the Federal Reserve Board, the U.S. equivalent of the new European Central Bank, controls the money supply and interest rates in a single economic and political entity. Most of its citizens share a common language and a national culture of mobility — social, economic and physical. When regional economies fail, as did the manufacturing Midwest in the 1970s and the Texas oil patch in the 1980s, many workers move to areas where jobs are more plentiful. A common fiscal policy also means that a region in recession will pay less in federal taxes and receive more in federal welfare benefits, further easing the blow of economic hardship.

Euroland, by contrast, is a patchwork of sovereign nations with distinct languages, cultures and histories that have more often been at war with each other than in search of common ground. Today, just one European in three speaks English, the most commonly spoken foreign language on the Continent, and just 15 percent of non-French Europeans speak French. [5]

In fact, when Germany emerged as the strongest economy in the EC in the 1970s and '80s, language and cultural differences prevented many jobless workers from southern Italy, Greece and other poor regions from moving to Germany, even after new policies favoring labor mobility made it possible for EU citizens to work anywhere in the union. This labor immobility, together with the lack of a common fiscal policy, makes it all the more likely that regional recessions will escalate, creating what economists call asymmetric shocks that monetary union alone cannot prevent.

"Just to have monetary policy and nothing else won't work," says Grahl of the University of North London. "It will be hard to get an efficient system if you don't coordinate fiscal policy with monetary policy.* But all that exists at the moment is a constraint on deficits. There are no procedures

---

* Monetary policy involves setting interest rates; fiscal policy deals with spending and taxing.

for coordinating fiscal policies or for aligning fiscal policy with monetary policy. The danger is that the monetary policy will be announced, and then each country will have to adapt its own fiscal policy without asking, or even being able to ask, what the implications of everybody's fiscal policies are for the macroeconomy."

Grahl supports expansion of the European Union's budget, which is now used primarily to pay agricultural subsidies to member farmers. A small portion of the budget is used to help compensate for unemployment or low income in economically depressed regions and to help Spain, Greece, Portugal and Ireland — the "poor four" — reach EMU eligibility. The EC budget would have to be about five times its current size and used mostly to help regions cope with economic downturns, Grahl says, to have a macroeconomic impact.

But expansion of the EU budget would require agreement among all 15 members, a prospect that seems less likely than consensus on monetary union. "The feeling at the moment is that Germany, which is the biggest paymaster, would want reform of the way in which the budget is financed before it would consider an expansion of the budget," Grahl says. "And there are some countries, including Britain, which are just flatly opposed to [budgetary] expansion and want to continue to have a small budget."

Other experts say the risk of asymmetric shocks under EMU have been overblown. "It's very hard to think of shocks that would hit just one national economy and not the others in the system because European economies are not terribly specialized," says Portes of the London Business School. "There's a lot of differentiation among regions in individual countries, such as the Northeast and Southeast of England, not to mention Scotland, where conditions are very, very different. We have a one-size-fits-all monetary policy, and yet somehow we have survived."

Some economists emphasize that while the EMU is limited to monetary union, EC members are continuing to build closer links in other policy areas that will enable them to overcome regional downturns. "Economic policy consists of more than monetary policy," says Cicogna of the Italian Embassy. "Policies related to budgets, competition, strengthening the Common Market and other instruments can all be used to deal with this kind of problem, and these are areas in which member countries are now improving coordination. So I don't see any incompatibility between the creation of a single monetary and anti-inflationary policy on the one hand and problems that may affect the various countries in different ways."

Whether the EMU will lead to closer economic or even political union is a matter of even greater controversy. Churchill's vision of a United States of Europe is still acknowledged as the ultimate goal of the 40-year-old process of European integration. "The construction of economic and monetary union is a step in a much broader vision whose goal is to strengthen the political links among the nations of Europe," says Cicogna of the Italian Embassy, reflecting his country's strong support of the process. "Certainly the direction in which public opinion is headed in Italy points to stronger ties with the rest of Europe, though how this will or can happen on an institutional level is hard to say."

Euroskeptics counter that the economic and political basis for

monetary union does not yet exist. "One of the bricks in the wall of Europe is the euro, but it won't stand because they are building on a foundation of sand," says Johnson of the Hudson Institute. A currency's success, he says, relies on confidence in

---

"Euroland will have a huge economy, massive reserves and a huge trade surplus. If it's a success, it ought to be the second currency behind the dollar, without any shadow of a doubt."

— Caesar Bryan, senior vice president, Gabelli Asset Management Co.

---

the issuer's political stability. "The Swiss franc is essentially the strongest currency in the world because people are confident about the stability of the Swiss government and the degree of gold backing. There's nothing backing the euro except the mixed basket of currencies, which includes not only the Deutschmark but the Spanish peseta, and that shakes people up."

Some critics predict that going ahead with EMU in the absence of

closer fiscal and political union dooms the euro to failure from the outset. "Political union must precede monetary union — that is what historical experience keeps stressing," writes Josef Joffe, an editor of the Munich daily newspaper *Süddeutsche Zeitung*.

"Nor is monetary union a kind of furtive shortcut to political union, as Europe's federalists might presume," Joffe continues. "Money, in fact, does not bind what pulls apart. The first thing secessionist states do is to print their own tender — as the American Confederacy did in 1861, as Slovakia did in 1993. Money, as every unhappy family knows, is a prime cause of discord and divorce." [6]

Does European monetary union threaten the United States?

The U.S. dollar has reigned as the world's leading currency for more than a half-century. Most international trade, including non-U.S. trade, is conducted in dollars, and foreign governments hold more dollars in reserve than any other currency. But the new euro, by essentially incorporating the currencies of 11 European countries — including the mighty Deutschmark — may be poised to challenge the dollar's supremacy. At stake is not only the competitive edge held by U.S. banks and other financial institutions and lower transaction costs for American companies but also the political clout that comes with ownership of the world's pre-eminent currency.

"If the birth of the single currency lives up to its expectations," writes Italian financial columnist Isabella Bufacchi, "Euroland will not only develop to resemble the U.S. market,

Visitors to Europe won't see the new euro currency until Jan. 1, 2002. But beginning in 1999, the euro will be used for non-cash transactions, such as stock and bond purchases. Coins valued at one euro, above, will be worth slightly more than $1.

but it may even aspire to dethrone the dollar and its financial products from their dominion, thus far uncontested, on a global scale. How? The EMU meets all the requirements to become one of the biggest and most efficient markets in the world for stocks, bonds and derivatives denominated in what could well be a currency of refuge." [7]

Some American analysts agree that the euro has the makings to challenge, if not eclipse, the dollar. "Euroland will have a huge economy, massive reserves and a huge trade surplus," writes Caesar Bryan, senior vice president of Gabelli Asset Management Co. in Rye, N.Y. "Inflation is very low. If it's a success, it ought to be the second currency behind the dollar, without any shadow of a doubt." [8]

Other economists dismiss the euro as a threat to the greenback's dominance. "The dollar is still the major trading currency because commodities that are traded worldwide, from oil to pork bellies, are denominated

in dollars at the end of the transaction," Johnson says. "Also, Europe is not a serious player in the Asian markets, and it's a non-player in South America," regions where dollar transactions dominate.

Not only the U.S. currency but also American companies may face stronger rivals as a result of the euro's arrival. Monetary union is forcing European companies to become more efficient, and thus potentially stronger competitors with U.S. companies for market share, both in the EU and abroad. Long before the euro's arrival, the pace of cross-border mergers between large European companies picked up in preparation to compete with U.S. giants in the global marketplace. Even longstanding rivals like the London and Frankfurt stock exchanges plan to start cooperating Jan. 4, the first day of trading in euros. [9]

But many American analysts say U.S. producers will flourish under the new currency regime, just as they have since the removal of internal trade barriers under the EU's single

market. "U.S. manufacturers already benefit enormously from the economies of scale in Europe," says Marino Marcich, director of international investments and finance at the National Association of Manufacturers. By providing "one-stop shopping" for U.S. producers, he says, the single market means that "You can take a product, and if you have market access to a country like Ireland, you can market the exact same product across borders in 14 other countries."

In this view, large American companies, especially multinationals already present in Euroland, will actually gain a competitive edge over their European rivals under the euro. That's because the process of privatization is still very much under way in Europe, where many of the largest companies still retain the inefficiencies of partial or total state ownership and have yet to penetrate markets outside their borders.

"Unlike large European companies, which are mostly single-state companies, U.S. multinationals are all multi-European national companies," says Ludolph of the International Trade Administration. "Because the euro will be more stable [than national currencies], there will be less cost associated with changes among the various currencies that a U.S. multinational deals in. So they really are in a position to reap most of the benefits of the single currency."

U.S. multinationals may also be better placed than their European competitors to take advantage of the increase in price "transparency" the euro will bring. Up to now, companies selling goods on the European market have been able to charge different prices among countries and hide the differences behind the veil of frequently adjusted exchange rates.

"Starting Jan. 1, companies will no longer be able to mask their lack of competitiveness behind the differences between, say, lire and marks,"

Ludolph says. "They will have to be able to explain to Italian and German customers what exactly is in the price, and price competition will begin in a serious way. Companies caught at high price levels will have to come down to whatever the average price is in Europe. With the euro, we will see the beginning of the kind of cost sensitivity that you see in the United States, where price is the primary factor in competition."

American multinationals may be well-prepared for the euro's arrival. But the same cannot be said for the majority of American exporters, who shipped more than $140 billion in goods and services to EU countries last year, accounting for a fifth of total U.S. exports. Since June, the Commerce Department has held seminars-around the country and in September created a Web site to help exporters deal with the change, including the need to shift their contracts from marks and francs into euros.

But only weeks before the euro goes into effect on Jan. 1, Ludolph says, "U.S. exporters are, as a practical matter, totally uninformed and unprepared for the euro. Most exporters really don't read the newspapers, so they're unaware that the euro is going to change the currency that they're going to be dealing with. When they start getting orders in euro, there will be quite a bit of turmoil."

On balance, however, the Clinton administration has concluded that the euro's benefits for the U.S. economy far outweigh its potential threat to the dollar's supremacy. In the administration's view, the benefits are twofold. "The euro would force Europe to make macroeconomic decisions that are more market-oriented," Ludolph explains, "and this would make Europe a stronger economic partner for the United States."

"Also," Ludolph continues, "instead of 15 members of the EU making decisions on exchange rates, there would be a single exchange-rate policy, one based on sound monetary and fiscal policy. We're really glad to see these governments adopting the same kind of structure that we have with the Federal Reserve Board." ■

BACKGROUND

Early Union Efforts

The euro is the end result of repeated efforts to coordinate Europe's economic policies that predate the postwar push toward European Union. More than 130 years ago, France established a monetary system that linked the franc with the currencies of Belgium, Bulgaria, Greece, Italy and Switzerland. The Latin Monetary Union was intended to tame the volatility of members' exchange rates, which had disrupted trade.

The union did not last. But efforts to stabilize Europe's exchange rates did, initially by fixing currencies to the gold standard. After World War II, calls for greater economic and political collaboration among the countries of Western Europe mounted. France and West Germany took the lead, creating the European Coal and Steel Community in 1952 to coordinate coal and steel production under a supranational authority. Belgium, Italy, Luxembourg and the Netherlands also joined.

Under the 1958 Treaties of Rome, the same six countries established the European Economic Community with the goal of removing barriers to the free movement of capital, products and people. Together with a third entity, the European Atomic Energy Community, these institutions were known collectively as the European Community (EC), or the Com-

mon Market. Britain, Ireland and Denmark joined the EC in 1973, followed by Greece in 1981 and Portugal and Spain in 1986. In 1990, German unification added an additional 18 million people to the 12-nation community.

In addition to broadening the EC's reach with new members, the community gradually strengthened the bonds linking them. In 1968 a new agreement removed all customs duties on trade within the EC, setting a common external tariff on imports to the community. The EC also adopted a common agricultural policy. In 1979, EC citizens elected the first European Parliament.

Searching for Stability

In 1944, a new system of fixed exchange rates was set up, supported by a newly created multilateral institution, the International Monetary Fund (IMF). Using the dollar as the dominant currency, the Bretton Woods system reduced the volatility of exchange rates and enhanced the postwar economic boom and expansion in world trade for the next 27 years.

At the same time, efforts grew to more closely integrate monetary policy within the EC, and in 1962 the European Commission first proposed establishing a single currency. In 1971, EC heads of government endorsed a plan drawn up by a committee of experts headed by Luxembourg Prime Minister Pierre Werner that called for full economic and monetary union with a common currency by 1980.

The Werner Report's strategy was thwarted the same year when President Richard M. Nixon suspended convertibility of the dollar into gold, causing the Bretton Woods system of fixed exchange rates to collapse. Left

Chronology

1950s-1960s

After World War II, Western European countries take steps to coordinate economic policy.

1952
The European Coal and Steel Community is set up to coordinate coal and steel production in France and Germany. Belgium, Italy, Luxembourg and the Netherlands also join.

1957
The same six countries sign the Treaties of Rome establishing the European Economic Community (EC), or Common Market, to remove trade barriers.

1968
A customs union goes into effect removing all duties on trade within the EC and setting a common external tariff on imports to the community. The EC also adopts a common agricultural policy.

1970s-1980s

Enlargement brings more Western European countries into the Common Market.

1971
President Richard M. Nixon abandons the Bretton Woods system of fixed exchange rates, resulting in chaos on European exchange markets and the creation of an exchange-rate system tying European curren-cies to the Deutschmark.

1973
The United Kingdom, Denmark and Ireland join the EC.

1979
A new European Monetary System is established to curb fluctuations in currency values. Community citizens elect the first European Parliament.

1981
Greece joins the EC, followed in 1986 by Portugal and Spain.

June 1988
EC members endorse a plan by Commission President Jacques Delors of France to achieve a single European market by 1992.

1990s-2000s

European integration proceeds with economic and monetary union.

1990
German unification adds 18 million people to the 12-member EC.

December 1991
Meeting in Maastricht, the Netherlands, EC members agree to establish a common currency and establish the economic criteria for countries wishing to join the monetary union.

January 1992
All internal border checks on the flow of people, goods, services and capital fall. The community renames itself the European Union (EU).

1995
Austria, Finland and Sweden join the EU, bringing the membership to 15 countries.

Dec. 12-13, 1997
Meeting in Luxembourg, the EU invites six countries — the Czech Republic, Cyprus, Estonia, Hungary, Poland and Slovenia — to become candidates for admission, but rebuffs Turkey, which first applied in 1963.

May 2, 1998
European heads of state meeting in Brussels agree that 11 EU member states will adopt the euro on Jan. 1, 1999. Greece fails to meet the criteria, and the United Kingdom, Denmark and Sweden choose not to join for the present. Wim Duisenberg, a former central banker from the Netherlands, is chosen to be the first president of a new European Central Bank.

Jan. 1, 1999
Eleven EU members will adopt a single currency, the euro, and hand over much of their power to make monetary and economic policy to the European Central Bank.

Jan. 1, 2002
Euro notes and coins are to be issued, replacing all national currencies in the 11 countries participating in monetary union within six months.

Wim Duisenberg of the Netherlands was chosen as the first president of the new European Central Bank.

to the vagaries of the marketplace, European currencies gyrated in value until 1972, when EC governments devised an alternative mechanism to stabilize them.

The new system, known as the "snake," tied currencies loosely to the mark, which by then had replaced the pound sterling as Europe's strongest currency, thanks in large part to Germany's strong anti-inflationary policy. But domestic policy differences, which caused broad swings in currency values, weakened the system. Britain, France and Ireland joined and then dropped the snake.

In 1979, EC members replaced the snake with the European Monetary System and established a new exchange-rate mechanism (ERM) that strictly limited fluctuations in currency values. Member countries agreed to take the policy steps necessary to keep their currencies within a narrow range of a central rate denominated in a new European currency unit (ECU), whose value was based

on the weighted average of all member countries' currencies.

But the new system was unable to prevent France and some other countries from repeatedly devaluing their currencies, and Britain and Italy eventually abandoned it. By 1993, EU members were forced to widen the allowable range of exchange-rate fluctuation.

Maastricht Treaty

By the early 1990s, the EC boasted 12 members and a complex of supranational institutions overseeing efforts to integrate Europe's diverse economies. But exchange-rate stability continued to elude the community. Dissatisfied with the ERM, EC members in June 1988 endorsed a plan by Commission President Jacques Delors of France to achieve a single European market by 1992. [10]

With the arrival of the "single market" in January 1992, EC members eliminated internal border checks on the flow of people, goods, services and capital. The community renamed itself the European Union and continued the process of enlargement by admitting Austria, Finland and Sweden in 1995, bringing the total membership to 15 countries. (Norwegians declined admission in a referendum.)

An integral part of Delors' plan was the creation of economic and monetary union as the first step toward political union. Included in the plan were common policies on foreign affairs, defense, justice and internal affairs. At the 1991 Maastricht conference, EC heads of government established five criteria for adoption of the single currency: a budget deficit of no more than 3 percent of GDP; a national debt of no more than 60 percent of GDP; stable currencies; and

limits on inflation and interest rates.

As governments worked toward meeting these strict conditions, EU leaders in 1995 set the Jan. 1, 1999, deadline for monetary union and replacement of the ECU with the new currency, which they dubbed the euro.

Britain, long the most vocal skeptic of European integration, opted out of the treaty and was joined later by Denmark, whose citizens rejected the single currency in a referendum, and Sweden. ∎

CURRENT SITUATION

Policy Differences

The ability of the 11 countries of Euroland to overcome deeply rooted economic problems has surprised the experts. Italy, for example, slashed its budget deficit from 11 percent in 1990 to less than 3 percent of GDP, as required by the Maastricht Treaty. They also have cut inflation and the ratio of government debt to GDP.

To achieve this performance, however, governments have had to make painful adjustments in public benefits and policies that have long been considered a right of citizenship. In addition, the same austerity measures that have enabled many countries to gain admission to the monetary union have blocked noticeable improvement in Europe's high unemployment rate. Unemployment averages 10.9 percent throughout the EU, ranging from a negligible 3.6 percent in Luxembourg to a severe 19.6 percent in Spain. Even as many Europeans welcome the euro's advent, the joblessness that has accompanied preparations for its arrival may undermine popular support for monetary union.

This is especially true in Germany, where government enthusiasm for the euro has never been matched by popular opinion. "Italy and the smaller states, such as Luxembourg, the Netherlands and Belgium, are very much in favor of the new currency," Miegel says. "But Germany, like France, is particularly hesitant. Germany has little history as a nation-state, so our economic situation, including our currency, means a lot to most Germans. For them, the mark is the symbol of Germany's resurrection after the Second World War as well as the symbol of identity when East and West Germany were united eight years ago. These are episodes in our history which are of great importance."

In exchange for giving up the mark, former Chancellor Kohl insisted that the European Central Bank adopt Germany's strict anti-inflationary monetary policy. But that may not satisfy popular opinion in Germany, Europe's economic powerhouse, where unemployment exceeds 11 percent of the work force.

Analysts attribute Kohl's defeat in September in part to concern about unemployment. His successor, Social Democrat Schroeder, promises to follow a political "Third Way" between traditional European socialism and American-style, free-market capitalism with a pledge to maintain Germany's generous welfare benefits while fostering industrial competitiveness.

But Schroeder's powerful finance minister, party leader Oskar Lafontaine, supports higher corporate taxes and berates the "casino quality" of free-market capitalism, alarming German business-men over the new government's true agenda. Schroeder has further unnerved corporate leaders by calling for a cut in the retirement age from 65 to 60, with no loss of Germany's generous mandated benefits, as a way to generate new jobs.

> "Italy and the smaller states, such as Luxembourg, the Netherlands and Belgium, are very much in favor of the new currency. But Germany, like France, is particularly hesitant."
>
> — *Meinhard Miegel, Director, Bonn Institute for Economic and Social Research*

Other governments, forced to adopt austerity measures to gain admission to the monetary union, face even more daunting problems. As unemployment topped 12 percent in the wake of efforts to reduce France's budget deficit, French voters last year replaced the ruling conservatives with a socialist government led by Prime Minister Lionel Jospin, who pledged to make job creation his main priority. In February, the National Assembly approved Jospin's initiative to shorten the workweek to 35 hours by 2000, in hope that more workers will be required to produce the same amount of goods and ser-vices. Jospin's job-creation efforts have begun to pay off, as unemployment dropped to 11.7 percent in September.

Dissatisfaction with high unemployment also helped bring down the government of Italian Prime Minister Romano Prodi, whose policies had forced the Italian economy into compliance with the Maastricht criteria. Prodi's successor, the former communist D'Alema, pledged that his center-left government would maintain Prodi's budget and other policies governing Italy's adoption of the euro.

But the fall of Prodi's government showed how concern over the country's 12.5 percent unemployment rate runs high, even in a country where popular support for the euro has thus far been strong. D'Alema himself predicted that his government's survival will depend on its ability to create jobs, and he pledged to pursue Prodi's earlier goal of shortening the workweek.

"In the final analysis, the hope is to be able to restore sustainable growth in Italy," Cicogna says. "Now that we have achieved financial and monetary stability, we have to try to get some dividends here at home with job growth. Unemployment is undoubtedly the No. 1 problem in Italy right now."

Skeptics Opt Out

A sign of weakness in Europe's support for monetary union remains the decision by the United Kingdom, Denmark and Sweden to opt out, at least for now. Disagreement over European integration has long dominated British politics, contributing to the 1990 resignation of Conservative Prime Minister Margaret Thatcher, who had reservations about the UK's place in the European Union, and the 1997 electoral victory of the Labor Party. Skepticism over monetary union continued to run so strong that even pro-Europe Conservative Prime Minister Tony Blair ruled out joining until after the next national election, expected to be held in 2001, and a referendum on monetary union shortly thereafter. Polls show a majority of Britons still opposed to adopting the euro. The government cited Britain's high interest rates as the main reason for its decision to postpone immediately adopting the euro and the fear that taking the steps needed to meet the membership criteria would destabilize the economy. That fear has continued as economic growth has since stalled, putting Britain out of sync with much of the rest of Europe. [11]

Unlike Germany, where opposition to the euro is based on the mark's symbolic value, British Euroskepticism has arisen mainly from a reluctance to yield sovereignty over its monetary policy and cast its lot irrevocably with the rest of Europe, a move some see as jeopardizing Britain's longstanding partnership with the United States.

"The sterling is a very weak currency," Grahl says. "We're always going to have to relate our policy either to the United States or to Western Europe. We can cut adrift from one, but only by attaching ourselves more closely to the other."

In Grahl's view, Britain will eventually adopt the euro, despite strong opposition among Conservatives and

their supporters, including media magnate Rupert Murdoch and his vast news empire. "Probably it will be more advantageous to link up with Western Europe than to base our policy on dollar interest rates," Grahl

> "The devastating American Civil War shows that a formal political union is no guarantee against an intra-European war."
>
> — *Martin Feldstein*
> *Professor of economics,*
> *Harvard University*

says, "because we have a lot more trade with Western Europe and because, typically, interest rates would be rather lower." ∎

OUTLOOK

Interest Rate Fight

On Jan. 1, 1999, the euro will be established as the official currency of the European monetary union. The new currency will be denominated in 100 cents to the euro, and its conversion rate in national currencies will be permanently set. Over the next three years, national currencies will still circulate, but all capital, foreign exchange and interbank markets will convert their operations to euros. Retail businesses will accept national currencies, but prices will be quoted in both national currency and euro values.

The final phase will begin Jan. 1, 2002, when euro notes and coins will be issued throughout Euroland. Over the next six months, retailers will have to accept both currencies, as national currencies are gradually withdrawn from circulation. On July 1, 2002, they will cease to be legal tender altogether, and the euro will stand alone.

Just weeks before the euro's introduction, disagreement over optimal interest-rate levels is dividing Euroland. Europe has finally begun to feel the effects of the financial crises in Asia and Russia, mainly in terms of reduced exports. The forecast for the region's economic growth next year has been lowered by a half-point, to just over 2 percent. [12] To help restore economic growth, a number of Euroland's leaders have started calling for a reduction in interest rates.

Meeting in Austria in late October, several EU leaders called for lower interest rates together with government programs to stimulate the economy. Their request was dismissed by Duisenberg as well as his likely successor, Trichet of France, as nothing more than politically motivated statements that Europe's central banks should ignore. More re-

At Issue:

Will monetary union help solve Europe's economic problems?

KLAUS FRIEDRICH

Chief economist, Dresdner Bank Group

From testimony before the House Banking and Financial Services Subcommittee on Domestic and International Monetary Policy, April 28, 1998.

*W*ith the growing globalization of markets, Europe has to seize every opportunity if it wants to compete successfully in global markets. . . . Competition between the three economic powers — Europe, the United States and Japan — will become even fiercer: New competitors, for example from fast-growing Southeast Asia, are entering the market. A large Economic and Monetary Union will increase Europe's growth, market and job potential, thereby strengthening its global, competitive position.

Competition within Europe will also stiffen. Germany has to face up to that challenge, too, while at the same time taking advantage of the opportunities a bigger market provides. A single currency will not only spare tourists and business travelers the inconvenience and cost of having to exchange their national currencies. An important direct effect will also be that companies operating in the European market will no longer have to deal with exchange-rate risks and hedging costs. This will make the flow of goods, services and capital more efficient, thereby pushing down prices.

Monetary union will also facilitate long-term investment planning; capital will flow more readily into areas where it can be used efficiently. Above all, the elimination of exchange rates will increase market transparency, which will particularly benefit small- and medium-sized firms. Price lists will become more transparent, and internal cost accounting will become easier. Finally, monetary union should step up the pressure on economic policy-makers to abolish existing protectionist mechanisms and to break up monopolies and rigid market structures within the [European Union].

EMU is the monetary counterpart to the liberalization of trade within the framework of the European single market. The elimination of trade barriers and the mutual recognition of technical norms and standards in the European single market are widening our continent's product markets. Hence, it seems only logical after the removal of physical impediments to trade to also provide the necessary monetary "lubricant" in the form of a single currency. Europe still needs to improve further as a business location, and the euro could act as a catalyst in this respect.

German companies in particular will benefit from monetary union. They have time and again been profoundly affected by the real overvaluation of the D-mark. . . . A single European currency will significantly reduce such exchange-rate-related competitive distortions, thereby strengthening the international competitiveness of German exporters.

Robert Dujarric

Research fellow, Hudson Institute, Indianapolis, Ind.

From Robert Dujarric, "Europe's Continental Drift," American Outlook, *summer 1998, pp. 60-62.*

*t*he new currency will create additional problems for the EU. . . . Optimists about [European Monetary Union] hope that it will lead to political union because a monetary union creates requirements for greater economic union. This notion, however, underestimates the resiliency of the nation-state in Europe. There is still no such thing as a "European people" or European solidarity. Note that whereas western German taxpayers transfer $75 billion annually (net) to eastern Germany, Germany's contribution to the EU is only $12 billion, and increasing it has become politically unacceptable.

It is probably wishful thinking to believe that a European Union could order massive transfer payments across borders of the sort common within nation-states. European integration efforts in the past half-century show that economic integration does not automatically create momentum toward political union. Europe has made enormous progress in economic integration, but on the political front there has been almost none. . . .

[M]onetary union will do very little to solve Europe's economic and social problems. It will not foster political union and is unlikely to increase the pace of necessary economic deregulation and reform. Moreover, the risks associated with EMU are very high. A failure of monetary union would create the most acrimonious intra-Western European dispute since the 1950s and could paralyze Europe for years as states disagreed over financial and economic matters while lacking institutional mechanisms through which to resolve them effectively. . . .

Eventually, Europe's governments will be unable to finance the continental welfare state as its costs rise faster than their ability to tax. This may well destabilize political systems when governments no longer have generous benefits with which to pacify the electorate, which could induce a protectionist, inflationary and anti-deregulation backlash. . . .

Continental Europe is rich, democratic and bourgeois. Decay and instability will not overturn its liberal democratic order, nor is war between Western European states conceivable. . . . It is probable, however, that Europe's economic and social woes will increase during the next 10 years and that its ability to help stabilize the regions of the former communist world in the Balkans, Eastern Europe and the former Soviet Union will diminish. That will increase possibilities for conflict in those regions because the former communist states need a dynamic, prosperous and strong European Union to help them make the transition to freedom.

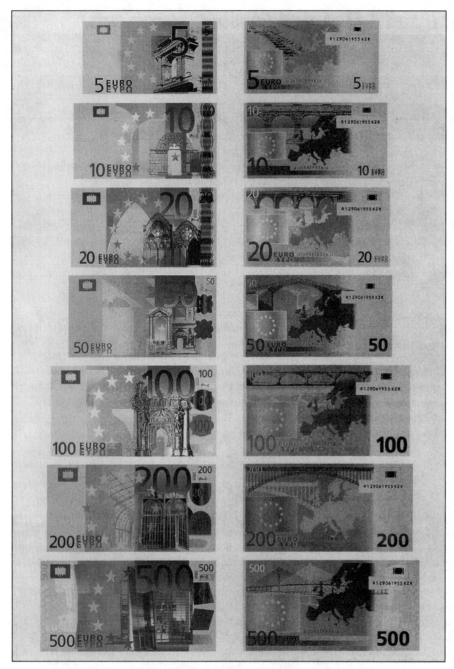

The new euro currency goes into general circulation in January 2002, and in July the German mark, Italian lira and other currencies will be withdrawn.

Italy cut its benchmark discount rate by a full percentage point in October, but that still left it at 4 percent, while Ireland's securities-repurchase rate stands considerably higher, at 4.9 percent.

Among Euroskeptics, Martin Feldstein, a Nobel Prize-winning economics professor at Harvard University, goes so far as to suggest that current differences over the relative importance of price stability and job creation and other issues may escalate under monetary union, in part because there is no acknowledged provision for countries to leave Euroland once they enter. "[C]ontrary to the hopes and assumptions of [French champion of European union Jean] Monnet and other advocates of European integration, the devastating American Civil War shows that a formal political union is no guarantee against an intra-European war," he writes. "Although it is impossible to know for certain whether these conflicts would lead to war, it is too real a possibility to ignore in weighing the potential effects of EMU and the European political integration that would follow." [13]

But supporters of the euro, including recent convert Portes of the London Business School, predict that the ongoing controversies over interest rates and job creation will soon be forgotten, as the euro's salutary effects on the European economy become apparent. Portes expects monetary union will provide a boost to capital markets in Europe, where companies have thus far relied mostly on bank loans to finance their business.

"You hear a lot of moaning about European labor markets," he says, "but there is increasing evidence that the major problem of the European economy is not over labor markets, but rather capital markets. We have lacked a single, broad, unified, liquid capital market in which firms can get away from the dead hand of bank

cently, German Chancellor Schroeder and his finance minister, Lafontaine, have joined the chorus, asking the Bundesbank, Germany's central bank, to lower its short-term rate of 3.3 percent. The same call has been heard in France, where the short-term rate also stands at 3.3 percent.

But not everyone endorses interest-rate drops. If Germany and France, whose interest rates serve as the standard for Euroland convergence, cut their rates, it will become that much harder for countries with higher rates, notably Ireland, Italy, Portugal and Spain, to stay in line.

financing and go into the markets."

Portes predicts the euro will permit the emergence of a thriving junk-bond market. "That kind of market doesn't exist here," he explains. "In Europe, it's only the big firms that can go into the capital markets, while the rest have to deal with the banks, and the banks are conservative."

As the capital market takes off, Portes predicts, big institutional investors will play the dominant role in financial markets, as in the United States.

"We will see the pension funds, insurance companies and asset managers take a pan-European view of their investment position and take on major roles in corporate governance and in exerting pressure on firms to improve their game," he says. "There will be integration of stocks markets, and this is really going to change the face of European business." ∎

Notes

[1] Speaking before a European Commission meeting held in Vienna, Austria, on Sept. 25, 1998.
[2] Eurostat, "New EUR 11: 'World's Greatest Trading Power,'" May 1, 1998; Eurostat is the EU's statistical branch.
[3] "European Commission Says 11 EU Member States Ready for Euro," *European Union News*, March 25, 1998.
[4] "The Global Giants," *The Wall Street Journal*, Sept. 28, 1998.
[5] See "Euro-Tongues Wag in English," *The Economist*, Oct. 25, 1997, p. 60.
[6] Josef Joffe, "The Euro: The Engine That Couldn't," *The New York Review of Books,* Dec. 4, 1997, p. 30.
[7] Isabella Bufacchi, "Le Borse degli Undici preparano l'attacco al trono di Wall Street," Il *Sole-24 Ore,* Sept. 28, 1998.
[8] Quoted by Christopher Gay and Sara Calian, "Ask the Pros," *The Wall Street Journal*, Sept. 28, 1998.
[9] See Dagmar Aalund, "What's the Euro?" *The Wall Street Journal*, Sept. 28, 1998.
[10] For background, see Mary H. Cooper, "Europe 1992," *The CQ Researcher,* June 28, 1991, pp. 417-440.
[11] See "Who Wants the Euro, and Why," *The Economist,* May 2, 1998, pp. 51-52.
[12] See Anne Swardson, "On the Verge of the Euro, a Continental Divide," *The Washington Post*, Nov. 7, 1998.
[13] Martin Feldstein, "EMU and International Conflict," *Foreign Affairs*, November/December 1997, p. 62.

FOR MORE INFORMATION

Delegation of the European Commission, 2300 M St. N.W., Washington, D.C. 20037; (202) 862-9500; http://www.eurunion.org. The information and public affairs office in the United States for the European Union provides statistics and documents on member countries and information on EU policies and programs.

Institute for International Economics, 11 Dupont Circle N.W., 6th floor, Washington, D.C. 20036; (202) 328-9000; www.iie.com. The institute conducts studies and makes policy recommendations on international monetary affairs. It has issued a number of studies on the effects of monetary union in Europe.

International Trade Administration, 14th St. and Constitution Ave. N.W., Suite 3850, Washington, D.C. 20230; (202) 482-3808; www.ita.doc.gov. A part of the Commerce Department, the ITA implements programs to promote world trade and monitors international developments affecting U.S. trade, including adoption of the euro.

Bibliography

Selected Sources Used

Books

Eichengreen, Barry, and Jeffry Frieden, eds., *Forging an Integrated Europe*, The University of Michigan Press, 1998.
In this collection of essays, economists and political scientists examine the potential for further European integration in the face of controversy over the degree of autonomy member states will retain.

Newhouse, John, *Europe Adrift*, Pantheon Books, 1997.
Newhouse, a consultant to the State Department, predicts that divisions within Europe over policy toward the Balkans, the decades-old feud between Greece and Turkey and other foreign policy issues will undermine the European Union's efforts to unify the continent.

Yergin, Daniel, and Joseph Stanislaw, *The Commanding Heights: The Battle Between Government and the Marketplace That is Remaking the Modern World*, Simon & Schuster, 1998.
Deregulation and privatization of industries worldwide are shifting power away from governments. In Europe, monetary union is accelerating the change as governments sell off unprofitable enterprises to help meet strict economic criteria for adopting the euro.

Articles

"An Awfully Big Adventure," *The Economist*, April 11, 1998, 22 pp.
This special survey of European monetary union examines the risks and potential benefits to Europe, the history leading up to the 1991 decision to adopt a single currency and the timetable for the euro's introduction.

Ash, Timothy Garten, "Goodbye to Bonn," *The New York Review of Books*, Nov. 5, 1998, pp. 41-43.
The September election of Social Democrat Gerhard Schroeder as Germany's new chancellor marks the beginning of a new era in Germany. The downfall of Helmut Kohl's 16-year Conservative government coincides closely with the replacement of the powerful Deutschmark by the euro and next year's move of the government from Bonn to Berlin.

Bergsten, C. Fred, "The Dollar and the Euro," *Foreign Affairs*, July/August 1997, pp. 83-95.
Unless the United States and the European Union cooperate to achieve a smooth transition from the dollar-denominated monetary regime, the new system created by the euro could create tensions between the two, sparking a round of trade protectionism that would disrupt world trade.

Feldstein, Martin, "EMU and International Conflict," *Foreign Affairs*, November/December 1997, pp. 60-73.
The Nobel Prize-winning economist warns that Europe is not ready for monetary union and that adoption of the euro will lead to disputes among European countries with different economic conditions that may spill over into neighboring countries outside the EU.

Fox, Justin, "Europe Is Heading for a Wild Ride," *Fortune*, Aug. 17, 1998, pp. 145-149.
Europe's businesses and citizens may be unprepared for the confusion and change that await them with the euro's introduction, beginning Jan. 1, 1999. Businesses will face unprecedented competition from rivals in other European countries, while unemployed workers may be unwilling to move abroad to find jobs.

Frieden, Jeffrey, "The Euro: Who Wins? Who Loses?" *Foreign Policy*, fall 1998, pp. 24-40.
The new European Central Bank may face conflicts in crafting monetary policy if some member countries slip into recession. Some groups, such as financial centers, stand to benefit from a strong euro, while workers and farmers would benefit from a weak euro, which would make European goods more competitive on world markets.

Joffe, Josef, "The Euro: The Engine That Couldn't," *The New York Review of Books*, Dec. 4, 1997, pp. 26-31.
A German journalist predicts that monetary union will not pave the way to political union in Europe: "Frenchmen and Germans don't want to be like the citizens of Michigan and New York; nor do Italians, Spaniards or Britons. They like Europe, but they like even better their national homelands, which have been around for one or two millennia. They don't speak each other's languages; they do not share each other's memories."

Malcolm, Noel, "The Case Against 'Europe,'" *Foreign Affairs*, March/April 1995, pp. 52-68.
A columnist for *The Daily Telegraph* of London opines that the costs of European integration outweigh any benefits. "'Europe,' he writes, "will stumble under the weight of its costs like a woolly mammoth sinking into a melting tundra."

Portes, Richard, and Hélène Rey, "The Emergence of the Euro as an International Currency," *Economic Policy*, April 1998, pp. 307-343.
Two British economists predict that the euro will end the dollar's uncontested dominance in world trade and financial markets, bringing political and economic benefits to Europe.

5 International Monetary Fund

MARY H. COOPER

They were known as the Asian tigers. Hong Kong, Singapore, South Korea and Taiwan had enjoyed such an economic boom that — together with Japan, Indonesia, Malaysia and Thailand — they had transformed East Asia into one of the world's fastest-growing regions and hottest destinations for foreign money.

Then, almost overnight, the tigers lost their roar. The beginning of the end came on July 2, 1997, when Thailand devalued its currency, causing skittish foreign investors to lose confidence in the country's economic prospects and withdraw their holdings.

Despite emergency infusions of cash from the International Monetary Fund (IMF) and other lenders, the flight of overseas capital spread throughout the region. Banks failed and economies fell like dominoes as investors pulled out of one Asian country after another.

As international investors grew increasingly pessimistic about emerging markets, the "Asian contagion" continued to spread. Last summer, it infected the Russian economy, and by September it was threatening Brazil and the rest of Latin America.

To many observers, the economic chaos claimed another potential victim: the IMF itself. In trying to calm the global economy, the low-profile agency was thrust into an acrimonious international debate over the way it had tried to stabilize the global financial system.

Indeed, the austerity methods the IMF used to staunch capital flight sparked criticism from some unexpected quarters. Harvard University economist Jeffrey Sachs, who had helped Russia dismantle its state-run economy, called the IMF the "Typhoid Mary of emerging markets, spreading recessions in country after country." [1]

From *The CQ Researcher,*
January 29, 1999.

And Joseph E. Stiglitz, chief economist of the World Bank, issued an unusually harsh assessment of the IMF's performance. Stiglitz suggested that the austerity measures required by the IMF — including the imposition of high interest rates — helped spread the Asian crisis even to well-managed economies. "Many countries that have . . . as reasonable economic policies . . . as you will find have been very adversely affected," he said. "The recognition that the contagion that occurs affects countries whether or not they have undertaken undue risks is a reality that has to be confronted." [2]

IMF Managing Director Michel Camdessus has defended the fund's actions, saying they will work over the long term. "The International Monetary Fund has come under heavy criticism in recent months both for its handling of global financial contagion and its proposals for defending against future crises," he wrote recently. "While many of the critics have offered constructive advice, at times the discourse has lost sight of the facts — and the true significance of the proposed remedies." [3]

Launched in 1945 to help stabilize the war-torn global economy, the IMF today provides short-term loans to its 182 member countries when they face temporary balance-of-payments problems caused by insufficient reserves of foreign exchange to pay off overseas creditors.

The IMF doesn't just hand out loans on demand but may require the recipient government to institute policy changes to improve its economy. In that way, the IMF seeks to ensure that the loan will be repaid and to reduce the risk of future crises. To help Mexico and other Latin American countries overcome a serious debt crisis in the 1980s, the IMF required higher interest rates to shore up investor confidence in local currencies, government spending cuts to reduce deficits and privatization of unprofitable state-owned enterprises. [4]

When the Asian financial crisis erupted in 1997, the IMF imposed similar conditions on governments that appealed for IMF loans. But the stringent spending cuts and high interest rates drove those troubled economies into further difficulties. Because businesses could no longer afford to borrow money, factories shut down and workers lost their jobs. Moreover, the region's already weak social programs were unable to prevent a sharp decline in living standards. Today, despite some signs of improvement, especially in Thailand and South Korea, recession afflicts the region, with depressed output, widespread unemployment and, in some cases, high inflation.

"The IMF has a difficult challenge in Asia," says Robert Manning, an Asia specialist at the Council on Foreign Relations. "They have put up more than $120 billion, and there has been no discernible uptick in the region's performance. But you have to consider another question. Where would the region be today without the IMF?"

The answer to that question, some critics say, is clear. "The world would be a lot better off without the IMF," says Mark Weisbrot, research director of the Preamble Center, an economic-policy think tank in Washington. Like other left-leaning critics, Weisbrot blames the IMF — and the

Economic Trouble in Developing Countries

Economic output plummeted throughout much of East Asia after Thailand devalued its currency in July 1997. The "Asian contagion" then spread to Russia and Brazil.

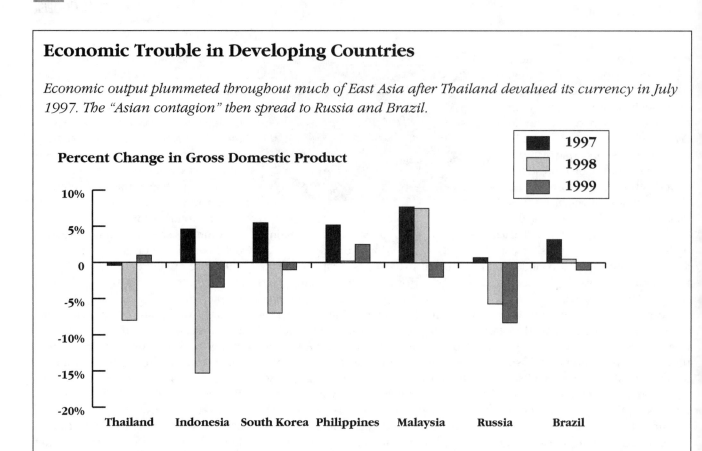

Percent Change in Gross Domestic Product

Legend: 1997, 1998, 1999

Countries: Thailand, Indonesia, South Korea, Philippines, Malaysia, Russia, Brazil

Source: International Monetary Fund

U.S. Treasury Department, its main ally — for impoverishing millions of already poor people in countries where it has required austerity measures in exchange for loans. "The IMF is like a medieval doctor who applies leeches and bleeds patients until they hopefully get better," he says, "but often they don't."

Opposition to the IMF's policies is no less scathing on the right, where critics charge that the fund undermines the workings of the free market by bailing out inefficient governments. "The idea that you need to pay for economic reforms has been proven time and time again to be incorrect," says Bryan T. Johnson, a policy analyst at the Heritage Foundation. "Transferring wealth from countries that have it to countries that don't have it is not a way to create and generate wealth in less-developed countries."

In this view, IMF lending poses a "moral hazard," a term insurance companies use to describe the risk that policyholders will fail to adequately protect their property once it is insured. Similarly, critics say, by holding out the promise of help to governments that fail to adopt sound economic policies, the IMF discourages countries from adopting such policies in the first place.

"The problem in these countries is that people aren't free to work" because their governments fail to embrace free-market policies, Johnson says. "Establishing economic policies that allow people to work doesn't cost money."

Voicing another common complaint from conservatives, many congressional Republicans have long decried what they see as the IMF's lack of accountability to the United States, its biggest donor. As evidence mounted that the

IMF's interventions in Asia and other regions had failed to resolve economic crises, lawmakers delayed action on the Clinton administration's request last year for $17.9 billion to help replenish the IMF's coffers. Congress finally approved the funding measure after attaching requirements that the IMF open more of its activities to public scrutiny.

Even fund officials acknowledge that changes are needed if the IMF can be expected to forestall economic crises in the future. "We can surely do better in reducing the frequency and intensity of emerging-market financial crises . . . than we have in the last five years," said American economist Stanley Fischer, the IMF's deputy managing director. [5]

In an unusual self-criticism, the IMF has admitted to mistakes in its handling of the crisis in Asia. "[B]oth the fund and outsiders erred in some ways that could have been avoided at the time," the agency conceded in a recent report. Moreover, earlier crises "might have led one to predict a much sharper slowdown in growth than was initially projected in the Asian crisis countries." [6]

Fischer added that the rapid spread of financial crises around the world in recent years "has led to the most serious rethinking of the structure of the international financial system since the breakdown of the Bretton Woods system in 1971" (*see p. 84*). The Clinton administration also has called for a "new architecture" to strengthen the system's ability to cope with the rapid flow of capital that has accompanied economic globalization (*see p. 90*).

As policy-makers consider revisions to the IMF and other institutions charged with ensuring the global economy's health, these are some of the questions they are asking:

Are the IMF's tough lending policies helping financially strapped countries?

Throughout its history, the IMF has advised governments receiving short-term loans on ways to improve their financial health. In the 1980s, the agency required indebted countries in Latin America to adopt strict austerity measures as a condition for receiving IMF loans. Since then, "conditionality" — requiring recipient governments to take steps to strengthen their economies before receiving loans — has been a prominent characteristic of IMF lending practices.

When Asian countries turned to the IMF for help in 1997, the agency's conditions for short-term loans included the familiar prescription handed out during the Latin American debt crisis: To shore up currency values and attract foreign capital, governments were required to raise interest rates. To reduce deficits, they were to cut government spending.

To raise revenues, they had to improve tax collection.

Unlike Latin America, however, Asia did not respond readily to the IMF's bitter medicine. Indeed, the region's economies sank into severe recession. Although the IMF now says it made some mistakes, it generally defends its policies in Asia as necessary to the region's recovery from the

financial crisis. "If you have cancer, chemotherapy doesn't make you feel better in the short term, but it may nevertheless be essential for a successful cure," explained Michael Mussa, director of the agency's research department. [7]

But many analysts now say that the IMF's "chemotherapy," which may work in countries with large trade and budget deficits, was overkill for Asia, where economic policies were generally sound. "These countries were growing at very healthy rates before the crisis," Weisbrot says. "They were running budget surpluses and had some of the world's highest savings rates. There is not any excuse in the world to try and put them through the wringer. It was completely outrageous."

Asia expert Manning agrees that the IMF's prescription for Asia was faulty, at least initially. "In the beginning of the crisis, they were almost

mechanically applying some of the formulas they'd used for Latin America," he says, "but the budget and other problems typical of Latin America didn't exist in Asia."

When its policies failed to help Asia's ailing economies, the IMF relaxed its conditions somewhat, resulting in some economic improvement, at least in Thailand and South Korea. "To the IMF's credit, they did revise their stance," Manning says. "Of course, that also raises the question of whether they knew what they were doing in the first place."

That question is particularly relevant, critics say, in the IMF's program for Russia, which last Aug. 17 devalued the ruble and defaulted on $40 billion in domestic treasury debt. [8]

When the Soviet Union collapsed in 1991, the IMF faced perhaps its most challenging task ever: helping Russia and the other successor republics enter the global free-market system by privatizing state-owned enterprises and opening their economies to foreign investment and trade.

Even after receiving billions of dollars from the IMF and other donors, the Russian economy remained in a shambles. Foreign trade had virtually ground to a halt, many profitable businesses were in the hands of criminals and the standard of living of ordinary Russians was arguably lower than at any time since World War II.

The IMF suspended its lending to Russia, raising further questions about the agency's ability to solve financial crises. "Russia is clearly the most destructive example of IMF policy failures," Weisbrot says, citing the halving of Russia's gross domestic product (GDP) and falling life expectancy over the past few years. "They have tried to transform this economy in the space of just a few years from a planned economy to their kind of textbook, idealized version of a market economy, and it's been a complete disaster."

How the IMF Works

Membership in the International Monetary Fund is voluntary and open to any country that controls its own foreign policy and agrees to abide by the fund's charter. Among other things, members promise to maintain uniform exchange rates. The IMF currently has 182 members, including Russia and other former Soviet republics. [1]

Central to the fund's mission is the smooth flow of money around the world, a flow that has increased in volume with the expansion of world trade and international investment. Because there are almost as many different currencies in circulation as there are IMF members, currency exchanges occur with virtually every shipment of goods across borders. [2] A wine merchant in Brazil, for example, wishing to buy a shipment of Chianti from an Italian vineyard would run into trouble if he tried to pay in Brazilian reals. But because both Italy and Brazil have made their currencies convertible as part of their commitment to the IMF, the transaction can take place after the merchant exchanges his reals for lire.

The IMF also acts as a kind of credit union. Upon joining, each country contributes a certain amount of money, called a quota subscription. The quota goes into a pool that the IMF draws from to lend to members in financial difficulty. The amount of the contribution, which is based on the country's annual economic output, determines how much it can borrow from the IMF. The quota amount also determines each member's clout in formulating IMF policy.

The United States, the world's largest economy, contributes the most — 18 percent of the total, or about $35 billion; the island nation of Palau, which joined in 1997, contributes the least, about $3.8 million. Likewise, the United States has the strongest voice in setting IMF policies, with more than 265,000 votes, or 18 percent of the total; Palau has 272 votes.

Each member has a representative and an alternate on the Board of Governors, the IMF's top policy-making group. Typically finance ministers or central bank heads, they meet annually. During the rest of the year, the board members relay their governments' positions on day-to-day IMF operations to members of the decision-making Executive Board in Washington. The board's chairman — currently Michel Camdessus of France — is also the IMF's managing director, who by tradition is not an American. (The president of the World Bank, the IMF's sister institution, is traditionally an American.) A staff of about 2,600 people from 122 countries, including battalions of economists, carry out IMF policies.

The fund's main objective is to prevent financial crises. "The IMF has a key role in crisis prevention," says Shailendra J. Anjaria, the fund's external relations director. "In fact, if the IMF does a good job with crisis prevention, it will not be called upon as frequently as it might otherwise to provide large financing packages. Prevention is better than cure. It's also less costly to prevent a fire than to fight a fire."

The main tool used by the IMF to prevent financial crises is surveillance, which it carries out by analyzing all member countries' economic data and suggesting any changes it feels will improve economic conditions. To make it easier to assess those conditions, the IMF recently adopted uniform standards members must use in reporting economic and financial data, including taxation and government expenditures.

"It is very important for the public and for markets to have a consistent and coherent notion of where the money is coming in and where it is going out," Anjaria explains. The IMF's aim, he says, is to "encourage countries to become more transparent and follow coherent standards that can be understood all over the world."

The IMF also has begun publicizing its assessments of economic conditions in member countries. "If markets are better informed, they can make better decisions and are not caught by surprise," Anjaria adds. As a result, "there is less destruction when there is a change in the situation than if the markets were caught by surprise."

When preventive measures fail and member countries encounter difficulties in paying overseas creditors, the IMF will provide short-term loans to help them meet their financial obligations on condition that they adopt economic policies prescribed by the IMF. Before the Asian crisis erupted in mid-1997, the fund provided five- and 10-year loans, each limited to the recipient country's quota. In 1997 it added a two-and-a-half-year loan. Although the new, short-term loan must be repaid earlier and carries a slightly higher interest rate than the other types, the amount is not limited to the recipient's contribution to the IMF. To date, South Korea, Russia and Brazil have received IMF credit under the new terms.

Very few countries have defaulted on IMF loans. Even Russia, which is behind on many of its foreign debts, is current on its IMF obligations. The reason, Anjaria explains, is that other lenders look to a country's record with the IMF before extending credit.

"Countries are very anxious to be current with the IMF," he says, "because if they didn't pay $1 billion back to the IMF, they wouldn't get $100 billion from other places."

---

[1] Material in this section is based on David D. Driscoll, "What Is the International Monetary Fund," September 1998, available on the IMF's Web site at www.imf.org.

[2] Eleven European countries recently adopted a single currency, the euro. For background, see Mary H. Cooper, "European Monetary Union," *The CQ Researcher*, Nov. 27, 1998, pp. 1025-1048.

In Russia, many critics say, the IMF compounded excessive optimism over the economy's potential for rapid change with a failure to perceive the political repercussions of its reform prescription. "The IMF didn't pay enough attention to how the actual policies they were pursuing were being implemented on the ground in Moscow," says Thomas Graham, a senior associate at the Carnegie Endowment for International Peace and a former U.S. diplomat in Moscow. "They came up with a program that they thought made sense from an economic standpoint but did not consider whether there would be sufficient political backing to get the various parts of the program approved by the Russian parliament. Therefore, a lot of things they proposed simply did not work out in reality because of opposition within the broader political framework of the population as a whole."

Particularly noxious to many Russians was the IMF's call for privatization of state-owned businesses and sweeping budget cuts in a country accustomed to generous government benefits. "I think most Russians now accept privatization as a necessity," Graham says. "But there were concerns about the way the program that was devised by the Russian government in consultation with Western advisers and the IMF played itself out in practice, the way it appeared to enrich a very small group of politically well-connected businessmen and financiers."

Shailendra J. Anjaria, the IMF's director of external relations, defends the IMF's program for Russia as a long-term effort that entails no less than the rebuilding of the nation-state and its institutions, which collapsed with the Soviet Union. "Those who felt that reforms could be achieved overnight will perhaps be disappointed," he says. "But that does

"While many of the critics have offered constructive advice, at times the discourse has lost sight of the facts — and the true significance of the proposed remedies."

— *Michel Camdessus, IMF Managing Director*

not mean that the reforms were not needed or are not needed now."

Critics see the IMF's role in Brazil, the latest victim of the international financial crisis, as equally destructive. "Brazil is going into a recession right now and largely as a result of policies imposing extremely high interest rates, of around 36-40 percent in a country where inflation is running at only 3-4 percent," Weisbrot

says. "If we had such policies [in the United States], we'd be in a depression today."

But here, too, IMF supporters say the criticism is misplaced. "The IMF does not impose policies," said C. Fred Bergsten, director of the Institute for International Economics, a nonprofit think tank in Washington. "It works them out with the countries. Brazil's high interest rates were put in place by Brazil a year ago. You can't blame it on the IMF." [9]

Is the IMF up to the task of dealing with financial crises on its own?

The seemingly relentless spread of the financial crisis from Asia to Russia and possibly to Latin America over the past year and a half has left many observers wondering whether the IMF is still able to do its job.

Computerized trading has made it increasingly easy for international investors to buy and sell stocks, bonds and other securities 24 hours a day, and liberalized markets have greatly expanded their access to countries around the world. While all this facilitates the free flow of capital by making it easier for investors to quickly move their money from one country to another, it makes it harder for the IMF to keep an eye on things and avert crises before it's too late.

"The reason that dealing with economic problems is more difficult today than it was 25 or 50 years ago is that the world is more integrated," Anjaria says. "Economies also are more integrated with each other, and there is a belief very strongly held in all parts of the world that markets

Did Malaysia Shoot Itself in the Foot . . .

When panicky investors began pulling their money out of one East Asian country after another in mid-1997, one nation refused to stand by and wait for disaster to strike. Malaysia simply slammed the door shut. On Sept. 1, 1998, it adopted currency controls that barred foreigners from withdrawing their funds for a year after investment and pegged the currency, the ringgit, to the U.S. dollar.

"The free-market system has failed and failed disastrously," declared Prime Minister Mahathir Mohamad. "The only way that we can manage the economy is to insulate us ... from speculators." [1]

Mahathir's solution to the Asian financial crisis dismayed the International Monetary Fund (IMF) and other supporters of global economic integration. It reminded them of the beggar-thy-neighbor policies of the 1930s, when countries refused to exchange their currencies, contributing to the international tensions that eventually ignited World War II. Preventing a repetition of that scenario was the impetus behind the IMF's creation 54 years ago and the gradual liberalization of international capital flows that followed.

"If the capital is well-used for productive investment rather than for real estate and other speculative investment, it adds to a country's wealth potential and improves its standard of living," says Shailendra J. Anjaria, the IMF's director of external relations. "The most important thing is that the capital flow be sustainable and stable." For countries to enjoy these benefits, he says, they must adopt sound economic policies and have strong, well-run financial institutions. "I don't think that there is any disagreement whatsoever that under those conditions capital liberalization is helpful and not hurtful." [2]

But some economists say that capital controls are a legitimate policy alternative, at least in situations like Malaysia's. Rather than allow the depletion of its capital reserves and accept the painful austerity measures linked to IMF loans, Malaysia sought to prevent its economy, already suffering its first recession in more than a decade, from plunging even further.

Indeed, private lenders, who have yet to return to much of Asia, recently extended a $1.35 billion loan to Malaysia. [3] That development cheers Mark Weisbrot, research director of the Preamble Center in Washington. "Here's a country that's already been put on the bad list by the IMF for adopting currency controls and had their bond rating reduced to near junk-bond status in world markets," he says. "They went to the big U.S. banks and told them to give them the loan or get out of their country, and it worked. It shows how much the IMF and these other colonial institutions really depend on the very active collaboration of the leadership of countries" that turned to the IMF for help as the crisis spread.

In addition to the new infusion of private loans, Malaysia has enjoyed low inflation, a widening trade surplus and rising consumption. But the jury is still out on the long-term impact of its currency controls. Industrial production declined in the third quarter of 1998, indicating a possible deepening of Malaysia's recession. [4]

In adopting capital controls, Mahathir may have taken his cue from China, which does not allow the free conversion of its currency although it is a member of the IMF. China's economic insulation from the economic collapse around it has enabled the economy to continue to grow, though perhaps not by the stunning 7.8 percent reported by the government for 1998. "The Chinese have control over their banking system, and they don't have massive foreign ownership of stocks," Weisbrot says. "They have all the tools they need to run their own economy."

While other Asian governments turned to the IMF for help and cut back public spending, China embarked on a stimulus program, including massive subsidies for construction and factory expansion. "Some of the things they're building won't be used for years, but so what?" Weisbrot says. "They're keeping their economy from sinking into the swamp that everyone else is sinking into. This is just because they're one of the only independent countries in the world."

Other experts say China is merely postponing an inevitable reckoning with economic reality. "China has a

must be kept open, even when there is a crisis."

The IMF has tried to improve its ability to prevent and cure financial crises by encouraging member countries to provide consistent and timely data on their economic conditions. (*See story, p. 80.*) Some economists call for expanding the agency's power as well. Billionaire investor George Soros has

proposed transforming the IMF into a global central bank, ready to bail out countries with much larger infusions of money than the IMF currently has at its disposal. [10]

Soros also has proposed the creation of an "international credit insurance corporation" to provide prompt infusions of capital into countries threatened by the kind of sudden withdrawal of pri-

vate capital experienced during the Asian crisis. This new entity would work much as a doctor gives a blood transfusion to an accident victim. "The most urgent need is to arrest the reverse flow of capital," Soros wrote. "That would ensure the continued allegiance of the periphery to the global capitalist system, which would in turn reassure the financial centers . . . and moderate the

... When It Adopted Currency Controls?

financial system as weak as any in Asia," says Robert Manning, a specialist on Asia at the Council on Foreign Relations. "Because they're so nervous about unemployment and instability, they're simply having the banks gin up more loans to state-owned enterprises. But they are digging themselves into an even deeper hole, and the next two or three years are going to be very dicey for China."

But as austerity measures have failed to quickly restore economic health to Asia, many economists are reconsidering the suitability of some form of currency controls. Massachusetts Institute of Technology economist Paul Krugman, for example, warns that the postwar liberalization of financial markets and move to full currency convertibility may have gone too far. "[I]n bringing back the virtues of old-fashioned capitalism, we also brought back some of its vices, most notably a vulnerability both to instability and sustained economic slumps," he wrote. "[I]t is hard to avoid concluding that sooner or later we will have to turn the clock at least part of the way back: to limit capital flows for countries that are unsuitable for either currency unions [such as the European Monetary Union] or free floating." [5]

Not all currency controls are the same, however. By adopting such strict controls after investors were already pulling out of Malaysia, Mahathir may have caused unnecessary long-term harm to the economy. "Malaysia stopped currency from leaving the country after it had already left," Manning says. "So instead of actually stopping currency from leaving, they're making it harder for currency to come in. Malaysia is using every trick in the book to get capital, but over the longer term it's not going to be very productive for them."

Many economists endorse the more modest controls adopted by Chile as a better way to discourage capital flight that stops short of scaring away investors interested in long-term investment. Instead of directly banning the withdrawal of foreign capital, Chile in 1991 began phasing in a tax on capital investments that were withdrawn from the country after less than one year. "Overall, the international system has an interest in creating a tax regime

that motivates capital to make long-term investments in the real economy, rather than one that rewards speculators for destabilizing currency markets," writes Ethan B. Kapstein, a political scientist at the University of Minnesota. But he warns against imposing the kind of strict controls that Malaysia has adopted. "This might make sense for some countries at particular moments in their development, but as a general rule it would do considerable harm to the world economy. It would freeze a good share of trade and investment flows, lowering growth rates and creating new sources of conflict." [6]

For the time being, capital controls have ceased to be a burning issue for some economists, who point out that even Chile abandoned its controls last fall. "The question of capital controls on inflows was a relevant issue for debate and discussion among economists at a time when there was a lot of capital sloshing around in the world," says Anjaria. But the amount of private capital invested in developing countries has shrunk dramatically since 1997, when it totaled $286 billion. "Today you're not going to worry about whether to keep capital out or not because none is coming in," Anjaria says. "So I think that debate for the time being can be put on the back burner, and what we can do is help countries build stronger financial systems so that they can deal with the flow of capital when capital does decide to return."

---

[1] Quoted by Sheila McNulty, "Mahathir Introduces Strict Currency Curbs," The (London) Financial Times, Sept. 2, 1998.

[2] For background, see also Shailendra J. Anjaria, "The Capital Truth," Foreign Affairs, November/December 1998, pp. 142-143.

[3] See "12 Banks to Lend Malaysia $1.35 Billion at a Low Rate," The New York Times, Dec. 30, 1998.

[4] See "Malaysia's Industrial Output Tumbled," The Wall Street Journal, Jan. 12, 1999.

[5] Paul Krugman, "The Return of Depression Economics," Foreign Affairs, January/February 1999, pp. 71, 74.

[6] Ethan B. Kapstein, "A Global Third Way: Social Justice and the World Economy," World Policy Journal, winter 1998/99, p. 33.

---

ensuing recession." [11]

In a similar vein, the IMF's Fischer has called for the agency to become the world's official "lender of last resort," making larger loans available to troubled countries than the fund currently can afford to make. To reduce the "moral hazard" of rescuing any needy government, Fischer recommends limiting IMF loans to

countries that follow sound economic policies. "These changes should not result in an increase in IMF lending," Fischer said. "For if the reforms succeed, there will be fewer international crises, and fewer occasions for crisis lending. And that, surely, is a goal we all share." [12]

Critics of IMF lending policies naturally look askance at proposals

to expand the agency's authority. "In an ideal world, it may be that we would need a central bank for the global economy if it did at least as good a job as the Federal Reserve does in the United States," says Weisbrot, who points out that Alan Greenspan, chairman of the U.S. central bank, is at least indirectly answerable to the American public for his policies. "But at the international level, institutions like the IMF are accountable only to the most powerful actors in the world economy, which are big corporations and the U.S. Treasury Department."

Weisbrot is far more supportive of alternative proposals to expand the role of regional, rather than global, institutions. Japan, for example, proposed the creation of a new Asian Monetary Fund, to be funded largely by Japan and limited to the countries of East Asia. "I'm very much in favor of that approach," he says. "Japan has an interest in economic growth throughout that region because that's where most of its exports go. It's much better than having one country control the whole world economy, as the United States does through the IMF." The regional approach is opposed by the United States and other developed countries that fear it would undermine the IMF's leadership role.

Some critics of the IMF say it should be abolished altogether. "The IMF and the World Bank believe they can stop these short-term economic crises by simply transferring wealth from institutions to countries that need it," says Johnson of the Heritage Foundation. "But that ignores the central reason why these countries have put themselves in a situation where there is little or no foreign investment coming in and why they aren't achieving economic growth. The reason is that those governments have bad economic policies."

Far from encouraging governments to improve their policies, in Johnson's view, IMF lending programs inevitably lead them to put off government spending cuts and other painful policy adjustments, in spite of the agency's strict conditionality. "If you look at all the major IMF recipients over the last 50 years, you will see that a country that becomes an IMF recipient is much more likely to become a long-term recipient of as-

sistance than countries that didn't get IMF aid," Johnson says. "Once you become a recipient of aid, you become addicted to it."

But most economists say that abolishing the IMF is not the answer to today's financial instability. Even Russia, which critics call the most conspicuous example of poor management by the IMF, may have benefited from the agency's technical assistance. "I think those who argue that Russia would be in better shape now without the IMF are wrong," says the Carnegie Endowment's Graham. "In the absence of an IMF, there would have been an even greater decline in economic activity, and the Russians wouldn't have the knowledge base they have now to apply to what is still a very difficult situation."

While acknowledging the need for some changes to the IMF in light of the changing global financial system, IMF spokesman Anjaria urges caution. "Because the Asian crisis had a strong element of contagion and spread unexpectedly, because the economic downturns were deeper than people initially expected and because some people were waiting for instant results, there was initially a flurry of frantic calls for reforming everything under the sun," he says. "I think that as the Asian situation stabilizes, people will be looking at reform in a more considered and reflective way." ■

BACKGROUND

Visionaries at Work

T he International Monetary Fund was founded as part of a new international system set up to help restore financial stability and expand

world trade in the aftermath of World War II. Meeting in Bretton Woods, N.H., in July 1944, delegates of the United States and 43 other countries devised a system of fixed exchange rates in which participating currencies were pegged to the dollar, which in turn was linked to gold. [13]

The IMF, which began operations in May 1946, was set up to monitor the new regime's performance and support the convertibility of member countries' currencies. Its founders hoped that it could prevent the kind of sudden variations in exchange rates that had made governments reluctant to allow their currencies to be exchanged for foreign currency and contributed to the tensions leading up to the outbreak of hostilities.

At the same time that the IMF was established, the International Bank for Reconstruction and Development, better known as the World Bank, was set up. The IMF's sister institution was created to provide assistance in long-term development, initially to war-torn Europe and later to developing countries. With a loan to Belgium in 1952, the IMF began extending short-term loans to member countries having trouble meeting their financial obligations to other members. The loans are made available on condition that the recipient country's government undertakes economic reforms to eliminate the causes of its balance-of-payments problem.

The global fixed-rate system collapsed in 1971, when President Richard M. Nixon abandoned the gold standard, allowing the dollar to fluctuate in value. However, the IMF continued to play an important role in the rapidly expanding global economy when member countries voted to enlarge its mandate. In addition to supporting the convertibility of exchange rates, the IMF began to more closely oversee economic policies that influence the balance of payments in member

Chronology

1940s-1960s
After World War II, industrial countries join in an effort to rebuild the international financial system.

July 1944
Meeting in Bretton Woods, N.H., delegates of 44 countries set the stage for establishing the International Monetary Fund (IMF), to oversee the system of fixed exchange rates based on the gold standard, and the World Bank, to assist needy countries with long-term development assistance.

Dec. 27, 1945
Twenty-nine nations sign the articles of agreement formally creating the IMF, which opens its headquarters in Washington, D.C., the following May.

1952
Belgium becomes the first country to receive a short-term loan from the IMF, to help it meet a temporary balance-of-payments problem. As a condition for the loan, the IMF requires Belgium to make policy changes to help prevent such problems from arising in the future.

———— • ————

1970s
Although the Bretton Woods system of fixed exchange rates falls apart, the IMF expands its role in stabilizing the global financial system.

1971
President Richard M. Nixon takes the dollar off the gold standard, allowing the currency's value to float against other currencies.

1980s
Debt crises in Latin America prompt the IMF to impose stricter conditions on its loans.

1982
After borrowing heavily from foreign banks to finance economic development, Mexico is unable to repay its loans on time, sparking a debt crisis that spreads throughout the region. In exchange for loans to Latin American countries, the IMF requires austerity measures, such as budget cuts and tax increases.

———— • ————

1990s
The rapid expansion of international capital investments poses a new challenge to the IMF's oversight role.

December 1991
With the Soviet Union's collapse, Russia and the other successor republics begin the difficult task of transforming their economies, with technical and financial assistance from the IMF.

July 2, 1997
The Asian financial crisis begins in Thailand when the government, short of foreign exchange, devalues its currency, the baht.

Aug. 20, 1997
The IMF arranges a $17.2 billion loan package for Thailand, requiring the government to curtail spending and adopt other austerity measures.

Oct. 31, 1997
The IMF arranges a $42 billion loan for Indonesia.

Dec. 3, 1997
The IMF arranges a $58 billion rescue for South Korea.

May 21, 1998
Indonesian strongman Suharto resigns after riots break out to protest the government's removal of price subsidies on consumer goods.

July 20, 1998
The IMF assembles $22.6 billion in loans for Russia, following an earlier $10 billion package.

Aug. 17, 1998
Russia devalues the ruble and defaults on some debts. The IMF suspends payments to Russia.

September 1998
Malaysian Prime Minister Mahathir Mohamad imposes strict capital controls to curb speculation on the country's currency. Chile abandons the tax on foreign investment it introduced in 1991, as the volume of private investment capital flowing to developing countries continues to plunge.

Oct. 21, 1998
President Clinton signs into law a $17.9 billion funding increase for the IMF. The measure calls on the IMF to provide more information on its operations.

Nov. 13, 1998
In an attempt to prevent the spread of the Asian crisis to Latin America, the IMF and the Clinton administration unveil a $41.5 billion loan package for Brazil.

Jan. 19, 1999
Days after devaluing the real, Brazil abandons the currency's fixed rate, relying on high interest rates to buoy its value.

Is Debt Relief the Answer?

Many developing countries are so deep in debt to foreign creditors that they are unlikely to free themselves without help. Some economists call on creditors to offer these countries some form of debt relief, either by stretching out repayment deadlines or by forgiving debt outright.

The IMF and the World Bank have identified 41 "highly indebted poor countries" (HIPC) that are unlikely to pay off their creditors without help (*see map*). The IMF has helped put together special debt-relief packages for seven of the HIPC countries — Bolivia, Burkina Faso, Ivory Coast, Guyana, Mali, Mozambique and Uganda — which owe foreign creditors, including the IMF, a total of $3 billion.

But the IMF accounts for only about 10 percent of outstanding debt in the poor countries it has singled out for relief. Its main role is getting the foreign governments, banks and other creditors to agree to the terms of debt relief. "The HIPC initiative has been a significant source of debt relief for the countries that have already been approved," says Shailendra J. Anjaria, the IMF's director of external relations. "In addition, similar mechanisms have been extended to take care of Honduras and Nicaragua," the two Central American countries that were hardest hit by Hurricane Mitch last fall.

Russia, which fell victim to the Asian financial crisis last August, also has asked for debt relief. The government of President Boris Yeltsin announced in January that it could pay only about half of its foreign debt obligations this year without help. But many economists warn that offering extensive debt relief to any but the poorest countries would backfire. They note, for example, that Russia's plight is not as hopeless as that of war-torn Mozambique.

"Don't forget that today the reality is that private flows of capital, including not only loans but also direct investment, which can boost developing country economies in a very healthy way, are far more important than official loans," Anjaria says. "If you create an artificial incentive for countries not to repay their debt on time, you're not going to be able to attract private capital."

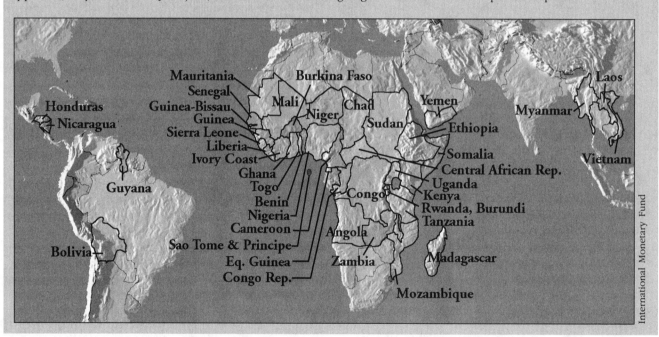

International Monetary Fund

countries and to provide policy advice as well as short-term loans to reverse imbalances.

The 1980s saw the expansion of private international lending, which was encouraged by President Ronald Reagan's downplaying of the IMF and other public institutions in favor of "the magic of the marketplace." But Reagan softened his antagonism toward the IMF when the 1982 Mexican crisis made it clear that private funding alone was insufficient to prevent a major economic disaster. The administration supported an $8.4 billion increase in the U.S. contribution to the IMF, which Congress approved in 1983.

The IMF played a key role in helping Mexico and other Latin American countries overcome the debt crisis, which threatened major commercial banks in the United States and other lending countries. To increase levels of foreign exchange needed to pay off their debts, the Latin American countries had to boost their exports and curb their imports. To this end they adopted sweeping reforms aimed at reducing government spending, raising taxes and raising interest rates to limit domestic borrowing. In Mexico and other countries where unprofitable state-owned enterprises contributed to budget deficits, privatization was another important element of the IMF's prescription for "structural adjustment."

To avoid widespread bank failures at home, the U.S. government provided short-term loans that enabled Mexico to pay off its immediate debts to banks. The IMF also provided some short-term financing, but its main role was to monitor the debtor nations' progress in improving their financial conditions. It was up to the debtor countries and their commercial bank creditors to negotiate new terms for the repayment of loans. In some cases, banks wrote off loans; in others, they accepted reduced payments.

The collapse of the Soviet Union and its allies in Eastern Europe in the early 1990s presented the IMF with a new challenge — providing technical assistance and funding to help successor governments in the region transform their state-run economies into free-market economies able to participate actively in the global trade system. The IMF funding went to so-called transition economies that accepted IMF advice on such matters as privatizing industries, setting up efficient tax-collection systems and adopting legal guarantees for foreign investors.

Crisis in Asia

The financial crisis that erupted in Asia in 1997 soon proved to be different from previous upheavals the IMF had dealt with. Runs on currencies in Mexico and other countries had been reversed after painful cuts in government spending and tax increases required by the IMF to qualify for its loans. Investor confidence was restored as sounder economic policies took effect, and foreign capital once again flowed into many countries receiving IMF loans, enabling businesses to expand and hire workers and consumers to purchase goods and services.

By 1997, however, the sheer volume of foreign capital investments and the ease with which investors could shift their money from one country to another had grown enormously. International capital flows from private sources to developing countries stood at $286 billion before the Asian crisis erupted, according to the IMF. That was far more than the capital coming from governments and multilateral institutions, which amounted to about $50 billion. Unlike foreign direct investments in production facilities, such as factories or power plants, capital investments in securities are highly liquid and can be quickly withdrawn at the first sign of trouble.

Among the most attractive targets for foreign investors since the early 1980s were the fast-growing, export-driven economies of East and Southeast Asia. Lured by the promise of high returns, investors largely ignored the warning signs of impending debt problems resulting from unrestrained lending and consumption throughout much of the region.

A favorite investment target was Thailand, even after it became clear that its currency, the baht, was overvalued. When the Thai government finally devalued the baht in July 1997, foreign investors, fearful that the booming economies of East Asia were primed for a fall, panicked and withdrew their money not only from Thailand but also from other coun-

tries, touching off a financial domino effect. The fall in value of currencies, real estate and stocks discouraged would-be private investors, driving away sources of new lending. The Asian contagion spread from Thailand to Indonesia, South Korea, Malaysia and the Philippines.

Battered East Asian countries tried to prop up their currencies by raising interest rates, hoping that investors seeking attractive returns would keep their money there. But these efforts failed to staunch the outflow of capital. Meanwhile, the high interest rates drove businesses into bankruptcy and workers into unemployment. Because most East Asian countries lacked the kind of social safety net that shields jobless workers from poverty in more developed countries, standards of living plummeted throughout the region. The crisis also deepened a recession in Japan, a key export market for the troubled Asian countries. [14]

IMF in Action

The IMF stepped into the Asian financial crisis with loan packages aimed at enabling the affected countries to pay off their most pressing debts. Those loans, which amounted to $57 billion for South Korea alone, came with the usual strings attached — mainly higher interest rates, cuts in government spending and higher taxes — in an effort to restore investor confidence and inflows of private capital.

But the IMF prescription failed to revive the Asian economies quickly, prompting criticism of the IMF for misdiagnosing the region's problems. The IMF later acknowledged that some of its conditions were too harsh and relaxed them somewhat.

Concerns about the IMF's effectiveness intensified on Aug. 17, 1998, when the Russian government devalued the ruble, dismissed the economic reformers who had worked with Western advisers since 1992 and imposed a 90-day moratorium on the repayment of foreign debts held by Russian banks. Russia's action caused stock markets around the world to plummet and prompted the IMF to cut off further payments to Russia, which had been mired in recession for more than six years. The IMF and other donors had provided billions of dollars to help Russia transform its economy, including a three-year, $10 billion IMF loan program in 1996 and a $22.6 billion rescue plan announced in July.

Another indication of the global financial system's vulnerability to sudden shifts of private capital came last fall, when the near collapse of a single U.S.-based hedge fund, Long-Term Capital Management, threatened to undermine the entire system. Fearing widespread panic if the $125 billion fund were allowed to default, the Federal Reserve Bank of New York arranged the fund's rescue by 14 banks and brokerage firms on Sept. 23.

By last fall, the financial crisis threatened to infect Brazil, whose currency, the real, was considered greatly overvalued. In September and October investors withdrew about $30 billion — more than a third of Brazil's hard-currency reserves. Because Brazil is Latin America's leading economic power and the eighth largest in the world, policy-makers feared that the spread of the Asian contagion to Brazil would infect the entire region and beyond.

To prevent that, the IMF and the Clinton administration put together a massive, $41.5 billion rescue package for Brazil, whose president, Fernando Henrique Cardoso, had recently won re-election on a cam-paign promise to drastically reduce the growing budget deficit. ∎

CURRENT SITUATION

U.S. Policy

Efforts to stem the global financial crisis have been led not only by IMF Managing Director Camdessus but also by U.S. Treasury Secretary Robert E. Rubin. Because voting in the IMF is based on the size of each member's contribution, or quota, the United States enjoys an 18 percent weighted vote in the 182-member fund. Because that is much more than any other single member — and because of the United States' traditional leadership role in the IMF — the United States has overwhelming influence over the organization's lending policies.

To many observers, the close working relationship between the IMF and the U.S. Treasury is symbiotic. The IMF enjoys the visible support of the holder of the world's leading reserve currency, the dollar, while the United States can advance its global economic interests behind the shield of a multilateral agency that acts on behalf of 181 other countries. "The critics don't seem to get it," Manning says. "The IMF is very useful to the United States because it lets somebody else do the dirty work."

But many critics contend that the IMF poses a threat to U.S. sovereignty by requiring the Treasury to pay billions of dollars to an organization that is not accountable to American taxpayers. Some conservatives also object to the IMF because they view it as meddling in the free market, which would fare much better, they say, if left to its own devices. In this view, countries that fail to adopt sound economic policies are lulled into complacency by the assurance of IMF assistance.

But criticism of the IMF is not limited to the right end of the political spectrum. "I'm opposed to the IMF because it's a completely unaccountable, colonial institution that plays an overwhelmingly destructive role in the world economy," Weisbrot says. "And I don't see them changing anytime soon."

Before Congress approved $17.9 billion in funding for the IMF last year, lawmakers held a series of hearings on IMF operations. As a result of these hearings, Congress required the IMF to make public more of its deliberations. For example, the funding bill calls for IMF materials to be made available for an annual audit by the U.S. General Accounting Office. It also requires the Treasury secretary and Fed Chairman Greenspan to certify that the IMF's leading members have agreed to support greater transparency in IMF operations, including the discussions leading up to policy-making decisions related to the fund's loan programs.

But there are limits to what the IMF can make public, Anjaria says, because member countries are loath to release all their current economic data for fear of frightening investors. "The IMF is dealing with very sensitive policy matters, such as external debt, exchange rates and interest-rate policy," he says. "I think a lot more can be done to improve transparency in these areas [after the fact], but during the decision-making process a certain degree of confidentiality will need to be maintained simply

At Issue:

Is the International Monetary Fund up to dealing with the financial crises of struggling countries?

ROBERT E. RUBIN
U.S. TREASURY SECRETARY

FROM TESTIMONY BEFORE THE HOUSE BANKING AND FINANCIAL SERVICES COMMITTEE, SEPT. 16, 1998.

*t*he United States has strongly supported the International Monetary Fund as the central institution in the effort to resolve the financial crises in Asia. The IMF programs have been focused on promoting reform in countries in crisis to address the problems that gave rise to the financial instability, combined with financial assistance if necessary. The IMF is the right institution to be at the center of this effort for three important reasons. First, it has the expertise to shape effective reform programs. Second, it can obtain reforms in crisis countries that no assisting nation could obtain. Finally, the IMF internationalizes the burden.

The IMF-led reform programs have been facing an unprecedented situation of enormous complexity. A number of countries have had great difficulties at the same time, and events in one country have greatly affected currencies, trade and investment flows and confidence in others. There have been enormous capital flows into countries with large amounts of private-sector debt and badly flawed financial sectors. There are no simple answers and no guarantees, and in our view, the judgments made by the IMF during this crisis have been largely sensible with subsequent adjustments as circumstances warrants. It is important to remember that problems in these countries are not a function of the IMF, but of the underlying crises.

Countries that have adhered to IMF-led reform programs — specifically the Philippines, Korea and Thailand — have begun to see signs of a return to stability. Although there is clearly a great deal of work yet to do, in Korea and Thailand, currencies have appreciated and interest rates have come down below pre-crisis levels. I have no doubt the situation over the past year would have been much worse without the work of the IMF. . . .

Russia, where the IMF has played an active role in trying to promote financial stability, is in great difficulty. . . . Russia made significant progress in reforming its economy over the last several years, particularly in privatization and trade liberalization. However, the Russian government this summer proved unable to adequately carry forward the necessary reforms. We all knew there was a real risk that this wouldn't work, but it was a risk well worth taking. . . .

Indonesia is another example of a country that simply did not take ownership of reform. In all countries in crisis, and this has been demonstrated throughout the past year, the politics of reform must keep pace with the policies of reform.

GEORGE SOROS
CHAIRMAN, SOROS FUND MANAGEMENT LCC

FROM TESTIMONY BEFORE THE HOUSE BANKING AND FINANCIAL SERVICES COMMITTEE, SEPT. 15, 1998.

*t*his hearing is very timely because the global capitalist system which has been responsible for the remarkable prosperity of this country in the last decade is coming apart at the seams. . . .

[One] major factor working for the disintegration of the global capitalist system is the evident inability of the international monetary authorities to hold it together. IMF programs do not seem to be working. . . . The response of the governments [of the seven leading industrial countries] to the Russian crisis was woefully inadequate, and the loss of control was quite scary. Financial markets are rather peculiar in this respect: They resent any kind of government interference but they hold a belief deep down that if conditions get really rough the authorities will step in. This belief has now been shaken. . . .

There is much talk about imposing market discipline, but imposing market discipline means imposing instability, and how much instability can society take? Market discipline needs to be supplemented by another discipline: Maintaining stability in financial markets ought to be the objective of public policy. This is the general principle that I should like to propose.

Despite the prevailing belief in free markets, this principle has already been accepted and implemented on a national scale. We have the Federal Reserve and other financial authorities whose mandate is to prevent a breakdown in our domestic financial markets and, if necessary, act as lenders of last resort. I am confident that they are capable of carrying out their mandate. But we are sadly lacking in the appropriate financial authorities in the international arena. We have the Bretton Woods institutions — the IMF and the World Bank — which have tried valiantly to adapt themselves to rapidly changing circumstances.

Admittedly, the IMF programs have not been successful in the current global financial crisis; its mission and its methods of operation need to be reconsidered. I believe additional institutions may be necessary. At the beginning of this year I proposed establishing an International Credit Insurance Corporation, but at that time it was not yet clear that the reverse flow of capital would become such a serious problem, and my proposal fell flat. I believe its time has now come.

because that is the practice in all countries at the national level, including the United States."

In any case, the reform measure may have little impact on IMF operations. "A lot of people may be surprised to learn that Congress can pass as many laws as it wants to [concerning the IMF]," Johnson says, "but there's no enforcement mechanism to back them up." The U.S. representative to the fund can exercise the power of "voice and vote" on the fund's executive board, but nearly all decisions are reached by consensus, and very few come to a vote. For that reason, Johnson says, "The IMF doesn't have to listen to anything the United States puts into law."

Indeed, some observers say Congress has little say at all in dealing with the global financial system. "Congress has become irrelevant," writes Robert B. Reich, Clinton's Labor secretary from 1993-97. For all the criticism of the IMF last year, Reich explains, Congress finally approved the funding increase. "They didn't want to be blamed for the global economy collapsing. But they don't know exactly what the IMF is doing with all that money or how it comes up with the strings it attaches." [15]

Is Asia Recovering?

Supporters of IMF policies today point to signs that the crisis in Asia may have bottomed out. "If you look at the performance of Thailand, Korea and Indonesia, there are many signs of stabilization and gradual turnaround," Anjaria says. South Korea, for example, has recently repaid, on schedule, $3.8 billion in loans from the IMF. Another sign of improvement in South Korea is the return of private capital; foreign investment in

the country reached a record $8.85 billion last year. [16]

The IMF now predicts that South Korea will turn last year's 5 percent decline in output into economic growth of more than 3 percent in 1999. Output in the other four countries in the region most affected by the crisis — Indonesia, Malaysia, the Philippines and Thailand — is expected to continue to decline, but only by 1.4 percent, compared with 10.6 percent in 1998. [17] "Clearly, there is a turnaround, and the economic formula which the IMF recommended is bearing fruit," Anjaria says. "In fact, the general conclusion that one can draw is that where countries implement sound economic policies and are serious about reforms, confidence returns faster than where they do not."

But critics say the IMF's assessment of Asian economies is far too rosy, particularly in the case of South Korea, where one of the goals of the IMF program was to lessen the influence of the corporate conglomerates known as *chaebols*. "You have to wonder if they know what they're talking about," Manning says, citing South Korea as an example of poor underlying economic conditions. "I'm not sure Korea has hit bottom yet because of its huge corporate debt. Because the banks are afraid that the whole financial system will go down, they continue to lend to the *chaebols*. As a result, the *chaebols* are actually playing a larger role in the Korean economy than they did before the crisis."

Unlike Latin America, Manning says, where earlier crises involved government-to-government debt, the Asian crisis primarily has involved private-sector loans to private-sector creditors. "So in countries like Indonesia, South Korea, Thailand, probably Malaysia and even Japan, you've got hundreds if not thousands of borrowers, and the challenge is how to

write off the debt and clear the books. You're not going to get significant amounts of capital coming back in until you sort that out."

As a result, Manning expects the crisis to continue to plague most of Asia for several years. "Beginning at the end of 1997, we're looking at three to five years, possibly longer in some cases," he says. Although Manning predicts that South Korea and Thailand may begin to grow later this year or next, "Indonesia is a basket case, it's on the edge of chaos, so it's going to be quite a while before they turn around."

Russia and Brazil

Russia remains mired in a deep recession and has seen private investment dry up since last August's ruble devaluation. But its long-term prospects are positive, in the IMF's view. "The unfortunate actions of Aug. 17," Anjaria says, "should not obscure from our vision the fact that Russia is a major economic power with a great deal of potential for economic growth, for improving the standard of living of its people and for contributing to world economic stability."

Some observers agree with the IMF's assessment of Russia's long-term prospects. "It would be a mistake to look at the past six or seven years as a total failure just because of what happened in August," Graham says. "The IMF did some valuable things for Russia by helping educate a whole layer of Russian officials as to how an advanced Western economy functions. If you look at where the country was seven years ago and compare that to where it is now, overall it is in better shape, at least in terms of knowledge of what it needs to do and eliminating some of the adverse aspects of the Soviet system. They've got a long way to go, but we all realized this intellectually in 1992. Then we became victims of our own enthusiasm and hoped that it would go much more rapidly than it did, which makes the situation now look much worse than it is, in fact."

Some critics dismiss the IMF's relatively optimistic assessment of current conditions because it ignores the impact of its policies on the poor in countries with IMF programs. "The impact in Indonesia is the worst of all," Weisbrot says. "The country is in a terrible depression, and there are people who are reduced to living on bark, leaves and insects." Indeed, following the May 1997 resignation of President Suharto, violence has erupted in several regions.

Even among countries that are thus far unaffected by the current financial crisis, Weisbrot says, adoption of IMF programs in the past has lowered living standards, especially for the poor. "In the 1960s and '70s, Mexico and other Latin American countries grew at a per capita rate of more than 3 percent," Weisbrot says. "Since the 1980s, those economies have been stagnant. So even by the IMF's own measure of success, which is economic growth, the era of structural adjustment has been a miserable, miserable failure."

Latin America's ability to avoid contagion by the current crisis depends on the outcome of Brazil's recent brush with financial ruin. The country's troubles sprang mainly from chronically high budget deficits and fears that it will be unable to pay its debts. Despite last fall's rescue package, put together by the IMF and the United States, the Brazilian government raised interest rates in a futile effort to retain foreign capital after the Brazilian Congress refused to approve some of President Cardoso's budget cuts. After a state governor

announced in January that his state would be unable to repay a loan to the federal government, investors pulled billions of dollars out of the country, severely depleting its foreign currency reserves.

In a desperate effort to staunch the outflow of capital, the Brazilian government announced on Jan. 13 that it had devalued the real. When that failed to buoy confidence in the currency, the government announced six days later that it had abandoned the real's dollar-pegged fixed rate and would allow the real to float on global markets, relying on even higher interest rates to buoy its value and attract foreign investors. But that move, strongly supported by the IMF and the Clinton administration, could result in a further devaluation of the real, touching off inflation and eroding living standards. Such a development would make it even harder for Cardoso to convince Brazilian lawmakers to approve the reform measures he says are needed to set the economy right.

Cardoso's move paid off on Jan. 20, when Brazil's lower house approved the most contoversial element of his austerity program, a pension-reform plan that was considered certain to win swift passage by the Senate. [18]

The specter of a Brazilian collapse bodes ill for the U.S. and European economies, which have been largely spared the ill effects of the ongoing crisis. Brazil alone buys 20 percent of U.S. exports and is the United States' 11th-largest market. A Brazilian recession would hurt American exporters, who have already seen a contraction in exports as a result of the recessions in Asia. Because other countries in Latin America have close economic ties to Brazil, it is likely that a crisis in that country would quickly spread throughout the region, further reducing demand for U.S. and European exports. ■

OUTLOOK

A 'New Architecture'?

Since the Asian financial crisis began a year and a half ago, many economists and politicians have called for a fundamental review of the global financial system and the institutions that oversee it. Computerization of financial markets, expansion of trade and the rapid integration of economies around the world, they say, have radically changed the global economy, leaving the IMF and other postwar institutions unable to ensure financial stability.

In addition to exercising its considerable leverage in the IMF, the Clinton administration has also called for restructuring of the global financial system to make it less vulnerable to the kinds of shocks it has received over the past 18 months.

"I have called on the world community to act to adapt the architecture of the international financial system for the new realities of the 21st century, the 24-hour-a-day, high-tech markets, with $1.5 trillion a day in currency exchanges," Clinton said in November. "That is many, many times the total value of goods and services traded in any given day. And that is at the bottom of a lot of the challenges we're facing today: How do we continue to support the necessary free flow of capital so that we can have the trade, the investments we need and avoid the enormous impact that a financial collapse can have when the money being traded on its own is so much greater than the total value of goods and services being traded or investments being made?" [19]

But critics say the administration has failed, in fact, to answer the very question Clinton posed, limiting itself to vague calls to come up with a "new architecture." "I think it's irresponsible to just say that as a throwaway line, as Rubin has done in several speeches," Manning says. "The real flaw is in short-term capital flows, where you've got some 25-year-old kid pushing buttons in New York or Singapore and taking down all sorts of currencies."

Some critics say the Clinton administration's failure to take a more active role in overhauling the global financial structure has undermined the United States' traditional leadership in this arena. "The Clinton administration has dropped the ball on this," says Johnson of the Heritage Foundation. "The first Bretton Woods conference was pushed by the United States, and we had a strong leadership position there. The administration has completely ignored this issue."

Meanwhile, British Prime Minister Tony Blair has called on the seven highly industrialized nations — the G-7 — to convene a contemporary version of the Bretton Woods conclave that created the IMF and World Bank. Some of the IMF's strongest critics would like to see such a conference abolish the fund and the bank altogether. "We need a multilateral institution in today's global economy, but I don't think it needs to be a money-lending institution," Johnson says. "It should be mainly a negotiating forum that allows countries to come together to reduce barriers to trade and investment."

But the IMF's Anjaria doubts that a new Bretton Woods-type conference would bring about such a radical overhaul of global financial systems. "As the Asian situation stabilizes, people will be looking at the issue of reform more calmly," he says. "One cannot look for instant solutions to these very complex issues. They will take time to resolve." ∎

FOR MORE INFORMATION

Council on Foreign Relations, 1779 Massachusetts Ave. N.W., Washington, D.C. 20036; (202) 518-3400; www.cfr.org/pl. This nonprofit research organization is among several groups studying proposals to strengthen the international financial system.

Heritage Foundation, 214 Massachusetts Ave. N.E., Washington, D.C. 20002-4999; (202) 546-4400; www.heritage.org. This think tank promotes free-market economic policies and is highly critical of the International Monetary Fund's role in the global economy.

Institute for International Economics, 11 Dupont Circle N.W., Washington, D.C. 20036-1207; (202) 328-9000; www.iie.com. This nonprofit, nonpartisan research institution is devoted to the study of international economic policy.

International Monetary Fund, 700 19th St. N.W., Washington, D.C. 20431; (202) 623-7000; www.imf.org. The 182-member multilateral organization provides loans to member countries facing balance-of-payment difficulties.

Preamble Center, 2040 S St. N.W., Washington, D.C. 20009; (202) 265-3263; www.preamble.org. This independent research and education organization studies a broad array of policy issues, including the impact of multilateral agreements on the world economy.

Notes

[1] Jeffrey D. Sachs, "With Friends like IMF...," The (Cleveland) Plain Dealer, June 6, 1998.
[2] Stiglitz spoke at a press briefing at the World Bank's Washington headquarters on Dec. 2, 1998.
[3] Michel Camdessus, "The IMF and Its Critics," The Washington Post, Nov. 10, 1998.
[4] For background, see David Masci, "Mexico's Future," The CQ Researcher, Sept. 19, 1997, pp. 817-840.
[5] Fischer spoke at a joint meeting of the American Economic Association and the American Finance Association in New York City on Jan. 3, 1999.
[6] Timothy Lane et al., "IMF-Supported Programs in Indonesia, Korea and Thailand: A Preliminary Assessment," International Monetary Fund, January 1999, p. 54.
[7] Mussa spoke at an IMF press conference on Dec. 21, 1998.
[8] For background, see David Masci, "U.S.-Russian Relations," The CQ Researcher, May 22, 1998, pp. 457-480; Mary H. Cooper, "Russia's Political future," The CQ Researcher, May 3, 1996, pp. 385-408 and Mary H. Cooper, "Aid to Russia," The CQ Researcher, March 12, 1993, pp. 217-240.
[9] Bergsten spoke on National Public Radio's "The Diane Rehm Show" on Nov. 19, 1998.
[10] George Soros, "To Avert the Next Crisis," The (London) Financial Times, Jan. 4, 1999.
[11] George Soros, The Crisis of Global Capitalism (1998), p. 176.
[12] Fischer spoke at a joint meeting of the American Economic Association and the American Finance Association in New York City on Jan. 3, 1999.
[13] Information in this section is based in part on Martin Feldstein, "Refocusing the IMF," Foreign Affairs, March/April 1998. For background, see also Mary H. Cooper, "Bretton Woods Forty Years Later," Editorial Research Reports, June 22, 1984, pp. 449-468.
[14] For background, see Christopher Conte, "Deflation Fears," The CQ Researcher, Feb. 13, 1998, pp. 121-144.
[15] Robert B. Reich, "Trial Ties Up Senate? Don't Worry, Congress Is Irrelevant," USA Today, Jan. 7, 1999.
[16] See "Foreign Investors Flock to Korea," The Wall Street Journal, Jan. 5, 1999.
[17] See International Monetary Fund, "World Economic Outlook and International Capital Markets: Interim Assessment," December 1998, p. 83.
[18] See Anthony Faiola, "Brazilian House Adopts Reform Bill," The Washington Post, Jan. 21, 1999.
[19] Clinton spoke at a meeting of the President's Export Council on Nov. 10, 1998.

Bibliography

Selected Sources Used

Books

Soros, George, "The Crisis of Global Capitalism [Open Society Endangered]," *Public Affairs*, 1998.

An international financier writes that the private capital flows that have made him a billionaire have grown to the point where the IMF is no longer able to prevent crises when investors suddenly withdraw their funds from a country. He proposes the creation of a new "international credit insurance corporation" to provide additional loans to developing governments that face liquidity crises.

Articles

Feldstein, Martin, "Refocusing the IMF," *Foreign Affairs*, March/April 1998, pp. 20-33.

A Harvard University economist criticizes the IMF for meddling excessively in the political affairs of governments that turn to it for short-term loans.

Fischer, Stanley, "The Asian Crisis and the Changing Role of the IMF," *Finance & Development*, June 1998, pp. 2-5.

The IMF's deputy managing director reviews the institution's transformation over the past half-century and its response to the current economic crisis. He calls for increased oversight of member-country policies to avert similar disasters in the future.

Krugman, Paul, "The Return of Depression Economics," *Foreign Affairs*, January/February 1999, pp. 56-74.

The author, an economist at the Massachusetts Institute of Technology, finds alarming similarities between the current economic crisis with the Great Depression of the 1930s. Continuation of the IMF's austerity measures, he writes, may bring about another global recession.

Madrick, Jeff, "The IMF Approach: The Half-Learned Lessons of History," *World Policy Journal*, fall 1998, pp. 39-55.

The best way to restore investor confidence in Asia and renew private capital flows to the region, writes Madrick, author of *The End of Affluence*, is to lower interest rates — not raise them as the IMF has required.

"Should the IMF Be Bigger or Smaller or Somewhere in Between?" *The Economist*, Oct. 10, 1998.

Calls for the IMF to become the world's "lender of last resort" by greatly increasing the amount of money member countries contribute to its lending pool would merely discourage governments from adopting painful but sound economic policies, the article suggests.

Wade, Robert, "The Coming Fight over Capital Flows," *Foreign Policy*, winter 1998-99, pp. 41-54.

The United States views the Asian crisis as the result of faulty policies in the countries involved. To many observers in Europe and Asia, however, it resulted from excessive liberalization of capital markets championed by the United States and the IMF. The author argues for a more permissive system that would allow for the coexistence of different types of national economic policies.

Reports and Studies

Bergsten, C. Fred, "Reviving the 'Asian Monetary Fund,'" *International Economics Policy Briefs*, Institute for International Economics, December 1998.

In 1997, Japan proposed the creation of an Asian Monetary Fund to help deal with the spreading Asian financial crisis. The idea was rejected because it was seen as a threat to the IMF's leadership role. The director of the Institute for International Economics proposes an Asia Pacific Monetary Fund to complement the IMF's work in the region by providing more effective oversight and intervention.

International Monetary Fund, *World Economic Outlook and International Capital Markets: Interim Assessment*, January 1999.

The fund issued this combined update of reports issued in the fall to reflect the "unusual turbulence" in financial markets that occurred in the final quarter of 1998. While it identified signs of recovery in a few countries hit by the Asian financial crisis, the report concludes that it is "premature to consider the difficulties to be over."

Johnson, Bryan T., and Brett D. Schaefer, "IMF Reform? Setting the Record Straight," *The Heritage Foundation Backgrounder*, Nov. 25, 1998.

Although the IMF funding measure signed into law last fall requires the IMF to provide more information about its activities, these analysts at the Heritage Foundation say it doesn't go far enough. They call on Congress to promote a new international conference aimed at reforming, if not eliminating, the IMF and its practice of "bailing out" governments with poor economic policies.

Lane, Timothy, et al., "IMF-Supported Programs in Indonesia, Korea, and Thailand: A Preliminary Assessment," *International Monetary Fund*, January 1999.

In this review of its lending policies in three of the hardest-hit Asian countries since 1997, the IMF admits to some mistakes in its handling of the region's crisis.

6 World Trade

MARY H. COOPER

The Qin Shi handbag factory in China's Guangdong Province employs about 1,000 workers to sew Kathie Lee Gifford handbags for Wal-Mart. They toil 12 to 14 hours a day, seven days a week. The workers share metal bunk beds in crowded dormitories. They are allowed outside the fenced compound for only one-and-a-half hours a day.

All this for an average wage of 3 cents an hour — about $3 for a 98-hour workweek. And that's the average. Almost half the workers earn nothing after deductions for room and board. [1]

With such low labor costs, Wal-Mart is able to sell the handbags in the United States for less than $10. In fact, the giant retailer finds overseas manufacturing so profitable that it imports more goods than any other U.S. firm. But it is hardly alone. Nike, RCA and Huffy are just a few of the U.S. manufacturers that lower their labor costs by making goods in China and other developing countries.

Before the House of Representatives voted to normalize trade relations with China last month, members debated more than such arcane matters as tariffs and import taxes. The most contentious issues were appalling working conditions like those at the Qin Shi factory, environmental pollution and the threat to American jobs posed by expanded U.S.-China trade.

World trade has emerged as a critical issue among American voters concerned about how opening up new markets affects ordinary people's lives — here and abroad. The last several months have seen the political debate spill onto the streets of

From *The CQ Researcher,*
June 9, 2000.

A 16-year-old girl makes Keds sneakers at a factory in China, which provides about 60 percent of all the shoes sold in the United States.

Seattle and Washington, D.C., in demonstrations that have rivaled in intensity the antiwar protests of the 1960s.

The protests have focused on the seemingly inevitable move toward a more global economy — the rapid expansion of international trade, the movement of multinational corporations to low-wage countries and the erosion of national boundaries by advances in telecommunications.

Critics — including labor leaders, human-rights activists and environmentalists — charge that globalization does little more than encourage corporations to relocate factories to countries with the cheapest labor and the weakest environmental laws. But proponents say that free trade, a hallmark of the so-called new economy, will be the key to raising living standards in developing countries, improving working conditions in authoritarian countries and protecting the environment on a global scale.

"The question is not whether trade works or is appropriate," says Jeff Faux, president of the Economic Policy Institute, a Washington, D.C., think tank. "Of course, it is both. The question is, 'What are the rules of this global economy?' Are we going to have rules that protect workers, human rights and the environment the way we have in

our own successful history?"

Free-trade champions, including the Clinton administration and business organizations, say such fears are unfounded. Not only will trade expansion, or "liberalization," establish new markets for American exports and thus create new jobs at home, they say, but opening countries like China to American business will inevitably open them to American values as well.

"With more than a billion people, China is the largest new market in the world," President Clinton said in welcoming the House vote. "Our administration has negotiated an agreement which will open China's markets to American products made on American soil — everything from corn to chemicals to computers. We will be exporting, however, more than our products. By this agreement, we will also export more of one of our most cherished values — economic freedom. Bringing China into the World Trade Organization and normalizing trade will strengthen those who fight for the environment, for labor standards, for human rights, for the rule of law." [2]

By granting permanent, normal trade relations (PNTR) with China, the House voted to relinquish its 21-year practice of approving China trade each year after reviewing the country's human rights record. (The Senate is expected to approve the measure by a wide margin this month.) As a result of the bilateral trade agreement reached last Nov. 15, Chinese imports will receive the same favorable tariff treatment the United States extends to all but a handful of countries subject to sanctions for political reasons, such as Cuba, Afghanistan and North Korea. [3]

In return, China agreed to open its markets to a broad array of U.S. farm,

Trade by China, Latin America Increased the Most

Exports from China increased by 15 percent from 1990 to 1998, nearly twice as much as the next-highest increase. Imports by China and Latin America increased the most during the period. Overall, Western Europe had more trade than any other region.

Growth in Value of Trade, 1990-1998

	EXPORTS		IMPORTS	
	Value (in $ Billions)	Percent Change 1990-98	Value (in $ Billions)	Percent Change 1990-98
World	$5,270	6%	$5,465	6%
North America*	897	7	1,152	8
Latin America	276	8	340	14
Western Europe	2,348	5	2,367	4
European Union	2,181	5	2,172	4
Africa	107	1	134	5
Middle East	137	0	144	5
Asia	1,293	7	1,086	5
Japan	388	4	280	2
China	184	15	140	13

Excluding Mexico

Source: World Trade Organization

industrial and telecommunications exports and reduce tariffs on those goods. The agreement, together with a similar pact China reached with the 15-member European Union shortly before the House vote, paves the way for China's entry into the 136-member World Trade Organization (WTO), the Geneva-based organization that oversees the global trading system.

In the view of free-trade supporters, history shows that eliminating barriers among countries hastens a fairly predictable process of economic development, one that moves from subsistence farming to industrialization, from authoritarian to democratic political systems and from poverty to modern living standards. "The economic evidence overwhelmingly suggests that other countries have had their wage levels rise over time because of trade," says Robert E. Litan, director of economic studies at the Brookings Institution, a Washington think tank. "Just look at countries that have been closed to trade — the Cubas, the North Koreas and, for that matter, Eastern Europe before the Berlin Wall fell. Countries that were closed obviously have done less well in terms of their wage growth than countries that have opened up. This is not rocket science; it's basic economics."

Likewise, trade boosters say that globalization helps the environment over time because history also shows that societies that are mired in poverty are too concerned about getting enough to eat to do much about curbing pollution.

"In the long term, trade makes everybody richer and better off," says Paul Portney, president of Resources for the Future, a Washington research organization. "When that happens, then people are going to pay attention to the environment."

But skeptics say one need look no further than the North American Free Trade Agreement (NAFTA) to understand how trade expansion has fallen short of those promises. [4] The agreement, which expanded an earlier free-trade area between the United States and Canada to include Mexico, was signed by Republican President George Bush and won congressional approval with Clinton's strong support in 1993. Supporters hailed the agreement as a way to hasten Mexico's economic development and create American jobs as demand for U.S. products rose with Mexican consumers' disposable income.

Less than a decade later, NAFTA is widely perceived as having not lived up to those expectations. Not only have American workers lost jobs as their employers moved production to lower-cost Mexican sites, but the anticipated boost in American exports to Mexico has failed to materialize as economic problems have persisted south of the border.

Additionally, the high concentration of polluting *maquiladoras*, or assembly plants on the Mexican side of the border that churn out goods for export to the United States, has grown even larger, aggravating air and water pollution in U.S. border states. The problems are so serious that a Clinton administration task force recently called for special federal assistance to the border region. [5]

The reason globalization has failed to spread its benefits, critics say, is that it has been promoted and carried forward at the behest of multinational corporations — and their political supporters — with an overriding interest in maximizing profits. Unlike the U.S economy, which is regulated by labor, health and envi-

U.S. Trade Deficit Mushroomed

The nation's balance of trade dropped from its high point, a $12 billion surplus in 1975, to a deficit of more than $271 billion in 1999. As barriers to global trade have fallen, trade has assumed growing importance to the U.S. economy. Supporters of trade liberalization say that encouraging the flow of goods, services and capital among nations benefits everyone, but labor unions say it encourages manufacturers to transfer operations overseas, costing Americans jobs and increasing the deficit.

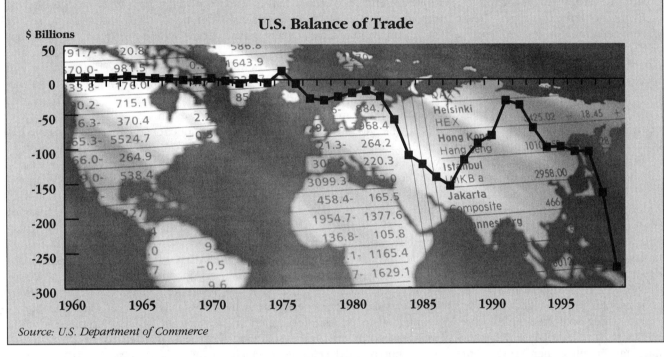

U.S. Balance of Trade

Source: U.S. Department of Commerce

ronmental laws, the global economy is relatively free of such regulatory safeguards.

Indeed, a central mandate of the institutions that govern international trade — the WTO, the International Monetary Fund (IMF) and the World Bank — is to remove obstacles to the international flow of goods and capital. The bank provides economic assistance to poor countries, while the IMF makes loans to countries that agree to make their economies more competitive. [6]

"We are now going to a global economy, but there's no global government, so the rules have been set by these narrow institutions, which are essentially driven by narrow economic and business interests," says Faux of the Economic Policy Institute.

"So-called free-trade agreements such as NAFTA, permanent normal trade relations with China and even the WTO itself are actually full of rules that protect investors, such as protections of intellectual property rights."

He and other critics are calling for trade agreements to include rules that guarantee workers' rights and help safeguard the environment.

When tens of thousands of demonstrators disrupted last fall's WTO meeting in Seattle, Clinton acknowledged the protesters' demands by proposing the creation of a working group on trade and labor within the WTO and promising to assess the environmental impact of future trade pacts. But the administration has since remained silent on the issue, and the trade agreement with China contains

none of the protections labor and environmental activists sought.

The China agreement is not the last word on the subject of labor and environmental standards, however. Unions, environmental organizations and human-rights activists promise to continue pressing for greater regulation of the world economy.

As policy-makers address the issue, these are some of the questions they are asking:

Is globalization good for American workers?

The United States is enjoying a period of unprecedented prosperity. Now in the longest expansion in history, the booming economy has led to skyrocketing stock prices, enriching many Americans who invested in companies producing computers, software and electronics equipment. Inflation, which historically rises with a booming stock market, has remained low, enabling policy-makers to maintain low interest rates and avoid — so far, at least — the boom-and-bust cycle that has marked industrial development in the past.

Even the federal budget deficit, once a seemingly permanent feature of the political landscape, has vanished under the wave of new tax revenues, leaving politicians arguing over how best to spread the largess. This technology-driven "new economy" has created instant millionaires of dot-com investors and increased the retirement security of millions of working Americans.

Trade has played a big role in America's prosperity. Since the end of World War II, the United States and other countries have reduced tariffs, the taxes on imported goods designed to protect domestic industries from foreign competition. Many countries also have negotiated bilateral and regional free-trade agreements, such as NAFTA, which eliminate tariffs altogether. Today, the value of U.S. exports and imports is equal to one-quarter of total U.S. economic output, more than twice the level just 40 years ago.

A key player in the global economy is the multinational corporation. Worldwide, some 60,000 multinationals and a half-million of their affiliates in various countries account for 25 percent of global output. U.S. multinationals employ about 20 million American workers and 8 million workers in other countries. Foreign multinationals with factories in the United States employ about 5 million Americans. [7]

Globalization has brought benefits to American workers — but at a cost. On the positive side, unemployment, at about 4 percent, is lower than at any time since the late 1960s. Low

inflation is protecting the value of workers' paychecks. And for workers with retirement accounts tied to the stock market, the booming economy has increased the prospects of a secure retirement.

But the news is not all good. After rising more than 2 percent a year from the end of World War II to the first energy crisis of 1973, Americans' wages on average have actually fallen over the past quarter-century when inflation is taken into account. Highly skilled workers have held their own, but the lowest-paid workers have seen their incomes plummet. As a result, the income gap between the richest and poorest Americans has widened. [8]

"There's no question that average wages rise as a result of international trade," says the Brookings Institution's Litan. "The only dispute is about whether trade hurts particular portions of the labor force." In his view, increased global trade probably has contributed slightly to the plight of low-income workers, but not nearly as much as immigration, which forces American workers to compete for low-skill jobs, and technological development, which favors skilled workers.

But even those disadvantages have faded since the early 1990s, Litan says. "During the Clinton years, the United States has enjoyed not only rapid economic growth at the average level, but the growth has been broadly distributed across all income classes," he says. "Not only have all workers shared in the prosperity, but throughout this period, the United States has become more and more involved with trade. So to the extent that there has been any depressing effect of trade on wages in the past, it certainly doesn't look like it's had much impact at all in the 1990s."

Some experts emphasize that free trade indirectly benefits all Americans, especially low-income workers, by making available cheap im-

ports, which generally depress prices for consumer goods across the board.

"Openness to imports has helped to keep inflation low, broaden choice and improve consumer prices, especially for basic household necessities," U.S. Trade Representative Charlene Barshevsky said. "This is especially important for the poorest families." [9] That was a strong selling point behind the Trade and Development Act, which Clinton signed into law on May 18. The measure will facilitate imports of low-cost clothing from poor countries in Africa and the Caribbean Basin. [10]

Critics charge that globalization has cost American workers dearly in terms of lost jobs and lower wages. They estimate that free-trade agreements such as NAFTA, for example, have cost hundreds of thousands of American jobs since 1993. "For working people in the United States, NAFTA continues to mean good-paying jobs moving to low-wage countries like Mexico," said Rep. Sherrod Brown, D-Ohio, a leading congressional ally of labor unions and critic of U.S. trade policy. "In 1994, NAFTA's supporters said we would see up to 200,000 new jobs created in the U.S. because of increased trade. Instead, NAFTA has led to the elimination of nearly 204,000 high-paying U.S. manufacturing jobs. [11]

Critics predict the China trade deal will worsen the U.S. trade deficit with China, which reached $69 billion last year, and bleed away even more U.S. jobs. "For every 10 percent increase in U.S. multinational investment in China over the last 20 years," Faux says, "Chinese exports to the United States have risen by 7.3 percent, and U.S. exports to China have decreased by 2 percent."

This lopsided trade pattern, he says, is the result of a deliberate strategy by U.S. multinationals to use China as a low-wage assembly area for products that they then turn around and export to the United States. "Forty percent of the bilateral trade deficit is made up of so-called 'tourist exports'," Faux says. "In this way, U.S. multinationals export raw materials or parts to a production platform in China for input into a good that will be re-exported back into the United States."

Are labor standards the best means of improving the lot of workers in poor countries?

U.S. labor unions are at the forefront of a campaign to include labor standards in both bilateral and multilateral trade agreements to protect foreign workers from exploitation. They contend that conditions in today's global economy mirror those in the United States at the turn of the last century, when rapid industrialization and interstate commerce expanded to create a truly national U.S. economy.

"The enormous transformation of the American economy at that time resulted in the vast movement of people from farm to factory and appalling labor conditions," says David Smith, director of policy for the AFL-CIO. Decades of union activism led to fundamental labor protections.

In 1935, Congress passed the National Labor Relations Act, or Wagner Act, protecting workers' rights to bargain collectively and form unions. Three years later, lawmakers approved the Fair Labor Standards Act, which barred child labor, established the minimum wage and required employers to pay time-and-a-half wages for overtime.

"Our history demonstrates that the process of development requires rules

like these," Smith says. "Improvements in working conditions in the United States did not happen because corporations wanted them. We had to establish rules of the game stipulating that you can't send an 11-year-old into the factory, you can't insist that men and women work more than 40 hours a week without overtime compensation and you must allow people who

Labor union activists at the U.S. Capitol in April denounce the landmark trade bill with China, which they fear threatens American jobs. Union officials say U.S. companies will move production to cheaper overseas factories.

work for you to freely associate and form a union if they wish to. We need those same kinds of rules in the international arena."

But government officials in many developing nations strongly oppose inserting labor standards into international trade rules. They argue that standards would place them at an unfair competitive disadvantage be-

cause they cannot afford to implement the kinds of workers' rights taken for granted in the industrial world.

"If you ask the trade ministers of many developing countries whether they want labor standards, they adamantly say no," Litan says. "The biggest opposition is the countries themselves. And given that, who in the hell are we to tell them what to do?"

But union supporters say the generic standards they propose need not discriminate against Third World countries. "We're not talking here about exporting the American minimum wage or the Fair Labor Standards Act," Smith says.

He and other proponents say the WTO should incorporate into trade pacts those core labor standards already espoused by the International Labor Organization (ILO), an agency established in 1919 to promote workers' rights. Chief among those standards are workers' right to organize and prohibitions on discrimination, child labor and prison labor.

"We're merely insisting that these basic labor rights ought to be honored," Smith says, "both because it reflects our values and because those standards provide a check on a global race to the bottom."

But some experts warn the push to include labor standards in trade agreements actually may worsen working conditions in developing countries.

"On the surface, it sounds easy to say that everybody should have these minimum standards as a condition for trading with them," Litan says. "But the reality is that a lot of Third World countries either don't have labor laws on their books or, if they do, they don't have the resources to

U.S. and Germany Lead Global Trade

The United States and Germany exported goods worth $1.2 trillion in 1998 and had imports valued at $1.4 trillion, leading the world.

Top 20 Trading Nations

COUNTRY	EXPORTS	
	Value (in $ Billions)	Share of World Market
United States	$682.5	12.6%
Germany	539.7	10.0
Japan	387.9	7.2
France	304.8	5.6
United Kingdom	272.9	5.0
Italy	242.3	4.5
Canada	214.3	4.0
Netherlands	198.7	3.7
China	183.8	3.4
Belgium-Luxembourg	178.5	3.3
Hong Kong	174.9	3.2
South Korea	132.3	2.4
Mexico	117.5	2.2
Singapore	109.9	2.0
Taiwan	109.9	2.0
Spain	109.0	2.0
Sweden	84.7	1.6
Switzerland	78.9	1.5
Russia	73.9	1.4
Malaysia	73.3	1.4

COUNTRY	IMPORTS	
	Value (in $ Billions)	Share of World Market
United States	$944.4	16.8%
Germany	466.6	8.3
United Kingdom	315.2	5.6
France	286.3	5.1
Japan	280.5	5.0
Italy	215.6	3.8
Canada	206.2	3.7
Hong Kong	186.8	3.3
Netherlands	184.2	3.3
Belgium-Luxembourg	166.5	3.0
China	140.2	2.5
Spain	132.8	2.4
Mexico	129.0	2.3
Taiwan	104.2	1.9
Singapore	101.6	1.8
South Korea	93.3	1.7
Switzerland	80.2	1.4
Sweden	68.2	1.2
Austria	68.2	1.2
Australia	64.7	1.2

Source: World Trade Organization

enforce them." Consequently, most work performed in developing countries is unregulated, he says, and "if we put trade sanctions on countries that fail to meet the standards, more of the labor forces of these countries would just go underground, and that would only make working conditions worse for them."

A better way to improve working conditions in the developing world, some free-trade supporters say, is to make it even easier for U.S. multinationals to set up shop there. Because many American firms with overseas factories pay higher wages and provide better working conditions than local employers, they can, by their very presence, raise the expectations of local workers, putting pressure on governments and companies to improve working conditions throughout the economy.

"We employ more than 450 people in our Chinese subsidiary, where salaries are far higher than the average Chinese wage," writes Microsoft Corp. Chairman Bill Gates. "Our compensation and benefits are helping to raise the standard of living." [12]

But the same cannot be said of many other U.S. firms currently producing goods in China. The National Labor Committee (NLC), a human-rights advocacy group, alleges that Nike, the Gap, Liz Claiborne, Kathie Lee Gifford/Wal-Mart and the Walt Disney Co. are among American firms that run sweatshops in China that force workers to toil under prison-like conditions to make such items as car stereos, bikes, shoes, sneakers, clothing, TVs, hats and bags for export to the United States. [13]

Critics charge that the WTO's exclusion of labor standards undermines the interests of workers everywhere. "When there are no ground rules for corporations concerning labor or human rights, a brutal 'race to the bottom' in wages and working conditions is triggered," write Lori Wallach and Michelle Sforza of Public Citizen's Global Trade Watch. "The country that can offer the cheapest production costs 'wins' by merit of production being moved there, but people working in that country — under horrific conditions and paid starvation wages — lose, as do the people in the competing countries. [14]

Don't look to China's dissidents to resolve the debate over labor standards. Harry Wu and Wei Jingsheng, who were persecuted at home before emigrating to the United States, pleaded with lawmakers to reject the China trade agreement on human-rights grounds. "The conditions described in [the NLC] report are rampant throughout China," Wu said. "Let's not pretend that American companies in China care about spreading democracy and human rights. They care about profits and business rights."

But Bao Tong, another prominent dissident who lives in Beijing, disagreed. "I appreciate the efforts of friends and colleagues to help our human-rights situation," he said. "But it doesn't make sense to use trade as a lever. It just doesn't work." [15]

Do existing trade rules undermine environmental quality?

With its central mandate to dismantle remaining barriers to interna-

tional trade, the WTO has no specific rules aimed at protecting the environment. Member governments are free to enforce whatever environmental laws they choose within their borders.

But if a country restricts trade with another country that it claims violates its own environmental laws, the WTO

Chinese dissident Harry Wu displays a poster of alleged Chinese human-rights abuses during a Teamsters rally in Washington, D.C., to oppose permanent normal trade relations (PNTR) with China.

can — and has — stepped in. On several occasions, the organization has ruled that trade restrictions imposed to protect the environment constitute unacceptable discrimination in international trade. [16]

The first challenge to U.S. environmental laws came soon after the WTO was launched, when Venezuela and

Brazil charged that a 1990 amendment to the Clean Air Act requiring oil refiners to make cleaner gasoline discriminated against their gasoline exports to the United States. In January 1996, a WTO dispute panel agreed. To avoid trade sanctions by Venezuela and Brazil, the Environmental Protection Agency (EPA) adopted a less stringent standard for gasoline contaminants.

The United States was the complainant in another prominent trade dispute, this one related to the U.S. cattle industry's practice of treating beef and dairy cattle with hormones. The European Union, sensitized to potential health hazards in their beef supply following Great Britain's "mad cow" scare, banned U.S. exports of hormone-treated beef. [17] In 1997 a WTO panel agreed with the U.S. position that its treated beef posed no risk to human health or the environment.

Perhaps the most controversial case challenging environmental-protection efforts came following a complaint by several Asian countries about a U.S. ban on imports of shrimp from countries that allow fishermen to catch shrimp using methods that kill endangered sea turtles. The turtles are protected under several multilateral environmental agreements, including the 1979 Bonn Convention on Protecting Migratory Species of Wild Animals. However, a WTO panel found the U.S. "turtle-safe" requirements an unacceptable violation of its nondiscrimination rule.

"Unfortunately, our predictions of a movement to the lowest-common denominator on environmental standards have come true," says Brent Blackwelder, president of Friends of the Earth. "Both under NAFTA and the WTO, there have been significant challenges to health and environmental regulations, and in a number of cases, the rulings have gone in favor of the polluter or the weaker standard."

Recent trade agreements, he contends, have been as detrimental to the environment as union supporters say they have been to global working conditions. "The corporate globalization that is going on right now is extremely damaging," Blackwelder says. "Trade agreements are empowering corporations all over the world to go to the utmost corners of the world and exploit resources in a most unsustainable manner."

Blackwelder, who serves on an advisory committee on the environmental impact of trade at the U.S. Trade Representative's office, decries the absence of environmental-protection standards in recent agreements, including the one with China. China is the world's biggest trader in animal parts from such endangered or threatened species as tiger and rhinoceros, and it is the main source of the Asian long-horned beetle, an invasive species that is already destroying trees in parts of the United States.

"There were many opportunities to get some understanding with China on curtailing its trade in endangered species and an agreement not to challenge our efforts to block invasive species," Blackwelder says. "China also is extremely polluted, and our pollution-control equipment could cut that in half. But the agreement was not written to deal with urgent issues like that. It's hard to imagine a greater hostility towards the environment from any administration than we've gotten from this one."

On Nov. 16, President Clinton issued an executive order requiring a review of how future trade agreements would affect the environment.

But he and other free-trade supporters insist that trade itself holds out the greatest promise for improving environmental quality throughout the world.

"We are committed to finding solutions which are win-win, that benefit both the economy and the environment — open trade and cutting-edge clean technologies, which I believe will be the next industrial revolution," Clinton said. [18]

Indeed, some observers say the inclusion of environmental standards in trade agreements may actually impede improvements in the global environment.

"I'm willing to consider having environmental issues raised in trade negotiations, but if they become a big obstacle and prevent further trade liberalization, then I think that in the long term we will have set the environment back, not forward," says Portney of Resources for the Future. "If you bollix up trade agreements too much with these issues, the poorer countries that would benefit from enhanced trade will grow less slowly than they would otherwise, and so they'll pay less attention to the environment than they would otherwise." ∎

BACKGROUND

Postwar Trade System

The foundation of the world-trade system in place today was laid 56 years ago at the remote New Hampshire mountain resort of Bretton Woods. Representatives of 44 countries met there in the final months of World War II to decide how best to shore up the world economy, laid to waste by conflict, and to protect it from the forces that had helped spark

the war in the first place.

Nazism and Germany's aggression against its neighbors in Europe did not arise in a vacuum — rather they came in the wake of severe economic hardship. As the Great Depression destroyed jobs at home, governments of the industrial powers enacted protectionist laws designed to keep out imports that might compete with domestic industries. For every trade barrier thrown up by one country, its trading partners erected retaliatory barriers, setting in motion a process that quickly brought international trade to a standstill and fueled political extremism that erupted in war.

History gave the conferees at Bretton Woods little hope for success. A similar effort to create an international forum for settling disputes, launched in the wake of World War I, had gone nowhere. Despite the ardent support of President Woodrow Wilson, Congress rejected U.S. membership in the League of Nations. Without the crucial imprimatur of the United States, by then a major economic and military power, the League was swept away in the turmoil that sparked World War II.

The decisions made at Bretton Woods proved more lasting. In an effort to prevent the wild swings in currency values that had contributed to financial instability in the 1930s, participants agreed on a fixed-rate exchange system in which the dollar's value was set at one-thirty-fifth of an ounce of gold and other currencies were "pegged" to the dollar.

To oversee the new fixed-rate system, they created the International Monetary Fund, composed of high-ranking government officials from each country that signed the agreement. * A sister organization, the In-

---

* Though the gold standard was later abandoned, the IMF continues to issue loans to countries with balance-of-payments difficulties.

Chronology

1930s Congress passes key labor laws.

1935
The National Labor Relations Act, or Wagner Act, guarantees workers' rights to bargain collectively and form unions.

1938
The Fair Labor Standards Act bars child labor, establishes the minimum wage and requires employers to pay time-and-a-half wages for overtime.

1940s-1960s
In the wake of World War II, international trade expands under the oversight of multilateral institutions.

May 19, 1948
Twenty-three countries meet in New Hampshire and later establish the General Agreement on Tariffs and Trade (GATT) to set rules governing international trade, the International Monetary Fund (IMF) to oversee exchange rates and the World Bank to assist economic development in poor countries.

1970s-1980s
Key environmental laws take effect in the United States.

1970
The Clean Air Act sets standards for major air pollutants in U.S. cities.

1972
The Clean Water Act requires the removal of pollutants from the nation's waterways.

1973
The Tokyo Round of trade negotiations among about 100 countries begins. The talks, which last for six years, result in an average one-third reduction in customs duties in the world's major industrial markets.

1988
The Trade and Competitiveness Act requires the president to retaliate against countries found to engage in unfair trade practices, such as "dumping" goods in the United States at below-market prices.

1990s-2000s
Trade expansion continues despite growing protests.

1993
Congress approves the North American Free Trade Agreement (NAFTA), expanding an earlier U.S.-Canadian free-trade area to include Mexico.

December 1994
Negotiations to extend NAFTA to all countries in the Western Hemisphere begin at the Summit of the Americas, held in Miami. Talks bog down after Congress refuses to renew the president's "fast track" trade negotiating authority.

Jan. 1, 1995
The World Trade Organization (WTO), founded by 135 countries to replace the GATT, begins operations, with the mandate of administering trade agreements and settling trade disputes.

January 1996
A WTO dispute panel rules that a 1990 amendment to the Clean Air Act requiring refiners to make cleaner gasoline discriminates against Venezuelan gasoline exports to the United States, prompting the Environmental Protection Agency to adopt a less stringent standard for gasoline contaminants.

1998
A WTO panel rules than a ban by the European Union on imports of hormone-treated beef from the United States violates trade rules because there is no proof that it threatens public health.

Nov. 15, 1999
China and the United States reach an agreement on bilateral trade expansion. The same month, violent demonstrations by globalization opponents disrupt a WTO meeting in Seattle.

Nov. 30 – Dec. 3, 1999
The ninth round of international trade negotiations takes place in Seattle amid massive protests.

May 18, 2000
President Clinton signs the Trade and Development Act, which opens U.S. markets to more goods from Africa, the Caribbean and Central America.

May 24, 2000
After a heated debate, the House approves the China trade bill, paving the way for China's acceptance into the WTO.

ternational Bank for Reconstruction and Development — better known today as the World Bank — was set up to help raise productivity and reduce poverty in developing countries and thus hasten their entry into the world trading system.

A third institution established at Bretton Woods was the General Agreement on Tariffs and Trade, or GATT. The clumsy acronym was chosen for what originally was intended to be simply an agreement until a permanent body, the International Trade Organization, could be established to oversee it. But Congress never approved the permanent body, leaving the GATT bureaucracy, headquartered in Geneva, as the only mechanism for setting the rules of international trade for the next 30 years.

The GATT, initially signed by 23 countries, was formally launched on May 19, 1948, with the mandate to promote the free trade of goods by supporting the elimination of tariffs, import quotas and subsidies that prevented or discouraged imports. Over the years, as the volume of trade and the number of signatories grew, the GATT underwent a number of revisions that were agreed to in multilateral trade talks, known as rounds. These generally lasted for a number of years and produced changes in the rules that gradually reduced allowable tariffs. The Tokyo Round, for example, involved about 100 countries, lasted from 1973-79 and resulted in an average one-third reduction in customs duties in the world's major industrial markets.

The United States, traditionally one of the strongest champions of free trade, came under pressure to curb imports in the 1970s, as the domestic auto, steel and other basic manufacturing industries lost market share to imports from Japan, Europe and other countries. With the 1974 Trade Act, Congress required the executive branch to monitor foreign trade practices and authorized the president to impose tariffs on countries found guilty of unfair trade practices.

Also in 1974, a separate agreement covering trade in textiles went

U.S. Trade Representative Charlene Barshefsky addresses the press at the World Trade Organization meeting in Seattle last November. Street protests forced the WTO to cancel its opening ceremony.

into effect. The Multifibre Arrangement, as it was known, sought to promote free trade in textiles but also allowed countries to retain certain protections for their textile industries, a sector that is especially vulnerable to low-cost competition from developing countries.

But as quickly as GATT members tore down tariffs and duties on imports, they often created less visible barriers to trade, such as import license requirements and government subsidies to prop up domestic industries threatened by imports. As a result, entire sectors of a country's economy, such as agriculture, textiles and the fast-growing service sector, remained largely off-limits to trade-liberalizing rules.

Frustrated by the practice of some exporters of "dumping" their goods in the United States at below-market prices, Congress passed the 1988 Trade and Competitiveness Act, which beefed up earlier legislation by requiring the president to retaliate against countries found to engage in dumping and other unfair trade practices.

To deal with those entrenched barriers to trade, GATT members launched another round of negotiations in 1986. Called the Uruguay Round after their location in Punta del Este, Uruguay, the negotiations went on for almost eight years. By their conclusion in 1994, the 125 member countries had agreed to expand the subject of trade rules beyond goods to include services and intellectual property as well. They also agreed to establish the WTO with a stronger legal mandate than the GATT to oversee the expanded trade regime.

As the GATT moved ahead with liberalized trade rules, the United States and other countries proceeded to eliminate remaining trade barriers through a series of free-trade agreements with individual countries or regions. In 1985, the United States signed a free-trade pact with Israel, followed in 1988 by the U.S.-Canada Free

Anti-Globalization Movement Unites Students and Unions

"**M**ake the global economy work! Stop corporate greed!" read the banner being carried down K Street in downtown Washington. A few minutes later, police in riot gear fired several canisters of tear gas to keep the protesters from getting any closer to the White House. When the crowd refused to disperse, armored personnel carriers moved in, and police handcuffed dozens of youthful demonstrators and carted them off to jail in yellow school buses.

The confrontation was one of many between demonstrators and law-enforcement officers that engulfed the capital for two days in mid-April. The catalyst was the annual meeting of the International Monetary Fund (IMF) and the World Bank, the global institutions that oversee exchange rates and provide economic assistance to developing countries, respectively. The same rallying cries had been heard at the violent protests in Seattle during a meeting of the World Trade Organization (WTO) last November.

"The WTO, the IMF and the World Bank are the main institutions that promote corporate greed," Drea, a young woman who had traveled from Montana for the April demonstration, told a reporter. "What's bringing all these people together is the recognition that globalization is just another way to allow multinational companies to exploit people all over the world. We can't just ignore what's happening and let them do it."

Washington hadn't seen such an outpouring of youthful outrage since the late 1960s, when antiwar demonstrators took to the streets. But the anti-globalization forces also seem to include a broader cross-section of the American public. Marching alongside the students were a number of veterans of earlier protests — middle-aged men and women with more than a few gray hairs. A group of elderly ladies wearing plastic rain kerchiefs said they had come from California to march and ask their congresswoman to vote against trade agreements that cost Americans jobs and gut U.S. environmental-protection laws.

But the biggest difference between the antiwar protests and the demonstrations against globalization may be the active participation by labor unions. In the 1960s, student protesters clashed not only with police but also with "hard hats," blue-collar workers who denounced the protesters as unpatriotic slackers.

"There's a new coalition today," says David Smith, director of policy at the AFL-CIO. "In both Seattle and Washington we saw young people, environmentalists and folks from the religious community marching together with trade unionists. This is a powerful and growing popular coalition."

Free-trade advocates wasted no time in dismissing the demonstrators as extremist kooks. A *Wall Street Journal* editorial described the Washington protesters as "this seeming circus — a smorgasbord of save-the-turtles activists, anarchists, egalitarians, Luddites and Marxists."[1] James Pinkerton, a columnist for *Newsday*, wrote of "pasty wastrels taking time off from their studies at Vassar to rage against the machine, their expensive orthodontia bared at the Kevlar-knuckled cops in riot gear."[2]

To Smith, such statements amount to little more than whistling past the graveyard. "I take some of the venom of our critics as a sign that we're on the right track," he says.

Indeed, says Brent Blackwelder, president of Friends of the Earth, multinational corporations will face even greater opposition in the future if they continue to ignore calls to protect the environment and workers' rights.

Police used tear gas and pepper spray to control crowds protesting the policies of the World Bank and International Monetary Fund during their meeting earlier this year in Washington, D.C.

"The huge demonstrations in Seattle and Washington provided a clear signal to the international globalization institutions that if they keep trying to do business as usual they're going to encounter an ever-growing storm of protest," he says. "People are not going to stand by and see their communities and their quality of life degraded by distant corporate powers. I certainly hope they get the message, because if things don't change I would predict that this is just the initial blip on the radar screen of a growing tidal wave."

---

[1] "Trade Junked," *The Wall Street Journal*, April 21, 2000.

[2] James Pinkerton, "Methinks They Doth Protest Too Much," IntellectualCapital.com, April 20, 2000.

Fair-Trade Movement Targets 'Unfair' Labor Practices

At the same time that the Clinton administration and other governments are doing their best to dismantle tariffs and other barriers to trade, citizens' groups and state and local governments are moving just as fast to put them back up again.

It's all part of a movement known generally as "fair trade," and it has the enthusiastic support of those who feel the current trend toward globalization is not the panacea for the world's problems that free-trade advocates say it is.

The initiative harkens back to the 1980s grass-roots campaign to isolate the South African government and its racist policy of apartheid by boycotting American companies doing business there. The effort paid off. Heeding the call of the Rev. Leon Sullivan, who wrote a corporate code of conduct for dealing with South Africa, many American firms pulled out of the country, providing an important impetus for apartheid's eventual repeal in 1991.

Today, fair-trade advocates are trying to put similar pressure on companies to ensure that products they import and sell to the American public are produced in ways that protect workers' rights and the environment.

The movement took root more than a decade ago in Europe, where some importers agreed to buy coffee beans from Central American farmers' cooperatives that distributed proceeds from coffee sales to the farmers themselves. Fair-trade coffee is now available in the United States as well, though it accounts for less than one-tenth of 1 percent of all the coffee consumed in this country.[1]

A more visible expression of the fair-trade movement is the current wave of campus boycotts of athletic shoes, clothing and equipment bearing college logos sold by companies that produce them in sweatshops in the United States and overseas.

The protest effort is coordinated by an international coalition called United Students Against Sweatshops. In 1997, the coalition launched a campaign encouraging students to force their colleges to take responsibility for

the conditions under which such products were made. Duke University completed a code of conduct for its suppliers last November, and Brown University followed suit in May.

"The goal of students across the country who are organizing around sweatshop issues is to create widespread change in an industry where insufficient wages and mandatory overtime are common," writes Sarah Jacobson, a coalition activist and a senior at the University of Oregon. "In many Third World and American apparel factories, there have been reports of intimidation of workers who try to speak out. And because it is easy for these factories to cut and run, vanishing across national borders and abandoning workers, many people are hesitant to organize unions or demand a living wage."

A number of state and local governments have selective-purchasing policies that prohibit them from doing business with companies that engage in objectionable practices. Many of these provisions are aimed at punishing companies that do business in countries with repressive governments, such as Myanmar, formerly Burma, and Nigeria. The city of Berkeley, Calif., for instance, has so many purchasing restrictions in place that the city government reportedly has trouble finding adequate supplies.[2]

On May 8, San Francisco went beyond such specific purchasing bans to become the first U.S. city to adopt a general resolution opposing unregulated economic globalization and supporting fair trade, socially responsible investment and sustainable and equitable economic development.

It is uncertain, however, whether other governments will follow suit. The World Trade Organization is considering new trade regulations that would find such fair-trade initiatives in violation of its non-discrimination rules.

[1] See John Burgess, "Deal Brews to Give Fairer Deal to Farmers," *The Washington Post*, May 13, 2000.

[2] See Miles A. Pomper, "Sanctions Slowdown," *Governing*, June 2000, pp. 28-29.

Trade Agreement. In December 1992, President Bush signed NAFTA, which expanded the North American free-trade area to include Mexico.

Hailed by its supporters as the most comprehensive regional free-trade pact ever negotiated, NAFTA became a lightning rod for critics who decried the absence of adequate protections for workers' rights and the environ-

ment. These issues were addressed in supplemental, or side, agreements. The North American Agreement on Labor Cooperation created a trinational secretariat in Dallas to field petitions regarding labor practices. The North American Agreement on Environmental Cooperation created a similar body based in Montreal to promote cooperation on improving environmental protection throughout the

continent. Congress eventually approved NAFTA in 1993, and President Clinton signed it into law.

World Trade Organization

By 1990, international trade accounted for an unprecedented

portion of global economic activity. (*See graph, p. 100.*) The volume of world trade was clearly outstripping the GATT's ability to oversee it. For that reason, 135 countries agreed in 1994 to replace the GATT with a new agency, the WTO.

Like its predecessor, the Geneva-based WTO was given the mandate to assure the freest possible flow of trade, administer trade agreements and act as a forum for trade negotiations. Unlike the GATT, it was granted a clear legal mandate to implement trade agreements and settle trade disputes between governments.

Under the new organization's dispute-resolution system, member countries can file complaints against other members with the WTO. If subsequent negotiations fail to resolve a dispute, the matter is turned over to a WTO panel of trade experts who issue a formal decision. A country found guilty of unfair trade practices can legally refuse to comply with the panel's ruling. But if it does, the WTO will allow the petitioner to retaliate with trade sanctions and other potentially costly penalties. Since 1995, more than 150 trade disputes have come before the WTO; of those, more than 100 are still in the process of adjudication or appeal.

From its opening on Jan. 1, 1995, the new trade organization chalked up early achievements reflecting the growing impact of the information-based "new economy" on global trade patterns. With a series of agreements in 1997, many WTO members agreed to lower customs duties on computer and software products, phase out barriers to foreign telecommunications investments and open their markets to foreign banks, securities firms and insurance companies.

Trade's growing importance to domestic prosperity prompted many countries that had shunned affiliation with the GATT to seek membership in the WTO. Among these was China,

whose government had encouraged limited foreign investment since the 1970s but resisted the broad liberalization of its vast markets.

On Nov. 15, 1999, China and the United States reached trade-expansion agreement that would facilitate China's entrance into the WTO. The United States agreed to suspend its annual review of China's human-rights record for renewal of China's most-favored-nation status. In return, China agreed to open its markets to a broad range of U.S. exports and investments.

The Clinton administration and other free-trade supporters had eagerly anticipated last fall's meeting in Seattle as the launch of a new round of talks that would continue the removal of trade barriers. But the ninth round of multilateral trade negotiations since Bretton Woods, known variously as the Seattle Round or the Millennium Round, got off to a shaky start as demonstrators insisted that trade liberalization not come at the cost of workers' rights and environmental protection.

Negotiators made little headway, leaving the resolution of several major issues for the future:

• Agriculture: Negotiators agreed to begin talks on reducing agricultural export subsidies. Although the European Union continues to protect member nations' farmers from cheap agricultural imports, it is not alone. The United States still subsidizes the production of sugar and other commodities. Trade in genetically modified foods, which the United States and some developing countries support amid skepticism in Europe, will be the subject of a new WTO study group.

• Services: Despite earlier agreements liberalizing trade in financial services, telecommunications and transport, many countries still bar imports of these services. U.S. efforts to start talks on sweeping changes

that would open up such trade fell short. Members agreed to the talks, but the goal will not be to end countries' right to exclude services.

• Dumping: Some countries want to make it harder for the United States to implement its anti-dumping laws, which bar imports that are sold below cost on the U.S. market.

• Technology: Members agreed to extend a moratorium in new tariffs on electronic transmissions across borders, but failed to agree on a new set of talks aimed at reducing tariffs on high-tech products.

• WTO transparency: Members agreed to make public WTO documents and decisions, but stopped short of opening up the dispute-resolution process or allow non-governmental organizations to participate in that process.

• Labor standards: Developing countries blocked a U.S. proposal to study the impact of trade on labor standards, arguing that such efforts could enable developed countries to bar Third World imports.

• Poor countries: Members agreed to allow poor, developing countries to phase in WTO requirements over three years. [19]   ∎

CURRENT SITUATION

New Trade Talks

Supporters of labor and environmental standards are now focusing their efforts at ongoing efforts to expand NAFTA to include other countries of the Western Hemisphere, beginning with Chile. Negotiations on a Free Trade Area of the Americas

(FTAA) began in earnest after the December 1994 Summit of the Americas, held in Miami.

But those talks have bogged down in large part because of Congress' refusal to renew the president's "fast-track" trade negotiating authority when it expired in 1994. Fast-track authority requires lawmakers to vote for or against trade agreements reached by the president within 90 days, with no amendments allowed. The lack of fast track, which Clinton requested and failed to obtain in both 1997 and 1998, has hampered his administration's ability to negotiate trade agreements. In its absence, the Chilean government is reluctant to sign an agreement that may be significantly altered by Congress.

Despite Congress' action, Clinton recently reiterated his determination to meet the goal of achieving a free-trade agreement covering all of North and South America by 2005. "You should not believe that because the legislation didn't pass, that the United States is any less committed to finishing the Free Trade Area of the Americas," he said, "or that, because it didn't pass, any agreement we make in the context of a Free Trade Area of the Americas is less likely to pass Congress." [20]

But union and environmental activists want to make sure than any future agreement the United States enters into contains specific standards to promote workers' rights and environmental quality. "As the administration negotiates the FTAA, they ought to negotiate an obligation to adhere to the ILO core labor standards," says Smith of the AFL-CIO. "That ought to be part of the deal, as well as any other deal that Congress approves."

Including such provisions in the FTAA would mean rewriting NAFTA because it relegated labor standards to side agreements with no enforcement measures. "Under NAFTA, if a Mexican company making goods for export to the United States decides to reduce its labor costs by shooting somebody who wants to start a union or otherwise suppress wages in ways that would be illegal in the United States, it will face no penalties," says the Economic Policy Institute's Faux. "We need to renegotiate NAFTA to force the Mexicans to abide by the core ILO labor standards, include a mechanism for increasing the minimum wage in Mexico as productivity increases and stipulate that violations of labor rights be punishable by trade sanctions."

Consumer Choice

As the debate over the inclusion of enforceable standards in trade agreements continues, there is renewed interest in expanding the use of product labels to promote environmental quality and workers' rights. By identifying products that are made using environmentally friendly methods and under acceptable working conditions, so-called eco-labels enable consumers to exert pressure on manufacturers directly.

"Given the concerns being raised on both the labor and the environmental side," says Portney of Resources for the Future, "one obvious thing we can do is harness market power and allow consumers to vote with their pocketbooks in deciding which conditions they want to see continued and which ones they don't want to see continued."

He advocates labeling as an especially effective tool for promoting environmental protection. "It deals with legitimate national concerns about products, for example the use of genetically modified organisms, which some countries object to." Many Europeans in particular are concerned about the potentially adverse health and environmental effects of so-called "Frankenfoods" and have staged demonstrations against importing such products from the United States. [21]

To be effective, however, labeling programs have to be backed up by a credible certification system. "If the program is self-certified, it's meaningless," Portney says. "You've got to have some organization that's respected for its objectivity. And of course it's also meaningless unless the standards set for qualifying for labels are strict enough to exclude producers that fall short of widely accepted consumer expectations."

Some eco-label programs call for government certification, such as the EPA energy ratings on appliances and the "dolphin-safe" label placed on cans of tuna caught using nets that don't trap and kill dolphins. But even when they are backed by certification, label programs are vulnerable to challenge under international trade rules. In 1991, GATT dispute panels ruled that the U.S. ban on imports of tuna from Mexico, associated with the dolphin-safe program, was illegal. "The dolphin-safe tuna program was great," Friends of the Earth's Blackwelder says, "but since it's come under attack as a result of trade agreements, the label is likely to become meaningless."

More recently, students on many campuses across the country have organized boycotts of Nike and other suppliers of athletic clothing bearing college logos made in Chinese sweatshops. (*See sidebar, p. 105.*) But labor activists say that approach is not enough to protect workers and the environment. "Certainly, well-informed consumers will vote with their feet, and we welcome that," the AFL-CIO's Smith says. "But it's not a substitute for the rule of law and the obligation of governments to adhere to core standards. If you thought that volunteerism would work, all you

At Issue:

Will the U.S.-China trade agreement help workers' rights?

CHARLENE BARSHEFSKY

U.S. Trade Representative

FROM TESTIMONY BEFORE THE SENATE BANKING COMMITTEE, MAY 9, 2000

*W*ith respect to reform within China, WTO [World Trade Organization] accession represents a potentially profound and historic shift, building upon — but going much further than — China's domestic reforms to date.

China's domestic reforms have reversed the most damaging policies of the Cultural Revolution and Great Leap Forward. WTO accession will accelerate and deepen this process, altering policies [that] date to the earliest years of the communist era. As it enters the WTO, China will:

• Permit foreigners and all Chinese businesses to import most goods into China;

• Reduce, and in some cases remove entirely, state control over internal distribution of goods and the provision of services;

• Enable foreign businesses to participate in information industries such as telecommunications, including the Internet; and

• Subject its decisions in all areas covered by the WTO to enforcement. . . .

These commitments are a remarkable victory for economic reformers in China. They will give China's people more access to information, and weaken the ability of hardliners in government to isolate China's public from outside influences and ideas. More deeply, they reflect a judgment that prosperity, security and international respect will not come from the static nationalism, state power and state control over the economy China adopted after the war, but that China's own interests are best served by the advancing economic freedom, engagement with the world and, ultimately, development of the rule of law inherent in the initiative President Truman began in 1948 with the founding of the GATT [General Agreement on Tariffs and Trade].

The WTO accession, therefore, has potential beyond economics and trade: as a means to advance the rule of law in China, and a precedent for willingness to accept international standards of behavior in other fields. That is why many Hong Kong and Chinese activists for democracy and human rights . . . support PNTR [permanent normal trade relations] and see WTO accession as China's most important step toward reform in 20 years. And it is why our support for WTO accession rests on a broader long-term commitment to human rights and freedoms, as well as new opportunities and strengthened guarantees of fairness for Americans.

HARRY WU

Executive director, Laogai Research Foundation

FROM TESTIMONY BEFORE THE SENATE COMMERCE, SCIENCE AND TRANSPORTATION COMMITTEE, APRIL 11, 2000.

*I*t has long been fashionable to think, "What is good for Wall Street is good for the United States." Globalization has greatly benefited multinational corporations, and it is true that PNTR [permanent normal trade relations] and WTO entry for China will further help these companies economically. But the other major beneficiary of China's entry into the [WTO] will be the Chinese Communist Party (CCP). The CCP maintains political and economic control in China, and WTO entry will not change that. . . .

Why do the Western capitalists want to rush into China? China has a population of 1.25 billion. This is a lucrative market. . . . But even more importantly, China has a huge, cheap and obedient labor force. In this country there are no free trade unions, all the men and women are controlled by one hand — the communist government. . . .

We've heard many politicians and business people say that doing business in China helps spread American values and business practices. It is true that Chinese businessmen are willing to learn how to be more efficient, but U.S. businesses in China will never be allowed to take steps to improve human rights that go against the fundamental policies of the Communist Party. The Chinese communist government is one of the worst human-rights violators in the world today. In China, there is a national "population-control" policy. . . . If a woman in an American company gives birth to a child without a permit, Chinese law says that she will be fired. There is nothing the American bosses can do. If Chinese workers want to organize an independent trade union in an American company in China, these people would be fired or even arrested. Again, there is nothing the American bosses can do. . . .

In 1994, the Clinton administration delinked human rights and trade. . . . Last month the State Department Human Rights Report admitted that the human-rights situation in China is worsening. The administration intends to introduce a resolution at the Human Rights Commission in Geneva this year. But why not take a stand in Washington, D.C., using our economic leverage? If foreign policy does not contain a moral basis, it is a typical appeasement policy.

From a human-rights standpoint, one can only hope this focus on trade agreements will not completely overshadow the long road that must be traveled towards democracy in China. Perhaps one day, the U.S. government will try to promote human rights in China with the same zeal that it runs after market access.

have to do is look at the history of industrial relations in this country and in Europe to understand that it won't. These things require a commitment by government. Otherwise, all you get is a race to the bottom."

Workers' Anxieties

Amid the emotional debate emanating from the streets of Seattle and Washington and from Congress regarding the China trade vote, opinion polls suggest that Americans are ambivalent about the impact of globalization on their lives.

On the China deal, for example, a recent Gallup Poll indicates Americans are slightly more likely to believe increased trade will benefit the U.S. economy (48 percent) than believe that it would hurt it (37 percent). But 57 percent said that increased trade with China would "mostly hurt" U.S. workers, as opposed to helping them (28 percent). [22]

The popular perception that trade is good for the economy but bad for job security suggests to some analysts that the government needs to beef up assistance to workers who are displaced by economic trends. "We do not handle displacement as well as we should," says Litan of the Brookings Institution. "We ought to do a lot more to promote retraining of workers during their working lives."

In addition, Litan proposes the creation of a new government program that would provide workers with "wage insurance." When workers lose employment and can only find lower-paying jobs, such a program would help make up the difference, encouraging workers to take inferior jobs temporarily and get training for better-paying jobs in the future.

The government also should offer better health insurance coverage for unemployed workers, Litan says. Under current law, displaced workers can receive 18 months' coverage under their former employers' health plans, but they have to pay the entire premium out of pocket.

"If you're a displaced worker today, you can get health insurance, but you can't pay for it," he says. "Subsidizing health insurance for the unemployed is a no-brainer. I'm mystified that the politicians haven't even discussed such a proposal." [23] ■

OUTLOOK

Gore's Balancing Act

The benefits of trade and globalization are one area where the two candidates for this fall's presidential election agree. Both Vice President Al Gore and George W. Bush, the Republican governor of Texas, supported the trade agreement with China and have consistently touted the advantages of globalization for the U.S. economy.

The Clinton administration's unequivocal endorsement of globalization has complicated Gore's standing with the American labor movement, however. Despite their steady decline in membership over the past three decades, unions hold the key not only to Gore's presidential bid but also to Democrats' hopes of regaining the majority of seats in the House. Unions and environmental groups welcomed Gore's strong endorsement last fall of Clinton's executive order requiring environmental-impact reviews of all trade agreements negotiated by the United States, a process Gore promised would "revolutionize the way the environment is dealt with in all future trade talks." [24]

But the emergence of the China trade agreement as the administration's top legislative priority this year forced Gore to straddle the line on that key issue. He declared his support for the trade bill even though it contained no environmental or labor standards and no formal assessment of its impact on those areas.

"I strongly support normal trade relations with China because I believe it is right for America's economy and right for the cause of reform in China," he said on May 22, just two days before the crucial House vote.

Many union leaders, who led the opposition to normalizing trade relations with a country they see as a major threat to American jobs, were outraged at Gore's position. Stephen P. Yokich, head of the United Auto Workers (UAW), said the union was "deeply disappointed" in Gore because he had "tried to have it both ways" on trade.

"Gore is holding hands with the profiteers of the world," Yokich said. He and other union leaders threatened to throw their support behind the presidential candidacy of consumer activist Ralph Nader, leader of the Green Party. Although the likelihood of a Nader victory is next to nil, a defection of union support to his cause could cost Gore critical votes in the West and Midwest, and perhaps the election.

That scenario became less likely, however, when AFL-CIO President John Sweeney renewed the federation's endorsement of Gore after losing its battle to defeat the China trade bill. "The vice president is not the president," Sweeney said, "and this was clearly the president's bill. We saw very little lobbying by the vice president." [25]

However they view the impact of trade on jobs and the environment, most observers agree that the concerns that have colored the debate about globalization did not end with the vote to normalize trade relations with China.

"Every economic system has a politics, and the global economy is going to be no different," says Faux of the Economic Policy Institute. "What we've seen in recent months is just the beginning of a global politics that will accompany a global economy." ∎

Notes

[1] National Labor Committee, "Made in China: The Role of U.S. Companies in Denying Human and Worker Rights," 2000.

[2] From remarks made at the White House on May 24, 2000. For background, see David Masci, "China After Deng," *The CQ Researcher*, June 13, 1997, pp. 505-528, and Kenneth Jost, "Democracy in Asia," *The CQ Researcher*, July 24, 1998, pp. 625-648.

[3] For background, see Kenneth Jost, "Future of Korea," *The CQ Researcher*, May 19, 2000, pp. 425-448, Mary H. Cooper, "Economic Sanctions," *The CQ Researcher*, Oct. 28, 1994, pp. 937-960, and David Masci, "Castro's Next Move," *The CQ Researcher*, Dec. 12, 1997, pp. 1081-1104.

[4] For background, see Mary H. Cooper, "Rethinking NAFTA," *The CQ Researcher*, June 7, 1996, pp. 481-504.

[5] See Glenn Kessler, "U.S. Task Force Targets Poverty Along Mexican Border," *The Washington Post*, May 26, 2000. For background, see David Masci, "Mexico's Future," *The CQ Researcher*, Sept. 19, 1997, pp. 817-840.

[6] For background, see Mary H. Cooper, "International Monetary Fund," *The CQ Researcher*, Jan. 29, 1999, pp. 65-88.

[7] Council of Economic Advisers, Economic Report of the President, February 2000, pp. 202-203.

[8] See Gary Burtless, Robert Z. Lawrence, Robert E. Litan and Robert J. Shapiro, *Globaphobia* (1998), pp. 1-3.

[9] Testifying Feb. 8, 2000, before the House Ways and Means Subcommittee on Trade.

[10] See Lori Nitschke, "Third World Trade Bill Likely to Have Limited Impact," *CQ Weekly*, May 6, 2000, pp. 1020-1027.

[11] From Rep. Brown's Web site, www. house.gov/sherrodbrown.

[12] Bill Gates, "Yes, More Trade with China," *The Washington Post*, May 23, 2000.

[13] National Labor Committee, "Made in China: The Role of U.S. Companies in Denying Human and Worker Rights," May 10, 2000. For background, see Kenneth Jost, "Human Rights," *The CQ Researcher*, Nov. 13, 1998, pp. 977-1000.

[14] Lori Wallach and Michelle Sforza, *Whose Trade Organization?* (1999), p. 174.

[15] Quoted by John Pomfret, "Dissidents Back China's WTO Entry," *The Washington Post*, May 11, 2000.

[16] For details on the WTO's approach to environmental issues, see Gary P. Sampson, "Trade and the Environment," in Miguel Rodriguez Mendoza, Patrick Low and Barbara Kotschwar, eds., *Trade Rules in the Making* (1999), pp. 511-524.

[17] See Suzanne Daley, "Rise in Cases of Mad Cow Disease Alarms Europe," *The New York Times*, May 7, 2000.

[18] Clinton spoke Dec. 1, 1999, before a meeting of trade officials attending the WTO meeting in Seattle.

[19] See Steven Pearlstein, "Key Negotiating Points," *The Washington Post*, Dec. 4, 1999.

[20] Clinton addressed a meeting of the Council of the Americas in Washington on May 2, 2000.

[21] For background, see Kathy Koch, "Food Safety Battle: Organic vs. Biotech," *The CQ Researcher*, Sept. 4, 1998, pp. 761-784.

[22] Jeffrey M. Jones, "Americans Think Increased Trade with China Will Help U.S. Economy but Hurt Workers," The Gallup Organization, May 17, 2000.

[23] For more information, see Burtless et al., *op. cit.*, pp. 127-155.

[24] From a statement issued on Nov. 17, 1999.

[25] Quoted in David S. Broder, "AFL-CIO Lauds Gore for Role in 'President's China Trade Bill,'" *The Washington Post*, May 26, 2000.

FOR MORE INFORMATION

American Federation of Labor-Congress of Industrial Organizations (AFL-CIO), 815 16th St., N.W., Washington, D.C. 20006; (202) 637-5000; www.aflcio.org. The union is the leading source of information on the impact of trade on U.S. jobs and on working conditions.

Friends of the Earth, 1025 Vermont Ave., N.W., Washington, D.C. 20005; (202) 783-7400; www.foe.org. This environmental-advocacy group supports the inclusion in international trade agreements of standards to protect the environment.

International Bank for Reconstruction and Development (World Bank), 1818 H St., N.W., Washington, D.C. 20433; (202) 473-1155; www.worldbank. org. The bank provides exhaustive information on environmental protection, agriculture, health and other conditions in the developing world.

International Monetary Fund, 700 19th St., N.W., Washington, D.C. 20431; www.imf.org. The IMF, established in 1948 to oversee exchange rates, is an excellent source of statistics on international trade.

International Trade Administration, U.S. Department of Commerce, 14th St. and Constitution Ave., N.W., No. 3850, Washington, D.C. 20230; Trade information: (800) 872-8723; Publications: (202) 482-5487; www.its. doc.gov. The ITA implements programs to promote world trade.

World Trade Organization, 154 rue de Lausanne, 1211 Geneva 21, Switzerland; 41-22-739-51-1; www.wto.org. The successor agency to the General Agreement on Tariffs and Trade (GATT), the WTO oversees the world-trade system and hears disputes among its 136 member countries.

Bibliography

Selected Sources Used

Books

Burtless, Gary, Robert Z. Lawrence, Robert E. Litan and Robert J. Shapiro, *Globaphobia: Confronting Fears about Open Trade*, **Brookings Institution, Progressive Policy Institute and Twentieth Century Fund, 1998.**

The authors address some common fears about globalization, including its impact on jobs, wages and environmental quality. They conclude that other forces, notably technological development, play a greater role in those areas and suggest that trade offers more benefits than costs over the long run.

Friedman, Thomas L., *The Lexus and the Olive Tree*, **Farrar Straus Giroux, 1999.**

Globalization is revolutionizing world markets, writes Friedman, a foreign-affairs columnist for *The New York Times*. At the same time, the rapid flow of goods, capital and information — symbolized by the Lexus — threatens the survival of local communities and culture, the olive tree of the book's title.

Mendoza, Miguel Rodriguez, Patrick Low and Barbara Kotschwar, eds., *Trade Rules in the Making: Challenges in Regional and Multilateral Negotiations*, **Organization of American States/Brookings Institution Press, 1999.**

Chapters by experts treat a broad range of trade issues, including the history of trade and efforts to reduce barriers; the authority of multilateral trade groups, such as the World Trade Organization (WTO), and regional agreements; and prospects for future pacts like the Free Trade Area of the Americas.

Wallach, Lori, and Michelle Sforza, *Whose Trade Organization? Corporate Globalization and the Erosion of Democracy*, **Public Citizen, 1999.**

This critique of the WTO examines its negative impact on the environment, food-safety standards, labor rights and economic development in the Third World. The head of Public Citizen is consumer advocate Ralph Nader, this year's presidential candidate of the Green Party.

Articles

"Vote for China's Freedom," *The Economist*, **May 20-26, 2000.**

Given the choice between opening China to trade, investment and outside information and the status quo, members of the House of Representatives should opt for openness as a way to improve workers' rights and economic development in the world's largest market.

Avery, Dennis T., "Clueless in Seattle," *American Outlook*, **winter 2000, pp. 31-34.**

Instead of protecting workers' rights and the environment, the author charges, the protesters who disrupted the WTO meeting in Seattle inadvertently undermined their own agenda by delaying further trade liberalization, which he contends offers the greatest promise of global progress.

Hornblower, Margot, "The Battle in Seattle," *Time*, **Nov. 29, 1999, pp. 40-44.**

Written before the WTO meeting in Seattle broke down amid violent street protests against globalization, this article reviews the trade organization's history and the agenda of the coming round of trade talks.

Licking, Ellen, "They're Here, and They're Taking Over," *Business Week*, **May 24, 1999.**

In the absence of natural predators to keep them in check, exotic species arriving in the United States on the hulls of cargo ships or embedded in shipping pallets threaten widespread environmental damage and exemplify the potential damage posed by free-trade agreements.

Noland, Marcus, "Learning to Love the WTO," *Foreign Affairs*, **September/October 1999, pp. 78-92.**

Free trade's critics charge that it enables corporations to exploit workers and foul the environment in the developing world. But the author, a senior fellow at the Institute for International Economics, says those accusations often are a cover for less noble, protectionist motives.

Reports and Studies

Burke, James, "U.S. Investment in China Worsens Trade Deficit," Economic Policy Institute, May 2000.

American manufacturers are building factories in China, where they exploit low-wage labor and add to the country's already serious pollution problems in order to make goods for export, largely back to the United States.

World Trade Organization, "Trade and Environment, 1999."

This exhaustive study examines the impact of trade on such worrisome environmental problems as global warming, deforestation and overfishing. The report concludes that government policies are needed to limit the environmental damage resulting from industrial development and trade.

7 Oil Production in the 21st Century

MARY H. COOPER

American motorists got a shock this year: After enjoying several years of cheap gasoline, they were suddenly faced with gas prices that in some parts of the country exceeded $2 a gallon.

Several factors produced this unhappy turn of events. In March 1999, the Organization of Petroleum Exporting Countries (OPEC) began curtailing its output of crude oil in an attempt to halt a glut of global oil supplies that had depressed prices to their lowest level in 30 years.* The move caught American refiners by surprise, leaving them with lower than normal inventories for the U.S. market. At least two major pipeline disruptions added to the shortage of gasoline in the Midwest, where the price boost was most pronounced.

Consumers were quick to blame oil companies, OPEC and the federal government's clean-air requirements for the price hike. Worried about the impact of oil prices on the outcome of this fall's elections, politicians were sensitive to their complaints. The Clinton administration launched a federal investigation into alleged price fixing by the oil companies, while the governors of Illinois and Indiana responded to consumer outrage by suspending the states' gas taxes.

All indications were that the price hike, which propelled the average price for a gallon of regular unleaded gas to $1.68 on June 19, was temporary. By late July, the average price had fallen to $1.60. But in some ways, this summer's gas shortage resembled earlier energy crises. It may also have served as a useful reminder to Ameri-

---

* OPEC members are Algeria, Indonesia, Iran, Iraq, Kuwait, Libya, Nigeria, Qatar, Saudi Arabia, the United Arab Emirates and Venezuela.

Originally published August 7, 1998.
Updated by Mary H. Cooper,
August 10, 2000.

Public Broadcasting Service

can consumers that the era of cheap oil will one day come to an end.

Just a quarter-century ago, OPEC had the United States and the rest of the industrialized world by the throat, and Saudi Arabian oil minister Sheik Zaki Yamani was as familiar to many Americans as their representatives in Congress. Saudi Arabia and the four other major Middle East members dominated OPEC, controlling more than a third of world oil production.

In October 1973, the oil cartel imposed a total embargo on its exports to the United States and the Netherlands for their support of Israel in the Yom Kippur War. Oil prices skyrocketed. The ensuing inflation and stagnant industrial output spilled over from the U.S. and Dutch economies to infect the entire industrial world. Stagflation became even more deeply entrenched after 1978-79, when the Iranian revolution sparked a second energy crisis and rise in oil prices.

The industrial world responded to OPEC's grip on world oil supplies by searching for alternative sources. By the 1990s, non-OPEC producers such as Britain, Mexico and Norway had enabled importers to reduce their oil dependence on the volatile Persian

Gulf. They also launched campaigns to reduce their consumption of oil by raising energy taxes and encouraging energy conservation through improved efficiency of automobiles and appliances. And they sought to develop alternatives to oil such as solar, wind and geothermal energy.

These efforts paid off in the next two decades. Largely by diversifying their sources of foreign oil, the United States and other major consumers have significantly reduced their vulnerability to oil price manipulations by OPEC. Technological advances in exploration and drilling equipment have enabled producers to discover new oil deposits, further relaxing pressure on oil prices posed by growing global demand for oil.

Worries about future energy crises diminished still further when oil reserves under and around the Caspian Sea were opened to outside development after the Soviet Union's collapse in 1991. The former Soviet republics of Azerbaijan, Kazakhstan and Turkmenistan that border the Caspian — and, to a lesser extent, their Central Asia neighbors Tajikistan and Uzbekistan — stand to reap enough earnings from oil and natural gas exports alone to launch them into the modern industrial era in the space of a few years.

"The Caspian is potentially one of the world's most important, new, energy-producing regions," said former Energy Secretary Federico Peña in 1998. "Although the Caspian may never rival the Persian Gulf, Caspian production can have important implications for world energy supplies by increasing world supply and diversifying sources of supply among producing regions of the world." [1]

The oil glut that began in 1997 provided the icing on the cake for oil consumers. But as this summer's gas price hike suggests, Americans would be foolish to gloat over their current

Getting Oil Out of the Caspian

Several new pipelines have been proposed to move oil from the landlocked Caspian republics to maritime ports for export. The U.S. favors lines running from Baku, Azerbaijan, to Ceyhan, Turkey, or from Baku to Georgia. Russia prefers a northern pipeline connecting to its own system or to its Black Sea port of Novorossisk. The pipeline sought by the Caspian republics, runnning south to the Persian Gulf, is opposed by the U.S. because it crosses Iran. The route planned by China across Kazakhstan is not controversial.

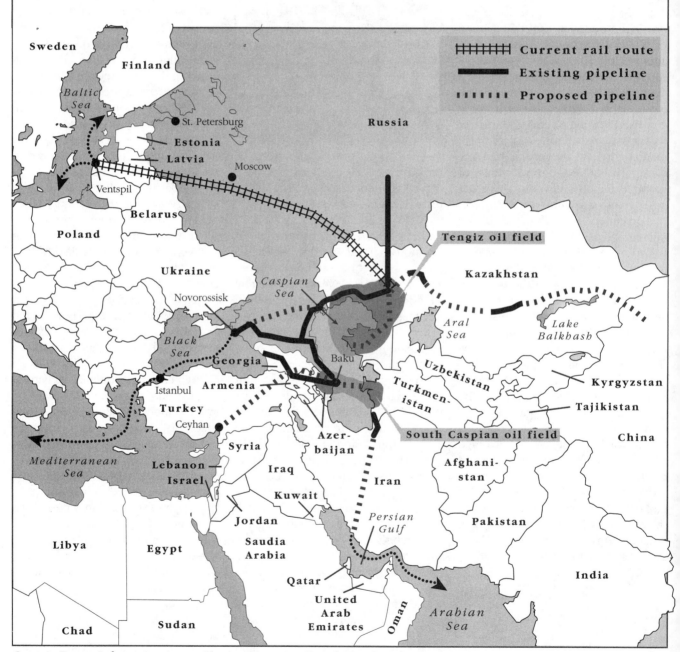

Sources: *Energy Information Agency, Fortune Magazine, Parade Magazine*

bounty. Even counting Alaska's prolific North Slope oil fields, domestic
reserves are falling. The United States
now imports more than half of its oil,
placing the country at added risk
from future disruptions of foreign
supplies. [2]

For all its promise, the Caspian
Sea region is far from coming on line
as a major source of non-OPEC oil.
The region's remoteness and legend-
ary political turmoil threaten to postpone or even scuttle the flow of oil
before production is fully under way.

Meanwhile, historically low gasoline prices have lulled American motorists into trading in their energy-
efficient sub-compact cars for gas-
guzzling sport utility vehicles, which
now account for almost half of
American new car sales. Programs to
develop alternatives to oil are losing
support in Congress, which has cut
the Energy Department's research
budget.

America's growing oil consumption also flies in the face of concern
that using oil and other fossil fuels is
causing a gradual but potentially
catastrophic warming of Earth's atmosphere. In December 1997, the
United States joined 167 other countries in agreeing to reduce fossil fuel
consumption. But in the current climate of energy abundance, support
for the Kyoto Protocol has stalled,
and the Senate appears highly unlikely to ratify the measure anytime
soon.

For much of the 1990s, OPEC
members were unable to agree on
production cuts to buoy prices. But
as consumers discovered this year, it
is too soon to write the organization's
obituary. OPEC has begun seeking
agreement from non-member producers to go along with its efforts to
buoy sagging prices. In March 1998,
Mexico agreed to join OPEC in cutting production, prompting some oil
experts to predict that other countries soon would join in. [3]

Crude Oil Prices Have Been Dropping

World crude oil prices dropped in the 1990s as members of the Organization of Petroleum Exporting Countries resisted OPEC efforts to limit their oil production. Discoveries of new oil sources in non-OPEC nations also have kept prices down.

(Dollars per barrel)

Source: Energy Information Administration, World Oil Markets 2000.

Even absent a further strengthening of OPEC's ability to manipulate oil prices over the short term,
some experts contend that the
break in oil prices that prevailed in
the 1990s will prove to be temporary. Colin J. Campbell, an oil-in-
dustry consultant in Geneva, Switzerland, and author of *The Coming
Oil Crisis*, predicts that prices will
rise when global oil production
reaches its peak, "within the first
few years of the next century." After
that, he predicts, demand for oil
will outpace its supply. "This will
be a fundamental turning point,
because until now we've always
had growing oil production," he
says.

As global oil deposits are depleted,
OPEC's Middle East producers could
be left in control of an increasing
portion of world reserves. "We can
expect another major price shock
around 2000," Campbell said two

years ago, "when the Middle East's
share of world reserves will be much
greater than it is now."

As Americans fire up their gas
guzzlers for summer outings, these
are some of the questions oil experts
are asking:

Has OPEC lost its control over global oil prices?

Through new discoveries and an
expanded membership, OPEC's oil
reserves have grown over the years.
The organization has reached beyond
its stronghold in the Persian Gulf —
still the main source of the world's oil
— to include far-flung producers such
as Indonesia and Nigeria. And OPEC's
undisputed leader, Saudi Arabia, retains its clout as the world's largest
oil producer.

But OPEC's grip over world oil production has slipped in the past 20 years,
largely as a result of its own actions.
When it set strict quotas in the 1970s

Getting Oil Out of the Caspian ...

Although some parts of the Caspian region and Central Asia do not hold promise as oil and gas producers, virtually every country in the vast area is likely to play a role in the industry's development. Some will serve as routes for pipelines or railroads and some, because of the threats they pose to the region's political stability, will retard progress. Here are the likely key players:

Armenia — In 1988, the largely Armenian population of Nagorno Karabakh, a province of Azerbaijan, began a six-year rebellion in an effort to become a part of neighboring Armenia. With support from Armenia, the rebels emerged victorious in 1994. Under the truce, Armenia was left in control of the province and other territory comprising 20 percent of Azerbaijan. Peace talks led by the United States, France and Russia, under the aegis of the Organization for Security and Cooperation in Europe, produced a compromise by which Nagorno Karabakh would be an autonomous province of Azerbaijan. After agreeing to these terms, rejected by the province's rebels, Armenian President Levon Ter-Petrossian was forced from office and replaced in March 1998 by Robert Kocharian, a Karabakh native who opposed the compromise. The U.S.-backed proposal to build a pipeline from Baku, Azerbaijan, to the Mediterranean port of Ceyhan, Turkey, would pass through Armenia.

Azerbaijan — Foreign oil companies have already invested heavily in the oil fields centered around the city of Baku. American companies Amoco, Exxon, Pennzoil and Unocal lead a consortium of 11 companies from eight countries — the Azerbaijan International Operating Company — that are drilling for oil for the first time in the country since it gained independence with the Soviet Union's collapse in 1991. President Heidar Aliyev, a former KGB general and member of the Soviet Politburo, took power in a 1993 coup against democratically elected Abullaz Elchibey. Aliyev has survived two attempted coups since then but remains a popular leader who has brought political stability despite the destabilizing effect of the war with Armenia, which ended with the occupation of a fifth of Azerbaijan's territory, including Nagorno Karabakh.[1] Azerbaijan subsequently imposed a trade embargo against Armenia. Under pressure from the Armenian Assembly of America, Congress passed a measure in 1992 barring economic aid to the Azeri government until it takes steps to lift the embargo. An amendment to the Freedom Support Act that provides aid to the former Soviet republics, Section 907, remains in effect despite growing opposition from the Clinton administration and many lawmakers who see it as an obstacle to ensuring U.S. access to Azeri oil.

Georgia — This former Soviet republic has been torn by fighting among several distinct ethnic communities after gaining independence in 1991. President Eduard Shevernadze, a former Soviet foreign minister, has survived two assassination attempts since assuming power in 1992. An oil pipeline links the Azeri oil fields at Baku and the Georgian Black Sea port of Supsa.

Iran — A longstanding oil producer of the Persian Gulf region, Iran also borders the Caspian's southern coast. Because the region's main oil and natural gas deposits lie north of the Iranian coast, Iran's main potential role in the Caspian Sea's oil industry is as a transport link. The Caspian oil producers back construction of a pipeline that would carry the region's oil through Iran to the Persian Gulf for shipment through the Strait of Hormuz to market. The United States, which maintains a unilateral embargo against Iran for its role in supporting international terrorism, adamantly opposes this route. For

---

that quadrupled oil prices, the cartel sparked a frantic search for alternative sources of oil by the industrial world, which depends on petroleum products for its economic survival.

With the exception of the United States, most industrial countries imported the bulk of their energy supplies. Using sophisticated technology, Britain and Norway soon located and began working oil deposits under the North Sea. *(See story, p. 123.)* The United States and other countries shifted much of their oil demand to these and other non-OPEC producers, which now account for about half of the oil export market. Russia and Norway now are the world's second- and third-largest exporters, after Saudi Arabia.

Until earlier this year, OPEC appeared to have lost its ability to set production quotas among its membership as a way to buoy prices, especially in the fall of 1998, when a global oil glut began depressing prices. As usual, Saudi Arabia took the lead, calling in March of that year for a cut in oil production of 1.2 million barrels a day. But with prices falling — and with them precious oil revenues — many members ignored their quotas and pumped as much oil as the market would bear.

Desperate to reduce output, OPEC has appealed to other producers, which are also feeling the pinch of falling oil revenues. Russia, which has the largest oil reserves of any non-OPEC country and badly needs oil revenues to stave off its deepening financial crisis, attended an OPEC meeting in 1998, giving rise to speculation that it might join the organization.[4] On June 4, 1998 the oil ministers of Saudi Arabia and Venezuela reached an agreement with Mexico to cut production by 450,000 barrels a day, beginning July 1. This agreement had some effect on prices, leading some observers to predict that

---

... Involves Many Actors, Many Ifs

now, some Caspian Sea oil is making its way indirectly through Iran via a swap arrangement by which oil is shipped to refineries in northern Iran, and an equivalent amount of Iranian oil is loaded onto tankers in the Persian Gulf for transport to market.

Kazakhstan — Though only a fraction of this vast and sparsely populated country's territory lies near the Caspian, it holds one of the region's most promising oil and gas deposits — the Tengiz Basin now under development by Chevron and other companies. China plans to build a 1,900-mile pipeline from the basin across Kazakhstan to Xinjiang, China. President Nursultan Nazarbaev, a former first secretary of the Kazakhstan Community Party, was elected after the country declared its independence from the Soviet Union in December 1991. Since then he has consolidated his power by eroding the country's limited representative government.

Kyrgyzstan — Considered to be the most democratic country in Central Asia, Kyrgyzstan is led by Askar Akaev, a former physicist who often quotes Thomas Jefferson. Elected president by the Supreme Soviet in 1990, Akaev won re-election in 1995. The country's oil potential is uncertain.

Russia — Like Iran, Russia stands to play a marginal role in the Caspian's oil production, but a crucial one in transporting the region's oil and gas to market. The first developer of the region's oil a century ago, Russia — and later the Soviet Union — largely abandoned the Caspian fields in favor of other domestic reserves to build its considerable oil industry. Today Russia transports Caspian oil by rail to the Baltic Sea and maintains other oil and gas pipelines, including one from Baku to its Black Sea port of Novorossisk. A proposed pipeline would also link the Tengiz oil field and Novorossisk.

Tajikistan — In 1997, Tajik President Imomali Rakhmonov and opposition forces signed a peace agreement ending a five-year civil war waged among the country's four regional tribes and between the secular government and Islamic militants. One of the poorest of the former Soviet republics, Tajikistan supports a thriving drug trade that has hampered efforts to improve the economy. [2]

Turkmenistan — Saparmurat Niyazov, a former Communist Party leader who became president in 1990, heads an oppressive regime based on a cult of personality. Known as Turkmenbashi — "head of the Turkmen" — Niyazov has banned opposition parties and presides over the legislature. Despite considerable reserves of natural gas and oil under and around the Caspian Sea, mismanagement of the economy has impoverished the country, which borders Afghanistan and Iran. The only existing export outlets for Turkmen gas is through Russian pipelines.

Uzbekistan — With almost 24 million inhabitants, Uzbekistan is the most populous country in the region. Cotton is the country's main product, but the government has announced plans to search for oil and gas under the polluted Aral Sea, drained of much of its water for irrigation. President Islam Karimov, a former communist leader, has introduced limited democratic reforms but faces the growing influence of Islamic militants.

---

[1] See Richard C. Longworth, "Boomtown Baku," *The Bulletin of the Atomic Scientists,* May/June 1998, pp. 34-38.

[2] See Martha Brill Olcott, "The Caspian's False Promise," *Foreign Policy,* summer 1998, pp. 94-113.

OPEC would turn more often to informal agreements of this kind in an effort to regain leverage over the market and stabilize prices around the historical norm of about $20 a barrel.

"OPEC is a major factor in determining world oil prices," said Edward H. Murphy at the time. He is the director of finance, accounting and statistics for the American Petroleum Institute (API), which represents U.S. oil companies. "They have succeeded in reducing production by about 2.1 million barrels a day, or 6 percent, since February. That is a significant factor that has prevented oil prices from falling even further. They're not back up to $20 a barrel, but they'd be a lot lower today in the absence of OPEC's production cuts."

A landmark agreement among OPEC members in March 1999 to restrict production helped propel the price of crude from its 12-year low of $10.72 a barrel in December 1998 to $32.72 on June 28, 2000. Fearful of causing a global recession that eventually would hurt the oil producers themselves by drying up demand for oil, Saudi Arabia unilaterally announced in July that it would increase its output enough to nudge the price of oil back below $30 a barrel.

Does U.S. foreign policy enhance Americans' access to foreign oil?

A fundamental, though infrequently recognized, goal of U.S. foreign policy has been to ensure the access of American businesses and consumers to foreign oil supplies, especially since 1971, when domestic oil production peaked and began its gradual decline. By 1996, the United States — once a leading exporter of crude — was for the first time forced to import half of its oil. Today, imports account for half of U.S. consumption. *(See graph, p. 118.)* As demand for oil continues to rise, the

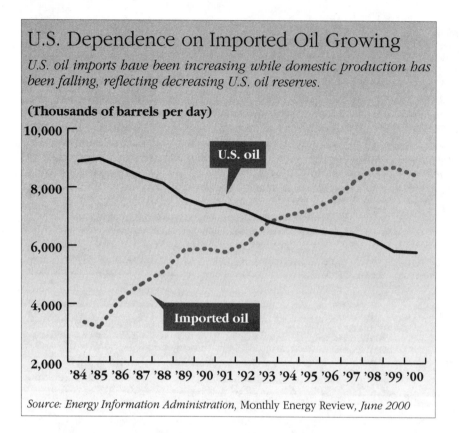

U.S. Dependence on Imported Oil Growing

U.S. oil imports have been increasing while domestic production has been falling, reflecting decreasing U.S. oil reserves.

(Thousands of barrels per day)

U.S. oil

Imported oil

'84 '85 '86 '87 '88 '89 '90 '91 '92 '93 '94 '95 '96 '97 '98 '99 '00

Source: Energy Information Administration, Monthly Energy Review, *June 2000*

United States will likely depend on imports for an ever-growing portion of its oil supply.

Like other industrialized countries, the United States has diversified its sources of foreign oil away from the Middle East since the energy crises of the 1970s. Today, Canada is the leading source of U.S. oil imports, followed by Venezuela. Although U.S. dependence on Persian Gulf oil has fallen from 24 percent of oil imports in 1991 to 21 percent today, the region will remain a vital oil supplier for years to come. But it is also one of the most politically unstable regions, the focus of 50 years of hostilities between Israel and its Arab neighbors and, for the past two decades, of militant Islamic fundamentalism.

Access to oil has figured prominently in the United States' activities in the Middle East throughout this period, most recently in the 1991 Persian Gulf War, when the United States led a United Nations military coalition that forced Iraq to withdraw from neighboring Kuwait. [5]

Of course, access to oil is not the sole U.S. strategic interest in the region. Even during the gulf war, the Bush administration stressed the need to repel Iraq's invasion of Kuwait to maintain the international rule of law. Because Iraq's leader, Saddam Hussein, was suspected of producing nuclear and biological weapons, the United States also sought and obtained Security Council support for a U.N. embargo against Iraq pending the completion of U.N. inspections of Iraqi arsenals. But the Clinton administration's "dual containment" policy toward Iraq and Iran — which together control 20 percent of the world's proven reserves — has implications for U.S. access to the region's oil exports. [6]

Iraq, with 112 billion barrels of proven oil reserves, is second only to Saudi Arabia, with 262 billion barrels. The embargo has exacted a heavy toll on Iraq, depriving it of oil rev-

enues and leaving many Iraqis without adequate food and medical supplies. In December 1996, the embargo was eased to allow Iraq to export just enough oil to pay for food and other essential supplies. This "oil-for-food" provision is to remain in place until the Iraqi government allows U.N. arms inspectors full access to weapons sites.

But some oil-importing countries, notably France, Russia and China, oppose continuing the embargo against Iraq indefinitely. Critics of the embargo welcomed U.N. Secretary General Kofi Annan's role in prodding Saddam Hussein to allow U.N. inspectors greater access to the country in February 1998. Annan signaled a softening of international attitudes toward Iraq by calling the Iraqi leader "a man you can do business with." For his part, Saddam has threatened to take unspecified action to break the embargo if it is not lifted. [7]

Indeed, Iraq is already expanding oil exports in defiance of the U.N. embargo. "The fact that Iraq continues to export sizable amounts of petroleum products illegally — and that the Iraqi government refuses to permit the U.N. to oversee or monitor these sales — strongly suggests that the proceeds from these sales are intended for non-humanitarian purposes," said Under Secretary of State Thomas R. Pickering in 1998. "We are currently seeking ways to make the Iraqi government accountable for this illegal traffic — or to end it through tougher enforcement measures." [8]

Critics say the U.S. efforts are doomed. "American policy [toward Iraq] is nothing more than the desperate embrace of sanctions of diminishing effectiveness punctuated by occasional whining, frequent bluster, political retreat and military paralysis," said Richard Perle, assistant secretary of Defense for international security during the Reagan administration.

Varied Sources Provide U.S. Oil Imports

U.S. oil imports come from a wide range of sources. Four of the top five providers are not Arab nations, and two of the five are not members of the Organization of Petroleum Exporting Countries (list at left). More than half the oil imported by the United States comes from non-OPEC members (list at right).

Top Five U.S. Suppliers	
(thousands of barrels per day)	
Canada	1,648
Venezuela*	1,480
Saudi Arabia*	1,452
Mexico	1,329
Nigeria*	777

OPEC vs. Non-OPEC Production	
(thousands of barrels per day)	
Arab OPEC	2,209
Other OPEC	2,501
Non-OPEC	5,799
Total	10,510

* OPEC members

Source: Energy Information Administration, Monthly Energy Review, *June 2000*

"The pressure to relax the sanctions, which has already pushed to more than $10 billion per year the amount of revenue Iraq is allowed from the sale of oil, will not subside and will almost certainly increase. The French, Russians and others will continue to agitate for the further relaxation of sanctions, and the United States will almost certainly make further concessions in this regard." [9]

U.S. policy toward Iran, whose 93 billion barrels of proven oil reserves place it fifth in the global ranking of oil powers, elicits similar concerns. Since the 1979 Islamic revolution, the United States has identified Iran as one of the world's leading supporters of international terrorism. With the Iran-Libya Sanctions Act, the United States unilaterally barred American and foreign companies from investing more than $20 million in Iran's energy sector.

But Iran is an important source of Persian Gulf oil, and several foreign companies have defied the ban. Under pressure from Europe, Clinton announced in May 1998 that he would not impose sanctions on three French, Russian and Malaysian companies that invested $2 billion in a natural gas field in Iran.

Meanwhile, U.S. oil companies are losing lucrative oil contracts to overseas competitors. "There's no question that unilateral sanctions against Iran are hurting U.S. companies," said Murphy of the API. "By preventing them from competing in those markets, the sanctions provide a relative advantage to foreign oil companies. That's a real concern of our members. Whether or not there's a fair foreign policy tradeoff, I can't say."

Some critics see a clear clash of interests between U.S. foreign policy in the region and U.S. energy security. "The United States' vilification of Iran, Iraq and Libya makes for strange policy," Campbell said, "especially when you understand we'll be dependent on these three places for oil before long."

The Clinton administration continues to defend its policy of containment toward Iran. "Unilateral sanctions have proven costly to U.S. business," conceded Assistant Secretary of State for Near Eastern Affairs Martin S. Indyk. "However, we believe that Iran poses threats so significant that we have no choice but accept these costs. Economic pressure has an important role in our efforts to convince Iran to cease its efforts to acquire weapons

of mass destruction and missiles and to support terrorism." [10]

The U.S. position toward Iran has shown signs of softening since the August 1997 election of President Mohammad Khatami, who has loosened somewhat the strict regime set in place by his militant predecessors by expanding press freedoms and establishing more cordial relations with countries in the Persian Gulf and Europe.

But, citing evidence that Iran's support of terrorism is unchanged, the United States officially has not changed its position on sanctions. On June 17, 1998, however, Secretary of State Madeleine K. Albright held out the possibility of a future improvement in bilateral relations. Although she refrained from proposing specific steps to normalize relations, Albright said, "Obviously, two decades of mistrust cannot be erased overnight. The gap between us remains wide. But it is time to test the possibilities for bridging this gap." [11]

The Caspian Sea region is another area where foreign policy goals may clash with those of energy security. "Our interest in the Caspian is not defined simply by the region's energy resources, but no one doubts their significance," said Stephen Sestanovich, special adviser to the secretary of State for the new independent states. "Energy could become a source of conflict, a lever of control or an obstacle to progress. Or it could become a ticket to prosperity and peace, a secure link to the outside world." [12]

The United States has played an active role in brokering peace talks in some of the region's simmering ethnic battles, such as those between the government of Azerbaijan and leaders of Armenian rebels who occupy the region of Nagorno Karabakh. It also has funneled economic and technical assistance — totaling $372 million in fiscal 1998 — to the newly independent countries of the region, which own potentially huge deposits of oil.

But an existing measure, Section 907 of the 1992 Freedom Support Act, bars the United States from extending this assistance to Azerbaijan. Enacted at the behest of the U.S. Armenian lobby, which claimed that the government of Azerbaijan subjected ethnic Armenians to human rights abuses, the measure has attracted widespread opposition since the extent of Azerbaijan's oil wealth has become more apparent. The Clinton administration also supports the measure's repeal.

Caspian Sea oil cannot reach consumers until a pipeline network is built linking the remote, landlocked region to seaports far away. *(See map, p. 114.)* The most direct route, and possibly the least expensive to construct, would pass through Iran to the Persian Gulf. But U.S. sanctions against Iran stand in the way of that option. Instead, the United States backs a multiple pipeline network that includes the so-called main export pipeline, which would pass through Georgia and NATO ally Turkey to the Turkish port of Ceyhan on the Black Sea, where the oil would be loaded onto tankers and shipped to markets via the Mediterranean Sea.

Some experts say the United States should ease its current opposition to the Iran pipeline option. "If the international oil companies working in Central Asia do not need to start construction of new pipeline routes immediately, the U.S. government should not lock the door prematurely against the prospect of a new pipeline transiting Iran," said Richard W. Murphy, senior fellow for the Middle East at the Council on Foreign Relations. "The routing of new pipelines will have profound political and economic implications for years to come." [13]

Will the United States be ready with alternative energy sources when the oil runs out?

As a finite resource, petroleum will not last forever. Estimates of how long the world has before the oil runs out vary widely. The United States is likely to run out far sooner than many major producers, however. Using about 7 billion barrels of oil products a year, the United States is the world's most voracious oil consumer. And it shows no sign of changing its energy habits. U.S. demand for oil is expected to grow by 20 percent by 2015. [14]

But the crunch is likely to come long before the world exhausts its oil supplies. "The idea of running out of oil, of when the last barrel comes out of the ground, is a red herring," Campbell said. "It misses the point. What's much more relevant is when world production will peak, and that will occur within the first few years of the next century." When that happens, Campbell predicts, oil consumers will be in for a major price shock as production slows.

Campbell says the United States may be especially ill-prepared for the next energy crisis. Even though U.S. oil production started declining in 1971, the United States was never seriously affected because it was able to import its oil from other countries. "This chapter is coming to an end because the other places, too, are

getting close to peak production," he said. "There's monumental ignorance in the government and among the public at large on this subject."

Other critics charge that the United States, by holding oil taxes below those of other consuming nations, has encouraged oil consumption with little concern for the consequences. [15] "Part of our energy policy seems to be to keep prices low," said George Yates, chairman of the Independent Petroleum Association of America, whose 8,000 members produce almost half of the nation's domestic crude. "But we have only about 3 million barrels a day worldwide of excess capacity, and that includes Iraq, which is officially out of production because of the embargo. That's a pretty slim margin. It's like operating a factory at 100 percent capacity — you can't go on forever like this."

The development of alternatives to oil has proceeded slowly in the United States. After the energy crises of the 1970s, the federal government funded research and development of renewable energy sources such as solar, wind, geothermal and biomass energy. [16] But as oil prices subsequently fell and Congress turned its attention to reducing the federal budget deficit, support for these efforts dwindled.

According to Energy Under Secretary Ernest Moniz, his department's budgets for energy research and development fell fivefold from 1978 to 1997; privately funded research has also declined. [17] Today, much of the U.S.-developed technology for renewable energy sources is being used more intensively in Europe and Asia — where oil products are heavily taxed — than in the United States.

"The effects of world dependence on Middle Eastern oil means that while the quoted market price per barrel is about $20, the costs associated with keeping shipping lanes open, rogue states in check and terrorists at bay may more than quadruple the price per barrel," said Sen. Richard G. Lugar, R-Ind., before the recent price rise. "Given these costs, the United States may pay more than $100 billion this year for oil from the unstable

Chronology

1960s *Oil production comes under the growing control of Middle Eastern producers.*

Sept. 14, 1960
Iran, Iraq, Kuwait, Saudi Arabia and Venezuela form the Organization of Petroleum Exporting Countries (OPEC).

1970s *An Arab embargo leads to oil crises that quadruple the price of oil.*

1970
Domestic oil production peaks at 11.3 million barrels a day in the United States, forcing it to gradually increase its dependence on imports.

October 1973
After OPEC raises oil prices by 70 percent, to $5.11 a barrel, Arab producers impose an embargo on oil exports to the United States and the Netherlands for their support of Israel in the Yom Kippur War. Oil prices soar above $17 a barrel.

1975
The Strategic Petroleum Reserve is created to protect the United States from interruptions in oil supplies. Congress sets fuel-efficiency standards for cars.

December 1978
The Iranian revolution disrupts Persian Gulf oil supplies, causing a second oil shock and deepening inflation in oil-consuming countries.

June 1979
OPEC raises the price of crude from $14.50 to as high as $23.50 a barrel. Gas lines form in the United States.

1980s *As oil production spreads outside OPEC, prices begin to fall.*

1980
The eight-year Iran-Iraq War begins, compounding the disruption in Gulf oil. By the following January, OPEC's oil price reaches $34 a barrel, more than 10 times the price in 1972.

1986
Oil prices fall to their lowest level since the first oil crisis in 1973.

1990s *OPEC's inability to control output leads to a global oil glut.*

Aug. 2, 1990
Iraq occupies Kuwait, cutting off 1.6 million barrels of oil a day from the world market. The U.N. imposes an embargo on Iraqi oil exports as well. Panic buying pushes oil prices up from $13 a barrel to $40.

1991
The United States leads a coalition of forces in the Persian Gulf War to drive Iraqi occupying forces out of Kuwait.

December 1991
The Soviet Union dissolves, and the newly independent countries of the Caspian Sea begin opening their oil reserves to exploitation.

1992
Congress passes the Freedom Support Act providing economic assistance to the former Soviet republics. Section 907 of the law prohibits the aid from going to Azerbaijan — a major oil producer — for abuses against ethnic Armenians.

1993
Chevron Corp. invests in Kazakhstan's vast Tengiz oil field, beginning the oil rush in the Caspian Sea region.

1996
The U.S. begins to import more than half the oil it consumes.

December 1996
An "oil-for-food" provision is added to the U.N. embargo against Iraq, allowing the country to export just enough oil to pay for food and other essential supplies. The same year, energy conservation pushes oil consumption in the industrial world below the peak level of 1978.

October 1997
The financial crisis in Asia curbs oil consumption in that part of the world, leading to a glut in world oil supplies.

March 1998
As oil prices plummet to their lowest levels in decades, OPEC reaches an unprecedented agreement with a non-OPEC oil producer — Mexico — to curtail production in an effort to keep oil prices from falling further.

March 1999
OPEC members agree to curtail oil output, propelling the price of crude to more than $30 a barrel by 2000.

Middle East. By contrast, the United States will spend less than $1 billion this year on energy research." [18]

Some analysts find little reason for concern about the United States' energy future. In their view, the technology that has enabled oil producers to discover new deposits and remove more oil from existing wells will continue to advance. "We've made tremendous advances that have made it cheaper to find and produce oil," said Murphy of the API. "If those continue, we're probably looking at oil availability for the indefinite future at today's prices or less."

When the oil crunch does come, Murphy predicts, the technology to provide cheap alternatives will be ready to take up the slack. "My feeling is that long before the use of petroleum is diminished, other sources will be there. In 10 years, all cars may be run with fuel cells instead of gasoline."

BACKGROUND

OPEC's Power Play

The United States was the world's dominant oil producer for the first half of this century. [19] Outside the United States, world production fell under the control of the world's major oil companies, known as the "Seven Sisters," which acquired the right to

A replica of the world's first oil well, drilled by "Colonel" Edwin L. Drake in Titusville, Pa., in 1859.

Public Broadcasting Service

extract oil from countries where they operated in exchange for royalties paid to the host governments. So great was their power over the markets that they were able to manipulate the price of crude from their extensive holdings in the Middle East. [20] By the late 1950s, however, they faced growing competition from independent companies and cut their prices.

Because they collected taxes based on oil prices, Persian Gulf countries where the Seven Sisters extracted oil were faced with falling revenues. On Sept. 14, 1960, representatives of Iran, Iraq, Kuwait, Saudi Arabia and Venezuela met in Baghdad, Iraq, and founded OPEC. The fledgling cartel froze oil prices to prevent further erosion in oil revenues. Other producer nations joined OPEC, including Qatar, the United Arab Emirates in the Persian Gulf region, as well as Algeria, Indonesia, Libya and Nigeria. Membership in the organization enabled these countries to set a minimum royalty to be paid by companies for the privilege of extracting oil from their territories. The organization's expansion also helped the Seven Sisters by making it harder for independent companies to undercut them in the host countries.

The new order in oil development began to unravel in 1969, when Libyan strongman Muammar el-Qadaffi forced Occidental Petroleum, an independent American operator in Libya, to cut production. Because Libyan oil was of high quality, it was in high demand, and the cutback created an oil shortage. OPEC decided to profit from the change by raising oil prices. In an effort to stabilize the market, OPEC and the oil companies agreed in 1971 to a new pricing system that allowed for prices to be negotiated every five years.

As Oil Runs Out, Technology Buys Time

The world's supply of "conventional" oil — oil that is easily recovered — is running short of demand. In little more than a decade, some experts predict, global demand will so far exceed supplies of conventional oil that price shocks will occur that may lead to recession or political turmoil.

Faced with this impending shortfall, oil companies are investing heavily in research to improve existing technologies and develop new ones. Some of the work is already paying off. According to Roger N. Anderson, director of petroleum technology research at Columbia University, recent advances in finding and extracting oil may raise world oil production by more than 20 percent by 2010. [1]

Recent advances in oil exploration and extraction include:

4-D Seismic Analysis — As oil and natural gas are extracted from underground deposits, the remaining oil and gas seeps into the layers of rock. Three-dimensional monitoring with seismic instruments helps identify the location of oil deposits but cannot follow the shifting of oil that occurs as the well's contents run down. Anderson and others have developed a "4-D" system that incorporates the added dimension of time and helps drillers determine where the rest of the oil is likely to settle. Recovering this otherwise lost oil can increase the output of a given field by as much as 15 percent. The new technology has been applied at about 60 oil fields worldwide over the past four years.

Steam and Gas Injection — Drillers traditionally abandon wells when the flow of oil slows to a trickle. But scientists now know that this often leaves behind more than half the oil in a given deposit. Pumping steam, natural gas or liquid carbon dioxide into seemingly dry wells can force the remaining oil through porous rock toward a neighboring well, where it can be extracted. Another technique involves pumping water below the deposit, which increases the pressure under the oil, forcing it to the surface. Although steam or gas injection increases oil recovery by up to 15 percent, the high cost of this technique often outweighs the oil's value.

Directional Drilling — Oil wells typically are drilled straight down into the ground. But new technology allows drillers to change direction thousands of meters below ground and bore horizontally through rock in search of deposits a mile or more away from the wellhead. Sensors near the drill bit can detect oil, water and gas by measuring the density of surrounding rock or by measuring minute changes in electrical resistance. Engineers at the surface monitor the drill's progress by computer.

Deep-Water Drilling — Most offshore rigs, such as those along the coasts of Texas and Louisiana, operate at relatively shallow depths. But new technology is enabling drillers to tap into oil deposits under deeper water — currently down to 1,700 meters. Unmanned submarines install equipment on the ocean floor to regulate the flow of oil at high pressure and prevent environmentally devastating blowouts. The oil is then loaded onto tankers at sea or piped ashore or to shallow-water platforms through underwater pipelines. Recently declassified U.S. Navy technology enables geophysicists to detect underwater oil deposits through the sheets of salt and basalt that often hide them from conventional seismic surveys. While deep offshore drilling is very expensive, it is expected to become more widely pursued as conventional oil deposits dry up. Deep-water platforms are already in use off the coast of Newfoundland, Canada, and more are planned for the Gulf of Mexico, the North Sea and the Atlantic Ocean off Brazil and West Africa.

Just how much impact technological advances can have on global oil supplies is a matter of heated debate. Oil companies are optimistic about technology's ability to extend the petroleum era for decades to come. "If you look at the available proved reserves, there are about 1 trillion barrels of oil still in the ground," said Edward H. Murphy, an economist at the American Petroleum Institute. "If we continue to produce 27 billion barrels a year as we do now, that means we have 37 years left." That deadline can be extended, Murphy says, by technological advances. "We only recover 40 percent of production out of a given field today," he said. "So there's substantial room for enhanced recovery."

There's a downside to technology's impact on oil production, however, especially for small domestic producers who depend on the slow but steady flow of oil from marginal wells. "Some technologies mean that the same reserves are depleted more quickly instead of maintaining production over a long period," said George Yates, chairman of the Independent Petroleum Association of America. "So while technology has had a very positive impact on this industry, it's also put more oil on the market, which exacerbates our problems."

Still other experts say technology can only delay for a short time the inevitable demise of our oil-based economy. "Deep-water drilling is capable of producing 100 billion barrels, or about five years of world demand," said Colin J. Campbell, a consultant in Geneva, Switzerland. "It's expensive, and it's viable only in giant fields." He foresees further development of oil deposits under polar ice in Alaska, Russia and Canada, as well as the large deposits of heavy oil in Canada and Venezuela. "But even that won't make a lot of difference," Campbell said. "Whatever the accumulated advances of technology can deliver ought to be incorporated into our estimates of existing oil reserves. It's not something you can keep adding to."

---

[1] Information in this section is largely based on Roger N. Anderson, "Oil Production in the 21st Century," *Scientific American,* March 1998, pp. 86-91.

Energy Crises of the 1970s

OPEC's new pricing system quickly fell apart, however. Oil was bought from companies in the open market for more than the established price, and OPEC members wanted to share in the profits. After the companies balked at their request, OPEC unilaterally raised the official price by 70 percent in October 1973, to $5.11 a barrel. The same month, the Arab producing countries imposed an oil embargo on the United States and the Netherlands for their support of Israel in the Yom Kippur War. The embargo was later replaced with a cutback in production by all Arab members except Iraq.

"Using oil supply as a political weapon was a new development in the industry and one that did great damage to OPEC's commercial credibility as a reliable supplier," writes Fadhil J. Chalabi, director of the Center for Global Energy Studies in London and acting secretary of OPEC from 1983-88. [21]

The production cutback reduced availability to all oil importers and led to a quadrupling of prices and the decade's first oil shock. The second shock came in the winter of 1978-79 following the Iranian revolution, which led to the ouster of Shah Mohammed Reza Pahlavi and his replacement by the Ayatollah Ruhollah Khomeini's militant Islamic regime.

The revolution caused a disruption of oil from the Persian Gulf that was compounded by the outbreak in 1980 of the Iran-Iraq War. By January 1981, OPEC's oil price had reached $34 a barrel, more than 10 times the price in 1972, before the first oil shock. Taken together, the shocks produced a windfall for OPEC members, whose oil revenues skyrocketed from less than $23 billion in 1972 to more than $280 billion by the end of the decade.

Oil Consumers React

But OPEC's bonanza days were numbered. The United States and other industrial countries reacted strongly to the gasoline rationing, long lines at the pump and double-digit inflation produced by the pro-

Part of the Caspian Sea oil-drilling installation built by Soviet leader Josef Stalin in 1949, about 40 miles east of Baku, Azerbaijan.

duction cutbacks and price increases. They launched a frantic search for alternative sources of oil and set about trying to reduce their dependence on oil imports by making more fuel-efficient cars, improving energy conservation and developing renewable energy sources.

Over time, the growth in demand for oil slowed. By 1995, industrial nations were consuming only 2 million barrels a day more than they had in 1975. "Put another way," wrote Chalabi, "oil consumption by OECD countries in 1996 was less than at its peak level in 1978, even though their [gross domestic product] had grown by 42 percent during the same period." [22]

The oil consumers' efforts to reduce their reliance on Middle East oil paid off most successfully in the development of new oil fields. Companies shifted their investments to non-OPEC countries such as Mexico and Canada, as well as Britain and Norway, where they developed new platform-drilling technology to exploit the vast deposits under the North Sea. High oil prices also made it feasible to tap the enormous reserves on Alaska's North Slope.

As a result of these efforts, OPEC's share of the global oil market fell by half, from 56 percent in 1975 to just 26 percent in 1995. Although non-OPEC countries possess only a quarter of the world's oil reserves, they now account for 60 percent of global production.

CURRENT SITUATION

OPEC's Dilemma

Despite the industrial nations' success in reducing their dependence on Middle East oil, OPEC has continued to reap enormous profits from oil exports. The revenues from oil sales have enabled many member countries to invest in other industries to help diversify their economies in preparation for the day when they will no longer be able to rely on petroleum exports.

But the glut in oil supplies that began in 1997 dealt a serious blow to countries that still depend heavily on oil exports, both within and outside OPEC. Even Saudi Arabia felt the pinch of falling oil revenues.

The economic crisis encouraged cheating on the part of some OPEC members, further undermining the organization's clout. Venezuela was said to be the most flagrant offender, and called on fellow OPEC members to abandon quotas altogether in favor of other strategies to win market share. Algeria, Iran, Libya and Nigeria also routinely ignored the production quotas to prevent further erosion of the oil revenues they depend on for economic survival. [23]

In a desperate effort to slow production, OPEC for the first time called on non-member producer countries to cooperate with its quota system. In March 1998, Mexico agreed to cut oil output, and Norway later agreed to curb production as well. Russia has expressed interest in joining OPEC and attended the organization's June 1998 meeting in Geneva as an observer. The March agreement sent oil prices up by 13 percent, to almost $17 a barrel. But prices soon dropped back to around $14, suggesting that the market was not confident that

OPEC could hold production down for long.

Some U.S. oil-company representatives supported OPEC's campaign to hold the line on output and prices. "I'm hoping that by including non-members, OPEC can exercise some

Oil companies are investing heavily in research to improve exploration and drilling technology, because conventional methods may be unable to meet demand in the near future.

restraint on oil production," said Yates of the Independent Petroleum Association. "Restraint, coupled with higher prices, will mean fewer oil wells being abandoned in the United States. It also means new wells will

be drilled to find additional oil, which will make us better able to meet demand in the future. OPEC's really the American consumer's friend right now."

But many analysts question OPEC's ability over the long term to control the global market, which has changed in fundamental ways over the past two decades. "What's dominating the market today is the advance of technology, which is having a significant impact on the industry's ability to explore and produce oil in areas they were forbidden from exploring before," said Murphy of the API. Another change is the willingness of countries such as Venezuela, where the oil business was once run by state-owned companies, to have foreign, private companies come in and produce their oil. Finally, the former Soviet republics in the Caspian may have a major impact on world markets when the region's oil starts to flow. "OPEC is a bystander in this region," Murphy said.

OPEC's difficulties have led some experts to predict its eventual demise. "OPEC, as such, is disintegrating," Campbell said. Indeed, OPEC members know that drastically raising prices to solve their current dilemma will backfire on them in the end. "They remember what happened after the last shock," he said, "and they fear that if they put up the price they will lose their market share, and if that happens that they will lose everything."

In Campbell's view, however, the five leading Middle Eastern producers — Iran, Iraq, Kuwait, Saudi Arabia and Abu Dhabi (one of seven emirates comprising the United Arab Emirates) — have nothing to worry about. "They don't realize that the situation is very different today," he said. He calculated that by about 2002 world production of conventional oil — that which is easily recoverable — would peak, sending prices upward once again.

"Unlike the 1970s, when a flood of new oil production followed the price shocks," he said, "there are very few new oil deposits being found, with the exception of the Caspian." Campbell predicted that Middle Eastern producers, with about half the world's remaining conventional oil reserves, will see their share of recoverable oil rise substantially by 2000.

At that point, he said, "the Middle Eastern countries will recognize their control."

Cheap Oil

Campbell's prediction appears to be borne out by the current oil price hike. Until this year, however, oil-producing countries, including the petroleum-rich kingdoms of the Middle East, were suffering as a result of low oil prices. Most depend on oil exports for the bulk of their revenue. Saudi Arabia saw its oil revenues drop from $43 billion to about $29 billion between 1997 and 1998. As a result, King Fahd's government was forced to borrow $2 billion from Saudi banks to fund public programs and cut its budget by at least 10 percent. [24]

The bad news for oil producers may have a silver lining over the longer term. As autocratic regimes in the Middle East are forced to reduce their generous health, education and welfare programs, social unrest may quicken the pace of economic and political reforms. Pressure for reform has surfaced in a number of the region's oil states, including Saudi Arabia and the other gulf states, as well as Syria and Iran. [25]

Oil producers outside the Middle East have had problems as well. Before the recent price rise, unexpectedly low oil revenues forced Mexico, a major source of U.S. oil imports, to undergo a number of painful spending cuts. Nigeria, in the midst of chronic political turmoil, faces an even graver plight. In this poor West African country, earnings from oil exports provide a vital buffer against widespread poverty. For Russia, low oil prices of recent years have only added to the country's serious economic crisis. Only Britain and Norway, with the most diversified industrial economies among the major foreign exporters, were able to absorb the loss of oil revenues without major disruption.

In the United States, which now imports more than half its oil, the recent spike in oil prices appears to have had little impact on energy consumption and the economy. Sales of gas-guzzling SUVs and other large vehicles continue apace, and inflation remains in check. The main beneficiaries of the price rise are U.S. oil companies, which have recovered from their poor financial performance of the late 1990s. Both Exxon Mobil Corp. and the Chevron Corp., the two largest U.S. oil companies, registered record earnings in the second quarter of 2000. [26]

Most analysts predict that oil prices will remain unstable for the foreseeable future, a trend that may discourage major new investments in domestic output. Low crude oil prices of recent years have dampened the incentive for oil companies to look for new domestic deposits and to maintain production in existing fields with marginal output. According to the API's Murphy, the number of drilling rigs used to search for oil and gas fell by 31 percent over the average used for that purpose in the 1990s. "This drilling data should, we believe, be of major concern to those interested in this country's energy future," he said. "Oil drilling at these rates is inadequate to maintain U.S. crude oil production levels, particularly in the lower 48 states." [27]

Many smaller American oil companies are in especially bad shape. As a group, the 8,000 independent oil companies suffered a 25 percent drop in revenues in 1998. These include many companies that extract natural gas as well as oil. Natural gas prices have been largely unaffected by the oil glut. "But some of our members produce only oil," explained Yates of the Independent Petroleum Association. "For them, the impact of low oil prices is extremely dramatic. You have to go back to the 1930s for corresponding prices, and then they had to call out the Texas Rangers to bring order to the market." *

Many small companies face bankruptcy. "The worst off are those with marginal production," Yates said. "There are thousands of these mom-and-pop operations." As large oil fields have run dry in the United States, many of the 500,000 wells operated by the association's members produce just two or three barrels of crude a day. "Most of these marginal wells could go on producing forever, but not at a loss, so they are being abandoned," Yates said. "This is a very serious issue, because the oil we don't produce domestically we have to import. And it's not just the oil producers who are affected,

---

* In 1931, an oil glut in Texas and Oklahoma drove down oil prices, prompting Texas Gov. Ross Sterling to send the Texas Rangers into the East Texas oil fields to enforce a production cutback.

At Issue:

Should the United States ease its sanctions against Iran to improve international access to Caspian Sea oil?

S. FREDERICK STARR

Chairman, Central Asia Institute, Nitze School of Advanced International Studies, Johns Hopkins University

FROM TESTIMONY BEFORE THE HOUSE INTERNATIONAL RELATIONS SUBCOMMITTEE ON ASIA AND THE PACIFIC, FEB. 12, 1998.

*t*wo presidential directives in 1995 and the Iran-Libya Sanctions Act of 1996 cut off all significant American and foreign investment in Iran's petroleum industry, including pipelines. The purpose was to pressure Iran into dropping its support for terrorism, abandoning programs to develop atomic weapons and [stopping its] meddling in the Middle East peace process. However laudable the aims, the burden of these measures falls disproportionately on Azerbaijan, Kazakhstan and Turkmenistan, for it prevents them from exporting their gas and oil by one of the obvious alternative routes to Russia, namely, Iran. The U.S. position has been to argue that this would not be in the Central Asians' own interest, but none of our friends there agree.

Now, let us suppose that the U.S. sanctions [remained] in place for a long time and [were] truly effective. Over time, so we have argued, planners and financial markets would adjust to this reality. They would construct the east-west pipeline and thus give Central Asians access to secure export routes bypassing both Iran and Russia.

But this is not happening. French, Indonesian and Russian firms are already investing in the construction of oil facilities and pipelines in Iran, and the U.S. seems disinclined to intervene against them. Iran itself is busy constructing a line linking Turkmenistan and Turkey. Turkmenistan and Kazakhstan have worked out swap deals with Tehran, by which Central Asia ships its crude oil to Iran's north and Iran then exports the same quantity of its own oil from the south. In short, the American quarantine of 1995-6 is not holding. . . .

[The United States could] adopt a "wait and see" posture toward Iran, one that would be cautious but less categorical than our current policy. It would replace an "all or nothing" approach with one that recognizes the existence of a large number of finely calibrated positions between these two extremes. . . . On balance, it seems to me that [this alternative] holds the most promise for achieving a balance between U.S. objectives in Central Asia, in the Caspian basin and in Iran. . . .

[I]t is no longer possible to treat U.S. policy toward Central Asia and toward Iran as totally separate from one another. Our Iranian policy, however just its goals, has a powerful and, for the most part, negative impact on our ability to achieve our stated objectives in Central Asia and the Caspian basin.

SEN. SAM BROWNBACK, R-KAN.

FROM TESTIMONY BEFORE THE SENATE FOREIGN RELATIONS SUBCOMMITTEE ON INTERNATIONAL ECONOMIC POLICY, EXPORT AND TRADE PROMOTION, OCT. 23, 1997.

*t*he countries of the South Caucasus and Central Asia — Armenia, Azerbaijan, Georgia, Kazakhstan, Kyrgyzstan, Tajikistan, Turkmenistan and Uzbekistan — are at a historic crossroads in their history: They are independent, they are at the juncture of many of today's major world forces, they are rich in natural resources and they are looking to the United States for support. . . .

First of all, these countries are a major force in containing the spread northward of anti-Western Iranian extremism. Though Iranian activity in the region has been less blatant than elsewhere in the world, they are working very hard to bring the region into their sphere of influence and economic control.

Secondly, the Caspian Sea basin contains proven oil and gas reserves which, potentially, could rank third in the world after the Middle East and Russia and exceed $4 trillion in value. Investment in this region could ultimately reduce U.S. dependence on oil imports from the volatile Persian Gulf and could provide regional supplies as an alternative to Iranian sources. . . .

The independence of the region could indeed well depend on the successful construction of pipelines on an east-west axis through non-Russian as well as non-Iranian territory. Both Russian and Iranian rhetoric on this issue shows clearly that these countries see the connection between pipelines free of Russian and Iranian control and their domination over the region. And it is no coincidence that we are seeing an intense rapprochement between these two countries.

Time is of an essence here. We have the opportunity to help these countries rebuild themselves from the ground up and to encourage them to continue their strong independent stances, especially in relation to Iran and the spread of extremist, anti-Western fundamentalism, which is one of the most clear and present dangers facing the United States today.

The window of opportunity has been closed even further by the recent investment by the French company Total . . . in the Iranian South Pars offshore gas field. It is vital that the [Clinton] administration hold strong on implementing existing sanctions and on discouraging our allies from following the despicable example of Total. If the floodgates open through Iran, the eastern Caspian will certainly fall into the Eastern sphere of dominance, and the South Caucasus will lose out on its opportunity to prosper as producer of oil and as a pivotal transit point from East to West.

because as imports grow, so does the trade deficit." In May 2000, the U.S. trade deficit hit a record $31.04 billion as imports grew and exports fell. [28]

Caspian Treasure

As petroleum deposits are depleted in coming years, prices are likely to rise more dramatically, formally ending the era of cheap oil. With few major new fields expected to be found, oil companies are in hot competition to develop the potentially huge reserves under and around the landlocked Caspian Sea, which lies between southern Russia and northern Iran. Estimates of the volume of crude oil in the region range up to 200 billion barrels — more than a quarter of the Middle East's reserves.

The region's oil has been known about for centuries. Marco Polo remarked on the seepage of oil around the Caspian Sea during his travels along the Silk Road, the ancient trade route between Europe and the Far East. Swedish businessmen Ludwig and Robert Nobel began developing oil fields in Baku, on the western coast of the Caspian Sea, more than 120 years ago. [29] The Soviet Union, with large oil reserves in other parts of the coun-

try, did little to develop the Caspian fields because most of the oil was trapped under water or salt formations and too hard to extract.

Modern technology now places the Caspian's oil within reach, and oil companies have descended on the sparsely populated region since 1991

New pipelines are needed to move crude oil from the landlocked Caspian Sea region to deep-water ports where it can be loaded onto tankers and shipped to markets.

©Digital Stock

to gain a foothold in what may be the world's last oil boom. One of the first Western companies in the region was Chevron Corp., which in 1993 began

investing in Kazakhstan's Tengiz oil field in and around the northeastern Caspian. Numerous other companies have since invested in the region as well. A consortium of other companies, including Exxon Mobil and eight other international companies recently discovered a mammoth deposit in the Caspian Sea field of Kashagan off the Kazak coast that may hold up to 50 billion barrels of oil. [30]

The main obstacle to the development of Caspian oil is the volatile political situation throughout the region. The Soviet Union's dissolution in 1991 transformed the former Soviet republics of Azerbaijan, Kazakhstan and Turkmenistan, which also border the Caspian, into independent countries. With no democratic tradition, ethnic divisions that rival those of the former Yugoslavia and virtually undeveloped economies, the Caspian is a region that journalist Richard C. Longworth described as "Bosnia with oil."

"In this oil-soaked cockpit, the prospects for both wealth and trouble are simply stupendous," he wrote. "The Caucasus is a land of ancient vendettas and warring tribes that makes the Balkans look straightforward by comparison, and the Caspian is where this bloody region meets Central Asia and the

Middle East. It's where Orthodox Christianity meets both Sunni and Shi'ite Islam, where Iranians traveling north have met Russians coming south. It's an area once ruled by Iran, then by Russia, now contested by Turkey, whose language and civilization dominate the region." [31]

Pipelines and Politics

The Caspian region's political turmoil exacerbates another significant obstacle to developing Caspian oil: transportation problems. Once the crude is extracted, it must travel thousands of miles to reach ports where it can be loaded onto tankers and shipped to markets. Some oil from the Tengiz field already reaches the Baltic Sea by rail. But rail shipment is expensive and increases the risk of oil spills. [32] The only alternative under consideration is to build pipelines. Three are already being developed. The problem is where to build the next ones.

China plans a 1,900-mile pipeline from Tengiz across Kazakhstan into China. But all the routes from the Caspian to Western markets have political drawbacks. The most direct route to open sea, and the one desired by the Caspian countries, is through Iran to the Persian Gulf. But the United States opposes that route because it would defy U.S. sanctions against Iran and make Caspian oil hostage to political instability in the gulf.

Although Secretary Albright waived the sanctions against three foreign companies that invested in Iranian oil fields in May 1998, the move apparently did not signal a change in policy. "We continue to oppose trans-Iran pipelines for Caspian energy exports in the strongest terms," said Sestanovich of the State Department. [33]

Russia has proposed a route that would carry oil from the eastern

FOR MORE INFORMATION

Energy Information Administration, U.S. Department of Energy, 1000 Independence Ave. S.W., #2G051, Washington, D.C. 20585; (202) 586-5214; www.eia.doe.gov. The EIA collects and publishes data on domestic production, imports, distribution and prices of crude oil and refined petroleum products.

American Petroleum Institute, 1220 L St. N.W., Washington, D.C. 20005; (202) 682-8042; www.api.org. This membership organization of U.S. producers, refiners, marketers and transporters of oil and related products provides information on the industry.

Independent Petroleum Association of America, 1101 16th St. N.W., 2nd Floor, Washington, D.C. 20036; (202) 857-4722; www.ipaa.org. Members are independent oil and gas producers and others involved in domestic oil and gas production.

International Energy Agency, 9, rue de la Federation, 75739 Paris Cedex 15, France; (33-1) 40.57.65.51; www.iea.org. Created in the wake of the energy crises of the 1970s, the IEA monitors global oil production and helps consumer countries coordinate strategies to avoid supply disruptions.

Caspian to the Russian port of Novorossisk on the Black Sea, which already serves as the terminus for an existing pipeline from Baku. Turkey opposes this and other new pipelines that would terminate at the Black Sea because the oil must then be shipped through the narrow Bosporus strait, which passes through Istanbul, to reach the Mediterranean. Some 4,000 tankers already pass through the 17-mile-long passage each year, negotiating four 45-degree turns on their way and posing the risk of disastrous oil spills. Another planned pipeline, linking Turkmenistan to Pakistan, is on hold pending resolution of Afghanistan's protracted civil war.

The Clinton administration supports a network of multiple oil and gas pipelines to make it less likely that a supply interruption in one would cut off the entire region's oil flow. It is pushing strongly for a pipeline stretching from the Caspian port of Baku, Azerbaijan, through Georgia to the Mediterranean port of Ceyhan in Turkey, a NATO ally.

The region's political turmoil leads some observers to question the ability of the Caspian region to meet the grow-ing global demand for oil. "The Caspian states are not necessarily plunging into a maelstrom in which corrupt regimes will be challenged either by secret drug lords or social unrest," wrote Martha Brill Olcott, a senior associate at the Carnegie Endowment for International Peace and professor of political science at Colgate University. "But the possibility of such chaos cannot be precluded. Each of these states faces difficult political transitions in the next five to 10 years, while peak oil production and the economic benefits that it promises are unlikely to be realized in the region until 2010." [34]

Other obstacles to the region's ascendance as a leading oil provider spring from its geological limitations. "The Caspian is the only place in the world right now with significant promise," Campbell said. "But there's been some exaggerated talk about its real potential." He estimates that the region may contain only 50 billion barrels. "Even that is stretching credibility a little bit," he says. "And that's if it comes in, which as of today is not something to count on."

With Caspian deposits perhaps equivalent in volume to those under the North Sea, Campbell said, offshore production could total up to 4 million barrels a day by 2025. "Although that's valuable and not to be dismissed," he said, "it's unlikely to make much of an impact on the peak of global oil production," which he says will occur within the next few years. ∎

OUTLOOK

Will Prices Rise?

OPEC surprised its critics in 1999 when it succeeded in curbing production output, eliminating the world oil glut and forcing the price of oil above $30 a barrel by 2000. They were aided by rising demand, as economic recovery took hold in Asia and the appetite for oil products continued to grow in the United States.

Gasoline prices in the United States peaked in mid-summer and appear likely to decline even more in coming months. Saudi Arabia is leading a call to increase OPEC output in an effort to prevent a global energy crisis.

Some economists predict that oil prices will continue to subside in the immediate future because the world has already begun to wean itself from petroleum products.

"The industrial world uses 42 percent less oil to produce an extra unit of [gross domestic product] than it needed in 1973," wrote Lester C. Thurow, an economics professor at the Massachusetts Institute of Technology. "Transportation still depends upon oil, but fuel cells look as if they are about to arrive. When they do, early in the next century, oil demand will begin to fall even in this, its primary market." As a result, Thurow predicted, oil "prices will be low for

the foreseeable future." [35]

Other experts are equally convinced that oil prices are headed in the opposite direction. In Campbell's view, the world is in for an oil shock that will make the energy crises of the 1970s pale in comparison. "There will be an initial price shock around 2000, with a doubling or perhaps a tripling of prices," he said in 1998. "Although the roof won't fall in overnight, long-term shortages will force a change in attitude about energy consumption."

The price rise will spur development of renewable energy sources, Campbell predicted. "But it's hard to picture this being done at a rate and a scale to enable renewables to act as substitutes for the way we've used cheap oil up to now."

In Campbell's view, the United States will play a crucial role in determining the global response to what he sees as the coming oil crisis. "There is an enormous danger that the United States, with its peculiar Middle East policies, may misunderstand this situation and perceive the price hikes to be a politically hostile act by Iran or Iraq," he said.

"But at the heart of the matter, the coming oil crisis isn't about politics; its simply about the distribution of a resource that events during the Jurassic Period dictated." ∎

Notes

[1] Peña testified April 30, 1998, before the House International Relations Committee. Peña announced on April 6 he would resign this summer, and President Clinton nominated U.N. Representative Bill Richardson as the next Energy secretary. The Senate Energy and Natural Resources Committee voted 18-0 on July 29 to approve Richardson's nomination. The Senate approved Richardson on July 31.

[2] For background, see Mary H. Cooper, "Oil Imports," *The CQ Researcher,* Aug. 23, 1991, pp. 585-608.

[3] For background, see Rodman D. Griffin, "Mexico's Emergence," *The CQ Researcher,*

July 19, 1991, pp. 497-520.

[4] For background, see David Masci, "U.S.-Russian Relations," *The CQ Researcher*, May 22, 1998, pp. 457-480, and Mary H. Cooper, "Russia's Political Future, *The CQ Researcher,* May 3, 1996, pp. 385-408.

[5] For background, see Patrick G. Marshall, "Calculating the Costs of the Gulf War," *Editorial Research Reports,* March 15, 1991, pp. 145-156.

[6] See James Kim and Chris Woodyard, "Glut Knocks Oil Costs Down, but It Won't Last," *USA Today,* Feb. 26, 1998.

[7] See "Saddam Seeks End to U.N. Embargo This Year," *The Washington Post,* July 18, 1998.

[8] Pickering testified May 21, 1998, before a joint hearing of the Senate Energy and Natural Resources and Foreign Relations committees.

[9] Perle testified at the May 21 hearing before the Senate Energy and Foreign Relations committees.

[10] Indyk testified May 14, 1998, before the Senate Foreign Relations Subcommittee on Near Eastern and South Asian Affairs.

[11] Albright spoke before the Asia Society in New York City. See Thomas W. Lippman, "Albright Offers Iran Possibility of Normal Ties," *The Washington Post,* June 18, 1998.

[12] Sestanovich testified July 8, 1998, before the Senate Foreign Relations Subcommittee on International Economic Policy, Export and Trade Promotion.

[13] Murphy testified May 14, 1998, before the Senate Foreign Relations Subcommittee on Near Eastern and South Asian Affairs.

[14] See Tad Szulc, "Will We Run Out of Gas?" *Parade Magazine,* July 19, 1998, pp. 4-6.

[15] For background, see Mary H. Cooper, "Transportation Policy," *The CQ Researcher,* July 4, 1997, pp. 577-600.

[16] For background, see Mary H. Cooper, "Renewable Energy," *The CQ Researcher,* Nov. 7, 1997, pp. 961-984.

[17] Moniz testified Feb. 5, 1998, before the House Commerce Subcommittee on Energy and Power.

[18] Lugar, chairman of the Senate Agriculture, Nutrition and Forestry Committee, spoke before the committee on Nov. 13, 1997.

[19] For background, see Cooper, *ibid.*

[20] Unless otherwise noted, information in this section is based on Fadhil J. Chalabi, "OPEC: An Obituary," *Foreign Policy,*

winter 1997-98, pp. 126-140.

[21] Chalabi, *op. cit.,* p. 130.

[22] *Ibid,* p. 133. The Organization for Economic Cooperation and Development represents the leading industrial nations.

[23] *Ibid,* p. 136.

[24] See Youssef M. Ibrahim, "Falling Oil Prices Pinch Several Producing Nations," *The New York Times,* June 23, 1998.

[25] See "When Gulf States Tighten Their Belts," *The Economist,* March 14, 1998, pp. 49-50.

[26] See "2 Oil Giants Register Record Earnings," *The New York Times,* July 26, 2000.

[27] Murphy spoke July 15, 1998, at an American Petroleum Institute press conference in Washington.

[28] See Edward Alden, "U.S. Trade Deficit Hits Record Levels in May: Reaches US$31B," *Financial Times,* July 26, 2000.

[29] For background on early oil development in the Caspian region, see Daniel Yergin, *The Prize* (1991), pp. 56-65. Another Nobel brother, Alfred, invented dynamite. Their father, Immanuel, invented the underwater mine.

[30] See Hugh Pope, "New Caspian Well Yields Substantial Oil and Gas," *The Wall Street Journal,* July 25, 2000.

[31] See Richard C. Longworth, "Boomtown Baku," *The Bulletin of the Atomic Scientists,* May/June 1998, p. 35.

[32] For background, see Mary H. Cooper, "Oil Spills," *The CQ Researcher,* Jan. 17, 1992, pp. 25-48.

[33] From July 8, 1998, testimony before the Senate Foreign Relations Subcommittee on International Economic Policy, Export and Trade Promotion.

[34] Martha Brill Olcott, "The Caspian's False Promise," *Foreign Policy,* summer 1998, p. 110.

[35] Lester C. Thurow, "Oil Prices No longer Hold Us Hostage," *USA Today,* May 26, 1998.

Bibliography

Selected Sources Used

Books

Adelman, M. A., *The Genie Out of the Bottle: World Oil Since 1970,* MIT Press, 1995.

The author, a leading petroleum economist, builds on his earlier analyses of the global oil trade with this review of events encompassing OPEC's rise to power over oil production and its more recent decline.

Campbell, Colin J., *The Coming Oil Crisis,* Multi-Science Publishing and Petroconsultants, 1997.

A former geologist for Texaco and Amoco predicts that global oil production will peak within the next few years. It is at this point, he writes, not when supplies are close to exhaustion, that oil prices will rise significantly.

Yergin, Daniel, *The Prize: The Epic Quest for Oil, Money & Power,* Simon & Schuster, 1991,

This sweeping history of the oil industry takes the reader from the first oil well in 1859 in Titusville, Pa., through the rise of OPEC and the West's reaction to the energy crises of the 1970s.

Articles

"Asia: The Cloning of America," *Energy Investor,* June/July 1998, pp. 2-3.

Despite its current economic crisis, Asia remains a leading consumer of oil. With rapid industrialization in much of the continent, Asia already uses 70 percent of all newly discovered oil, and its demand for oil can only be expected to grow in coming decades.

Chalabi, Fadhil J., "OPEC: An Obituary," *Foreign Policy,* winter 1997-98, pp. 126-140.

A former OPEC official writes that the formerly omnipotent cartel will continue to lose its control over global oil production and prices because oil-consuming countries have found alternative sources of oil. To survive, the organization's members must introduce economic reforms and change its quota system to reflect changes in the global oil market.

Coy, Peter, Gary McWilliams and John Rossant, "The New Economics of Oil," *Business Week,* Nov. 3, 1997, pp. 140-144.

The authors conclude that today's low oil prices may continue for decades as technological advances make it easier than ever to produce oil.

Longworth, Richard C., "Boomtown Baku," *The Bulletin of the Atomic Scientists,* May/June 1998, pp. 34-38.

Political turmoil in the oil-rich countries bordering the Caspian Sea makes the region the equivalent of "Bosnia with oil," writes journalist Longworth. U.S. policies, especially those favoring Armenian separatists in Azerbaijan, work against U.S. oil companies' efforts to develop the region's oil.

Olcott, Martha Brill, "The Caspian's False Promise," *Foreign Policy,* summer 1998, pp. 94-113.

A Colgate University professor of political science describes the obstacles to oil development in the Caspian Sea region, the most promising new source of oil today. Poverty, ethnic rivalries and economic mismanagement since the region gained independence with the Soviet Union's collapse in 1991 may derail plans for large-scale oil exports.

"Preventing the Next Oil Crunch," *Scientific American,* March 1998, pp. 77-95.

Four articles describe the problems associated with falling oil reserves. Technological advances will stretch out the petroleum age, but price hikes are likely as oil reserves drop and extraction becomes increasingly costly.

"When Gulf States Tighten Their Belts," *The Economist,* March 14, 1998, pp. 49-50.

The collapse in oil prices since early this year has drastically curtailed revenues in the rich kingdoms of the Persian Gulf. Because they depend so heavily on income from oil exports, these countries are having to reduce spending on social programs and hasten economic reforms.

Reports and Studies

Energy Information Administration, Petroleum Supply Monthly, May 1998.

This publication of the U.S. Department of Energy provides updated statistics on global oil supplies and imports and exports, as well as prices and a breakdown of oil products. Historical tables show changes in supplies and prices since the early 1980s.

International Energy Agency, *Oil Market Report,* July 9, 1998.

The Paris-based IEA, created in response to the 1970s' energy crises, monitors the global oil market and helps consuming countries overcome supply disruptions. The latest report concludes that the current oil glut and low prices are likely to continue until consumer nations draw down their record high oil stocks.

8 China Today

Last October, the People's Republic of China threw itself a party the likes of which hadn't been seen in Beijing in years.

The mammoth event featured a five-mile-long parade that snaked past President Jiang Zemin and other government leaders gathered in Tiananmen Square to celebrate the PRC's 50th anniversary. Some 90 floats depicted the communist state's recent achievements, from its growing industrial might and improved standard of living to its victories in the Olympics.

But the parade also was intended to showcase China as an up-and-coming military power, a point dramatically made by the more than 10,000 white-gloved soldiers and 400 tanks and other military vehicles. (*See sidebar, p. 139.*)

The display of military might was calculated, says James R. Lilley, a resident fellow at the American Enterprise Institute. "They want us to know that they're not going to be pushed around," he says. "Their intention is clear: neutralize American power in the region and press their territorial claims."

Pressing territorial claims has been a priority for China in recent years. On June 30, 1997, the British followed the dictates of a 19th-century treaty and returned Hong Kong to the PRC. Two and half years later, China took back the island of Macao from another former colonial power, Portugal.

But one major prize remains: Taiwan. Unlike Hong Kong and Macao, the island is a de facto independent state, run by a democratically elected government. Bigger than the state of

From *The CQ Researcher*,
August 4, 2000.

A huge portrait of Sun Yat-sen, founder of the Republic of China, looms over the mammoth parade in Beijing's Tiananmen Square last Oct. 1 celebrating the 50th anniversary of the People's Republic of China.

Maryland, modern Taiwan was founded in 1949 by China's former leader, Chiang Kai-shek, and his Nationalist Party. Chiang and the Nationalists — losers in the civil war that brought the Communists to power — set up a parallel state and proclaimed themselves the legitimate government of all of China.

Until the 1970s, the United States accepted Taiwan as the sole representative of China. But President Richard M. Nixon's groundbreaking visit to the mainland in 1972 set in motion a shift in American policy. Today, the United States recognizes the Communists on the mainland as the legitimate government of China. It also adheres to what is known as the "one China" policy, which maintains that Taiwan should reunite with the mainland, though by peaceful means. [1]

Some experts contend that the "one China" policy is misguided and should be discarded in favor of one that respects the wishes of Taiwan's 26 million people. "Unlike [mainland] China, Taiwan is a democracy, and we need to respect and back up whatever decision [it] makes," says Gary Schmitt, executive director of the Project for the New American Century, a Washington, D.C., think tank that promotes

American global leadership. That includes the right to be independent, he says. [2]

Schmitt and others argue that instead of pushing Taiwan into the arms of the PRC, the United States should be telling the government on the mainland that it will defend the island's right to decide its own fate.

But others say that such a move would be terribly irresponsible and not in America's interests. "Our relationship with China is one of the cornerstones of U.S. foreign policy, and siding squarely with Taiwan would destabilize that relationship and the whole region," says Richard Haass, director of foreign policy studies at the Brookings Institution.

"One China" is a viable strategy, according to Haass, because it "allows Taiwan to continue in its present state without antagonizing the Chinese."

Haass and others also argue that mainland China is becoming a more open society, making the prospect of reunification at some point in the future much more appealing to Taiwan. "Economic changes have already transformed China for the better and will continue to do so," Haass says.

Indeed, those who believe that China is becoming a more open society contend its expected entry into the World Trade Organization (WTO) next year should accelerate the process of liberalization. [3]

"Membership will ultimately make China a more transparent society, one that is more accountable to its people," says David Shambaugh, director of the China Policy Program at George Washington University.

The WTO is a multinational coalition that works to lower barriers to international trade. Supporters of China's entry into the organization argue that increased trade will spur economic growth, creating a middle class that will come to expect greater personal liberty and political freedom.* In addition, supporters say, WTO membership will integrate China further into the world community, pushing the country to adopt international standards, like respect for the rule of law and human rights.

But Margaret Huang, program director for Asia at the Robert F. Kennedy Memorial Center for Human Rights, argues that WTO membership actually may make the Chinese Communists more, not less, repressive. According to Huang, as freer trade forces the government to cede control over the economic sphere, it may feel the need to tighten its hold over political activity. "They may feel more threatened and crack down," she says.

As events in China unfold, here are some of the questions experts are asking:

Should the United States continue to support the "one China" policy?

For the mainland, the meaning of "one China" is simple: Taiwan is a renegade province that must eventually return to the fold. In fact, for most of its 50-year existence, the government in Taipei also envisioned full reunification, though with a Nationalist government at the helm.

But Taiwan now views the "one China" concept more ambiguously. Chen Shui-bian, the island's recently elected president, has said "one China" could have a range of meanings, presumably from some sort of

---
* A landmark China trade bill approved by the House in May would end the annual congressional review of China's trade status, which is partly based on China's improvements in human rights, and grant the Beijing government permanent normal trade relations as part of its accession to the WTO next year. The proposal has overwhelming support in the Senate and is expected to pass easily on the final vote in September.

loose association to complete reunification. But Chen, the first non-Nationalist to hold Taiwan's presidency, has not publicly stated his own definition of the term. [4]

Until recently, there was a lot of ambiguity in how the United States publicly viewed the relationship between Taiwan and China. In 1972, the year Nixon made his trip to China, the United States stated that it "acknowledges that all Chinese on either side of the Taiwan Strait maintain there is but one China and that Taiwan is part of China." [5] In other words, America simply affirmed the view held by both sides without saying anything more.

Even in 1979, when the United States officially shifted diplomatic recognition from Taipei to Beijing, the meaning of "one China" remained nebulous.

But in 1998, President Clinton peeled away some of the ambiguity. While on a visit to Shanghai, the mainland's largest city, he asserted what became known as the "three no's," rejecting the idea of Taiwanese independence, two Chinas or membership for the island in any international organizations that require statehood. [6]

"This was a big mistake for the Clinton administration because we put our cards on the table, we picked a side," says Stephen Yates, a senior policy analyst at the Heritage Foundation, a conservative think tank. "When you say 'one China' and spell out what that means the way Clinton did, you're implying that you want reunification as an outcome and are basically accepting Beijing's argument."

Instead, Yates says, the United States should drop the "one China" policy and simply push for a peaceful resolution of the situation. "This should be about process, not outcome," he argues.

Others favor more openly siding with Taiwan. "Supporting the 'one China' policy is living in the past be-

cause the situation has changed so dramatically since that policy was developed," says Schmitt of the Project for the New American Century. "Taiwan is now a democracy and, frankly, I don't think [its] heart is in this," he says, referring to the prospect of reunifying with the mainland.

Schmitt says the United States needs to "break out" of its current policy and fully back and defend, with military force if necessary, Taiwan's right to self-determination. "We need to make it clear that it's unacceptable for Beijing to do anything to force Taipei into accepting something [it doesn't] want," he says.

But other China experts think that jettisoning "one China" is foolhardy and dangerous. "One China" is the only policy that will bring any resolution to this problem," says George Washington University's Shambaugh. "An independent Taiwan has no future."

Supporters of "one China" contend that if the United States were to publicly abandon the policy, Taiwan's security would be seriously compromised, even with American support. "Taiwan's long-term security cannot be achieved just through weapons but must come through some sort of accommodation with the People's Republic of China," says David M. Lampton, director of China Studies at the School for Advanced International Studies (SAIS) at Johns Hopkins University.

According to Lampton, mainland China's vast population advantage over Taiwan (1.3 billion people vs. 23 million) and close proximity to the island mean that it will be a serious threat to Taiwan as long as it wants to be. And, Lampton, says, China is unlikely to relinquish its claim to the island anytime soon.

"If China went democratic tomorrow," he says, "[it'd] be as tough on Taiwan as [it is] today because this is a great nationalist issue."

Finally, supporters say, "one China" is the best policy for the United States

Inside the World's Most Populous Nation

Former Chinese leader Mao Zedong once likened his vast nation to "another United Nations." The world's most populous country dwarfs tiny Taiwan, off the southeast coast. China has 31 provinces and two special administrative regions, the islands of Hong Kong and Macao. The largest province is Xinjiang, about three times the size of Spain. The most populous province, Sichuan, has more than 110 million residents, about the same as Japan. China's largest city, Shanghai, has 11 million people. Many provinces, including Guangdong, Hubei, Shandong, Jiangsu and Hunan, all have 50-100 million people, similar to such countries as France and Mexico.

While China is more than 90 percent Han Chinese, each region does have its own cultural and economic flavor. Guangdong, in the south, is known for its freewheeling ways and burgeoning economy. Shanghai is China's cultural and financial center. A number of provinces, like Tibet and Xinjiang, have large pockets of non-Chinese ethnic groups and have been designated as "autonomous regions." Nonetheless, separatist movements are active in both provinces.

While China's 1.3 billion people make up more than one-fifth of the world's population, they only occupy one-fifteenth of the Earth's land. And, since much of the Western part of the country is sparsely inhabited, due to the harsh terrain and climate, more than two-thirds of China's people are crowded into the more prosperous eastern part of the country.

China's Golden Coast

GDP per capita, 1998
- $250-500
- $500-750
- $750-1,000
- $1,000+

Source: China Statistical Yearbook

500 km

Sources: China Statistical Yearbook, The Economist

because U.S. relations with the mainland are much more important than those with Taiwan. "If we changed this policy, we would cause a serious and fundamental crisis with China," says Nancy Bernkopf Tucker, a professor of history at Georgetown University. "Doing so with such a huge and important country cannot be in the national interest."

Will membership in the World Trade Organization lead to a more open society in China?

Sometime next year, the People's Republic of China will almost certainly join the WTO. Admission will be a major victory for China's Communist government, which spent the last 13 years negotiating terms of entry with the United States and other Western countries.

The WTO is a 135-nation trading club whose members agree to reduce barriers to international commerce. In its bid for membership, China has agreed to significantly lower tariffs on industrial and agricultural goods and reduce existing restrictions on foreign investment.

Supporters of China's application say it will accelerate the country's efforts to develop a modern market economy. U.S. Trade Representative Charlene Barshefsky and other WTO boosters also argue that entry will help China become a more open society. WTO membership will help make China "freer, more open to the world and [more] responsive to the rule of law than it is today," Barshefsky said in May. [7]

"When you inject the seed of capitalism in a place, it naturally breeds openness everywhere," says William

Morley, chief lobbyist for the U.S. Chamber of Commerce, which supports WTO membership for China. Once you give the people economic freedom, they'll begin to want more personal freedom."

Morley predicts that WTO membership will help create a solid middle class that will quickly develop a sense of its rights. "Once people begin enjoying the fruits of their labors," he says, "they inevitably start to demand a greater say in other areas, like politics." And that, adds the Heritage Foundation's Yates, "expands the amount of pressure on the government to become more open and democratic, and to guarantee personal freedom."

Supporters also argue that WTO membership will force China to begin to respect the rule of law, a human rights linchpin in any society. "[WTO membership] will get them much more involved in rules-based behavior," says Johns Hopkins' Lampton, "because without it they won't be able to operate in the international arena."

First, Lampton argues, China will have to develop a more reliable court system to deal with business-related issues such as commercial transactions and intellectual property. But eventually, he says, the openness and reliability will spill over into other areas. "Once you develop a core of people who rely on due process in one realm, they begin to expect it in others," he says.

Finally, WTO supporters contend, freer trade will bring an influx of new ideas and information, via the Internet and a host of other mediums. "This will bring greater access to informa-

tion, especially information from the West," Morley says. "They will become accustomed to the Western way of doing things, and this will have a profound impact on them."

How profound? No one knows, of course. But according to the American Enterprise Institute's Lilley, the influx of new ideas and information from the outside "could very well help to undermine the current system."

House Minority Whip David Bonior, D-Mich., cautions that accession to the WTO may not ultimately

Farmers shovel fertilizer onto a wheat field outside Beijing. Despite China's aggressive push toward modernization and manufacturing, more than two-thirds of its 1.3 billion people still live in rural areas.

be a positive force for change. "Contrary to the assertions of WTO cheerleaders, the hidden hand of the marketplace will not automatically bring about democratic reforms or social progress," Bonior wrote recently. He argues that it was organized protest, not the marketplace, that won Americans greater labor and other rights in the 20th century. [8]

Indeed, some experts say entry into the WTO might shrink political freedoms. "I think things are going to get worse because the government will tighten political control as it loses

more and more authority in the economic sphere," says the Robert F. Kennedy Center's Huang. "There will be more arrests, more crackdowns, more harassment of labor organizers and human rights workers."

Huang predicts additional curtailment of rights and liberties as the opening of the economy leads to massive worker dislocation and other social tensions. "WTO [membership] will lead to millions being laid off as they privatize state-run industries," she says. "The sudden presence of all of these unemployed workers and other changes are going to lead to social upheaval, which will force the government to crack down even more" (see p. 139).

And some argue that China will probably try to segregate the system used for international business from the rest of the country's legal infrastructure. "They may well be able to guarantee that commercial law reaches certain standards without changing the way, say, human and labor rights are handled," says Mike Jendrzejczyk, Asia director for Human Rights Watch, an advocacy group that favors China's admittance to the WTO. "My guess is that they'll try." ∎

BACKGROUND

East Meets West

Until relatively recently, China took little interest in the outside world.

Chronology

Secure in its venerable culture and society, the so-called Middle Kingdom usually ignored the world beyond its borders.

Even when the Chinese did venture out, their actions would have seemed alien to Western explorers, conquistadors and adventurers. In the early 15th century, for example, Adm. Cheng He took Chinese naval expeditions as far as East Africa. Cheng was not seeking new lands to conquer or even plunder, however. His mission was "to make 'the whole world' into voluntary admirers of the one and only center of civilization." [9]

But China could not remain closed to the outside world forever, and when European powers took an interest in it in the 19th century, the nation was wholly unprepared.

The first major opening came in 1840, when a British fleet arrived in southern China to force the repeal of measures that had outlawed the lucrative, British-controlled opium trade. Outgunned by the English on sea and land, the Chinese swallowed a peace treaty that not only permitted the opium trade but also ceded Hong Kong to the British and opened five ports to foreigners.

The rest of the 19th century was equally difficult for China. Forays by France, Russia and Japan, in addition to Britain, were common. The foreign meddling, coupled with internal strife, weakened the state tremendously.

In 1911, China's last imperial dynasty, the Qing, fell, and a republic was proclaimed under Sun Yat-sen, a Western-educated reformer. But Sun's republic quickly disintegrated into chaos as independent warlords fought for control of the country.

After World War I, Sun's Nationalist Party, known as the Kuomintang, began working to reunite China. Under Sun's successor, Chiang Kai-shek, and aided by the growing Communist Party, the Nationalists began

1900-1939
China's last imperial dynasty topples.

1911
The last Qing emperor abdicates, and Nationalist Party leader Sun Yat-sen becomes president of the new Republic of China.

1927
Civil war begins between the Communists and Nationalists.

1934
The defeated Communists go on "The Long March" into northern China.

———— • ————

1940-1974 The
Communists defeat the Nationalists for control of China.

Oct. 1, 1949
The Communists proclaim the People's Republic of China. Chiang and the Nationalists escape to Taiwan.

1960
Mao taps Deng Xiaoping and other pragmatists to reverse the economic damage caused by an experiment in socialism.

1966
Mao launches "The Cultural Revolution" to eliminate Western influence, killing millions.

1972
President Richard M. Nixon visits China; the U.S. recognizes the Communist government.

1975-Present
Mao is replaced by reformers Deng and Jiang.

1976
Mao dies. Deng launches economic reforms.

1979
President Jimmy Carter resumes full diplomatic relations with the People's Republic and breaks ties with Taiwan.

1989
Pro-democracy protests in Tiananmen Square in Beijing are brutally suppressed by Deng. Jiang Zemin becomes Deng's handpicked successor.

1996
China fires practice missiles near Taiwan; the U.S. dispatches two aircraft carriers to the area.

February 1997
Deng dies; Jiang takes over.

June 30, 1997
Britain returns Hong Kong to China.

Dec. 20, 1999
Portugal returns Macao.

February 2000
China threatens to use military force against Taiwan if the island indefinitely delays reunification talks.

May 2000
Chen Shui-bian becomes president of Taiwan and accepts the "one China" policy.

creating a unified Chinese state.

In 1927, Chiang broke with his Communist allies. Although the Nationalists controlled most of the country, the Communists established a substantial military and even administrative presence in parts of China.

Japanese aggression in Manchuria beginning in 1931 distracted the Nationalists. But in 1934, Chiang refocused his attention on the Communists, routing them in most areas under their control. The scattered Communist army retreated for nearly two years, fighting its way through western China to Shaanxi Province in summer 1936. Known as "The Long March," the odyssey established Mao Zedong as the leader of the Communists. [10]

In 1937, Japanese aggression turned into a full-scale invasion of northern and eastern China, prompting the Nationalists and Communists to bury their differences and confront the Japanese together. But Japan's modern military quickly occupied much of the country.

Chairman Mao

After World War II, Chiang and Mao began fighting again. This time, the Communists were stronger. Mao's genius for organizing had enabled the party and its military wing, now called the People's Liberation Army (PLA), to grow tremendously during the war years. [11]

Chiang's undisciplined army was no match for the well-organized PLA, and by 1949 the Nationalists were in severe trouble. On Oct. 1, the Communists formally established the People's Republic of China, and Chiang and about 200,000 followers fled to Taiwan.

During the first decade of his rule, Mao turned China into a socialist state. Agriculture was collectivized and industry was nationalized. China's first five-year plan, in 1953, set out to develop heavy industry, using the Soviet Union as a model. At the same time, Chinese society became more structured and, for many, more inhospitable. For example, peasants and workers were organized into brigades, while many artists, professionals and businessmen were persecuted as enemies of the party. In 1958, the transformation was accelerated in what came to be known as "The Great Leap Forward," which lasted for two years.

Throughout the first decade of Communist rule, China maintained close relations with the Soviets. China's entry into the Korean War against the United States in 1950 strengthened the tie. But as the 1950s came to a close, Sino-Soviet relations grew colder because of ideological differences and territorial disputes. The freeze would last for three decades.

By 1960, Mao and other Chinese leaders recognized that the Great Leap had been a failure. The economy was in a state of crisis. In response, a new group of pragmatic leaders arose, including Deng Xiaoping. They improved the economy by allowing farm and factory managers more control over production. At the same time, Deng strengthened the Communist Party. [12]

Mao, sensing he was being edged from power, began a campaign against what he said were China's increasingly "capitalist" tendencies. During the so-called Cultural Revolution (1966-1976), Mao purged his political opponents, including Deng. Millions of people were killed, including many of China's leading thinkers, politicians and professionals. Many other educated people were sent to remote parts of China to be "re-educated" through manual labor.

Secure once again, Mao, during his remaining years eschewed the bold — and often disastrous — steps that characterized the first 20 years of his rule. A major exception was the building of better relations with the United States, fostered by President Nixon's historic 1972 trip to China. At the time, each country saw the other as a valuable ally against the Soviet Union.

Deng Takes Over

By the time Mao died in 1976, Deng had been rehabilitated. Mao's trusted lieutenant, Premier Zhou Enlai — himself a pragmatic modernizer — had brought Deng back in 1973 to once again help restructure Chinese society.

But Zhou had died eight months before Mao, leaving a huge leadership vacuum. After a relatively brief struggle for power with Mao's widow and her key supporters (known as the Gang of Four), Deng became paramount leader.

Deng quickly launched a series of ambitious reforms. Collective agriculture was scrapped in favor of the old system of family-run farms. Private enterprise, once illegal, was encouraged, leading to the rapid creation of a new business class. China's market was opened to foreign trade and investment.

Important non-economic changes also were undertaken. Couples were restricted to one child to reduce China's huge population, and diplomatic relations were established with the United States and other Western countries.

In the political arena, though, there was a marked absence of change. The Communist Party retained control of the government and restricted citizens' liberty. The limits on freedom of speech and assembly were dramatically revealed to the world in 1989, when tens of thousands of democracy supporters gathered in Beijing's Tiananmen Square to demand change. After vacillating for a number

China Beefs Up Its Military

For the United States, the 1991 war against Iraq vindicated more than a decade of spending on high-tech armaments. Equipped with so-called smart bombs, Patriot surface-to-air missiles and powerful M-I Abrams tanks, American forces led by Gen. Norman Schwartzkopf dispatched Saddam Hussein's military in a matter of days.

But for China's political and military leadership, the conflict over Saddam's invasion of Kuwait was a wake-up call, many defense experts say. "They were very impressed with U.S. power and realized that their military was decades behind ours," says Harvey Feldman, a senior fellow at the Heritage Foundation's Asia Studies Center.

Since then, the Chinese have been trying to catch up, embarking on a massive effort to buy and develop new weapons and professionalize their military. "They clearly want to be able to challenge U.S. power in the Pacific," says James R. Lilley, a resident fellow at the American Enterprise Institute.

Throughout the 1990s, China's military budget has steadily increased, usually growing by 10 percent or more each year.[1] At the same time, President Jiang Zemin ordered the military to divest its substantial business holdings, which at one point comprised an estimated 20,000 companies employing 16 million people. Profits from these businesses — which included hotels, farms and factories — were used for military purposes. But Jiang worried that China's generals were becoming more concerned with the bottom line than combat readiness.

In some military areas, the Chinese have made substantial progress in recent years. For example, they have developed intercontinental ballistic missiles capable of hitting the West Coast of the United States, as well as other possible adversaries such as Russia, India and Japan. "By next year, they should be able to hit any target in our country," Feldman says.

In addition, the Chinese have made strides in efforts to miniaturize nuclear weapons — aided by stolen U.S. technology, American officials charge. "This allows them to put more than one [nuclear] warhead on their long-range missiles," Feldman says.

In most military areas though, China still lags far behind the United States. For instance, while the 3-million-strong People's Liberation Army is the world's biggest fighting force, many of its troops still use weapons from the 1960s and '70s. And training and tactics are also still antiquated. The navy, and to some extent the air force, fare little better by comparison. "They're still completely out of our league," Feldman says. "In an all-out engagement, we would destroy them."

The Chinese are trying to close the gap by buying sophisticated weapons from abroad, especially from the Russians. They already have purchased two Russian *Sovremenny*-class destroyers with the Sunburn anti-ship missile, one of the most effective weapons of its kind. "This is a particularly bad development, because these missiles can threaten our [aircraft] carriers," Lilley says. "They are difficult if not impossible to defend against," says Michael Pillsbury, a Department of Defense consultant on the Chinese military.

In addition, Beijing has bought a number of Russian fighter planes, including the SU-27 and the more advanced SU-30MK. While these aircraft are a substantial improvement over the rest of China's aging air force, they cannot effectively stand up to F-16, F-18 and other front-line American fighter planes, many experts say.

Actually, the Chinese do not expect these and other weapons purchases to put them on a military par with the United States any time soon, Feldman says. Instead, he says, the Chinese just want to be powerful enough to deter the U.S. from intervening if China were to attack Taiwan, which it has threatened to do if the island declares independence.

"Their short-term goal is to be able to hold us off long enough to destroy the military and economic capability of Taiwan," he says. "And you know, I think they're getting there."

---

[1] Figures cited in Frank Gibney Jr., "Birth of a Superpower," *Time*, June 6, 1999.

of weeks, the government violently crushed the protest, killing thousands, according to some reports.[13]

Tiananmen tarnished the regime's image abroad and at home but had little impact on China's reforms or its rapidly growing economy. By the time Deng died in 1997, China had been transformed from an isolated country with an inefficient state-run economy into an economic powerhouse that many say will be a superpower in the next century.[14]

But Deng's passing also left political uncertainties, including whether party elite would accept his hand-picked successor, Jiang Zemin.

Unlike Mao and Deng, Jiang was not a founding member of the Communist Party. Moreover, he had not served in the military and consequently lacked strong support within the all-powerful PLA.

Still, Jiang has established a relatively strong power base, placing people loyal to him in important government posts. The smooth takeover of Hong Kong and Macao under Jiang's watch, coupled with China's continued economic growth during the Asian financial crisis, also helped ease uncertainties about his leadership. ∎

CURRENT SITUATION

Economic Growth

During the early 1990s, China's economy defied gravity. In 1992, for instance, the gross domestic product (GDP) rose a phenomenal 14 percent. Average growth for the decade was an impressive 10 percent. [15]

Deng's market-opening reforms had brought a vibrant and brash form of capitalism to China, transforming the lives of hundreds of millions.

But economic gravity is a powerful force, and in the second half of the 1990s it returned, although not with enough force to stall the economy. From 1995 to 1999, GDP growth steadily slowed, from 10 percent to 7 percent. [16] During this time, however, most developing economies in East Asia were spiraling into a deep recession.

Still, government spending has fueled much of the growth over the last three years, which in turn has driven up China's budget deficit. "They can't keep pumping up the economy with government stimulus," says Nicholas Lardy, a senior fellow at the Brookings Institution and an authority on China's economy. "What they're doing is ultimately unsustainable," he says, noting that 50 percent of government spending now goes to debt repayment.

Growth also has been sustained by overproduction, experts say. Between 1990 and 1998, an estimated 40 percent of the increase in GDP

was due to the production of products that were not needed and not sold. "They've built up huge inventories that just go into warehouses," Lardy says. "Last year they produced 30 million televisions and sold 20 million, leaving the remaining 10 million in inventory."

Economic Problems

Moreover, the economy still needs more structural reform. Beijing continues to have a huge presence in many commercial areas, a vestige of once-pervasive communism. Most economists believe the government controls between one-quarter and half of the means of production, making everything from telecommunications equipment to autos.

Economists generally agree that a large share of the state-owned businesses are inefficient holdovers, often employing too many workers making products not up to market standards. "Many of them are just not competitive and are losing a lot of money," says Gary Jefferson, a professor of economics at Brandeis University in Waltham, Mass.

Under premier and economic czar Zhu Rongji, the government has been steadily selling off state-owned businesses. "They've made real progress in shrinking the state's presence in the economy," Jefferson says.

Lardy agrees but feels that Rongji has not moved fast enough, out of the legitimate fear that accelerated privatization will put millions of Chinese out of work and could lead to social upheaval. "They clearly need to speed up the pace here because it's such a terribly inefficient use of resources," he says.

The inefficient state sector is also creating another problem. "Because many of these state enterprises are in

financial difficulty, they are putting an enormous strain on the banking system," Jefferson says. Indeed, an estimated 75 percent of the loans made by China's four biggest state banks go to government enterprises. [17] Many of these loans will never be repaid, as both the bankers and company managers well know, Jefferson says. But lending continues because the banks are directed by the government not to let these money-losing firms slide into bankruptcy, he says.

The banking problem is already enormous, Lardy says. As of last year, up to 40 percent of the banking system's $1 trillion in outstanding loans were deemed unrecoverable, largely because of lending to the state sector. [18] "Unless something is done to change this," he says, "the financial system may collapse."

Still, Jefferson sees the overall economic picture as positive. "If international growth rates continue, I predict that China will continue to grow in a stable way," he says, citing healthy exports and continued high levels of foreign investment.

In addition, Jefferson says, China's imminent WTO membership will open the country's markets to more competition, forcing the government to "further accelerate efforts to reduce state participation in the economy. They'll have to move forward rapidly with this if they want to compete." ∎

OUTLOOK

Political Change?

In May, President Jiang announced the latest in a long line of efforts to rejuvenate the Chinese Communist

At Issue:

Should Congress link passage of permanent normal trade relations (PNTR) with China to guarantees on human rights reforms?

MIKE JENDRZEJCZYK
Washington director, Asia Division,
Human Rights Watch

FROM TESTIMONY BEFORE THE HOUSE COMMITTEE ON
INTERNATIONAL RELATIONS, MAY 10, 2000

China has lobbied for several years for an end to
the annual review of its trade status under the
Jackson-Vanik amendment of the Trade Act of
1974, and as part of the World Trade Organization
(WTO) deal President Clinton has pledged to give China
permanent normal trade relations status. . . .

Congress should set concrete, meaningful and realistic
human rights conditions that China must meet before
receiving PNTR. The president should be required to certify
that these conditions have been met, and this could happen
any time following China's accession to the WTO.

For example, China should be required to:
• Ratify the two United Nations human rights treaties
it has signed: the International Covenant on Civil and
Political Rights . . . and the International Covenant on
Economic, Social and Cultural Rights;
• Take steps to begin dismantling the huge system of
"re-education through labor," which allows officials to
sentence thousands of citizens to labor camps each year
for up to three years without judicial review;
• Open up Tibet and Xinjiang to regular, unhindered
access by U.N. human rights and humanitarian agencies,
foreign journalists and independent monitors. . . .

Getting China to meet these conditions is possible, if
the administration engages in the kind of intensive, high-
level negotiations with Beijing it conducted to finalize the
trade agreement last November. In light of the failure of
the U.N. in Geneva to censure China, it is even more
imperative that Congress and the administration agree on
meaningful human rights conditions on PNTR as one of
the few remaining sources of serious leverage.

To replace the annual trade-status review, we would
strongly support creation of a new mechanism, such as a
special commission appointed jointly by Congress and the
executive branch along the lines of what Rep. [Sander M.]
Levin, [D-Mich.,] has proposed. This commission should
issue a report annually on China's compliances with
international human rights and labor rights norms.

But this should be more than a pro forma process, or
it will have no real credibility. Legislation establishing the
commission should require a vote by Congress on the
commission's findings and recommendations for U.S.
bilateral and multilateral policy initiatives. . . .

WILLARD WORKMAN
Vice president for International Affairs,
U.S. Chamber of Commerce

WRITTEN FOR *THE CQ RESEARCHER*, JULY 2000

Using trade as a weapon does more than hurt the
working people, farmers and business of the United
States — it reduces our economic and social
influence abroad. We don't just export goods, we export
American ideals.

Throughout the United States and around the world,
individual liberty and free enterprise go hand in hand. By
their very presence and operations, American companies and
the expatriate communities that depend on them contribute
mightily to economic, political and religious freedom in their
host countries. Continuing U.S. company presence abroad is
critical to the inculcation of American civic values.

The U.S. business presence in China has resulted in
greater job choice for workers, higher wages and living
standards, better workplace safety and health standards,
improved education and training opportunities and a host of
other benefits sought by workers in the United States, China
and all over the world. And as hundreds of millions of
Chinese people continue to migrate from the interior to the
coastal regions to take advantage of these imported economic opportunities, the potential for expanded U.S.
economic, social and cultural influence will be historic.

These workers will make more money, read more
Western books and periodicals and receive greater exposure
to Western ideals of social, economic and political reform
than their compatriots who remain isolated. Unilateral
restrictions on U.S. firms in China not only imperil U.S.
competitiveness in that country but also compromise a
principal source of human progress for nearly one-fourth of
the world's people.

No moral person can countenance the atrocities that are
committed around the world against our fellow human
beings, whatever the political, economic, social or religious
pretext. Basic human rights are core American values. (We
believe just as strongly in the need to combat other man-
made scourges, such as terrorism, weapons proliferation and
drug trafficking, that plague us.)

But history demonstrates that unilateral economic sanctions not only fail to address these concerns but also make
heroes out of the regimes we target and impede, rather than
advance, the cause of freedom in those countries.

For all of these reasons — plus the fact that U.S. economic and national security interests demand it — Congress
should approve PNTR now.

Party. Jiang's plan, spelled out in a 74-page booklet issued to party cadres, is known as "The Three Represents."[19] According to the president, the party must "always represent the development needs of China's advanced social productive forces, always represent the onward direction of China's advanced culture and always represent the fundamental interests of the largest number of Chinese people."[20]

Jiang reasons that if the party follows his simple advice of devoting itself to the Chinese people, it will prosper long into the future, regardless of economic and other changes taking place.

But many China-watchers claim that "The Three Represents" has the more immediate goal of shoring up the party's stature enough to counter any calls for a multiparty system or some milder form of political liberalization.

"They understand that they have to change if they want to stay in power," says George Washington University's Shambaugh. "They know that they have to root out corruption and become more responsive, more accountable to the people."

Indeed, by all accounts, corruption and other abuses have lowered the party's stature in the eyes of most ordinary Chinese. Protests and even violent riots are not uncommon, especially in the countryside, where poor farmers are often overtaxed by corrupt, local party officials.

Some experts say the Communists may be able to transform themselves sufficiently to retain enough popular support to hang on to power in the coming decades. "Assuming this party stays in power, it will be a very different party in 20 years," says Georgetown's Tucker. "The next generation of leaders will be more internationalist in their thinking and more open to new ideas."

But Brandeis University's Jefferson doubts that "The Three Represents" or any other efforts will restore the party's esteem in the eyes of the people. In the coming decades, he predicts, the Communists will no longer be the undisputed and sole political force in China. "The most likely scenario is that they will evolve much like South Korea or Taiwan has, in the sense that you'll see the ruling party slowly being pressured to allow more and more room for the opposition until there is a real multiparty system," Jefferson says.[21]

The Heritage Foundation's Yates sees a different path to the same outcome. "They will be incapable of changing and will lose power," he says. "I just don't think that they'll transform themselves into some sort of European-style socialist party that allows for competing voices."

The Robert F. Kennedy Center's Huang agrees: "The government will continue to crack down on its citizens and then will lose its mandate and be overthrown."

But Schmitt of the Project for the New American Century is betting that Jiang and the Communists may well hang onto power without significant political liberalization. "They're very determined not to let go, and they've learned a lesson from [Mikhail S.] Gorbachev," whose efforts to promote more political freedom led to the breakup of the Soviet Union and the fall of the Communists.

Schmitt reasons that if China's Communists continue to improve the standard of living (as they have for 20 years), they should be able to keep a lid on efforts to change the country's political system.

"Look, if [Cuban Communist leader] Fidel Castro can hang onto power for 40 years and provide little or nothing to his people," Schmitt asks, "why can't the Chinese Communists go on for decades with a growing and vibrant economy?" ■

Notes

[1] For background, see Kenneth Jost, "Taiwan, China and the U.S.," *The CQ Researcher*, May 24, 1996, pp. 457-480.

[2] For background, see Kenneth Jost, "Democracy in Asia," *The CQ Researcher*, July 24, 1998, pp. 625-648.

[3] For background, see Mary H. Cooper, "World Trade," *The CQ Researcher*, June 9, 2000, pp. 497-520.

[4] John Pomfret, "Taiwan Leader Accepts 'One China' Idea," *The Washington Post*, June 29, 2000.

[5] Quoted in Larry M. Wortzel, "Why the Administration Should Reaffirm the 'Six Assurances' to Taiwan," The Heritage Foundation, March 16, 2000.

[6] *Ibid.*

[7] Speech before the Bretton Woods Committee, a nonpartisan membership group that supports the World Bank and International Monetary Fund, May 16, 2000.

[8] Quoted in David Bonior, "Free for All," *The Washington Post*, Nov. 27, 1999.

[9] Daniel J. Boorstin, *The Discoverers* (1983), p. 192.

[10] Frederica M. Bunge and Rinn-Sup Shinn (eds.), *China: A Country Study* (1981), p. 27.

[11] *Ibid.*, pp. 27-30.

[12] *Ibid.*

[13] Harry Harding, *A Fragile Relationship: The United States and China Since 1972* (1992), pp. 216-224.

[14] For background, see David Masci, "China After Deng," *The CQ Researcher*, June 13, 1997, pp. 505-528.

[15] Karby Leggett, "China Sees a Solid Jump in Growth," *The Wall Street Journal*, July 11, 2000.

[16] *Ibid.*

[17] Cited in Dominic Ziegler, "Now Comes the Hard Part," *The Economist*, April 8, 2000.

[18] Cited in Hugo Restal, "Is China Headed for a Crash?" *The Wall Street Journal*, Sept. 2, 1999.

[19] "The Three Big Thoughts," *The Economist*, June 17, 2000.

[20] Quoted in *Ibid.*

[21] For background, see Kenneth Jost, "The Future of Korea," *The CQ Researcher*, May 19, 2000, pp. 425-448.

Bibliography

Selected Sources Used

Books

Bernstein, Richard, and Ross Munro, *The Coming Conflict with China*, Alfred A. Knopf, 1997.

Veteran journalists Bernstein and Munro argue that China and the United States are headed toward ever worsening relations and possibly war. The problem is that China wants to become the dominant power in Asia and sees America's presence in the region as the primary obstacle.

Soled, Debra E. (ed.), *China: A Nation in Transition*, CQ Press, 1995.

A writer with a special interest in Asia provides a useful introduction to China detailing its history, economy, society, and foreign policy.

Articles

"Can China Change?" *The Economist*, Oct. 2, 1999.

The article asks whether China can continue to develop economically without corresponding political changes. It concludes that if China is to become a more open society, it will almost certainly do so in spite of rather than because of the Communist Party.

Gibney, Frank, "Birth of a Superpower," *Time*, June 7, 1999.

Gibney details China's efforts to modernize its poorly equipped military.

Jost, Kenneth, "Taiwan, China and the U.S.," *The CQ Researcher*, May 24, 1996, pp. 457-480.

A slightly dated but enlightening report argues that Taiwan's surging economic self-confidence and China's increasing assertiveness pose difficult policy choices for the United States.

Lilley, James, and Arthur Waldron, "Taiwan is a 'State.' Get Over It," *The Wall Street Journal*, July 14, 1999.

Lilley and Waldron contend that treating Taiwan as a de facto independent country is the best way for China to bring about reunification.

Masci, David, "China After Deng," *The CQ Researcher*, June 13, 1997.

A report on issues facing China nearly two decades after Deng Xiaoping initiated economic reforms.

Pomfret, John, "Dissidents Back China's WTO Entry," *The Washington Post*, May 11, 2000.

Pomfret details support for China's membership in the World Trade Organization by members of the country's dissident community.

Ziegler, Dominic, "Now Comes the Hard Part," *The Economist*, April 8, 2000.

Ziegler predicts extraordinary and beneficial changes in the country's economy, but he is less certain about China's future political landscape.

Reports and Studies

Wortzel, Larry M., "Why the Administration Should Reaffirm the 'Six Assurances' to Taiwan," The Heritage Foundation, March 16, 2000.

Wortzel, director of the foundation's Asian Studies Center, argues that the United States should work harder to reassure Taiwan and stop trying to "appease" China.

FOR MORE INFORMATION

Council on Foreign Relations, 58 E. 68th St., New York, N.Y. 10021; (212) 734-0400; www.cfr.org. The nonpartisan research organization studies international issues.

Heritage Foundation, Asian Studies Center, 214 Massachusetts Ave. N.E., Washington, D.C. 20002; (202) 608-6081; www.heritage.org. Conducts research and provides information on trade, military policy and other issues that concern the United States and Asia.

Human Rights Watch, 1522 K St., N.W., Suite 910, Washington D.C. 20005; (202) 371-6592; www.hrw.org. The nonpartisan organization monitors human rights violations worldwide.

Project for the New American Century, 1150 17 St., N.W., Suite 510, Washington, D.C. 20036; (202) 293-4983. The educational organization supports American global leadership.

Robert F. Kennedy Memorial Center for Human Rights, 1367 Connecticut Ave., N.W., Suite 200, Washington, D.C. 20036; (202) 463-7575; www.rfkmemorial.org. Investigates and reports on human rights around the world.

U.S.-Asia Institute, 232 E. Capitol St., N.E., Washington, D.C. 20003; (202) 544-3181. Conducts research and sponsors overseas visits and conferences to foster greater cooperation and understanding between the United States and Asian countries.

9 Population and the Environment

MARY H. COOPER

Two hundred years ago, an English cleric named Thomas Robert Malthus wrote an essay that would forever change the secure view people had of their place on Earth. Like other animal species, Malthus wrote, humans can reproduce faster than the natural resources they require to survive. As a result, he postulated, humans eventually would overwhelm the environment, possibly resulting in their extinction.

"Famine seems to be the last, the most dreadful resource of nature," Malthus wrote. "The power of population is so superior to the power in the Earth to produce subsistence for man, that premature death must in some shape or other visit the human race." [1]

Malthus wrote his treatise in response to the prevailing optimism of the time, which saw population growth as an unqualified boon to mankind. The Marquis de Condorcet, a French mathematician and pioneering social scientist, and William Godwin, an English social philosopher, held that man was perfectible, headed toward a future free of all evil, discomfort and disease. As mankind approached immortality, Godwin predicted, population growth would cease altogether because sexual desire would be extinguished.

Two hundred years later, the debate continues — but amid profound changes. In Malthus' day, there were fewer than 1 billion people on Earth. More recently, global population has mushroomed, growing from 1.6 billion to almost 6 billion in the 20th century alone, numbers that surely would have been taken by 18th-century thinkers as confirmation of the Malthusian nightmare. But technological changes, equally unimaginable to observers at the dawn of the Indus-

From *The CQ Researcher,*
July 17, 1998.

Reuters/Corinne Dufka

trial Revolution, have vastly increased global food supplies, giving credence to Malthus' optimistic critics. [2]

What hasn't changed over the past two centuries is the distance separating the two sides in the ongoing debate over human population. On the one side are Malthus' intellectual heirs, dubbed doomers or Cassandras. They see the continuing rise in global population as a recipe for disaster. The crash will come not only because of food shortages, they say, but because of myriad insults to the environment humans exact by their sheer numbers. *(See graph, p. 160.)*

"I certainly think we face an environmental crisis, whether it amounts to a Malthusian outcome or not," says Leon Kolankiewicz, coordinator of the Carrying Capacity Network, which promotes sustainable development. Rather than the global collapse of food supplies that Malthus envisioned, Kolankiewicz foresees any number of localized crises, similar to that which may have struck Easter Island in the Pacific Ocean, whose inhabitants are believed to have died out after exhausting the island's natural resources.

"For a time, people can exceed the long-term carrying capacity for an area, but this eventually leads to collapse," he says. "In a given region, if not the world, not only will the population collapse, but there also will be such damage to the natural capital — the resources that sustain life — that for a long time to come the environment will no longer be able to support human life."

On the other side of the debate are Godwin's successors — the boomers or Pollyannas — who say more people mean a larger pool of human ingenuity to discover new ways to thrive on planet Earth. They point to the successes of the Green Revolution, an international drive to increase crop yields in the 1950s and '60s, as evidence that humans will always come up with a technological fix to accommodate their growing numbers.

Several new developments have colored the population debate in recent years. One is the discovery that human activities — especially in the developed world — affect the atmosphere, long considered a relatively inexhaustible asset of Earth's environment. When scientists demonstrated that the release of chlorofluorocarbons from man-made coolants and aerosols had eroded Earth's protective ozone layer, world leaders agreed in 1992 to ban the chemicals.

More recently, scientists have concluded that burning fossil fuels may cause a gradual but potentially catastrophic warming of the atmosphere. Fear of so-called global warming resulted in last December's agreement in Kyoto, Japan, to curb the burning of oil, coal and natural gas.

Malthus' supporters point to these and other strains on the environment as signs that human population has exceeded Earth's "carrying capacity," its ability to sustain life indefinitely.

Childbearing Is Greatest in Africa and Asia

The fertility rate — the average number of children that women in a country have — is generally higher in Africa and Western Asia and lower in North America, Europe and Eastern Asia. In the future, according to United Nations projections, small differences in childbearing levels will result in large differences in global population. If women average a moderate two children, population would rise to 11 billion in the 21st century and level off. If women average 2.5 children, population would pass 27 billion by 2150. But if the fertility rate fell to 1.6 children, population would peak at 7.7 billion in 2050 and drop to 3.6 billion by 2150.

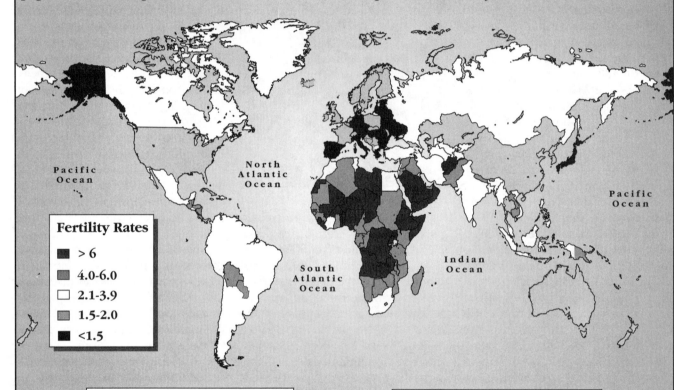

Fertility Rates
- > 6
- 4.0-6.0
- 2.1-3.9
- 1.5-2.0
- <1.5

The 10 Highest Fertility Rates	
Gaza	7.4
Yemen	7.3
Angola	7.2
Oman	7.1
Ethiopia	7.0
Somalia	7.0
Uganda	6.9
Western Sahara	6.9
Burkina Faso	6.9
Togo	6.8

The 10 Lowest Fertility Rates	
Hong Kong	1.1
Latvia	1.2
Bulgaria	1.2
Czech Republic	1.2
Russia	1.2
Italy	1.2
Spain	1.2
Greece	1.3
Slovenia	1.3
Estonia	1.3

Source: "1998 World Population Data Sheet," Population Reference Sheet

Other signs include the rapid disappearance of plant and animal species as humans settle in once-remote parts of the world, a sharp decline in certain fish from overfishing, water shortages as agriculture and industry outpace existing water reserves and land degradation resulting from the relentless spread of agriculture onto land that is ill-suited to cultivation.

Although these strains have not yet precipitated a global environmental collapse, ecologists say we are living on borrowed time. "There is tremendous momentum in population growth," says Brian Halweil, a research fellow at the Worldwatch Institute, which studies global environmental problems. "Even if the total fertility rate were now at replacement level, world population growth would still be a problem." *(See map, p. 146.)* Halweil points to regions that are fast approaching a food crisis, such as the Nile River basin, whose current population of 110 million is expected to more than triple to 380 million by 2050. "With so many people being added," he says, "the per capita availability of resources will zoom down."

It's not that women are having more babies than their grandmothers. In fact, fertility rates have fallen in much of the world, especially where women have gained access to education and economic opportunities that make bearing large numbers of children less attractive. What has happened is that more children now survive to adulthood, thanks to vaccines, improved hygiene and more reliable food supplies.

Optimists in the population debate point to other statistics to refute Malthusian predictions of impending doom. While population growth continues, the rate of growth has slowed considerably in recent years as births in a growing number of countries are falling below 2.1 children per couple — the "replacement level," below

which population begins to decline. This trend has forced the United Nations Population Division to lower its projections of future population growth. Under the "low" variant of its most recent projection, the U.N. agency expects human population to peak at 7.7 billion around the middle of the next century before starting a slow decline. Under its "high" variant, however, there would be 27 billion people on Earth by 2150, with no end of growth in sight.

But some optimists in the debate focus on the low numbers and conclude that the real threat today is the prospect that there will be too few people in coming decades — a virtual birth dearth.

"Predictions of a Malthusian collapse have been vastly exaggerated over the last few decades and continue in the face of new evidence that fertility rates are falling worldwide," says Steven W. Mosher, president of the Population Research Institute, in Falls Church, Va. "This is happening not only in the developed world but also in many developing countries, such as Thailand and Sri Lanka, which are already below replacement level, so that their populations will shortly be declining. The world's population will never double again."

Indeed, say optimists in the population debate, the real problem humanity faces is the coming loss of population, especially in Europe, where births have fallen far below replacement level. *(See story, p. 154.)* Ironically, Italy — homeland of the Vatican, contraception's archenemy — has the lowest fertility rate in the world: Each woman has an average of just 1.2 children in her lifetime. "If you built a fence around Europe, which has an average fertility rate of 1.35, the last European would turn out the lights in 300 years," Mosher says. "If current trends continue, the continent's population would go from 860 million today to zero."

But the Cassandras say it's too soon to start mourning the loss of

European civilization. For one thing, they say, no one can predict with any certainty how many children future generations of people will choose to have. Moreover, because of high birthrates in earlier decades, the large number of women entering their child-bearing years will ensure that population continues to grow despite falling fertility rates. The fastest growth will come in the very countries that are least able to support more people — poor countries of sub-Saharan Africa and South Asia. "Population dynamics are like a supertanker," says Robert Engelman, director of the program on population and the environment at Population Action International. "They don't go from zero to 60 in 30 seconds, and they don't stop so fast either. So while total population growth has slowed more than demographers had expected, it's wrong to say the trend is irrevocable or permanent."

For 200 years, worldwide food production defied Malthusian predictions of global starvation. But now there are ominous signs that worldwide grain production will be unable to keep up with the population growth that is expected to continue for at least the next several decades. According to Worldwatch President Lester R. Brown, impending water shortages will soon force China to begin importing vast quantities of grain to feed its 1.2 billion people. This will drive up grain prices, Brown predicts, leaving developing countries in Africa and elsewhere unable to import enough to meet their food needs. The result: Malthus' nightmare.

"The jury's still out on Malthus," said Robert Kaplan, author of numerous articles on population and environmental issues. "But 200 years later, some people still agree with him. I think that's his ultimate success." [3]

In this bicentennial of Malthus' essay, these are some of the key questions being asked about population growth and the environment:

Will World Population Keep Climbing?

The world's population reached nearly 6 billion in 1997, more than double the 1950 level.

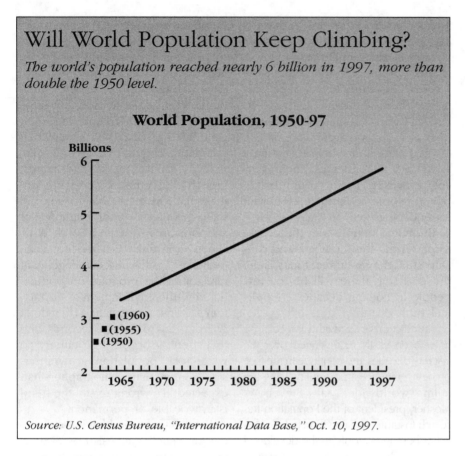

World Population, 1950-97

Source: U.S. Census Bureau, "International Data Base," Oct. 10, 1997.

Can agricultural productivity increase without causing irreversible damage to the environment?

In the 1950s and early '60s, a time of unprecedented high population growth in the developing world, demographers and policy-makers in the industrial countries realized that global food supplies — much provided by exports from developed nations — would soon fall short of demand. Agricultural researchers embarked on an urgent project to develop better-yielding grains in an attempt to avert widespread famine.

The results of this effort, later dubbed the Green Revolution, were stunning. Hybrid strains of rice, wheat and other grains were developed that produced more food per plant and shortened maturation periods so that more than one crop could be cultivated each growing season. In some instances, crop yields tripled.

The Green Revolution's success leads some experts to conclude that further advances in agronomy will suffice to feed the world's growing population. According to Mosher of the Population Research Institute, researchers at the United Nations' Food and Agriculture Organization (FAO) are confident that, even using current technology, enough food could be produced to feed as many as 14 billion people — well above most projections of Earth's population at its peak.

"There is a curious dichotomy between the world's political leaders, who are talking famine, and the researchers who are running the numbers," Mosher says. "The experts aren't being listened to by their own political bosses." In his view, the reason no one is listening to scientists who are confident in the world's ability to feed so many more people comes down to self-interest. "Popu-

lation programs have been generously funded for the past 30 years, and there are a lot of researchers who have benefited from these programs and don't want to see them ended," he says. "As the Chinese would say, they don't want to see their own rice bowls broken."

While other experts agree that further improvements in food production are possible, they worry about the environmental effects of intensifying agriculture much beyond current levels. "I suspect that there is more the Green Revolution can do, that there are more opportunities to increase the yield of a set unit of land," says Engelman of Population Action International. "The important point is that almost all agricultural experts agree that the vast majority of all food will be produced on land we're now cultivating. There just isn't a whole lot of new farmland out there."

Intensifying output on existing farmland can only continue so long before the land is seriously degraded, Engelman warns. "I worry that we may not be able to increase output generation after generation without irrevocably damaging the resources we depend on for food." These include the soil, fresh water and the whole complex of systems that produce food, including organisms in the soil that facilitate the uptake of nutrients in plants.

Each year, an estimated 25 billion metric tons of nutrient-rich topsoil are blown or washed away, largely as a result of intensive agriculture. The soil that is left is denser, making it less able to retain water and allow root penetration. Irrigation produces another problem, salinization, or the buildup of salt and other waterborne minerals in the soil, which can destroy the land's productivity over time.[4] According to David Pimentel, an agricultural expert at Cornell University, soil degradation poses an even more serious threat to the environment than global warming. "It takes 500 years to produce one inch of soil," he said. "Erosion is a slow, gradual problem, but considering that 99 percent of our food comes from the land, it's one that's basic to the survival of the food system."[5]

Besides depleting the soil, irrigation and other modern agricultural techniques pose additional environmental hazards. "Inherent in Green Revolution technologies is the dependence on greater quantities of water, pesticides and fertilizers," says Kolankiewicz of the Carrying Capacity Network. "The environmental effects of this kind of agriculture are numerous and far-reaching, including pesticides that can be bioaccumulated and affect whole species and the drawdown of aquifers and depletion of stream flows by irrigation. So we're already robbing Peter to pay Paul."

Drawing on his experience as a Peace Corps volunteer in Latin America during the 1980s, Kolankiewicz also points to the damage caused as more and more marginal lands are brought into cultivation. "Very steep land is being stripped of trees because of the desperate need for food, population growth and inequitable land distribution," he says. "In many countries the best land for sustainable agriculture is owned by just a few people, who hold it idle, raise cattle on it or grow grain for export."

Some experts see a way out of this quandary through a more efficient global economy. "In an ideal, future world, there would be a number of places where people farming today would trade their labor for food produced elsewhere," says Nicholas Eberstadt, a Harvard University demographer and scholar at the American Enterprise Institute for Public Policy Research. "The environmental implications of such specialization are positive, however, because marginal lands would be under less pressure" from cultivation.

But a key condition for this outcome, Eberstadt says, is broader access to property rights. Environmental degradation occurs "when nobody feels they

own a common resource, and everyone feels they can plunder it," he says, citing desertification in the Sahel in southern Sahara — caused by trying to turn marginally productive land into farmland — and severe industrial pollution in China, where property rights are severely limited. "Both a clear and rational framework of property rights and a more relaxed regimen of international trade could be facilitating mechanisms for ensuring sustainable food supplies in the future."

Should the U.S. government support international efforts to curb population growth?

The United States has led the industrialized nations in funding programs that provide family-planning services to developing countries since the late 1960s. At that time, the U.N. Population Fund was set up to coordinate programs aimed at slowing rapid population growth. The federal government provides funding through the U.N. fund as well as through the U.S. Agency for International Development (AID), which helps other governments and non-governmental organizations (NGOs) in voluntary family-planning projects that provide information, services and supplies to communities throughout the world.

U.S. population assistance has been controversial, however. Anti-abortion activists charge that many overseas programs are coercive, forcing women to be sterilized or undergo abortions against their will. China's one-child policy — the toughest population-control policy in the world — has been especially criticized for allegedly forcing pregnant women who already have a child to have abortions, even late in pregnancy.

In response to the critics, President Ronald Reagan initiated the so-called Mexico City policy — named for the 1984 international population conference. Federal law already barred the use of U.S. funds to pay for abortions performed under international family-planning programs. Reagan took the

ban a step further, issuing an executive order that prohibited federal funding of any NGO involved in abortion activities, even if U.S. funds were not used specifically to pay for abortions.[6]

As one of his first acts after taking office, President Clinton reversed the Mexico City policy, sparking a renewed debate over funding of international population programs. Supporters of these programs say they are largely responsible for the fall in fertility rates over the past three decades. "These programs are absolutely effective," says Carl Haub, senior demographer at the Population Reference Bureau. "A lot of countries can't get started [on cutting population growth] without outside help."

While many countries with high population growth can afford to pay for family-planning clinics, medical personnel and supplies such as birth control pills and condoms, U.S.-funded AID personnel help governments coordinate their programs, Haub says. "AID personnel provide continuity in countries with unstable local governments," he says. "They basically keep the ball rolling by providing the social marketing needed, especially in illiterate societies where it's hard to educate people on how to use birth-control methods like the pill."

Critics say that despite the existing ban on funding programs that provide abortion services or abortion-related lobbying or research, part of the $385 million AID budget earmarked for family-planning services inevitably finds its way into such programs. "Population-control programs in Third World countries involve various forms of coercion," says Mosher, who spent a year studying life in a commune in China in 1979, as the one-child policy there began to be enforced. "China is the worst case in terms of the sheer number of women who are brutalized, but it's not alone," he says. His institute has documented instances of abuse in 38 countries, including sterilizations performed

High Fertility Means Low Development

Regions with high fertility rates like Africa and Latin America have a lower per capita gross national product (GNP) and greater annual population increases than more developed areas, such as North America and Europe. Indeed, Europe's 1.4 fertility rate is below the replacement level, and its population is declining by 0.1 percent a year.

Major Regions of the World

	Population mid-1998 (millions)	Natural Population Increase (Annual %)	Projected Population (millions) 2010	2025	Total Fertility Rate	1996 GNP Per Capita
World	5,926	1.4%	6,903	8,082	2.9	$5,180
More Developed Nations	1,178	0.1	1,217	1,240	1.6	20,240
Less Developed Nations	4,748	1.7	5,687	6,842	3.3	1,230
Africa	763	2.5	979	1,288	5.6	650
North America	301	0.6	333	376	2.0	27,100
Latin America & the Caribbean	500	1.8	591	697	3.0	3,710
Oceania	30	1.1	34	40	2.4	15,430
Asia	3,604	1.5	4,235	4,965	2.8	2,490
Europe	728	-0.1	731	715	1.4	13,710

Source: "1998 World Population Data Sheet," Population Reference Bureau, 1998

without informed consent, coerced abortions and unhygienic conditions in clinics.

"In countries like Mexico, Peru, Bangladesh and Indonesia, agents of the state are going to people's homes and telling women what they should do," Mosher says. "Imagine U.S. Health and Human Services agents coming to your home and telling you to take contraceptives. You would be outraged, yet this is the nature of population-control campaigns overseas."

But supporters of continued U.S. funding of international family-planning programs point instead to the gradual fall in fertility rates as evidence that women are voluntarily embracing the opportunity to have fewer children. "There's almost nothing rational about the debate over whether the United States is somehow contributing to abortions overseas," Engelman says. "We see the fall in fertility rates in developing countries as great news. It shows that population assistance is having the impact it was designed to have — more women are wanting fewer children."

Haub fears that the recent warnings about the dangers of population decline in the industrialized world will further erode support for U.S. funding of population programs. "This trend most definitely can have an effect on people's opinions about these programs," he says. "But fertility trends in Europe have absolutely nothing to do with trends in developing countries, which have very young populations and account for 80 percent of world population and 98 percent of the population growth."

Haub points to Mali, where the fertility rate has remained unchanged from around 7 children per woman for the past decade or more. "It's ridiculous to say that fertility rates in Africa are plummeting." Indeed, AID surveys suggest that more than 100 million married women in developing countries have an unmet need for family-planning information and contraceptives. [7]

But support for population programs remains weak in Congress, where the abortion controversy remains the primary focus of the debate on population. In April, for example, Congress added a stipulation to a State Department authorization bill (HR 1757) to pay nearly $1 billion in back dues to the U.N. that would bar U.S. aid to any international groups that lobby for abortion rights. President Clinton threatened to veto the measure. [8]

Some experts say the abortion debate in Washington undermines the progress made by family-planning efforts to date. "The U.N. estimates that if there isn't an immediate stepping up of international family planning there will be 3 billion more people in 50 years," says Halweil of Worldwatch. "That's 9.5 billion people by 2050. But reports that the population explosion is over, combined with pressure from groups that oppose abortion, are eroding domestic support for international family-planning efforts."

Should immigration be limited to protect the U.S. environment from overpopulation?

Like most industrialized countries, the United States has experienced a decline in fertility rates in recent decades, as the postwar baby boom was replaced with the baby bust of the 1970s and '80s. Today, American women have, on average, 2 children. That's slightly below the 2.1 level demographers identify as replacement level fertility, since it allows for the replacement of both parents, with a small allowance for children who die before reaching adulthood.

But the U.S. population, now 270 million, is expected to grow almost 50 percent by 2050, to 387 million. [9] With fertility rates steady among native-born American women, experts say the increase is largely due to immigration. More than 800,000 immigrants legally enter the United States each year (1.1 million, if illegal immigrants are included). That level

is almost triple the average annual immigration of 255,000 from World War II until 1970.

Almost as controversial as using abortion to control population growth is cutting immigration levels to slow environmental degradation. Indeed, although many environmental groups identify population growth as a threat to the environment, and most population growth in the United States today is a result of immigration, few of these organizations actually advocate capping immigration levels.

Earlier this year, the Sierra Club, one of the oldest and most respected environmental groups in the United States, ignited controversy among its members: It asked whether the group should abandon its neutrality on immigration or advocate caps on the number of people admitted each year in the interest of protecting the environment from the effects of overpopulation. When the votes were counted in April, the membership chose by a 3-to-2 margin to continue to stay out of the immigration quagmire altogether.

"This is a resounding defeat for a misguided policy," said Carl Pope, the Sierra Club executive director and a strong proponent of the group's neutral position on immigration. "Through this vote, our members have shown they understand that restricting immigration in the United States will not solve the environmental problems caused by global overpopulation. The common-sense solution to overpopulation is birth control, not border patrols." [10]

But supporters of immigration caps say the vote was little more than a politically correct cop-out encouraged by the group's leaders, who fear alienating the Hispanic and Asian immigrant population of California, its main political base. "There's no way we can stabilize population without reducing immigration," says Kolankiewicz, a Sierra Club member who was involved

in the effort to bring the issue to the vote. "The Sierra Club tried to step very delicately around a very controversial domestic issue. But it's duplicitous to suggest that with continued international family-planning measures we'll be able to stabilize our population."

Over the past 45 years, Kolankiewicz says, U.S. immigration levels have quadrupled at the same time global fertility has declined by 40 percent. "We have the right and the responsibility to control our own population," he says.

While acknowledging the link between population growth and environmental degradation, some experts dispute the value of capping immigration levels in the United States. Of the 800,000 foreigners who legally enter the United States each year, all but about 120,000 gain entry because they are related to current residents or citizens. A significant reduction in immigration levels, says Haub, "would mean we'd have to tell the people who are already legal residents they can't bring over their immediate relatives. That's a political impossibility."

For its part, the Clinton administration has not taken a clear position on the issue of immigration's impact on the environment. A 1996 report by a White House task force concluded that "reducing immigration levels is a necessary part of population stabilization and the drive toward sustainability." [11] But the president recently defended immigration, calling immigrants "the most restless, the most adventurous, the most innovative and the most industrious of people."

Clinton condemned "policies and ballot propositions that exclude immigrants from our civic life" and praised the United States' tradition as an immigrant nation. "Let me state my view unequivocally," Clinton said. "I believe new immigrants are good for America." But he sidestepped the question of whether current immigration levels are appropriate. ■

BACKGROUND

A Radical Idea

When Malthus launched the ongoing debate over population growth in 1798, Europe was on the threshold of a radically new era. The Industrial Revolution was just getting under way, opening the way for dramatic shifts in Europe and North America from an agricultural to a modern industrial economy.

Malthus graduated from Cambridge University and later became an Anglican priest. In 1805 he became what is considered the world's first professor of political economy, a position he held at the college of the East India Company until his death in 1834.

The essay that made him famous arose from a friendly argument with his father over man's place in the world. Daniel Malthus espoused the optimistic view that prevailed at the time — no doubt inspired by the rise of democracy and technological progress — that man's ability to improve his lot is unlimited.

Two philosophers were the main purveyors of this view. In France, the Marquis de Condorcet welcomed the revolution in his country as evidence of mankind's ceaseless progress toward perfection. Even after he was imprisoned for criticizing the new Jacobin constitution, Condorcet never lost his optimism. Before starving to death in prison, he completed his writings, which were published posthumously in 1795. [12]

In England, social philosopher William Godwin shared Condorcet's views. In "An Enquiry Concerning Political Justice, and Its Influence on General Virtue and Happiness" (1793), Godwin took Condorcet's utopian thinking even further, calling for the abolition of all governmental and social institutions, including religion, school and family. All such associations, Godwin wrote, were oppressive and would no longer be needed when mankind reached its inevitable goal of perfection. At that point, he predicted, population growth would cease to be a concern. "The men who exist when the earth shall refuse itself to a more extended population will cease to propagate, for they will no longer have any motive, either of error or duty, to induce them. In addition to this they will perhaps be immortal." [13]

In refuting Condorcet and Godwin, Malthus argued that the notion that all people can live in ease and comfort defies laws of nature. Because population will always tend to grow faster than food supplies and other natural resources required for human survival, he wrote, humankind will always be afflicted with "misery and vice," such as war, famine, disease and abortion. "Famine seems to be the last, the most dreadful resource of nature," Malthus wrote. "The power of population is so superior to the power in the earth to produce subsistence for man, that premature death must in some shape or other visit the human race." [14]

Godwin's prediction that population growth will cease as people stop reproducing, Malthus wrote, defies another of the "fixed laws of our nature." "[T]owards the extinction of the passion between the sexes, no progress whatever has hitherto been made," he wrote. "It appears to exist in as much force at present as it did two thousand or four thousand years ago. . . . Assuming, then, my postulata as granted, I say that the power of population is indefinitely greater than the power in the earth to produce subsistence for man." [15]

Malthus modified his views slightly in later essays on the subject, suggesting that population growth could be slowed somewhat by delaying marriage and childbirth. But his basic thesis that there are natural limits to population growth was to greatly influence thinkers of his time and later. Charles Darwin acknowledged a debt to Malthus in devising his theory of evolution, published in 1859. Karl Marx, who published *Principles of Political Economy* the same year, denounced Malthus as a pawn of conservatives because his theory ruled out the Marxist ideal of the classless society. [16]

20th-Century Concerns

Record population growth in the 1960s and '70s sparked renewed interest in Malthus. The burgeoning environmental movement also raised concern about the effect of population growth on fossil fuel supplies and other natural resources. As in Malthus' time, optimists dismissed such worries, arguing that technological advances would provide for virtually limitless numbers of people.

Throughout this century, no voice has been more influential in rebutting Malthus than the Roman Catholic Church. In 1968, Pope Paul VI declared in an encyclical, "Humanae Vitae," that "each and every marriage act must remain open to the transmission of life," effectively banning all forms of birth control short of abstention. Population growth is not the problem among poor nations, the pope implied, but poor government and a lack of social justice. He called for humanity to undertake "the efforts and the sacrifices necessary to insure the raising of living standards of a people and of all its sons."

The same year the encyclical was

Chronology

1700s *The debate over the impact of population growth begins.*

1793
English social philosopher William Godwin calls for the abolition of all governmental and social institutions as oppressive obstacles to human perfection. He predicts that population growth will eventually cease.

1795
Posthumously published writings by the Marquis de Condorcet, a French philosopher, argue that mankind is evolving toward perfection.

1798
Thomas Robert Malthus, an English cleric, warns in *An Essay on the Principle of Population* that unlimited population growth will overwhelm food supplies.

————— • —————

1950s-1960s
The Green Revolution greatly increases crop yields, quelling fears that famine will halt Earth's rapid population growth.

1960
The International Rice Research Institute (IRRI) is created to increase rice yields. Research eventually leads to a doubling and tripling of yields, averting famine in Asian countries with high population growth.

1968
Pope Paul VI issues an encyclical entitled "Humanae Vitae," banning all artificial methods of birth control and ensuring the Roman Catholic Church's position as the most influential opponent of international population-control efforts.

————— • —————

1970s *Record population growth renews Malthusian fears, while China launches its controversial one-child policy.*

1971
The Consultative Group on International Agricultural Research (CGIAR) is set up to coordinate the improvement of food production worldwide. Its 16-member research organization helps boost crop and fish yields.

————— • —————

1980s *U.S. support for overseas family-planning programs wanes amid anti-abortion sentiment.*

1980
Stanford University biologist Paul Ehrlich bets University of Maryland Professor Julian Simon that commodity prices will rise as a result of population growth. Ten years later, Ehrlich loses the bet to Simon, who argues that technological progress will increase commodity supplies and lower prices.

1984
President Ronald Reagan initiates the so-called Mexico City policy — named for the population conference held there — prohibiting federal funding of any non-governmental organization involved in abortion activities.

1990s *Forecasters alter their future projections in the wake of an unexpected slowing of population growth.*

January 1993
Shortly after taking office, President Clinton overturns the Mexico City policy.

1996
A White House task force calls for curbs on immigration to stabilize the U.S. population and protect the environment.

November 1996
The World Food Summit sets a goal of cutting in half the number of undernourished people on Earth from 800 million to 400 million by 2015.

————— • —————

2000s *Population growth is expected to continue, albeit at a slower pace.*

2000
After a century of rapid growth, Earth's population is expected to reach 6 billion, up from 1.6 billion in 1900.

2050
The population of the United States is expected to reach 387 million, up from 270 million in 1998. According to the United Nations Population Division's "middle" variant, world population is expected to peak at 7.7 billion before starting a slow decline.

Falling Fertility Rates Threaten ...

The population debate usually focuses on the impact of overpopulation on food supplies, health and the environment in developing countries. But scores of developed nations face an equally ominous threat: dwindling populations caused by low fertility.

Falling fertility rates have helped slow population growth throughout the world in recent years, but in some 50 countries the average number of children born to each woman has fallen below 2.1, the number required to maintain a stable population. Nearly all of these countries are in the developed world, where couples have been discouraged from having large families by improved education and health care, widespread female employment and rising costs of raising and educating children.

Conservative commentator Ben Wattenberg and others who question the value of family-planning programs have seized on this emerging trend to shift the terms of the population debate. "Never before have birthrates fallen so far, so fast, so low, for so long all around the world," Wattenberg writes. "The potential implications — environmental, economic, geopolitical and personal — are both unclear and clearly monumental, for good and for ill." [1]

According to Wattenberg, the implications are particularly dire for Europe, where the average fertility rate has fallen to 1.4 children per woman. (See map, p. 604.) Even if the trend reversed itself and the fertility rate returned to 2.1, the continent would have lost a quarter of its current population before it stabilized around the middle of the next century. With fewer children being born, the ratio of older people to younger people already is growing. "Europe may become an ever smaller picture-postcard continent of pretty old castles and old churches tended by old people with old ideas," Wattenberg writes. "Or it may become a much more pluralist place with ever greater proportions of Africans and Muslims — a prospect regarded with horror by a large majority of European voters." [2]

Some European governments are clearly concerned about the "birth dearth" in their midst. With fewer children being born, they face the prospect of shrinking work forces and growing retiree populations, along with slower economic growth and domestic consumption. Italy, whose fertility rate of 1.2 children per woman is among the lowest in the world, stands to suffer the most immediate consequences of shrinking birthrates. "Italy's population will fall by half over the next half-century, from 66 million now to 36 million," says Steven W. Mosher, president of the Population Research Institute. "The Italian government warns that the current birthrate, if it continues, will amount to collective suicide."

Like Italy, France and Germany have introduced generous child subsidies, in the form of tax credits for every child born, extended maternal leave with full pay, guaranteed employment upon resumption of work and free child care. Mosher predicts that the European Union will likely extend these and other policies to raise birthrates throughout the 15-nation organization in the next couple of years because all members are below replacement level.

"Humanity's long-term problem is not too many children being born but too few," Mosher says. "The one-child family is being chosen voluntarily in many European countries like Italy, Greece, Spain and Russia, which are already filling more coffins than cradles each year. Over time, the demographic collapse will extinguish entire cultures."

Although it is most pronounced in Europe, the birth dearth affects a few countries in other parts of the world as well. Mosher calculates that Japan's population will fall from 126 million today to 55 million over the next century if its 1.4 fertility rate remains unchanged. The trend is already having a social and cultural impact on the country.

"In Japan, which boasts the longest lifespans of any country in the world, it's now common for an elderly

issued, Stanford University biologist Paul Ehrlich issued an equally impassioned plea for expanded access to birth-control services in *The Population Bomb*. In this and other warnings about the dangers of population growth, Ehrlich and his wife, Anne, also a Stanford researcher, predicted that the resources on which human survival depends would soon run out. "Population control is absolutely essential if the problems now facing mankind are to be solved," they wrote. [17]

At the same time, Worldwatch's

Brown began warning of an impending food crisis. "As of the mid-1970s, it has become apparent that the soaring demand for food, spurred by both population growth and rising affluence, has begun to outrun the productive capacity of the world's farmers and fishermen," he wrote. "The result is declining food reserves, skyrocketing food prices and increasingly intense international competition for exportable food supplies." [18]

The voices of alarm were dismissed by some free-market economists,

who, echoing Godwin's view of man's perfectibility, asserted that human ingenuity would resolve the problems of population growth. The late Julian Simon, a professor at the University of Maryland, declared that Earth's natural resources will never be completely exhausted because human intellect, which is required to exploit them, is infinite. [19] To prove his point, Simon bet Paul Ehrlich that between 1980 and '90 the prices of several minerals would fall as technological progress raised their supply. Ehrlich bet that growing resource scarcity,

... Dire Consequences for Europe

person to hire a family for a day or a weekend to experience family life and enjoy interaction with young people," Mosher says. "It's sad to have to rent a family for a weekend, but this is a way of life that is no longer available to the Japanese because the country is dying."

The birth dearth has geopolitical implications, as well. "As the population plummets, you can say goodbye to Japan as a world power," Mosher says. "And this trend is very hard to reverse. Every young couple would have to have three or four kids to stop the momentum, and that's not going to happen."

Apart from encouraging childbirth, the only way governments can halt population loss is to open the doors to immigrants. In the United States, where the 2.0 fertility rate is just below replacement level, the population is growing by 160,000 people a year, thanks to immigration.

While immigration has always played a prominent, if controversial, role in the United States and Canada, it is a far more contentious issue in the rest of the developed world. Most European countries have more homogeneous societies than those of North America, and deeply entrenched resistance to immigration, especially by people from non-European countries, has fueled support for right-wing politicians like France's Jean-Marie Le Pen. Anti-immigrant sentiment has occasionally escalated into violence, such as the firebombings of housing for Turkish "guest workers" in Germany during the 1980s.

Still, immigration has become more acceptable throughout much of Europe in the past decade, and many of the "guest workers" who come from North Africa, Turkey and other places in search of jobs have stayed and even gained citizenship. "Immigrants are continuing to move to Europe, bringing their cultures and their religions with them," Mosher says. "Intermarriage also is increasing." Japan has been much less hospitable to foreigners.

"Immigration is a very sensitive subject in Japan," Mosher says, "and it is unlikely to be used in the short term to address the growing shortfall of workers there."

Advocates of population-control programs dismiss the concern over shrinking birthrates. "We are delighted to see falling birthrates in our lifetimes, and will continue to encourage the trend," says Robert Engelman, director of Population Action International's program on population and the environment. "I don't want to minimize the problems associated with aging populations. But because this is a slow process, societies will have plenty of time to adjust to the economic and political stresses by increasing immigration from parts of the world where population will continue to rise for some time."

Of course, immigration will be a viable solution to depopulation only as long as humanity continues to grow in number in other parts of the world. Those who worry about falling population point to the United Nations' most conservative projections, which suggest that global population could begin to shrink as early as 2040. But others see little cause for concern.

"If world population starts to fall in 2040, so what?" Engelman asks. "Please identify the danger of population decline that starts at a level much higher than today's and at worst may bring population down to levels seen earlier in the 20th century. There's only so much fresh water, so much atmosphere to absorb the waste greenhouse gases we inject into it every day, so much forest, so much land that can be cultivated. When you consider the enormity of these problems, there's nothing to be afraid of with gradual population decline."

[1] Ben J. Wattenberg, "The Population Explosion Is Over," *The New York Times Magazine*, Nov. 23, 1997, p. 60.

[2] *Ibid.*

stemming in part from population growth, would drive prices up. Simon won the bet.

Green Revolution

Acting on concerns that rising populations in developing countries were outstripping the world's capacity to produce enough food, leaders of NGOs, foundations and national governments launched an international agricultural-research effort to avert famine. In 1960, the International Rice Research Institute (IRRI) was created to increase the yield of rice, the basic food for more than half the world's population. Within a few years, IRRI developed the first of several dwarf breeds that enabled farmers to grow more rice on limited land, using less water and fewer chemicals.

Under the leadership of the Consultative Group on International Agricultural Research (CGIAR), set up in 1971, biologists and agronomists from 16 research centers around the world have since produced hundreds of hybrid strains of staple grains, such as rice, wheat and corn. They have recently extended their efforts to improve yields of potatoes, fish and other basic foods.

These efforts have been so successful that they are known as the Green Revolution. Indeed, although world population has almost doubled since 1961, per-capita food production has more than doubled. The FAO estimates that people in the developing world consume almost a third more calories a day than in the early 1960s. As a result, experts say, there are fewer deaths from

Population Programs Depend ...

The International Conference on Population and Development, held in Cairo, Egypt, in 1994, laid out a formula for stabilizing the world's growing population. Adopted by 180 nations, the plan called for improvements in women's health and job opportunities and greater access to high-quality reproductive health care, including family planning.

As the following examples show, countries that embraced the Cairo conference's "program of action" are at varying stages in population planning, due to varying levels of development, status of women and religious beliefs:

China — In 1971 Mao Zedong acknowledged the threat posed by China's more than 850 million people and launched a family-planning policy urging later marriage, increased spacing between children and a limit of two children per couple. The policy was later intensified into the radical "one-child" policy, which attracted international condemnation for its practice of forced abortions. The policy has since been relaxed, however. According to firsthand reports, it never covered most of rural China, where many families have three or more children. Still, the fertility rate has plummeted, from 5.8 children per woman in 1970 to 2 today. China's 1.2 billion people makes it the most highly populated country in the world. [1]

India — In 1951 India launched the world's first national family-planning policy. Although almost half of the nation's married women use family planning, and birthrates have come down, most of the slowdown has come in the more developed southern part of the country. "The real story in the past 20 years has been in the large illiterate states of the north known as the Hindi belt," says Carl Haub, senior demographer at the Population Reference Bureau. "In Uttar Pradesh, with a population of 150 million people, women still have an average of five children." That compares with 3.9 children for the country as a whole. With 989 million people, India today is the second most populous country in the world. With an annual growth rate of almost 2 percent — twice that of China — India may surpass China by 2050. [2]

Pakistan — Just across India's northwestern border, Pakistan has been much less aggressive in its population program. The fertility rate has fallen only slightly, from 6.6 children per woman in 1984-85 to 5.6 children today. A number of factors have contributed to the slow fall in fertility, including official indifference, inadequate funding of population programs and the country's Islamic traditions, which grant women little status, give men the leading role in family decisions and place a high value on sons. [3]

Bangladesh — When Bangladesh won independence from Pakistan in 1971, it had roughly the same population — 66 million people — and the same population growth rate — 3 percent a year — as Pakistan. But the new leaders of Bangladesh, unlike Pakistan, made family planning a top priority. As a result of a sweeping education program and widespread distribution of contraceptives, the fertility rate has dropped from more than 6 children per woman to three. Today, the population of Bangladesh is 120 million, compared with 140 million in Pakistan. [4]

Thailand — Population-control advocates consider Thailand a major success story. Its strong government program is credited with raising contraceptive use from 8 percent to 75 percent of couples over the past 30 years. As a result, the fertility rate has plummeted from 6.2 to 2 births per woman, slightly below the replacement level of 2.1. The relatively high status of Thai women, an extensive road network facilitating access to health clinics and low child mortality are cited as reasons for the program's success. [5]

Rwanda — Since the bloody civil war in 1994, when as many as 750,000 Tutsis were slaughtered by rival Hutus, members of both tribes have set about what one doctor calls "revenge fertility" — a competition to procreate in

famine and malnutrition than ever before. [20] The famines that have occurred in the past 35 years, such as those in Ethiopia and Somalia in the 1980s, and now in Sudan, have been largely the result of war and civil unrest rather than scarcity of global food supplies.

A little-mentioned side effect of the Green Revolution, however, was the environmental damage that accompanied the astonishing increase in crop yields. Some of the new strains were more susceptible to insect infestation than traditional breeds. Pesticide use in rice production, for example, increased sevenfold, threatening the safety of water supplies. Some insects have developed resistance to the chemicals, resulting in yet heavier pesticide use. Green Revolution crops also require fertilizer, in some cases up to 30 times the amount used on traditional crops. With prolonged use, fertilizers can damage the soil. Finally, because many new plant strains require irrigation, the Green Revolution has been accompanied by increased erosion and water run-off, further harming land productivity.

"The reduced productivity requires added fertilizer, irrigation and pesticides to offset soil and water degradation," write David Pimentel and Marcia Pimentel of Cornell University. "This starts a cycle of more agricultural chemical usage and further increases the production costs the farmer must bear." [21] ∎

... On Wide Range of Factors

what is among Africa's most densely populated countries. With fertility at about 7 children per woman and population growth of 3.5 percent, the population of this impoverished country roughly the size Maryland is expected to grow from 7.2 million people today to 25 million by 2030. [6]

Kenya — Although it was one of the first African countries to introduce family-planning services, Kenya saw its fertility rate continue to grow for some time, from 5.3 children per woman in 1962 to 8 children per woman by 1977. In 1982, however, the government strengthened the program, providing community-based services in isolated areas that have increased the use of contraceptives among rural populations. As a result, the fertility rate has fallen to 4.5 children per woman — a rate that ensures continued population growth for decades but one that places Kenya well below the average rate of 6 children per woman in all of sub-Saharan Africa. Kenya's success in lowering fertility rates is now being mirrored in several other countries in the region, including Zimbabwe, Ghana, Nigeria and Senegal. [7]

Tunisia — Since 1957, Tunisia's population has doubled from 4 million to 8 million. While that's a huge increase, it pales in comparison with neighboring Algeria, which also started out in 1957 with 4 million inhabitants but now is home to 57 million. The difference, according to journalist Georgie Ann Geyer, is culture. "Thirty percent of the budget in Tunisia goes to education," she said. "Also, population control is part of the culture." [8] The government population program provides free family-planning services in most parts of the country, and mobile units serve rural areas. The program also is sensitive to religious customs: Rather than urging new mothers to use birth control methods right after delivery, for example, health personnel schedule a return visit to hospital 40 days later — the day new mothers return to society from seclusion, according to Islamic custom. [9]

Iran — Since the 1979 Islamic revolution, Iran's

population has jumped from 35 million to 60 million, fueled in part by official encouragement for large families. In 1993, the government adopted a strict family-planning program that encourages vasectomy and other means of birth control — though abortion remains illegal in most cases — and denies subsidized health insurance and food coupons to couples with more than three children. As a result of these efforts, the population growth rate has dropped from 4 percent a year in the 1980s — among the highest in the world — to about 2.5 percent in 1996. [10]

Peru — To stem its 2.2 percent annual increase in population, the government of Peru in 1995 stepped up its population-control program, with the additional goal of raising the status of women in the country. Since then, the program has come under fire, as health workers are accused of offering gifts to illiterate women to undergo sterilization in often unhygienic conditions. [11]

---

[1] See Mark Hertsgaard, "Our Real China Problem," *The Atlantic*, November 1997, pp. 96-114.

[2] See "India's Growing Pains," *The Economist*, Feb. 22, 1997, p. 41.

[3] Population Reference Bureau, "Pakistan: Family Planning with Male Involvement Project of Mardan," November 1993.

[4] See Jennifer D. Mitchell, "Before the Next Doubling," *World Watch*, January/February 1998, pp. 20-27.

[5] Population Reference Bureau, "Thailand: National Family Planning Program," August 1993.

[6] See "Be Fruitful," *The Economist*, Feb. 1, 1997, p. 43.

[7] See Stephen Buckley, "Birthrates Declining in Much of Africa," *The Washington Post*, April 27, 1998.

[8] Geyer spoke at "Malthus Revisited," a conference held May 8-9, 1998, by the Warrenton, Va.-based Biocentric Institute, which studies ways to enhance the quality of life for all peoples.

[9] See Population Reference Bureau, "Tunisia: Sfax Postpartum Program," March 1993.

[10] See Neil MacFarquhar, "With Iran Population Boom, Vasectomy Receives Blessing," *The New York Times*, Sept. 8, 1996.

[11] See Calvin Sims, "Using Gifts as Bait, Peru Sterilizes Poor Women," *The New York Times*, Feb. 15, 1998.

CURRENT SITUATION

Population Explosion

The 20th century has seen by far the fastest population growth in human history. For the first million years or so of man's existence on Earth, global population probably did not exceed 6 million — fewer than New York City's current population. With the beginning of agriculture some 10,000 years ago, population expanded gradually until it approached 1 billion by 1700 and 1.6 billion by 1900. Population growth never exceeded 0.5 percent a year over that 200-year period. [22]

By 2000, global population is expected to reach 6 billion. The unprecedented population explosion of the 20th century peaked in the 1970s, when the growth rate reached 2 percent a year. It has since slowed, thanks to improved access to family-planning information and contraceptives and expanded educational and employment opportunities for women in developing countries.

As couples become less dependent

on children to help in the fields and take care of them in old age, the value of large families decreases. The same medical advances that helped fuel the population explosion by reducing infant mortality also enable couples to have fewer children in the knowledge that they will survive to adulthood.

As a result of these changes, fertility rates of most developing countries are following those in industrialized countries, where fertility rates have fallen dramatically in recent decades. As more people move to the cities, the cost of raising children — housing, food, clothing and schooling — is a powerful inducement to reducing family size. "Birthrates in a large number of countries in the developing world, except for Africa, Pakistan and some countries in the Persian Gulf, have come down to a degree," says Haub of the Population Reference Bureau. "The big question is whether they will come down to the 2.1 level seen in developed countries. That would bring the population growth rate to zero."

But while fertility rates are slowly falling in many developing nations, the population momentum of the earlier boom ensures that population growth will continue in these countries for years to come. While population growth rates have dropped in industrial nations, in the developing world more than 2 billion young people under age 20 are entering or will soon enter their childbearing years, according to the Population Reference Bureau. This trend is especially significant in sub-Saharan Africa, the region with the highest fertility rate in the world — an average of 6 births per woman. With 45 percent of the inhabitants of sub-Saharan Africa age 15 or younger, population growth will likely continue, no matter what the birthrate may be in the next few decades. [23]

The difference in fertility rates between industrialized and developing countries has implications for the future. Today, there are four times as many people in developing countries as in industrial countries. Because 98 percent of global population growth is taking place in developing countries, that gap is likely to widen. If current trends continue, many industrial nations will soon begin to lose population, especially young, working-age people. [24] As developing countries struggle to support and employ their growing number of youth, many more young people from the developing world may migrate to other regions, including the developed countries.

Norman Myers of Oxford University, in England, puts the number of "environmental refugees" at 25 million, primarily in sub-Saharan Africa, China, the Indian subcontinent, Mexico and Central America, who are fleeing drought, erosion, desertification, deforestation and other environmental problems.

"The issue of environmental refugees is fast becoming prominent in the global arena," Myers writes. "Indeed it promises to rank as one of the foremost human crises of our times." Myers foresees increased resistance to immigration in industrial nations. "Already migrant aliens prove unwelcome in certain host countries, as witness the cases of Haitians in the United States and North Africans in Europe. No fewer than nine developed countries, almost one in three, are taking steps to further restrict immigration flows from developing countries." [25]

Environmental Impact

As global population continues to mount, so does the strain on the environment, as people move into previously uninhabited areas and consume ever-increasing amounts of natural resources. In recent times, the first signs of population's impact on the environment were regional food shortages in the 1960s and '70s. Initially, the Green Revolution resolved the shortages by introducing high-yield grains and innovative farming techniques. But the more intensive methods of agriculture required to boost food production in many parts of the world have since produced environmental damage of their own. "You can't fertilize crops without fresh water," says Halweil. "If you increase fertilizer use, you have to increase water use. As a result, large areas of Latin America, Africa and China are now suffering water shortages."

Another result of intensified irrigation and fertilizer use is the buildup of salt and other minerals that are left in the soil after the water evaporates. After prolonged irrigation, land also tends to become waterlogged and no longer suitable for growing plants. Even before land degradation sets in, there are limits to the benefits of fertilizers. "You can't just keep putting fertilizer on the land indefinitely," Halweil says. "Eventually the yield increases cease."

With economic development, more people around the world are consuming poultry, beef, pork and other meat products. As demand for such foods rises, cattle ranches are occupying land once used for agriculture, pushing farmers onto marginal lands such as steep hillsides and virgin forests. The deforestation that results, most evident recently in tropical South America and Africa, promotes erosion and has been implicated in global warming.

Biologists recently warned that a "mass extinction" of plant and animal species is now taking place, the result of human destruction of natural habitats. [26] Even the oceans are showing signs of strain from population growth. Overfishing and pollution have caused sudden decreases in fish catches, prompting temporary bans in many fisheries that only a few decades ago seemed limitless. [27]

Population growth has also been accompanied by air and water pollution. While developed countries have made strides in these areas, industrializing countries are facing mounting problems.

At Issue:

Has economic development proved Malthus wrong?

JAMES P. PINKERTON
Lecturer, Graduate School of Political Management, The George Washington University

JOHN F. ROHE
Attorney and author of A Bicentennial Malthusian Essay *(1997)*

*i*n 1798, a 32-year-old minister from England published, anonymously, a 54,000-word "Essay on the Principle of Population." In it, he argued that "the power of population is indefinitely greater than the power in the Earth to produce subsistence for man." And so, he concluded in his famous formulation, "Population, when unchecked, increases in a geometrical ratio. Subsistence increases only in an arithmetical ratio." Neither the author nor his essay stayed obscure for long. Yet for all the renown of Thomas Robert Malthus, it is hard to think of an idea that has been simultaneously more influential and more wrong.

On the bicentennial of his famous treatise, Malthus lives on as adjective; a Nexis database search for the word "Malthusian" just in the last year found 138 "hits." Indeed, Malthusianism has become an intellectual prism for explaining the world, like Marxism or Freudianism — even for those who have read little or nothing of the original texts. Just as Marxists explain everything as a consequence of class structure or Freudians interpret behavior by identifying underlying sexual impulses, so Malthusians start with an inherent presumption of scarcity and impending doom. And so Malthus stands as the patron saint of pessimists, those who see the glass as half-empty, not half-full. As he wrote then, his view of the world had "a melancholy hue."

Interestingly, the first Malthusians were on the political right. The landed gentry from which Malthus sprang looked upon the swelling population of the big cities with fear and even loathing . . . .

Today's Malthusians, of course, are on the environmental left. Once again, the dynamic is that many among the elite look upon their fellow humans as liabilities. And once again, they have been mostly wrong.

The leading Malthusian today — if you don't count Vice President Al Gore — is Stanford Professor Paul Ehrlich. His landmark book, *The Population Bomb*, published in 1968, began with an alarm. "The battle to feed all humanity is over," he declared, predicting worldwide famine. A more recent book, *The Population Explosion* (1990), co-written with his wife Anne, carries on the same doom-gloom argument. Praising, of course, the memory of Malthus, the Ehrlichs prescribe a long list of control on virtually every aspect of human activity . . . .

Ironically, toward the end of his life, Malthus altered his views. In "Principles of Political Economy" (1820) he acknowledged that economic growth would improve the prospects of the populace. But as so often happens, the original outrageous assertion is remembered forever, while the subsequent revision, even if it is closer to the truth, fades away quickly.

*p*hilosophers at the dawn of the Industrial Revolution . . . suggested that prosperity and wealth were dependent on more people. In his essay, "Of Avarice and Profusion" in 1797, William Godwin states, "There is no wealth in the world except this, the labor of man . . . ." While serving as an ordained priest in the Church of England, Thomas Robert Malthus questioned these findings. He pondered basic mathematical principles. If parents had four children, and if the population continued to double every generation, the exponential progression would be as follows: 2, 4, 8, 16, 32, 64, 128, 256, 512, 1024, 2048. The numerical surge becomes explosive. Malthus determined a finite planet could not accommodate perpetual growth . . . .

Thomas Robert Malthus unlocked the door to one of nature's best-kept and most formidable secrets. He discovered a universal law of biology. For every plant and animal, there are more offspring than the ecosystem can sustain. And we are just beginning to grapple with the ethical dilemma resulting from his humbling conclusion: This universal law even applies to us.

The view from a seemingly lofty perch on nature's food chain can be deceptive. We enjoy but a brief reprieve from universal biological principles. The prescient message of a pre-scientific era has not been rendered obsolete by modern technology.

Our planet now experiences a daily net population gain of 250,000 people (total births minus deaths), and approximately 1.3 billion go to bed hungry every night. Several hundred thousand slip beyond the brink of malnutrition every year.

While the Earth's natural capital is systematically dismantled, efforts to discredit Malthus persist. For example, Julian Simon claims the world's resources can continue to accommodate human growth for 7 billion years! By then, the unchecked human biomass would fill the universe.

Efforts to discredit Malthus do not always plummet to such overt absurdities. Subtle efforts to refute him are exhibited every time a politician promises to add more exponential growth to the GNP. Proponents of growth are implicitly found in every financial report, business forecast and economic news publication. An abiding faith in growth has become the unexamined conviction of our age. Notions of sustainability are not on the table. The talismanic affinity for growth is an implicit rejection of Malthus . . . .

We were not exempt from the laws of biology unveiled by Thomas Robert Malthus in 1798. And we are not exempt now. At the bicentennial anniversary of his essay, Malthus deserves recognition for predicting the cause of today's most pressing concerns and most challenging ethical challenges. We discredit him at our peril.

Developed Nations Use the Most Resources

The United States accounts for only 5 percent of the world's population but uses a third of its paper and dumps three-quarters of the hazardous waste. Similarly, other developed countries account for a small fraction of Earth's population but use the largest percentage of its metals and paper.

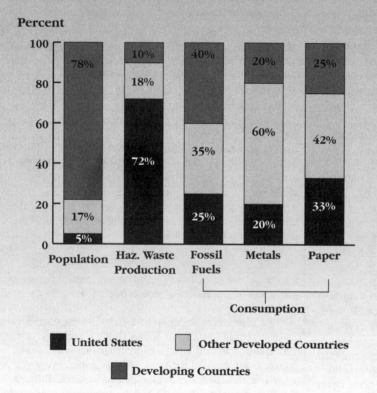

Share of Population, Waste Production and Resource Consumption

Sources: "New Perspectives on Population: Lessons from Cairo," Population Bulletin, March 1995; Natural Resources Defense Council

the Rhine River and has greatly improved air quality. Mankind is capable of creative solutions."

Even more controversial is the link between population growth and global warming. Consumption of coal, oil and natural gas has been implicated in the gradual heating of the atmosphere that scientists fear will cause melting of polar ice caps, rising water levels and flooding of crowded coastal areas. Warming may also speed desertification and the spread of malaria and other insect-borne diseases. Although carbon-fuel consumption can be expected to continue to rise with economic development, many scientists predict that the growth in human population alone will increase demand for these fuels until cheap alternatives are developed.

But optimists in the population debate firmly reject this argument. "The odd suggestion that babies are somehow responsible for pollution tends to be the mindset of people who blame problems on the sheer number of people who exist," says Mosher, reflecting the view of many critics of the Kyoto Protocol, which was endorsed last December by the United States and 167 other countries. "But this view is wrong and was also rejected at Kyoto.

When the developed countries asked developing countries to further decrease their total fertility rates as part of the treaty, they were rejected outright, and rightly so. There is no necessary connection between the number of children being born and the level of carbon dioxide in the air."

Critics also charge that the global-warming theory rests on shaky scientific evidence. Consequently, they oppose U.S. participation in the treaty, which they say would cost more than 3 million jobs as businesses curb production to comply with its requirement to cut carbon emissions. The Clinton administration, which strongly supports the treaty, faces an uphill battle in the

China, for example, which uses coal for industry, as well as for heating and cooking, has among the worst air pollution in the world. Taiyuan, in northern China, has seven times as much particulate matter as Los Angeles, by far the most polluted city in the United States. Beijing and other Chinese cities are also blanketed by pollutants. [28]

Optimists in the population debate reject the notion that population growth

by itself causes environmental damage. "I don't think there is a direct link between population and the environment," says the Population Research Institute's Mosher, who blames misguided government policies. "You can create environmental problems in a lightly populated country by failing to control pollution, just as you can have a very clean environment in a densely populated country, such as Germany, which is cleaning up

Senate, which must ratify it by a two-thirds majority before it will take effect in the United States. [29] ■

OUTLOOK

Grain Crunch?

For the past several decades, the Green Revolution has largely discredited the Malthusian prediction of imminent collapse of the global food supplies needed to feed a rapidly expanding population. But the environmental degradation that has continued apace during that time may have laid the groundwork for just such a calamity in the not too distant future. According to Worldwatch, rapid industrialization in China is reducing the supply of water farmers use to irrigate their grain crops. Because 70 percent of the grain consumed by China's 1.2 billion inhabitants comes from irrigated land, the diversion of water for industrial use may soon force the country, now largely self-sufficient, to start importing grain.

Because of its sheer size, China would quickly overwhelm the global supply of grain, driving up prices and forcing less affluent grain-importing countries, such as those of sub-Saharan Africa, out of the market. The result, Worldwatch warns, would be widespread famine. "For the 1.3 billion of the world's people who live on $1 a day or less, higher grain prices could quickly become life threatening," write Brown and Halweil. [30]

Brown has made similarly dire predictions in the past that have proved wrong, drawing the scorn of optimists in the Malthusian debate. But now, the situation he describes is sufficiently alarming to have drawn the attention of the U.S. National Intelligence Council, which calls

for greater U.S.-China cooperation in agricultural production and technology. Brown and Halweil endorse the idea.

"If the world's two leading food producers can work closely together to protect their agricultural resource bases, while the world works to stabilize population," they write, "it will benefit not only each of those countries, but the rest of the world as well." [31]

Although the implications of China's water shortage are especially alarming, it is hardly the only country faced with competing demands on dwindling water supplies. According to Population Action International, some 80 percent of the world's population lives in countries facing problems with fresh water supplies. Population growth will lead to more widespread water shortages, the group predicts, heightening the risk of conflict over water supplies in areas such as the Tigris-Euphrates basin, where water rights are already a source of tension among Iraq, Syria and Turkey. [32]

Meanwhile, the CGIAR continues trying to ward off famine with further improvements in crop yields as well as fish and meat production. In an effort to halve the number of undernourished people on Earth to 400 million by 2015 — the goal set by the World Food Summit in November 1996 — the international research organization is studying the potential of bioengineering as the next weapon in its arsenal to continue the Green Revolution into the next century. [33]

Consumption to Blame?

Today's consumer society has added a new twist to the warning issued by Malthus about inadequate food supplies. Latter-day Malthusians warn that the economic systems prevalent in most of the world today can only accelerate that end by encouraging consumption of resources without regard to its impact on the environment. In the United States, advertise-

ments promise consumers that buying an endless array of products will bring greater happiness. With the end of the Cold War and the demise of the Soviet Union, the Western model of economic life is being pursued throughout most of the world.

Some experts say the combination of population growth and rising consumption do not threaten Earth's carrying capacity. "The long-term trend for inflation-adjusted prices of commodities has been going down, not up," Eberstadt says. "This suggests to me that natural resources are less scarce today than they were when there was less demand. In any case, we're heading toward a knowledge-and-service economy, so the direction of our development is less resource-intensive and more reliant on human skills. That gives me hope that we may be able to manage our resource demands in the future."

But many environmentalists say Malthus' nightmare will become reality that much sooner if the rest of the world adopts the consumption-based model developed in North America and Western Europe. In their view, economic growth has become a fundamental, but flawed, barometer of well-being. "Every news report, every business forecast assumes that growth is good and that more growth is better," says attorney John F. Rohe, author of the 1997 book *A Bicentennial Malthusian Essay*. "But the issue is not how we grow. It's how we can develop sustainably." *(See At Issue, p. 159)*

In this view, current efforts to protect the environment fall far short of the changes that are required to ensure sustainability. "People wonder whether the economy can continue to grow if we stop excessive consumption of oil and polluting goods," Halweil says. "They say we can shift to solar energy, fuel cells and biodegradable plastics. But the answer isn't having a hybrid-fuel car in everyone's garage. It's having fewer people driving and more taking public transportation."

The only answer to having more people on the planet, Halweil says, is to drastically cut consumption. "We are addicted to consumption, and we have to be slowly weaned off it," he says. "I don't know what it will look like, but the economic system will have to be different if the environment is to be protected." ∎

Notes

[1] Thomas Robert Malthus, *An Essay on the Principle of Population* (1798), cited in Philip Appleman, ed., *An Essay on the Principle of Population* (1976), p. 56. For background, see "World Hunger," *The CQ Researcher*, Oct. 25, 1991, pp. 801-824.

[2] See "Population Growth," *The CQ Researcher*, July 16, 1993, pp. 601-624.

[3] Kaplan spoke at "Malthus Revisited," a conference held May 8-9, 1998, by the Warrenton, Va.-based Biocentric Institute, which studies ways to enhance the quality of life for all peoples.

[4] See Population Action International, *Conserving Land: Population and Sustainable Food Production*, April 1995.

[5] Pimentel spoke at the May conference on Malthus (see above).

[6] See "International Population Assistance," *Congressional Digest*, April 1997.

[7] See "What Birth Dearth? Why World Population Is Still Growing," *Population Action International Fact Sheet*, 1998.

[8] See "Clinton Uncaps Veto Pen As State Department Bill Clears," *CQ Weekly*, May 2, 1998, pp. 1167-1168.

[9] See James P. Smith and Barry Edmonston, eds., *The New Americans* (1997), p. 95.

[10] Quoted in William Branigin, "Sierra Club Votes for Neutrality on Immigration," *The Washington Post*, April 26, 1997.

[11] President's Council on Sustainable Development, "Task Force Report on Population and Consumption," 1996, p. iv.

[12] Condorcet's last work was *Esquisse d'un tableau historique des progrès de l'esprit humain.*

[13] Quoted in Gertrude Himmelfarb, "The Ghost of Parson Malthus," *Times Literary Supplement* (London), Jan. 23, 1998.

[14] Malthus, *op. cit.*, p. 56.

[15] *Ibid*, p. 19-20.

---

[16] For more information on Malthus and his time, see David Price, "Of Population and False Hopes: Malthus and His Legacy," *Population and Environment*, January 1998, pp. 205-219. See also Keith Stewart Thomson, "1798: Darwin and Malthus," *American Scientist*, May-June 1998, pp. 226-229.

[17] Paul R. and Anne H. Ehrlich, *Population Resources Environment* (1972), quoted in Appleman, *op. cit.*, p. 240.

[18] Lester R. Brown, *In the Human Interest* (1974), quoted in Appleman, *op. cit.*, p. 243.

[19] See Julian Simon, *The Ultimate Resource* (1981).

[20] See "Environmental Scares: Plenty of Gloom," *The Economist*, Dec. 20, 1997, p. 20.

[21] David Pimentel and Marcia Pimentel, "The Demographic and Environmental Consequences of the Green Revolution," *The Carrying Capacity Briefing Book* (1996), p. XII-101.

[22] *Ibid.*, p. XII-97.

[23] Population Reference Bureau, *1998 World Population Data Sheet*, May 1998.

[24] See Michael Specter, "Population Implosion Worries a Graying Europe," *The New York Times*, July 10, 1998, p. A1.

[25] Norman Myers, "Environmental Refugees," *Population and Environment*, November 1997, pp. 175-176.

[26] See William K. Stevens, "One in Every 8 Plant Species Is Imperiled, a Survey Finds," *The New York Times*, April 9, 1998.

[27] See "The Sea," *The Economist*, May 23, 1998, Survey section, pp. 1-18.

[28] See Elisabeth Rosenthal, "China Officially Lifts Filter on Staggering Pollution Data," *The New York Times*, June 14, 1998.

[29] See "Fresh Focus on Global Warming Does Not Dispel Doubts About Kyoto Treaty's Future," *CQ Weekly*, June 6, 1998, pp. 1537-1538.

[30] Lester Brown and Brian Halweil, "China's Water Shortage Could Shake World Food Security," *Worldwatch*, July/August 1998, p. 10.

[31] *Ibid.*, p. 18.

[32] See Tom Gardner-Outlaw and Robert Engelman, "Sustaining Water, Easing Scarcity: A Second Update," *Population Action International*, Dec. 15, 1997.

[33] See Consultative Group on International Agricultural Research, "Nourishing the Future through Scientific Excellence," Annual Report 1997.

Bibliography

Selected Sources Used

Books

Appleman, Philip, ed., *An Essay on the Principle of Population: Thomas Robert Malthus*, W.W. Norton, 1976.

This volume contains not only the writings of Malthus and his contemporaries but also those of 20th-century thinkers who joined the debate over Earth's ability to support a rapidly growing population in the 1970s.

Brown, Lester R., Michael Renner and Christopher Flavin, *Vital Signs 1998: The Environmental Trends That Are Shaping Our Future*, W.W. Norton, 1998.

Among the trends featured are population growth and grain yields, two essential ingredients in the Malthusian prediction of famine. Though population growth has slowed, it continues, and further increases in grain yields may be hampered by dwindling water supplies.

Easterbrook, Gregg, *A Moment on the Earth: The Coming Age of Environmental Optimism*, Penguin Books, 1995.

The author claims that prevailing concerns over a number of environmental issues are overstated. The recent slowing of population growth, he writes, marks the beginning of an era when man's impact on the environment will be insignificant: "Human overpopulation, which environmental orthodoxy today depicts as a menace of unimaginable horror, will be seen by nature as a minor passing fad."

Rohe, John F., *A Bicentennial Malthusian Essay: Conservation, Population and the Indifference to Limits*, Rhodes & Easton, 1997.

The author attributes many of today's problems, from famine to road rage, to the same overpopulation that concerned Malthus 200 years ago. Compounding the problem, he writes, is the quest for economic growth regardless of its impact on natural resources.

Articles

Ashford, Lori S., "New Perspectives on Population: Lessons from Cairo," *Population Bulletin*, March 1995.

The International Conference on Population and Development, held in September 1994 in Cairo, Egypt, produced a list of goals for family-planning programs. This article presents an overview of these programs around the world and identifies policies that have had the most success in reducing population growth.

Brown, Lester R., and Brian Halweil, "China's Water Shortage Could Shake World Food Security," *Worldwatch*, July/August 1998, pp. 10-18.

Rapid industrialization and population growth are depleting China's water supplies so fast that the country's farmers may soon be unable to meet domestic food needs. If China is forced to buy its grain, global grain prices will rise, perhaps beyond the means of poorer developing countries that depend on imports to meet their food needs.

Hertsgaard, Mark, "Our Real China Problem," *The Atlantic*, November 1997, pp. 97-114.

During a trip through rural China, the author found that the country's infamous one-child policy has been largely abandoned and that continuing population growth is compounding China's serious environmental pollution.

Mann, Charles C., "Reseeding the Green Revolution," *Science*, Aug. 22, 1997, pp. 1038-1043.

The Green Revolution prevented widespread famine in recent decades, but many scientists worry that the potential for increasing crop yields is reaching its limit. Bioengineering and other breakthroughs may provide the tools to achieve another major leap in agricultural productivity.

Price, David, "Of Population and False Hopes: Malthus and His Legacy," *Population and Environment*, January 1998, pp. 205-219.

The author, an anthropologist at Cornell University, presents an excellent overview of the life and times of Thomas Robert Malthus on the bicentennial of his essay on population and the relevance of his ideas to modern concerns about Earth's carrying capacity.

Smail, J. Kenneth, "Beyond Population Stablization: The Case for Dramatically Reducing Global Human Numbers," *Politics and the Life Sciences*, September 1997.

A Kenyon College anthropology professor opens a roundtable presentation by 17 population experts who support greater efforts to curb population growth.

Reports and Studies

Gardner-Outlaw, Tom, and Robert Engelman, Sustaining Water, Easing Scarcity: A Second Update, Population Action International, 1997.

Water supplies are threatened in many parts of the world by rising population. By 2050, the authors report, at least one person in four is likely to live in countries that suffer chronic or recurring water shortages.

Population Reference Bureau, *World Population Data Sheet: Demographic Data and Estimates for the Countries and Regions of the World*, 1998.

This pamphlet presents a country-by-country assessment of population, fertility rates, life expectancy and other statistics that help demographers forecast future population growth trends.

10 Saving the Rain Forests

DAVID HOSANSKY

In Indonesia, desperate fishermen burn lush forests to trap turtles, which they sell for food in Hong Kong and other Asian ports. In Ivory Coast, impoverished peasants invade state-owned nature preserves, burning and cutting trees to carve out small farms. In Brazil, cash-strapped landowners hack away at the last remnants of the Atlantic rain forest to create pasture and cropland.

The world's last rain forests are vanishing. Despite a determined international campaign waged for years by an array of conservation and government organizations, the irresistible forces of population growth and rural poverty are consuming the lush tropics as never before.

The crisis has intensified in recent years, with unprecedented fires destroying millions of pristine acres in Latin America and Asia and economic crises spurring governments to scrap environmental protections and open up more forests to development. And now, portending more destruction, Asian logging firms are beginning operations in Latin America, and U.S. oil companies are surveying the Amazon.

"All indications are that the extent and rate of loss are increasing," says Bruce J. Cabarle, director of the World Wildlife Fund's global forest program. "There may be positive indications in terms of the political dialogue, but in terms of action on the ground, we haven't seen that yet."

Scientists fear that the loss of the forests will have major worldwide consequences, including global climate change and the massive extinction of plant and animal species. In tropical areas, floods and droughts are having catastrophic effects where trees no longer protect the soil. In Nicaragua, the entire side of a de-

From *The CQ Researcher,*
June 11, 1999.

nuded volcano collapsed during Hurricane Mitch in 1998, burying 2,000 subsistence farmers in an avalanche of mud. [1]

Already, more than half of the forested belt around the tropics — once about 5.5 million square miles — has been lost. [2] Pristine tropical forests in West Africa, Madagascar, the Philippines and Brazil have been reduced to less than 10 percent of their natural areas. India has virtually no original forests remaining. [3]

Moreover, scientists estimate that at least 34 million acres of tropical forests are still being cleared yearly due to the insatiable global demand for land, timber, crops and such valuable commodities as gold and oil; millions more acres are partially logged. [4]

In the early 1990s, amid much publicity about the need to save the rain forests, the pace of deforestation appeared to slow somewhat. [5] But then came massive forest fires in 1997 and '98 and an economic crisis that spurred indebted individuals and governments to strip the forests anew. In Indonesia, for example, the government began clearing millions of acres for oil-palm plantations, and village traders showed up in the

capital, Jakarta, selling rare monkeys in tiny cages for pets. Brazil slashed funds for rain forest preservation as part of a fiscal-austerity package to win overseas loans.

"It's going to take a lot to slow the current rate of destruction," says Randy Curtis, director of conservation finance and policy at The Nature Conservancy's Latin American/Caribbean division. But, he adds, "We don't have any choice, so we just have to keep churning forward."

Deforestation is hardly unique to the tropics. For thousands of years, human progress in Europe and other temperate regions has gone hand-in-hand with clearing land. But the uniqueness of tropical ecosystems suggests that destroying rain forests may have tragic consequences.

Rain forests play a vital role in regulating water flow and stabilizing soil. Take away the trees, which act as sponges, and the land is vulnerable to flooding and erosion in the wetter months, and to drought in the dry season.

Perhaps nowhere have the effects of tree-cutting been as severe as in Haiti, a once lush country that loses an estimated 36 million tons of topsoil each year and is slowly turning into a desert. Caught in a maelstrom of economic and political turmoil, Haiti may portend the future for other severely deforested countries from the Philippines to El Salvador. [6]

To make matters worse, rain forest soil generally is too poor to grow crops for more than a few years, forcing farmers to constantly clear new land — until no more is left. Ivory Coast, which has cleared most of its forests for cocoa and coffee plantations, faces imminent economic disaster because the soil is expected to give out. "The situation is dramatic," said Jean-Michel Pavy, a World Bank biodiversity expert. "We are talking about a matter of years." [7]

The toll has been greatest on the indigenous people who have inhabited the forests for hundreds or even thousands of years. Many tribes have been wiped out entirely because of disease, battles with settlers and the loss of their traditional homelands.

But the effects of deforestation are also reaching the United States and other wealthy nations. Since rain forests are thought to harbor about half the world's species of plants and animals, researchers worry that destruction of the globe's genetic library will hamstring efforts to create new medicines and more productive crops.

In addition, the forests act as "carbon sinks," absorbing some of the excess carbon that is pumped into the atmosphere by industry. Thus, clearing the rain forests is likely to aggravate global warming, possibly causing coastal flooding and unpredictable weather patterns.

"We cannot escape the effects of global climate change, biodiversity loss and unsustainable resource depletion," the U.S. Agency for International Development (AID) warns. "The quality of life for future generations of Americans will in no small measure be determined by the success or failure of our common stewardship of the planet's resources." [8]

On the surface, the causes of deforestation appear fairly straightforward. Logging companies, including multinational firms with little interest in the long-term health of the forests, strip the forests of mahogany and other valuable trees. Local farmers penetrate the forests on logging roads, while plantation owners clear swaths of forest for cocoa, coffee and other crops. Cattle ranchers use the land for pasture.

"The pattern in Latin America is well-established," said Anthony Coates, deputy director of the Smithsonian Institution's Tropical Research Institute in Panama. "A road goes in, the loggers and farmers move in, they slash and burn and then move on to repeat the process." [9]

In addition, miners are swarming to the Amazon and other rain forests in search of gold and other minerals, and oil companies increasingly are exploring the vast reserves beneath Latin America's forests.

But more complex factors are also at work in developing countries, including overpopulation, poverty, inequitable land distribution, corrupt or inefficient government agencies and burgeoning debt. The destruction is being driven both by impoverished people who exploit forest resources simply to survive, and by corporations and wealthy planters seeking to meet the worldwide demand for lumber, crops and minerals.

Not surprisingly, straightforward conservation strategies have failed to stem the tide. Protected preserves, for example, are often invaded by slash-and-burn farmers who view them as unnecessary playgrounds for the rich. "I have 10 children and we must eat," said Sep Djekoule, an Ivory Coast farmer. "There is no way they can keep me away from my livelihood." [10]

Efforts by affluent nations to protect the forests often have met with failure. Throughout the decade, a World Bank policy against giving loans for logging projects in virgin forests failed to stop companies from finding other funding sources. A 1998 initiative by the Group of Seven leading industrialized nations, or G-7, to fund 90 percent of a $250 million rain forest conservation project in Brazil had a rocky start when the government, in the midst of a fiscal austerity program, temporarily turned down the money. [11]

"You're dealing with places with a lot of human misery, a lot of economic problems," says Mark Plotkin, president of the Amazon Conservation Team, in Arlington, Va.

Undaunted, environmental organizations are working with government agencies on a three-pronged offensive to save as least a portion of the forests. Their main tactic is to place land in protected preserves that are overseen by local conservation organizations or government agencies. About 5 percent of Earth's rain forests currently are off-limits to development, but biologists believe that figure must be at least doubled if a substantial portion of rain forest animals and plants are to be saved from extinction. In 1998, Conservation International scored a major success in South America when it persuaded Suriname to put one-tenth of its area off-limits to development. [12]

Second, environmentalists want to increase the economic value of rain forests so there will be more profit from leaving them alone than destroying them. They have helped turn several rain forest preserves into ecotourism destinations. They are persuading tropical countries to subsidize forested states that supply drinking water to cities, thus encouraging them to preserve the forests, which soak up precious water. They also are working with power companies in the United States and other industrialized countries that are beginning to contribute money to forest preservation efforts aimed at slowing down global warming.

Third, environmentalists are advising industries how to minimize the impact of development. Loggers, for example, are encouraged to avoid denuding steep hillsides by cutting only selected trees. And coffee growers are urged to grow coffee under the rain forests' natural canopy, instead of clearing forests to create coffee plantations. Increasingly, consumers are becoming interested in "rain forest-friendly" products.

But these are imperfect strategies. Developing countries frequently lack either the desire or the means to protect parks from poaching or legal development. Moreover, making a profit from an intact forest is so elusive that some economists believe it is a losing battle. And it remains unclear whether logging and other such activities can be conducted without badly damaging the forest.

Still, environmentalists are cheered by the growing worldwide concern over deforestation. Brazil, the Philippines and other nations have recently imposed partial or total bans on logging old-growth forests The World Bank committed itself to helping establish 125 million acres of forest preserves and 500 million acres of "sustainable" forestry projects. And in a widely publicized announcement in 1998, Brazilian President Fernando Henrique Cardoso promised to put 10 percent of the country's rain forests — 240,000 square miles — into protected preserves. [13]

Even though it is not clear how much more parks and laws will help — after all, 70 percent of tropical forest logging in Brazil already is done illegally — the United Nations Food and Agriculture Organization predicts the situation will improve. "There is a global commitment to improving the management of forests," it says in a 1999 report. [14]

As efforts intensify to save the rain forests, conservationists and officials must confront these questions:

Are the rain forests doomed?

The Rev. Gerald Hanlon, a priest in Peru, recently described the environmental destruction around him — a new highway slashed through a once pristine ecosystem, trees cut down to fire a brick kiln, a lake polluted by a timber mill. Doubtful of

Threatened Frontier Forests of South America

Large-scale resettlement and agricultural and resource development projects claimed much of the 645,000 square kilometers of forest lost in South America between 1980 and 1990. However, the continent still retains vast areas of frontier forest, or large tracts of original forest cover. Logging currently is the main threat to the continent's tropical and temperate frontier forests.

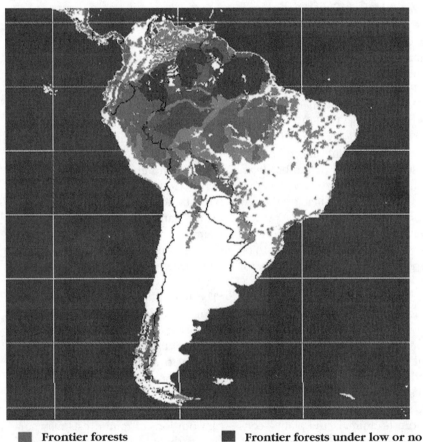

■ **Frontier forests under medium or high threat**

■ **Frontier forests unassessed for threat**

■ **Frontier forests under low or no threat**

■ **Non-frontier forests**

Source: World Resources Institute, May 1999

the Amazon's survival, Hanlon pledged to leave a small piece of forest near his own house untouched. "If I live to a great age and all this passes into history," he wrote, "at least I shall be able to say that I once saw the rain forest." [15]

Many scientists share Hanlon's pessimism. The world's population — now about 6 billion — is growing yearly by about 90 million people. The unprecedented growth subjects the forests to hordes of slash-and-burn farmers and subsistence hunters, swelling cities and creating ever-increasing demand worldwide for lumber, palm oil, coffee and other tropical products. At the current rate of destruction, the forests have perhaps 50 years left, after which there may be just a few remnants left in national parks and steep, inaccessible regions. [16] Fire, which has devastated forests in recent years, may destroy most of the remaining tropical tracts even sooner, taking with it millions of species of plants and animals, many still undiscovered.

"We're destroying our biodiversity," said Garo Batmanian, head of the Brazilian office of the World Wildlife Fund. "Humanity is becoming poorer." [17]

Underscoring the grim outlook, a joint European research group, Tropical Ecosystem Environment Observations by Satellites (TREES), concluded in 1998 that conservationists should consider abandoning efforts to save "hot spots" — areas rich in biodiversity that are threatened by development — and focus instead on the few remaining areas that are not yet facing encroachment. "The pressures to remove the forests are too great to be stopped," said study coordinator Frederic Achard. [18]

Even the last great areas of virgin rain forest, including large tracts in the Amazon and Congo, are coming under growing pressure by multinational logging companies that have already cleared most of the original forests in Southeast Asia.

To save a significant portion of the rain forests' animals and plants, conservationists are pressing developing countries to put at least 10 percent of the remaining forests in protected preserves. "What makes the most sense is to first protect what's left," says Plotkin of the Amazon Conservation Team.

Even if they meet their 10 percent goal, scientists predict an extraordinary wave of extinctions. That's because the destruction of just 50 percent of a forest tends to cause the immediate loss of 10 percent of its species and the gradual extinction of countless additional plants and animals. [19] Many undiscovered species are thought to have already disappeared, and such familiar rain forest creatures as orangutans are becoming perilously rare.

But figuring out the rate of extinction when only 10 percent of a rain forest is saved may be an irrelevant exercise. At present, just 5 percent of the forests are designated as protected, and the pace of creating new parks in the tropics has diminished. Some experts conclude that, in the end, no more than about 7 percent of Earth's rain forests will be protected unless there are major policy changes. [20]

Even more problematic, many existing forest preserves are "paper parks" that are virtually unguarded. Governments lack the resources to patrol them, and impoverished residents view them as unreasonable barriers to development. In "protected" lands in Southeast Asia, for example, poachers hunt the few remaining rhinoceroses for their horns and deplete the rivers by fishing with dynamite, poison and electric shocks. "The final bulwark erected to shield tropical nature from extinction is collapsing," warned a 1997 study. [21]

Parks aside, conservationists are rushing to minimize the effects that logging, oil extraction and other activities would have on the surviving rain forests. They believe that significant portions of rain forests may survive with only moderate damage if companies are willing to use such techniques as leaving intact strips of trees along rivers and on hillsides and transporting mining equipment by helicopter instead of building roads. In addition, the conservationists are trying to promote more environmentally benign uses of the rain forests.

"You want to preserve both areas that are very rich in species and being cleared very rapidly, and also save intact areas," says Dirk Bryant, a senior associate with the World Resources Institute. "That way, you can maximize biodiversity."

Conservation organizations are scoring some notable victories. Mobil Oil Corp., for example, consulted with Conservation International when conducting preliminary oil explorations in a biologically rich section of the Peruvian Amazon without substantially damaging the environment. The company cleared minimal forest areas, used small underground seismic charges instead of drilling exploratory wells and took steps to prevent watershed contamination.

Due to the growing awareness worldwide about the importance of biodiversity, environmentalists say they may yet be able to preserve significant portions of the rain forest. "Overall, I am very optimistic," said Glenn Prickett, vice president of corporate partnerships for Conservation International. "I think you have a new generation of leaders who recognize the environmental problems and the very valuable assets they have in these untouched areas."

But every environmental victory seems to be accompanied by a setback. A new policy in China, for example, to ban most logging is merely creating more demand for Indonesian lumber. A policy initiative in Brazil to put 10 percent of the rain forests into preserves has been thrown into doubt by the need for budget cuts.

Even though saving the rain forests may be in the long-term interest of humanity, it has little short-term economic appeal to impoverished countries that need the forests to sustain their swelling populations. Duke University biologist John Terborgh warns that, despite the best efforts of conservation-minded leaders, "There are going to be a few successes and more than a few failures."

Can people profit from rain forests without destroying them?

In a landmark 1989 article, Yale

University economist Robert Mendelsohn and two fellow researchers advanced the bold claim that more money could be made by collecting plants in the rain forests than by destroying them. They demonstrated that fruits, nuts, latex and wild chocolate on a 2.5-acre plot in the Peruvian Amazon could produce a net profit of $422 and, over time, generate two to three times the per-acre return earned by cattle ranchers. [22]

The article helped spark a new school of thought among environmentalists: The best way to save the rain forests was to demonstrate the potential profits of leaving them intact. As Harvard University biologist Edward O. Wilson wrote in his 1992 book, *The Diversity of Life*: "The race is on to develop methods to draw more income from the wild lands without killing them, and so to give the invisible hand of free-market economics a green thumb." [23]

Unfortunately, conservationists early in the decade who pushed the benign harvesting of natural forest products found themselves facing two problems: Few rain forests contain products of great economic value. And second, when there are valuable products, the harvesting tends to be so intense that it degrades the environment. The Peruvian example seems to be an exception — profitable in part because the land studied was along a river that provided a natural transportation route.

"If something is worth doing at a fairly low intensity of operation," says economist David Simpson, a fellow at Resources for the Future, "it's even more worth doing at a high intensity of operation, which would definitely cause environmental impacts."

Consider some of the rain forests' most well-known agricultural products. Coffee, which grows wild under the rain forest canopy, is now grown more profitably on cleared plantations. Rubber, which continues to be tapped from trees in the Amazon by workers scratching out a subsistence living, is more economically grown on Asian plantations or produced synthetically. Trees can be harvested without widespread damage to the environment, but much higher prof-

The Nature Conservancy is working with local environmental organizations to protect and manage more than a million acres in Ecuador's vast Condor Bioreserve.

its result when less environmental care is taken.

The very diversity of the rain forests is an economic barrier, since the one species that produces a desirable fruit or other product is often mixed in with dozens or hundreds of other plant species. "Rather than grabbing some nuts from one tree and going off 100 yards and finding the next tree, people just line them up in a field," says Ohio State University agricultural economist Douglas Southgate.

To be sure, there are niches for non-forest timber products. In Peru, for example, local people sell seeds

from native trees to organizations planning reforestation projects. But such activities tend to generate either just enough revenue to preserve a relatively small section of land or so much revenue that crowds of harvesters clear away the non-profitable plants, gradually altering the ecosystem. "What people tend to do is sort of weed out the other things, so you end up with something like an orchard," Southgate says

Refusing to be deterred, however, conservationists in recent years have come up with more innovative and promising incentives to preserve rain forests. One of the most touted is "carbon sequestration," which takes advantage of the ability of forests to store vast amounts of carbon dioxide and reduce the effects of global warming. Companies in industrialized countries, hoping to earn carbon "credits" to offset their greenhouse gas emissions, pay developing countries to set aside tracts of forest. In one of the most notable instances, an agreement between U.S.-based energy companies, environmental groups and government officials led to the protection of about 1.5 million acres in Bolivia, including the expansion of the spectacular Noel Kempff Mercado National Park.

Drinking water also is emerging as a possible source for profits. Rain forests act as natural sponges, storing groundwater that is needed by growing cities in developing countries. Since destroying forests for plantations or industrial operations would mean losing the water, governments are experimenting with different ways of encouraging the preservation of watershed areas. In Brazil, for ex-

Most Original Forests Have Disappeared

Only about one-fifth of the world's original forest cover remains in large, relatively undisturbed tracts, or frontier forests.

Region	Original Forest (000 KM²)	Total Remaining Forest (Frontier and Non-Frontier Forest) (000 KM²)	Total Frontier Forest (000 KM²)	Frontier Forest as a Percentage of Total Original Forest
Africa	6,799	2,302	527	8%
Asia	15,132	4,275	844	6%
Central America	1,779	970	172	10%
North America	10,877	8,483	3,737	34%
South America	9,736	6,800	4,439	46%
Europe	4,690	1,521	14	0.3%
Russia	11,759	8,083	3,448	29%
Oceania*	1,431	929	319	22%
World	**62,203**	**33,363**	**13,500**	**22%**

* Oceania consists of Papua New Guinea, Australia and New Zealand

Source: "The Last Frontier Forests," World Resources Institute, 1997

ample, 5 percent of the sales tax collection in Parana is earmarked for municipalities with sources of drinking water, thereby rewarding them for keeping the water-producing areas uncontaminated. [24]

Another economic incentive is using rain forest plants for pharmaceutical purposes. More than half the prescription drugs used in the United States are derived from natural sources, and researchers believe that clues to curing such diseases as cancer and AIDS may be found in the rain forests. Several U.S. pharmaceutical companies are investing millions of dollars in rain forest research, even working with local officials to preserve natural areas. (*See story, p. 171.*)

In recent years, ecotourism also has become an incentive to preserving rain forests. (*See story, p. 172.*) Travelers who want to visit undisturbed places helped preserve portions of the African savanna, and

conservationists believe the same approach can work for rain forests. Costa Rica, for example, has preserved about 25 percent of its land and is becoming an increasingly popular destination for tourists seeking pristine beaches and forests.

However, no economic incentives are surefire barriers to deforestation, and some even have environmental drawbacks. Carbon sequestration, for example, may simply encourage large companies to keep polluting. "It's a risky strategy," says the World Wildlife Fund's Cabarle. "There's no way you can create enough forest to even begin to compensate for the amount of carbon we're pumping out."

Moreover, recent economic studies indicate that so-called bioprospecting by pharmaceutical companies pays too little economic return in this age of synthetically produced drugs to justify setting aside huge sections of virgin forest. And

ecotourism sometimes spawns environmentally damaging development while doing little to help the lot of impoverished local communities. [25]

The situation is frustrating for scientists who say rain forests contain a wealth of riches that could enhance everyday life. Harvard's Wilson cites hundreds of tropical fruits, grains and tubers that are savored by local people but not marketed worldwide. And Plotkin has devoted his life to working with traditional medicine men, or shamans, uncovering numerous promising remedies, such as a painkiller from the skin of a poison-dart frog.

Despite the mixed marketing results, many conservationists still believe that economics is the key to saving the rain forests. "In the final analysis," Plotkin says, "they are going to have to pay for themselves."

Are wealthy nations contributing to tropical deforestation?

Visiting Brazil in 1997, President Clinton announced that the United States would contribute $10 million to a program to protect the rain forests. But the following year, Brazilian officials cut the program as part of a budget austerity deal, worked out with U.S. approval, to get a much-needed $41.5 billion loan package from the International Monetary Fund. [26]

Stephan Schwartzman of the Environmental Defense Fund denounced

Bioprospecting Has Yet to Strike It Rich

With its pink, five-petaled flowers, the rosy periwinkle of Madagascar looks like just another pretty tropical plant. But it produces two alkaloids that are highly effective in treating children with lymphocytic leukemia and adults with Hodgkin's disease — two of the deadliest forms of cancer. [1]

The rosy periwinkle is just one of many plants that have been used for medicinal purposes. A recent study sponsored by the National Institutes of Health and other agencies found that 40 percent of the most commonly prescribed drugs were developed from natural sources. [2] These range from traditional painkillers such as aspirin to the potent anti-cancer drug Taxol, which is derived from the bark of the Pacific yew tree. This year, researchers are looking at Australian frog secretions that contain antibacterial properties and a compound from the bark of a Samoan tree that may help with AIDS treatments. In addition, scientists who have found evidence that the AIDS virus was originally contracted from chimpanzees in African forests believe the same forests hold the key to treating the disease.

There are doubtless far more cures waiting to be found in tropical rain forests and other natural places: Of the approximately 1.8 million species that have been catalogued on the planet, only a minute fraction have been closely examined for their medicinal value. And biologists believe that tens of millions more may yet be discovered — more than half of them in tropical rain forests. These species can yield leads for promising drugs, insecticides or other products because they produce highly complex molecules, such as plant toxins that repel insects.

"Certainly the destruction of the rain forests would jeopardize our future discoveries," says David G. Corley, a tropical-species researcher at Monsanto Corp. "Our future ability to bring innovative products to the market and meet human needs depends on biodiversity."

As recently as the early 1990s, environmentalists viewed the search for natural medicines, or bioprospecting, as perhaps the most promising incentive to stop deforestation. When pharmaceutical giant Merck & Co. struck a million-dollar deal with Costa Rica in 1991 to search for usable new species, it appeared at last that there was an economic reason, as well as a social imperative, to save the forests. Two years later, the National Institutes of Health and other government agencies launched a $12 million grants program to evaluate tropical species and work with indigenous people who use natural products for medicine.

Although these initiatives have developed promising research leads, they have yet to produce a single drug in the marketplace. Instead, like so many other conservation initiatives, bioprospecting is failing to live up to the early expectations, and some former advocates of the approach, such as Shaman Pharmaceuticals, now are pulling back.

One problem is economics. It is so rare to find an organic sample with important medicinal properties — an estimated one in 250,000 samples will lead directly to a commercial drug — and it takes so long to develop a product from such a sample — often 10-20 years — that many drug companies are reluctant to make large investments in the process. [3] Moreover, each square mile of protected tropical rain forest has so many unexamined plant and animal species that there is little economic incentive to set aside vast new regions.

Another problem is the divisive issue of who should profit from bioprospecting. Since developing countries contain a major portion of the world's biological resources, they want considerable compensation for their plants and animals. Finally, there is also a trend in the pharmaceutical industry toward synthetic compounds, which can be screened at a rate of close to 100,000 molecules a day to check for possible medicinal effects. [4]

Small wonder, then, that economists warn against relying on bioprospecting to save the rain forests. "To be sure, society as a whole, either now or in later years, might attach a very high value to the lives saved because specimens can be gathered in the wild," economist Douglas Southgate writes. [5] "But none of this has much of an impact in the marketplace."

More promising, some researchers say, is the use of tropical species for research into better food supplements or the development of more productive crops. Indeed, a wild species of Mexican maize, nearly extinct when examined in the 1970s, is being used to develop disease-resistant types of corn.

As for the health-care industry, the increasing emphasis on using new techniques should help develop drugs much more quickly. But scientists still believe that the natural world could give invaluable guidance when it comes to developing entire new classes of treatment. The problem, they warn, is that the rate of extinction is increasing just as they are developing more sophisticated techniques to study plants and animals for their medicinal values.

"The greatest tragedy," says Joshua Rosenthal, program director of biodiversity at the National Institutes of Health's Fogarty International Center, "is that there is so much we don't even know that we're losing."

---

[1] Edward O. Wilson, *The Diversity of Life* (1992), p. 283.

[2] Interview with Joshua Rosenthal, program director of biodiversity at the National Institutes of Health's Fogarty International Center.

[3] Janet N. Abramovitz, "The Complex Realities of Sharing Genetic Assets," *Nature*, April 9, 1998.

[4] "Ethnobotany: Shaman Loses Its Magic," *The Economist*, Feb. 20, 1998, p. 77.

[5] Douglas Southgate, *Tropical Forest Conservation* (1998).

Ecotourism Offers Exotic Travel and Hope

The opportunities appear limitless: hiking in Costa Rica, birdwatching in the Amazon, canoeing down a remote African river or just relaxing in a spacious tent cabin under the rain forest canopy. For countless nature-starved travelers, such activities have an irresistible appeal.

Ecotourism is booming. Exact statistics are hard to come by, but ecotourism has become a multibillion-dollar industry in the United States, where most tour operators are based. Outdoor magazines are filled with ads for adventure and natural history trips to every continent, even Antarctica.

For environmentalists struggling to save the remaining rain forests, ecotourism offers salvation. Environmental activists tell stories of pristine patches of forest snatched at the last moment from chainsaws or bulldozers by investors seeking to make money while saving the environment. In Ghana, a tourism project that involved the creation of a visitor center, canopy walkway and trails at Kakum National Park was credited with generating 2,000 local jobs and saving much of the forest from logging and farming. It won the British Airways Tourism for Tomorrow awards. In Brazil's Atlantic region, climbers used bows and arrows to shoot ropes over 100-foot-high trees to build a canopy walkway, creating a park for tourists and ensuring an intact habitat for such rare species as the golden-faced lion tamarind.

"Ecotourism is probably one of the best options we have," says Oliver Hillel, who oversees ecotourism initiatives for Conservation International and helped set up the Brazilian reserve.

But far from being a reliable tool, ecotourism often has damaged the very thing it was designed to save. In a Mexican cloud forest reserve for monarch butterflies, for example, crowds of visitors litter the grounds and sometimes trample the butterflies. And in Ecuador's famed Galapagos Islands, tourism revenues have sparked a sevenfold population increase since 1960, spawning crime and pollution, along with a wave of invasive species such as wasps and fire ants that are threatening the local ecosystems. "Tourism is a curse in disguise," an island scientist told *National Geographic*. [1]

Indeed, there may be something of a contradiction in bringing people to natural areas in order to keep them undisturbed. Even in the United States, the Grand Canyon and other popular national parks are affected by millions of visitors and bumper-to-bumper traffic. In developing countries with little tourism experience, the impact can be devastating. Megan Epler Wood, president of the nonprofit Ecotourism Society in Bennington, Vt., cites areas of Nepal where all the trees were cut to provide firewood for trekkers, and unspoiled Costa Rican coastal areas that were bought by foreign developers. [2]

Still, Wood and other ecotourism advocates say the new industry on balance has been a positive force. A prime example is Costa Rica, which has set aside 25 percent of its land for preservation partly because of the huge influx of tourist dollars.

Seeking to curtail the negative impacts of travel in natural areas, the Ecotourism Society runs programs to

Ghana's Kakum National Park features a walkway above the forest canopy.

Lamb Studios/Conservation International

the agreement as "an insignificant step towards balancing Brazil's budget and a giant step toward the destruction of Brazil's ecological patrimony."

Even though Brazilian officials restored much of the funding early in 1999, the effectiveness of their environmental programs remained in question because of the ongoing need for budget cuts. "The [budget] crisis has made me even more pessimistic about the future of the environment here," said Paulo Paiva, a Brazilian environmental official. [27]

The episode in Brazil illustrates the complex role that the United States and other wealthy nations play in tropical deforestation. On one hand, government and corporate leaders contribute millions of dollars toward rain forest conservation. And concerned consumers pitch in by buying such products as Ben & Jerry's Rain Forest Crunch ice cream, which teach tour operators about environmentally friendly practices, such as working closely with local people, limiting the amount of travelers on each trip and using rustic facilities with such features as kerosene lighting instead of electricity. Wood believes that tour operators are becoming better environmental stewards. Travelers looking for environmentally aware tour operators can check the group's Web site, www.ecotourism.org.

"The capability of delivering sustainable development benefits in all these biologically diverse rain forests is great," Wood says. "It is one of the main choices for local people in the rain forests. They find it more compatible with the existing natural environment than other forms of development."

Still uncertain, however, is whether the tourism potential for rain forests compares with East Africa, where conservation efforts have been spurred by worldwide interest in seeing large animals in the wild. But trekking through the rain forest, where many creatures live hidden in the dense canopy, may be less alluring.

Some also wonder whether it is possible to provide facilities that satisfy the tastes of less intrepid tourists without degrading the fragile rain forest ecosystem. "There's not a whole lot of money to be made from a handful of people who are willing to rough it and willing to be eaten by wild animals or bitten by mosquitoes as opposed to staying in a luxury hotel," says David Simpson, an economist at Resources for the Future. Too often, he adds,

the formula for drawing tourists is: "Spray DDT and kill mosquitoes; get rid of predatory animals; build a road; build a nice hotel."

Conservation International's Hillel, however, says it is possible to strike a balance between the needs of travelers and the goal of environmental protection. Ideally, he says, an ecotourism destination is divided into different zones, including a developed area with hotels, an accessible natural area with trails and rustic accommodations and a mostly untouched wilderness area. Furthermore, at least 30 percent of the tourism revenues should go to local people, who can operate the facilities and work as guides.

Perhaps the biggest benefit of ecotourism is that it can motivate local people to protect their resources, Hillel says. He cites an example in Bolivia, where poor residents who used to scratch out a living from illegal logging and hunting are now making money from an ecotourism lodge and emerging as the most effective defenders of a nearby preserve.

"In this area, you can imagine the government doesn't carry a lot of weight," Hillel says. "But when the community says 'Don't do it,' this is something that the people really respect."

[1] Peter Benchley, "Galapagos: Paradise in Peril," *National Geographic*, April 1999, p. 30.

[2] Megan Epler Wood, "Monitoring the Global Challenge of Community Participation in Ecotourism: Case Studies and Lessons from Ecuador," The Nature Conservancy and U.S. AID, 1998.

uses Brazil nuts and cashews collected by indigenous people in the Amazon to promote non-destructive uses of the forest.

On the other hand, U.S. economic and trade policies sometimes indirectly accelerate the rate of deforestation. And consumers, who use prodigious quantities of lumber, oil, coffee and other products also spur more tropical development.

"A major force [behind deforestation] is the growing demand for forest products, stoked mainly by rising affluence," writes Janet N. Abramovitz, senior researcher at the Worldwatch Institute. "Today, less than one-fifth of the world's population living in Europe, the United States and Japan consumes over half the world's industrial timber and more than two-thirds of its paper," she wrote in a 1998 report. "To reduce their consumption and waste by even a small fraction

would ease pressures on forests significantly." [28]

To be fair, governments and conservation organizations in Europe and the United States spark the creation of new rain forest preserves every year and encourage loggers and industrial companies to minimize the environmental effects of their actions. And the governments of developing countries are hardly blameless, since they regularly sponsor initiatives to clear land for farming and housing.

But despite pledges on all sides to preserve the rain forests, economic policies by wealthy nations often cause more environmental damage. For example, the International Monetary Fund (IMF) — which is controlled primarily by the U.S. and other wealthy nations — regularly pressures debt-burdened countries to cut their budgets, including environmental programs, to qualify for loans. In

one recent case, Indonesia ended restrictions on foreign investment to clear forestlands as part of a $43 billion agreement with the IMF. [29]

"The IMF has the idea that they have the answer to any macroeconomic question, and the impacts on people and the environment are basically secondary," says environmentalist Marijke Torfs, who worked with Friends of the Earth and other organizations in 1998 to try to cut U.S. funding for the IMF.

The debt-burdened countries face further pressure to exploit their natural resources to pay off the debts. The four countries with the most rain forest — Indonesia, Congo, Brazil and Peru — owe the United States about $5 billion. The huge debt has spurred calls in Congress to forgive part of the debt to encourage rain forest preservation. In the meantime, Indonesia is burning millions of acres of untouched forest to create palm oil, rubber and coffee plantations to shore up the economy.

Consumer demand also fuels deforestation. In Latin America, so many trees have been felled to create coffee plantations that migratory songbirds are losing vital winter habitat. As consumers of fully one-third of the world's coffee, Americans contribute to such environmental degradation.

"When coffee is produced in a way that's not sustainable, it pollutes streams, it gets rid of forest cover, it increases erosion and reduces the amount of carbon dioxide the plants take out of the air," said Russell Greenberg, director of the Smithsonian Institution's Migratory Bird Center in Washington. [30]

The situation recalls an earlier wave of deforestation in the 1960s and '70s, when U.S. demand for beef contributed to the conversion of vast Central American rain forests into ranchlands. Now that large oil reserves are being found in the Amazon, oil imports by the United States, Europe and Japan may indirectly spur more deforestation.

Because the causes of deforestation are so complex, the United States sometimes can hardly avoid contributing to the problem. By propping up the price for domestically grown sugar, for example, Washington has undermined a main export market for the Philippines, causing tens of thousands of displaced Filipino sugarcane workers to stream to upland forests where they engage in slash-and-burn farming.

Sometimes, however, the U.S. role is more direct. Indigenous people in Ecuador sued Texaco Inc. over its part in oil operations that spilled as much as 19 billion gallons of toxic waste into the environment. The company, which is no longer operating in Ecuador, paid $40 million for an environmental cleanup but claims

much of the damage was caused by other companies. [31]

"Our life in the Amazon is being twisted and ruined," Humberto Piaguahe, leader of the 400-member Sequia tribe of Ecuador, told reporters. We are being done in by the contamination. We are disappearing." [32]

Conservationists looking for a silver lining believe they can harness the U.S. economy to help the environment, rather than create more harm. For example, the Audubon Society and the Migratory Bird Center believe consumers can encourage reforestation efforts by buying only shade-grown coffee. Since 1996, shade-grown coffee advocates have made uneven progress, partly because the beans tend to be more expensive.

But the advocates won a convert in 1999 when the Rainforest Café chain announced it would sell only shade-grown coffee and encouraged other restaurants to adopt the policy. "This is environmentally friendly," says company President Kenneth Brimmer. "It's part of what Rainforest stands for." ■

BACKGROUND

A Profusion of Life

The tropical rain forests that have spurred worldwide conservation efforts girdle the globe, mostly between the Tropic of Cancer and the Tropic of Capricorn. They are the richest ecosystems on Earth, believed to harbor at least one-half of the estimated 30 million or so organisms on the planet. Scientists still struggle to explain how rain forests regulate local weather patterns and spawn such a profusion of life. Along with the boreal forests of Canada and Russia, they are the largest remain-

ing intact forests, since most of the original temperate forests in the United States, Europe and Asia have been cleared.

Stepping into a tropical rain forest is a memorable experience. It is like walking into the semidarkness of a long tunnel, for the overhead canopy is so thick that it blocks most of the sunlight from hitting the forest floor. Tree trunks typically reach straight up 100 feet or higher before branching out, their interwoven limbs sheltering the forest from harsh drying winds and nurturing a consistently humid climate.

Scientists believe the rain forests began developing during a warm, moist period about 200 million years ago. The vegetation typically requires at least 80 inches of annual rainfall and thrives in equatorial regions where the average temperature is 75 degrees. [33] Powerful entities that create their own weather systems, the forests send up columns of white vapor after a rainfall that form brooding clouds, diffusing the sunlight and eventually releasing more rain on the trees.

When most people think of rain forests, what they have in mind are lowland forests. These are the most prolific of the world's plant communities, with profusions of hanging vines and creepers that wind around and sometimes connect giant evergreens that soar 200 feet or higher. In *Heart of Darkness*, Joseph Conrad described the foreboding sense of journeying on a river into such a rain forest in Africa: "Going up that river was like going back to beginnings, when vegetation rioted . . . and the trees were kings." [34]

The largest intact lowland forests are in the Amazon and Zaire river basins. But fragments of once extensive lowland forests still exist in Southeast Asia, Central America and West Africa.

At higher altitudes, tropical mountains are covered with montane rain

Chronology

1970s
The World Bank and regional development banks provide loans to developing countries for massive projects that result in widespread deforestation. Demand by U.S. consumers for beef spurs the "hamburgerization" of Central America.

1977
Amid mounting alarm over rain forest loss, an environmental movement in Kenya begins employing women to plant trees in deforested areas.

1980s
The pace of deforestation accelerates, with as much as 1.8 percent of the rain forests destroyed yearly.

1980
The "Global 2000" report, commissioned by President Jimmy Carter, identifies deforestation as the biggest environmental threat for the next two decades.

1982
Brazil, with World Bank funding, launches the vast Polonoroeste project, a controversial road-construction and resettlement campaign in the Amazon basin.

1984
Brazil completes the Tucurui Dam, spanning 12 miles on the Tocantins River, a tributary of the Amazon. It floods 800 square miles of virgin forest.

Mid-1980s
As a result of a relocation project in Indonesia, 2.5 million Javanese inhabit the undeveloped outer islands. More than 1.7 million forested acres are cleared, the highest deforestation rate in Southeast Asia.

1985
World Bank helps launch the Tropical Forestry Action Plan with the goal of establishing sustainable forest management in every tropical country.

December 1988
Brazilian rubber tapper Chico Mendes is assassinated following his extensively publicized campaign to curtail forest clearing in the Amazon.

1990s
Threats of global warming heighten concern about deforestation. The annual loss rate of tropical rain forests dips early in the decade before sharply increasing in the late 1990s.

1990
The Group of Seven leading industrialized nations (G-7) agree to work with Brazil to develop a $250 million pilot program for rain forest conservation. Funding is delayed for years due to bureaucratic red tape and disagreement over how to disburse the money.

1991
Amid concerns that sustainable forestry goals are spurring new rates of destruction, the World Bank withdraws support from the Tropical Forestry Action Plan and institutes a policy of no new loans for tropical logging.

1993
Foresters, timber companies and environmental groups from around the world launch the Forest Stewardship Council with the goal of certifying logging operations that minimize environmental damage.

1994
The newly created Global Environment Facility, a multilateral group that works closely with the U.N. and the World Bank to promote environmental initiatives, receives pledges of $2 billion from 34 nations to aid worldwide conservation programs.

1997-1998
Fires destroy millions of acres of pristine rain forests in Mexico, the Amazon and Indonesia due to droughts caused by El Niño.

April 1998
Brazilian President Fernando Henrique Cardoso creates four protected rain forest areas, totaling more than 1 million acres, as part of a commitment to triple the amount of protected Amazon land by 2000.

June 17, 1998
Suriname announces it will set aside one-tenth of its land for conservation purposes.

July 29, 1998
President Clinton signs legislation to forgive some debts of developing nations that undertake conservation initiatives. Congress provides no funding for the plan in 1998 but considers a $50 million appropriation in 1999.

February 1999
Preliminary figures from Brazil indicate that deforestation in the Amazon increased by almost 30 percent from 1997 to 1998.

forests, sometimes called "cloud forests" because of the mists that engulf the treetops. The height of the canopies of these forests decreases as the elevation increases. Lichens hang like beards from the upper branches of the gnarled and twisted trees, and the floor is covered with damp, green mosses. Another type of rain forest is the mangrove forest, which flourishes along sheltered shores in tropical regions.

Tropical rain forests cover about 3 million square miles, or 6 percent of Earth's land surface, and contain a greater variety of life than any other region. [35] Harvard's Wilson counted 43 different species of ants on a single tree in the Amazon — about the same number of ant species in all of Great Britain. [36] Whereas an entire temperate forest may contain only a handful of tree species, a single acre of rain forest can boast more than 100. [37] In Borneo, home to one-third of the world's flowering plants, a few acres of rain forest contains more species of trees than all of Europe. [38]

But this web of life is so fragile that, in some cases, a single species of plant can be pollinated by just one type of insect. In perhaps the most remarkable case of this interdependence, there are about 900 species of fig trees in the world and 900 species of tiny wasps that pollinate them — one for every species. [39]

Rain forests are so complex that researchers divide them into vertical strata, each containing multitudes of plant and animal species. On the forest floor are networks of fungi and swarms of insects, along with such unusual creatures as the bird-eating tarantula. The next layer up, the understory, is composed of shrubs, immature trees and dwarf palms that are laden with orchids and other epiphytes — plants that grow on other plants — and bound with a profusion of woody vines that reach toward the sun.

It is the top layer, the canopy, that has most intrigued naturalists in recent years. Bathed in strong sunlight and bursting with fruits, nectars and seeds, the canopy supports the spectacular animals that most people associate with rain forests — agile monkeys, brightly colored toucans, gliding geckos, sluggish sloths — as well as uncounted species of insects. Many canopy inhabitants spend their whole lives in the trees, hidden from observers on the ground.

The canopy shelters most of the species in the rain forest, and possibly the majority of all life forms on Earth. In fact, scientists are revamping their theories about species diversity because of the rain forest canopies. Until the early 1980s, scientists believed there were no more than a few million species in the world — perhaps 5 million at most. [40] But then they began exploring the canopy with a new technique, fogging the foliage with a biodegradable pesticide and counting the insects that fell. Fogging enabled Smithsonian entomologist Terry Erwin to count more than 650 beetle species in a single tree in Peru and as many as 60,000 insect species in a 2.5-acre plot in Ecuador. Now many scientists believe there are as many as 30 million species in the world, although estimates range from 10 million to 100 million. [41]

Disastrous Schemes

For thousands of years, forest-dwellers wove themselves into the diversity of rain forest life. Although few relics survive from the early inhabitants — wooden arrowheads, woven baskets and other natural materials quickly rot in the tropics — anthropologists believe the first people in the rain forests lived off fish and game as well as fruits, nuts and tubers. In fact, anthropologists say that

some peoples — the Pygmies of Africa, the Semang of Malaysia and others — gradually evolved smaller statures that made it easier to move through the dense brush and to climb trees. [42]

Scientists believe the early inhabitants may have relentlessly hunted some species into extinction, such as giant kangaroos and marsupial wolves in New Guinea and Australia. However, the indigenous people lacked the sophistication, or the desire, to destroy the rain forests. To this day, their farming techniques are held up as models of sustainable agriculture, in part because they relied on so many crops that they did not deplete any single source.

The first major assaults on the rain forests were launched in the early to mid-19th century by European and North American nations seeking hardwood, rubber and other commodities. But it was not until the middle of this century, when tropical populations began to boom, that the rain forests began suffering widespread destruction.

Seeking to relieve overcrowding, developing countries conceived disastrous schemes to move poor people out of the cities and into the sparsely populated forests. Brazil's ambitious and ill-fated Operation Amazonia, for example, destroyed large swaths of rain forest to make room for the country's new capital, Brasilia, and a network of roads linking the coast to the interior. The government also built dams, created gigantic colonization projects in the Amazon and encouraged environmentally damaging cattle and mining operations. Similarly, Indonesia in the 1980s moved 2.5 million landless people to underdeveloped islands, clearing forests at a higher rate than anywhere else in Southeast Asia. [43]

By 1990, Earth's tropical rain forests had shrunk to little more than half of their original area of 5.5 million square miles, with about 1.8

percent more cleared each year and environmentalists warning that the ancient forests could not endure more than another few decades. Yet, much of the cleared land proved of little value to the new inhabitants, because the soil of rain forests is often too poor to sustain farming for more than a few years.

Amid warnings of catastrophic damage to the global environment, conservation organizations and national governments began seeking to stem the tide in the 1980s and '90s. The World Bank cut off funding for logging projects in undisturbed forests; a consortium of nations set up a $1.3 billion global environmental fund and U.S. government agencies worked to set aside land and to explore the rain forests for possible medicinal uses. Across the world, conservation groups and indigenous peoples joined forces to plant trees in deforested areas, create preserves and popularize sustainable uses of the forest, such as harvesting fruits and latex.

But they were too late to save many of the indigenous peoples who had lived in the rain forests for millenniums. Beset by disease, pollution and settlers determined to kill them for their land, at least 90 Amazon tribes have been wiped out of existence this century — nearly one per year. [44] In the latest setback, a pilot program to survey Brazil's rain forest and mark off 40,000 square miles for indigenous people is threatened by the Brazilian economic crisis.

The worldwide conservation efforts also may be failing to preserve the forest plants and animals. Wilson estimated in 1992 that the destruction of the rain forests was dooming at least three species to extinction every hour, or about 27,000 a year. "Clearly, we are in the midst of one of the great extinction spasms of geological history," he wrote. [45]

Despite such warnings, the defor-

estation has continued. If Wilson's estimate was correct, the world has lost about 189,000 species in the seven years since he published his book. ■

CURRENT SITUATION

Government Initiatives

As a deeply divided Congress this year debates plans to cut taxes and boost spending, Republicans and Democrats are finding themselves in agreement on at least one issue: Appropriating money for rain forests.

President Clinton's fiscal 2000 budget proposes spending $50 million on a much-touted plan to forgive debts by developing nations in exchange for those nations undertaking certain conservation efforts. Congress passed the plan overwhelmingly in 1998, but provided no funding for it.

The proposed "debt-for-nature" swap builds on earlier U.S. initiatives and brings together an unusual group of political leaders, including Clinton and one of his arch-rivals, House Budget Committee Chairman John R. Kasich, R-Ohio. It is perhaps the most closely watched rain forest initiative in Washington in years, winning praise from Nature Conservancy President John C. Sawhill as "a means for preserving millions of acres of tropical forests."

The unlikely sponsor of the plan is Rep. Rob Portman, R-Ohio, a conservative best-known for his work on the Ways and Means Committee. Portman, who does not serve on the Resources Committee and has almost no experience on environmental bills,

usually focuses on such matters as pension reform, tax collection methods and restricting the ability of Congress to impose mandates on state and local governments. But he is an avid kayaker and outdoorsman who has visited the rain forest in Costa Rica, and he believes preserving the rain forests should be a major U.S. priority. "By protecting these far-off tropical forests," he says, "we are also protecting our own air quality, food supply and the medicines we use to cure disease."

Portman believes the legislation can spur major conservation efforts without costing U.S. taxpayers much money. He notes that about half of the world's tropical forests are located in four countries — Brazil, Congo, Indonesia and Peru — that have more than $5 billion of outstanding U.S. debt. Given their economies, they are unlikely to repay much of the debt anyway. So, he asks, why not forgive it in exchange for such initiatives as the creation of funds to preserve and restore forested areas? "This is one case where, for a very small subsidy, there can be a huge return," he says. "It's a common-sense approach to a major problem that affects all of us, not just the countries that have tropical forests."

In addition to the $50 million this year, the plan would spend $125 million in the two years on the debt-for-nature swaps. [46]

But with lawmakers pursuing competing plans to cut taxes, boost military spending and shore up the Social Security and Medicare trust funds, it remains uncertain whether they will find the money for the rain forest initiative. Indeed, rain forest conservation efforts generally have received limited attention in Congress. In recent years, for example, funding for AID programs to protect rain forests have either remained stable or slightly declined. At present, the agency spends about

$15 million to $20 million annually on forestry initiatives.

On the other hand, the United States is stepping up initiatives with other industrialized nations. It joined more than 30 other nations in pledging a total of $2.75 billion in 1998 to the Global Environment Facility, a multilateral group that works closely with the United Nations and the World Bank to promote environmental initiatives worldwide. Of that money, $300 million or more is expected to be spent assisting countries to protect their rain forests.

The G-7, meanwhile, has launched additional initiatives throughout the decade, including pledging most of the funding for a $250 million pilot project to save the remaining Brazilian Amazon. President Clinton in October 1997 promised an additional $10 million, saying: "We share Brazil's determination to conserve the Amazon, one of the world's most wondrous and biologically diverse environmental habitats."

But facing an economic crisis, Brazil cut much of its environmental budget in 1998, leaving the fate of the new program in doubt. Also uncertain is whether President Cardoso will follow through on his 1998 pledge to set aside 10 percent of the rain forest, or 240,000 square miles.

Market-Based Solutions

Even as world leaders appear stymied over rain forest conservation efforts, country music is moving to bridge the gap. Gibson Musical Instruments in Nashville, Tenn., has released a new line of guitars made from wood that is harvested using environmentally friendly techniques

and certified by the Forest Stewardship Council. Although guitar makers normally rely on mahogany and other rare tropical woods, they are concerned about the growing scarcity of certain woods.

"If we keep using the forests at the rate we're currently doing and not paying any attention to maintaining them, there won't be any more left," says Gene Nix, a Gibson wood specialist.

While Washington officials focus on the rain forest battle overseas, some environmentalists are looking for success in the consumer products arena. They believe that a key to saving the rain forests will be generating consumer demand for environmentally friendly versions of wood, coffee and other rain forest products. And consumers appear to be on their side: a poll cited by the Rainforest Alliance showed that 66 percent of consumers would switch brands to favor corporations that demonstrate environmental responsibility. [47]

Many businesses are trying to cultivate images as environmental stewards. After protests by the Rainforest Action Network, for example, retailing giant Home Depot promised early this year to emphasize selling wood that is harvested from carefully managed forests. Similarly, Seattle-based Starbucks entered into a three-year

agreement with Conservation International (CI) in 1999 to help farmers grow coffee in the shade of forest canopies, instead of cutting down trees. The partnership will focus initially on coffee growers adjacent to one of the world's most threatened and environmentally diverse ecosystems: the El Triunfo Biosphere Reserve in Chiapas, Mexico.

"Starbucks and CI share an interest in ensuring that coffee production does not harm the world's rich and fragile tropical forests," said Starbucks President Orin Smith.

At the forefront of the lumber effort is the Mexico-based Forest Stewardship Council, an international organization that certifies well-managed forests and their wood products. To win certification, a logging company must do minimal harm to animal habitats and local cultures. Logging must be limited to a pace that allows a forest to replenish itself. Since its founding in 1993 by a coalition of logging companies and environmental organizations, the council has certified more than 37 million acres worldwide. [48]

"It allows consumers to make an intelligent choice and choose products that come from well-managed forests," says Richard Donovan, president of SmartWood, a Vermont-based conservation organization that works with the council to certify wood.

The idea seems to be gaining acceptance in the logging community. Even though unrestricted logging techniques can frequently be more economical, Donovan said that 200 logging operations around the world have become certified, with the loggers in many cases approaching the environmental community, rather than the other way around. "They feel they either want to do it for their own

A ground orchid reflects the rich biodiversity of the rain forest in East Madagascar.

O. Langrand/World Wildlife Fund

At Issue:

Is it economically viable to look for natural cures in rain forests?

JOSHUA ROSENTHAL

Program Director for Biodiversity, Fogarty International Center, National Institutes of Health

WRITTEN FOR *THE CQ RESEARCHER*, MAY 1999.

ompounds derived from plants, animals and micro-organisms always have been and will continue to be important sources of medicinal agents. Forty percent of all drugs approved by the FDA between 1983 and 1994 were derived from natural products. Currently, major new pharmaceuticals derived from natural products are in clinical trials for treatment of extreme pain, cancer, AIDS, malaria, obesity, Alzheimer's and heart disease, among other therapeutic needs.

Tropical forests contain more than half of the species on the planet. These rich ecosystems historically have been an important source of many of these drugs, and yet we have analyzed only a tiny fraction of their species for pharmaceutical potential. In recognition of this potential the National Institutes of Health, most of the world's major pharmaceutical companies, hundreds of biotechnology companies and many other public and private organizations support natural products discovered from rain forests. Most scientists believe that it pays to look for natural cures in rain forests.

Perhaps a more debatable question is whether new drugs from tropical forests will pay for conservation of these endangered habitats. It would be unrealistic to depend on any single income source to counter the enormous economic pressures responsible for tropical forest destruction, and most conservation programs employ a variety of approaches.

In fact, we have seen already that combining drug-discovery research with conservation — bioprospecting — can be very powerful. This year the government of the small Amazonian country of Suriname set aside 4 million acres of tropical rain forest for preservation. In part, this occurred because supporters in Suriname were able to point to an active bioprospecting program in their country that is yielding a variety of benefits to local communities as well as scientific and government institutions. In the process, a piece of rain forest has been conserved that provides all of us with many benefits, including potentially new treatments for diseases, replenishment of global oxygen supply, recreational opportunities and many others.

Perhaps the greatest irony of today's dramatic rates of tropical deforestation and associated species extinction is that this process coincides with explosive growth in our scientific and technical ability to explore and develop the biochemical riches of those forests. Discovery of new medicines is not the only reason for, nor the singular means of, preserving these unique, irreplaceable treasures — just one of the best we have.

R. DAVID SIMPSON

Fellow, Resources for the Future

WRITTEN FOR *THE CQ RESEARCHER*, APRIL 1999.

ome people argue that every time we lose biodiversity-rich habitat we lose a treasure trove of potential cures for AIDS or cancer or a disease yet-to-be-identified. Since cures depend on having as many leads as possible, so the argument goes, we must conserve as many genes, species and ecosystems as we can. If pharmaceutical researchers only realized how much money they could be making from biodiversity, the argument concludes, they would conserve habitat.

Regrettably, the argument doesn't hold water. Saving more tropical rain forests will have little effect on the chance of finding the next miracle drug or of making a bundle.

Economically speaking, a species' value lies in the added chance it creates that researchers will find what they are looking for. With millions and millions of species in existence, sources of useful products are either so common as to be redundant, or so rare as to make discovery unlikely. Either way, the sheer numbers of wild plants and animals available to sift through mean no wild area is worth much as the potential source, say, of a chemical that will treat cancer.

Research by Resources for the Future has shown that pharmaceutical companies would be willing to pay, at most, only a couple of dollars per hectare to preserve some of the most imperiled, biodiverse regions on Earth. The money to be made isn't enough to overcome the pressures for metropolitan expansion in such "hot spots."

One needn't appeal only to rarified economic theory to see that the economic case for biodiversity preservation through bioprospecting remains bleak. The British science journal *Nature* documented the dearth of ventures as the cover feature of its April 9, 1998, issue. The rush of interest, contracts — and, eventually, revenue — that many early advocates hoped for has failed to materialize.

Biodiversity does matter — for commercial, ecological, esthetic, ethical and spiritual reasons. No substitute exists for it as a whole. Still, bioprospecting is no key to conservation. In terms of profit, preservation for the purpose rarely beats out other land-use options. In terms of success in finding useful products, this enterprise doesn't depend on the vastness of virgin habitat. By insisting otherwise, we may be diverting attention — and funds — from more promising conservation strategies.

The Limits of Reforestation

The volcanic island of Krakatoa was about the size of Manhattan and covered with lush rain forests before its eruption in 1883. But all life and most of the island was destroyed in an explosion that was of such force — equivalent to about 100-150 megatons of TNT — that the resulting airwave circled the Earth seven times, stirred seas as far away as France and created ash-colored sunsets worldwide for years. A series of tidal waves killed some 40,000 people on the nearby islands of Java and Sumatra. [1]

As for Krakatoa, it virtually ceased to exist. All the explosion left behind were four fragments — small lifeless islands covered with volcanic ash up to more than 300 feet deep. Naturalists working in nearby Indonesia began surveying the island, wondering if it would reveal how a rain forest emerges from total destruction.

It soon became clear that the islands were not destined to remain devoid of life. Just nine months after the explosion, a French expedition discovered a single animal: a microscopic spider. It apparently had floated in on a strand of silk. [2] Other forms of life gradually arrived, including insects and the seeds of plants that were carried by wind and water from islands 25 miles away. Just 10 years after the eruption, explorers found a few saplings; by the 1920s, the island was largely covered by forest. [3]

But nature has yet to entirely recover. Few of the new trees are found in the mature rain forests of Java and Sumatra, and recent surveys have found just five species of butterflies. It may be hundreds or even thousands of years before the forest, sustained by a cycle of numerous species of insects and birds scattering the pollen and seeds of a great variety of plants, recovers its former luxuriance. Still, the island's thick tree cover "offers testimony to the ingenuity and resilience of life," according to Harvard University biologist Edward O. Wilson. [4]

For conservationists dismayed by the current worldwide destruction of rain forests, Krakatoa offers both hope and caution. Certainly, nature is a resilient force, and rain forests that are partially logged or used for small-scale slash-and-burn farming can recover. In some cases, small clearings may help rare species that have trouble contending with dominant tree competitors.

On the other hand, badly damaged rain forests may take centuries to regain their onetime glory, and rain forest land that is cleared altogether for such activities as cattle ranching may never grow a wealth of plants again. Furthermore, even minor deforestation can cause the extinction of endemic species.

For all their profusion of growth, rain forests are far more fragile than the temperate woods in the United States and Western Europe. In temperate zones, the soil typically contains the nutrients necessary for life and remains hospitable to trees.

But rain forests are a very different type of ecosystem. Nutrients and carbon are generally stored in the tissue and dead wood of vegetation, while the soils tend to be heavily acidic and poor. Although some rain forest soils are rich with volcanic minerals, they are more commonly so sandy that scientists sometimes refer to the areas as "wet deserts." Moreover, the seeds of tropical trees tend to be fragile, germinating within weeks instead of lying dormant for long periods until the right conditions of temperature and humidity occur, as do seeds in temperate regions.

"In some areas, where the greatest damage is combined with low soil fertility and no native forest exists nearby to provide seeds, restoration might never occur without human intervention." Wilson wrote. "Ohio, in a word, is not the Amazon." [5]

There are other worrisome indications that much of the rain forests will never come back, even if large-scale restoration efforts are attempted. The forests interact in mysterious ways with the weather, bringing down the rain that they need for sustenance. Cutting down trees reduces humidity, potentially drying the land. Also, heavily logged forests tend to lose their genetic variation, resulting in trees that may be more susceptible to disease and stunted growth. A recent study indicated that trees left standing in pastures can dominate the reproduction in remnant forests, creating a "genetic bottleneck," because the seeds from the pasture are more easily spread by birds and other animals. [6]

Because of such barriers, conservation organizations focus on warding off destruction before it happens. To be sure, they point to minor restoration projects, such as tree-planting programs that create natural corridors for wildlife to move from one patch of forest to another. But the sense generally is that once a rain forest is destroyed, there is little hope it can return.

"Once they're lost, they're gone," says Bruce J. Cabarle, director of the World Wildlife Fund's global forest program. Noting that the rain forests have been evolving steadily since the last Ice Age 8,000 years ago, he adds: "It would be inconceivable to think we could re-create that."

---

[1] Edward O. Wilson, *Diversity of Life*, (1992), p. 16.

[2] *Ibid*, p. 19.

[3] Mark Collins, *The Last Rain Forests* (1990), p. 51.

[4] Wilson, *op.cit.*, p. 23.

[5] *Ibid*, p. 274.

[6] University of Georgia press release, July 2, 1998. The study is by Prof. James Hamrick.

internal credibility reasons or there's a market for it," he said.

Some environmentalists, however, have misgivings about whether it makes sense to focus on sustainable logging. With scientists struggling to understand the basic biology of rain forests — the growth rate of different species and the ways in which seeds are dispersed and pollinators work — conservationists disagree over what methods may be used to log a forest without greatly damaging it. In fact, reports by Conservation International warn that repeatedly logging a forest for one species of tree, such as mahogany, can create severe ecological damage, especially if logging companies clear out competing vegetation to spur growth of the desired tree. A more effective approach, according to CI researchers, would be to purchase already logged areas that may cost as little as 5 percent of the pre-logging price. [49]

But Donovan believes it is possible to strike a balance between the demand for lumber and the need to protect forests. To ensure an adequate level of protection, he said the Forest Stewardship Council may request a complete logging ban in such areas as steep hillsides where there is a chance of severe erosion or where the last vestiges of a rain forest may harbor endangered species. "Every forest is different, and you have to look at the circumstances," he said. "It's got a great potential for success." ∎

OUTLOOK

A Question of Money

Loggers, cattle ranchers, plantation owners, developers and miners— all have been blamed for the destruction of the rain forests. But even if they were to stop their activities tomorrow, British environmentalist Norman Myers believes it would do little to save the forests. He identifies the growing number of landless peasants, desperate to feed their families, as the driving force behind clearing away trees.

In the Philippines, for example, he says forested areas have dropped from about two-thirds of the nation's land area in 1945 to one-sixth or less at present. Landless peasants, driven from the fertile lowlands by rapid population growth and the concentration of agriculture into large farms and plantations, have migrated by the millions to formerly unpopulated upland forests. Using machetes and matches, farmers desperately try to clear a few acres of land and stave off starvation for another couple of years.

The number of slash-and-burn, or shifting, farmers in the developing world has been estimated at between 200 million and 600 million — meaning they could account for as many as one-in-10 people on the planet. "Shadowy figures to Western eyes, they are precipitating the most rapid global change in land use in history," Myers warned. [50]

For all their efforts to set aside preserves and persuade multinational corporations to adopt environmentally friendly practices, conservationists know they cannot turn the tide without confronting poverty and population growth. Already estimated at 6 billion, the world's population is projected to surpass 10 billion by the year 2050. [51] As the flood of people exhausts the nutrient-poor soil of the rain forests and exposes the land to more erosion and watershed contamination, the poverty can only become more intense.

To compensate, some analysts believe developing countries should try to improve their crop yields from existing farmlands. Since the rain forests tend to be too poor for sustained farming, agricultural economists such as Southgate of Ohio State University say the focus should be on making existing farmland more productive, thereby alleviating food shortages and the need to clear more land. In addition, they promote such initiatives as agroforestry — using land for crops, pasture and trees — and the creation of tree plantations so loggers will have little incentive to blaze roads into remote areas.

But such proposals are not without a downside. More intensive agricultural methods can harm the environment because of soil erosion and possible water contamination by fertilizers and pesticides.

Others call for more emphasis on creating preserves and patrolling them to stop illegal logging and poaching. Two professors at the Center for Tropical Conservation at Duke University, Randall Kramer and Carel van Schaik, recently concluded that law enforcement should be "a fact of life" in many parks, since that may be the surest way to guarantee the long-term survival of vital ecosystems — and perhaps the future well-being of nearby communities. [52]

But it is not clear whether parks can be fully protected, even with vigilant patrols. Noting that Salvadoran peasants pushed their way into Honduras and the United States despite the best efforts of law enforcement, Southgate asked: "If rural people who are desperate to support themselves and their families pay little heed to national frontiers, how much respect are they ever likely to show for park boundaries?" [53]

Similarly, Southgate and others question the long-term benefits of such economic gambits as carbon sequestration and a tax structure offering incentives for conserving land

and water. Unless both the poor as well as the wealthy profit from conservation, the rain forests will continue to be besieged.

In the end, the solution may come down to money. If the industrialized nations believe it is in their best interests to save the rain forests, they may have to dig into their budgets and pay for it. "What you have to do is provide enough money to make it worthwhile for people who normally destroy the forests not to destroy the forests," said economist Simpson of Resources for the Future. "Basically, you've got to pay them off." ∎

Notes

[1] "Devastation of Denuded Hillsides," *Los Angles Times*, Nov. 22, 1998.

[2] Mark Collins, *The Last Rain Forests* (1990), p. 96.

[3] Randall Kramer, Carel van Schaik and Julie Johnson, *Last Stand* (1992), p. 19.

[4] United Nations Food and Agriculture Organization, "Report on the State of the Forests," 1997.

[5] *Ibid*.

[6] "As Trees Go, Haiti Becomes a Caribbean Desert," *Reuters*, Dec. 15, 1998.

[7] Glenn McKenzie, "West Africa Faces Grim Choice; Ivory Coast Families Killing Precious Rain Forests for Lucrative Crops," *Chicago Tribune*, Feb. 15, 1999, p. 4.

[8] From AID's Web site, www.info. usaid.gov/environment, April 6, 1999.

[9] "Canal Ecology Endangered; Rain Forest Needs More Protection," *The Washington Times*, Jan. 13, 1999, p. A1.

[10] McKenzie, *op. cit.*

[11] Diana Jean Schemo, "Brazil Slashes Money for Project Aimed at Protecting Amazon," *The New York Times*, Jan. 1, 1999, p. A9.

[12] Kramer et al, *op. cit.*, p. 32.

[13] Schemo, *op. cit.*

[14] Cambridge International Forecasts, February 1999.

[15] Gerald Hanlon, letter to *The Guardian*, Feb. 14, 1999.

[16] Kramer et al, *op. cit.*, pp. 16, 19.

[17] Diana Jean Schemo, "Data Show Recent Burning of Amazon is Worst Ever," *The New York Times*, Jan. 27, 1998, p. A3.

[18] Fred Pearce, "No Hope for Rain Forests," *Fort Lauderdale Sun-Sentinel*, Nov. 1, 1998, p. 28A.

[19] Kramer et al, *op. cit.*, p. 21

[20] *Ibid*, p. 23.

[21] Carel Van Schaik, John Terborgh and Barbara Dugelby, "The Silent Crisis: The State of Rain Forest Nature Preserves," in Kramer et al, *op. cit.*, p. 64.

[22] Douglas Southgate, *Tropical Forest Conservation* (1998), p. 45.

[23] Edward O. Wilson, *The Diversity of Life* (1992), p. 283.

[24] "Water, We Can Care For It!", The Nature Conservancy, p. 5.

[25] Janet N. Abramovitz, "The Complex Realities of Sharing Genetic Assets," *Nature*, April 9, 1998.

[26] The Associated Press, Nov. 25, 1998.

[27] Anthony Faiola, "Killing the Forest for the Trees," *The Washington Post*, March 23, 1999, p. A11.

[28] Worldwatch Institute, *Taking a Stand*, (1998), pp. 7-8, 32.

[29] Fred Pearce, "Economy Turns Turtle," *The Guardian*, Feb. 25, 1999, p. 7.

[30] Sara Silver, The Associated Press, Dec. 15, 1998.

[31] "Reinventing the Well," Conservation International, p. 18, and National Public Radio, Feb. 7, 1999.

[32] Richard Pyle, The Associated Press, "Texaco Says Ecuadorian Indian Lawsuit Doesn't Belong in U.S. Courts," Feb. 2, 1999.

[33] Roger Thompson, "Requiem for Rain Forests?" *Editorial Research Reports*, Dec. 20, 1985, pp. 945-964.

[34] Collins, *op. cit.*, p. 14.

[35] *Ibid*, p. 96.

[36] *Ibid*, p. 13.

[37] *Ibid*, p. 39.

[38] Karen Catchpole, "Welcome to the Jungle," *Escape*, April 1999, p. 44.

[39] Laura Tangley, *The Rain forest* (1992), p. 46.

[40] *Ibid*, p. 37.

[41] Virginia Morell, "The Variety of Life," *National Geographic*, April 1999, p. 16.

[42] Collins, *op. cit.*, p. 93.

[43] Mary H. Cooper, "Saving the Forests," *The CQ Researcher*, Sept. 20, 1991, pp. 681-704.

[44] Tangley, *op. cit.*, p. 98.

[45] Wilson, *op. cit.*, p. 280.

[46] Testimony before House Appropriations Subcommittee on Foreign Operations, Export Financing and Related programs, March 1, 1999.

[47] Rainforest Alliance fact sheet.

[48] *Ibid*.

[49] Laura Tangley, "Sustainable Logging Proves Unsupportable," *U.S. News & World Report*, June 29, 1998, p. 63.

[50] Norman Myers, "Pushed to the Edge," *Natural History*, March 1999, p. 20.

[51] Kramer et al, *op. cit.*, p. 16.

[52] *Ibid*, p. 215.

[53] Southgate, *op. cit.*, p. 149.

FOR MORE INFORMATION

Conservation International, 2501 M St., N.W., Suite 200, Washington, D.C. 20037; (202) 429-5660; www.conservation.org. CI promotes rain forest preservation through economic development, including the exchange of debt relief for conservation programs that involve local people.

World Resources Institute, 10 G St. N.E., Suite 800, Washington, D.C. 20002; (202) 729-7600; www.wri.org. WRI is an independent center for policy research and technical assistance on global environmental and development issues.

World Wildlife Fund, P.O. Box 97180, 1250 24th St., N.W., Washington, D.C. 20037; (202) 293-4800; www.wwf.org. WWF conducts scientific research and analyzes policy on environmental and conservation issues and supports projects to promote biodiversity and save endangered species and their habitats.

Worldwatch Institute, 1776 Massachusetts Ave., N.W., Washington, D.C. 20036; (202) 452-1999; www.worldwatch.org. This research organization focuses on interdisciplinary approaches to solving global environmental problems.

Bibliography

Selected Sources Used

Books

Collins, Mark, ed., *The Last Rain Forests*, Oxford University Press, 1990.
A beautifully illustrated book that details the life of the rain forests, including the people who live there and the many plant and animal species that make these forests. The book also discusses the reasons for deforestation and urges action to save the forests.

Kramer, Randall, Carel van Schaik and Julie Johnson, eds., *Last Stand*, Oxford University Press, 1992.
This collection of essays by economists and conservationists about the myriad threats facing the rain forests includes a final chapter on strategies to save the forests.

Southgate, Douglas, *Tropical Forest Conservation*, Oxford University Press, 1998.
This academic treatment of the main economic issues facing Latin America's forests contains in-depth analyses of such conservation strategies as bioprospecting, ecotourism, marketing of non-timber forest products and more intense agricultural use of already-cleared land.

Tangley, Laura, *The Rainforest*, Chelsea House, 1992.
A leading environmentalists has written an easy-to-read introduction to the rain forests. Tangley discusses the devastating effects of deforestation on local people and the environment, and proposes alternatives to destroying them.

Wilson, Edward O., *The Diversity of Life*, Harvard University Press, 1992.
In this landmark book, one of the world's leading biologists warns that the Earth may face a massive extinction of plant and animal species unless major conservation steps are undertaken. Wilson focuses much of his discussion on the rain forests, detailing the many ways that they can enrich future generations if left intact.

Articles

"The Complex Realities of Sharing Genetic Assets," *Nature*, April 9, 1998.
A series of articles examining the economic and scientific issues of trying to use plant and animal species to create new drugs.

Morell, Virginia, "The Variety of Life," *National Geographic*, February 1999.
This package of five articles captures the stunning diversity of Earth's plant and animal species and spells out the threat of a major wave of extinctions.

Pearce, Fred, "Playing with Fire," *New Scientist*, March 21, 1998.
A detailed examination of the causes and devastating consequences of forest fires in Indonesia.

Reports and Studies

Bryant, Dirk, Daniel Nielsen and Laura Tangley, "The Last Frontier Forests," World Resources Institute, 1997.
This landmark report and concludes that just 20 percent of the Earth's original forest cover still remains in large, relatively undisturbed tracts.

Forests for Life, World Wildlife Fund, 1998.
The fund's annual global forest report summarizes major conservation efforts as well as environmental threats and forest destruction.

Gordon, Debra L., Marianne Guerin-McManus and Amy B. Rosenfeld, "Reinventing the Well," Conservation International, 1997.
This report by a conservation group that seeks to minimize the environmental effects of industrial development in the Tropics focuses on oil development. It provides case studies of companies that have used "best practices" to protect the environment as well as examples of the environmental and social damage caused by careless industrial development.

State of the World's Forests, United Nations Food and Agriculture Organization, 1999.
A biannual report that surveys deforestation and conservation initiatives worldwide. Despite finding evidence of continuing deforestation, the report concluded that more and more countries were taking steps to protect their forests. The report is perhaps the most widely quoted source for statistics on the destruction of rain forests and other types of forests, but environmentalists believe it understates the crisis facing forests by reporting only on areas that have been entirely cleared of trees, rather than areas that have been just partially cleared.

Wood, Megan Epler, "Meeting the Global Challenge of Community Participation in Ecotourism: Case Studies and Lessons from Ecuador," The Nature Conservancy, 1998.
The president of the Ecotourism Association analyses the benefits as well as the drawbacks of ecotourism, with specific recommendations about how to make travel more environmentally friendly in Ecuador.

11 Democracy in Asia

KENNETH JOST

When political change came to the world's fourth most populous nation this spring, it arrived with stunning speed.

On May 20, an estimated 1 million Indonesians, mostly youths, rallied in the central square of Yogyakarta, a large university city on the south Javan coast. They listened to speaker after speaker call for the resignation of President Suharto, the country's autocratic, longtime leader.

"We expected that the struggle could linger on for several months before we could push Suharto," recalls Mohtar Mas'oed, an activist and senior lecturer at Gadjah Mada University, who attended the rally.

Less than 20 hours later, however, the former general went on television and abruptly ended his 32-year rule over the sprawling chain of islands.

"It was very surprising for us when he decided to step down by himself," Mas'oed says.

In truth, Suharto had little choice. He had amassed billions of dollars for himself, his family and his political cronies after taking power in a 1965 coup. But as he hunkered down in the presidential palace in Jakarta, the capital, members of parliament and his Cabinet deserted him, along with the leader of Indonesia's powerful military.

A turbulent year of economic collapse and political turmoil — climaxed by the killing of six students at Jakarta's Trisakti University eight days earlier — had left Suharto, at age 76, with virtually no support.

The killing of the students sealed Suharto's fate, says Nasir Tamimi, deputy chief editor of the newspaper *Republika*. "People were very angry," he recalls. Five hundred people were killed in rioting in Jakarta over the

From *The CQ Researcher,* July 24, 1998.

next three days — forcing Suharto to cut short a trip to Egypt in a fruitless effort to calm the country and keep his office.

But William Liddle, a professor at Ohio State University and an expert on Indonesia, says that Suharto's demise was due more broadly to public discontent over the collapse of the economy in the wake of the financial crisis that swept Asia beginning last July. [1] The economic woes also heightened public resentment about the system of corruption and cronyism that had allowed Suharto and his family to amass a fortune estimated at $30 billion to $40 billion in a country with an annual state budget in 1997 of about $30 billion.

"It's the economy, stupid," Liddle says, recalling the slogan from President Clinton's 1992 campaign. Suharto "really did depend on that economic base. And there was the family favoritism: He just let [his children] do whatever they wanted."

Suharto yielded the presidency to his vice president, B.J. Habibie, a Western-educated aeronautical engineer, who removed some of Suharto's

close associates from the Cabinet and promised to institute political reforms. But he also disappointed the country's unseasoned reform movement by announcing an election schedule that called for parliamentary balloting in mid-1999 and the election of a new president at the end of the year.

"Some observers think he's not going fast enough," says Donald Emmerson, a professor of political science at the University of Wisconsin in Madison who visited Indonesia in June. Even so, Emmerson says that Habibie is "comfortable with the ideology of democracy" and has been "extremely adroit" in managing a delicate political situation.

But Emmerson and other experts stress that Indonesia's path of political reform depends most on Habibie's ability to manage a dire economic situation. Poverty and unemployment have soared in the year since Indonesia's rupiah first plunged in value last July. Last year, the International Monetary Fund (IMF) put together a $43 billion bailout package only to see Suharto balk at its terms. Now the IMF estimates that Indonesia's gross national product will decline 10 percent this year — in stark contrast to the 6.6 percent average annual growth between 1985 and 1994.

Political reform in Indonesia would represent a major gain for advocates of democracy in Asia. But the uncertainty about the outcome matches the mixed assessments that human rights advocates in the United States make about the path of democratization in the region.

"There have been major gains in the past year, but I wouldn't say this is an overall trend," says Mike Jendrzejczyk, Washington director for the Asia division of Human Rights Watch.

Charles Graybow, an Asia specialist at the conservative-leaning human rights group Freedom House, sees both "bright spots" and "setbacks" in Asia

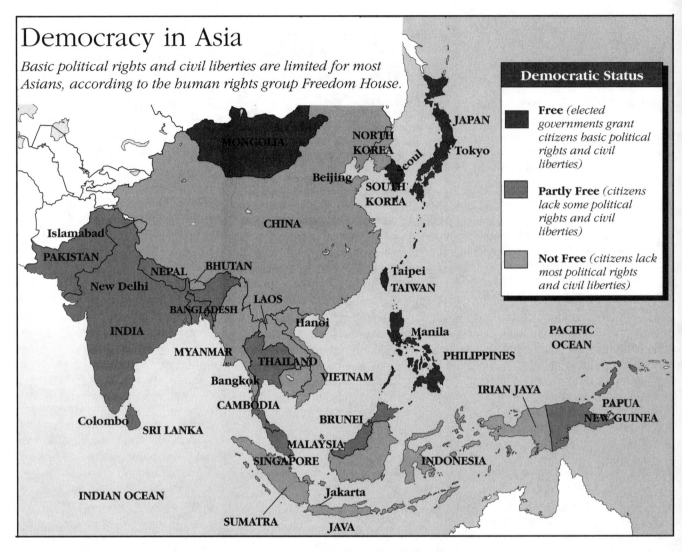

Democracy in Asia

Basic political rights and civil liberties are limited for most Asians, according to the human rights group Freedom House.

Democratic Status

- **Free** *(elected governments grant citizens basic political rights and civil liberties)*
- **Partly Free** *(citizens lack some political rights and civil liberties)*
- **Not Free** *(citizens lack most political rights and civil liberties)*

over the past decade. Many countries with formal democratic processes, he says, still have "weak" institutions, such as political parties, labor unions, business groups and so forth.

On the plus side, advocates of democracy point to moves toward freer political systems in such countries as South Korea, Taiwan and Thailand in East and Southeast Asia and in Bangladesh, Nepal and Pakistan in South Asia. *(See chart, p. 188.)* But the military regime in Myanmar, the former Burma, remains intractable; the elections being held in Cambodia on July 26 are widely viewed as rigged by the country's dictator, Hun Sen; the "dominant party" democracies in such coun-

tries as Malaysia and Singapore show few signs of welcoming free political competition; and political change is expected to be slow, at best, in China, much less in the region's other communist countries. [2]

Still, one former Clinton administration official is optimistic about the long-term prospects for reforming Asia's undemocratic political systems. "Political liberalization is definitely spreading in Asia," says Catharin E. Dalpino, a guest scholar at the Brookings Institution who served as deputy assistant secretary of State for human rights in President Clinton's first administration.

On the other hand, Larry Diamond,

editor of the *Journal of Democracy* and a senior research fellow at the Hoover Institute at Stanford University, is less optimistic. "I see, frankly, a region where there's maybe growing popular aspirations but not a rising tide that would be likely to lead to new democratic transitions," says Diamond, who spent the last year as a visiting scholar at the Academia Sinica in Taiwan.

The goal of democracy — pushed by human rights groups and the United States — is not universally shared. Over the past two decades, a few Asian leaders and Western scholars have contended that democratic government may be incompatible with Asian culture and economic growth.

Human rights advocates scoff at this so-called "Asia-values" debate. "It's said that ordinary Asian citizens prefer order and stability and that they're not really interested in participating in politics," Graybow says. "But what we've seen is that when Asian citizens have the opportunity to participate, they do. The voter turnout, when citizens feel that there is a choice, tends to be very high."

Amartya Sen, an Indian economist, also debunks the claimed linkage between economic growth and closed political systems. "If you look merely to economic growth, there's nothing to indicate in general that authoritarian governments do better than non-authoritarian countries," says Sen, a former professor at Harvard University and now master of Trinity College, Cambridge University, in England.

As experts debate the impact of President Clinton's recent trip to China, and the chances for political reform in Indonesia, these are some of the questions being asked:

Does "Western-style" democracy conflict with "Asian values"?

Since gaining independence from British colonial rule, Malaysia and Singapore have had governments that were democratic in form but widely viewed as undemocratic in practice. Both countries have been ruled continuously by a single political party or coalition, and both governments place what the U.S. State Department calls in Singapore's case "formidable obstacles" in the path of political opponents. [3]

Despite the criticism — or perhaps because of it — the longtime leaders of the two countries have helped spark an international debate over the role of democracy in Asia. In speeches, writings and interviews, Malaysia's prime minister, Mahathir bin Mohamad, and Singapore's Lee Kuan Yew, who served as prime

minister for 31 years and since 1990 has continued to wield influence as "senior minister," have defended their countries' political system as better suited for "Asian values" than so-called Western-style democracy.

"Asian societies are unlike Western ones," Lee remarked in one widely noted interview. In Lee's view, Western societies exalt individual interests over the collective good while Asian culture looks more to the best interests of society as a whole. A free-for-all-democracy, he told *The Wall Street Journal*, would produce a "tinderbox kind of society" for Singapore. Malaysia's Mahathir has similarly warned against the risk of allowing "pedantic notions of democracy" to result in "an excess of freedom." "To Asians," Mahathir says, "democracy does not confer a license for citizens to go wild." [4]

Human rights advocates in and outside Asia insist that the supposed tension between democracy and Asian values reflects a misunderstanding of both concepts. Asian cultures are not as hostile to democracy as the theory assumes, they say, and Asian peoples have demonstrated in many countries that they are willing to work and sacrifice for popular self-government.

"It would be a mistake to think that in Asia people haven't been willing to sacrifice a great deal to have democracy established and guaranteed," Professor Sen says.

Sen says that ancient Hindu and Buddhist writers emphasized the importance of individual freedom and tolerance and that the common depiction of Confucianism as valuing administrative efficiency over individual freedom is oversimplified. In recent history, he says, Asians in many countries have demonstrated "a strong commitment" to democracy — despite resistance first from colonial powers and then from home-grown authoritarian governments.

Still, some political scientists do see a distinctive Asian model of

democratic government — a so-called dominant party system that minimizes political competition for the sake of social order and economic growth. In his influential book, *The Third Wave*, Harvard political scientist Samuel Huntington called it "democracy without turnover" and said it represented "an adaptation of Western democratic practices, to serve not Western values of competition and change, but Asian values of consensus and stability." [5]

Lucian Pye, a political scientist at the Massachusetts Institute of Technology, likens the current dominant-party systems in Asia to China's Nationalist Party in the early 20th century, which envisioned a "tutelary role" for itself in creating democratic government. Today, Pye says at least some of the dominant-party systems — including South Korea's and Taiwan's — deserve credit for promoting both economic growth and democratic development. [6]

Asia's economic growth during the past two decades, in fact, created a receptive climate for the "Asia-values" theory. Growth was particularly strong in countries that limited political rights, like Indonesia, Singapore, South Korea and Taiwan. With an economic crisis sweeping through Asia over the past year, however, advocates of democracy are arguing that semiauthoritarian governments actually threaten economic development.

"This has really spelled the death knell for the Asia-values argument," says Freedom House's Graybow, "because it shows that authoritarian governments may have brought some illusion of stability, but in the long run you need openness and accountability to have sustainable economic growth."

Singaporean leaders defend their political system as democratic and bristle at the recurrent criticisms from the State Department in its annual human rights report, and from human rights groups. "What Asians object to

Democracy Eludes Many Nations in Asia

Country and Population	Type of Government	Political Conditions
East Asia		
China 1.2 billion	*Communist one-party*	*Chinese Communist Party "holds absolute power, has imprisoned nearly all active dissidents, uses the judiciary as a tool of state control and severely restricts freedoms of speech, press, association and religion."*
Japan 125.8 million	*Parliamentary democracy*	*Liberal Democratic Party government weakened by economic crisis, but no credible opposition party.*
Mongolia 2.3 million	*Presidential-parliamentary democracy*	*Formerly communist Mongolian People's Revolutionary Party recaptured presidency in June 1997 because of discontent with economic "shock therapy" program enacted by reformist coalition elected in 1996.*
North Korea 23.9 million	*Communist one-party*	*"Most tightly controlled country in world"; Kim Jong Il, son of the late longtime leader Kim Il Sung, formally assumed leadership in October 1997*
South Korea 45.3 million	*Presidential-parliamentary democracy*	*Election of opposition leader Kim Dae Jung as president in December 1997 caps decade-long political liberalization; National Security Law still used to curb contacts with North Korea.*
Taiwan 21.4 million	*Presidential-legislative democracy*	*Democratic transition consolidated by 1996 elections, but ruling Kuomintang Party maintains political advantages through control of media, business interests.*
South Asia		
Bangladesh 119.8 million	*Parliamentary democracy*	*June 1996 elections were freest in country's history, despite violence and irregularities; but parliamentary boycotts and other confrontational political tactics make normal legislative operations impossible.*
Bhutan 0.8 million	*Traditional monarchy*	*King wields absolute power; government arrested monks and civilians in 1997 to curb support for pro-democracy movement*
India 942 million	*Parliamentary democracy*	*Fairest elections in country's history in 1996 produced fractured parliament with no consensus on major issues; weak rule of law and social tensions contribute to widespread violations of civil liberties.*
Nepal 23.2 million	*Parliamentary democracy*	*Parliamentary government in place since end of absolute monarchy in 1991 is fragmented, but human rights conditions have improved*
Pakistan 133.5 million	*Presidential-parliamentary democracy*	*Nawaz Sharif led Pakistan Muslim League to victory in February 1997 election, then consolidated power in showdown in December with president, supreme court; democratic institutions weak, corruption widespread.*
Sri Lanka 18.7 million	*Presidential-parliamentary democracy*	*Political institutions "severely tested" by civil war, ethnic tensions, partisan violence; government put forth proposal in 1997 to end ongoing civil war with Tamil separatists.*
Southeast Asia		
Brunei 0.3 million	*Traditional monarchy*	*Sultan serves as prime minister and, along with inner circle of relatives, holds "absolute power."*
Cambodia 10.9 million	*Monarchy, constituent assembly*	*Co-premier Hun Sen regained total power after 1997 coup; "bleak" prospects for fair vote in 1998 elections*
Indonesia 207.4 million	*Dominant party (military-dominated)*	*"Turbulent year" in 1997 included violent parliamentary election campaign, crackdown on dissidents and student leaders, ethnic and sectarian violence due to frustration over corruption, and financial crisis; [President Suharto was forced out of office in 1998 and was replaced by Vice President B.J. Habibie].*

Country and Population	Type of Government	Political Conditions
Laos 5 million	*Communist one-party*	*One-party state controlled by Lao People's Revolutionary Party; some elements of state control relaxed in recent years.*
Malaysia 20.6 million	*Dominant party*	*Government has "significant control" over media, uses security laws to limit freedom of expression and chill political activity; judiciary subject to government influence in sensitive cases.*
Myanmar 46 million	*Military*	*"Effectively a garrison state ruled by one of the most repressive military regimes in the world."*
Papua New Guinea 4.3 million	*Parliamentary democracy*	*Elections marred by irregularities and violence; democratic institutions tested by fiscal pressures, corruption and challenge of nation-building in diverse country.*
Philippines 72 million	*Presidential-legislative democracy*	*Free elections marred by vote-buying and fraud; official corruption rampant; populist Vice President Joseph Estrada was front-runner in presidential race [elected, May 1998]*
Singapore 3 million	*Dominant party*	*Authoritarian People's Action Party crushed opposition in January 1997 election; government chills dissent through civil defamation suits, security laws and other harassment of opponents and journalists.*
Thailand 60.7 million	*Parliamentary democracy (military-influenced)*	*New constitution adopted in September 1997 aimed at rooting out corruption and establishing greater accountability in wake of public protests over economic crisis; new prime minister in office since November heads eight-party coalition.*
Vietnam 76.6 million	*Communist one-party*	*Vietnamese Communist Party rules nation as Leninist state with "tight control of all political, economic, religious and social affairs"*

Source: Freedom in the World: the Annual Survey of Political Rights and Civil Liberties, 1997-98, *Freedom House; updates from news accounts are bracketed*

is U.S. arrogance and self-righteousness," says Tommy Koh, an ambassador-at-large in Singapore's Ministry of Foreign Affairs and executive director of the Asia-Europe Foundation.

Professor Sen acknowledges that the Asia-values debate reflects anti-Western, anti-imperialist feelings among some Asians. "There was a tendency," he says, "to reject your rule, reject your authority and reject your values, too." But he says the persistent efforts by democracy movements throughout Asia show that democracy has universal appeal.

"The fact that people continue to agitate for political rights and individual freedom indicates that people do have an intrinsic interest in freedom without regard to economic development," Sen says. "That applies as much to Asia as to anywhere else."

Should the United States do more to encourage democracy in Asian countries?

When Secretary of State Madeleine K. Albright attended last year's meeting of the Association of Southeast Asian Nations (ASEAN), she urged Asian leaders to join the United States in pressuring Myanmar's military government to allow political reforms. "We must insist that we work together to promote conditions that will lead toward true democracy," Albright told the nine-nation group on July 27.

The response was polite but noncommittal. "It is for ASEAN to decide what we will do," said Malaysia's foreign minister, Abdullah Ahmad Badawi, "and we will bear in mind the views of Ms. Albright and others." [7]

The tepid reaction to the call for pressuring an evidently authoritarian

regime in a relatively small country gives one measure of the difficulties the United States faces in trying to encourage democratization in Asia. The United States' professed commitment to democratic change is simply not shared by countries in the region — not by the communist regimes of China, North Korea and Vietnam; not by countries that themselves have less than completely democratic political systems; and not even by the big democracy that is the United States' major ally in the region, Japan. [8]

Meanwhile, human rights advocates and Republican lawmakers give the Clinton administration no more than middling grades for its efforts to promote democracy in the region. The administration, in the view of these critics, was slow and half-hearted in adopting economic sanc-

Indonesia: A Country Profile

• INDONESIA

At a Glance

- **Area:** 735,510 sq. mi.
- **Population:** 207.4 million
- **Religion:** *86.9% Muslim, 9.6% Christian, 1.9% Hindu, 1% Buddhist, 0.6% traditional*
- **Major Ethnic Groups:** *Javanese (45%), Sudanese (14%), Madurese (8%), Coastal Malay (8%), Chinese (3%)*
- **Literacy Rate:** *83.8% (1995)*
- **Life Expectancy:** *62.7 years*
- **Labor Force:** *81,446 million*

With the exception of Jendrzejczyk, most observers say the U.S. sanctions on Myanmar — which no U.S. allies have supported — are having little, if any, effect. "We either have to persuade our European allies to go along and isolate the Burmese regime," Diamond says, "or else we need to pursue other means of pressuring for change in Burma."

The United States can take some credit for helping bring democracy to Asian countries in the past. The U.S. put the Philippines on a slow path toward self-government after seizing the islands as a colony from Spain at the turn of the century. It introduced democracy into occupied Japan after World War II and pressured European powers to yield up their colonies — for example, in Indonesia.

Today, however, the impetus for democratization comes from Asian peoples themselves. "It's inaccurate to imply that we jump-started any of these transitions," Dalpino says. "The Asians jump-started them themselves, which is the way it ought to be."

Is Indonesia on the road to a successful transition to democracy?

On May 23, in his first speech to Indonesians after assuming the presidency, Habibie sent ambivalent signals about his commitment to political change by promising to undertake "gradual and constitutional

tions against the Myanmar regime, has given little emphasis to human rights in other countries and has simply abandoned any pretense of pressuring China to grant political and human rights to its 1.2 billion people.

"The administration's track record in Asia on human rights and democracy is very mixed," says Jendrzejczyk of Human Rights Watch. "In some ways, the administration has positioned itself to keep human rights and democracy issues very much in the background while focusing very much on economic and security concerns."

Clinton's policy of "engagement" with China has drawn criticism from human rights groups on the left and the right. "The administration hasn't made a powerful push for the rule of law in China," Graybow says. "It's

possible to promote human rights and commercial interests at the same time," he says.

Elsewhere in the region, the administration manages to draw flak alternately for being too timid in pushing human rights issues or for being too assertive. Jendrzejczyk, for example, criticizes the administration's belated decision to impose economic sanctions on Myanmar. "They waited until the very last minute when pressure from Congress became almost unbearable," he says.

Some Indonesia experts, however, say Albright made a mistake by publicly calling on Suharto to step down prior to his resignation. "Indonesians are very nationalistic," Liddle says. "It's a very delicate situation."

In any event, the U.S. influence on events in Asia is easy to exaggerate.

reforms." [9] Habibie's background was itself ambivalent. He was an engineer who had attended school and worked in Europe but also advanced politically and prospered financially under Suharto.

Since taking office, Habibie has instituted some significant changes — for example, permitting new political parties and freeing some political prisoners. But Indonesians and outside observers are divided about Habibie's commitment to thorough-going changes — and about his own prospects for holding on to power.

"He is now perceived as going with the reformists," Tamimi says. "He has established a style where a president is just like any other citizen."

But Muhammed Hikam, a political scientist at the Indonesian Institute of Sciences, is less impressed. "Unfortunately, Habibie can do only so much," Hikam remarked during a visit to the United States last month with other members of the International NGO [non-governmental organizations] Forum on Indonesian Development.

Hikam says Habibie and his family are still linked to the corruption and favoritism of the Suharto regime. "He is not talking about reform within himself," Hikam says, "so he's still lacking moral credibility."

U.S. experts on Indonesia have similarly mixed views about Habibie. Emmerson calls him "extremely cosmopolitan" and "able to bridge gaps." Liddle is more critical. "He is a very arrogant person," he says.

Even so, Liddle credits Habibie with a real commitment to reform. "I think he's serious," Liddle says, "because without it he simply can't govern. He has to get some kind of political legitimacy."

The prospects for change are also clouded by weaknesses within Indonesia's reform movement, which has only limited political experience and no unifying platform or individual leader. "The problem of the reform movement is basically structural," Hikam says. "It has had no real political platform that is shared by all reform groups in Indonesia, including the students."

Liddle also fears that pro-democracy sentiment might fade if the government is unable to right the economy and restore political order. "These people are not used to the typical to-and-froing of democracy," he says. "If it looks to most of the middle class that the new government is not able to control the forces erupting in society, people will turn to the military very quickly again."

Other observers fear the military may unilaterally intervene to slow or prevent political changes. "The fragmented pro-reform forces and the economic disaster will bring new temptation for the military to step in," says Goenawan Mohamad, an editor of the pro-democracy newspaper *Tempo*.

For his part, though, Tamimia believes both the government and pro-democracy groups are on a path toward reform. "People and the government are starting to talk with each other," he says. "That didn't happen for 40 years."

As for Habibie, the economy may hold the key to his political fortunes. "The economy is bad and unlikely to get better," Emmerson says. "Whoever is president is likely to suffer, and that is going to hurt Habibie."

On the other hand, Tamimi says, "If Habibie's successful in making democracy a reality, and if he's successful in establishing the economic situation, people will follow him."

Despite the problems and uncertainties, observers and advocates in Indonesia and the United States voice a measure of cautious optimism about the prospects for democracy there.

"Now people are starting to make a program, to talk with each other," Tamimi says. "It will take time, but I think we are on the right track."

"There's a golden moment of opportunity here," Liddle says. "Indonesia could create a democracy here if it just seizes the moment." ■

BACKGROUND

East Meets West

Asians had relatively little experience with democracy before the arrival of European explorers, traders and colonizers in the 15th century. Asian societies — from sophisticated China and Japan to the less developed kingdoms and sultanates of the Indian subcontinent, the Malay Peninsula and the East Indies — were mostly hierarchically organized and governed. Asia has been late to develop the kind of representative assemblies, popular elections and written constitutions that comprise what is sometimes called "Western-style" democracy.

Hierarchical tendencies were reinforced by the region's dominant religions: Buddhism and Hinduism, both of which predated Christianity, and Islam, which spread through much of Asia beginning in the seventh century. Some scholars find democratic strains in Buddhism and Hinduism by focusing on the rulers' obligation in both religions to govern wisely and with the consent of his subjects. But historically, both Buddhism and Hinduism have been associated with elitist, authoritarian ruling systems. Similarly, Confucianism, the Chinese school of political thought that dates from the sixth century before Christ, contains some germs of democratic theory — for example, the right of the people to depose an unjust ruler. In practice, however, it, too, came to be associated with authoritarian rulers. [10]

The European powers also did little to prepare their Asian colonies for self-government until the very end of the colonial period. Spanish and Portuguese sailors were the first Europeans to explore the region, followed by Dutch traders in the 17th century, the British in the 18th and the French in the 19th. Developing trade was the first and most important objective; ruling colonies was an afterthought and nation-building did not make the agenda until the 20th century, if then. [11]

Of the major European colonies, only India had begun to take shape as a nation by 1900. France ruled what is now Vietnam as two disconnected colonies: Tonkin in the north, Cochin-China in the south. Britain had "organized" the Malay Peninsula into federated states, unfederated states and the "Straits Settlements." The Dutch East Indies was a geographic location, not a political entity. The 20th century saw some moves toward education and self-government in Asia — so-called enlightened policies — but they were typically limited. In Indonesia, for example, only 230 native-born Indonesians had college educations in 1942. [12]

Asia's largest countries that escaped colonization — China and Japan — did make some early moves toward democracy. In 1890 Japan adopted a constitution modeled on the Prussian charter, with a bicameral Diet including an elected lower house and a Cabinet of advisers to make decisions to be issued in the emperor's name. Competitive political parties developed by the 1920s, and the prime minister and Cabinet became responsible to the Diet. But in the 1930s the military took power, repressed democratic processes and led the nation into war first in China and then throughout East Asia.

In China, Western-trained Sun Yat-sen led a revolutionary movement that sought to unify China under a federal republic. But democratic impulses proved weaker than warlordism and communism. The Nationalist Party —

the Kuomintang or KMT — emerged as the leading power in the elections of 1912 but came to be dominated by local warlords more interested in protecting their power bases than in establishing democracy. The Chinese Communist Party split from the KMT in the 1920s, joined in unsteady alliance during the war with Japan but then gained power after a four-year civil war following the Japanese surrender in 1945.

It was the Japanese who ousted the European powers from most of their Asian colonies, embarrassing the white rulers with their easy conquests of the East Indies, Indochina and the British-ruled territories, including the supposedly impregnable Fortress Singapore. The Japanese occupiers encouraged anti-imperialist and pan-Asian sentiment even while subjugating the native peoples. At war's end, the colonial rulers expected to return. As author John Keay writes, however, the colonies were "reoccupied" but "never retaken." [13]

Paths of Independence

Nationalist movements gained strength in Asia before and during World War II and immediately challenged the European powers' attempt to return after the war's end. Over the next two decades, the British, Dutch and French were ousted and independence won in India (1947), Burma (1948), Vietnam (1954) and Malaya (1957, renamed Malaysia in 1963). Meanwhile, the United States had imposed a U.S.-style constitution on the defeated Japanese. Democratic government took hold in Japan, but elsewhere in Asia ethnic, religious, economic and ideological divisions stunted the growth of democracy and helped bring authoritarian regimes to power. [14]

India's democratic movement began with the formation of the National Congress Party in 1875, which first advocated self-government, then independence from Britain. The movement came to be led by Mohandas K. Gandhi, an Indian lawyer whose masterful political organizing and strategy of civil disobedience forced Britain to cede independence after the end of World War II. The movement toward independence, however, unleashed violence between the majority Hindus and minority Muslims, resulting in partition and the establishment of Pakistan as a Muslim homeland. Burma, ruled by Britain as part of India, had been moving toward separation before the war and gained its own independence in 1948.

In Indonesia, a nationalist movement also had been forming under Sukarno, who founded the Indonesian National Party (PNI). He encouraged strikes and non-cooperation with Dutch authorities and was imprisoned or exiled for most of the 1930s. During the war, he collaborated with the Japanese while other nationalists opposed the occupiers. As the war was ending, Sukarno and his colleagues declared Indonesia's independence. [15]

During four years of fighting and diplomatic maneuvering, the Dutch sought to preserve their rule by decentralizing power through a federal structure. The nationalists rejected the idea and fought a guerrilla war that, combined with diplomatic pressure from the United States and the United Nations, forced the Dutch to yield. Queen Juliana gave her formal assent to independence in December 1949. The new constitution called for a parliamentary democracy, with the first post-independence national elections to be held in 1955. In defiance of nationalist sentiments, the Dutch remained on the eastern half of New Guinea while Portugal still ruled the eastern half of the smaller island of Timor.

In Indochina, the nationalist movement was led by Ho Chi Minh, who (under the name Nguyen Ai Quoc) had presided over the founding meeting of the

Chronology

Before 1945
Asia has limited experience with democratic forms before colonialism; European powers do little to prepare their colonies for self-government.

1890
Japan establishes democratic constitution, the first in Asia.

1935
Britain provides limited self-government for India, but move does not satisfy independence movement.

1945-1965 *Era of European colonialism ends; most of the newly independent nations adopt some form of parliamentary democracy, but many come to be dominated by one party or yield to military rule.*

1947
Japan adopts U.S.-style constitution, providing for parliamentary democracy under constitutional monarch; India gains independence from Britain; Pakistan is established as Muslim homeland.

1949
Indonesia gains independence from the Netherlands; Communists come to power in China.

1954
France is ousted from Indo-China; Vietnam is partitioned between communist and pro-West governments.

1963
Malaysian Federation is established as independent nation, ending British colonial era in Southeast Asia; Singapore is ousted from federation two years later.

1965-1989 *U.S. fights protracted war in Vietnam but fails to prevent communist victory; Cold War politics shapes U.S. ties with authoritarian regime.*

1965
Sukarno is ousted in Indonesia; Suharto comes to power.

1979
U.S. recognizes People's Republic of China, downgrades relations with Taiwan.

1986
Philippines President Ferdinand E. Marcos ousted, succeeded by human rights activist Corazon Aquino.

1989
Chinese military suppresses pro-democracy rally at Tiananmen Square, killing hundreds.

1990s *With end of Cold War, democratization gains prominence in U.S. diplomatic agenda; democracy activists step up efforts in Asia, with uneven results.*

1990
Burmese military government nullifies election won by National League for Democracy.

1991
Burmese pro-democracy leader Aung San Suu Kyi awarded Nobel Peace Prize; military coup in Thailand; king forces coup leader to resign in 1992, paving way for return of democracy.

1993
Cambodia holds first election under 1991 Paris peace agreement, resulting in coalition government; Japan's Liberal Democratic Party yields power after losing parliamentary election.

1995
U.S. and Vietnam re-establish diplomatic relations; Malaysia's ruling coalition wins electoral landslide, with opposition party reduced to nine seats in parliament.

1996
Congress Party defeated at polls in India, but Hindu nationalist party falls short of majority; Taiwan holds first popular election for president; Bishop Carlos Belo and Jose Ramos-Horta, activists for East Timorese self-determination, are awarded Nobel Peace Prize.

1997
Singaporean opposition parties reduced to two seats after parliamentary elections; Hong Kong reverts to China; opposition leader Kim Dae Jung elected president of South Korea.

1998
Hindu nationalist party again leads coalition government, but wins only one-fourth of seats in Indian parliament; Suharto is ousted in Indonesia; his successor as president, B.J. Habibie, promises reforms, elections in 1999; President Clinton visits China; Cambodian elections, scheduled for July 26, are widely criticized as weighted in government's favor.

Indonesia's Year of Living Turbulently

May 1997 Ruling Golkar party wins sixth consecutive victory in parliamentary elections on May 29; more than 200 people die in riots before balloting.

July 1997 Rupiah closes down 5 percent on July 21 (about 2,500 to the dollar) in the wake of the July 2 devaluation of the Thai bhat.

October 1997 International Monetary Fund (IMF) announces three-year, $33 billion loan package to stabilize Indonesia's economy; accord follows President Suharto's agreement to institute reforms in banking and elsewhere.

Suharto

January 1998 Rupiah plunges to more than 9,000 to the dollar, prompting panic-buying for food and staples; Suharto, in new accord with IMF, promises Jan. 15 to end system of patronage favoring his children and friends.

March 1998 IMF delays first $3 billion installment of aid package on March 6 as Suharto balks at reforms; Suharto re-elected president March 11 by People's Consultative Assembly; after swearing-in, as many as 10,000 students protest at Gadjah Mada University in Yogyakarta, burning an effigy of the president.

May 1-10, 1998 Suharto is quoted May 1 as ruling out reform before end of five-year term in 2003; student protests held throughout Indonesia next day; rioting follows on May 5 as fuel and energy prices rise after government cuts subsidies.

May 11-20, 1998 Six students killed May 12 after police open fire on protesters at Jakarta's Trisakti University; 500 people die in rioting over next three days concentrated in Jakarta's wealthy ethnic Chinese neighborhoods; Suharto, after returning from Egypt May 15, announces May 19 he will hold new elections and not run for president again; behind the scenes, military chief Gen. Wiranto pressures Suharto to step down immediately.

May 21-31, 1998 Suharto announces immediate resignation May 21; Vice President B.J. Habibie is sworn in as successor; Gen. Wiranto removes Suharto's son-in-law from military command May 22; Habibie drops key Suharto associates in new cabinet named May 23 and promises "gradual and constitutional reforms," but says on May 25 that elections may not be held before mid-1999.

June 1998 IMF commits additional $4-$6 billion to aid package June 24; Habibie announces five-year action plan on human rights on June 25; the next day he proposes to release East Timorese rebel leader Jose Xanana Gusamo in exchange for recognition of Indonesian sovereignty; Gusamo says no deal.

Habibie

July 1998 National Golkar party conference July 9-11 elects Habibie-backed candidate Akbar Tanjung as party leader in secret ballot; rupiah drops to more than 14,000 to the dollar.

Vietnamese Communist Party in Hong Kong in 1930. The French responded to a campaign of hunger marches and commandeering of local estates with an air and ground offensive; many party activists were arrested, and Ho himself was later held by British authorities in Hong Kong. He was reported to have died in detention, but in fact escaped, eventually to Moscow, and returned to lead the nationalist movement during World War II. The French, like the Dutch, had expected to resume their colonial rule, but — despite fitful U.S. support — left Indochina after the 1954 defeat at Dien Bien Phu. Two decades later, Vietnam was unified under communist rule after the U.S. failed in its efforts to preserve a pro-American regime in the south.

The nationalist movement was weaker in what became Malaysia, in part because of the mix of native Malays and ethnic Chinese Malayans. Britain also proved more adroit in countering a communist-dominated insurgency with a mixture of military and political responses. With the insurgency deemed defeated, Britain granted independence to Malaya in 1957 while continuing to hold Singapore and its possessions on the island of Borneo: the sultanates of Sabah and Sarawak. Singapore, with its majority-Chinese population, was added to what became the Malaysian Federation in 1963 — balanced by the addition of the predominantly Malay populations of Sabah and Sarawak. But the Malay-dominated government ousted Singapore two years later out of concern that its Chinese population would threaten the ethnic Malays' political control.

Asian-Style 'Democracy'

Democratic forms, including regular elections and representative assemblies, took hold in most of the non-communist Asian countries after the colonial period ended. But from India to Japan and in most of the smaller countries in between, the political systems were dominated by single parties. Political rights were generally protected in some of the countries, including India and Japan, but less so in many others, including Indonesia, Malaysia, Singapore, South Korea and Taiwan.

Indonesia, according to Huntington, was the most authoritarian of these supposedly democratic countries.[16] The only free election in the nation's history, in 1955, gave four parties roughly comparable power in the parliament: Nationalists, Communists and two Muslim parties. Four years later, Sukarno, who served in the largely ceremonial role of president, joined in a coup with the military, which also chafed under the political fragmentation and its own limited role. The coup returned Indonesia to the strong presidential system of the short-lived 1945 constitution. "Guided democracy," Sukarno called his new system. "Far more guided than democratic," Emmerson says.

Sukarno, according to Liddle, sought to reduce his dependence on the military by aligning himself domestically with the communists as he also took on a leading role internationally as spokesman for the nonaligned nations. Communist-instigated unrest climaxed in the assassination of six Indonesian generals in 1965, most likely by leftist officers. The coup enabled Maj. Gen. Suharto to assume control of the military and lead a crackdown on the communists, depicted later by the film "The Year of Living Dangerously."

Suharto began his 32-year rule by restating the five principles that Sukarno had proclaimed in 1945 — monotheism, humanitarianism, unity, democracy and justice. He also eventually reduced the number of recognized parties to just three: the governing Golkar party and two opposition parties. Suharto was assured of re-election by the People's

Consultative Assembly, since he effectively controlled 500 of its 1,000 seats. And the army buttressed Suharto's power by suppressing any signs of political opposition.

Elsewhere in East and Southeast Asia, one-party rule proved almost as durable despite somewhat greater political freedom. In Malaysia, the ruling National Front has dominated every election since 1971. In Singapore, Lee's People's Action Party has held even greater sway.

Meanwhile, South Korea and Taiwan also were effectively ruled by single parties, thanks in part to periods of martial law justified by the threats posed by their communist neighbors, North Korea and mainland China. In Thailand, a period of relative democracy in the 1970s produced a degree of political disorder that a military-dominated government sought to control in the 1980s with authoritarian measures. In neighboring Burma, on the other hand, the military strongman Gen. Ne Win crafted a new constitution in 1974 that made his Burma Socialist Program Party the only recognized party.

Of the former European colonies, India was the most auspicious in its early years of democracy. Its first prime minister, Jawaharal Nehru, an ally of Gandhi's in the independence struggle, also proved skillful in the practical politics of democracy. But his daughter, Indira Gandhi, who succeeded to the post in 1966, stirred harsh criticism when she assumed virtually dictatorial powers from 1975 to 1977 and was widely blamed for politicizing the judiciary and civil service and permitting corruption to flourish at the local level. Her son, Rajiv, showed even less political talent in his years as prime minister after his mother's assassination in 1984. Throughout, however, India continued to hold regular national elections, and the Congress Party peacefully yielded power when it failed to maintain its majority position in 1977 and 1989.

'People's Power'?

Over time, Asia's authoritarian and semiauthoritarian governments bred domestic pro-democracy and human rights movements. In some countries they gained sufficient strength to challenge the regimes at the polls; elsewhere, they had to focus on mass protests, court challenges and pleas for international support. Meanwhile, the collapse of the Soviet Union and the end of the Cold War freed both the United States government and conservative U.S.-based groups to give greater emphasis to human rights and democracy as a diplomatic and political goal abroad.

The first demonstration of the potential impact of these Asian pro-democracy movements came in the Philippines, where longtime President Ferdinand E. Marcos was forced from office in 1986. Marcos, elected in 1965, imposed martial law in 1971 and ruled with an iron hand for the next 15 years. The assassination of opposition leader Benigno Aquino in 1982 helped galvanize the "People's Power Movement," which rallied behind his widow, Corazon. By 1985, when Marcos had all but lost his grip on power, President Ronald Reagan passed the word that there would be no U.S. intervention for its longtime ally. Marcos went into exile in Hawaii, and Corazon Aquino was installed as president and later elected in her own right.[17]

Events in the Philippines may have inspired challenges to the military regime in Burma, too, but the effort backfired. The military in 1988 installed a new ruling body, the State Law and Order Restoration Council, which proceeded simultaneously to suppress popular dissent and set elections for 1990. When the opposition National League for Democracy emerged as the winner — despite the house arrest of its leader, Nobel Peace Prize-winner Aung San Suu Kyi — the government ignored the results.[18]

Other military-dominated regimes

Indonesia's Troubled Rule Over East Timor

Indonesia invaded and then annexed East Timor 22 years ago to eliminate a potential threat to its stability. Instead, Indonesia's often violent rule over the tiny former Portuguese colony fueled an independence movement and eventually became a major diplomatic embarrassment for President Suharto.

Now, with Suharto's resignation, some observers see the possibility of resolving the issue. "The political transition in Indonesia has opened up the political middle ground," says Donald Emmerson, a political scientist at the University of Wisconsin in Madison.

Indonesia's new president, B. J. Habibie, is willing to discuss some measure of autonomy for East Timor, whose 600,000 residents occupy the eastern half of an island about the size of Maryland.

East Timorese independence advocate Jose Ramos-Horta, who shared the 1996 Nobel Peace Prize, has suggested that a referendum on East Timor's status could be held not immediately — as the movement has demanded — but five years from now.

Emmerson, a longtime student of Indonesian politics, thinks that a delayed vote offers something to both sides in the dispute. "The independence movement is realizing that it makes no sense politically to insist on a referendum tomorrow," he says. As for the Indonesian government, he continues, "the longer the time before the referendum, the more time Indonesia has to build a sense among the East Timorese that they belong in Indonesia."

The current-day dispute is a legacy of arbitrary boundaries drawn by European colonial powers centuries ago. [1] Portugal and the Dutch East India Trading Company established trading posts on opposite ends of the island, which lies near the coast of Australia at the southern end of the major chain of Indonesian islands.

The Indonesian national revolution after World War II brought the Dutch-ruled western half of the island into the new nation, but Portugal retained control of its colony — which, unlike Muslim-dominated Indonesia, was predominantly Roman Catholic. Portugal began to decolonize only decades later, in the 1970s, when a long-ruling dictatorship fell to a socialist-led opposition.

By then, the East Timorese people were themselves divided between three forces: an avowedly leftist independence movement, Fretilin (the Revolutionary Front for Independence of East Timor); the more elitist Timorese Democratic Union (UDT), which favored gradual independence and some continuing ties to Portugal; and a group favoring incorporation within Indonesia: the Timorese Popular Democratic Association, known by the acronym Apodeti.

Fretilin, with the largest amount of support, stirred fears in Jakarta and in Washington of a communist stronghold in the Indonesian archipelago. When a civil war broke out in August 1975, Portugal sided with Fretilin, Indonesia with Apodeti. On Dec. 7, Indonesia invaded East Timor. Historian M.C. Ricklefs says the invasion — supported by the U.S. — may have resulted in as many as 60,000 civilian casualties.

Indonesia formally annexed East Timor in July 1976, as Fretilin retreated to the hills. William Liddle, a political scientist at Ohio State University who visited East Timor in January, says the Suharto government brought "a lot of material progress" to the island — roads, schools, health centers and so forth. But the military presence remained — and continued to exact a heavy toll in deaths and injuries. "There was an awful lot of random, wanton killing," Liddle says.

In the worst such incident, Indonesian troops killed up to 200 East Timorese at the funeral of a separatist sympathizer in 1991. Subsequently, Fretilin rebel leader Xanana Gusma was sentenced to 20 years in prison.

Awarding the Nobel Peace Prize to Ramos-Horta and Bishop Carlos Belo in 1996 helped gain international support for East Timor. U.S. policy, however, continued to recognize East Timor as part of Indonesia.

Liddle thinks Habibie's offer to talk about autonomy may only embolden the independence movement. Emmerson, however, thinks the East Timorese may be cautioned by the current economic crisis in Indonesia and the region.

The political calculations in Jakarta are also multisided. Resolving the issue may appeal to Habibie, Emmerson says, but he also has bigger political problems.

Catharin E. Dalpino, former deputy assistant secretary of State for human rights, notes that any change in East Timor could encourage anti-Jakarta sentiment in other areas, notably Irian Jaya. Indonesia incorporated Irian Jaya, which occupies the western half of the former New Guinea, in 1969 after administering the former Dutch colony for the United Nations for seven years.

For now, Dalpino thinks Habibie's willingness will encourage more pro-independence demonstrations on East Timor. "It will kick up more dust," she says. But, she adds, "there's probably more hope for a mid-term to long-term solution."

---

[1] For background, see M.C. Ricklefs, *A History of Modern Indonesia since c. 1300* (2d ed., 1993); *The Washington Post*, July 10, 1998, p. A27.

---

in East Asia, however, did yield to domestic pressure or outside events during the 1980s and '90s.

In South Korea, the government, on the eve of hosting the Olympic Games, agreed to a new constitution and popular elections in 1988; the balloting left the governing Democratic Justice Party in shaky control and boosted the opposition Party for Peace and Democracy. Today, the longtime opposition leader Kim Dae Jung — imprisoned or exiled for years by the military government — serves as the country's president after a narrow election victory in December.

Taiwan began a decade-long path toward democracy in 1986 when its president, Chiang Ching-kuo decided to lift martial law, ease press censorship and permit political parties. After his death in 1988, constitutional reforms were carried forward by his successor, Lee Teng-hui, who went on to win Taiwan's first popular election for president in 1996.

In Thailand, the military upset a fragile balance between democracy and authoritarianism by seizing power from the elected government in 1991. After parties aligned with the military won a narrow victory in elections in March 1992, the leader of the coup, Gen. Suchinda Kraprayoon, tried to put the prime minister's post under military control. Public protests followed, and eventually King Bhumibol Adulyadej forced Suchinda's resignation and a new beginning of democratization.

Suharto's Final Days

There were few signs of democratization in Indonesia, however, as late as last year. Suharto's hold on power appeared secure, thanks to a rigged electoral system, the military's support and impressive economic growth. Leading up to the May 1997 parliamentary election, Suharto had engineered the ouster of the head of the Indonesian Democratic Party (PDI) and banned any discussion of a possible alliance with the other recognized party, the Muslim United Development Party. The result: The governing Golkar political bloc secured its largest majority ever — about 73 percent of the vote. [19]

When the rupiah fell last July, however, Asia's economic crisis caught up with Indonesia — and Suharto. The IMF eventually pledged up to $43 billion in bailout aid but insisted on stringent fiscal

conditions that included eliminating subsidies on critical consumer goods. When the rupiah fell further in January, Indonesians took to the streets to protest rising prices; by spring, pro-democracy students were calling for Suharto's ouster.

Suharto might have survived, nonetheless, but for the deaths of six students at Jakarta's Trisakti University on May 12. The shootings fueled more unrest and destroyed any remnant of Suharto's credibility with key military and political leaders. Publicly, armed forces chief Gen. Wiranto criticized the calls for Suharto's resignation, but privately he was scripting his removal. Suharto on May 19 promised to hold new elections and step down at some unspecified future date. But two days later, deserted by the military and by his Cabinet, Suharto announced his resignation on television "as of the reading of this statement." He named Habibie as his successor. [20] ■

CURRENT SITUATION

Building Democracy

Four days after taking office, Habibie announced a "national action plan" on human rights. The plan called for the government to ratify international human rights accords, publicize human rights policies and give "top priority" to implementing human rights provisions.

The initiative was "very big news" to journalist Tamimi, who attended the session. "I'm satisfied because he has signed all these international agreements on human rights," Tamimi says. "So now Indonesia has joined the rest of the world."

But in the two months since Habibie's

accession, both the government and its opponents have found that the path to political change is treacherous.

Habibie has drawn criticism both within and without Indonesia for the new election schedule. "The longer you have Habibie in power without democracy, the Indonesian crisis will be worse and worse," says political scientist Hikam.

"International confidence will be increased by holding an election for the Indonesian people to choose both a president and a representative assembly — and much sooner than the schedule" outlined by Habibie, says Human Rights Watch's Jendrzejczyk.

For its part, the reform movement appears unprepared to offer the country a unified platform or a strong alternative to Habibie. "It's been 40 days now, and we still don't know what to do with this," Mas'oed, the Gadjah Mada lecturer and activist, remarked recently.

Habibie scored a significant political victory earlier this month with the election of his executive secretary, Akbar Tanjung, to head the ruling Golkar party. Akbar was elected by secret ballot, 17-10, at the end of the party's special three-day conference July 9-11 in Jakarta; he defeated a Suharto-backed candidate, Edy Sudrajat, a former armed services chief. After winning, Akbar told reporters he would reform Golkar and "rid it of nepotism, corruption, and collusion." [21]

Tamimi says the party gathering was a "big victory for democracy" because of the first-ever direct election of the chairman. He also believes that Akbar himself rather than Habibie may prove to be the long-run winner from the meeting. "It pushes him toward being a prominent political figure," Tamimi says. "If Indonesia is becoming a real democracy, he will be in the best position to put himself forward as a candidate for president."

Habibie continues to gain generally positive reviews from Indonesian and U.S. observers. "Habibie has without a doubt surprised his critics," Emmerson said after the Golkar meeting. Tamimi, however, is more cautious about Akbar. "He was a part of the Suharto system," Tamimi says. Asked if he doubts Akbar's commitment to reform, Tamimi pauses before answering: "We should give him the benefit of the doubt."

Among the government's opponents, the prevailing picture is disarray. More than 30 political parties had registered as of mid-July, stirring fears of electoral fragmentation. Tamimi, however, expects the opponents to sort themselves out by next year's elections. He sees five major opposition parties: two predominantly Muslim parties, one modernist, the other traditional; a nationalist party; a party for Christians and other religious minorities; and a social democratic party. None of the parties is likely to win a majority, Tamimi says, and the opponents could gain enough strength to put together a coalition to deny Golkar a role in a new government.

Meanwhile, the economy remains the dominant issue for Habibie. In his speech to Golkar, Habibie conceded that the government's economic reforms had yet to yield "concrete results." [22] But even after acknowledging the country's lackluster financial markets and other problems, Habibie was optimistic. "In reality, the country has huge natural resources, manpower, experience, institutions and strong determination to come out of the crisis," he said.

Democracy in India

Fifty years after India became the world's most populous democracy, President K.R. Narayanan called the anniversary "a golden moment in the history of India and the world." But Narayanan also acknowledged that democracy's record in India has been mixed. [23]

"I am painfully aware of the deterioration that has taken place in our country ... in recent times," Narayanan said on Aug. 15, 1997. He pointed to the ill treatment of women and low-caste Indians; the lack of adequate education, health care and clean water; and the "criminalization of politics."

Throughout India, the anniversary turned into "a very somber celebration," recalls Sumit Ganguly, an Indian political scientist at Hunter College of the City University of New York. "People focused more on India's shortcomings. There was a great deal of soul-searching."

Political events have also raised concerns about India's democracy outside the country. The rise of Hindu nationalism as a political force has rekindled worries about the sectarian divisions in Indian society. The Hindu nationalist Bharatiya Janata Party (BJP) emerged as the leading vote-getter in parliamentary elections in 1996 and early this year but fell short of a majority. Today, the BJP's leader, Atal Behavi Vajpayee, leads a shaky coalition government. Some observers fear that the government decided to test nuclear weapons in May in part to strengthen its domestic political support.

Ganguly acknowledges concerns about the commitment to democracy among some BJP members. "There are some people who have some fascist orientation, and I don't use that term loosely," he says. But he also says that "countervailing forces" limit the influence of the party's more extreme elements. Freedom House's Graybow agrees. "Hopefully, [the party] will be moderated by having to form a coalition with others," he says.

India's commitment to democracy has also been tested by the secessionist movement in predominantly Muslim Kashmir. Ganguly, author of a new book on the problem, says the Indian government has practiced "calibrated but ruthless" repression

against the insurgents; the U.S. State Department similarly cites what it calls "serious human rights abuses" by government forces in Kashmir and neighboring Jammu. [24]

Despite those shortcomings, Sunil Khilnani, an Indian who teaches politics at Birkbeck College, University of London, says democracy has taken root in the Indian consciousness. "As an idea, it's been an enormous success," says Khilnani, author of a new book assessing Indian democracy. "There's no one in India today who questions democratic politics, whether they're on the right or left, rich or poor. There's a general feeling that democracy is the only way for India." [25]

Conflicted Democracies

India's neighbors, however, have had less success with democracy. Pakistan has had military rule for more than half its half-century of independence. [26] Democracy was restored in 1988, but the military still wields great influence. In addition, Islamic fundamentalists pressure the government on religious issues, ethnic and regional divisions run deep and political and economic corruption persist. The country's president resigned in December after complaining that Prime Minister Nawaz Sharif had politicized the judiciary while defending himself against corruption charges.

Bangladesh, the former East Pakistan, also has had frequent periods of military rule since independence in 1971. But Graybow lists Bangladesh among emerging democracies in the 1990s, and the State Department credits the country with a relatively free multiparty system.

Sri Lanka, on the other hand, had a strong tradition of democratic practice predating its independence from

At Issue:

Has the Clinton administration done a good job of promoting democracy in Asia?

CATHARIN E. DALPINO
*Guest Scholar, The Brookings Institution, former deputy
assistant secretary of State for human rights*

WRITTEN FOR THE CQ RESEARCHER, JULY 21, 1998.

Crafting effective U.S. strategies to promote democracy in Asia is difficult in today's policy environment. The lingering sense of triumph over the collapse of Soviet communism has encouraged a Eurocentric approach to political change and an exaggerated estimate of the power of external actors, even superpowers, to direct democratic transitions. Moreover, some politicians and the press recall only the moments of dramatic resolution — the fall of the Berlin Wall — and therefore view democratization as a sprint. In reality, it is a marathon.

The strength of the Clinton administration's approach to Asia is its willingness to play a strong supporting role in helping Asians find their own democratic solutions to political problems, despite domestic pressure at times for more dirigiste or high-decibel policies.

U.S. assistance programs in the Philippines to decentralize power and strengthen civil society have helped that country stay the democratic course. In Mongolia, democracy-assistance programs paid off in 1996 when parliamentary elections turned the communists out of power. Equally important, the defeated party took its place on the back bench without protest.

Clinton administration support to Indonesia's struggling non-governmental sector and to the National Human Rights Commission has helped to build the foundation for a democratic transition with Suharto's departure.

The administration's response to democratic backsliding in Cambodia last July was firm, but appropriately nuanced. Support was increased to Cambodian human rights organizations while aid to the government itself was suspended. U.S. pressure has kept the Cambodian seat vacant at the United Nations, pending a democratic resolution to the conflict. With U.S. urging, the Association of Southeast Asian Nations (ASEAN) pressed Hun Sen to agree to elections.

The success of the most important Clinton administration policy in Asia — to promote political liberalization in the Leninist states — can't be measured for years. Requests in the fiscal year 1999 budget, for programs such as the president's Rule of Law Initiative for China, are realistic first steps that will help to change the relationship between state and society in these countries. Paradoxically, our ability to encourage eventual democratization in China and its Leninist neighbors will depend upon our willingness to leave Cold War models and methods behind.

MIKE JENDRZEJCZYK
Washington Director, Human Rights Watch, Asia Division

WRITTEN FOR THE CQ RESEARCHER, JULY 21, 1998

the Clinton administration has tried to balance competing agendas in Asia, generally placing the highest priority on economic and security interests rather than on human rights and democratization. The results are decidedly mixed.

While enthusiastically promoting an agenda of free trade and open markets, the administration has been slow to see the linkage between the meltdown of Asian economies and growing aspirations in many countries for more open, accountable governance, the rule of law and an end to corruption. And in countries like China and Vietnam, it has been willing to abandon potentially effective policies and sources of leverage, relying instead on the market to eventually produce political change.

Indonesians trying to jettison repressive institutions and a political culture created over more than 30 years are now eager for change. They are clearly looking for U.S. support that goes beyond aid to non-governmental organizations or humanitarian assistance, as vital as that may be. They want U.S. support for a speedier transition and creative help in solving longstanding human rights problems such as East Timor.

Citizens of Burma and Cambodia, struggling under military rule or trying to restore democracy, believe that by withholding legitimacy — and funding by international financial institutions — the U.S. can create the political space they urgently need. They've already waited years to peacefully exercise their basic rights and feel they can ill afford to wait much longer.

Next week's meeting of the Association for Southeast Asian Nations (ASEAN) in Manila will provide an interesting window on the shifts under way in the region. Thailand and the Philippines have publicly called for the abandonment of "constructive engagement" (i.e. not interfering in the internal affairs of other nations) as an outmoded approach. They propose instead a policy of "flexible engagement" in order to deal with destabilizing problems, including the lack of progress in democratization.

In this rapidly evolving environment, the United States should not place its major emphasis on long-term rule-of-law programs alone, or on the instincts of "visionary" leaders such as Jiang Zemin, as Clinton called the Chinese president. And while being careful not to impose "American values" or solutions, the Clinton administration should clearly articulate more effective bilateral and multilateral policies that can aid Asia's crucial transitions.

Putting Myanmar on the Political Map

When U Zarni came to the United States 10 years ago, he expected to get a degree in education and return to his native Burma. But today he leads a coalition of other Burmese expatriates working within the United States for economic sanctions against his country. Their goal is to pressure the military government to permit the restoration of democracy.

"We put Burma on the map of international politics," Zarni says of the Free Burma Coalition, which he founded in 1995. "We as a grass-roots campaign brought Burma to American and international households."

The effect of the coalition's work, however, is sharply disputed. In 1997, Congress passed and President Clinton signed into law an economic-sanctions bill prohibiting U.S. companies from making new investments in Myanmar, as the military government renamed the country. Zarni says one state — Massachusetts — and 20 municipalities have passed broader sanctions measures that cut off trade with any companies operating in Myanmar. [1]

Zarni and other human rights advocates believe the sanctions are having an effect. "The junta itself admitted that they are reeling from the effects of American sanctions," says Zarni, now a graduate student at the University of Wisconsin in Madison.

As evidence, Zarni cites recent comments by a member of the ruling council, Brig. Gen. D.O. Abel, to *Leaders* magazine, an international business-oriented publication. Abel said that American companies are "holding off" investing in Myanmar because of the sanctions and that the sanctions are having an effect on other multinational companies. "Any Japanese companies that are operating here in Myanmar cannot operate in the state of Massachusetts," Abel said. "They and other multinational companies don't want to invest here because they are afraid of retaliation from the United States."

Zarni says the sanctions have led some 25 multinational companies — including Pepsico, Texaco, Heineken, Levi Strauss, Liz Claiborne and Eddie Bauer — to pull out of Myanmar. Two big U.S.-based oil companies — Arco and Unocal — are still there, however. Unocal is joint-venturing with a French and a Thai company on a $1.2 billion gas pipeline.

Policy-makers and foreign policy experts generally dismiss the effects of the sanctions as minimal. "We don't have sufficient leverage on Myanmar to force change from the outside," says Catharin E. Dalpino, a guest scholar at the Brookings Institution and former deputy assistant secretary of State for human rights in the Clinton administration. "And we haven't been able to get our allies, both Asian and European, to join with us."

Clearly, though, Zarni's group has raised awareness of Myanmar's military government inside the United States. The coalition operates an Internet site (www.freeburma.org) with up-to-date news and pro-democracy information. The coalition also used its boycott of Pepsi Cola to good effect. "Third-graders were boycotting Pepsi because their teachers were teaching them about human rights," Zarni says. [2]

Some other Asian expatriate groups also have lobbied within the United States to try to influence U.S. policy toward their native countries — most notably Chinese groups, such as the Independent Federation of Chinese Students and Scholars. The Washington-based group has helped organize protests in the United States against the Chinese government.

Generally, though, the groups' impact on policy appears to be relatively minimal. Until recently, at least, Asian-Americans have tended to shy away from domestic U.S. politics, and their numbers have been too small to have much influence except in a few areas. The influence of expatriate groups is inherently limited by their divided attention between the United States and their home country. An earlier Burmese group, for example, the Committee for Restoration of Democracy in Burma, is less visible in the United States because it concentrates on helping students and others inside Burma. And, as U.S. policy toward China illustrates, partisan politics and broad economic interests usually carry more weight in government decision-making than pro-democracy lobbying from ethnic or expatriate groups.

Zarni cut off ties with his family still in Myanmar — parents and seven siblings — to protect them from repercussions from his work in the United States. He has been granted political asylum in the United States, but he still hopes to return. "When the country is free," he says, "I intend to go back."

[1] For background, see *The Christian Science Monitor*, Jan. 29, 1998, p. 6.

[2] For further background, see *The New York Times*, April 8, 1997, p. A18, and *The Chronicle of Higher Education*, Feb. 14, 1997, p. A43.

Britain in 1948 that has been tarnished by protracted ethnic violence between the Sinhalese majority, mostly Hindu, and the predominantly Buddhist Tamil minority. The government's refusal to grant Tamil demands for more autonomy sparked a civil war that has raged since 1983. A measure of political order returned in the 1990s, but the government has yet to craft a political settlement acceptable to the separatist Tamils.

Meanwhile, Japan — arguably the region's most successful democracy — is in turmoil. "The Japanese political leadership is floundering," says Ellis Krauss, an expert on Japan at the University of California-San Diego. The Liberal Democratic Party (LDP) fell from power in 1993, regained control of the government in 1996, but — in the midst of an economic recession — suffered a stinging rejection at the polls in elections earlier this month. Prime Minister Ryutaro Hashimoto immediately resigned.

Even before Japan's economic problems surfaced, however, the government gave the United States only scant encouragement in efforts to promote democracy in Asia. "Japanese foreign policy is far more pragmatic" than U.S. policy, Krauss says. "It tends to be based on a more narrowly defined self-interest." ∎

OUTLOOK

Change and Resistance

When he ended his nine-day trip to China earlier this month, President Clinton emphatically predicted the eventual rise of democracy in Asia's largest country. But Clinton also acknowledged "powerful forces resisting change" in China. And he dodged a reporter's question asking whether he expected to see democracy in China in his lifetime. [27]

Similarly, in most of Asia's nondemocratic countries. There are stirrings of democracy, but the democratic forces face strong resistance from well-entrenched governments — whether they be communist, military or one-party regimes.

"We see growing pressure for democratic change" in Asia, says the Hoover Institute's Diamond. In most of the region, though, "it's hard to discern movement" toward democracy, he says.

Other U.S. observers and advocates are somewhat more optimistic. Brookings' Dalpino predicts "a series of quiet watersheds" in several Asian

countries over the next few years. Daniel Steinberg, director of the Asia studies program at Georgetown University, even sees gradual political liberalization in Asia's most authoritarian countries.

"We're talking about the rise of alternative centers of power, which means the state is less centralized than it once was," Steinberg says. "That's happening even in China. And on the economic side, you're getting people making economic decisions without reference to the state."

The likelihood of democratic change in China remains sharply disputed. The government is encouraging villages to hold elections for local offices, but there is no movement toward electing leaders at the national level. When the *Journal of Democracy* gathered 10 experts earlier this year to offer predictions about the potential for democratization in China over the next decade, the optimists outnumbered the pessimists, but they all hedged their bets. [28]

Among Asia's other communist regimes, Vietnam and Laos have both adopted some market-oriented reforms, and both countries held national elections last year. But the State Department reports little progress toward political liberalization. In North Korea, the government has ruled out any political or economic liberalization.

Myanmar's military regime similarly shows no easing up. "Nothing's changed there," says Steinberg, who visited Myanmar earlier this summer. "They will have a civilian government at some point in the indefinite future, but it will be militarily controlled." Malaysia's and Singapore's dominant-party governments also show no signs of liberalizing political rights or, for now at least, losing popular support.

On the subcontinent, Pakistan continues to have elements of repression and arbitrary rule despite democratic forms. Bangladesh witnessed a peaceful change of government after elec-

tions two years ago, but political violence and electoral fraud persist. And Sri Lanka's civil war continues to mar its record in democratic government.

The bright spots for advocates of democratization are relatively few, but significant. "We've seen some nice consolidation of democracy in Thailand, in the Philippines, in South Korea," Dalpino says. Nepal has held four relatively free elections since political parties were legalized in 1990. Mongolia is making what the State Department calls good progress toward democracy in its transition from a communist regime. And India and Japan remain relatively secure in their democracies despite domestic political turmoil.

The U.S. role in encouraging democratic developments, most observers say, is limited but still significant. Diamond, for example, credits the Clinton administration with standing behind the Thai government as it instituted political reforms. He and others also stress the importance of the less visible U.S. support, including financial assistance, for associations, labor unions, human rights organizations and other elements of so-called civil society. "These are micro-type linkages," Diamond says, "part of the ongoing, more prosaic process of building democracy."

Many of these organizations are funded through the National Endowment for Democracy, which Diamond notes has a difficult time getting funding every year on Capitol Hill. "It's been one of the great success stories of U.S. foreign policy," he says, "but it has to fight for its existence every year."

Meanwhile, the biggest question mark for the moment is Indonesia, which must institute political reform and economic revival simultaneously. Mas'oed fears the economic problems may temper popular support for reform. "The common people tend to think more about food than about the reform movement now," he says.

"That's a problem."

After watching the Golkar conference, however, Tamimi was optimistic about the prospects for democracy. "This is very good for democracy," he says. "If the ruling party gives this good example, others will follow. When you disagree, there is no other way but through voting — no more manipulation." ∎

Notes

[1] For background, see Christopher Conte, "Deflation Fears," *The CQ Researcher*, Feb. 13, 1998, pp. 121-144.

[2] For background, see David Masci, "China After Deng," *The CQ Researcher*, June 13, 1997, pp. 505-528, and Patrick G. Marshall, "New Era in Asia," *The CQ Researcher*, Feb. 14, 1992, pp. 121-144.

[3] U.S. Department of State, *Country Reports on Human Rights Practices for 1997*, March 1998, p. 900.

[4] Fareed Zakaria, "Culture Is Destiny: A Conversation with Lee Kuan Yew," *Foreign Affairs*, March/April 1994, pp. 109-126; *The Wall Street Journal*, June 25, 1996, p. A1; Mahathir Mohamad and Shintaro Ishihara, *The Voice of Asia: Two Leaders Discuss the Coming Century* (1995), pp. 82-83.

[5] Samuel P. Huntington, *The Third Wave: Democratization in the Late 20th Century* (1991), p. 306.

[6] Lucian Pye, "Dominant Party Democracies in Asia," in *Democracy in Asia and Africa* (1998), pp. 69-72. For background, see Kenneth Jost, "Taiwan, China and the U.S.," *The CQ Researcher*, May 24, 1996, pp. 457-480.

[7] See *The New York Times*, July 28, 1997, p. A3; *The Washington Post*, July 30, 1997, pp. A1, A19. ASEAN includes Brunei, Indonesia, Laos, Malaysia, Myanmar, the Philippines, Singapore, Thailand and Vietnam.

[8] For background, see Mary H. Cooper, "U.S.-Vietnam Relations," *The CQ Researcher*, Dec. 3, 1993, pp. 1057-1080.

[9] For excerpts, see *The New York Times*, May 23, 1998, p. A8.

[10] See Yoneo Ishii, "Buddhism"; Werner Menski, "Hinduism"; and Winberg Chai and May-klee Chai, "Confucianism," in *Encyclopedia of Democracy* (1995).

[11] Some background is drawn from John Keay, *Empire's End: A History of the Far East from High Colonialism to Hong Kong* (1997).

[12] Donald K. Emmerson, "Indonesia," in *Democracy in Asia and Africa* (1998), p. 86.

[13] Keay, *op. cit.*, p. 212.

[14] Background drawn in part from individual country articles in *Democracy in Asia and Africa* and Keay, *op. cit.*.

[15] For background, see Emmerson, *op. cit.*; Keay, *op. cit.*, pp. 32-35, 247-269.

[16] Huntington, *op. cit.* For background, see Emmerson, *op. cit.*; William Liddle, "Indonesia," in *Comparative Governance* (1992);

M.C. Ricklefs, A *History of Modern Indonesia Since c. 1300* (1993).

[17] For a detailed account, see Raymond Bonner, *Waltzing with a Dictator: The Marcoses and the Making of American Policy* (1987).

[18] See Aung Cin Win Aung, *Burma: From Monarchy to Dictatorship* (1994).

[19] See State Department, *op. cit.*, pp. 784-785.

[20] For accounts of Suharto's fall, see *Far Eastern Economic Review*, June 4, 1998, pp. 21-26; *Newsweek*, June 1, 1998, pp. 34-43; *Time*, June 1, 1998, pp. 60-63.

[21] Quoted in *The New York Times*, July 12, 1998, p. A8.

[22] Quoted in *The Washington Post*, July 10, 1998, p. A31.

[23] See *The New York Times*, Aug. 15, 1997, p. A13. For a retrospective on India's 50 years of independence, see John F. Burns, "India's Five Decades of Progress and Pain," *The New York Times*, Aug. 14, 1997, p. A1.

[24] State Department, *op. cit.*, p. 1637. See Sumit Ganguly, *The Crisis in Kashmir: Portents of War, Hopes of Peace* (1998).

[25] See Sunil Khilnani, *The Idea of India* (1998).

[26] For background, see John F. Burns, "Pakistan's Bitter Roots, and Modest Hopes," *The New York Times*, Aug. 15, 1997, p. A1.

[27] For edited transcript of the Clinton news conference, see *The Washington Post*, July 4, 1998, pp. A20-21.

[28] "Will China Democratize?" *Journal of Democracy*, January 1998, pp. 3-64.

Bibliography

Selected Sources Used

Books

Democracy in Asia and Africa, CQ Books, 1998.
  This reference work includes articles by leading Asia scholars assessing the status of democracy in Asia and Africa. Each article includes a short bibliography. Additional articles on Buddhism, Hinduism and Confucianism can be found in *The Encyclopedia of Democracy* (CQ Books, 1995).

Ishida, Takeshi, and Ellis S. Krauss (eds.), *Democracy in Japan*, University of Pittsburgh Press, 1989.
  Essays by 13 experts evaluate political, social and economic democracy in Japan as of the end of the 1980s.

Keay, John, *Empire's End: A History of the Far East from High Colonialism to Hong Kong*, Scribner, 1997.
  Keay, a British scholar, provides a readable survey of Dutch, English, French and American colonialism in East Asia beginning in the 17th century but focusing on the period 1930-1975.

Khilnani, Sunil, *The Idea of India*, Farrar Straus Giroux, 1998.
  Khilnani, a political scientist at the University of London's Birkbeck College, provides an evocative picture of Indian political culture since independence. The book includes a 25-page bibliographic essay.

Liddle, William, "Indonesia," in Philip Shiveley (ed.), *Comparative Governance*, McGraw-Hill, 1992.
  Liddle, a professor of political science at Ohio State University, contributes an overview of Indonesian politics and government to this political science text.

Ricklefs, M.C., *A History of Modern Indonesia Since 1300* (2d ed.), Stanford University Press, 1993.
  This authoritative history traces events in Indonesia from the arrival of Islam in the 14th century and colonization by the Dutch in the 17th century through independence and the Sukarno and Suharto eras. The book includes detailed source notes, maps and a 25-page bibliography. Ricklefs is a history professor at the Australian National University in Canberra.

Steinberg, David I., *The Future of Burma: Crisis and Choice in Myanmar*, University Press of America, 1990.
  Steinberg, now a professor at Georgetown University, wrote this account of the 1988 military coup and its aftermath immediately before the national elections in 1990, which were nullified by the military regime. The book includes a short list of suggested reading, including Steinberg's *Burma: A Socialist Nation of Southeast Asia* (Westview Press, 1982). For more recent books by a pro-democracy Burmese journalist now living in the United States, see Aung Chin Win Aung, *Burma: From Monarchy to Dictatorship*, Eastern Press, 1994; *Burma and the Last Days of General Ne Win*, Yoma Publishing, 1996.

Tharoor, Shashi, *India: From Midnight to the Millennium*, Arcade Publishing, 1997.
  Tharoor, a United Nations official who has lived outside India for most of his life, writes what he describes as a "paean" to India that nonetheless sharply criticizes the country's political system for producing corruption and instability. The book includes a four-page chronology covering 1947 through April 1997 and a seven-page glossary.

Reports and Studies

Freedom House, *Freedom in the World, 1997-1998*, 1998.
  The 610-page volume includes country-by-country assessments of political and economic freedoms covering events through Jan. 1, 1998. The volume includes a global overview essay and regional essays on East Asia and South Asia.

Human Rights Watch World Report 1998: Events of 1997, December 1997.
  Human Rights Watch's most recent annual report, covering events through 1997, includes featured essays on 10 Asian countries.

U.S. Department of State, *Country Reports on Human Rights Practices for 1997*, March 1998.
  The State Department's most recent annual report provides detailed country-by-country assessments of human rights, civil liberties, political rights, protections against discrimination and workers' rights.

FOR MORE INFORMATION

The **U.S. State Department's** annual *Country Report on Human Rights Practices* can be found online at www.state.gov.; (202) 647-4000.

Here are private organizations that follow human rights issues in Asia:

Freedom House, 1319 18th St., N.W., Washington, D.C. 20036; (202) 296 5101; 120 Wall St., 26th floor, New York, N.Y. 10005; (212) 514-8040; www.freedomhouse.org. The human rights organization publishes a biennial volume, *Freedom in the World*, with country-by-country assessments of political and economic freedoms.

Human Rights Watch, 350 5th Ave., 34th floor, New York, N.Y. 10018; (212) 290-4700; 1630 Connecticut Ave., N.W., Suite 500, Washington, D.C. 20009; (202) 612-4321; www.hrw.org. The human rights organization publishes periodic reports and an annual volume, *Human Rights Watch World Report*.

12 Human Rights

KENNETH JOST

The jungle in eastern Congo was so thick, Roberto Garretón recalls today, that you could not thread a needle through the trees. But after making his way through the dense foliage, the Chilean human rights lawyer came upon a clearing that was "upholstered with stones."

Garretón, guided to the site by a refugee from neighboring Rwanda, recognized the site as a mass grave — evidence of massacres committed by the rebel forces that controlled much of what was then called Zaire. The rebel leader, Col. Laurent Kabila, had heatedly denied allegations of mass killings. Now Garretón, on a United Nations mission to investigate the accusations, had proof before his eyes.

"Here was the grave where they buried their dead," Garretón says. "You have people telling you that there had been massacres there, and you have a person telling you, 'I buried them here.'"

Garretón's 16-page report on his discoveries, submitted to the United Nations Human Rights Commission in April 1997, was the first independent confirmation of atrocities being committed by Kabila's rebels as they sought to topple the government of longtime strongman Mobutu Sese Seko. Less than six weeks later, the rebels took over the capital city of Kinshasa and installed Kabila as the head of a new government. In one of his first actions, Kabila declared Garretón persona non grata and ordered him out of the country.

In the 18 months since then, Garretón has continued in his role as the United Nations' so-called "special rapporteur" on the situation in Congo — supervising, in absentia, a team of U.N. investigators that has remained in the country but under significant limitations imposed by Kabila's government.

From *The CQ Researcher,*
November 13, 1998.

Reuters

The U.N.'s critiques of human rights practices in Congo have not stopped the killings or had any noticeable effect on Kabila's policies. But the reports prepared by Garretón and a growing number of other U.N. special rapporteurs investigating human rights issues have helped document abuses around the world and may have helped improve human rights practices in some countries. (*See story, p. 214.*)

The mixed record helps explain why the international human rights community has mixed feelings as it prepares this year to mark an important milestone: the 50th anniversary of the Universal Declaration of Human Rights. The declaration, adopted by the United Nations General Assembly on Dec. 10, 1948, was the first comprehensive international charter of individual freedoms (*see p. 215*). It set the stage for dozens of major human rights treaties and the creation and later expansion of a United Nations apparatus that has sought to set human rights standards for individual countries to follow; assist governments in improving human rights conditions; and investigate, document and deter violations.

Human rights conditions have vastly improved in much of the world

since 1948, advocates and policymakers agree. But with gross human rights abuses fresh in mind — as seen most recently, for example, in the wartime killings of civilians in Congo and Kosovo — human rights groups are tempering their celebrations with somber notes.

"We think that as we look back over 50 years, many of the promises have not been delivered," says Pierre Sané, secretary general of Amnesty International.

"Human rights groups are reluctant to talk about celebrating," says Kenneth Roth, executive director of Human Rights Watch. "There's so much left to be done."

On the positive side of the ledger, human rights advocates and experts list the development and broad acceptance of a growing body of international standards. "Fifty years ago, there were many, many governments that viewed human rights as interference in their internal affairs," says Roth. "That excuse is utterly discredited today."

A second major accomplishment is the growth of the human rights movement itself — not only international groups like Amnesty International and Human Rights Watch but also domestic organizations that operate in relatively free countries and in countries with more repressive regimes. "Today, you find human rights groups in almost every country in the world," says Roth. "Only the most repressive countries lack an indigenous human rights organization today."

Despite those accomplishments, human rights advocates acknowledge that the U.N. and advocacy groups have often been powerless to prevent the most blatant instances of human rights violations or to ensure compliance from governments that profess commitments to human rights.

"We see in the 1990s genocide in

Universal Declaration of Human Rights

The broadly phrased Universal Declaration of Human Rights covers civil and political rights (Articles 3-21) and social and economic rights (Articles 22-27). The United Nations General Assembly adopted the declaration 48-0, with eight abstentions, on Dec. 10, 1948.

Article 1 — All people 'born free and equal in dignity and rights.'

Article 2 — Everyone entitled to all freedoms set forth 'without distinction of any kind.'

Article 3 — Right to life, liberty, and security of person.

Article 4 — No slavery or servitude.

Article 5 — No torture or 'cruel, inhuman or degrading treatment or punishment.'

Article 6 — Right to recognition everywhere as a person before the law.

Article 7 — Equal protection of the law against 'any discrimination' and 'against any incitement to such discrimination.'

Article 8 — Right to effective remedy by competent national tribunals for violations of fundamental rights.

Article 9 — No arbitrary arrest, detention, or exile.

Article 10 — Right to a fair and public hearing by an independent and impartial tribunal in criminal cases.

Article 11 — Presumption of innocence until proved guilty in a public trial with 'all guarantees necessary for [a] defense.'

Article 12 — No 'arbitrary interference' with privacy, family, home or correspondence; no 'attacks' on 'honor or reputation.'

Article 13 — Freedom of movement and residence within national borders; right to leave and return to one's country.

Article 14 — Right to seek and enjoy in other countries asylum from prosecution, but not from non-political crimes.

Article 15 — Right to a nationality.

Article 16 — Men and women 'of full age' have a right to marry and found a family, without limitation due to race, nationality, or religion.

Bosnia and Rwanda right in front of our eyes," Sané says, "with total inaction by the international community."

'We are going through a very isolationist, complacent period in our history," Roth says, "where it's been all too difficult to mobilize attention to problems in Kosovo, Afghanistan, Congo or China.

"Human rights principles are broadly accepted, but human rights are nonetheless violated widely," Roth says.

The United Nations has been deeply involved in human rights since its founding in 1945. The Universal Declaration — 30 articles long — was one of the U.N.'s first major accomplishments. But the declaration was not binding, and it took another two decades to draft the two major human rights covenants: the International Covenant on Civil and Political Rights and the International Covenant on Economic, Social and Cultural Rights.

Most of the major U.N. treaties have been ratified by more than 100 countries each, but human rights groups note that the United States has failed to ratify many of them because of opposition within Congress and from conservative advocacy groups. "The United States has been one of the most reluctant countries to allow itself to be bound by international law," says Richard Reoch, who was an official with Amnesty International in London for 23 years before leaving in 1993 to head an environmental advocacy group.

Critics, however, say that the U.N. treaties are often vague or overly ambitious or

Article 17 — Right to own property 'alone or in association with others.'

Article 18 — Right to freedom of thought, conscience, and religion, including freedom to change one's religion or belief; right to manifest one's religion or belief in 'teaching, practice, worship and observance.'

Article 19 — Right to freedom of opinion and expression, including freedom 'to seek, receive and impart information and ideas through any media and regardless of frontiers.'

Article 20 — Right to freedom of peaceful assembly and association.

Article 21 — Right to take part in the government of one's country, 'directly or through freely chosen representatives'; equal access to public service; 'periodic and genuine elections' held by 'universal and equal suffrage' and secret vote.

Article 22 — Right to social security and to 'realization ... of the economic, social and cultural rights indispensable for [one's] dignity' through national and international efforts and 'in accordance with the organization and resources of each State.'

Article 23 — Right to work, 'free choice of employment,' 'just and favorable conditions of work,' and 'protection against unemployment'; 'equal pay for equal work'; right to form and join trade unions.

Article 24 — Right to 'rest and leisure,' including 'reasonable limitation of working hours' and 'periodic holidays with pay.'

Article 25 — Right to a standard of living 'adequate for the health and well-being of [one's self] and [one's] family,' including food, clothing, housing and medical care; right to 'security' in event of unemployment, disability, sickness, or old age; all children entitled to protection whether born in or out of wedlock.

Article 26 — Right to education, including free education 'at least in elementary and fundamental stages'; compulsory elementary education; parents have 'a prior right to choose the kind of education' for their children.

Article 27 — Right to 'freely participate' in cultural life; right to protection of 'the moral and material interests' resulting from one's scientific, literary, or artistic works.

Article 28 — Everyone entitled to a social and international order in which rights set forth can be realized.

Article 29 — Everyone has duties to the community; rights and freedoms can be limited only to secure 'due recognition and respect' for rights of others and for 'the just requirements of morality, public order and the general welfare.'

Article 30 — Nothing in Declaration gives any state, group or person right to take action aimed at destruction of any of listed rights.

both and that the U.N. has proved to have little power — or political will — to enforce them anyway. "As a rule, the treaties are less important than either the willingness of private-sector groups to organize and fight and raise hell and of governments to be willing to make an issue about human rights even when that makes for diplomatic discomfort," says Joshua Muravchik, a self-described neoconservative human rights expert at the American Enterprise Institute.

The U.N. has moved to strengthen its human rights machinery in recent years, however. The most visible of the changes came in 1994 when then Secretary General Boutros Boutros-Ghali created the post of High Commissioner for Human Rights to direct the U.N.'s work in the area. The current commissioner, Mary Robinson, former president of Ireland, has been both visible and outspoken since assuming the post in September 1997.

As for the human rights groups, they are often criticized for taking an overly simplistic view of how to achieve their goals. "They tend to demand that these rights be respected instantly, without taking into account the longer processes of liberalization and democratization," says Catharin Dalpino, a visiting scholar at the Brookings Institution who served as deputy assistant U.S. secretary of State for human rights in President Clinton's first term. "Their lack of patience, or lack of realism, weakens their position."

U.S. Faulted on Executions, Police Practices

The murder case against Dwayne Allen Wright for a 1989 killing spree that left four people dead proceeded through Virginia courts much like other capital punishment cases. After his conviction and sentence to death, his final plea for executive clemency was rejected. On Oct. 14, 1998, he was executed in the electric chair.

For human rights groups, though, the Wright case put Virginia in the unsavory company of only five countries besides the United States — Iran, Nigeria, Pakistan, Saudi Arabia and Yemen — that defy international standards by executing people for offenses committed as juveniles.

The use of the death penalty against juvenile offenders is one of several issues that the human rights group Amnesty International is highlighting in a yearlong campaign against what it calls "a persistent and widespread pattern of human rights violations" in the United States.

"The United States prides itself as being a human rights leader," William Schulze, executive director of Amnesty International-USA, told a Washington, D.C., news conference to kick off the campaign on Oct. 7. "If our own house is not in order, that voice is diminished, less powerful."

But a prominent neoconservative human rights expert sharply attacked Amnesty for putting the United States in the same league as non-democratic countries with notorious records on human rights.

"In the interest of a false objectivity, they go about a distortion of reality," says Joshua Muravchik, a fellow at the American Enterprise Institute. "It's nonsense, and it does grave harm to the cause of human rights."

Amnesty launched the campaign by publishing a 150-page report that criticized the United States for "entrenched and nationwide police brutality," "physical and sexual abuse of prisoners" and the rising number of people executed and awaiting execution on death rows around the country. "It is time for the USA to deliver rights for all its people," the report concludes. [1]

On capital punishment, Amnesty noted that the International Covenant on Civil and Political Rights prohibits the death penalty for juvenile offenders. In ratifying the treaty, the United States added a number of so-called "reservations," including one to allow continued use of the death penalty for crimes committed by juveniles.

Wright, who was 17 years old at the time of the 1989 killings and had a history of mental illness, was the thirteenth person executed in the U.S. since 1990 for murders committed while they were juveniles. [2] In declining to commute the death sentence, Virginia Gov. James S. Gilmore III made no reference to the issue of executing juvenile offenders.

Amnesty's report said that police in the United States often use excessive force against suspects and that complaint procedures are "inadequate or wholly absent in some areas." Schultze and others at the news conference in particular criticized the growing use of electroshock devices — so-called "stun guns" — to control suspects, saying they inflict serious injury and their long-term effects are not known.

The National Association of Chiefs of Police dismissed the report as unfair. "Most U.S. law officers act in appropriate accordance with the intense level of danger their responsibilities present," the group's director, Gerald Arenberg, said in a statement. He also defended the use of stun guns. "It's actually one of the better devices, if used properly," Arenberg told The Associated Press.

The report also faulted prison conditions in the United States, saying that facilities are overcrowded, abuse of prisoners common and legal safeguards inadequate. It specifically criticized the housing of juveniles with adult offenders and the use of shackles for women prisoners in labor or while giving birth.

Muravchik said Amnesty's critique showed an anti-law enforcement bias. "Only in a lawful society are rights protected," he said after being given a summary of the issues raised. "A system of law entails restraints and punishments aimed at lawbreakers."

In releasing the report, however, Amnesty's international secretary-general, Pierre Sané, said the United States was lagging on human rights.

"Human rights practices in the United States have not kept pace with the evolving standards of decency," Sané said. "If the United States does not clean its own house," he added, "its credibility among the general population of the world will be tarnished."

---

[1] Amnesty International, *United States of America: Rights for All*, October 1998.

[2] *The New York Times*, Oct. 15, 1998, p. A19.

President Clinton himself was widely expected to put a strong emphasis on human rights in foreign policy, but advocacy groups are generally disappointed with his record in office. They complain, for example, of his decision midway in his first term to delink human rights and trade in dealing with China. More recently, they have sharply attacked the administration's refusal to approve a draft treaty completed this summer to establish an international criminal court. (*See "At Issue," p. 219.*)

Despite these controversies, the human rights community is likely to put aside some of those differences next month as they commemorate the Universal Declaration's 50th anniversary. Afterward, however, here are some of the issues that will continue to generate debate:

Is it realistic to expect all countries to comply with the Universal Declaration of Human Rights?

When the United States led the way in drafting and promulgating the Universal Declaration of Human Rights, racial segregation was still pervasive in America, women had few legal protections against discrimination, and the rights of criminal defendants were often ignored in police stations and in courtrooms. Today, countries with even graver human rights problems are among the nations that have endorsed the Universal Declaration and ratified many of the treaties written to implement its provisions.

The gap between rhetoric and reality gives critics and skeptics ample opportunity to question the value of the Universal Declaration. "Anyone who wants to damn it can do so by stressing the hypocrisy, the apathy, and the degree to which for the major powers human rights has been tucked into a larger framework of more material interests, like national security and economic matters," says Harvard Law School Professor Henry Steiner.

"It's worth celebrating, but with the understanding that the problems out there remain pretty much the same as they were 50 years ago," says Charles S. Lichenstein, a former deputy U.S. ambassador to the United Nations in the early 1980s and now a distinguished fellow at the conservative Heritage Foundation in Washington.

Human rights groups and advocates say that even though the declaration itself did not establish any binding obligations, it has helped reshape attitudes among governments and among the peoples of the world. "It established a common standard for all mankind," Steiner says.

"It was valuable to be able to say that this is something that is accepted everywhere, more or less," says Muravchik.

Some human rights experts, however, question the practical value of the declaration. "It's a fine goal, but the Universal Declaration is not in itself a roadmap," says Dalpino. "It does not begin to suggest how countries get to that level of recognition of human rights."

Dalpino sees greater value in the more specific provisions of the various U.N. treaties that have been negotiated since 1948, such as the two major covenants on civil and political rights and economic, social, and cultural rights. She says that even though many countries, including the United States, attach significant reservations to the treaties, ratification helps by giving domestic groups a standard to hold the government accountable to. In addition, some of the treaties, such as the covenant on civil and political rights, require countries to provide periodic reports on their compliance with the provisions. "That's very helpful internally too," Dalpino says.

Many conservatives, however, sharply attack the treaties, especially the covenant on economic rights and the more recent Covenant on the Rights of the Child. "The economic and social covenant seems to me to be very questionable," Muravchik says. "It boils down to saying that every country should be a relatively well-off country in which everyone shares the benefits. The problem is there's no way to decree that, there's no way to just make that happen."

Despite the limitations, liberal human rights experts maintain that the Universal Declaration remains valuable today in setting forth standards for all countries to be held to. "There are certain things that a government should refrain from doing, to refrain from transgressing moral values that are held around the world," says Roth of Human Rights Watch. "And if a government is determined to transgress them, the world has a duty to speak out against it."

These experts insist that the declaration's influence can be seen both in real events and in people's attitudes toward freedom around the world. "A discourse has been introduced that over 50 years has become so rooted that it cannot be uprooted," Steiner says.

"The fundamental themes show in the People's Republic of China. They showed in the breakup of the Soviet Union. They showed in the Velvet Revolution [in Czechoslovakia]. They show in the conflict in Nigeria. They showed in South Africa," Steiner continues. "It's in the air. More than in the air, it's in people's psyches."

Has the United Nations been effective in promoting international human rights?

The 50 years since the adoption of the Universal Declaration have witnessed the end of colonialism, the collapse of most of the world's communist regimes, and the gradual, if fitful, spread of democracy in the developing world. The United Nations' role in these developments is debatable: some advocates and experts credit it with helping to promote the spread of human rights, while others regard its impact as minimal or even counterproductive.

The U.N.'s principal human rights organ, the Human Rights Commission, was created in 1946 and now consists of 53 countries serving rotating three-year terms. The commission meets annually at its headquarters in Geneva, and the weeklong sessions serve as a forum for debating human rights issues, often focused on individual countries.

Some experts say those debates have been useful in promoting debate and encouraging progress on human rights in specific countries. "If you look at international relations in 1998, and if you compare it to 1948, there's much more attention to human rights," says David Forsythe, a law professor at the University of Nebraska. "Human rights violators are under much greater pressure. So, in the long run, the U.N. Human Rights Commission has been quite important in

Major U.N. Human Rights Treaties

The United Nations adopted two major human rights treaties in 1966 and five others since then along with an optional protocol to abolish the death penalty. The United States has ratified only three of the treaties.

Treaty	Date Adopted	Number of Countries to Ratify	U.S. Position
International Covenant on Economic, Social and Cultural Rights	1966	138	Signed; not ratified
International Covenant on Civil and Political Rights	1966	140	Ratified, 1992
CCPR: Optional Protocol #2 [Abolition of death penalty]	1989	92	No action
International Convention on the Elimination of All Forms of Racial Discrimination	1966	151	Ratified, 1994
Convention on the Elimination of All Forms of Discrimination Against Women	1979	162	Signed; not ratified
Convention against Torture and Other Cruel, Inhuman or Degrading Treatment or Punishment	1984	109	Ratified, 1994
Convention on the Rights of the Child	1989	191	Signed; not ratified
International Convention on the Protection of the Rights of All Migrant Workers and Their Families	1991	9	No action

Source: U.N. Commission on Human Rights

keeping this discourse on human rights fairly salient."

Other experts, however, say the Human Rights Commission's debates have been too political — slanted against Western countries and Israel, for example, while failing to confront human rights issues in communist countries or dictatorial regimes in the Third World.

"The U.N. has been a fudge factory," says Muravchik. "Every single one of the most vicious and most abusive governments in the world has served as a member of the Human Rights Commission: Cuba, Iraq, Syria, China, the Soviet Union, and on and on," he continues. "It's just

meant that the U.N. arena has not been a very fertile one for the advancement of human rights."

Dalpino says she sees no evidence that the Human Rights Commission's resolution process has been linked to any positive action in the countries being considered. "It tends to back abusive countries into a corner, and certainly doesn't do anything to make them want to liberalize," she says. "They're feel-good exercises and rather costly ones."

Most human rights groups, however, want the U.N. commission to be more willing to censure countries with poor records on human rights.

Roth complains, for example, of the commission's repeated refusal over the past several years to approve a resolution — supported by the United States up until this year — criticizing China for its human rights practices.

"Under any objective standard, China would have been repeatedly condemned," Roth says. "But China has been able to cajole or bribe several governments to oppose any condemnation effort, and this year even the U.S. government was willing to succumb to that bribery."

Reoch says the weaknesses are built into the U.N. system. "The United Na-

Probes Cover Torture, Children, Racism

United Nations human rights investigators — variously called special rapporteurs, special representatives or independent experts — are currently conducting inquiries in 12 individual countries and examining 19 broad "thematic" issues in countries throughout the world. The U.N. Human Rights Commission also provides advice, such as how to run a fair election, through technical-cooperation programs in four countries.

Country-specific investigations

Afghanistan • Burundi • Congo • Equitorial Guinea • Iran • Iraq • Myanmar • Nigeria
Palestinian territories occupied since 1967 •
Rwanda • Sudan • Territory of the former
Yugoslavia

Technical-cooperation programs

- Cambodia
- Haiti
- Somalia
- Chad

Thematic investigations

Racism, racial discrimination and xenophobia • Extrajudicial, summary or arbitrary executions • Freedom of opinion and expression • Impact of armed conflict on children • Independence of judges and lawyers • Internally displaced persons • Mercenaries • Religious intolerance • Sale of children, child prostitution and child pornography • Torture and other cruel, inhuman or degrading treatment or punishment • Illicit movement and dumping of toxic waste • Violence against women • Effects of foreign debt • Restitution, compensation and rehabilitation for victims of grave violations of human rights • Extreme poverty • Education • Right to development • Working group on arbitrary detention • Working group on enforced or involuntary disappearances

Source: United Nations Commission on Human Rights

tions is nothing more than a club of governments," the former Amnesty official says. "It's often like asking the police to police themselves. In some ways, it's a miracle that it has produced the level of human rights commitment that it has produced."

Human rights groups are encouraged, however, by changes at the United Nations over the past few years — in particular, by the appointment of a high commissioner for human rights after more than a decade of lobbying for the post. The first high commissioner, Ecuadorean diplomat José Ayala Lasso, was criticized as weak and ineffectual in the position, but Robinson has drawn wide praise when she was appointed and since then. "It now has

better leadership," says Roth.

In addition, human rights groups and experts say that what Roth calls the U.N.'s "fact-finding capacity" has improved over the past few years. Currently, the Human Rights Commission has some 31 special rapporteurs at work: 12 on individual countries and another 19 on such broad themes as torture, judicial independence, and extrajudicial executions and disappearances.

Dalpino, the former Clinton administration official, says that in addition to providing factual documentation of human rights conditions, the special rapporteurs can often achieve positive results in the countries they are investigating. "They negotiate with the host government to a

certain extent," she says. "The report-writing is the end of a process. It tends to be less confrontational."

Human rights groups have also applauded the increased attention to human rights within the U.N.'s peacekeeping machinery, as in Bosnia and Rwanda. "The Security Council now deals with human rights on a regular basis as linked to peace and security issues," says Forsythe. Human rights groups want to see more money for the U.N.'s human rights machinery, and they complain about the limitations on the two U.N.-established war crimes tribunals for the former Yugoslavia and Rwanda.

Overall, however, human rights groups and experts say they are encouraged by the U.N.'s recent moves.

"International relations is fundamentally different in the 1990s on human rights, and the U.N. is frequently at the center of these activities," Forsythe concludes.

Has the Clinton administration done enough to support human rights around the world?

As the human rights community prepared last year to begin observing the Universal Declaration's 50th anniversary, President Clinton went before an audience of diplomats and activists to affirm the United States' commitment to the cause. "Advancing human rights must always be a central pillar of America's foreign policy," Clinton said at the Dec. 9 speech at the Museum of Jewish Heritage in New York City.

The Clinton administration's record on human rights, however, has been sharply criticized from all sides of the political spectrum. Conservatives and liberals alike say the administration has failed to back up its rhetorical commitment with concrete action to promote human rights from issues ranging from China and Bosnia to land mines and the proposed international criminal court for war crimes.

"Terrific rhetoric, no follow-through," says Lichenstein. "The Clinton administration never follows through. All it does it make threats, and now the threats are empty because the bad guys are pretty clear in their head that we don't mean it."

"Bill Clinton uses human rights like a bad cook uses spices," says Schultze of Amnesty International-USA. "He sprinkles a little bit of human rights on foreign policies when he wants to make them look good."

Conservatives and liberals have joined in sharply criticizing the administration's policies toward China. They fault Clinton for his decision midway in his first term to delink human rights and trade with China and for the decision this year to drop the effort at the U.N. Human Rights Commission to censure China. The administra-

tion has also been criticized for not doing enough to try to apprehend war crimes suspects in the former Yugoslavia, including Yugoslav President Slobodan Milosevic.

Liberal groups have also focused on the administration's stance on the land mine treaty and the international criminal court. In its annual report last December, Human Rights Watch charged that the administration had "actively obstructed" the effort to create the international tribunal and renewed the criticism this summer after a U.N. conference reached agreement on a draft treaty to be submitted to countries for ratification.

The administration has stoutly defended its record on the various issues. It has contended that its policy of "engagement" with China is more likely to produce human rights improvements than a more confrontational stance. It has also insisted that NATO peacekeeping troops should not have been given the additional responsibility of actively searching out war crimes suspects in the former Yugoslavia. And, when the Human Rights Watch report came out last year, State Department spokesman James Rubin said it was "obviously ridiculous" to accuse the U.S. of obstructing the international criminal court. [1]

Even so, the United States found itself in a small minority in July when the U.N. conference completed work on a treaty to create the new court. The conference, held in Rome, ended with a 120-7 vote in favor of the draft treaty.* The United States exerted strong pressure at the conference to modify the agreement, but the changes were rejected in a lopsided 113-17 vote.

Afterward, Rubin said the treaty was "deeply flawed and will produce a flawed court." He complained that the proposed court would subject U.S. service personnel to "politically motivated or ill-consid-

---

* The seven countries that voted against the treaty were China, Iraq, Israel, Libya, Qatar, the United States and Yemen.

ered or unjustified prosecutions." Among the changes the United States sought unsuccessfully was one that would have allowed countries ratifying the treaty to bar prosecutions of their nationals for war crimes or crimes against humanity for the first 10 years after creation of the court.

Human rights advocates have continued to sharply criticize the U.S. stance — contrasting it with the U.S. role in creating the two special U.N. war crimes tribunals for the former Yugoslavia and Rwanda. "It's OK for Yugoslavs, it's OK for Rwandans, but not for Americans," says Forsythe. "There's a real double standard there."

Despite those criticisms, administration officials insist that the United States has been — and remains today — at the forefront of the effort to promote human rights around the world. "I think that if you look around the world and you ask the people of the world which nation they look to as the beacon for human rights, democracy and freedom, there's no question the answer will be the United States," Rubin remarked last year. [2] ∎

BACKGROUND

Universal Rights

The Universal Declaration of Human Rights represents the first comprehensive effort to establish global standards for individual freedoms, but the idea of "natural rights" began to emerge in the so-called Age of Enlightenment in the 17th and 18th centuries. The English philosopher John Locke and the French thinkers Montesquieu, Rousseau and Voltaire all articulated natural rights theories that influenced the writing of such national rights charters as the English

Chronology

Before 1940
Political philosophers develop theories about universal human rights.

1919
League of Nations is founded after end of World War I, but proves unable to prevent a second world war.

———— • ————

1941-1965 *The United Nations adopts a non-binding "declaration" of human rights, then spends nearly two decades drafting two major treaties.*

1948
United Nations General Assembly adopts Universal Declaration of Human Rights, 48-0, with eight abstentions, on Dec. 10. Convention on the Prevention and Punishment of the Crime of Genocide is approved a day earlier.

1950
Council of Europe adopts U.N. adopts European Convention of Human Rights.

1952
General Assembly adopts Convention on Political Rights of Women.

1961
Amnesty International is founded.

———— • ————

1965-1980 *Two major international covenants are approved by General Assembly and take effect.*

Dec. 21, 1965
International Convention on the Elimination on All Forms of Racial Discrimination is adopted by U.N. General Assembly.

1966
U.N. General Assembly on Dec. 16 adopts the International Covenant on Economic, Social and Cultural Rights and the International Covenant on Civil and Political Rights; treaties come into force in 1976.

1975
Human rights provisions are included in Helsinki accord signed by 35 Western and Eastern European countries, as well as the Soviet Union, United States and Canada.

1978
U.N. Human Rights Commission appoints special rapporteur (investigator) on human rights conditions in Chile.

Dec. 18, 1979
Convention on the Elimination of All Forms of Discrimination against Women.

———— • ————

1980s *Use of special rapporteurs is expanded to more countries.*

1981
U.N. General Assembly adopts non-binding declaration against religious intolerance and discrimination.

1982
Special rapporteur on summary executions is appointed.

1984
International convention against torture is adopted by General Assembly on Dec. 10.

1989
General Assembly adopts Convention on the Rights of the Child; also adds optional protocol for abolition of death penalty to International Covenant on Civil and Political Rights.

———— • ————

1990s *Human rights components are added to U.N. peacekeeping operations.*

1993
Security Council creates war crimes tribunal for former Yugoslavia; World Conference on Human Rights held in Vienna; General Assembly approves post of high commissioner for human rights.

1994
José Ayala Lasso is appointed by Secretary General Boutros Boutros-Ghali as first high commissioner for human rights; Security Council creates war crimes tribunal for Rwanda.

1997
Lasso resigns amid criticism; Secretary General Kofi Annan names as his successor Mary Robinson, former president of Ireland; President Clinton calls human rights "central pillar" of U.S. foreign policy.

1998
U.N. conference completes draft of resolution to create International Criminal Court, with United States opposed; Universal Declaration celebrates its 50th anniversary on Dec. 10.

U.N. Investigators Uncover Harsh Conditions . . .

Nigel Rodley had been told that the use of leg irons, or "bar fetters," was common in Pakistani jails. So two days before he was to inspect the Lahore central jail in 1996, he urged the country's minister of justice to end the practice.

But Rodley, then an English lawyer serving as the United Nations' "special rapporteur," or investigator, on "torture and other cruel, inhuman or degrading treatment or punishment," didn't find a single inmate in irons on his visit. When he talked with the inmates in confidence, however, they told him that 300 sets of shackles had been removed the previous night.

Rodley asked officials to see the jail's registry. There, carefully recorded, was evidence that many of the inmates had been "awarded" bar fetters and that some had been shackled for months at a time. Jail officials admitted their ruse. Today, the Pakistani government says it is abolishing the practice.

The episode provides an unaccustomedly clear example of a positive result achieved by the U.N.'s human rights machinery. For the most part, though, Rodley, now a professor at the University of Essex, acknowledges that the work rests "pretty much on an act of faith that doing something is likely to be better than doing nothing."

"What effect one has on this or that particular case, one doesn't know," says Rodley, who worked for Amnesty International for 17 years and has served as the U.N.'s special rapporteur on torture since 1993. "One just intuits that the drip, drip, drip of pressure eventually erodes the resisting stone of the torturers."

Rodley is one of 31 people — mostly law professors or longtime human rights lawyers — currently directing U.N. human rights investigations either as special rapporteurs, special representatives or independent experts. Twelve are investigating individual countries; the other 19 are dealing with broad thematic issues. In addition, the U.N. Human Rights Commission has technical-cooperation programs with Cambodia, Chad, Haiti and Somalia.

The history of such U.N. human rights investigations dates to the 1960s, according to Rodley, when ad hoc groups of experts — as they were formally called — were created to examine human rights issues in southern Africa (1967) and the Israeli-occupied territories (1968). The U.N. created a special rapporteur on Chile in 1978 — the first formal use of that title — five years after Gen. Augusto Pinochet came to power in a bloody civil war.

Broader, thematic investigations were created in the 1980s: a working group on involuntary disappearances (1980), followed by a special rapporteur on summary executions (1982). The special rapporteur on torture was created in 1985, one year after the U.N. General Assembly adopted the international convention against torture.

Rodley's position is unusual in that it deals with individual allegations of torture as well as broader investigations. The special rapporteur is authorized to receive so-called urgent appeals in cases where an individual is being detained under circumstances that indicate a risk of torture; letters are then sent under Rodley's signature to the authorities asking for assurances that no ill treatment will occur. Specific allegations of

Bill of Rights (1688) and the French Declaration of the Rights of Man and the Citizen (1789). Their writings also influenced such Americans as Thomas Jefferson and James Madison and through them the writing of the Declaration of Independence (1776) and the U.S. Bill of Rights (1791).

Before World War II, however, the few international treaties on human rights issues dealt only with specific issues, such as the 1817 treaty to ban the slave trade and the Geneva accords of the late 19th and early 20th centuries governing the conduct of war and the treatment of prisoners of war. The International Labor Organization, created along with the League of Nations after the end of World War I, approved a treaty in 1930 restrict-

ing the use of forced labor. But the League of Nations itself did little work on human rights questions and proved unable as well to prevent a second world war.

The horrors of World War II convinced the international community of the need for concerted action to prevent aggressive war and violations of human rights by totalitarian governments. [3] The United Nations Charter, signed in San Francisco on June 26, 1945, established the U.N.'s major bodies for international consultation and peacekeeping but contained only a few, general references to human rights. The charter, however, included a provision that the Economic and Social Council create a Commission on Human Rights with

instructions to draft a comprehensive charter of individual freedoms for the General Assembly to consider and vote on.

Eleanor Roosevelt, widow of President Franklin D. Roosevelt, took the lead in the two-year effort to draft and adopt the declaration. The movement took inspiration in part from President Roosevelt's famous Four Freedoms speech in January 1941; it also built on the writings and advocacy of human rights activists in a number of other countries. Several of those served on the 18-member commission, including France's René Cassin, Lebanon's Charles Malik and Chile's Hernán San Cruz. Mrs. Roosevelt was elected chairman, a post she held through 1952.

... And Sometimes Bring About Change

torture can also be investigated in individual cases, but Rodley says the money and staff available for such investigations is "egregiously limited."

Finally, Rodley, accompanied by a small number of staff members, visits individual countries to examine conditions. Within the past year, for example, Rodley visited Russia, where he says he found "unbelievably barbaric conditions in places of pretrial detention." He has also visited Rwanda and several countries in Latin America, including Colombia and Mexico. One limitation: Rodley cannot visit an individual country without an invitation. Among the countries that have declined to issue invitations are the world's two most populous nations: China and India.

The reports by U.N. investigators often provoke negative reactions in the countries being examined. When a special rapporteur visited the United States to study the death penalty, some federal and state officials refused to see him; Senate Foreign Relations Committee Chairman Jesse Helms, R-N.C., called the mission "an absurd U.N. charade." The report, issued April 6, criticized the United States for the unfair, arbitrary and racist use of capital punishment. [1]

In another investigation, the United States refused, along with most other industrial countries, to provide information to the special rapporteur on the illicit movement and dumping of toxic wastes. African countries pushed for the creation of the post in 1995, saying that the export of toxic wastes to the continent threatened Africans' rights to life and health. But U.S. officials argued the investigation marginalized the significance of human rights. An initial report, nonetheless, identified the United States, along with Germany, Australia, Great Britain and the Netherlands, as the largest exporters of toxic wastes. [2]

The Human Rights Commission sometimes uses the reports in drafting and approving resolutions critical of individual countries or broad practices. The commission, for example, has passed several resolutions urging the new government in Congo to improve human rights conditions there. So far, the reports and resolutions appear to have had little effect on the government of President Laurent Kabila.

Even so, Roberto Garretón, the Chilean human rights lawyer serving as special rapporteur for Congo, says his experiences during the struggle against the Pinochet government demonstrate that the U.N.'s human rights work can have "enormous political and moral importance."

"I was a lawyer against the dictatorship for 16 years," Garretón says. "I never won a trial. I never liberated a prisoner. I was never able to convict a torturer. But we always won, twice a year" — referring to resolutions by the General Assembly in New York and the Human Rights Commission in Geneva.

"To the dictatorship and its ambassadors, this was what most annoyed them," Garretón continues. "We photocopied the reports and distributed them throughout the country, so that people could see that the truth was recognized somewhere."

[1] *The New York Times,* April 7, 1998, p. A17.

[2] *The New York Times,* April 5, 1998, p. A10.

The final declaration emerged from two major drafting sessions by the commission and detailed debates and voting by the General Assembly in Paris in August 1948. The commission worked through a host of drafting questions and political mine fields: Anti-colonial countries, for example, forced the inclusion of a paragraph stating that "no distinction" was to be made between individual rights in independent countries and those recognized in "non-self-govering" territories. The commission intended to draft binding treaties at the same time, but that goal proved to be overly ambitious — and, in fact, was not completed until 1954. But the declaration went before the General Assembly on Dec. 10, 1948, and won approval on a 48-0 vote, with eight countries (Saudi Arabia, South Africa and Soviet-bloc countries) abstaining and two countries not present.

The drafters of the declaration cheered its adoption. Mrs. Roosevelt predicted it might become "the international Magna Carta of all mankind." Some other human rights advocates, however, professed sharp disappointment with the declaration's generality and its lack of binding provisions. When the Economic and Social Council was discussing plans in 1949 to mark the first anniversary of its adoption, the observer from the International Law Association said the best way to celebrate the Universal Declaration of Human Rights was to forget it. [4]

Writing the Covenants

The United Nations approved the first of the more than 60 binding human rights treaties in force today on Dec. 9, 1948, the day before the adoption of the Universal Declaration. The Convention on Genocide — approved by the General Assembly without dissenting vote — sought to prevent a recurrence of anything like the Nazi Holocaust; it prohibited the killing, serious injury, or forced relocation of members of any national, ethnic, racial, or religious group "with intent to destroy" that group "in whole or in part" A second treaty followed just four years later: the Convention on the Political Rights of Women, a bare-bones document guaranteeing women the right to vote, hold public office, and exercise other public functions "on equal terms with men."

By contrast, the effort to put into effect the sweeping provisions of the Universal Declaration took more than a quarter-century. The Commission on Human Rights itself took six years to produce drafts of two covenants — not one, as originally contemplated. The General Assembly decided in 1951 to divide the two treaties because of the significant differences between the two types of rights: civil and political rights could be expressed in more nearly absolute terms and enforced by courts, while social and economic rights needed to be phrased in aspirational terms and their achievement depended mostly on legislative and executive branches than on the courts.

The two covenants follow the Universal Declaration's general structure, but both are significantly longer: 31 articles for the economic and social rights covenant, 53 for the one on civil and political rights. Some of the civil rights are prescribed as absolutes: the prohibition against slavery, the right "to have or to adopt" a religion, and the mandatory notice to a criminal defendant of the charges brought. Many others, however, contain significant qualifications. The right to counsel in criminal cases, for example, applies "in any case where the interests of justice so require" (Article 14). And the right to freedom of expression may be restricted "for respect of the rights and reputations of others" or "for the protection of national security or of public order, or of public health and morals" (Article 19).

The covenant on economic and social rights opens in explicitly aspirational terms: it calls on each signatory country to take steps "to the maximum of its available resources, with a view to achieving progressively the full realization of the rights" specified. Some provisions are nonetheless stated as absolutes — for example, the "right to social security, including social insurance." Working mothers are to be accorded "paid leave" or "leave with adequate social security

---

The Convention on Genocide — approved by the General Assembly without dissenting vote — sought to prevent a recurrence of anything like the Nazi Holocaust

---

benefits" during "a reasonable period before and after childbirth."

Most of the provisions, however, recognize inherent limits on a government's ability to put them into effect. The covenant, for example, requires universal free primary education but only the "progressive introduction" of free secondary education (Article 13). It calls on states to recognize "the right of everyone to the enjoyment of the highest attainable standard of physical and mental health" (Article 12). And it calls on signatory countries to use their own resources and "international cooperation" to provide "adequate food,

clothing, and housing" (Article 11).

Even after the drafting was completed in 1954, approval of the two covenants took another 12 years. The General Assembly adopted both treaties without dissenting vote on Dec. 16, 1966. It also approved an "optional protocol" to the civil and political covenant aimed at strengthening the enforcement powers of the Commission on Human Rights. In its earliest years, the commission had declined to consider individual complaints of human rights violations; by the mid-1950s, it agreed to consider specific incidents but kept any deliberations confidential.

The new protocol provided that countries could agree to permit citizens to file a so-called communication with the commission alleging a violation of any of the covenant's provisions; the commission was then empowered to "examine" the communication, in closed meetings, and "forward its views" to both the individual filing the complaint and the government concerned. There were again no dissenting votes on the protocol, but a substantial number of countries — 38 — abstained.

Stronger Machinery

Another decade passed before the two human rights treaties were ratified by the specified minimum number of countries — 35 — to come into force. [5] The United States did not ratify the covenant on civil and political rights until 1992 and so far has only signed but not ratified the covenant on economic and social rights. In the meantime, the General Assembly has gone on to approve several other major human rights covenants, including a treaty banning torture (1984), prohibiting "all forms" of discrimination against women (1988), and establishing rights for children (1989).

In addition to these international treaties, the U.N. had also used economic sanctions to deal with two specific human rights issues: the denial of political rights to black Africans by white minority governments in Rhodesia and South Africa. The U.N. Security Council voted to impose sanctions against Rhodesia on the same day that the General Assembly approved the two human rights covenants in 1966. The campaign against apartheid took form in an international convention approved by the General Assembly in 1973 that defined South Africa's system as a "crime against humanity." The Security Council followed in 1977 with an arms embargo against South Africa, though it stopped short of broader economic sanctions. The U.N.'s measures are credited, even by critics of economic sanctions, with playing some role in the eventual creation of representative democracies in Zimbabwe and South Africa.

The priority that the U.N. attached to the South Africa issue attested to the growing power of the African and Asian countries that gained independence in the decolonization period of the 1950s and '60s. The emergence of the so-called Third World ended the United States' dominance of the U.N. Critics of the U.N. contend that the shift resulted in an anti-Western bias reflected, for example, in opposition to Israel and a double standard toward human rights issues in many non-aligned nations and the communist bloc.

In an evaluation written at the end of the 1980s, Forsythe agreed that the Human Rights Commission devoted disproportionate attention to apartheid and to Israeli practices in the territories it occupied after the 1967 Arab-Israeli War. But he also said that the United States has been guilty of a double standard — for example, focusing far more attention on Cuba than on the death squads in El Salvador, a U.S. ally. [6]

More broadly, Forsythe contended, many Third World countries had come to show more genuine support for human rights issues despite a continuing concern about non-intervention in internal affairs. He noted that since 1978 the Human Rights Commission had been publishing a list of countries that had been the subject of human rights complaints. Despite a lack of specifics, the list has become more balanced over time, he wrote. He also found evidence of greater balance and greater resolve in the work of other U.N. human rights organs as well as in the General Assembly itself.

As one example, Forsythe noted a General Assembly debate in 1982 between competing resolutions sponsored by Cuba and Ireland on the relative importance of collective or individual rights. While the Cuban resolution passed with only one no vote — from the United States — many non-aligned countries then followed by joining the U.S. and other Western countries in adopting the second resolution as well — in effect, giving equal priority to individual rights.

The end of the Cold War eased the ideological divisions that had complicated the U.N.'s human rights work. By the end of the 1980s, the U.N.'s human rights machinery itself was also expanding. Besides receiving reports from individual countries, the Human Rights Commission had also begun to appoint independent experts — so-called special rapporteurs — to investigate claims of human rights violations both in specific countries, such as Chile and Iran, and on general subjects, such as religious persecution.

Human rights activists were disappointed by the General Assembly's continued refusal to create the post of High Commissioner for Human Rights. But as the 1990s began, the U.N.'s prospects for a stronger and more coherent approach to human rights appeared to be better than at any time in its history.

New Post Created

The United Nations continued to build its human rights machinery through the 1990s — in particular, with the creation of the high commissioner post in 1993. In addition, the U.N. broadened the human rights agenda by creating two special war crimes tribunals and by moving to incorporate human rights initiatives in peacekeeping operations. The two tribunals, however, have struggled against an array of difficulties, from limited funding to the difficulty of apprehending suspects in the former Yugoslavia. And human rights activists were generally disappointed with the low-key approach taken by the first high commissioner, José Ayala Lasso, who served for three years until resigning last year to become his country's foreign minister.

The General Assembly adopted the resolution establishing the high commissioner's post in December 1993 following a recommendation from a worldwide conference on human rights in Vienna in June. [7] The Clinton administration helped ensure passage by giving the proposal higher priority than the U.S. had done in the past. In an important concession to developing countries, the resolution included a clause reaffirming "the importance of promoting a balanced and sustainable development for all people." The resolution provided that the high commissioner would serve a four-year term, hold the rank of under-secretary general, and be responsible for improving the "coordination, effectiveness, and efficiency" of all U.N. human rights activities.

Upon his appointment, Lasso was viewed with suspicion by human rights groups because he had served in Ecuador's military government in the 1970s. When he resigned, he was given some credit for consolidating the office and for dispatching U.N.

monitors to Rwanda to try to stop the massacres there. But he was also criticized for having refused to speak out about human rights abuses, even in private. "He had no clout behind him except his moral voice, which he refused to use," says Roth. By contrast, Secretary General Kofi Annan was widely praised for picking Robinson for the post and for promising to integrate human rights issues into the range of the U.N.'s work.

The creation of the U.N. war crimes tribunals for the former Yugoslavia in 1993 and Rwanda in 1994 stemmed from the worldwide revulsion over the documented evidence of widespread killings of civilians and other human rights violations in those two conflicts. [8] The tribunals were the first courts ever created by the United Nations to try individuals for war crimes: the victorious Allies had conducted the trials of German and Japanese officials after World War II. Their work has been slow. So far, the tribunal for the former Yugoslavia — sitting in The Hague, Netherlands — has won only three convictions; the court for Rwanda — which sits in Ashura, Tanzania — has taken one guilty plea and not held any trials.

Meanwhile, an increasing number of U.N. special rapporteurs were working — and producing detailed reports — on a growing agenda of human rights issues. "Over the past five years [the Human Rights Commission] has developed an enhanced fact-finidng ability," Roth says. In addition, the commission was examining with greater care reports that individual countries were supposed to file on their compliance with human rights treaties. Forsythe said the accountability process sometimes paid off. "Human rights reports indicate that a number of states have changed their domestic legislation when questioned," he says.

Forsythe sees a more dramatic potential for change in what he calls the U.N.'s recent blending of human rights and security issues. In addition

to the two war crimes tribunals, Forsythe notes that the Security Council has authorized what he calls "complex peacekeeping" operations in Cambodia and El Salvador — deploying peacekeeping forces at the same time that human rights teams were dispatched to help supervise elections. "The new peacekeeping is designed to create a liberal democratic peace," he says. "In places like El Salvador and Cambodia, it's worked fairly well." ∎

CURRENT SITUATION

Enter Mary Robinson

The 40-year-old civil war in Colombia has claimed more than 120,000 lives and has been marked by pervasive human rights abuses by the government and paramilitary forces on one side and the leftist guerrillas on the other. So the international human rights community was cheered last year when the United Nations Commission on Human Rights opened an office in the capital city of Bogotá to help demonstrate the worldwide concern about conditions there.

But when the U.N.'s high commissioner for human rights, Mary Robinson, visited Colombia last month, she got dramatic reminders of the limits on the international body's ability to control events. In the days before her visit, some 56 people were killed by a rebel bombing of an oil pipeline, and the vice president of the country's largest trade union was assassinated outside his home. Robinson herself received a

telephone call warning that a bomb had been placed in the hotel where she was to attend a seminar on protecting human rights defenders.

Robinson issued statements condemning both of the incidents, and the seminar went ahead as scheduled. The 54-year-old former president of Ireland also went ahead with the rest of her schedule, which included meetings with Colombia's president, Andres Pastrana, and other ranking officials, including the country's human rights ombudsman. They assured Robinson that the government intended to implement a "national action plan" on human rights. Robinson was "happy to hear of that commitment," says spokesman José Diaz.

After one year in office, Robinson has collected a few other, similar assurances of cooperation on human rights issues, most notably in a 10-day visit to China in September. Chinese leaders used the visit to signal their intention to sign the International Covenant on Civil and Political Rights and to sign a letter of understanding with the U.N. Human Rights Commission requesting technical assistance on human rights matters. Robinson told an end-of-trip news conference that she was "interested in the awareness of and willingness to admit human rights problems among China's leaders." [9]

Robinson has traveled widely in the 14 months since assuming the U.N.'s top-ranking human rights post on Sept. 12, 1997. The other trouble spots she has visited include Cambodia, Iran, and Rwanda. She has also spoken out on a range of issues — for example, calling the civil war in Algeria an "intolerable" catastrophe and criticizing the pace of executions in the United States. [10]

In appointing Robinson, Secretary General Kofi Annan charged the one-time human rights lawyer not only with strengthening the U.N. Human Rights Commission itself but also with streamlining and coordinating human rights functions throughout the U.N. In a speech at Oxford University two months after taking office, Robinson appeared to agree

At Issue:

Should the United States join the proposed International Criminal Court?

HELEN DUFFY

Counsel to the Campaign for an International Criminal Court at Human Rights Watch

CHARLES M. LICHENSTEIN

Distinguished Fellow, The Heritage Foundation; deputy U.S. ambassador to the U.N., 1981-1984

*t*he International Criminal Court contributes to American foreign policy objectives in a number of ways. First, it's the most important development in human rights since the Universal Declaration of Human Rights 50 years ago. The new court will be able to hold perpetrators of genocide, crimes against humanity and serious war crimes personally to account. For the victims and survivors of future atrocities, the court will offer justice. And for those who commit heinous crimes, and hitherto have done so with impunity, the court will signal that they can no longer act without fear of prosecution. In and of itself, promoting human rights is obviously a central tenet of U.S. foreign policy.

At the same time, the court will have some good practical effects. It will encourage, even pressure, domestic courts to investigate and prosecute the worst human rights crimes themselves. Far from being a Hydra-headed harbinger of world government, the court should actually strengthen domestic court systems. This will fill an important practical gap in humanitarian law enforcement internationally.

Moreover, this kind of proactive judicial enforcement by national courts and the international court might forestall the next Rwanda or Yugoslavia.

So what's the problem? Clinton administration representatives have insisted on ironclad guarantees that no American would ever be prosecuted without U.S. government approval. That would gut the court's effectiveness. At the Rome conference finalizing the court's statute, other delegations conceded to U.S. demands for extremely strong guarantees against unwarranted prosecution and for multiple checks and balances on prosecutorial discretion and judicial decisions. All of these provisions were sufficient to satisfy France and the United Kingdom, among other close allies.

But not the United States. In Rome, the final vote was 120-7, with the U.S. delegation finding itself in the embarrassing company of Iraq, China, Libya and other frequent enemies of human rights.

If the United States wants to write the rules of international behavior, it also has to play by them. Washington seems to think that it can dictate the terms of institutions such as the International Criminal Court without actually participating in them. The next round of talks on the International Criminal Court will take up some critically important questions, such as the rules of evidence and procedure. The United States has key contributions to make to this debate. But those contributions will not count for much if Washington continues a policy of hostility to the court.

*t*he short answer is, of course not. Not yet at any rate, and probably not at all. But I propose a fair and reasonable trade-off. If proponents of this triumph of good intentions can show me that an International Criminal Court (ICC) would likely bring Slobodan Milosevic to the bar of justice, and mete out some appropriate punishment, I vow to become its principal advocate — reserving the right to recommend major revisions in the court's processes.

The jurisdiction of the court embraces genocide, aggression, and an undifferentiated category of "crimes against humanity." With Hitler, Stalin, and Mao Tse-tung gone, who better than Milosevic to test the court's efficacy?

Obviously, though, it is not the absence of an ICC that leaves Milosevic free to commit genocide. It is the absence of political will on the part of some of the court's most ardent founding state parties: the United Kingdom, Canada and Germany, to name a few. In the language of the street, it is the absence of guts.

The United States, equally lacking in guts, at least has not yet compounded the hypocrisy by signing on to the Treaty of Rome. As soon as 60 countries do sign on, the ICC is in business.

It is scary to note, moreover, that the ICC as proposed would trash the constitutional protections of Americans who might get caught up in its limitless reach. The court itself will be the sole judge of whether it will defer to the prior jurisdiction of judicial systems party or non-party to the treaty. The court would be its own prosecutorial arm and its own appellate branch.

It is one thing to suggest that "there oughta be a law" or, in this case, a court. Maybe there ought to be a way of policing the boundaries of civilization against genocide and "crimes against humanity." But the terms would have to be defined with precision, legal procedures put in place, and institutions established — all within the context of a broad consensus about the purposes of the undertaking, the legitimacy, and the limits of the processes and institutions, and with protections against abuse.

In fact, there already is such a way, and it is called democracy or the democratic ethos. That is the necessary foundation. The institutional elaboration follows.

It may be that, if present trends toward democratization were to continue and strengthen, an International Criminal Court would be one of its byproducts. When the world is ready for an ICC, that is to say, it may not need one.

Mary Bourke Robinson:
United Nations High Commissioner for Human Rights

Born: May 21, 1944.

Education: Bachelor's and law degrees, Trinity College, Dublin, 1967; master of law, Harvard University, 1968.

Career in Ireland: Member of Irish Senate (1969-89), Dublin City Council (1969-75); law professor, Trinity College (1969-75); twice defeated in elections for the Dail, major chamber in Irish Parliament; president of Ireland, 1990-1997 — first woman to hold position.

Human rights activities: Special rapporteur to European regional meeting on human rights, 1993; first head of state to visit Rwanda in aftermath of genocide there; appointed U.N. High Commissioner for Human Rights by Secretary-General Kofi Annan on June 12, 1997; took office, Sept. 12, 1997. As high commissioner, Robinson supervises the Geneva-based U.N. Center for Human Rights and 22 field offices, with about 300 employees and an annual budget of $21 million in regular U.N. funds and about $30 million in additional, voluntary payments by governments.

Source: U.N. Commission on Human Rights

with criticisms of the U.N. bureaucracy as "being out of touch and, certainly, of being resistant to change." In the same speech, she had a downbeat assessment of the U.N.'s accomplishments on human rights.

"Count up the results of 50 years of human rights mechanisms, 30 years of multibillion-dollar development programs and endless high-level rhetoric," Robinson said, "and the global impact is quite underwhelming." [11]

Robinson has not been visibly daunted by the scope of her assignment or the number of obstacles. In a speech in Sweden last month, for example, she complained that human rights efforts were hampered by a "compartmentalized" international system and endorsed what is called "mainstreaming" human rights issues into other international organizations,

including the two major lending institutions, the International Monetary Fund and the World Bank. In the same speech, Robinson made clear that her view of human rights extends beyond civil and political freedoms to include economic issues. "If we are serious about the right to life, we must equally be serious about the right to food, health care, education and shelter," Robinson said. [12]

Human rights groups generally cheered Robinson's appointment. Today, they are still positive, but cautious. "She is much more willing to be outspoken," says Human Rights Watch Executive Director Roth. But, he adds, "To some degree the jury is still out."

Concrete results, though, are still hard to find. Winifred Tate, a fellow with the Washington Office on Latin

America, an advocacy group, says the establishment of the U.N. human rights office in Colombia "demonstrated concern" about the situation, but she notes that so far it has filled only six out of 12 budgeted staff positions.

"Unfortunately, the situation [in the country] has not improved," Tate adds. "That's not something you can expect."

Seeking Justice

Augusto Pinochet came to power in Chile in a bloody civil war in 1973 and ruled the South American country with an iron hand for the next 17 years before making way for a democratic government and retiring with what he thought was immunity from prosecution. But last month Pinochet was arrested in London under a warrant issued by a Spanish judge investigating the former leader's role in abduction, torture, and murder of political opponents.

Pinochet's arrest by British police on Oct. 16 touched off a vigorous debate not only in the countries directly involved — Chile, Britain, and Spain — but throughout the world. Supporters of the move hailed the effort to bring Pinochet to justice as vindication for the victims and a signal to other repressive leaders around the world. Critics said it risked reopening political tensions in Chile and deterring future dictators from leaving office peacefully for fear of criminal prosecutions years later. [13]

The debate is now on hold pending an appeal of a British court's Oct. 28 ruling that Pinochet has immunity from civil or criminal prosecution in England because he was a head of state during the events in question. Regardless of the outcome, though, Pinochet's case dramatizes the growing effort to bring human rights violators to justice either in national courts or through the use of international law and international tribunals.

So far, those efforts have produced relatively meager results, at least in terms of prosecuting high-ranking officials. National courts typically lack the resources or institutional strength to carry out legal proceedings. "There are always going to be all sorts of local and political pressures for courts within the country not to take the lead on these issues," says Michael Posner, executive director of the Lawyers Committee for Human Rights. Posner notes as one example that six one-time members of the ruling Argentine military junta were among those convicted for their parts in the so-called "dirty war" against suspected leftists in the late 1970s and early '80s, but they were given presidential pardons in late 1990. [14]

An alternative is represented by the South African Truth and Reconciliation Commission, which was established to investigate political crimes committed by the former apartheid government as well as by the African National Congress before the creation of a multiracial democracy in 1994. The commission had the power to issue an amnesty for crimes up to and including political assassinations, but only if an individual testified truthfully about his or her role in the offenses. The commission's final report, issued Oct. 29, strongly criticized both the government and the anti-apartheid movement for their actions during the liberation struggle. "Atrocious things were done on all sides," the report said.

Posner says the Spanish judge's actions represent a largely untested idea of prosecuting someone in a national court for offenses committed in another country. Over the past decade or so, however, U.S. courts have recognized civil claims in suits brought under a 1789 law, the Alien Tort Claims Act, against officials of foreign governments by victims of torture or other political offenses. A 1995 law also allows federal prosecutors to bring criminal charges in U.S. courts against foreign torturers if they are found in the United States. So far, no prosecutions have been brought under the law, and the few judgments won in civil suits have proved difficult to collect.

Those difficulties have led human rights advocates to turn to the idea of international tribunals for prosecuting the most serious offenses: genocide, crimes against humanity, and war crimes. Even as the U.N. was creating the two special war crimes tribunals for the former Yugoslavia and Rwanda, human rights groups and experts were trying to hammer out an agreement on a permanent international court. The draft treaty approved in Rome on July 17 calls for a court of 18 judges, each from a different country and serving nine-year terms, and a full-time prosecutor with authority to initiate cases. The maximum punishment that could be imposed would be life imprisonment.

The Clinton administration initially supported creating the court, but came to oppose the proposal taking shape because of what the Defense Department saw as the risk that U.S. military personnel might be prosecuted for war crimes. To guard against that possibility, the U.S. wanted prosecutions to be initiated by the U.N. Security Council, where the U.S. has a veto. It also opposed a final provision that allows citizens of a country to be brought before the court even if it has not ratified the treaty.

Human rights advocates minimize the risk that Americans would ever be prosecuted before the new court. They note that the treaty calls for the tribunal to take a case only if the country's own courts cannot or will not prosecute. They also say that despite the U.S. position, the treaty is likely to be ratified in the relatively near future by the number of countries — 60 — needed to bring the court into existence. "We're now a couple of years away, probably three to four years at most, from 60 countries ratifying the treaty," Posner says. ∎

OUTLOOK

Universal Rights?

China has gone to great lengths over the past month to try to improve its human rights image in international circles. It signed the International Covenant on Civil and Political Rights on Oct. 5, hosted an international human rights symposium the same week, and issued official communiqués afterward stressing its support for the Universal Declaration of Human Rights on the occasion of its 50th anniversary.

The declaration "plays an important role in promoting the development of the cause of human rights in the world," Chinese President Jiang Zemin said in a letter to U.N. Secretary General Annan publicized Oct. 22. But even as Jiang's letter was being released, the government was reported to be cracking down on political debate by closing a democracy-minded think tank and barring distribution of a book on political reform. The incidents showed that "sharp limits on what is permissible continue to exist," the U.S. State Department declared. [15]

China is far from the only country where human rights words are not matched by deeds. "Many governments subscribe to the [Universal Declaration] only nominally, but don't respect it at home," Roth says.

Robinson sounded a similar note in her annual report to the U.N. General Assembly. "The last 50 years has generated much hope," Robinson told the assembly's so-called Third Committee on Nov. 4. "Yet, I am afraid that in terms of practical reality of how human rights are lived, we must admit that the vision of the Universal Declaration is still far from reality."

Despite the unfulfilled promise on

such basic human rights issues as ensuring religious freedom or preventing torture, the United Nations is making its human rights agenda both broader and more ambitious. One recent initiative deals with the rights of indigenous people. In her report last week, Robinson stressed economic concerns. "The elimination of poverty and social exclusion may well be the most important human rights objective of the coming century," she said.

At the same time, Robinson told the General Assembly that the commission may not be able to carry out its responsibilities without "additional resources" for the coming year. The budget approved for the commission in 1997 allotted $42.2 million from regular U.N. funds for the two-year period 1998 and 1999. The commission also received voluntary contributions from member countries totaling about $31 million for 1998. "Further improvement would be at risk if resources remain inadequate," Robinson said.

Some critics see the emphasis on economic issues as a distraction from more genuine human rights concerns. "If you say every citizen should have a decent home to live in, I can't imagine that there's anyone who disagrees with that aspiration," Muravchik says. "But if you're saying this is a right, then what exactly do you mean by that?"

Liberal human rights experts sharply disagree, saying that the critique reflects a bias of the affluent West. "If you're talking to someone from the global South, they don't agree that economic rights are marginal," Forsythe says. "They don't agree that right to food, shelter, health care are in any way inferior to the civil and political rights that are well known in the West. If you're starving, don't have adequate nutrition or health care, then a lot of the civil and political rights become quite marginal."

Despite the differences and disagreements, human rights experts are generally optimistic about the future as they prepare to mark next month's historic milestone.

FOR MORE INFORMATION

Amnesty International, USA, 322 Eighth Ave., New York, N.Y. 10001; (212) 807-8400; www.amnesty-usa.org.

Human Rights Watch, 350 Fifth Ave., 34th floor, New York, N.Y. 10018; (212) 290-4700; 1630 Connecticut Ave., N.W., Suite 500, Washington, D.C. 20009; (202) 612-4321; www.hrw.org.

Lawyers' Committee for Human Rights, 333 Seventh Ave., 13th floor, New York, N.Y. 10001; (212) 845-5200; www.lchr.org.

United Nations Commission on Human Rights, Palais Wilson, Room 2-016, 1211 Geneva, Switzerland; [011] 41-22-917-1239; www.unhchr.ch.

United Nations, Development and Human Rights Section, Department of Public Information, The United Nations, Room S-1040, New York, N.Y. 10017; (212) 963-1234; www.un.org.

"There is an unstoppable momentum in this area," says Reoch, the former Amnesty International official. "There is a growing expertise in international human rights. The number of countries that are signing up for international treaties is increasing. The pressure on the U.N. to be effective in this area is increasing. And more and more and more governments are facing increasing pressure at home."

"I think we're seeing in the last 50 years only the start of a human rights revolution," he concludes. ∎

Notes

[1] See *The New York Times*, Dec. 5, 1997, p. A13.
[2] *Ibid.*
[3] Background on the drafting and adoption of the Universal Declaration, drawn from *The United Nations and Human Rights, 1945-1995* (1995), pp. 5-28; John P. Humphrey, *Human Rights and the United Nations: A Great Adventure* (1984), pp. 12-77. For background on the U.N., see Mary H. Cooper, "United Nations at 50," *The CQ Researcher*, Aug. 18, 1995, pp.729-752.
[4] Humphrey, *op. cit.*, p. 75.
[5] For evaluations of the U.N.'s work, see Patrick James Flood, *The Effectiveness of UN Human Rights Institutions* (1998), pp. 31-48,

116-132; David P. Forsythe, *The Internationalization of Human Rights* (1991), pp. 55-86.
[6] Forsythe, *op. cit.*, pp. 65-69.
[7] See Flood, *op. cit.*, pp. 118-124, 156-159 (text of resolution). Flood, a retired career foreign service officer, served in the U.S. mission to the Human Rights Commission in Geneva during the 1980s.
[8] For background, see Keneth Jost, "War Crimes," *The CQ Researcher*, July 1995, pp. 585-608.
[9] See *The New York Times*, Sept. 16, 1998, p. A8.
[10] Some background drawn from a profile by Craig Turner, "At Swords' Point With Repression," *Los Angeles Times*, July 2, 1998, p. A1. For a biography, see John Horgan, *Mary Robinson: A Woman of Ireland and the World*, Roberts Rinehart, 1998.
[11] Mary Robinson, "Realizing Human Rights," Romanes Lecture, Oxford University, Nov. 11, 1997.
[12] Mary Robinson, "Human Rights: Challenges for the 21st Century," First Annual Dag Hammarskjold Lecture, Uppsala, Sweden, Oct. 1, 1998.
[13] For opposing points of view, see Diane F. Orenthicher, "Putting Limits on Lawlessness," *The Washington Post*, Oct. 25, 1998, p. C1; Adrian Karatnycky, "Pinochet's Rights and Ours," *The Wall Street Journal*, Oct. 26, 1998, p. A23. Orenthlicher is a professor of international law at American University's Washington College of Law; Karatnycky is president of Freedom House, a human rights organization.
[14] See *The New York Times*, Dec. 31, 1990, p. A4.
[15] See *The New York Times*, Oct. 28, 1998, p. A1.

Bibliography

Selected Sources Used

Books

Eide, Asbjorn, Gudmundur Alfredsson, Göran Melander, Lars Adam Rehof and Allan Rosas (eds.), *The Universal Declaration of Human Rights: A Commentary,* **Scandinavian University Press, 1992.**

The book proceeds from a brief history of the writing of the Universal Declaration of Human Rights to a chapter-by-chapter exposition of each of its 30 articles. Each chapter contains a list of references. Eide, the lead editor, is director of the Norwegian Institute of Human Rights; the other editors each represent other Scandinavian countries: Iceland, Sweden, Denmark, and Finland, respectively.

Flood, Patrick James, *The Effectiveness of UN Human Rights Institutions,* **Praeger, 1998.**

Flood, a retired U.S. foreign service officer, provides an overview and three case studies to examine the effect that United Nations' human rights bodies have had in improving human rights conditions. The book includes chapter notes, texts of some recent U.N. resolutions or instruments and a six-page bibliography.

Forsythe, David P., *The Internationalization of Human Rights,* **Lexington Books, 1991.**

Forsythe, a professor of political science at the University of Nebraska, gives an overview of the growing acceptance of human rights at the international level. Each chapter includes detailed source notes; there is also a six-page list of basic research and reference sources.

Hannum, Hurst, and Dana D. Fischer (eds.), *U.S. Ratification of the International Covenants on Human Rights,* **Transnational Publishers, 1993.**

The book provides legal and political perspectives on the issues created by the United States' consideration of the two major human rights treaties: the international covenants on civil and political rights and economic, social and cultural rights. Hannum is a professor at the Fletcher School of Law and Diplomacy, Tufts University; Fischer is a U.S. foreign service officer.

Humphrey, John P., *Human Rights and the United Nations: A Great Adventure,* **Transnational Publishers, 1984.**

Humphrey, a Canadian law professor who served as the first director of the United Nations' division on human rights, provides a personal memoir of the U.N.'s human rights work in its first two decades.

Steiner, Henry J., and Philip Alston, *International Human Rights in Context: Law, Politics, Morals,* **Clarendon Press, 1996.**

This comprehensive law school textbook covers the theoretical and historical background of international human rights law; human rights institutions and processes; the role of nation states in protecting and enforc-

ing human rights; and some current topics, including proposals for an international criminal court. Steiner is a professor at Harvard Law School and founder of the school's human rights program; Alston is professor of international law at the European University Institute in Florence and has served as chairman of the U.N.'s Committee on Economic, Social and Cultural Rights. The book includes a six-page bibliography.

***The United Nations and Human Rights:* 1945-1995, The United Nations: Department of Public Information, 1995.**

The book traces the history of the United Nations and human rights from the drafting of the U.N. Charter and the adoption of the Universal Declaration of Human Rights through the adoption of the various international human rights treaties and the integration of human rights components in current U.N. peacekeeping efforts. The book includes a six-page chronology and texts of nearly 100 U.N. resolutions, declarations or conventions on human rights from 1945 through 1994. Texts of major human rights treaties can also be found in Ian Brownlie (ed.), *Basic Documents on Human Rights*, Clarendon Press, 1992.

Reports and Studies

Jost, Kenneth, "Religious Persecution," *The CQ Researcher,* **Nov. 21, 1997, pp. 1009-1032.**

The report covers issues of religious persecution around the world, focusing in particular on the campaign against alleged mistreatment of Christians.

Jost, Kenneth, "War Crimes," *The CQ Researcher,* **July 7, 1995, pp. 585-608.**

The report, written as the United Nations' war crimes tribunal for the former Yugoslavia was about to begin its first trial, traces the development of international law regarding war crimes and the events leading to the establishment of the two U.N. tribunals — one dealing with Bosnia, the other with Rwanda.

Articles

Frum, David, "The International Criminal Court Must Die," *The Weekly Standard,* **Aug. 17, 1998, p. 27.**

Frum strongly argues against creation of the proposed International Criminal Court.

Stanley, Jonathan, "Focus: International Criminal Court — A Court That Knows No Boundaries?", *The Lawyer,* **Aug. 11, 1998, p. 8.**

This 1,200-word article in a British legal publication analyzes the proposed international criminal court from a supportive perspective. It also provides an address for the Web site maintained by the coalition campaigning for the new court: www.igc.apc.org/icc.

13   Women and Human Rights

MARY H. COOPER

The following stories are not for the faint of heart:

- In India, a 10-year-old girl is rescued by a flight attendant who notices her crying. She had been sold by her father for $240 to the 60-year-old Saudi Arabian man sitting next to her.

- In Kenya, 300 boys at a boarding school rape 71 girls in the girls' dormitory. "The boys never meant any harm against the girls," the vice principal explains. "They just wanted to rape."

- In Ireland, courts refuse to let a 14-year-old girl who was raped by her best friend's father travel to England to have an abortion. Only when she threatens suicide does Ireland's Supreme Court relent.

- In the United States, a 51-year-old woman is stabbed to death by her former boyfriend as she waits inside a courthouse to extend a protective order. Two previous harassment charges against the man had been dropped.[1]

Fifty years after the United Nations Declaration of Human Rights established the world's first comprehensive charter of individual freedoms, violence against women and girls still remains a problem of global dimensions.[2]

Much of the violence is linked to ethnic and religious conflicts that have erupted in the 1990s. After the Soviet Union and other communist governments within its sphere of influence collapsed, longstanding differences among religious and ethnic populations burst forth into brutal conflict. In Bosnia-Herzegovina, once part of Yugoslavia, Bosnian Serbs systematically raped and impregnated Muslim women as part of their program of "ethnic cleansing" to drive Muslims out of the country during the 1992-95 Bosnian war.

Ali Jarekji/Reuters, March 29, 1999

Ethnic Albanian refugees are reporting similar incidents committed against women fleeing the Yugoslavian province of Kosovo. Rape, mutilation and enslavement of women and girls also are common instruments of war in ongoing African civil conflicts in Rwanda, Sierra Leone and Algeria.

Human rights experts say that some of the most egregious acts have occurred in countries that have adopted Islamic law, or *Shari'a*, as the basis of their judicial systems. The most blatant violations of women's rights under Islamic law are being committed by the militant Taliban movement, which has gained control over most of Afghanistan in that country's ongoing civil war. Afghan women are held as virtual prisoners in their homes and subjected to severe punishment and even death for such minor offenses as appearing outside unescorted by a close male relative. Women fare only somewhat better in some of the more affluent Islamic countries, such as Saudi Arabia, where women are held to a strict dress code, barred from driving and often murdered by male relatives for committing adultery.

Millions of women and girls also are subjected to traditional practices that have been internationally condemned as human rights violations. A common practice in much of Africa subjects girls to painful coming-of-age rites involving the surgical removal or alteration of their genital organs. Defended as "female circumcision" by proponents of the practice, it has been condemned as "female genital mutilation" by the United Nations and human rights organizations around the world.

Even in countries where laws offer official protection from abuse, women face violence at home, from wife-burning in India, to "honor killings" of rape victims in the Middle East, to the trafficking in girls and women in Asia. Indeed, human rights groups say that violence against women is common in the United States and many other countries that officially champion human rights and offer women legal protections against violence such as wife battering and sexual abuse of female inmates.

According to the U.N. World Health Organization (WHO), most violent acts are perpetrated by husbands or other male relatives. In fact, WHO says that as many as half the women in the world have been raped or otherwise physically abused by their partners at some time in their lives. "The perpetrators of violence against women are almost exclusively men," the agency reports, and "women are at greatest risk of violence from men they know." Moreover, WHO reports, in many cases, women have nowhere to turn for help. "The response of many professionals and social institutions has been to either blame or ignore the victim."[3]

But the news is not all bad. An international women's rights movement has gathered strength in recent years, building support for interna-

From *The CQ Researcher*,
April 30, 1999.

tional efforts to stop the violence and successfully pressuring governments to pass protective laws. In addition to the Universal Declaration of Human Rights, the United Nations has adopted several conventions aimed specifically at protecting women and children. Last year, the International Criminal Tribunal for Rwanda was set up and for the first time in history legally designated rape as a war crime. The court also convicted a former local official, Jean-Paul Akayesu, of sexual violence in Rwanda's 1994 genocide and sentenced him to life in prison.

Governments around the world also are taking steps to enforce women's rights. Last year, for example, Taiwan required police to file criminal charges in rape or sexual-abuse cases, and Egypt's supreme court upheld a 1996 ban on female genital mutilation. [4]

"Throughout the world, parliaments are still male-dominant, as are heads of state, but they are listening much more today to the call for women's rights," says Urban Jonsson, regional director of the U.N. Children's Fund (UNICEF) for Eastern and Southern Africa. "We have a long way still to go, but there is a sensitivity to these issues from within governments now that was not there before."

Nonetheless, according to WHO, women between the ages of 15 and 44 are more likely to die or be disabled as a result of violence than of cancer, malaria, traffic accidents and even war. Violence against women often does not end with the act itself. Especially in Africa and other regions where AIDS is rampant, female rape victims are doubly traumatized. "More and more women and girls are being infected with HIV [the human immunodeficiency virus] as a result of coerced relationships," said James Gustave Speth, administrator of the U.N. Development Program, which seeks to eradicate poverty and promote economic development in the Third World. "An estimated nine of every 10 new HIV infections result from such relationships." [5]

The United States presents an ambivalent face to the world community when it comes to women's rights. The Clinton administration is a strong advocate of women's rights. In 1994, at President Clinton's urging, Congress established the office of senior coordinator for international women's

Holding a sign that reads "No More Violence Against Women," Maria Lopez protests with 500 other women's rights activists at the National Assembly building in Tegucigalpa, Honduras.

AP Photo/Eugene Hoshiko/Nov. 23, 1995

issues within the State Department. Secretary of State Madeleine K. Albright and first lady Hillary Rodham Clinton have been vocal champions of women's rights in international forums.

But the administration has been unable to convince the Senate to ratify the U.N. Convention on the Elimination of All Forms of Discrimination Against Women, commonly referred to as CEDAW. "The fact that the United States Senate has not seen fit to recommend ratification of CEDAW shows how out of touch the U.S. Congress is with women's lives," says Rebecca Cook, an American citizen and law professor at the University of Toronto.

Signed 20 years ago by President Jimmy Carter, the convention has since been ratified by 163 countries. "I don't think the Senate realizes yet that half of the world's population is composed of women who have very significant problems in society," Cook says, "or that CEDAW has really been the international bill of rights to address some of the social justice questions that women are facing not only in the United States but also internationally."

Opposition to CEDAW stems in part from concerns that the agreement would require the United States to adopt the Equal Rights Amendment to the Constitution. First proposed in 1923 and finally passed by Congress in 1972, the ERA failed to win ratification by the states. Opponents to CEDAW also include anti-abortion activists who fear the treaty would undermine their efforts to overturn the right to an abortion, enshrined by the U.S. Supreme Court's 1973 ruling in *Roe v. Wade*.

"Time has shown that 'family-planning' rhetoric means access to abortion services," declared Concerned Women for America, a conservative group in Washington, D.C. "Ratification of CEDAW could easily be used as a precedent to broaden the scope of abortion in the United States." [6]

But women's rights activists in the United States say that the controversy over abortion should not be allowed to cloud U.S. efforts to protect women's rights. "I think it's a distortion to give this much visibility to the abortion issue," says Joan Dunlop, former president of the International Women's Health Coalition and a prominent advocate of international women's rights. "The future of the next century is going to be the struggle to grapple with threats to the environment, human rights, economic development and health." She is trying to organize a "new constituency" of American women who would come up with innovative ways to combat these "four horsemen of the Apocalypse."

Dunlop and other activists have a long way to go, however. On March 8, International Women's Day was observed with great fanfare around the world, as it has been for more than 80 years. Government leaders made speeches, rallies were held and merchants hawked gifts to mark the occasion. [7]

But in the United States, Secretary's Day receives more attention than Women's Day, which once again passed largely unnoticed this year. A U.N. videoconference entitled "A World Free of Violence Against Women," featuring U.N. Secretary-General Kofi Annan, actress Julie Andrews and CNN anchor Judy Woodruff, was broadcast around the world but received little or no mention in the U.S. press. "This was a really powerful and impressive event concerning violence against women around the world," Dunlop says. "But it was totally inadequately reported in the United States. It was an outrage that the press failed to pick this up."

As activists and policy-makers confront violence against women around the world, these are some of the issues they are considering:

Should the United States be more tolerant of female genital alteration and other traditional practices of immigrant communities?

As a nation of immigrants, the United States has accommodated the religious and cultural practices of many societies. But the recent growth of non-European immigrant populations that wish to continue performing female genital alteration ceremonies challenges the limits of American tolerance. [8]

Known as "female circumcision" by its proponents and condemned as "female genital mutilation" by its detractors, the practice is a common coming-of-age rite in about 28 African countries and a few countries in the Middle East and Asia, including Egypt, Oman and Yemen. Most commonly, it involves excision of the clitoris and labia minora, but an estimated 15 percent of the cases also involve infibulation, in which the remaining flesh is sewn together, leaving only a small opening through which urine and menstrual blood can pass.

The World Health Organization and other international organizations place halting female genital alteration near the top of their list of priorities in combating violence against women. "Female genital mutilation (FGM) is a deeply rooted, harmful traditional practice that has serious health consequences for girls and women, especially in its severe forms," states WHO, which estimates that 130 million girls and women alive today have undergone some form of the operation. "Female genital mutilation reinforces inequality suffered by girls and women in the communities where it is practiced and must be addressed if their health, social and economic development needs are to be met." [9]

The issue is at the heart of a high-profile deportation proceeding involving a woman from Ghana who says she fled to the United States because she feared that her tribe's leaders were about to cut her genitals. Denied refugee status by an immigration judge and the Board of Immigration Appeals, Adelaide Abankwah has been detained at the Wackenhut Detention Center in Queens, N.Y., for more than two years. A Manhattan appeals court is scheduled to conduct a final hearing on the case on May 3. [10]

Opponents of FGM argue that it constitutes a violation of universally recognized human rights. "My position is very clear," says Jonsson, whose area of responsibility in UNICEF includes 23 countries of Eastern and Southern Africa. "I very strongly believe in some basic moral minimum standards, and I will not defend any compromise on our work against female genital mutilation."

Immigrant communities in the United States, Britain and other industrial countries are challenging the international condemnation of FGM, which they see as a violation of their right to carry on an integral part of their cultural heritage. This clash of views erupted into a local controversy in Seattle in 1996 after a Somali woman admitted to Harborview Medical Center, a public hospital, for routine delivery was asked whether she wanted her baby, if a son, circumcised. She answered, "Yes, and also if it's a girl." [11]

Doctors and hospital administrators discussed ways they might accommodate the mother's request, which was supported by the local community of Somali immigrants, while honoring their professional ethics, and decided on a minimal, "symbolic" procedure involving a small cut in the baby's clitoris but no removal of tissue.

News of the hospital's decision leaked out, provoking a national outcry among women's rights advocates. Then-Rep. Patricia Schroeder, D-Colo., in a letter to the hospital director, challenged the legality of its decision and concluded that "this apparent push for such a barbaric procedure by a respected, mainstream medical establishment both baffles and horrifies me." [12] The public outcry against the hospital's proposal was so strong that the hospital ultimately backed down and refused the woman's request.

To some legal scholars and supporters of multiculturalism, the Seattle experience reveals a deep-seated bias in the United States against non-Western cultural practices. "The rhetoric of FGM and mutilation ought to be prohibited from civilized discourse," says Richard A. Shweder, a cultural anthropologist at the University of Chicago. "It represents African mothers as barbarians who are trying to mutilate their children. It starts the discussion with the assumption that they are bad mothers and we are good mothers. That to me is like starting a discussion about abortion by saying you're in favor of murdering innocent life."

Far from an oppressive practice imposed on girls by men, Shweder says female genital alteration is performed almost exclusively by women, often on adolescent girls who anticipate the event as an accepted rite of passage into adult society. "The image that many people have is that there is some brutal, patriarchal male grabbing a women and pulling her outside into the back yard screaming and kicking and using a razor blade to deprive her of her sexuality," he says.

While it is undeniably painful, he says, so too is the male circumcision that often is carried out by the same societies as a coming-of-age ritual. "This is not a case of societies picking on women," he says. "Male circumcision ceremonies at adolescence are common all over the world. It would be a rarity to find a society that circumcises girls but doesn't also circumcise boys."

Shweder is among a group of scholars who are studying ways U.S. laws affect ethnic customs among immigrants in conjunction with the

Social Science Research Council in New York City. He says the campaign to ban female genital alteration in immigrant communities resembles an earlier campaign to ban male circumcision by Jewish immigrants. "One of the things that is most troubling about the current rhetoric is that it reproduces exactly the anti-Semitic rhetoric that tagged Jews as barbaric mutilators of infant babies," he says. Since then, male circumcision has become a common practice in U.S. hospitals, for Jews and non-Jews alike, even though the health benefits of this operation are apparently negligible. [13]

"Male circumcision is an irreversible change of the boy's body done without his consent," Shweder says. "Why do we allow it? I think because we feel it's minor enough that we choose to bow to parental rights, including the parents' religious freedom and cultural rights."

Opponents to FGM are undeterred by such arguments. "I see no reason why we in UNICEF would in any way legitimize a practice we condemn in Africa just because some of the same people move to other countries such as the United States," says Jonsson.

Indeed, American activists for women's rights reject the notion that immigrants such as the Somali woman in Seattle express the dominant views of their societies on this issue. "We feel without any reservation that this is a fundamental human rights violation," says Jessica Neuwirth, an international lawyer and president of Equality Now, a women's rights group in New York City. "We also find that our view is shared by African activists in every country where FGM is practiced." Neuwirth points to a grass-roots campaign in Senegal, which resulted in the passage last year of a law banning FGM. "We have great respect for culture in all contexts, but there has to be a line that you draw which has to do with violence and

harm," she says. "We can't tolerate practices just because someone thinks they're 'cultural.'"

Is Islam inherently more oppressive toward women than other religions?

The Taliban's treatment of women has drawn international attention to the plight of women and girls in many Muslim countries that have adopted Islamic law, or Shari'a, as the basis of their legal and judicial systems. Citing religious scripture that emphasizes the different roles of men and women in Muslim society, governments in much of the Islamic world hold women in subservient positions, forcing them to wear cumbersome robes, denying them full access to public life and in some cases subjecting them to outright violence.

In Afghanistan, the most extreme case of female subjugation under Islamic law, women must don a "burqa," a dark robe with only a small, heavy mesh opening to see through, before venturing out of the house. Roving police physically punish any woman who calls attention to herself even by wearing shoes that squeak or click on the pavement. Worse punishment awaits a woman who is not escorted by a close male relative.

The many Afghan women whose fathers, husbands or brothers have died in the country's ongoing civil war live under virtual house arrest. They are even denied a view of the outdoors, as the windows of houses where women live must be painted over to prevent them from being seen from the street.

Afghan women are no longer allowed to work outside the home. Because male doctors are not allowed to care for females, this means that women and girls are routinely denied health care, even emergency operations such as appendectomies or cesarean sections. Female mortality is rising, partly from an increase in suicides by severely depressed women. Perhaps worst of all, girls may no longer go to school or even be taught at home. This means that if and when the veil of Islamic law finally lifts from Afghanistan, about half the population may be illiterate and unable to function in modern society.

Some aid workers in Afghanistan dispute the severity of conditions among women, especially outside the capital, Kabul. "Definitely women in Afghanistan are suffering tremendous abuses; their human rights are not being respected," said Judy Benjamin, head of the Women's Commission for Refugee Women and Children. "But you need to put this in the context of what's happened to the country in the past two decades. Much of the grief and poverty is a result of conflict and war, not a result of the Taliban. There is suffering and poverty, but in most of Afghanistan people will say the Taliban have brought peace and security." [14]

But many women's rights advocates say the situation is intolerable. Moreover, they say, women fare only somewhat better under Shari'a law adopted in other Muslim countries. "What's happening to women in Afghanistan is really just devastating," says Mahnaz Afkhami, an international women's rights advocate and president of the Sisterhood Is Global Institute, a women's rights organization in Bethesda, Md. "But right after Afghanistan comes Saudi Arabia, where there is full gender apartheid. Of course, Saudi Arabia is a rich country, so women at least get services such as health care.

Poor countries that try to maintain separate services can't afford to have full services given by females, so there often are not enough facilities, not enough nurses and no female doctors."

But even the harshest critics of female oppression in some Islamic societies say that women and girls can thrive as practicing Muslims. "The way Shari'a law is now being incorporated into legal systems is gener-

Seita, a young Kenyan woman, recovers after her genital-alteration ritual. The photo was part of a series on female circumcision that won the 1996 Pulitzer Prize for feature photography.

AP Photo/Newhouse News Service, Stephanie Welsh

ally very oppressive, but it needn't be," says Afkhami, herself a Muslim and a former minister of state for women's affairs in Iran, whose 1979 revolution installed the first modern state based on Islamic law.

"There are perfectly wonderful passages in the Koran and other religious texts of Islam that support women's rights," she says. "The prophet's wife, for example, was also his employer and a highly respected figure in the community. "At the beginning of Islam a woman could be like that," Afkhami says. "Current laws are just patriarchal ways of keeping women down by using religion as a pretext."

Not only is there nothing in Islam that inherently violates women's rights, but Muslim women thrive in some countries that have not incorporated Shari'a law into their judicial systems. The Muslim state of Qatar in the Persian Gulf allowed women to both vote and run for public office when it held its first-ever elections in March. In Turkey, where Islam is the predominant religion, women are actually fighting the secular government's ban on wearing head scarves in schools and other state institutions. And in Pakistan, female government officials resigned en masse to protest a bill now before parliament that would make Shari'a law the law of the land.

"There is a huge diversity of ways of expressing yourself as a Muslim," Afkhami says. "In India there are some 100 million Muslim women who go around with bare midriffs, and they are perfectly fine Muslims, just as are those who are covered head to foot. It is a mistake to think that the only authentic Muslim women are the ones who are veiled and crouching in the corners of cities in the Muslim societies."

Countries that have adopted Islamic law are not the only ones that oppress women in the name of religion. Activists cite the denial of women's right to reproductive freedom in Ireland, Chile and other predominantly Catholic countries that ban abortion and limit access to contraceptive services as other examples of religious oppression.

"We should oppose not just Islamic laws, but also Judaic and Christian laws that violate the precepts of gender equality," says Neuwirth. "Our standard of measurement is the basic principles of human rights set forth in the Universal Declaration, which have been reaffirmed by the Convention on the Elimination of All Forms of Discrimination Against Women. World governments have signed on to these, at least in principle, and we want to hold them to that commitment."

Is the United States doing enough to promote international women's rights?

Most women's rights activists give the Clinton administration high marks for its efforts to advance the cause of international women's rights. In 1994 the administration requested and Congress created a separate position of senior adviser for women's rights in the State Department.

Since taking office in 1996, Secretary of State Albright has become a forceful spokesperson for the international women's rights movement. "I believe that of all the forces that will shape the world of the 21st century, this may be the most important," she said in 1998. "From the tiniest village to the largest city, surmounting every barrier of geography, language, ethnicity and background, the movement to unleash the full capacities and energies of women and girls is gaining strength." [15]

The administration's most vocal advocate of women's rights has been first lady Hillary Rodham Clinton. As the U.S. representative at the U.N. Fourth World Conference on Women in 1995 in Beijing and other meetings on the issue, Mrs. Clinton has been outspoken in her support for efforts to end violence and oppression aimed at women and girls. Singling out the Taliban's treatment of Afghan women as "the egregious and systematic trampling" of women's rights, Mrs. Clinton recently told a U.N. gathering: "It is no longer acceptable to say that the abuse and mistreatment of women is cultural. It should be called what it is — criminal." [16]

The Clinton administration's vocal

First lady Hillary Rodham Clinton greets Mary Leslie-Bryant, a survivor of domestic violence, at the opening of a battered women's shelter in Cincinnati, Ohio, on July 27, 1998.

Reuters/John Sommers

support of women's rights stands in stark contrast to the Senate's failure to ratify CEDAW. The treaty formally codifies women's equality and promotes women's inclusion in all areas of public life. It provides a universal definition of discrimination and sets clear guidelines for signatory countries to combat forms of discrimination such as violence against women and unequal pay.

Signed in 1979 by President Carter, the treaty would have to be approved by a two-thirds majority to win final ratification. But it has languished in the Senate ever since amid opposition of conservative lawmakers who say it would jeopardize U.S. sovereignty by forcing the United States to change its laws on such controversial issues as equal pay and abortion rights — although the treaty does not provide the right to abortion.

In 1994, when the Democrats had a majority in the Senate, the Foreign Relations Committee approved CEDAW and sent it to the full Senate.

"The minority recognizes the unfortunate prevalence of violence and human rights abuses against women around the world," said Sen. Jesse Helms, R-N.C., and other minority opponents of the treaty, "and we share the majority's strong support for eliminating discrimination against women. We are not persuaded, however, that [CEDAW] is a proper or effective means of pursuing that objective. Indeed, we fear that creating yet another set of unenforceable international standards will further dilute respect for international human rights norms."

Since becoming Foreign Relations chairman, in 1995, Helms has kept CEDAW from being considered by the committee, much less by the full Senate. Although Helms and other Senate conservatives have said little about the treaty, conservative activists are outspoken in their objections to what they see as its threat to American values. CEDAW, writes Phyllis Schlafly, head of the conservative Eagle Forum, "would require us to follow U.N./feminist dictates about 'customs and practices,' 'social and cultural patterns of conduct of men and women,' 'family education,' and even revision of textbooks." Schlafly also rejects the U.N. Convention on the Rights of the Child, another treaty that has yet to be taken up by the Senate, as a document that "would bring about massive U.N. interference in family life, education, day care, health care and standard of living." [17]

But human rights activists and development experts say the failure to ratify CEDAW has undermined not only the well-being of women around the world, but the United States' credibility as well. "Most people see the United States as a powerful nation, and certainly if the most powerful nation in the world doesn't agree that creates a bad precedent for women's rights around the world," says Jonsson of UNICEF. "It also is not good for the United States' image as a champion of human rights when it stands with Somalia as the only countries that have failed to ratify CEDAW."

Several lawmakers, including Sen. Russell D. Feingold, D-Wis., and Rep. Lynn Woolsey, D-Calif., have issued impassioned calls for the treaty's ratification. But so far, the push to ratify CEDAW is largely limited to isolated voices in Congress and resolutions by a handful of city governments, such as San Francisco.

"My impression is that the Clinton administration strongly favors ratification of CEDAW," Neuwirth says. "But at the same time, it's really clear that the stumbling block is in the Senate, especially in the person of Sen. Helms. The notion that people who even pay lip service to the idea of the rule of law can be unwilling to accept ratification of CEDAW is very difficult to accept."

Some activists say that Americans tend to assume they champion human rights based on the country's track record in establishing democratic institutions and advancing the civil rights of African-Americans and other minorities. "The civil rights law is in fact much more limited in scope

than the human rights language and principles," says Dunlop. "We don't really understand what human rights are in this country. Instead, we see abuses of women's rights as isolated incidents rather than as a continuum with the whole issue of human rights."

Other activists point to the public preoccupation with the president's affair with Monica Lewinsky for most of the past year as another indication of U.S. lawmakers' failure to acknowledge the widespread violations of women's rights around the world. "The fact that Congress and the press wasted a whole year on bedroom ethics as opposed to violence against women shows just how completely out of touch they are," says Cook. "As disgraceful as the Lewinsky affair was, the fact remains that Congress could have spent their time better by addressing issues that could make a real difference to women's lives." ∎

BACKGROUND

Catalog of Horrors

Since the 1970s, the international women's movement has emerged from the campaign for human rights as a separate and forceful voice. It was largely responsible for the U.N. endorsement of CEDAW, the convention on children's rights and other documents that guarantee, on paper at least, the rights of girls and women to live free from discrimination and violence. At the 1993 U.N. World Conference on Human Rights, activists won recognition that women's rights are analogous to human rights. And at the 1995 U.N. Conference on Women in Beijing, governments

agreed that all efforts to improve women's status must be founded not only on the need to improve human health and well-being but specifically on the need to respect women's rights.

"What's significant about the international movement to combat violence against women is that it has sensitized us to all kinds of discrimination against women, whether it takes the form of physical violence or government neglect," says Cook of the University of Toronto. "Whatever form it takes, we're now sensitized to the fact that discrimination against women is no longer acceptable."

Despite this progress, violence continues to be a part of everyday life for women and girls in many parts of the world. "In 1998 violence against women remained one of the most intractable violations of women's human rights," reports Human Rights Watch, an international, nonpartisan organization that monitors human rights violations worldwide. "In various forms it persisted in times of peace as well as in times of conflict. The perpetrators were as likely to be private actors as public officials. Women were beaten in their homes by intimate partners; raped and otherwise sexually assaulted during times of internal conflict by soldiers; sexually assaulted by law enforcement personnel while in their custody; raped in refugee camps by other refugees, local police or the military; and targeted for sexual violence based on their low social status." [18]

These are among the more common forms of violence against women and girls:

Repression under Islamic law — The Taliban's mistreatment of women tops the Clinton administration's list of violent offenses against women's rights. Albright has branded as "despicable" the governing movement's practice of "gender apartheid." [19]

Even under the leadership of President Mohammed Khatemi, a "moderate" cleric, Iran continues to impose strict rules over women's lives under that country's Islamic law. Since 1979, when it became the first country to adopt Shari'a law in modern times, Iran has forced women to respect a strict dress code, called hijab. The long coat and *chador*, or scarf, must cover the entire body except part of the face.

Like the Taliban, Iran's version of Islamic law segregates women from men in schools, buses, mosques and even hospitals. Although Iranian women are allowed to appear in public with men who are not close relatives, they fall under the authority of their fathers or other male relatives. Under Iranian law, men are allowed to practice polygamy, may divorce more freely than women and prevail in most child custody disputes. [20]

The imposition of Islamic law is especially jarring to women in Iran in light of the strides they had made before the revolution. "Women in Iran were some of the more advanced in the Third World and began feminist activism at the turn of the century," says Afkhami. "The revolution completely put a stop to that, and all the laws that had been worked for so hard were canceled as the government quickly adopted the most fundamentalist interpretation of Islam." The minimum age for marriage for girls was reduced from 18 to 8-1/2, death by stoning became the punishment for female adulterers and men were granted the unilateral right of divorce.

Women strongly supported the candidacy of Khatemi, who gained further support in March when his moderate allies won most of the seats in municipal elections. But his attempts to restore some freedoms for women have run into opposition from the parliament, which is controlled by the conservative clergy.

In the past year, health services have been segregated, making it hard for women to receive even emergency health care, and publishers have been barred from featuring pictures of women, even when fully veiled, on magazine covers. "The atmosphere is a little more open in Iran today," Afkhami says. "But there is a lot of struggle going on inside the country, and it's still a very dangerous situation for women."

Even some Islamic countries that have not adopted many of the strict rules imposed under Shari'a law still tolerate violent practices against women that are part of the male-dominant traditions of the Arab world. In rural Pakistan, women are often killed for marrying against their fathers' wishes, and female adulterers are routinely stoned to death. As part of a terror campaign aimed at destabilizing the secular government, Islamic militants in Algeria target women for rape, kidnapping and forced prostitution.

In Jordan, as in other Muslim countries, women who commit adultery are often murdered by brothers or other close male relatives who defend the practice as essential to preserving the family's honor. Even rape victims are subjected to such "honor killings." The practice is illegal, and Jordanian women, including Princess Basma, sister of the late King Hussein, have marched in protest against honor killings. But police and judges remain generally sympathetic to the killers, who typically either are not prosecuted or receive light sentences. Women who fear they may be targeted for honor killing often have no choice but to seek protective custody in prison to stay alive. [21]

Female genital mutilation (FGM) — Performed as a coming-of-age ritual, FGM involves partial or total removal of the external female genitalia or other injury to the genital organs for cultural or other non-medical reasons. Even in its least invasive forms, the changes brought by FGM are irreversible. FGM is widely practiced in much of sub-Saharan Africa, as well as in Egypt, Oman, Yemen and some other countries of the Middle East. Although a number of predominantly Muslim countries condone FGM, it is not unique to Muslim societies. Numerous African tribes perform it — either at birth or as a coming-of-age ceremony — and consider a woman unworthy of marriage unless she has undergone the rite at some point in her life.

"In some societies, this procedure is seen as a statement about the woman's civility," Shweder says. "By doing this you're cutting out what they view as animalistic because from their point of view it's only animals that would be driven by sexual desire. In some societies they think female circumcision improves the esthetics of the body, that by smoothing it out they're making it more attractive."

Marriage prospects are an important reason parents subject their daughters to FGM. "No responsible mother in these societies would willingly fail to circumcise her daughter for fear that people would think of the girl as a prostitute, as someone who has no control over her sexuality," Shweder says.

Although some legal experts and anthropologists argue that FGM should be tolerated, at least in its less extreme forms, most advocates for women's rights and international organizations are unequivocally opposed to the practice. The World Health Organization, for example, established a special working group to combat the practice in July 1995.

Women's rights activists in some countries have successfully lobbied

Chronology

1940s *The first efforts toward international women's rights are launched.*

1946
The United Nations establishes the Commission on the Status of Women to promote women's rights around the world.

———— • ————

1970s-1980s
The international women's rights movement goes into high gear.

1972
Congress passes the Equal Rights Amendment, but it fails to win ratification by the states.

1973
The U.S. Supreme Court's 1973 ruling in *Roe v. Wade* upholds the right of American women to obtain an abortion.

Dec. 18, 1979
The U.N. General Assembly adopts the Convention on the Elimination of All Forms of Discrimination Against Women (CEDAW).

1979
A revolution in Iran ushers in the first modern state based on Islamic law.

July 17, 1980
President Jimmy Carter signs CEDAW and sends it to the Senate, which fails to ratify it. Since 1995, the treaty has not made it out of the Senate Foreign Relations Committee, chaired by Sen. Jesse Helms, R-N.C.

1990s *Violence against women and girls becomes the main focus of the international women's movement.*

1992
As part of their campaign of "ethnic cleansing," aimed at driving all Muslims from Bosnia, Bosnian Serb forces systematically rape and impregnate Muslim women and girls.

1993
The U.N. World Conference on Human Rights adopts the Vienna Declaration, which holds that "the human rights of women and the girl-child are an inalienable, integral and indivisible part of human rights." The General Assembly adopts Resolution 48/104 recognizing the need to focus on domestic violence.

1994
At the behest of President Clinton, Congress establishes the office of senior coordinator for international women's issues within the State Department. . . . The 1994 Violence Against Women Act provides federal funding of battered women's programs and interstate enforcement of protective orders issued to batterers to stay away from their victims. . . . Hutu troops target Tutsi women and girls for sexual assault during a genocidal civil war in Rwanda.

1995
The Taliban militia emerges as a key force in the civil war in Afghanistan. The fundamentalist Islamic movement later deprives women of their human rights.

July 1995
The U.N.'s World Health Organi-

zation (WHO) establishes a special working group to combat "female genital mutilation."

Sept. 4-15, 1995
Delegates to the Fourth World Conference on Women in Beijing recognize that the status of women has advanced but that inequalities and obstacles remain.

1996
Madeleine K. Albright, the U.S. representative to the United Nations, is appointed secretary of State and becomes a forceful spokesman for the international women's rights movement.

1998
Ivory Coast and Togo ban female genital mutilation. . . . To mark International Women's Day on March 11, President Clinton announces a $10 million increase in funding to combat violence, a joint U.S.-European Union campaign to combat trafficking of women from and through Central Europe and the former Soviet Union and stepped-up efforts through the U.S. Agency for International Development to help victims of domestic violence.

1999
Senegal bans female genital mutilation. . . . Amnesty International documents widespread sexual abuse of female inmates in the United States. . . . Republican and Democratic lawmakers introduce competing legislation aimed at combating international trafficking in women and children. . . . The 4th U.S. Circuit Court of Appeals in Richmond, Va., rules on March 5 that the Violence Against Women Act is unconstitutional. The ruling denies women the right to sue their attackers in federal court.

for abolition of FGM. In Egypt, where an estimated 97 percent of the women have been circumcised, a 17-year campaign to ban the practice prevailed on Dec. 28, 1997, when the country's supreme court sustained an earlier ban. [22] In 1998, Ivory Coast and Togo also passed laws banning FGM, as did Senegal in January of this year.

Burkina Faso is taking an even more aggressive stand against the practice. "Burkina Faso has the most active program," Neuwirth says. "The government not only has supported a legislative ban on FGM but also set up an active hotline people can call to alert the police if they hear of suspicious behavior in their neighborhood."

In other countries, however, FGM is still broadly tolerated. For example, the government of Nigeria — Africa's most populous country — publicly opposes the practice but has taken no legal action to ban it, despite a grass-roots campaign by private groups. About a third of Nigerian households of all ethnic and religious groups practice the procedure. [23]

Trafficking in women and girls — According to the State Department, as many as 2 million women and girls are bought and sold each year, generally for the purpose of forced labor, domestic servitude or sexual exploitation. [24] Just as criminals control the export and import of illegal drugs, traffickers in women and girls generally belong to well-organized criminal organizations that control most of this multibillion-dollar industry. They often deceive their victims with promises of employment as nannies, models or waitresses in foreign countries where they are

subsequently forced into virtual slavery. If they have been smuggled into the country, the victims may fear reporting their condition to the authorities.

Trafficking in girls is especially common in East and South Asia, where impoverished parents sell daughters for cash to buy food for the rest of the family. A major source of women and girls today is North Korea, where starving families re-

Posters calling attention to domestic violence are being displayed in Massachusetts in 32 state domestic violence agencies and on transit trains.

portedly sell their daughters to Chinese traffickers for $800-$1,500. Although they are often bought by Chinese farmers as wives, many end up as prostitutes. [25]

Despite a law banning trafficking in women, more than 7,000 women and girls are smuggled into India from Nepal and other neighboring countries each year for India's booming sex trade. According to the Coalition Against Trafficking in Women,

made up of private human rights organizations, some 100,000 Filipino girls are sold each year as "entertainers" to Japan's sex industry, some 2 million Thai women and children — out of a total population of 60 million — are prostitutes, and 200,000 Bangladeshi women and girls are being held in sexual bondage in Pakistan. [26]

Young girls in Ghana are subjected to another kind of trafficking. Called *trokosi*, this involves a family's donation of a young daughter to a priest as a way to appease the gods for crimes committed by members of the family. The girl becomes the priest's property and is used as a maid or farmhand until puberty, when she is exploited sexually as well. Last year the Ghanaian parliament criminalized ritual enslavement of any kind.

Secretary of State Albright has launched a diplomatic initiative to counter the trafficking of girls and women, which she calls "one of the fastest-growing criminal enterprises in the world." "After all," she said, "if we believe in zero tolerance for those who sell illegal drugs, shouldn't we feel even more strongly about those who buy and sell human beings?" [27]

In March 1998, the United States and the European Union launched a joint information campaign to combat the trafficking of women from and through Central Europe and the former Soviet Union, especially Ukraine and Poland. Traffickers have used these countries both as sources of victims and as transit points for smuggling women and girls from Eastern Europe and Asia.

Rape as a weapon of terror — Although the sexual assault of women and girls trapped in combat zones has

International Groups Fight Violence With Education

Since the 1970s, a number of governments and private, non-governmental organizations have launched programs to advance the status of women around the world. Their activities were spurred by efforts to curb population growth in the developing world, which skyrocketed in the 1950s and '60s as a result of childhood vaccination campaigns and improvements in health care and sanitation. Overpopulation threatened to undermine widespread advances in agricultural output and economic development, which industrial countries and multilateral institutions such as the World Bank had supported through foreign aid programs.

Initially, the population-growth programs provided contraceptives, family-planning counseling and, in some cases, abortion services. But support for such programs waned in the 1980s under pressure from opponents of abortion and other forms of birth control.

Even supporters of population programs soon realized that their efforts were not enough to slow population growth. As long as the developing world relied mainly on farming for their livelihoods, the incentives for having large families would persist because children were viewed as vital assets as field hands and caregivers for infants and the elderly.

Increasingly, women's rights advocates have identified improvements in women's education and social services as essential to improving standards of living throughout the Third World. Policy-makers also recognized the need to focus development assistance specifically on women. In 1974, the U.S. Agency for International Development (USAID), for example, created its Office for Women in Development to help ensure that assistance programs integrate women more fully into local economies.

The change in priorities within the women's rights movement gained widespread support following several international meetings sponsored by the United Nations that brought together activists from around the world. In 1994, 179 countries participating in the U.N. International Conference on Population and Development in Cairo, Egypt, agreed to integrate into population programs the broader goals of fostering human and economic development and improving quality of life, particularly for women and girls. That theme was reiterated at the Fourth World Conference on Women, held in 1995 in Beijing. A follow-up meeting to the Cairo conference, held in February 1999 in the Hague, Netherlands, reinforced international support for improved access to family planning, gender equality and stabilization of world population. Also in February, representatives of 17 countries meeting in Mexico City under the auspices of the U.N. Children's Fund

(UNICEF) endorsed the right of women to receive quality health care and participate in decisions affecting their well-being.

The Clinton administration strongly endorses the integration of women's rights and population programs. "If there is one achievement that I hope we can [someday] look back on," said first lady Hillary Rodham Clinton at the Hague forum, "I hope it will be that we have created an environment in which more children are wanted who come into our world in the next century, and where pregnancies are planned, and where women are given their rightful place in all of their societies." [1]

In his budget request for fiscal 2000, President Clinton asked for increased funding for USAID and restoration of the U.S. contribution to the U.N. Population Fund (UNFPA). Congress has cut USAID funds for population and reproductive health assistance by a third since 1995, and in 1999 Congress eliminated funding of UNFPA altogether.

More recently, international women's rights groups have identified violence as the most basic and pervasive violation of women's rights. "The chief organizing principle of the international women's movement today is violence against women," says Joan Dunlop, former president of the International Women's Health Coalition in New York City and a leader of the women's rights movement. "By that I mean all forms of violence, not just domestic violence or battering."

In some respects, the struggle against violence is far more challenging than any fight the women's movement has undertaken before because situations that activists consider to be abusive are often accepted as normal in many societies, such as pregnancy among girls and young teenagers.

"We've always thought that adolescent, unwanted pregnancy would go away if we could just provide contraceptive services and sex education," says Rebecca Cook, a professor of women's health and human rights law at the University of Toronto. "Now we understand that up to 20 percent of the pregnancies in some countries are a result of abusive sex, particularly by older men against younger women."

Stopping such unwanted pregnancies is not just a matter of stopping forcible sex, hard as that may be, through tougher criminal penalties for rape. "Sometimes it happens because older men have such an influence over younger women that they are able to set conditions that include sex," Cook says.

---

[1] From an address before the Hague International Forum, Feb. 12, 1999.

been one of the nightmarish hazards of modern warfare, the systematic use of rape as a weapon intended to strike terror in civilian populations is a more recent phenomenon. Bosnian Serb forces shocked the world in the early 1990s when they rounded up Muslim women and girls for the sole purpose of raping them — and in some cases intentionally impregnating them — as a means of "ethnic cleansing," or driving all Muslims from the country. [28]

"Rape was never considered as a war crime during the Nuremburg trials," says Cook of the international proceedings against Nazi war criminals. "But the fact that rape is being prosecuted as a war crime at the international tribunal for the former Yugoslavia shows how far we have gone toward being sensitized to the fact that rape and forced pregnancy — using a woman's body for purposes that the government is pursuing — are forms of violence against women that constitute war crimes."

Even when it is not condoned by government forces, rape is used by participants in civil conflicts as a weapon to harm or drive out ethnic minorities. During last May's riots in Indonesia following the resignation of President Suharto, hundreds of ethnic Chinese women and girls were raped by poor residents who resent the Chinese for their economic well-being. [29]

Recent civil conflicts in Africa have also been marked by the systematic rape of women and girls. In their armed struggle against the secular government of Algeria, Islamic extremists target women, raping, mutilating and often kidnapping young women who are held as sex slaves. In Sierra Leone, wracked by civil war for the past nine years, rebel forces are raping and mutilating women and children by hacking off their arms and legs. Hutu troops targeted Tutsi women and girls for sexual assault during the 1994 genocide in Rwanda. Refugee camps offered

little protection from the violence: Rwandan women fleeing that country's genocide in 1994 reported repeated incidents of rape at the hands of other refugees.

Wife-burning — While the reports of rape and mutilation in Africa have horrified the world, some development experts say the plight of women is even worse in India and the other countries of South Asia. "Women are subordinated, exploited and targeted for violence all over the world, but the way women are perceived in families and communities in South Asia makes their situation especially bad," says Jonsson, who spent five years in the region with UNICEF. "In some parts of Bangladesh, for example, a traditional practice has it that when a husband finds his wife no longer attractive enough he arranges for her to be raped in the presence of their son, and the community will react by immediately killing her."

South Asian women have long been victimized by the region's traditions regarding marriage and the family. Because girls are viewed as less valuable than boys, some impoverished families defy existing laws by committing infanticide of baby girls and selling young daughters into marriage or prostitution. More than half the women in the northern Indian state of Rajasthan were married before they turned 15, according to one recent survey. [30]

The tradition of providing dowries also leads to violence. In the typical dowry dispute, a groom's family members harass a woman whose family they believe has not provided a sufficient dowry. This harassment sometimes ends in the woman's death, which family members try to portray as a suicide or kitchen accident. Last year alone, the Indian government reported 3,260 "dowry deaths," in which women were doused with kerosene and ignited.

The practice is so entrenched in some areas that courts are required to presume that the husband or his family is responsible for every unnatural death in the first seven years of marriage when there is evidence of harassment. [31] In 1997, newspapers in Lahore, Pakistan, reported more than four incidents a week of "stove burnings," in which most of the victims died. In Bangladesh, sulfuric acid is often used to kill or disfigure women and girls. [32]

Domestic violence — Wife-beating remains a common practice throughout the world. Even in the United States and other industrial countries that have taken steps to combat battering by strengthening criminal penalties against batterers and offering special shelters and counseling to help victims and their children, domestic violence continues to take a heavy toll, especially among women. Cultural traditions that are tolerant of wife-beating persist in some industrial countries, such as Poland, where a proverb says, "If a man does not beat his wife, her liver rots." [33] Similar attitudes have prevented women from gaining protection from batterers in Russia as well. [34]

In many developing countries around the world, where cultural traditions condone or tolerate battering, the situation is even worse. Despite their popular image as gentle, carefree societies, the Pacific Island countries have notoriously high rates of domestic violence against women. Papua New Guinea is reported to have the world's highest. [35]

A number of countries have recently taken steps to combat domestic violence. Turkey, for example, last year enacted a family protection law making spousal abuse illegal. But some laws merely ignore the problem. In some Latin American countries, a rapist may win immunity from prosecution if he offers to marry the

Abortion Issue Ignites Controversy

Few women's rights issues are more controversial than access to abortion services. In the United States, the controversy has only intensified since a woman's right to an abortion was upheld by the Supreme Court's landmark *Roe v. Wade* decision in January 1973. U.S. abortion clinics have been fire-bombed, doctors and other clinic personnel assassinated and women harassed for trying to end their unwanted pregnancies. Bowing to anti-abortion sentiments, many states have imposed restrictions on abortion, and Congress has barred funding overseas population programs that provide or promote abortion services. And now, every January, anti-abortion and pro-choice activists march on the Supreme Court to demonstrate their convictions on the issue.

Many countries have highly restrictive policies on abortion. In Nepal, obtaining an abortion carries a prison sentence of 20 years. In Peru, where abortion is illegal, poor women have been forcibly sterilized as part of a government-sponsored plan to reduce population growth. [1] And Ireland, Cambodia, Sudan and other countries prohibit the procedure except to save the woman's life.

But the promotion of women's rights in international agreements has strengthened the hand of pro-choice activists in many countries. While rejecting abortion as a preferred method of birth control, both the 1994 International Conference on Population and Development in Cairo, Egypt, and the Fourth World Conference on Women in Beijing in 1995, concluded that safe access to abortion services fell within the spectrum of human rights and social justice. The Beijing Platform for Action also condemned "forced pregnancy" as a violation of women's rights. Although the term describes the practice of intentionally impregnating civilian women in conflict, now recognized as a war crime, it may also describe the denial of abortion services to women who want to terminate unwanted pregnancies.

"Forced pregnancy describes not only denial of legal abortion when pregnancy follows rape but also state denial of abortion services when pregnancy termination is requested on other indications," conclude the authors of a recent survey of abortion legislation. "It imposes an unparalleled burden on women. No other circumstance requires unwilling individuals to provide the resources of their bodies for the sustenance of others — for instance, as organ, bone marrow or blood donors — and legal compulsion that they do so would quickly be condemned as a human rights violation." [2]

It is just such a broad interpretation of women's rights that has prompted anti-abortion activists to vehemently oppose U.S. ratification of the U.N. Convention on the Elimination of All Forms of Discrimination Against Women (CEDAW), signed by President Jimmy Carter in 1979. According to Concerned Women for America, a conservative group in Washington, the treaty's provision ensuring access to family-planning services "could easily be used as a precedent to broaden the scope of abortion in the United States. [CEDAW] was written in the late 1970s, and time has shown that 'family-planning' rhetoric means access to abortion services. That construction is consistent with feminist thought, which says that pregnancy is the only major difference between men and women. In the feminist view, pregnancy hampers women and lessens their ability to compete equally with men, so abortions must be available to all women as an equality measure." [3]

Only the United States and Somalia, which has long been torn by civil conflict, have failed to ratify CEDAW among the 163 signatories to the convention. Indeed, international trends suggest that the growing recognition of women's rights has been accompanied by increased tolerance of abortion. According to a recent survey, 26 countries have liberalized abortion laws over the past decade, while only four have restricted them. [4]

---

[1] See Christina Lamb, "Peru Condemned over Mass Sterilisation Abuses," *Sunday Telegraph* (London), Jan. 10, 1999.

[2] Rebecca J. Cook, Bernard M. Dickens and Laura E. Bliss, "International Developments in Abortion Law from 1988 to 1998," *American Journal of Public Health*, April 1999, pp. 582-583.

[3] Concerned Women for America, "Exposing CEDAW," April 3, 1997.

[4] Cook, et al., *op. cit.*

---

victim and she accepts his proposal. [36]

In Southeast Asia and many countries of Africa where AIDS has reached epidemic proportions, domestic violence is a major contributor to the deadly disease's spread. "For millions of girls and women worldwide, it is clear that violence, AIDS and human rights abuses are expe-rienced as three strands of the same traumatic reality," said Peter Piot, executive director of UNAIDS, a U.N. program. Because woman in many of these societies have few rights, he said, "they often cannot insist on fidelity, demand condom use or refuse sex to their partner, even when they suspect or know that he is already infected himself." [37]

Because women are more susceptible to HIV infection from sexual intercourse than are men, the incidence of AIDS among women is rapidly rising. In Malawi, for example, females ages 15 to 24 are six times more likely to be HIV-positive than men. [38] ∎

CURRENT SITUATION

U.S. Domestic Violence

The campaign against domestic violence in the United States took off in the 1970s as part of the fledgling women's liberation movement. Since then, hundreds of shelters and legal-assistance networks for battered women have been set up around the country. Victims of domestic violence can call local hotlines and take refuge in shelters maintained by local governments and private women's groups at undisclosed locations. There, women receive counseling, medical care for themselves and their children and help finding work so that they can gain the financial independence that is necessary for many victims to escape from abusive relationships.

As a result of this nationwide effort, thousands of lives that would have been lost to domestic violence have been saved. But ironically, most of the beneficiaries have been men, the most frequent perpetrators of spousal abuse.

According to a recent nationwide study, the number of men killed by their female partners has dropped by more than two-thirds, to around 400 a year, since the mid-1970s, while the number of women slain as a result of domestic violence has remained high, at more than 1,000 a year. The study's authors concluded that because domestic violence programs focus on helping women change their lives, by leaving abusive partners, they are less likely to kill their abusers than before. [39]

The campaign against domestic violence has prompted governors around the country to grant clemency to more than 150 battered women imprisoned for killing or assaulting their abusers. [40] Congress has also tried to combat domestic violence by increasing the price attackers must pay, beyond the existing criminal penalties. The 1994 Violence Against Women Act provided federal funding for battered-women programs and authorized interstate enforcement of protective orders issued to batterers to stay away from their victims. Total funding has amounted to more than $1.6 billion over six years for police and victim service initiatives.

The law also gave victims of rape and domestic violence the right to sue their attackers for violating their civil rights. That right was undermined in March, however, when the 4th U.S. Circuit Court of Appeals in Richmond, Va., invalidated the provision in the states under its jurisdiction — Virginia, West Virginia, Maryland and the Carolinas. The court found that such suits are not allowed under the Constitution, which limits Congress' power to open federal courts to questions unrelated to interstate commerce. The ruling means that domestic violence victims may sue their attackers under state tort laws, which may be more restrictive than the federal law. [41]

Abuse of Prisoners

Mostly as a result of mandatory sentencing provisions included in the "war on drugs," the number of women incarcerated in the United States has skyrocketed, from fewer than 40,000 in 1985 to more than 130,000 in 1997. According to Amnesty International, the incidence of sexual abuse and other forms of violence against female inmates has increased accordingly. The human rights group has documented incidents in which women were raped by male prisoners after being placed in men's units, abused by prison guards and shackled to their beds while giving birth.

"I was ready to give up my liberty," said Robin Lucas, a former inmate at the Federal Correctional Institution for Women in Dublin, Calif. "Not my soul; not my human dignity." Lucas and two other women, who were repeatedly raped by male inmates allowed into their cells, eventually received $500,000 in damages from a lawsuit against the Federal Bureau of Prisons. Similar cases have been reported throughout the country. [42]

In many cases, Amnesty found, states have failed to enforce existing laws protecting women from sexual abuse. But 12 states actually have no laws prohibiting sexual contact between women inmates and guards. The group has mounted a campaign in support of legislation to protect women from such abuse. "Most of the women in our prisons are convicted of non-violent offenses," said William F. Schulz, executive director of Amnesty International USA. "A nation that fails to ensure human rights for its own citizens loses the moral authority to press for human rights around the world, and puts its own welfare in jeopardy. The United States must not be such a nation." [43] ∎

OUTLOOK

Clinton's Initiatives

The Clinton administration continues to champion women's rights both at home and internationally. In January, for example, the president

At Issue:

Should the United States ratify the Convention on the Elimination of All Forms of Discrimination Against Women?

REP. LYNN WOOLSEY, D-CALIF.

FROM FLOOR SPEECH BEFORE THE HOUSE OF REPRESENTATIVES, MARCH 10, 1999.

i rise to ask my colleagues in the House of Representatives to take a stand for women. In honor of Women's History Month, I am reintroducing a resolution urging the Senate to ratify the United Nations Convention on the Elimination of All Forms of Discrimination Against Women, known as CEDAW. The convention holds governments responsible for first condemning and then working to eliminate all forms of discrimination against all women. This agreement establishes rights for women not previously subjected to international standards including political laws, including employment law, including education and health care.

CEDAW was approved by the United Nations General Assembly 19 years ago to codify women's equality — 19 years ago. Since then more than 160 nations have ratified CEDAW. Also, more than two-thirds of the U.N. members have gone on record dedicating themselves to ending state-sanctioned discrimination against women and girls. The one glaring exception is the oldest democracy in the world, the United States.

Mr. Speaker, since 1994 the president has repeatedly submitted this treaty to the Senate, where it has languished in the Committee on Foreign Relations. The position of the United States as an international champion of human rights has been jeopardized by its failing to consider and ratify CEDAW. Worse yet, our failure to act strips the United States of its ability to sit on an international committee established in the treaty to ensure that nations are adhering to the treaty's guidelines.

This action sends a message loud and clear to women in this country and all over the world. The message is that we are unwilling to hold ourselves publicly accountable to the same basic standards of women's rights that other countries apply to themselves This is despite the fact that since federal and state laws already prohibit many forms of discrimination against women, the United States could ratify the convention without changing domestic law.

The president, the secretary of State, Madeleine Albright, and national and international women's groups have expressed their commitment to CEDAW. Let us ratify CEDAW this year and make the 21st century the first century in the history of humanity where women do not know government-sanctioned discrimination.

CONCERNED WOMEN FOR AMERICA

"EXPOSING CEDAW: THE UNITED NATIONS CONVENTION ON THE ELIMINATION OF ALL FORMS OF DISCRIMINATION AGAINST WOMEN," APRIL 3, 1997. POSTED AT WWW.CWFA.ORG.

c oncerned Women for America strongly opposes the passage of the U.N. Convention on the Elimination of All Forms of Discrimination Against Women (CEDAW). This treaty is not necessary and would complicate the laws of the United States. . . .

The more than half a million members of Concerned Women for America find the provisions of this document very disturbing. What this treaty proposes is social engineering under the guise of "human rights."

According to Article VI, Section 2 of the U.S. Constitution, treaties supersede all federal and state laws. When they wrote the Constitution, our Founding Fathers believed that any treaty that was ratified should be, in effect, constitutional. Any treaty should line up with the principles of the Constitution and our republican form of government. CEDAW fails to meet this criterion on many grounds. Therefore, the Founding Fathers certainly would have rejected it.

Unfortunately, today's Supreme Court does not use strict constitutional interpretation as its measure, and often neither does Congress nor the president. CWA is therefore convinced that, if CEDAW is ever ratified, the federal government would treat it as a constitutional treaty, allowing CEDAW to supersede all federal and state laws. . . .

First and foremost, CEDAW's failure to define discrimination shows that the treaty is not about equality, which women in the United States already have. CEDAW is really about the promotion of the radical feminist agenda, which refuses to recognize any legitimate distinctions between men and women. . . .

The gender feminist movement has not been able to widely enact their legislation — gender re-education, comparable worth, the destruction of traditional family definitions and a federal Equal Rights Amendment — so they are using a United Nations treaty to mandate their agenda.

Women in the United States have the right to vote. They are fully participating members of society and are protected by the federal Civil Rights Code and the Equal Employment Opportunity Commission (EEOC), as well as state civil rights codes and state employment commissions.

The Convention on the Elimination of All Forms of Discrimination Against Women is flawed. It must not be ratified by the United States Senate. At its best, CEDAW is unnecessary. At its worst, CEDAW sells out America's families.

announced plans to spend $14 million to help close the gap between men's and women's wages and called on Congress to toughen the enforcement of equal-pay laws. When the 1963 Equal Pay Act took effect, American women earned 58 cents for every dollar a man earned. Today, women earn about 75 cents on the dollar. "When a woman is denied equal pay, it doesn't just hurt her," Clinton said. "It hurts her family, and that hurts America." [44]

Clinton has also stressed the importance of advancing international women's rights. "We cannot advance our ideals and interests unless we focus more attention on the fundamental human rights ... of women and girls," the president said. "We are putting our efforts to protect and advance women's rights where they belong — in the mainstream of American foreign policy." [45]

Clinton has taken a number of steps to combat violence against women around the world. On March 11, 1998, International Women's Day, the president announced a $10 million increase in funding of international programs to combat violence against women, a State Department initiative with the government of Ukraine to combat trafficking of women and stepped-up efforts through the U.S. Agency for International Development to help victims of domestic violence through the establishment of crisis centers and hotlines overseas.

Another focus of the administration's efforts to promote women's rights is a program to fund Afghan women's grass-roots organizations that are trying to resist the Taliban movement's bans on women's rights to work and receive education. The administration last year provided funds to support groups in Afghanistan fighting against the Taliban, with the particular aim of training Afghan women in health care and economic development.

Lawmakers are divided over ways to combat trafficking in women and children, a major focus of the administration's efforts to improve women's rights. Rep. Christopher H. Smith, R-N.J., has proposed legislation that would toughen penalties for trafficking of women and children for the international sex trade and bar most U.S. economic assistance to countries that fail to prohibit or adequately enforce laws to stop this activity.

Sen. Paul Wellstone, D-Minn., backs a broader initiative that would help as many as 100,000 women who are smuggled into the United States each year and forced to work as domestic servants under slavelike conditions. His bill would allow such women to stay in the United States under temporary visas while they seek asylum or sue their employers. [46]

Meanwhile, Clinton continues to call on the Senate to approve ratification of CEDAW. Last year, he announced that "obtaining Senate advice and consent to the ratification of CEDAW is a top administration priority during this session of Congress. I am also announcing my goal of having the full Senate act on CEDAW this year, which marks the 150th anniversary of the first women's rights convention at Seneca Falls, N.Y." [47]

Clinton's support of women's rights has not been enough to overcome opposition to the treaty by the Republican-led Congress, however. "Without a doubt, the administration's support is laudable, but the fact remains that the United States hasn't ratified the women's convention, the children's convention or other significant international human rights conventions," Cook says. "And unfortunately, that means that the United States is not a member of those clubs at a time when they are developing important international norms in these areas. It makes you wonder whether the members of Congress have ever stepped outside the Beltway, not to mention outside the borders of the United States." ∎

Notes

[1] Examples cited by Equality Now, a women's rights organization in New York City, at www.equalitynow.org.

[2] For background on the charter, see Kenneth Jost, "Human Rights," *The CQ Researcher*, Nov. 13, 1998, pp. 977-999

[3] World Health Organization, "Violence Against Women," August 1996.

[4] See Human Rights Watch, *World Report 1999* (1999), p. 429.

[5] From a message commemorating International Women's Day, March 8, 1999. For background, see Mary H. Cooper, "Women and AIDS," *The CQ Researcher*, Dec. 25, 1992, pp. 1121-1144.

[6] Concerned Women for America, "Exposing CEDAW," April 3, 1997.

[7] For background, see Charles S. Clark, "Feminism's Future," *The CQ Researcher*, Feb. 28, 1997, pp. 169-192.

[8] See Barbara Crossette, "Testing the Limits of Tolerance as Cultures Mix," *The New York Times*, March 6, 1999.

[9] World Health Organization, "Female Genital Mutilation," WHO Fact Sheet No. 153, April 1997.

[10] See Ginger Thompson, "Asylum Rule Urged for Sex-Based Persecution," *The New York Times*, April 26, 1999.

[11] This case is discussed at length in Doriane Lambelet Coleman, "The Seattle Compromise: Multicultural Sensitivity and Americanization," *Duke Law Journal*, February 1998, p. 717.

[12] Quoted in *Ibid*.

[13] The American Academy of Pediatrics recently declared that male circumcision provided few if any health benefits. See Eric Fidler, "Pediatricians Group: No Significant Benefits to Circumcision," The Associated Press, March 2, 1999.

[14] Quoted by Sharon Waxman, "A Cause Unveiled," *The Washington Post*, March 30, 1999.

[15] Madeleine Albright, "Advancing the Status of Women in the 21st Century," U.S. Department of State Dispatch, August 1998, p. 10.

[16] Mrs. Clinton addressed a meeting of the U.N. Trusteeship Council on March 3, 1999.

See Elisabeth Bumiller, "First Lady Speaks on Women's Issues at U.N.," *The New York Times*, March 5, 1999.

[17] Phyllis Schlafly, "Clinton's Power Grab Through Executive Orders," Jan. 20, 1999, posted on the Eagle Forum's Web site at www.eagelforum.org. The children's convention, which has been ratified by 191 governments, aims to protect children's human rights.

[18] Human Rights Watch, *op. cit.*, pp. 428-429. Unless otherwise noted, information in section is based on this report.

[19] Quoted in Peter Beaumont, "West's Women Are Sex Objects. Ours Have Dignity, Says Taliban," *The Observer*, March 8, 1998.

[20] For background, see David Masci, "Reform in Iran," *The CQ Researcher*, Dec. 18, 1998, pp. 1097-1120.

[21] See Lisa Beyer, "The Price of Honor," *Time*, Jan. 18, 1999, p. 55.

[22] "New and Old: A Survey of Egypt," *The Economist*, March 20, 1999, p. 17.

[23] U.S. Department of State, *Country Reports on Human Rights Practices for 1998*, Feb. 26, 1999.

[24] U.S. State Department, "Trafficking in Women and Girls — An International Human Rights Violation," fact sheet released March 10, 1998.

[25] See John Promfret, "For Some Food, North Koreans Deal Daughters," *The Washington Post*, Feb. 12, 1999.

[26] "Crackdown Urged on Exploitation of Women, Children in Prostitution," Deutsche Presse-Agentur, Jan. 29, 1999.

[27] Albright, *op. cit.*

[28] For background, see Kenneth Jost, "War Crimes," *The CQ Researcher*, July 7, 1995, pp. 585-608.

[29] Human Rights Watch, "Indonesia: The Damaging Debate on Rapes of Ethnic Chinese Women," 1998.

[30] John F. Burns, "Though Illegal, Child Marriage Is Popular in Part of India," *The New York Times*, May 11, 1998.

[31] U.S. Department of State, Global Human Rights 1998.

[32] Sisterhood Is Global Institute, "Acid Attacks on Women and Girls in Bangladesh," fact sheet issued March 7, 1999.

[33] Jane Perlez, "Dark Underside of Polish Family Life," *The New York Times*, May 8, 1998.

[34] See Human Rights Watch, "Russia: Too Little, Too Late: State Response to Violence

FOR MORE INFORMATION

Amnesty International USA, 600 Pennsylvania Ave. S.E., 5th Floor, Washington, D.C. 20003; (202) 544-0200; www.amnesty-usa.org. Amnesty monitors prison conditions around the world and urges fair and prompt trials for all political prisoners. It has documented extensive sexual abuse of female inmates in the U.S.

Concerned Women for America, 1015 15th St. N.W., Suite 1100, Washington, D.C. 20005; (202) 488-7000; www.cwfa.org. A conservative organization that opposes abortion and U.S. ratification of U.N. treaties promoting women's rights.

Equality Now, P.O. Box 20646, Columbus Circle Station, New York, N.Y. 10023; (212) 586-0906; www.equalitynow.org. A human rights group that helps women's groups in the developing world and immigrant women in the United States.

Feminist Majority Foundation, 8105 West Third St., Los Angeles, Calif. 90048; (323) 651-0495; www.feminist.org. A women's rights group that is leading a campaign publicizing the repression of Afghan women by the Taliban, an Islamic fundamentalist movement.

Human Rights Watch, 1630 Connecticut Ave. N.W., Suite 500, Washington, D.C. 20009; (202) 612-4321; www.hrw.org. This international, nonpartisan organization monitors human rights violations worldwide and has launch-ed a special campaign to promote women's rights.

Sisterhood Is Global Institute, 1200, Atwater Ave., Suite 2, Montreal, QC, Canada H3Z1X4; (514) 846-9366; www.sigi.org. This nonprofit group produces and circulates educational manuals and research papers publicizing issues of concern to women, especially those in Muslim societies.

United Nations Development Fund for Women, 304 East 45th St., 15th Floor, New York, N.Y. 10017; (212) 906-6400; www.unifem.undp.org. UNIFEM promotes women's rights around the world and is a leader of the campaign to publicize and combat violence against women and girls.

Against Women, December 1997.

[35] "South Pacific Nations to Study Rampant Wife-Beating Assaults," AP Worldstream, Jan. 26, 1999.

[36] *Ibid.*

[37] U.S. State Department, Human Rights Report for 1998.

[38] "Violence, AIDS Pose Joint Threat to Women," The Associated Press, March 4, 1999.

[39] See Brooke A. Masters, "Domestic Violence Programs Save Men's Lives, Study Says," *The Washington Post*, March 14, 1999.

[40] See Minouche Kandel and Kenneth J. Theisen, "Women Who Wait for Justice," *The San Francisco Chronicle*, Nov. 27, 1998.

[41] See Brooke A. Masters, "Appeals Court Rejects Part of Gender-Violence Act," *The Washington Post*, March 6, 1999.

[42] Amnesty International, " 'Not Part of My Sentence' — Violations of the Human Rights of Women In Custody," March 1999.

[43] Speaking at a news conference in New York City March 4, 1999.

[44] From the president's weekly radio address. See Sandra Sobieraj, "Clinton Aims to Close the Gender Wage Gap," *The Des Moines Register*, Jan. 31, 1999. For background, see Mary H. Cooper, "Income Inequality," *The CQ Researcher*, April 17, 1998, pp. 346-369.

[45] From a speech on international human rights delivered Dec. 10, 1997.

[46] See William Branigin, "A Different Kind of Trade War," *The Washington Post*, March 20, 1999.

[47] From a letter to Senate leaders dated March 11, 1998.

Bibliography

Selected Sources Used

Books

Fernea, Elizabeth Warnock, *In Search of Islamic Feminism: One Woman's Global Journey*, Anchor Books, 1998.

A professor of Eastern and Middle Eastern studies at the University of Texas, Austin, describes the wide diversity of living conditions and attitudes toward women's rights from interviews of Muslim women in Islamic countries as well as the United States.

Articles

Beyer, Lisa, "The Price of Honor," *Time*, Jan. 18, 1999, p. 55.

Female adulterers and even rape victims in Jordan and other countries of the Middle East continue to be murdered by male relatives who defend such "honor killings" despite campaigns by women's activists to end the practice.

Cook, Rebecca J., Bernard M. Dickens and Laura E. Bliss, "International Developments in Abortion Law From 1988-1998," *American Journal of Public Health*, April 1999, pp. 579-586.

This review of worldwide abortion laws finds that over the past decade 26 countries have liberalized access to abortion, while four have added new restrictions.

Martin, William, "The Christian Right and American Foreign Policy," *Foreign Policy*, spring 1999, pp. 66-80.

Religious conservatives, long suspicious of the United Nations, have vehemently opposed the platform of the 1995 U.N. World Conference on Women in Beijing as placing too much emphasis on reproductive freedom and depicting marriage and motherhood in a negative light.

Moshavi, Sharon, "Behind the Scarves, the Second Sex Seethes," *Business Week*, Feb. 23, 1998, pp. 30G-30J.

Encouraged by the reformist views of President Mohammed Khatami, Iranian women are cautiously challenging the restrictive policies imposed since the 1979 Islamic revolution in that country.

Sarkar, Tanika, "Women in South Asia: The Raj and After," *History Today*, September 1997, pp. 54-59.

Women in India have new rights — they gained citizenship in 1947, the practice of *suttee* — suicide of widows upon their husbands' deaths — has been banned and widows have been allowed to remarry. But a backlash against women's rights has eroded the status of women throughout the subcontinent.

Toubia, Nahid, "Female Circumcision as a Public Health Issue," *The New England Journal of Medicine*, Sept. 15, 1994.

As the number of immigrants from African and Middle Eastern countries grows in the United States, many communities wish to continue the traditional practice of "female circumcision" but run into resistance from public health officials and human rights activists who decry the practice as a violation of women's rights.

Reports and Studies

Afkhami, Mahnaz, Greta Hofmann Nemiroff and Haleh Vaziri, *Safe and Secure: Eliminating Violence Against Women and Girls in Muslim Societies*, Sisterhood Is Global Institute, 1998.

This training manual assists Muslim women to identify sources of violence in the family and society, publicize instances of violence and influence governments to eliminate gender-based violence.

Amnesty International, " 'Not Part of My Sentence:' Violations of the Human Rights of Women in Custody," March 1999.

Mandatory sentences introduced as part of the war on drugs in the United States have resulted in a dramatic increase in the number of female inmates. This report documents pervasive sexual abuse of women by male inmates and guards throughout the prison system.

Human Rights Watch, *World Report* 1999, 1998.

The New York City-based organization reports continuing gains in international human rights over the past year, such as the creation of the International Criminal Court. But many governments continue to deny equal rights for women or enforce existing laws aimed at promoting them.

Human Rights Watch, *Russia: Too Little, Too Late: State Response to Violence Against Women*, December 1997.

Violence against women is pervasive in Russia, but law-enforcement agencies routinely deny women their right to equal protection under the law by failing to prosecute violence against women.

U.S. Agency for International Development, *From Commitment to Action: Meeting the Challenge of ICPD*, February 1999.

This report assesses progress made since 1994, when participants at the International Conference on Population and Development in Cairo agreed to provide universal access to reproductive health information services by 2015.

14 Islamic Fundamentalism

DAVID MASCI

When Iranians went to the polls in February, the turnout was high — more than 80 percent — but so were the stakes. Voters weren't just picking a new parliament but resolving a showdown between reformers and proponents of the nation's strict Islamic rule.

In a surprising show of strength, the reformers won 70 percent of the seats, dealing a stunning rebuke to the hard-line Muslim clerics who have been running Iran for two decades. Afterwards, while the winners celebrated, the losers engaged in soul searching — up to a point.

"We will not change our principles or positions," declared Mohammad Reza Bahonar, a prominent conservative who lost his seat in parliament, "but it is natural that we should reconsider our policies and methods." [1]

The election of moderates in Iran surprised many Westerners. After all, isn't this the country that shocked the world in 1979 when radical Muslim clerics overthrew the government? Didn't Iran hold 52 American Embassy personnel hostage for 444 days? And doesn't Iran, to this day, encourage people to chant "Death to America" at political rallies?

To the United States and its allies, Iran is the quintessential example of religious orthodoxy taken to an extreme, more associated with its *fatwa* (death sentence) against British novelist Salman Rushdie than democracy. Other rigidly Islamic states, Sudan and Afghanistan among them, are viewed in much the same way. The United States bombed both nations in 1998 after they were linked to anti-American terrorism.

Clergymen at the Masourmeb shrine in Qum, Iran, wait in line to vote in last February's parliamentary elections, in which reformers dealt a blow to the strict Islamic government.

AP Photo/Kamran Jebreili

The terrorist bombings of the U.S. embassies in Nairobi, Kenya, and Dar es Salaam, Tanzania, and the World Trade Center in New York City represent the essence of Americans' fear of Islamic fundamentalism: unbending hostility to the West, crippling religious intolerance and a penchant for violence, both at home and abroad.

And yet, unlike most other Muslim states — including Egypt and other U.S. allies in the Middle East — fundamentalist Iran allows its citizens to choose freely among candidates with competing agendas. Many experts on the Middle East cite Iran's open elections as proof that Islamic fundamentalism and democracy can peacefully coexist. In fact, giving voters a chance to choose candidates who oppose the status quo, they say, is the ultimate test for a democracy. But others maintain that democ-

racy is inherently impossible for a fundamentalist state like Iran, mainly because many questions that would normally be debated in the political arena have been answered by Islam's holiest book, the *Koran*.

"For [fundamentalists], the truth is knowable, and so there is no need to discuss it in an open forum," says Daniel Pipes, director of the Middle East Forum, a think tank in Philadelphia. "That strikes me as undemocratic."

He notes that Mohammad Khatami may be president but real power lies with "supreme leader" Ayatollah Ali Khamenei, who controls the military and other organs of power, including press censorship.

But John Esposito, a professor of religion and international affairs at Georgetown University, is among those who argue that orthodox Islam is not inherently undemocratic. Many references in the *Koran* and other revered Islamic writings support the notion of representative democracy, he says.

"We assume democracy is impossible in a place like Iran," Esposito explains, "but it's actually the secular countries in the Muslim world, many of which, like Egypt, are allied with us, that are undemocratic."

Esposito and others also argue that because the West has misjudged Islamic fundamentalism, Americans, in particular, have "terribly exaggerated" the threat that fundamentalists pose to U.S. security. Much of the exaggeration is due to the news media's tendency to focus only on fundamentalists when there is a bombing, they say.

"They have oversimplified everything to do with Islam," says Shaul Bakhash, a professor of Middle Eastern history at George Mason Univer-

From *The CQ Researcher,*
March 24, 2000.

Fundamentalism in the Islamic World

After Christianity, Islam is the world's largest religion, with more than 1.2 billion followers. Forty countries are primarily Muslim, and more than 20 others have sizable Islamic minorities. In 11 of those nations, Islamic fundamentalists play major roles in political and social life:

1. Algeria: Islamic guerrillas have been fighting the government since 1991, when elections were cancelled to thwart a takeover by fundamentalists. Recently, a more aggressive military strategy and a government amnesty offer to the guerrillas have reduced the fighting.

2. Tunisia: Economic growth and a tough state-security apparatus have kept the country relatively free of fundamentalist political activity since the 1980s, when the government outlawed al-Nahda, the main Islamic party.

3. Sudan: The survival of the Islamic system established in 1989 by Hassan al-Turabi was thrown in doubt last year after President Omar el-Bashir removed Turabi as Speaker of parliament. Meanwhile, the civil war between the Muslim north and Christian and Animist south continues.

sity in Fairfax, Va. The reality, Bakhash and others say, is that few fundamentalists actually want to harm the United States. And those that do, he argues, pose only a "minuscule threat" to America, which after all is the world's most powerful nation.

In addition, Bakhash and others say, antagonism among Islamic fundamentalists toward the United States — largely due to U.S. support for Israel — has been significantly reduced in the 1990s by the Middle East peace process. "Because the Palestinians and Syrians are talking to the Israelis, things are not as tense as they once were," says Michael Salla, a professor of international relations at American University.

But hostility toward the United States is seen by others as ingrained in fundamentalist thinking. David Wurmser, a research fellow at the American Enterprise Institute (AEI), contends that fundamentalists desire nothing less than the fall of the West. "I think they see themselves as ideo-

logical opposites and say, 'It's either us or them.'"

In addition, Wurmser and others argue that fundamentalists, far from posing an insignificant threat, have killed many Americans both in the United States and abroad.

"These are dangerous people, and we ignore them at our own peril," says James Phillips, a research fellow at the Heritage Foundation.

As Americans try to understand Islamic fundamentalism, here are some of the questions being asked:

Is Islamic fundamentalism compatible with democracy?

Most people in the Islamic world do not live under democratic governments. From the sheikdoms of the Persian Gulf to the vast deserts of North Africa, the hallmarks of an open society, like fair elections and respect for the rule of law, are in scant evidence.

There are exceptions. A number of nations, like Jordan and Turkey, have

elected parliaments and permit a degree of pluralism. And Indonesia, the world's largest Muslim country, just overturned decades of secular, authoritarian rule and replaced it with a freely elected parliament and president.

Yet these nations are not full democracies, at least in Western terms. For instance, in Turkey, possibly the most westward-looking Muslim country, the political and cultural rights of Kurdish citizens (fully one-fifth of the population) have been severely curtailed. In addition, in 1997, a democratically elected government led by the fundamentalist Welfare Party was forced from power by the Turkish military. Still, Turks at least have had some say in who governs their country.

More typical are nations like Egypt and Tunisia, which have democratic trappings, including an elected president and parliament, but not much real democracy. In Egypt, for example, few opposition candidates are

4 Egypt: President Hosni Mubarak has cracked down on violent, anti-government fundamentalists. But he has also tried to give religion a more prominent role in society in an effort to accommodate moderate fundamentalists.

5 Saudi Arabia: The monarchy in Saudi Arabia, birthplace of Mohammad, founder of Islam, governs the country using religious principals, including *Shariah*, which punishes theft with amputation and other crimes with beheading.

6 Jordan: Until recently, the fundamentalist Islamic Action Front had been boycotting elections to protest a 1997 law aimed at curtailing the party's power. Last year, after King Hussein died and his son Abdullah took the throne, the Front decided to participate in elections again.

7 Turkey: The moderate fundamentalist Welfare Party won enough votes in 1996 to head a coalition government. But the Turkish military later forced Welfare from power, leaving secular parties to form a new government.

8 Iran: Islamic fundamentalists have governed since overthrowing the shah in 1979. Earlier this year, reformers won about 70 percent of the vote in parliamentary elections.

9 Afghanistan: The ruling Taliban have imposed strict Islamic law, or *Shariah*, over most of the country. Afghani seminary students formed the Taliban and took control of the government in a lightning military campaign in 1995-96.

10 Pakistan: Fundamentalists are a potent political force. Until last year's military coup removed him from office for alleged corruption, Prime Minister Nawaz Sharif was trying to bolster his political standing by replacing Pakistan's secular legal code with *Shariah*.

11 Indonesia: The world's most populous Muslim country has a tradition of religious tolerance, although recently there has been violence between Muslims and Christians. President Abdurrahman Wahid is a moderate fundamentalist.

permitted to run, ensuring that the ruling National Democratic Party dominates the legislature. Meanwhile, President Hosni Mubarak, who was re-elected (unopposed) to a fourth six-year term last year, maintains a large state security apparatus to control the opposition. [2]

Egypt's authoritarian model has been duplicated in various degrees throughout the Muslim world, prompting many analysts to question whether Islam and democracy can coexist. The question becomes even more acute when one looks at Islamic fundamentalism.

When fundamentalism grew into a mass political movement in the 1970s and '80s, Western analysts feared that a new generation of repressive theocrats would make traditional Muslim strongmen like Mubarak look as democratic as Thomas Jefferson. And such fears have been borne out in a number of places. Fundamentalist regimes in Sudan and Afghanistan are brutal and undemocratic.

But in Iran, considered the progenitor of all fundamentalist governments, an experiment is under way to show that muscular Islam and democratic traditions are not incompatible. Iran has an elected president and parliament, or *Majlis*. And, unlike Egypt and many other Muslim states, voters in Iran are not required to rubber stamp the ruling party's choice. In the parliamentary elections in February and the 1997 presidential contest, Iranians chose candidates who were not favored by the religious establishment.

Many scholars say that the election results in Iran prove that Islam and democracy are compatible. But others argue that many aspects of a religiously based political system like Iran's make real democracy impossible. "They are trying to square a circle," says AEI's Wurmser.

To begin with, they argue, fundamentalist regimes are by their very nature undemocratic because much of the government's structure and policy is based on the *Koran*, as well as Islamic law, or *Shariah*. (*See story, p. 247.*) Both sources are thought to come directly from God and hence are hard to question. "The whole essence of Islamic fundamentalist ideology is that truth is derived from the will of Allah, which means that there can never really be free debate on most issues since an answer already exists," Wurmser argues.

Moreover, Wurmser and others say, when a question arises over whether an answer is correct, it is clerics more than politicians who are relied upon to provide the answer. "It's very much like medieval Europe with its church dogma," Pipes says. "Many things just aren't open for general discussion."

And like medieval Europe, they say, Iran and the other fundamentalist regimes directly combine politics and religion, something considered anathema by most democratic states. "When you don't have separation of church and state, there can never be an equality of competing voices since one point of view is more valid than others," says Lawrence Davidson, an associate professor of history at West Chester University, in West Chester, Pa. "That's not what democracy is about."

All of this leads to a system that, at best, will be rigged in favor of the status quo. Even in Iran, Davidson and others point out, many powerful governing institutions are not democratic in any way. "All of the levers of power — military, judiciary, the economy and control over the press — are in the hands of Khamenei and the mullahs," Pipes says.

As for the parliament, its authority is very limited and not as democratic as it might seem at first blush. "The *Majlis* is not really freely elected because all candidates must be approved by the authorities before they can run," Pipes says. To win this approval, a candidate must show that he or she firmly supports the ideals of the Iranian revolution. Before the election earlier this year, for instance, hundreds of mostly liberal candidates were disqualified.

But others say that results of recent elections in Iran prove that a government run by fundamentalists can be democratic. "Iran is a democracy primarily because the [parliamentary] election turned out the government-backed candidates and that only could have happened in a real democratic state," says Stephen Pelletiere a professor of national security strategy at the Army War College in Carlyle, Pa.

Pelletiere and others also argue that while screening candidates might not be entirely fair, every democracy

tips its hat to the establishment. "Of course, the system is rigged to some extent to favor the powers that be, but so is every democratic system," he says. "Look at the United States," Pelletiere adds, pointing to campaign finance laws that many claim stack the deck in favor of incumbents.

Those who believe that democracy and Islam can coexist also dis-

Smoke billows over the heavily damaged U.S. Embassy in Nairobi, Kenya, on Aug. 7, 1998, after a bomb killed at least 247 people, including 12 Americans. Authorities blamed the attack on Islamic terrorists linked to Osama bin Laden, a wealthy Saudi fundamentalist based in Afghanistan.

count the idea that a strict separation of church and state is necessary in a democratic system. For instance, they point to Israel, which has a state religion — Judaism — but is still considered a democracy.

Supporters of this idea also point out that strict adherence to Islam does not preclude the development of

democratic institutions. They note, for example, that the Koran and other important writings can be interpreted to support democracy. "There is a tradition in Islam of consultation, a concept known as *ijma*, or consensus, that is used to justify a parliamentary form of government," says Georgetown University's Esposito.

Gary Sick, a professor of Middle Eastern politics at Columbia University, agrees. "A good Muslim can be committed to Islam and to democratic reform because there is plenty of evidence in the *Koran* and the *Shariah* for democratic forms of government," he says. "There is no missing 'democracy gene' in Muslims."

Indeed, Sick and others argue, it is not Islam that is preventing fundamentalist regimes like those in Afghanistan from democratizing, but more mundane concerns.

"These regimes don't want democracy for the same reason that other authoritarian governments don't: They don't want to lose power," he says "That's politics, not religion."

Do Americans exaggerate the dangers Islamic fundamentalism poses to U.S. security?

When many Americans think of Islamic fundamentalism, they think of terrorism and other acts of violence — and not without some justification. For much of the last 20 years, fundamentalist extremists have kidnapped, hijacked and killed Americans both overseas and at home.

Indeed, when U.S. officials speak of fundamentalist countries, regardless of the context, the specter of terrorism is often invoked. For example, at a Washington conference on American-Iran relations on March

What Do Fundamentalists Want?

There is no word in Arabic for fundamentalism. "The closest that we have is *usuliyan*, which means principalist," says Ebrahim Moosa, an associate professor of religion at Stanford University.

In fact, says Bahman Baktiari, a political science professor at the American University in Cairo, Islamic fundamentalism is a purely Western construct, "used to describe the rise of Islamic forces in the Middle East."

Moreover, Baktiari says, "this movement is not homogeneous." From North Africa to Asia, fundamentalists have different views about how to build a good Islamic society. For instance, in Iran, women can attend school, drive, vote and even hold public office. By contrast, women in Taliban-controlled Afghanistan can't."

Still, several common assumptions and principals underlie almost all fundamentalist, or Islamist, movements. Indeed, like orthodox movements within other faiths, Islamic fundamentalism took hold because of what some Muslims see as a crisis of epic proportions — namely, the state of confusion and decay in the Muslim world. The answer, they believe, is to return religion to its proper place of importance in society.

"God has not forsaken Muslims," the fundamentalists often say, "rather Muslims have forsaken God." [1]

A millennium ago, Islam was the foundation of the most dynamic civilization in the world. While the Christian West was still trying to recover from the fall of the Roman Empire, Arabs throughout North Africa and the Levant were building a sophisticated and energetic culture. But after several hundred years of prosperity, the Muslim world went into decline, increasingly beset by the military, economic and cultural power of Europe and, later, the United States. To make matters worse, Islamic fundamentalists say Muslim countries have been shamelessly forsaking their own glorious culture and replacing it with shallow, if not obscene, Western notions.

The first step on the road to reversing this decline, fundamentalists say, is to cast off Western music, literature and other influences.

"They want to do away with Michael Jackson and Madonna, this hedonistic culture that has been imposed on them," says Seyyed Hossein Nasr, a professor of Islamic studies at The George Washington University.

Fundamentalists also want to re-examine Western institutions and law. "The idea of the all-powerful state, which now exists in most Muslim countries, is also Western and alien to Islam," Nasr says. "Fundamentalists want peace and security like everyone else, but they don't want a government that meddles in their lives so much."

In place of Western culture and institutions, fundamentalists call for a return to a society based on Islam at all levels. "This is about Islam being part of public norms, in the political, economic and cultural spheres," Moosa says.

For the individual, this means finding homegrown alternatives to Western imports. "We need to reassert our identity," Nasr says. "And so instead of reading, say, a French book or an American book, we need to be looking to our own literature."

Music, fashion, cuisine, architecture and other aspects of culture must also reflect the influence of Islam. "Islamicizing society means a lot of things, from getting rid of pornography to making women wear chador [a head scarf to cover one's hair] to banning alcohol," says Daniel Pipes, president of the Middle East Forum in Philadelphia.

On the political level, a return to Islam entails infusing public institutions with religion. "All public life in Islam is religious, being permeated by the experience of the Divine," writes Hassan al-Turabi, who in 1989 engineered Sudan's experiment with an Islamic government. "Its function is to pursue the service of Allah as expressed in a concrete way in the *Shariah*, the religious law." [2]

But the meaning of the *Koran*, is, to some degree, dependent on who is reading it. "There are many different ways to interpret the *Shariah*," Moosa says. "Each group calibrates their reading of things based on local conditions."

In rough-and-tumble Afghanistan, for instance, the Taliban interpret the texts rather harshly. "But Iran is more cosmopolitan," Moosa says, "and it does not see things in such a Draconian way."

---

[1] Lawrence Davidson, *Islamic Fundamentalism* (1998), p. 83.

[2] Quoted in *Ibid.*, p. 127.

17, Secretary of State Madeleine K. Albright announced the easing of economic sanctions against Iran. But she still noted pointedly to the audience of academics and diplomats that "innocent Americans and friends of America have been murdered by terrorist groups that are supported by the Iranian government."

The assault on U.S. citizens and interests by Islamic militants began in 1979, when Iranian students (with their government's blessing) occupied the U.S. Embassy in Tehran and held 52 Americans hostage for 444 days. In the 1980s, Islamic militants were very active, most notably kidnapping and in some cases killing Americans

in Beirut throughout much of the decade. The worst of these incidents occurred in 1983, when 241 U.S. Marines died after a suicide bomber destroyed their barracks. [4]

In 1993, fundamentalist violence arrived on U.S. shores when a 1,000-pound bomb exploded in a garage underneath New York's World Trade

Center killing six and injuring over 1,000. [5] In August 1998, 257 people were killed — including 12 Americans — when U.S. embassies in Kenya and Tanzania were bombed by agents thought to be working for Osama bin Laden, a Saudi Arabian fundamentalist operating out of Taliban-controlled Afghanistan. [6]

Some Middle East experts see these and other similar incidents as proof of the need to maintain a watchful eye on Islamic fundamentalists throughout the world. "We've been repeatedly burned by these people, and so it's hard to exaggerate the threat they pose to us," Phillips says.

For one thing, Phillips and others argue, fundamentalists see themselves in direct conflict with the United States and other Western powers. "Their objective is nothing less than the total destruction of the West," says AEI's Wurmser. "They see no room for peaceful coexistence."

The desire to destroy the West, Wurmser and others say, stems from a perception held by many fundamentalists that Western, particularly American, ideas and values will destroy Islamic society. "Khomeini called the United States 'the Great Satan' in the sense that the devil destroys you by tempting you," Phillips says. "They understand the allure of Western culture and see it as a terrible evil."

But others say fundamentalists are feared primarily because they are misunderstood. "We have a tendency to simplify things and group them together to make them easy to understand," Bakhash says. "That has certainly happened here."

Such simplification is driven in part by America's allies in the Muslim world, like Egypt and Turkey, who promote the idea that all fundamentalists are violent. "These regimes find it convenient to label [fundamentalists] as dangerous extremists because it allows them to crack down on

them without being criticized by the West," Esposito says.

The news media are also culpable, Esposito argues. "The media only deal with fundamentalists when there's a bomb involved," he says. "No wonder Americans think they're all terrorists, when they bother to think about them at all." The reality, he and others claim, is that the vast majority of Islamic fundamentalists are peace-loving people of faith.

Finally, many Middle East experts argue, even violent fundamentalists are incapable of actually threatening U.S. security. "This is not China or Russia we're talking about," Bakhash says. "These are small groups and small states capable of creating small amounts of mischief, nothing more."

Pelletierre agrees: "To say that Osama Bin Laden is a threat to us is ridiculous, given that we're the most powerful nation on Earth, and he's one forlorn individual hiding out in a godforsaken place like Afghanistan."

But Phillips, Wurmser and others dispute the notion that fundamentalists are not a valid threat to American security. "These are very nasty people who are capable of doing very nasty things," Phillips says. "I mean, look at how many people they killed in the African embassy bombings," he adds. [7]

And the problem isn't just with terrorists, they point out. Countries like Iran and Sudan have repeatedly been accused of aiding or even directing these violent groups. Other states in the Muslim world, while not directly assisting Islamic terrorists, do offer tacit support to these groups. "Many Muslim governments don't dissociate themselves from this bad behavior," Wurmser says, "and so they are in a sense responsible for it."

If the United States and her allies dismiss the threat posed by these groups and their backers, they do so at their own peril, Phillips argues. "Look, we're going to get burned again by these people," he says. "It's better

to try to deal with this reality than to ignore it." ∎

BACKGROUND

An Islamic Revival

The history of Islam, like that of most major faiths, is replete with attempts to return the religion to its roots, usually in response to some sort of crisis. The most recent strain of fundamentalism has its roots in a calamity of the 19th century: the triumph of European colonialism. By the beginning of the 20th century, all of Muslim Africa and most of the Islamic lands of Central and South Asia had European overlords.

Muslims responded to this new reality in two ways. Some called on their brothers and sisters to imitate European ways in an effort to replicate European power. These "Westernizers" wanted to build secular societies where Islam and politics were separate. But others argued that European methods should only be used in the context of Islam. According to Davidson, the "Islamic modernizers" viewed Western political, educational and other models as a means to "revive" Islamic civilization, not supplant it with a European substitute. [8]

As the 20th century dawned, the Westernizers, with European support, began to gain the upper hand. This trend gathered speed after World War I, when the breakup of the Turkish-based Ottoman Empire created a series of new Muslim states, such as Iraq, Jordan and Saudi Arabia. As would happen with decolonization in Africa a half-century later, the new countries were drawn up by Westerners with little attention paid to the

Chronology

different peoples who would have to live together in these new political entities. In fact, the basic concept of a nation-state, as conceived in the West, flies in the face of Muslim tradition, which stresses a collective identity based on Islam. [9]

The breakup of the Muslim world into nation-states further accelerated after World War II, when French and British colonies in North Africa and elsewhere gained independence. In most cases secular, Western-influenced elites ran these new countries.

During these years, a number of other influences came to the fore, most notably Arab nationalism and socialism. But by the late 1960s these and other secular models began to fray as Muslims became disenchanted with governments that were increasingly corrupt and unable to improve people's lives.

It was at this time that fundamentalism began to seriously compete for the hearts and minds of many Muslims. The fundamentalist movement had existed for some time, but on a grass-roots and largely humanitarian level. Throughout the Islamic world, Muslim societies had been working for decades to provide everything from health care to religious and cultural education in tens of thousands of neighborhoods and communities. [10] Now the influence of this loose, informal network started to grow.

In 1979, fundamentalist Islam scored its first major political victory when Shah Mohammad Reza Pahlavi of Iran was overthrown by a popular uprising inspired and led by a leading Muslim cleric, Ayatollah Ruhollah Khomeini. In place of the secular, pro-Western Shah, Khomeini created a theocracy, asserting in 1979 that "there is not a single topic of human life for which Islam has not provided instruction and established norms." [11]

The Iranians sought to stoke the fires of Islamic revolution throughout the Muslim world. In Lebanon, for instance, they provided military and

1960s-1970s
Government corruption and inefficiency in the Muslim world lead to disenchantment and rising fundamentalism.

1967
Israel wins the Six-Day War, prompting much soul searching among Muslims.

1970
Egyptian President Gamal Abdel Nasser, the father of modern Arab nationalism, dies.

1977
Gen. Zia ul-Haq overthrows Pakistan's civilian government and introduces Islamic law.

1979
Fundamentalists in Iran overthrow the ruling Shah.

1980s *The Iranian revolution inspires many strict Islamic movements throughout the Muslim world.*

1980
Hezbollah (Party of God) is founded in Lebanon.

1981
Islamic militants assassinate Egyptian President Sadat.

1989
After a coup, Hassan al-Turabi establishes an Islamic government in Sudan.

1990s *Islamic fundamentalists suffer setbacks.*

1990
Islamic fundamentalists win 32 seats in Jordanian parliament.

1992
Algeria aborts national elections to thwart Islamic fundamentalists, sparking civil war.

1993
Islamic militants bomb the World Trade Center in New York City killing six people.

1994
The Taliban begin a military campaign to unify Afghanistan and establish an Islamic state.

1995
The Welfare Party in Turkey forms an Islamic government, but is ousted by the military.

May 1997
Reformer Mohammad Khatami is elected president in Iran.

November 1997
Islamic extremists kill 58 tourists in Luxor, turning many Egyptians against fundamentalists.

1998
Saudi fundamentalist Osama Bin Laden is linked to the bombing of two U.S. embassies in Africa.

1999
Hassan al-Turabi is removed as Speaker of Sudan's parliament.

February 2000
Reformers allied with Khatami win convincingly in Iran.

March 17, 2000
Secretary of State Madeleine K. Albright lifts some economic sanctions against Iran.

other assistance to Hezbollah (Party of God), which is still fighting to establish an Islamic state. But more than providing direct aid, Iran inspired Islamic fundamentalists everywhere, from the Muslim Brotherhood in Egypt and Jordan to the Islamic Salvation Front in Algeria.

And Iran was not the only country to establish a fundamentalist government. In 1989, a military coup in Sudan overthrew a civilian government and established a new regime led by Hassan al-Turabi, an Islamic fundamentalist and law professor.

In Afghanistan, a group of ultra-orthodox Muslims, the Taliban, came to power in 1996 after nearly 17 years of war following invasion by the Soviet Union in 1979. The Taliban instituted a particularly strict brand of *Shariah*, forcing women to be fully covered in public and denying them access to education. In addition, TV, film and music were banned. [12] ∎

CURRENT SITUATION

Struggle for Power

Every Muslim country from Morocco to Indonesia has its share of Islamic fundamentalists. In most of these states, fundamentalism is a potent political and cultural force. And in a few nations, like Saudi Arabia, Iran and Afghanistan, fundamentalists have actually come to power. Fundamentalists in Iran and Afghanistan took control by overthrowing the existing order, while their counterparts in Saudi Arabia have been the existing order.

Other countries, like Jordan and Pakistan, have accommodated orthodox Islamic political movements by allowing them to compete in elections. In Jordan, for instance, the Muslim Brotherhood won enough seats in parliamentary elections to join the governing coalition in 1991. [13]

But not all countries have accommodated Islam at the ballot box. Some states, fearful of violent revolution, have suppressed fundamentalist movements. Algeria and Egypt used their militaries to keep fundamentalists at bay.

In Algeria in 1991, the government canceled national elections after the first round of voting because a fundamentalist party, the Islamic Salvation Front, was poised to take power.

The Egyptian government has also been cracking down on fundamentalists, although less severely. Unlike Algeria, Egypt has never even scheduled, let alone held, an election that would give Islamic fundamentalists a chance to win any real power. And while it has not fallen into civil war, the nation has at times been wracked by fundamentalist-inspired violence. For instance, in 1997, radicals killed 58 foreign tourists in Luxor. [14]

Some Middle East experts see the crackdowns, especially in Algeria, as a necessary response to a valid threat. They argue that Algeria's Islamic Salvation Front never would have submitted itself to another vote if it had come to power in 1991. "The Islamists in Algeria weren't democrats and were only using the election to take power," says George Mason's Bakhash. "They almost certainly wouldn't have allowed themselves to be turned out by the electorate."

In addition, Bakhash and others say, the militants in Algeria attempted to create violent unrest in an effort to overthrow the government. "These are very dangerous groups we are talking about," says Jeffrey Kemp, director of regional strategic programs

at the Nixon Center. "They have killed a lot of people over the years."

As a result, some experts say, the Algerian government had no choice but to use violence to suppress violence. "They did exactly the right thing in Algeria when they crushed the Islamist rebels," Wurmser says, adding that the government should have introduced "rapid economic and political liberalization" at the same time. "That's really where they failed, and that's why [the war] is still going on."

Even in Egypt, where radicals were less of a threat than in Algeria, suppression of the more violent elements was necessary, some analysts say. "The Egyptian response was correct, because they focused on crushing the most dangerous fundamentalists while working to retain the support of other religious people," Phillips says. "Most fundamentalists in Egypt, especially after Luxor, now realize how dangerous the most violent elements within their movement are and have come to support the government's efforts against them."

But others say that violent reactions by these regimes, especially in Algeria, have been misguided and much too heavy-handed. "The [Algerian] Islamic Salvation Front was a diverse, broad-based group that was participating in the democratic process, and the military brutally suppressed them and drove them underground," says Georgetown's Esposito. "Only then did they resort to violence."

Those who oppose the crackdowns also argue that it is premature to assume the worst about Islamic fundamentalists. "One cannot say how one group will behave once in power, but the Islamists have not received a fair hearing on this issue," says Bahman Baktiari, a professor of political science at the American University in Cairo. Baktiari points out that it was the government, not the fundamentalists, who acted in an undemocratic manner when they

At Issue:

Should the United States try to establish closer ties with the Taliban regime in Afghanistan?

LAWRENCE DAVIDSON
Associate professor of history, West Chester University, West Chester, Pa.

WRITTEN FOR *THE CQ RESEARCHER*

yes

d iplomatic relations establish lines of communication between governments. They allow for the promotion and protection of national interests, including trade, assistance of citizens abroad, cultural interchange and the encouragement of mutually acceptable standards of behavior. Historically, diplomatic relations also have facilitated the settling of disputes between countries, short of war. Thus, it can be argued that diplomatic relations are most necessary and useful when exercised between states with significant differences.

This argument supports a position that the United States should have diplomatic relations with the Taliban regime in Afghanistan. The Taliban have demonstrated that they control most of the territory of Afghanistan, and they have established governing institutions for that land. Assuredly, their policies are not to our liking, particularly on human rights.

If we had diplomatic relations, we could more effectively communicate our disagreement with Taliban policies and encourage more acceptable ones. There is plenty of precedent for this. The United States has, in the past, and continues today, to have diplomatic relations with less than friendly countries governed by regimes with poor human rights records. In many cases, our government uses the argument above to defend having these relations.

What has the absence of diplomatic relations with Afghanistan accomplished for the United States? Have we been able to influence the Taliban in any positive way? Some American leaders have suggested applying economic penalties against Afghanistan rather than establishing and working through diplomatic relations. However, this approach has two flaws. First, in Afghanistan we have a regime that is ideologically and religiously committed to principles that are more important to them than economics. Economic sanctions are unlikely to sway the leadership.

Second, as is tragically clear from the case of Iraq, the use of economic sanctions can have a devastating impact on the general population of the country against which they are imposed. That means that, as perpetrators of such a strategy, the human rights record of the United States becomes as dismal as those we oppose.

U.S. national interests can only benefit from the establishment of diplomatic relations with Afghanistan. Doing so cannot harm them. Nor are there any good alternatives for bringing positive pressure to bear on the Taliban regime. Diplomatic relations should therefore be established.

YEHUDIT BARSKY
Director, Division on Middle East and International Terrorism, The American Jewish Committee

WRITTEN FOR *THE CQ RESEARCHER*

no

w hile diplomatic relations are the essence of statecraft, there are particular instances where limiting the level of diplomatic ties between states is useful for encouraging changes in foreign policy. In the case of Afghanistan, the current U.S. policy of withholding official recognition of the Taliban government sends a strong message that Afghanistan must change its current policy of providing shelter for Osama Bin Laden and other terrorists.

The singular focus of the Taliban's foreign policy since its takeover of Afghanistan in 1996 has been achieving international legitimacy. The only countries that have recognized the Taliban are Saudi Arabia, the United Arab Emirates and Pakistan. Contrary to the perception that Afghanistan has been treated as a pariah by the United States are the numerous contacts between American representatives and the Taliban. That same year, the Clinton administration dispatched then U.N. Representative Bill Richardson to Afghanistan to help persuade the Taliban and their political opponents to hold direct negotiations in an effort to end their civil war.

Contacts have increased over the past two years, particularly because of Afghanistan's continued sheltering of bin Laden. From the U.S. perspective, the discussions have focused on extraditing bin Laden and dismantling his Al-Qa'ida organization and other terrorist groups.

Other concerns include the development of Afghanistan over the past few years as the world's No. 1 producer of opium, and human rights issues such as the banning of education for women. Thus far, the Taliban have rejected the U.S. extradition request, and relations with Afghanistan have been downgraded to include the imposition of U.N economic sanctions.

Bin Laden's stated goal is to carry out acts of war against Americans. He has demonstrated his capability to send operatives from Al-Qa'ida to mount such attacks. Since the Taliban claim to control most of Afghanistan, they bear responsibility for the continued operation of bin Laden's organizational infrastructure, which they assert is independent of their regime.

Throughout its contacts with Afghanistan, the United States has withheld official recognition of the Taliban to tell them that they cannot have it both ways. They can demonstrate that they control their territory and turn over bin Laden, thus opening the door to official recognition, or continue on the path toward increased isolation.

cancelled an election they thought they were going to lose. "So which one is legitimate?" he asks. "A government that rejects the results of an election if they don't like it or the argument that if the Islamists win they will violate the process?"

Even if the fundamentalists had anti-democratic tendencies, the government still should have allowed them to take power, Esposito says. "The Front was in no position to run away with democracy because the military always had the power to step in and restore the status quo." ■

OUTLOOK

A Spent Force?

The last five years have not been good ones for fundamentalists. In Iran, the conservative clerics are under increasing challenge. Meanwhile, secular governments in Egypt, Tunisia and even Algeria have largely suppressed political Islam. Fundamentalists also seem on the defensive in Sudan, where the nation's premier Islamist, Speaker of the Parliament Turabi, recently was forced from power. Even the monarchy in peaceful Saudi Arabia is thought to be vulnerable, as an increasingly westernized population calls for more personal freedom and democracy.

"Extremist political Islam has failed because it has not been able to deliver the goods anywhere it has been in power," says the Nixon Center's Kemp. "People in the Islamic world, especially young people, realize that this romance with the past doesn't make their lives better."

Kemp and others say that the disenchantment is especially evident in

Iran. "It's clear to everyone that people in Iran don't like the mullahs and no longer accept the government's rationalization that their problems are caused by the United States and the West," says AEI's Wurmser.

This rejection is a troubling development for fundamentalists, Kemp and Wurmser say, because Iran's 21-year theocratic experiment has been an inspiration to fundamentalists around the world.

Strict Islamic governments in other countries, notably Afghanistan and, until recently, Sudan, are faring even worse than their counterparts in Iran. Sudan's experiment with fundamentalism has made the East African country a pariah. Meanwhile, the Taliban regime in Afghanistan has done virtually nothing to improve the lot of the people.

But others argue that while fundamentalists in certain states may be in trouble, fundamentalism itself is unlikely to disappear any time soon.

"Fundamentalism will never be a spent force because there will always be people in the Muslim world who will want to apply the *Koran* to everyday life," says American University's Salla. "In every country where the government isn't able to provide its citizens with the services they need, there will be fundamentalism because religious thinkers usually offer utopian solutions to problems, and that is very appealing to desperate people."

Others agree that while fundamentalism is not about to fade away, it already is transforming itself from a violent movement. "The enthusiasm for revolution throughout the Islamic world of the 1970s and '80s is gone," Dunn says. "They are starting to focus less on the top and more on the bottom, on grass-roots efforts aimed at making society more religious."

So far, this strategy seems to be working, says Michael Dunn, editor of the *Middle East Journal*. "Coun-

tries with secular governments are more religious than they were even 20 years ago," he says. "And so these movements, instead of being revolutionary, are becoming evolutionary, pushing for incremental change."

Efforts to bring Islam more into everyday life generally have not been resisted by these secular countries, even those that tried to crush Islamic radicals. For instance, Dunn says, Egypt and Tunisia are trying to accommodate the increasingly religious nature of society by building more mosques and taking into account the religious implications of new policies.

This new spirit of accommodation is likely to lead to a kinder, gentler form of fundamentalism in the future, Georgetown's Esposito says. "I see Islamic fundamentalism becoming much more progressive, much more tolerant." ■

Notes

[1] Quoted in Susan Sachs, "Many Iranian Conservatives Lose Seats," *The New York Times*, Feb. 23, 2000.

[2] "Mubarak Reelected With 94% of Vote," *Los Angeles Times*, Sept. 28, 1999.

[3] "The People Against the Mullahs," *The Economist*, Feb. 19, 2000.

[4] Mary H. Cooper, "Combating Terrorism," *The CQ Researcher*, July 21, 1995, pp. 633-656.

[5] *Ibid.*

[6] Pamela Constable and Kamran Khan, "Suspect Links Embassy Blast To Saudi Exile," *The Washington Post*, Aug. 17, 1998.

[7] *Ibid.*

[8] Lawrence Davidson, *Islamic Fundamentalism* (1998), p. 11.

[9] *Ibid.*, p. 12.

[10] John Eposito, *The Oxford History of Islam* (1999), p. 656.

[11] Quoted in Dan Diller (ed.), *The Middle East* (1994), p. 219.

[12] Esposito, *op. cit.*, p. 560.

[13] "Islam's Arab Backlash," *The Economist*, Nov. 27, 1999.

[14] John Daniszewski, "Islamic Group Taunts Egyptian President After Massacre," *Los Angeles Times*, Nov. 21, 1997.

Bibliography

Selected Sources Used

Books

Davidson, Lawrence, *Islamic Fundamentalism*, Greenwood Press, 1998.

Davidson, an associate professor of history at West Chester University, has written a clear and insightful introduction to Islamic fundamentalism. In addition to explaining its history and importance, Davidson includes a generous appendix of primary documents, from selections from the Koran to a speech by Iran's Ayatollah Ruhollah Khomeini.

Diller, Daniel (ed.), *The Middle East*, Congressional Quarterly Press, 1994.

A slightly dated but still useful guide to the politics and culture of the Middle East, including a number of chapters that deal with Islamic fundamentalism.

FOR MORE INFORMATION

The Center for Muslim-Christian Understanding, Georgetown University, 37th & O Sts., Washington, D.C. 20057; (202) 687-8375; www.cmcu.net. The center's purpose is to achieve a better understanding between Islam and Christianity and between the Muslim world and the West.

Middle East Institute, 1761 N. St. N.W., Washington D.C. 20036; (202) 785-1141; www.mideasti.org. The institute seeks to broaden knowledge of the Middle East through research, conferences and seminars.

Muslim Public Affairs Council, 923 National Press Building, 529 14th St. N.W., Washington, D.C. 20045; (202) 879-6726; www.mpac.org. The council represents the interests of Muslims in the United States.

The Nixon Center, 1615 L St. N.W., Suite 1250, Washington D.C. 20036; (202) 887-1000; www.nixoncenter.org. The center conducts research on foreign policy issues through the prism of American national interest.

Washington Institute for Near East Policy, 1828 L St. N.W., Suite 1050, Washington D.C. 20036; (202) 452-0650; www.washingtoninstitute.org. The research and educational organization promotes debate on Near East policy.

Esposito, John L. (ed.), *The Oxford History of Islam*, Oxford University Press, 1999.

Esposito, a professor of religion and international affairs at Georgetown University, has put together a series of essays chronicling the history of Islamic civilization from the days of Mohammad to the present. Esposito's own contribution, a chapter on contemporary Islam, explains the impact of today's fundamentalist movement on the Muslim world.

Mackey, Sandra, *The Iranians: Persia, Islam and the Soul of a New Nation*, Plume Press, 1998.

Mackey, an Atlanta-based expert on the Middle East, provides an in-depth look at the Iran of yesterday and today. Her chapters on the Iranian revolution and its aftermath are detailed and insightful.

Articles

"Islam's Arab Backlash: Defeated in Battle, Ignored in Politics, Islamists May be Gaining Ground in Arab Society," *The Economist*, Nov. 27, 1999.

The article argues that fundamentalists in many countries have given up dreams of revolution in exchange for a strategy of suffusing society with Islamic strictures.

"The People Against the Mullahs," *The Economist*, Feb. 19, 2000.

The piece focuses on Iran to illustrate the challenges of trying to establish a democratic system within a strict Islamic state.

Burns, John F., "A Time of Testing for Islamic Zeal," *The New York Times*, Feb. 20, 2000.

Journalist Burns argues that Islamic fundamentalism faces the possibility of decline, as voices of moderation grow louder in Iran, Lebanon and other nations where fundamentalist fervor is waning.

Masci, David, "Reform in Iran," *The CQ Researcher*, Dec. 18, 1998.

Masci explores the political and cultural landscape in Iran soon after the election of moderate President Muhammad Khatami.

Rieff, David, "Millimeter by Millimeter," *Newsweek*, Jan. 1, 2000.

Rieff says that President Khatami of Iran is not trying to change that country's theocratic system, as many believe, but save it through reform. He argues that a good parallel is the Soviet Union's Mikhail Gorbachev, who tried to reform his country in an effort revitalize communism, not destroy it.

15 Assisting Refugees

DAVID MASCI

O n the dusty road to Gisenyi, just inside Rwanda, 200,000 bedraggled people were at last nearing home.

"You could see this river of humanity, with all of their belongings on their heads and their kids straggling along," recalls Samantha Bolton, an aid worker. "Most of them were barefoot and exhausted."

The next day, says Bolton, communications director for Doctors Without Borders USA, another 150,000 people made the trek.

The people returning to Rwanda last November were Hutus. In 1994, by the hundreds of thousands, they had been chased out of Rwanda by an army of rebel Tutsis, a rival ethnic group. Now the Tutsis were pushing the Hutus back into Rwanda by forcibly closing the refugee camps in Zaire.

Thousands of refugees who had fled to Zaire would never come home. Many children and older people had died of starvation or cholera during the exodus from Rwanda. Others had been killed in the camps by thugs and extremists from their own tribe. Tens of thousands more had died in Hutu-Tutsi fighting that flared up last year in Zaire. *

Throughout the crisis, the United Nations High Commissioner for Refugees (UNHCR) and other aid groups scrambled, often with questionable success, to help. Many of the world's most powerful nations seemed in a quandary about whether to get involved at all, fearful of becoming too entangled in the horrific chaos.

As shocking and tragic as it has been, the situation in Rwanda and

---

By early December, more than 1 million of the 1.5 million Hutu refugees in Zaire had returned to Rwanda. Many of the half-million Hutus who had sought refuge in Tanzania also returned.

From *The CQ Researcher,*
February 7, 1997.

Remco Bohle

Zaire represents nothing more than the planet's latest refugee crisis, sandwiched between the festering upheavals in Bosnia and the next catastrophe yet to appear on the evening news.

Actually, many international experts say, the world is experiencing a level of conflict and population displacement rarely seen in human history. And, they warn, crises are becoming so commonplace that the world community can ignore them only at its own peril. Georgetown University Professor Charles Keeley predicts that multiethnic strife will force many states to collapse in coming decades, leading to still greater chaos.

The last decade has been especially volatile. While the United States, China, Germany and other global powers have been at peace through most of the post-World War II era, the developing world has seen a steady rise in war and civil strife. With the Cold War coming to an end, human misery and displacement became increasingly common in poorer countries, such as Somalia, Liberia and Burma. Since 1980, the estimated number of refugees in the world has

roughly tripled, rising from 5.7 million to 15.3 million in 1996. The number of people displaced within their own countries is even higher, topping 20 million by most estimates. [1] (*See story, p. 264.*)

The refugee increases generally have not been tied to one cause. In the past, a cataclysm on the scale of World War II or the partitioning of India would create millions of refugees for a relatively short period of time. But today, refugee crises are a series of small, constant blips on the world's radar screen, with many crises being precipitated by old ethnic conflicts that flare up periodically.

The growing plight of refugees has generated an unprecedented increase in the size and number of aid groups. The UNHCR, once a small agency that provided legal assistance to refugees seeking asylum in post-World War II Europe, aided more than 27 million people in 1995. (*See graph, p. 265.*) In addition, there are now hundreds of non-governmental relief organizations (NGOs) — including CARE, the Red Cross and Doctors Without Borders.

Besides trying to provide food and shelter, UNHCR and other organizations are searching for new and innovative ways to prevent or at least mitigate the number of refugees. They also are focusing more attention on aiding displaced peoples after they have been repatriated, to decrease the chance that they will leave their homes again.

But some observers find fault with the aid efforts, and even question the motives of the aid groups themselves. A number of refugee experts argue that UNHCR may have done more harm than good in Rwanda and Zaire by blindly providing assistance to all Hutus who crossed into Zaire in 1994. The problem, they say, is that among the refugees was a large group of militants who were responsible for the genocidal slaughtering — often by machete — of more than 500,000

Tracking the World's Refugees

There are an estimated 35 million displaced people around the world, including 15 million refugees and 20 million displaced within their own countries, according to the United Nations High Commissioner for Refugees. The major refugee crises are highlighted on the map.

Major Displaced Populations

Afghanistan: More than half of all Afghan refugees have been repatriated since 1992, but roughly 2.5 million Afghans remain in Pakistan and Iran.

The Caucasus: Within the Russian Federation, more than 1.5 million people have been displaced in Armenia, Azerbaijan, Georgia and Chechnya in recent years. Although an uneasy peace has returned to some of these areas, many displaced persons are unable or unwilling to return to their homes.

Liberia: Civil war has displaced an estimated 1.5 million Liberians, half of whom have fled to neighboring countries such as Sierra Leone and Guinea.

Mozambique: About 1.7 million refugees have returned to Mozambique from six neighboring nations following the end of civil war in 1992. Millions of land mines hinder efforts to rebuild Mozambique.

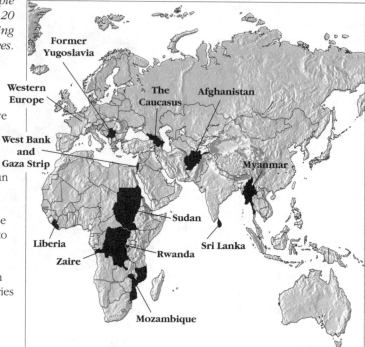

Myanmar: Fewer than 50,000 of the 250,000 people who fled from Myanmar (formerly Burma) in 1991 and 1992 remain in Bangladesh, which has closed its borders to further refugee flows.

Rwanda/Zaire: In late 1996, about 1.5 million Rwandan Hutus returned to their homeland after spending more than two years in refugee camps in Tanzania and Zaire. Estimates vary widely, but it is believed that more than 200,000 Rwandans remain in Zaire. These refugees fled east into the jungles of Zaire, largely out of the reach of most aid groups.

Sri Lanka: Most of the more than 100,000 refugees who fled to India have returned since 1992. But hundreds of thousands of Sri Lankans continue to be displaced internally as a result of the continuing civil war.

Sudan: Due to the continuing civil war between the Muslim north and largely Christian south, almost 500,000 Sudanese remain refugees in Uganda, Zaire and other nations. Another 4 million Sudanese have been internally displaced by the conflict.

Former Yugoslavia: More than 2.5 million people were displaced by the civil wars that rocked the republics of the former Yugoslavia. The vast majority of these displaced persons come from the republic of Bosnia-Herzegovina, where most have not been able to return home despite a peace agreement between the warring sides negotiated in November 1995 in Dayton, Ohio.

West Bank and Gaza Strip: Around 2.8 million people are registered with the United Nations Relief and Works Agency, which cares for Palestinian refugees. Whether they will return to the West Bank and Gaza Strip must be addressed in upcoming negotiations between Israel and the Palestinian Authority.

Western Europe: Since the early 1980s, more than 5 million applications for refugee status have been submitted in Western Europe. Recent tightening of asylum laws in most European countries has led to a marked decrease in applications. In 1995, for instance, fewer than 300,000 persons applied for asylum, compared with 700,000 in 1992.

Note: Displaced persons are defined as those who have been forced from their homes; refugees are displaced persons who have fled across international borders. More than 27 million displaced people are being assisted by UNHCR.

Tutsis and moderate Hutus. The Hutu extremists used the refugee camps as de facto military bases and treated the refugees as hostages.

Some cynics among the critics even say that UNHCR and the NGOs see it in their interest to create and perpetuate refugee crises. More starving children with bloated bellies on the evening news means more donations and government funding.

Aid groups call such views ridiculous. But they admit to owing their increased visibility, in no small part, to the news media, even as they fault the media for their short attention span and for ignoring many countries in turmoil. In the final analysis, they acknowledge, the media play the key role in making the global community aware of humanitarian needs.

Citizen awareness is crucial, aid experts say, and not just because it leads to charitable donations. Governments are more inclined to address a problem halfway around the world, they say, if their citizens call for action. Even then, nations in a position to help are often loath to do more than offer money. Many U.S. lawmakers, among others, are apprehensive about sending soldiers into harm's way to aid refugees or others in need, unless a key American interest is threatened. For example, they say, the Persian Gulf War was really about protecting U.S. access to Saudi Arabian oil, not saving Kuwait from Saddam Hussein's plundering troops.

Aid officials argue that affluent world powers like the United States should, in the interests of humanity and global peace, send troops to protect refugees and aid workers. UNHCR officials say they were rebuffed when they asked the major powers to send soldiers to the refugee camps in Zaire to separate the Hutu extremists from the legitimate refugees. UNHCR officials also say the international community's refusal to help left the agency with no choice but to assist everyone, good and bad, in the camps, in order to prevent innocent refugees from starving.

A young Rwandan Hutu refugee climbs into a truck for a ride back to Rwanda from Burundi in August 1996.

Reuters/Corinne Dufka

"If we had not started feeding them immediately, many people would have starved to death," says Soren Jessen-Petersen, director of UNHCR's New York City office.

As refugee advocates, politicians and others debate how to best respond to crises like the one in Zaire, these are some of the questions being asked:

Do the methods used by UNHCR and private relief organizations to help refugees actually make matters worse?

The crisis in the great lakes region of Eastern Africa has rocked the UNHCR to its foundations. Never before has the agency faced such a difficult and chaotic situation on such a vast scale.

In the second half of 1994, an estimated 2 million Rwandans, mainly from the Hutu tribe, fled into Zaire and Tanzania. The flight was triggered by a rebel army of Tutsis, which unseated the country's Hutu-led government.

The coup by the Rwandan Patriotic Front (RPF) was triggered, in turn, by the massacre earlier in 1994 of Tutsis and some moderate Hutus by Hutu extremists. The death toll in what has come to be known as the "Rwandan genocide" is estimated at about 800,000. [2]

When the RPF took control of Rwanda, the Hutus involved in the killings fled. Hundred of thousands of innocent Hutus followed the extremists into exile after being told that they would be targets of Tutsi retribution despite their innocence.

Critics of UNHCR say that it made egregious strategic mistakes at almost every step during the crisis in Zaire, revealing the organization's outmoded, institutional mindset. In particular, they say, UNHCR and the NGOs that support its work immediately moved to feed and care for all the Rwandan refugees streaming across the border, without considering the consequences.

Michael Maren, the author of a recent book highly critical of international aid efforts, contends that UNHCR, however unintentionally, provided aid and comfort to the perpetrators of the genocide when it set up camps for the Hutus. [3] "The Hutu leaders ran the camps and essentially controlled the distribution of aid," he says. In addition, says Maren, a former field worker for the U.S. Agency for Inter-

UNHCR to the Rescue

The United Nations High Commissioner for Refugees (UNHCR) coordinates the world community's efforts to assist and resettle refugees. Based in Geneva, Switzerland, the High Commissioner is nominated by the Secretary-General of the United Nations and elected by the General Assembly every five years. Sadako Ogata of Japan, the agency's eighth High Commissioner, took office on Jan. 1, 1991, but served a foreshortened three-year term. Her mandate was renewed for the full five years in 1994 and will expire at the end of 1998.

The UNHCR's budget and activities are monitored by a group of 50 U.N. member governments, including all of the major powers, known as the Executive Committee.

Roughly 2 percent of UNHCR's $1.4 billion budget, or $25 million, is provided by the U.N. to cover the agency's administrative costs. The remainder of the agency's funding is provided voluntarily by U.N. member states. Last year, 32 of the more than 170 U.N. members contributed.

Until recently, UNHCR worked largely to aid refugees after they had found asylum, often by providing legal assistance. In some cases, the agency aided the repatriation of displaced persons back to their country of origin after the danger that had forced them to flee had subsided.

Today, the agency's mandate is much broader. Since the 1970s, UNHCR has worked around the world to provide assistance to people who have recently been displaced, instead of waiting for them to reach a third country of asylum. As of last year, UNHCR maintained 255 offices in 118 countries.

national Development, the legitimate refugees were completely controlled by the Hutu killers, giving them enormous leverage with the international community. "The aid groups weren't feeding refugees," he says, "they were feeding hostages."

Instead of setting up camps, Maren says, the UNHCR and the NGOs should have provided services to Hutus in Rwanda. "The agencies should have told them: 'You cross the border, you're on your own,' " he says.

Stephen Stedman, a professor of African Studies at Johns Hopkins University's School of Advanced International Studies, agrees. He argues that if UNHCR had not assisted the Hutu refugees, they ultimately would have returned to Rwanda. This in turn would have denied the Hutu extremists the benefits they derived from the refugee camps.

Stedman also criticizes UNHCR and the NGOs for ignoring their own guidelines. "There are international conventions on what a refugee is, and it is very clear that they cannot be fleeing a country because they committed crimes; cannot be armed; and cannot use their refugee status to reconstruct an armed force," he says. [4]

But others say that the UNHCR made

the best of a bad situation. They argue the Hutus so feared for their lives that they would not have returned to Rwanda. If they had stayed, and UNHCR had remained aloof, mass starvation and disease would have resulted.

"What could we have done?" asks Harlan Hale, assistant director for food and logistics at Atlanta-based CARE. "Our humanitarian imperative is to minister to people who are at risk." Those who think that it would have been better in the long run to let some Hutus starve wouldn't feel that way "if it was one of their kids out there," Hale adds.

It is easy to ponder better strategies after the fact, when you don't have to make snap decisions, says Jessen-Petersen. "More than 1 million people fled, and we had to provide life-saving assistance within 72 hours, something that is not very easy when you're in the African bush," he says.

Jessen-Petersen says that it took UNHCR four to six weeks just to stabilize the situation to the point where his agency could begin considering issues beyond providing basic assistance. "Once we got our head above water, we understood that we had a monster on our hands," he says.

UNHCR decided that the only way to

tame the monster — the Hutu militants — was to disarm them or drive them from the camps. "The UNHCR knew that the camps contained a lot of killers, and they advocated a police force to separate out the killers from the refugees," says Jeff Drumtra, a policy analyst at the U.S. Committee for Refugees, an advocacy group in Washington. But the appeal fell on deaf ears, according to Drumtra and others. "There was simply no interest in doing this."

UNHCR supporters say that the unwillingness of the United States and other donor nations to commit the forces necessary to separate the extremists left the agency with limited options. "It was a horrible situation, and we faced it alone," says Marie Okabe, a senior UNHCR liaison officer in New York.

Others say that the donor countries' inaction allowed them to blame the UNHCR for anything that went wrong. Instead of taking action, Drumtra says, donor nations assuaged their consciences by pouring money into UNHCR to run the refugee camps in Zaire and Tanzania. UNHCR became "a fig leaf for their own lack of political will," he says.

After it became apparent that no military help was forthcoming, UNHCR officials say they tried to exert more control over the camps by breaking them down into smaller, more manageable units and by distributing food directly to those deemed to be legitimate refugees. But these efforts were stymied by the Hutu militants, who retained a firm hold on the populations in the camps.

Finally, UNHCR hired 1,500 members of the notoriously corrupt Zairian military to provide security in the camps. The intention, Jessen-Peterson says, was to create "a minimum of security" for legitimate refugees inside the camps. But the tiny force proved ineffective against the estimated 50,000-60,000 members of the Hutu militia. "In the end," Jessen-Peterson says, "nothing worked."

Bolton at Doctors Without Borders agrees that UNHCR was in a difficult situation after the refugee camps in Zaire had been established. But she also says the agency made other, big mistakes before the refugee crisis even occurred. "We had two weeks notice before the refugees crossed the border," she says, but "when they arrived no camps had been set up yet."

Bolton says UNHCR should have used the two-week window to set up many small camps, making it harder for militant Hutus to organize and control the refugees. "They had camps with 250,000 people, which you never do," she says, "because you're always going to have militarization."

But Jessen-Petersen and others say that with so many refugees crossing into Zaire at the same time, it was not logistically possible to break them into small groups while providing food and medical assistance.

Some critics also charge that many of the aid groups that responded to the crisis in Zaire can be criticized for more than shortsightedness. For instance, Maren says, UNHCR and other aid groups perpetuated this and other crises largely out of institutional self-interest. "NGOs don't want to shut down camps because they have a bureaucratic structure built up around these projects," he charges, adding that "there is very little accountability in the aid business, and that leaves lots of room for fat."

This is not true, Hale says. While he admits that groups like his receive more money — in the form of outside donations and UNHCR payments — during well-publicized crises, NGOs do not try to perpetuate disasters in order to improve their balance sheets, nor do they focus only on those situations that catch the public's eye. "It's not a question of helping some refugees and not others," he says, referring to those disasters that receive media attention and those that do not. "We distribute assistance based solely on need."

Should American military personnel be sent overseas to help refugees if it exposes them to danger?

The use of American troops to provide food and other aid to displaced people has become relatively common. In the last few years, U.S. soldiers have been sent to help people in Somalia, Haiti and Bosnia. In November, President Clinton said he would send American troops to Zaire and only reversed that decision after he determined that the situation had improved.

Still, Americans and their leaders are generally wary of committing troops to humanitarian missions in far-off lands. (See "At Issue," p. 269.) As chairman of the Joint Chiefs of Staff, Gen. Colin L. Powell was an influential advocate for sending American forces rarely, and only when the mission's goals were clear and the use of overwhelming force made the chances of success high.

Much of the reluctance about using force stems from the nation's painful experience in Vietnam, where a small number of American military advisers grew to a half-million combat troops in a matter of years. More recently, Americans watched in horror in 1993 as news reports showed a dead American serviceman in Somalia being dragged through the streets of Mogadishu.

The incident produced what has been dubbed the "Somalia Syndrome," or lawmakers' and the military's fear of sending troops overseas if the possibility exists for even a few casualties. [5] "They really got burned in Somalia, and they don't want to see any more body bags coming home," Bolton says.

Still, many refugee advocates argue that there are times when troops simply must be sent, particularly to protect refugees and aid workers. For instance, it is widely thought that the

Iraqi Kurds enter a refugee camp in Silopi, Turkey, in September 1996 after being evacuated from North Iraq.

Reuters

Africa Now Has the Most Refugees

Far more displaced persons in Africa than Asia are being assisted by the U.N. High Commissioner for Refugees, mainly due to recent civil wars in Africa and the resolution of refugee problems in Asia stemming from the Vietnam War and upheavals elsewhere in the region. In the decade from 1985-95, the number of UNHCR-assisted refugees and other displaced persons in Africa increased nearly fourfold; the number increased almost tenfold in Europe, primarily because of the crisis in the Balkans.

Number of People Assisted by the UNHCR

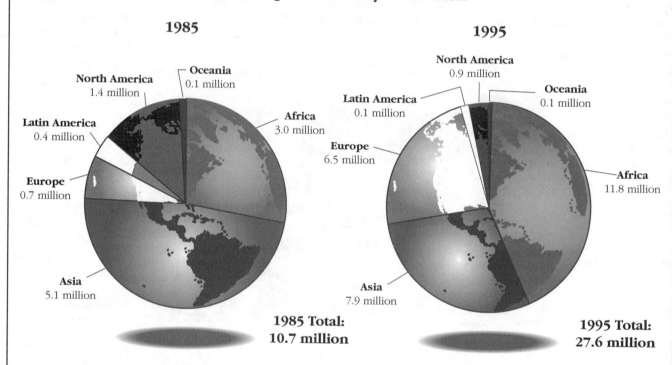

1985

Oceania
0.1 million

North America
1.4 million

Latin America
0.4 million

Africa
3.0 million

Europe
0.7 million

Asia
5.1 million

**1985 Total:
10.7 million**

1995

North America
0.9 million

Oceania
0.1 million

Latin America
0.1 million

Europe
6.5 million

Africa
11.8 million

Asia
7.9 million

**1995 Total:
27.6 million**

Source: United Nations High Commissioner for Refugees, The State of the World's Refugees, 1995

international community should have sent solders to drive Hutus who had participated in the Rwandan genocide out of the refugee camps.

"We had situations where Hutu soldiers just came into hospitals in the camps and shot patients dead," Bolton says. And, Bolton points out, refugees are not the only victims of such violence. Over the last five years, scores of aid workers have been killed in Somalia, Burundi and other hot spots. As recently as Feb. 4, five U.N. workers investigating human rights abuses in Rwanda were

ambushed on a country road and shot to death. And in December, six International Red Cross workers in Chechnya were murdered in their beds.

While refugee advocates generally favor multiethnic forces, they argue that some situations demand a U.S. military presence if the intervention is to be effective. CARE's Hale notes that the U.S. has more heavy-lifting capacity, access to intelligence and sheer firepower than any other nation on Earth. Steven Hansch, a senior program officer at the Refugee Policy Group, agrees: "In cer-

tain circumstances, our armed forces are the only ones who can do the job."

But, Hansch says, the Somalia syndrome has set "such a conservative threshold of pain" that the nation won't send soldiers anywhere unless the mission is risk free. "We are chickens about this," Hansch says.

According to many refugee advocates, this attitude has soured other nations on working with the U.S. to resolve international problems. "We need to show that we are willing to be a player, that we stand for something," Hale says.

But others argue that the United States military has done more than its share in humanitarian crises, pointing to the deployments in Haiti in 1994 and in Bosnia the following year. "We're doing this too routinely, and it's starting to become the norm," says Eugene B. McDaniel, president of the American Defense Institute, a Washington think tank.

Others question sending American soldiers under any circumstances. "Why should it always be the United States that answers the global 911 call?" asks Lionel Rosenblatt, executive director for Refugees International. Rosenblatt and others say that military leaders should be especially wary of sending troops into countries where warring factions are still fighting and civil society has broken down.

In addition, McDaniel says, "Our troops are for defending our country and its national interests," not feeding refugees in a country halfway around the world. This means defending the industrial world's access to oil — as was done during the 1991 Persian Gulf War — but not protecting combatants in Bosnia from each other, McDaniel says. "It's degrading to send our soldiers to those places on those missions," he says.

But Michael Clough, a research associate at the Institute of International Studies at the University of California-Berkeley, calls the argument put forward by McDaniel and others "nonsense." Clough says the United States and other industrialized countries have a clear interest in solving humanitarian and refugee crises around the world. "First, we have an interest in ensuring that places like Africa don't collapse," he says, adding that "by 2025, 30 per-

cent of the world's population will live in Africa, and you just can't write off a part of the world that big."

Another reason rich countries cannot ignore poorer states, Clough says, stems from the fact that large numbers of refugees will eventually reach the shores of European nations and the United States. In addition, he argues, there needs to be stability in the developing world if the global economy is to continue to expand.

But there may be a way to satisfy both McDaniel and Clough. Rosenblatt

STAHLER

SEND MORE CNN COVERAGE

© JEFF STAHLER reprinted with permission of Newspaper Enterprise Association, Inc.

is among those who propose the establishment of a permanent United Nations rapid deployment force to intervene in humanitarian crises. While the proposal has received some tepid support from the United States and other powers, no action has been taken on the idea, and its prospects are uncertain, at best. [6]

Does media coverage of refugee crises lead to aid decisions based on emotion and public opinion rather than reasoned policies?

Many in the refugee community argue that the media, despite their flaws, have served refugees well. They say that few people would ever learn about the plight of refugees anywhere if it were not for journalists on the

scene, and the dramatic, heart-wrenching images they bounce off satellites and into homes around the world. Such publicity is vital, they say, because the U.S. and other developed nations are typically reluctant to respond to an overseas crisis unless a sizable number of its own citizens call for action.

"On balance, I'd say that the media are a positive force, because when CNN or some other news crew is there, governments will follow," Rosenblatt says.

Drumtra of the U.S. Committee for Refugees agrees. "CNN drives policy simply by deciding where they are going to set up the cameras," he says.

By the same token, Drumtra adds, the media have a responsibility to do more than just show up at the occasional disaster. In general, he says, print and broadcast media outlets need to broaden their coverage to include more parts of the world. "The mission of journalists is to inform people about their world," he says, "and if they don't inform people of the activities of all the countries around the world, then they are failing in that mission."

In fact, others say, many catastrophes are simply ignored. For example, while the world in October and November was given repeated updates on the crisis in Zaire, few media outlets reported on a veritable roll call of other African nations with huge numbers of displaced persons. Among the most severely afflicted were Sudan, where a civil war has been raging since 1983 and an estimated 4 million people are internally displaced; another half-million Sudanese refugees were believed to be living in Uganda, Zaire, Ethiopia and other neighboring nations. Another victim of civil war, Liberia, had an estimated 120,000 refugees and 1 million internally displaced persons. [7]

Critics also say that the media's short-term coverage of situations leads to poorly considered policy that often seems designed only to assuage the conscience of the viewing public. "You get a very selective coverage of the worst disasters at a time when nothing constructive can be done about them," says Stedman at Johns Hopkins. "People say, 'Make the pictures go away,' and policy-makers respond to that," he says, adding that "when the pictures go away, everyone thinks that the problem must be solved."

But others say that it is unrealistic to expect the news media to cover so many stories for so long. Newspapers and television stations "only have so many columns or minutes on the air," says CARE's Hale, "and there are over 100 conflicts in the world." Instead, "it's our job to keep awareness of issues alive by doing more outreach and public education." ∎

BACKGROUND

Modern Aid Movement

For as long as there have been wars, persecutions and natural disasters, people have been forced to flee their homes. One of the first great works of ancient literature, the Bible, is replete with stories of people being displaced, from Adam and Eve, who were cast out of Eden, to the 40-year wanderings of the ancient Hebrews after slavery in Egypt to the Babylonian Captivity.

The fall of Rome in the 5th century AD led to 500 years of displacement on a scale never before seen. Waves of invaders swept through Western Europe and the Mediterranean basin scattering millions of people. Arab and Mongol invasions followed, also uprooting millions. [8]

Massive population displacements often have driven important historical events. The early European settlement of North America, for example, was precipitated by groups like Quebec's Huguenots, New England's Puritans and Maryland's Catholics, all of whom fled religious persecution in their homelands.

While refugees have always been a part of history's landscape, it was not until the 20th century that institutions were created to ease their plight. The first such organization was established in 1921, when the League of Nations named Norwegian explorer Fridjof Nansen as High Commissioner for Refugees to assist those fleeing the Russian Revolution. [9]

Impact of World War II

The modern refugee movement, like much of today's world, grew from the ashes of World War II. The allies actually began assisting displaced persons even before the war ended. In 1943, they established the United Nations Relief and Rehabilitation Agency, which for the next four years aided citizens of occupied countries who were liberated by the allies as they pushed the Germans back. [10]

By the time the war in Europe was over in May 1945, millions of people had been displaced. Millions more became refugees in the months following the war's end after ethnic German populations were expelled from Poland, Czechoslovakia, Hungary and other Eastern European countries.

The war's end also brought the beginning of decolonization, creating new refugee crises. For example, in 1947, the British pulled out of India. The subsequent division between Muslim Pakistan and largely Hindu India led to the displacement of more than 10 million people. [11]

During this period, a number of temporary refugee agencies were established by the great powers under the auspices of the United Nations, including the International Refugee Organization in 1947. But it was not until 1951 that the UNHCR came into being.

U.N. Involvement

On Jan. 1, 1951, the United Nations High Commissioner for Refugees (UNHCR) began operations. With a budget of just $300,000, the agency was given a mandate to seek "permanent solutions for the problems of refugees." In practice, this meant providing mostly legal assistance to persons who had reached a country of asylum. [12]

The scope of the work actually undertaken by UNHCR in those early years was far more limited than that of its immediate predecessors. The United States and other great powers had spent billions of dollars repatriating and resettling refugees during and directly after World War II. A farreaching UNHCR, they feared, could become an expensive proposition, especially if refugee problems in the developed world ever mirrored those of Europe during the 1940s.

In addition to establishing UNHCR in 1951, the U.N. also adopted the Convention Relating to the Status of Refugees, which created the legal underpinnings for the new agency's work. The convention defined refugees as people who left their homeland "owing to a well-founded fear of being persecuted for reasons of race, religion, nationality, membership in a particular social group or political opinion." [13] The all-encompassing definition grew out of a desire to protect the kinds of victims who had been persecuted by the Nazis, such as Jews and communists.

While the convention obligated sig-

Chronology

1920s-1940s

The first organized efforts to aid refugees are launched following international crises such as the Russian Revolution and World War II.

1921
League of Nations appoints a High Commissioner for Refugees to assist people fleeing the Russian Revolution.

1943
United Nations Relief and Rehabilitation Agency is created to aid the millions of people displaced by the allies as they push the Germans out of occupied Europe.

1947
British withdrawal from India leads to division between Muslim Pakistan and largely Hindu India, displacing at least 10 million people.

1948
The United Nations adopts the Universal Declaration of Human Rights, giving all persons the right to "life, liberty and the security of person."

---•---

1950s-1970s

The modern refugee regime is established with the creation of the United Nations High Commissioner for Refugees (UNHCR) and the adoption of the Convention Relating to the Status of Refugees.

1950
U.N. General Assembly creates the UNHCR to provide legal assistance to European refugees seeking asylum. The organization begins operation on Jan. 1, 1951.

1951
The Convention Relating to the Status of Refugees is adopted, requiring signatory nations to offer haven to refugees displaced from Europe before 1951.

1967
U.N. protocol is adopted applying the 1951 Refugee Convention to all refugees, regardless of their country of origin or the date of their displacement.

1975
The end of the Vietnam War sparks the beginning of a huge outflow of refugees from Indochina that will continue into the 1990s.

1979
Soviet Union invades Afghanistan, sending 3 million refugees into Pakistan. UNHCR helps to coordinate food and other emergency assistance to the displaced Afghans.

---•---

1980s-1990s

Large-scale refugee assistance and resettlement programs become more commonplace as the Cold War winds down. UNHCR expands its mandate beyond providing emergency assistance to trying to prevent or mitigate refugee flows.

1980
Congress passes the Refugee Act of 1980, overhauling U.S. refugee admissions policy.

1989
Berlin Wall, the pre-eminent symbol of the Cold War, falls. Less than two years later, the Soviet Union disintegrates into 15 independent and often chaotic states.

1991
Kurdish rebellion in northern Iraq displaces 1.5 million people. The international community responds by creating a Kurdish "safe haven" in Iraq. UNHCR expands its mandate to provide aid beyond traditional emergency assistance to include the reconstruction of villages.

1992
Civil war breaks out in the former Yugoslavian state of Bosnia-Herzegovina, displacing millions. Use of the "safe haven" strategy in 1995 fails to protect Bosnian Muslims from Serbian persecution.

1994
Two million Rwandan Hutus flee into Zaire and Tanzania. UNHCR efforts to assist the refugees are hampered by Hutu extremists, who dominate refugee camps set up by the agency.

1995
Immigration and Naturalization Service (INS) issues regulations calling for a larger, better trained staff to handle asylum cases and requiring the INS to handle cases within six months.

1996
Thousands of Hutus who fled from Rwanda are forced to return home after rival Tutsis disband the refugee camps. Immigration Control Act of 1996 revamps procedures to handle asylum requests more quickly and requires applicants to file requests for asylum within a year of arriving in the United States.

Internal Displacement Now Gets More Attention

Today, in a recent turnabout in refugee affairs, there are more people displaced within their own countries than beyond the borders of their homelands. Estimates of the number of internally displaced persons run as high as 30 million, or roughly twice the number of refugees in the world.

But the United Nations High Commissioner for Refugees (UNHCR) devotes the bulk of its time and resources to assisting refugees, who are defined as those displaced outside of their own countries. The agency's legal mandate requires it to care for refugees, not internally displaced people.

Under the UNHCR's charter, the High Commissioner has the authority to act on its own to assist refugees without seeking further U.N. permission. But UNHCR can help internally displaced persons only after the General Assembly, Security Council or some other principal body of the United Nations requests its assistance. [1]

Even when the agency gets U.N. permission, protecting the internally displaced can be difficult, because UNHCR and other aid organizations must often obtain the permission of the host government to intervene. In Sudan, for example, where a brutal 13-year civil war has internally displaced an estimated 4 million people, aid agencies often have had trouble receiving permission from the government and the rebels to help the victims of the conflict. Other countries with large populations of internally displaced citizens, notably Turkey and Burma, also limit international access by aid agencies.

Despite the obstacles, UNHCR is becoming more and more involved in assisting the internally displaced. "Most of the world's conflicts are now internal," says Soren Jessen-Petersen, director of UNHCR's New York office. "We would be totally irrelevant in today's world if we weren't involved in these internal conflicts."

An internal displacement problem of immense scale has been presented by the countries of the former Yugoslavia, where most displaced people remained within state boundaries. UNHCR was asked by then-U.N. Secretary-General Javier Perez de Cuellar to coordinate relief efforts

throughout that shattered country. In Bosnia, the agency provided assistance to many who had never left their homes. "This was a real departure for us because we were dealing with besieged people," says Marie Okabe, a UNHCR spokesperson in New York.

In the future, experts predict, an even greater share of the world's displaced persons will remain within their own countries. Roberta Cohen, a guest scholar at the Brookings Institution, traces the internal displacements to the fact that more and more countries will be unraveling internally in the post-Cold War world.

But Cohen and others worry that UNHCR may not be adequately positioned to deal with the new challenge. "UNHCR has stretched its mandate to help the internally displaced," she says, "but it's not enough." To be as effective as possible, she says, the agency must expand its mandate to directly cover the internally displaced, so that it can act rapidly on its own.

Many refugee advocates, Cohen among them, say that a state actually forfeits its right to be left alone when it neglects or abuses its people. "[S]tate sovereignty can no longer be defined negatively as a barricade against external involvement," writes Francis M. Deng, former Sudanese ambassador to the United States. "It must be recast as primarily a positive concept of responsibility toward the citizens and all those falling under the jurisdiction of the state. It is precisely by discharging those responsibilities that a state can legitimately claim sovereignty." [2]

Cohen, who is an expert on the problems facing the internally displaced, agrees. "The international community is moving toward the notion that sovereignty does not give you carte blanche to do whatever you want to your own people," she says. "There is a growing acceptance of the idea that when there is a humanitarian crisis, the international community must come in."

[1] United Nations High Commissioner for Refugees, "International Legal Standard Applicable to the Protection of Internally Displaced Persons: A Reference Manual for UNHCR Staff," 1996, p. 1.

[2] Francis M. Deng, "These Borders Are Not Sacred," Op. Ed. article in *The Washington Post,* Dec. 20, 1996.

natory states to offer haven to refugees, it covered only those persons who had been displaced before 1951. In addition, signatories were given the option of ignoring refugees outside of Europe. The U.N. removed those limits in 1967.

The 1967 change came in response to a trend that had been accelerating since the mid-1950s: the decline of the refugee problem as a uniquely European phenomenon. By the 1970s,

European refugees, with the exception of occasional escapees from the Soviet bloc, were a thing of the past. Most refugees were now coming from Africa and Southeast Asia. [14]

UNHCR's New Mandate

Until the late 1970s, the agency dealt with refugee movements after they had happened. In other words, once a group had left their country

and become refugees, UNHCR would then step in to try to help them either settle in the asylum country, resettle elsewhere or return to their country of origin. Little was done to aid refugees as they were fleeing their homeland. For example, UNHCR played no role in resettling the 7 million refugees that flowed into India from Bangladesh when that nation was created in 1972.

In the late 1970s though, things began to change. During that time, the world witnessed three large refugee crises simultaneously in Thailand, Afghanistan and Ethiopia. In Afghanistan, the 1979 Soviet invasion forced 3 million Afghans into Pakistan. The agency, in conjunction with the Pakistani government, provided food and other assistance to the refugees.

The magnitude of the Afghan crisis and others led the international community to look increasingly to UNHCR for leadership in organizing the care and protection of such huge, displaced populations. With the new responsibility came growth. From 1970 to 1980, UNHCR's budget ballooned from $8 million to almost $500 million — with 1,700 employees and more than 80 field offices around the world. [15]

Throughout the 1980s, the agency continued to grow. In addition, UNHCR solidified its role as the lead refugee agency by helping to coordinate relief to refugees around the world, from Central America to the horn of Africa.

Rise in Refugees

The number of people cared for by UNHCR has risen dramatically in recent years. In 1990, for example, 15 million refugees and other displaced persons were receiving some sort of help from the agency. That number had almost doubled, to 27.5 million, by 1995. * [16]

Much of the increase in refugees is linked to the end of the Cold War. Before the Soviet Union collapsed in 1989, many nations were held together, albeit tenuously, by the struggle between the two superpowers. The rivalry pushed the superpowers to give massive amounts of arms

---

* There are a total of 35 million refugees and other displaced people throughout the world, including those being aided by UNHCR, according to the U.S. Committee for Refugees.

Refugee Profile Undergoes Change

In the early 1990s, the number of refugees being aided by the U.N. High Commissioner for Refugees (UNHCR) began dropping while the number of other displaced people rose dramatically, particularly in the Balkans, Central Africa and parts of the former Soviet Union. Displaced persons are those who have been forced from their homes, including people displaced within their own countries and war-affected populations; refugees are displaced persons who have fled across international borders.

People Being Assisted by UNHCR, 1975-1995

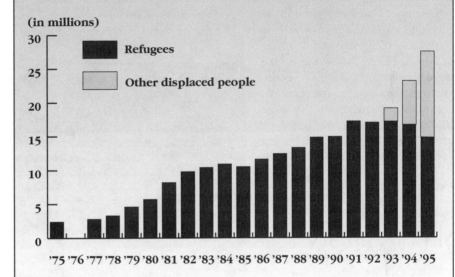

Note: No figure is available for 1976.

Source: United Nations High Commissioner for Refugees, The State of the World's Refugees, 1995

---

and aid to states that would not have been considered strategically important under different circumstances. When the aid was reduced, and in many cases eliminated, in the early 1990s, many countries quickly began unraveling, allowing ethnic, religious and political tensions that had been held in check to burst into the open. In the former Soviet Union alone, there were conflicts or civil wars in the republics of Georgia, Armenia, Azerbaijan, Tajikistan and Moldova and the Russian province of Chechnya.

"Conflicts spiraled out of control," says the Refugee Policy Group's Hansch, because "the hatreds, animosities and weapons were still there without the puppet masters to rein them in." Liberia, Yugoslavia, Somalia and other hotbeds of conflict virtually disintegrated as nation states. The resulting chaos displaced millions.

The first real post-Cold War test for UNHCR and other aid agencies came early in 1991 in northern Iraq. An uprising by ethnic Kurds following Saddam Hussein's defeat in the Persian Gulf War led to reprisals by the Iraqi government that displaced 1.5 million people, most of whom were trying to cross into neighboring Turkey or Iran. In an effort to stop the exodus as well as to prevent Iraq's brutal suppression of the Kurdish revolt, the United States and some of its allies against Saddam established a "safety zone" over part of the Kurdish area. UNHCR coordinated efforts to provide emergency relief for the displaced. In addition, the agency immediately began a massive reconstruction program to ensure that people would have adequate shelter by the time cold weather arrived. [17]

"Iraq was a real watershed," says Kathleen Newland, a senior associate at the Carnegie Endowment for International Peace. By setting up the safe haven and focusing on reconstruction, she says, the international community "was trying to be more proactive. There was a new attitude here: We need to do more than just try to feed people." ∎

CURRENT SITUATION

Preventive Action

Throughout the early 1990s, the new, proactive policy known as preventive action became the cornerstone of UNHCR's strategy. So far, however, it has enjoyed only limited success. In Bosnia, for example, the use of safe havens failed to protect the Muslim population from the genocidal killing known as "ethnic cleansing."

Even in northern Iraq, where the safe haven enabled the Kurds to establish a de facto state, the area has been riven by internal strife. In late 1996, in fact, Iraqi government troops actually invaded the safe haven — albeit briefly.

Since the 1970s, UNHCR has worked to assist refugees after they flee their homelands. But recently, the agency has been trying to change its approach to dealing with humanitarian crises.

"For many years, UNHCR and its operational partners waited for refugees to cross an international border before providing them with protection and assistance," High Commissioner Sadako Ogata wrote in 1995. By shifting some of its focus to preventive action, Ogata continues, the agency is becoming "equally concerned with conditions in actual and potential refugee-producing states." [18]

Preventive action is predicated on the notion that UNHCR can stop refu-

Countries Taking the Most Refugees	
Country of asylum	Number of Refugees (in thousands)
Iran	2,236.4
Zaire	1,724.4
Pakistan	1,055.0
Germany	1,004.6
Tanzania	883.3
Sudan	727.2
USA	591.7
Guinea	553.2
Cote d'Ivoire	360.1
Ethiopia	348.1
Armenia	304.0
Burundi	300.3
China	287.1
Uganda	286.5

gee flows before they start by closely monitoring tense situations; using diplomacy and conflict resolution to defuse pending crises; and providing more economic and social assistance to improve conditions in poor areas.

"In areas where there are obvious danger signals and risks for population movements, we have tried to go in and work with the authorities and private organizations to analyze the risks and find ways to prevent them," Jessen-Petersen says. "If we can't manage the risks, then we set up structures to manage such movements, should they happen."

In Somalia in 1992, for example,

"We went into villages where people were at risk and provided aid to prevent them from moving," he says, rather than "allowing people to move hundreds of kilometers under horrendous conditions in which they will die, just to find food."

Preventive action also entails paying more attention to refugees after they are repatriated. "Our task is to help people feel a level of confidence that they can reconstruct their lives without feeling like they're living on the edge any more, with one foot over the border," says Anita Parlow, a UNHCR spokesperson.

By working closely with other U.N. entities and NGOs, UNHCR helps restore basic services, such as roads, schools and hospitals, to the areas where refugees will be returning. In addition, Parlow says, the agency tries to create and sustain international support for the repatriation to give returnees a sense that they are not facing their challenges alone. "This means a lot to people," she adds.

But many observers outside UNHCR think that for the time being, preventive action is often little more than a nice idea when efforts are not backed by the broader international community, which they say is often the case. "It's good that UNHCR raises the issue," Drumtra says. "But ultimately, it comes down to the political will of the big powers."

Drumtra and others say that the UNHCR and other aid organizations do not have the resources and clout to take the unilateral actions required to really make preventive action workable. "UNHCR has very little running room of its own," Drumtra says, adding that "their budget and staff are already stretched to the limit."

U.S. Refugee Policy

The United States long has prided itself on being a haven for those in need. But many refugee advocates say that when it comes to taking in displaced persons, the U.S. doesn't live up to its self-image. [19]

Refugees can enter the United States either by being processed through the refugee admissions system or by requesting asylum. If a refugee's application for admission to the U.S. is approved, the refugee is provided with assistance by federal, state and private agencies. Each year, the president sets a limit on the number of refugees who can be admitted under this procedure. In fiscal 1996, the cap was set at 90,000, down from 110,000 the year before. This fiscal year, the number has dropped even further, to 78,000. [20]

The current system of annual refugee caps was established under the Refugee Act of 1980. The law requires the president each year to consult with Congress on the proposed number of refugees to be admitted. This is more than a formality since Congress in turn appropriates funds needed to help resettle the refugees.

The act also requires the administration to set, within the overall number, an admissions ceiling by region. Traditionally, the lion's share of refugee admissions has come from Eastern Europe (particularly countries of the former Soviet Union) and Southeast Asia. For instance, in fiscal 1997, 48,000, or more than half the total refugee admissions to the U.S., will come from Eastern Europe. By contrast, only 7,000 refugees from Africa will be admitted. [21] The policy, established during the Cold War, is intended to help Jews and other religious minorities from the former Soviet Union as well as those persecuted by the authoritarian regimes in Vietnam and other parts of Indochina.

Many refugee and immigration experts argue that the current admissions system is outmoded and needs to be changed. "We're doing it for domestic reasons [to satisfy] ethnic politics and because we still have a Cold War

mentality," says Georgetown's Keeley. He and others say that the current system, which is vigorously defended by powerful ethnic lobbies, is too rigid and numbers-oriented. "We need to be more flexible about the numbers," he says, adding that refugee admissions should be dictated more by circumstances than politics.

Others say that regional ceilings should be done away with entirely and replaced with a system based on need alone. "We need to restrict refugee resettlement to those people who have no other options," says Mark Krikorian,

Where Most Refugees Are From	
Country of Origin	Number of Refugees (in thousands)
Afghanistan	2,743.6
Rwanda	2,257.0
Liberia	794.2
Iraq	702.1
Somalia	535.9
Eritrea	422.4
Sudan	398.6
Burundi	389.2
Bosnia-Herzegovina	321.2
Vietnam	307.0
Azerbaijan	299.0
Angola	283.9
Sierra Leone	275.1
Mozambique	234.5
Chad	211.9

executive director of the Center for Immigration Studies. Krikorian points out that most of the Jews from the former Soviet Union and the Southeast Asians being admitted today as refugees are not really refugees as defined by international law. For example, he notes, Jews in the former Soviet republics no longer face institutional prejudice, and they have the option of emigrating to Israel.

But the Carnegie Institute's Newland warns against making hasty policy changes. While she wants a more flexible refugee admissions system that "can better respond to refugee flows," she is not entirely ready to scrap the current rules. In the case of Soviet Jews, for instance, "there is still a tremendous amount of anti-Semitism in the former Soviet countries," Newland says. She adds that "many [Jewish] people coming to the United States have relatives here, and so going to Israel is more difficult."

Asylum Policy Changes

S omeone fearing persecution can also enter the United States by requesting asylum. In such cases, the person arrives in the United States either legally or illegally and asks for asylum. That request will be granted if the person can demonstrate a well-founded fear of being persecuted at home due to race, religion, nationality, political opinion or membership in a particular social group. [22]

Unlike refugee admissions, there is no limit to the number of people who can be granted asylum. In 1996, 22 percent of all adjudicated cases (13,368 persons) were granted asylum. [23]

U.S. asylum policy, which is based on the Immigration and Nationality Act of 1952, has been altered several times. The most recent changes, in 1995 and 1996, were aimed at both streamlining procedure and stiffening requirements.

The Immigration and Naturalization Service (INS) issued regulations, effective Jan. 1, 1995, that mandated a larger, better trained staff to handle asylum cases and required the agency to rule on an asylum request within six months. In addition, the Immigration Control Act of 1996 provided for expedited procedures at points of entry in an effort to quickly reject and send back those without a solid claim. In addition, the new law required those applying for asylum to do so within one year of arriving in the United States.

INS officials say the new rules have substantially reduced the number of new claims for asylum. In fiscal 1996, the number of asylum applications fell sharply to 49,447, from 74,888 the year before. [24]

Changes in the asylum law are also coming from the courts. Refugee advocates have succeeded in expanding the number of categories for refugee status to include people suffering from discrimination based on their gender, sexual orientation or resistance to coercive population-control methods. For instance, in June 1996, the Board of Immigration Appeals granted asylum to a woman from Togo who had fled to avoid genital mutilation, a common practice throughout much of Africa. [25] People who have been persecuted because they are homosexual and those who refuse to obey China's one-child policy have also been granted asylum in the last few years.

The trend toward flexibility troubles Krikorian, who argues that the concept of asylum is being extended way beyond its traditional boundaries by feminist, gay rights and other advocacy groups. Such organizations are interested in using asylum as a legal tool to help "their favorite class of victims," Krikorian says, whether they deserve asylum or not. "Political asylum can't simply be a way for people in unfortunate circumstances to come to the United States," he says.

Instead, Krikorian says, asylum needs to be reserved for those who are being persecuted based on their beliefs. "If there is a basis for claiming that all women in the Third World who are suffering from [discrimina-tion] deserve asylum, then this could apply to all Muslim women, all African women and all Chinese women and could potentially turn into a flood of people," Krikorian adds. That would ultimately turn the American people against the idea of asylum, he says, and force Congress to impose severe limits on the practice that would hurt legitimate asylum seekers.

But Newland argues that there is a difference between genital mutilation and more common forms of discrimination against women in the Third World. "It's absurd to think that, say, all Saudi Arabian women will be eli-

Russian refugees from Grozny, Chechnya, flee the city last August after Russian troops threatened to renew bombing.

gible for asylum because they are not allowed to drive," she says.

In addition, Newland says, "the United States is not in any danger of being overrun by any one group," because, contrary to Krikorian, it is very hard to make a case for entering the country under the asylum laws. Georgetown's Keeley agrees, adding that the asylum laws would likely be changed if there were any signs that huge numbers of people were going to be able to use them to enter the country.

"Asylum and refugee policy is done for the state," he says, "and if that policy weakens the state, then it will be changed."

■

OUTLOOK

More Refugees Likely

Journalist Robert Kaplan has predicted that more and more people will be displaced both inside and outside of their countries in the coming decades. According to Kaplan, the chaos and anarchy that now permeate much of the developing world today will only spread, further destroying civil society in many countries and uprooting millions of people. [26]

While most refugee experts consider Kaplan to be overly pessimistic, many do agree that in some places, particularly Africa, things are likely to get worse before they get better.

"I'm afraid we're going to see more foreign crises," says CARE's Hale, adding that the developed world is helping to lay the groundwork for future tragedies by reducing foreign aid and by requiring many Third World governments to impose economic austerity on their people in the name of free market reform.

Others blame at least part of the problem on the nation-state system, which is becoming harder and harder to sustain in many parts of the post-Cold War world. "We assume that once a state is founded, it will always

At Issue:

Should American military personnel be used to help provide assistance to refugees?

STEVEN HANSCH

*Senior program officer, Refugee Policy Group,
Washington, D.C.*

WRITTEN FOR *THE CQ RESEARCHER*, JANUARY 1996.

t he U.S. armed forces often can provide critical assistance in refugee and emergency situations that complements the efforts of less well-equipped private voluntary agencies. Because of its tremendous infrastructure of equipment, the military can save lives in situations where the rest of the international humanitarian community falls short.

In recent years the efforts of our Army, Air Force, Navy and Coast Guard have saved tens of thousands of innocent civilians abroad, through rescue at sea (for example, Bangladesh), evacuation (Iraq), airlift of water pumps (Zaire) and assistance in delivery of food aid (Somalia).

Far too much is made of the perceived risks to our military personnel in humanitarian emergencies. Most humanitarian operations proceed quietly and without risk. Specific incidents in Lebanon and in Somalia are the exceptions, repeatedly abused by isolationists as grounds for retreating from any effort to provide aid — in effect, conceding victory to terrorists. Far less publicized are the military's numerous successes — in rescuing boat people at sea, providing security in complex emergencies, rehabilitating roads and wells, designing telecommunications systems and providing laboratory facilities in tropical epidemics.

Oddly, of all the agencies involved in emergency relief, only the military is routinely kept back because of concerns about security threats: It is ironic that those Americans who voluntarily enlist in the military and are paid to be prepared to accept combat risks are claimed by some to be less expendable than the American doctors, nurses and other humanitarians who are so much more routinely involved in the world's problem spots and incur significantly higher casualty rates per person than do military personnel.

Per capita, more American and European civilians were injured or killed in Somalia than the troops that were sent in. But the killing of the heroic civilian trying to save lives rarely makes headlines. Casualties to Americans volunteering with charitable groups like CARE, Catholic Relief Services and the International Rescue Committee count for little among isolationist policy analysts, but they count for a lot among millions of Americans who sponsor their heroic efforts.

Of course, we should deploy our foreign aid and diplomatic resources to facilitate resolution of problems. And flexing our military might will rarely be pivotal in these long-term arrangements. But that's a different matter. If lives are immediately at stake, most Americans would agree that the military should be involved and, where appropriate, lead the charge.

DOUG BANDOW

Senior fellow, Cato Institute, Washington, D.C.

WRITTEN FOR *THE CQ RESEARCHER*, JANUARY 1996.

y et another crisis has flared overseas. The images never change — starving people fleeing murder, rape and war. Only the victims are different.

Such conflicts cry out for Western involvement. Some people propose military intervention to stop conflict. A few even advocate de facto colonialism to remake failed societies. All treat their proposal as the only moral course of action.

However, none of these strategies is likely to succeed. At least not at a cost acceptable to the American people, who would be doing the paying and dying.

First, sending in the Marines would not automatically bring peace to shattered lands. This is a lesson that we should have learned from Lebanon and Somalia. Bitter conflicts around the world are not a consequence of, say, sunspots. Rather, they grow out of ethnic, religious and tribal hatreds, many of which go back centuries.

Of course, some people merely hope to stop the killing, obviously a worthy goal. But treating symptoms rather than causes is unlikely to save many lives. At best, intervention would create a temporary cease-fire likely to break down once the outside forces depart. Far worse is the possibility of Americans finding themselves dying in a civil war, as they did in Lebanon a decade ago. And, if Washington followed a consistent policy of humanitarian intervention in today's world of tragedy, U.S. soldiers could end up involved in a dozen or more conflicts simultaneously.

Moreover, the long-term Western occupation of poorer lands is no option. Remaking failed societies is an extraordinarily ambitious task for even the most arrogant social engineer. Casualties among the occupying forces would be inevitable, as warring factions coalesced against outsiders. Even average foreign citizens, the supposed "beneficiaries" of U.S. intervention, would likely grow to resent their new overlords.

Finally, for Washington to become Globocop would violate the government's duty toward the 18-year-old Americans who actually have to enforce a de facto empire. What right have Washington policy-makers to risk the lives of soldiers who joined the military in order to defend the U.S. when that nation's security is not at stake? There is nothing humanitarian about sending other people off to fight and possibly die, however attractive the end.

Americans like to solve problems, but not every crisis, however tragic, is soluble. Unfortunately, we simply aren't capable of putting dissolving nations back together. Nor would it be right to compound foreign tragedies by making casualties of our fellow citizens.

UNHCR Scores a Win in Mozambique

With no end in sight to refugee crises in so many places — Rwanda, Bosnia and Afghanistan to name just three — stories of successful repatriations may seem like an aid worker's faraway dream. But not every refugee problem remains unresolved. In Guatemala, Lebanon and, most dramatically, in Mozambique, many displaced citizens have been able to return to their homes.

Since 1992, in the largest organized repatriation ever undertaken in Africa, an estimated 1.7 million refugees and 4 million internally displaced people have returned home to Mozambique.

Refugee experts say that things went right in Mozambique because a number of pieces fell into place. Most important, the civil war that had been raging for 16 years ended in 1992, giving refugees their first reason to go home. That conflict, between the Marxist government and the RENAMO rebel group, had killed more than 500,000 people and displaced roughly one-quarter of Mozambique's 16.5 million people. [1]

The war wound down in part because the primary supporters of the government and the rebels, the Soviet Union and South Africa, respectively, withdrew their patronage. In addition, according to Samantha Bolton, communications director for the aid group Doctors Without Borders USA, everyone was ready for peace. "The sides were just so exhausted that they stopped fighting," she says. Another reason for the truce, she says, was Mozambique's limited natural resources. "In Mozambique there is nothing to fight over, unlike Angola, where the war has dragged on because there are gold and diamonds," Bolton says.

After the fighting had stopped in Mozambique, the situation further improved after both sides agreed to a peace treaty that allowed for power sharing within a democratic framework. "This was very important in terms of the assurances it gave refugees who were thinking of returning," says Soren Jessen-Petersen, director of the United Nations High Commissioner for Refugees' New York office. The public reconciliation convinced many displaced people that the peace would hold, he says. (By contrast, many people displaced as a result of the conflict in Bosnia did not return to their homes, because the peace accord signed by the warring factions in December 1995 was perceived as tenuous.)

Once the peace accord was signed in Mozambique, UNHCR and other aid groups began repatriating the nearly 2 million refugees who had fled the country. According to Jessen-Petersen, the task was daunting for a number of reasons. First, the refugees were displaced throughout six countries: South Africa, Tanzania, Malawi, Zambia, Zimbabwe and Swaziland. [2] Such widespread dispersion required UNHCR to deploy 41 heavy trucks to help transport refugees who were particularly far from their villages. [3] Others returned by rail and boat, but most Mozambicans went home on foot.

To make matters worse, Mozambique, a poor country to begin with, had been ravaged by the prolonged war. It was extremely important that the refugees' return be accompanied by the rehabilitation of their communities, Jessen-Petersen says. To aid the rehab work, UNHCR funded more than 800 small-scale development projects throughout the country, ranging from efforts to repair roads, bridges and other infrastructure to meeting basic community health and education needs. In addition, returnees were given enough food for 10 months as well as basic supplies like plastic sheeting for temporary shelter. UNHCR also distributed 190,000 seed kits and more than 900,000 agricultural tools to help the 90 percent of the refugees who were returning to farms to become self-sufficient. [4]

The repatriation reached its peak in 1994, when UNHCR estimates that some 17,000 refugees were returning home each week. The two-and-a-half-year operation cost almost $1.2 billion. The refugee agency has largely pulled out of Mozambique, and its mandate there now is to provide emergency assistance, not long-term development.

But if UNHCR's success in the country is to be sustained, the land-mine problem will have to be solved. During the war, both sides placed a vast number of mines throughout the country — possibly as many as 10 million. According to the U.S. Committee for Refugees, land mines still kill at least 40 people and injure scores more each month in Mozambique. Efforts by the United Nations and others to remove the mines continue, but progress is painstakingly slow. [5]

Another challenge is the economy. Decades of war and mismanagement have left Mozambique the world's poorest nation, with an annual per capita income of $60.

These and other remaining problems leave refugee experts cautiously optimistic. "I'd say things have gone right there, so far," Bolton says.

[1] United Nations High Commissioner for Refugees, *The State of the World's Refugees 1995*, p. 174.

[2] *Ibid.*

[3] Andrew Meldrum, "Repatriating the Refugees," *Africa Report*, March-April 1994, p. 46.

[4] U.S. Committee for Refugees, "World Refugee Survey 1996," p. 59.

[5] *Ibid.*

exist, and that is simply not true," says Keeley. Multiethnic states, such as those in Africa, are "a recipe for disaster." He predicts that "there will be a lot of weak, imploding states in the near future," which will lead to further population displacement.

At the same time, Hale says, the humanitarian-relief community is getting better at assisting those in need. "NGOs are now specializing in providing specific services — Doctor

Without Borders for medicine, Oxfam with supplying water and CARE with food distribution and camp management." The new division of labor, he says, is making NGOs faster and much more efficient providers of relief.

"We're seeing attempts to consolidate the lessons of the past," says Bolton of Doctors Without Borders. But while she believes that UNHCR and other groups will continue to hone their technical skills, the politics of each new situation will continue to prove challenging. "There are no formulas with this because the dynamic is always different," she says.

But one factor will remain constant, Keeley says ruefully: "Like the poor, refugees will always be with us." ■

FOR MORE INFORMATION

United Nations High Commissioner for Refugees, New York Liaison Office, United Nations, United Nations Plaza, New York, N.Y. 10017; (212) 963-6200; www.unhcr.ch. As the world's leading refugee aid organization, UNHCR coordinates relief efforts in scores of countries.

Doctors Without Borders USA, 6 East 39th St., 8th Floor, New York, N.Y. 10016; (212) 679-6800; www.dwb.org. This organization provides medical assistance to refugees and others in need, ranging from surgery to nutrition and sanitation programs.

U.S. Committee for Refugees, 1717 Massachusetts Ave., N.W., Suite 200, Washington D.C. 20036; (202) 347-3507; www.refugees.org. The committee monitors refugee crises and reports its findings to the public.

CARE, 151 Ellis St. N.E., Atlanta, Ga. 30303; (404) 681-2552; www.care.org. CARE aids refugees and other displaced persons through the delivery of food and other emergency assistance.

Refugees International, 1705 N St., N.W., Washington, D.C. 20036; (202) 828-0110; www.refintl.org. This group lobbies on behalf of refugees and works with the U.N., governments and humanitarian relief organizations to assess refugee crises and come up with workable solutions.

Notes

[1] U.S Committee for Refugees, "World Refugee Survey 1996," pp. 4-6.

[2] "Death Shadows Africa's Great Lakes," *The Economist,* Oct. 19, 1996, pp. 45-47.

[3] Michael Maren, *The Road to Hell: The Ravaging Effects of Foreign Aid and International Charity* (1996). Maren served as a field worker in Somalia for the U.S. Agency for International Development. He also has worked overseas for Catholic Relief Services and as a Peace Corps volunteer.

[4] For background, see "War Crimes," *The CQ Researcher,* July 7, 1995, pp. 585-608.

[5] For background, see "Foreign Policy and Public Opinion," *The CQ Researcher,* July 15, 1994, pp. 601-624.

[6] See Walter Clarke and Jeffrey Herbst, "Somalia and the Future of Humanitarian Intervention," *Foreign Affairs,* March/April 1996, p. 84.

[7] U.S Committee for Refugees, *op. cit.,* pp. 4-6.

[8] See Brian Tierney and Sidney Painter, *Western Europe in the Middle Ages,* 300-1475 (1983), p. 66.

[9] Gil Loescher, *Beyond Charity: International Cooperation and the Global Refugee Crisis* (1993), pp. 37-40.

[10] *Ibid.,* pp. 46-51.

[11] See Paul Johnson, *Modern Times, From the Twenties to the Nineties* (1991), p. 474.

[12] Loescher, *op. cit.,* pp. 87-88. For background, see "United Nations at 50," *The CQ Researcher,* Aug. 18, 1995, pp. 729-752.

[13] United Nations, *Treaties and International Agreements Registered or Filed and Recorded with the Secretariat of the United Nations,* Vol. 189 (1954), p. 137.

[14] For background, see "New Era in Asia," *The CQ Researcher,* Feb. 14, 1992, pp. 121-144; and "Democracy in Africa," *The CQ Researcher,* March 24, 1995, pp. 241-264.

[15] Loescher, *op. cit.,* pp. 87-88.

[16] United Nations High Commissioner for Refugees, *The State of the World's Refugees* (1995), p. 247.

[17] *Ibid.,* pp. 117-118.

[18] *Ibid.,* p. 8.

[19] For background, see "The New Immigrants," *The CQ Researcher,* Jan. 24, 1997, pp. 49-72.

[20] "FY 95 & 96 Refugee Admissions and FY 96 & 97 Ceilings," *Refugee Reports,* Sept. 30, 1996, p. 16.

[21] *Ibid.*

[22] Bill Frelick and Barbara Kohnen, "Filling the Gap: Temporary Protected Status," *Journal of Refugee Studies,* December 1995, p. 340.

[23] Immigration and Naturalization Service, Asylum Division.

[24] *Ibid.*

[25] David Wheeler, "Harvard Program Helps Change the Law," *The Chronicle of Higher Education,* July 5, 1996.

[26] Robert Kaplan, "The Coming Anarchy," *The Atlantic Monthly,* February 1994, p. 44.

Bibliography

Selected Sources Used

Books

Harrell-Bond, B.E., *Imposing Aid: Emergency Assistance to Refugees,* Oxford University Press, 1986.
Though somewhat dated, the author's dissection of the international community's response to refugee crises is still pertinent. In addition, she examines many aspects of refugee situations that are rarely discussed, ranging from fertility rates among displaced women to the practice of taxing refugees.

Loescher, Gil, *Beyond Charity: International Cooperation and the Global Refugee Crisis,* Oxford University Press, 1993.
Loescher, a professor of international relations at Notre Dame University, traces the development of the modern refugee movement around the world. In addition, he focuses on more recent attempts by the international community to aid refugees, from efforts to provide emergency assistance to current asylum policies.

Maren, Michael, *The Road to Hell: The Ravaging Effects of Foreign Aid and International Charity,* Free Press, 1996
Maren, a former aid worker turned free-lance writer, asserts that humanitarian aid generally does more harm than good. In addition, he accuses private aid organizations of perpetuating refugee and other crises in order to continue to attract private donations and government grants.

United Nations High Commissioner for Refugees, *The State of the World's Refugees 1995: In Search of Solutions,* Oxford University Press, 1995.
This is the most recent edition of UNHCR's annual reports on its accomplishments for the year before and its goals for the future. The book details the agency's efforts to assist refugees around the world, including case studies of some of the countries where UNHCR is currently operating.

Articles

Clarke, Walter, and Jeffrey Herbst, "Somalia and the Future of Humanitarian Intervention," *Foreign Affairs,* March/April, 1996.
The authors explore the failed military intervention in Somalia and its impact on the willingness of developed nations to send soldiers on future relief missions.

"Death Shadows Africa's Great Lakes," *The Economist,* Oct. 19, 1996.
The history and issues behind the ethnic strife that has led to so much death and displacement in Rwanda and Burundi are examined in detail. Of special interest, the article explains how German colonization in the late 19th century reinforced the existing dominance of the Tutsi tribe over the more populous Hutus and sowed the seeds for inter-tribal conflict in the two nations.

Krikorian, Mark, "Who Deserves Asylum?" *Commentary,* June 1996.
Krikorian, executive director of the Center for Immigration Studies, criticizes recent efforts by feminists, gay rights activists and others to expand the definition of a refugee for purposes of qualifying for asylum. Krikorian argues that letting more people enter the country under the asylum laws will undermine the entire system and ultimately hurt refugees entitled to protection in the United States.

Rieff, David, "Camped Out: Why Rwanda Invaded Zaire," *The New Republic,* Nov. 25, 1996.
Rieff, a senior fellow at the World Policy Institute at the New School for Social Research, argues that UNHCR and other aid agencies made huge mistakes when they set up refugee camps for Rwandan Hutus streaming into Zaire. Rieff asserts that the situation in Rwanda may alter the international community's opinion on the efficacy of humanitarian aid.

Reports and Studies

U.S. Committee for Refugees, *World Refugee Survey 1996,* Immigration and Refugee Services of America, 1996
An invaluable resource guide, compiled by a refugee advocacy group, that assesses the situation for refugees and other displaced people in almost every country in the world. In addition to the nations directly affected by human displacement, the book also examines the refugee policies of the United States and other developed countries.

16 Global Refugee Crisis

MARY H. COOPER

Rahman Rexhepi escaped Kosovo with his life. His brother was not so lucky. For weeks he had been escorting ethnic Albanian children to school in the village of Shtimje, amid intense Serbian harassment. But as he walked home one day, Rexhepi says, his brother was stopped by Officer Lubica, a local Serbian policeman, taken away and shot.

"After five days we found my brother's body," Rexhepi says. "The Serbs would only allow a few of us to bury him in a shallow grave, and they threatened to kill us all if we didn't get out of there fast."

After a cursory graveside service, Rexhepi joined the thousands of other ethnic Albanians last spring trekking into the limbo that is the growing world of refugees. Rexhepi ended up in the teeming refugee camp at Brazda, in neighboring Macedonia. But he longs to return home.

"Now I just want to go back to Kosovo to dig a proper grave for my brother," he says. "But I won't return until it's safe."

Yugoslav President Slobodan Milosevic's campaign of "ethnic cleansing" — his grotesque euphemism for the massacres and mass deportation of Kosovo's ethnic Albanians — has produced Europe's worst refugee crisis since World War II.

On June 2, after more than two months of bombing, NATO called a cease-fire after Milosevic agreed to withdraw his forces from Kosovo. By then, about 860,000 Kosovars had fled to neighboring Albania, Macedonia and Montenegro, where more than half found refuge with local families. Most of the others ended up in camps managed by the United Nations High Commissioner

From *The CQ Researcher,*
July 9, 1999.

for Refugees (UNHCR) and non-governmental organizations (NGOs) such as the Red Cross and Doctors Without Borders. *

The steady flow of refugees forced out of Kosovo quickly made the camps overcrowded. In late April, more than 25,000 refugees were packed into the Brazda camp, designed to accommodate 12,000, and the stench of human waste filled the air. The residents had to stand in long lines for food, and the risk of outbreaks of cholera and other deadly, contagious diseases rose with the coming summer heat. (*See story, p. 280.*)

But for all their misery, Brazda's denizens can count themselves lucky on at least one score. "These are some of the best-off refugees in the world," says Barnett R. Rubin, a Kosovo specialist at the Council on Foreign Relations in New York City. "They're in good health, they have enough food, they have communications and transportation — all those things that refugees in Africa and other regions don't have. They're poor by European standards, but they're not poor by world standards."

---

* Albania and Macedonia are independent countries, Macedonia having won its independence from Yugoslavia in 1991. Milosevic is president of the Federal Republic of Yugoslavia, which comprises the republics of Montenegro and Serbia and the previously autonomous provinces of Kosovo and Vojvodina.

The Kosovars are only a fraction of the world's estimated 13 million refugees — people who have fled their countries because they feared persecution based on race, religion, nationality, social group or political opinion. Many fled from war or other armed conflict. Both Hutu and Tutsi tribesmen fled Rwanda during the civil war and genocide that killed a half-million people in 1994. More than 400,000 people have fled the civil war that has ravaged Sierra Leone for more than seven years. About 100,000 ethnic Nepalese refugees from southern Bhutan have languished in camps in Nepal for the past 10 years, with no relief in sight. [1] (*See map and story, pp. 274-275.*)

"With the end of the Cold War, we had expected that there would be less conflict," says Panos Moumtzis, spokesman for the Washington, D.C., office of the UNHCR, which is based in Geneva, Switzerland. "Instead, we have seen more conflicts within countries, and the number of refugees has increased dramatically."

Refugees have always been the victims of civil strife, war and famine, but it was not until after the end of World War II, when hundreds of thousands of civilians were displaced, that world leaders decided to deal systematically with their plight. On July 28, 1951, the United Nations adopted the Convention Relating to the Status of Refugees, which stipulated the rights of refugees to safety and humane treatment. At the same time, the U.N. created the UNHCR to oversee humanitarian relief efforts to support refugees until they were able to safely return to their homelands or find asylum in third countries.

But the recent increase in refugee flows is challenging that system. The problem stems in part from the apparent willingness of national leaders

Half of All Refugees Are Palestinians, Afghans and Iraqis

Roughly half of the world's 13 million refugees are Palestinians, Afghans and Iraqis. Forty nations have produced at least 10,000 refugees; 15 nations have more than 200,000 refugees.*

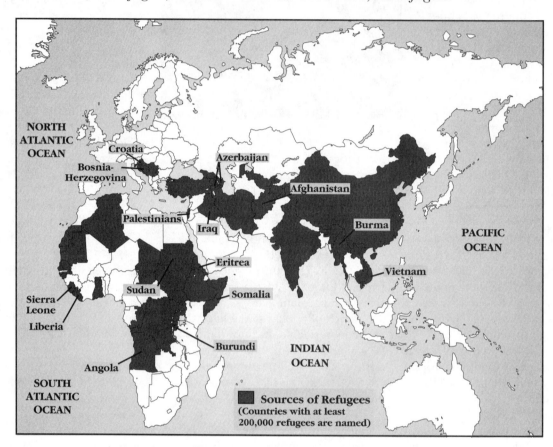

Principal Sources of Refugees as of Dec. 31, 1998

Palestinians	3,740,000	Azerbaijan	218,000	Mauritania	30,000
Afghanistan	2,600,000	Armenia	180,000	Georgia	23,000
Iraq	552,000	Congo/Kinshasa	136,000	Congo/Brazaville	20,000
Sierra Leone	480,000	Yugoslavia	133,000	Chad	16,000
Somalia	421,000	China (Tibet)	128,000	India	15,000
Sudan	352,000	Bhutan	115,000	Tajikistan	15,000
Bosnia and Herzegovina	345,000	Sri Lanka	110,000	Laos	12,000
Eritrea	322,000	Western Sahara	105,000	Rwanda	12,000
Liberia	310,000	Cambodia	51,000	Turkey	12,000
Croatia	309,000	Uzbekistan	45,000	Uganda	12,000
Angola	302,000	Algeria	40,000	Ghana	11,000
Burundi	281,000	Ethiopia	38,000	Guinea-Bissau	10,000
Vietnam	281,000	Iran	30,000	Senegal	10,000
Burma	238,000				

Note: Serbia's "ethnic cleansing" operation in Kosovo produced more than 860,000 ethnic Albanian refugees, but most returned home after the NATO bombing campaign ended on June 2.

* Refugees are defined as people who have fled their countries because they feared persecution based on race, religion, nationality, social group or political opinion.

Source: U.S. Committee for Refugees

Third World Is Home to Most Refugees

To many Americans, the word "refugee" has been defined in recent months by the poignant images and shocking stories reported from the Balkans. An estimated 860,000 ethnic Albanians fled Kosovo, but they represent only a fraction of the 13 million refugees scattered around the world, many living in even more appalling conditions than those found in Balkan refugee camps. In no region of the world is the refugee situation more dire than in Africa, where ethnic turmoil and civil wars in several countries have created more than 7 million refugees. The following nations each have produced at least 300,000 refugees:

Palestinians — Repeated Arab-Israeli conflicts over the past half-century displaced millions of Palestinian Arabs. Even today, more than 3.7 million Palestinians live as refugees throughout the Middle East and North Africa. In some host countries, where they are seen as a threat to sovereignty, Palestinian exiles have been attacked, notably in 1982 when extremists massacred refugees inside their camps in southern Lebanon.

Afghanistan — Two decades ago, a Soviet invasion in support of a communist regime sparked a civil war that continues even today, 10 years after the last Soviet troops withdrew and the militant Islamic Taliban took over much of the country. At its peak, the conflict uprooted as many as 6.2 million people, more than 2.6 million of whom still live in exile, mostly in neighboring Pakistan and Iran.

Iraq — Government persecution of ethnic Kurds has prompted hundreds of thousands to flee to neighboring Turkey in the 1990s. They and other refugees of the Persian Gulf War and its aftermath bring the total refugee population from Iraq to more than a half-million, most of whom are living in Iran, Syria, Saudi Arabia and Western Europe.

Sierra Leone — Some 405,000 refugees fled to Guinea and Liberia after rebel forces began terrorizing the population last year by hacking off the limbs of adults and children. West African peacekeeping troops retook the capital, Freetown, from the Revolutionary United Front in January, but the country remains embroiled in a civil war that began more than six years ago.

Somalia — The largest group of African refugees comes from Somalia, where a civil war beginning in January 1991, combined with prolonged drought, forced almost a million people, many of them seriously malnourished, to flee to neighboring countries. About 400,000 went to Kenya alone. In 1992 the United Nations High Commissioner for Refugees (UNHCR) began a relief operation inside Somalia to help refugees return and discourage further outflows. Almost a half-million Somalis remain outside the country, most in Ethiopia and Kenya.

Sudan — Africa's largest country has been ravaged by more than three decades of civil war between the Arab-dominated government, which controls the north, and secessionist rebels, mostly non-Muslim blacks, in the south. Nearly 2 million of the country's 30 million inhabitants have died in the conflict, and another 4 million have fled. More than 350,000 remain outside Sudan, mostly in impoverished neighboring countries such as Uganda, Congo and Ethiopia.

Bosnia-Herzegovina — After nearly four years of war with Yugoslavia ended with the Dayton Peace Agreement of December 1995, more than a million Bosnian refugees were scattered among some 25 host countries. In 1996 the UNHCR launched its Bosnia repatriation program, one of the largest the agency has undertaken. There are still a half-million Bosnian refugees — both Serbs and Muslims — and more than 800,000 displaced persons in Bosnia-Herzegovina itself, most of whom cannot return to their home villages because they are now under the control of a hostile ethnic group.

Liberia — After as many as seven years in exile, more than 200,000 Liberian refugees from one of the continent's most brutal civil wars returned home last year. But despite the peace process that began in 1996, 475,000 Liberians remain outside their homeland, uncertain about its safety and economic viability. Liberia's economy is being further strained by the arrival of hundreds of thousands of refugees from civil war in neighboring Sierra Leone.

Croatia — More than 340,000 refugees from Croatia's civil war, mostly ethnic Serbs, have yet to return home. Most are in Yugoslavia and Bosnia-Herzegovina. As in Bosnia, repatriation has been slowed by the reluctance of refugees to return to their homes, which are controlled by hostile ethnic groups.

to use civilians as pawns in their own political agendas. Milosevic's campaign against ethnic Albanians, for example, sprang from his revocation of Kosovo's autonomy 10 years ago and escalated after fighting broke out between Serb forces and the insurgent Kosovo Liberation Army (KLA).

But Milosevic carried the exploitation of refugees to a new level.

"The expulsion of refugees and internally displaced persons in the former Yugoslavia was an integral part of Serbian military strategy," says Roberta Cohen, a specialist in refugee issues at the Brookings Institution, a Washington, D.C., think tank. "The Serbs first started carrying out their ethnic cleansing campaign as a counterinsurgency strategy, and then used it as a form of collective punishment. It was also a way of changing the demographics of the area."

Milosevic has also used the hordes

Most Refugees in U.S. Are From Vietnam, U.S.S.R.

U.S. refugee policy in recent years has reflected the nation's efforts to contain communism. As a result, most of the million and a quarter refugees admitted to the United States since 1985 were from the USSR and Vietnam. Fewer than 10 percent came from Latin America and Africa.

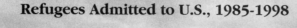

Refugees Admitted to U.S., 1985-1998

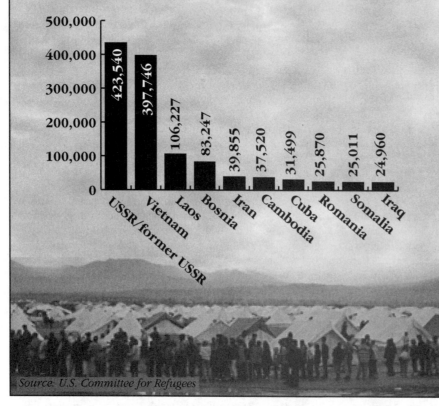

Source: U.S. Committee for Refugees

claim asylum in other countries.

NATO's decision to launch the first military offensive in the alliance's history was among the most innovative approaches to aiding the refugees. "This is the first time in recent history where the military forces that have been combatants in the conflict have also been playing a humanitarian role in the context of a UNHCR relief program, which is a supposedly neutral forum," says Kathleen Newland, a specialist in international migration policy at the Carnegie Endowment for International Peace in Washington. "I don't think they really had any choice because the refugee situation was absolutely desperate, but it did unquestionably cast doubt on the neutrality of the humanitarian effort, which is the cornerstone of humanitarianism as we have known it in the post-World War II setting."

NATO's involvement has also added tremendously to the overall cost of the refugee relief effort in the Balkans, which amounts to some $10 million a week in Macedonia alone. Some observers fear the high costs may backfire by causing the public to worry that the efforts to aid refugees in other parts of the world could spiral upward at a time when funding for such programs is already low.

"Even apart from the military involvement, the relief effort [in the Balkans] is a very expensive proposition because the logistics make this a difficult region to operate in," says Shep Lowman, vice president for policy at Refugees International. He says humanitarian programs to help refugees from Sierra Leone, Rwanda and Angola are badly underfunded. "It certainly has drained away some of the funds that would be available for other refugee programs," Lowman says. "On the other hand, it may also have renewed people's understanding of how tough it is to be a refugee."

The deployment of NATO and Russian peacekeepers in Kosovo marks a

of impoverished refugees to destabilize Albania and Macedonia, undermining their ability to challenge Yugoslavia's dominance of the Balkan region. "These refugees have been used as proxy armies to destabilize neighboring countries once they're forced out," Cohen says. "I'm sure there are some other cases where you have deliberate government policy to displace people for particular ends, but it's especially blatant here."

The mounting global refugee crisis is forcing governments, U.N. agencies and NGOs to develop innovative ways to aid the refugees. Because they usually flee with little but the clothes on their backs, refugees require prompt humanitarian assistance to obtain the basic needs for survival — food, water, shelter and health care. They often need help locating family members lost in the chaos of flight. Like the Kosovars, whose identification papers were systematically destroyed before they crossed the border, many refugees lack basic documents needed to prove their citizenship and new phase in the relief effort in the Balkans. But the nightmare for these refugees is far from over.

As policy-makers assess the relief efforts for Kosovo's refugees and their possible implications for other refugees, these are some of the questions being asked:

Should U.S. military forces be used to respond to refugee crises?

The 1990s have seen an expansion of U.S. military involvement in efforts to ease the plight of refugees. Since 1948, American soldiers have served in numerous multinational peace operations under the aegis of the United Nations to keep the peace and provide the security needed for refugees to return to their homes. Today, U.S. forces serve as peacekeepers in several countries, including Bosnia and Mace-donia, as well as the recently assembled NATO-led force in Kosovo, dubbed KFOR.

But the use of American soldiers in peace operations is often controversial, especially when it exposes troops to danger in places that critics say pose little threat to vital U.S. national interests. U.S. troops account for only 7,000 of the 50,000-member multinational peacekeeping force that began entering Kosovo on June 11 under U.N. authorization. But opposition to any involvement of American ground troops can still be heard in Congress.

"The administration grossly miscalculated the [Yugoslav] response, and the result was a humanitarian disaster," said Assistant Senate Majority Leader Don Nickles, R-Okla., re-ferring to the devastation wrought by the 11-week NATO bombing campaign. "If the administration calls this 'winning,' then what we're winning is that we get to occupy Kosovo at the cost of billions of dollars, and we get to be in Kosovo for no telling how long." [2]

Some critics express concern that committing U.S. forces to Yugoslavia has set a dangerous precedent for future refugee crises. "The United States does not have the resources or

Members of the Kosovo Liberation Army surrender weapons to British members of the NATO peacekeeping force in late June near Pristina, Kosovo.

Reuters/Radu Sigheti

the willpower to function as a global policeman with endless involvement in far-flung conflicts, civil wars and sectarian feuds," writes Kim R. Holmes, an analyst at the Heritage Foundation in Washington. "The United States should not risk the lives of American troops, deplete the already underfunded defense budget and reduce its ability to meet other security commitments unless vital national interests are at stake." [3]

U.S. forces also have become more heavily involved in humanitarian efforts to help the growing tide of refugees. As the flow of refugees from Kosovo developed into a flood in late March, for example, UNHCR and private organizations turned to American and other NATO troops to help build camps to house them.

"When massive numbers of people flee, the military is usually better equipped to build the necessary infrastructure in terms of food, water and sanitation than the civilian-sector agencies, which just don't have the resources or capacity to quickly move that much equipment and supplies," says John Fredriksson, associate executive director of the U.S. Committee for Refugees. "So a regime has developed in the last five to eight years whereby the civilian agencies tend to work very closely with the humanitarian response teams of the military to address these disaster situations in the early days."

In the early 1990s, military involvement in humanitarian relief was controversial. Pentagon officials saw such involvement as an inappropriate blurring of roles and a distraction of soldiers from their military duties. Criticism of the practice mounted in October 1993, after 18 American soldiers were killed during an operation in Somalia, where millions of Somalis displaced from their homes by a civil war were starving. Humanitarian agencies also have viewed the involvement of military forces in their relief operations as a threat to their strictly neutral stance in any situation that gives rise to refugees.

As refugee flows have grown in recent years, however, opposition to the military's involvement in relief operations has mellowed somewhat. "I think the non-governmental sector has come to terms with the fact that the military is usually the best

Many Seek Asylum, But Few Are Chosen

Persons from other countries seeking admittance to the United States to avoid persecution are classified as either asylum-seekers or refugees. Those still outside the United States are defined as refugees; applicants are considered asylum-seekers when application for refuge is made at a U.S. port of entry or after entry to the United States. Both categories are treated the same under the law.

Since 1991, the Immigration and Naturalization Service (INS) has maintained eight offices around the country, staffed by 300 members of the Asylum Officer Corps, to process asylum applications. So-called affirmative asylum applicants, who file voluntarily, are not placed in detention while their applications are considered. If applications are rejected, the individuals may reapply if they are later placed in removal proceedings before an immigration judge. Illegal aliens cannot be granted asylum by asylum officers but are referred to an immigration judge, who can consider their asylum claims.

Aliens who are placed in removal proceedings may apply for asylum as a way to avoid deportation. These so-called defensive asylum applicants may be detained for being in the United States illegally until an immigration judge rules on their asylum claims. The 1996 Illegal Immigration Reform and Immigrant Responsibility Act requires that aliens who arrive at a U.S. port of entry without legitimate travel documents also be detained and placed in expedited removal proceedings. Those who claim they fear persecution if turned away are interviewed by an INS asylum officer and, if their claims are accepted, are referred for ordinary removal proceedings in which they may apply for asylum before an immigration judge. But they must remain in detention pending adjudication of their cases.

INS district directors have the authority to parole, or release, an alien in proceedings from detention on humanitarian or other grounds. The asylum process is often slow: By the end of 1998 there were more than 360,000 asylum applications pending with the INS.[1]

Under the 1980 Refugee Act, the number of refugees and asylum-seekers eligible for admission to the United States and the nationalities eligible for refugee status are determined yearly by the president and Congress. The annual ceiling — currently 78,000 — is divided among five regions:

- Africa (12,000)
- East Asia (9,000)
- Europe (48,000)
- Latin America/Caribbean (3,000)
- Near East/South Asia (4,000)
- Unallocated spots (2,000); in addition, unused spots from one region may be transferred to another region where the demand exceeds the limit.

To apply for admission, a person must be of an eligible nationality, submit to an interview and file for refugee status. Refugee applicants usually are interviewed after they have fled their native country. However, the U.S. refugee program operates three in-country screening programs in Cuba, Vietnam and Russia. The Russia program processes applicants from all countries of the former Soviet Union.

Reacting to reports of forced abortions under China's "one-child" population policy, Congress in 1996 expanded the claim of persecution related to political opinion to include threats related to coercive population-control programs and limited the number of refugees or asylees admitted under this provision to 1,000 a year.

Once admitted to the United States, refugees may not be forcibly returned to their country of origin if they demonstrate that their lives or freedom would be put at risk.

[1] U.S. Committee for Refugees, Worldwide Refugee Information, www.refugees.org.

equipped to deal with an emergency situation such as what we saw in Yugoslavia," Fredriksson says. "What is important is that as the situation stabilizes the military must hand over the operations of these camps and programs to the civilian sector. I think the military would want that, too."

But NATO's latest campaign marked an escalation of U.S. military involvement in refugee relief efforts. Not only did American soldiers help build the camps in Macedonia and Albania and join KFOR, but U.S. pilots took the lead in bombing targets in Serbia, with the stated aims of stopping the ethnic cleansing and restoring the Kosovo refugees to their homes.

At its conclusion, President Clinton called the bombing campaign an unqualified success. "This victory brings a new hope that when a people are singled out for destruction because of their heritage and religious faith and we can do something about it, the world will not look the other way," the president declared. "In Kosovo we did the right thing. We did it the right way. And we will finish the job." [4]

Critics have charged that the campaign did more harm than good by destroying buildings and other infrastructure and also killing numerous civilians in the inevitable accidents the military calls "collateral damage." Indeed, Viktor Chernomyrdin, Russia's special envoy for Kosovo, charged that the United States sabotaged its stated goal of helping the refugees by systematically destroying the very homes they hoped to return to. "More bombing makes it pointless to plan a return of refugees," he charged at the height of the bombing campaign. "What will they come back to — homes in debris, without electricity or water?. . . Thus the bloc is headed for a Pyrrhic victory, whether the conflict ends with the Serbs capitulating or an invasion of Yugoslavia.

"The campaign will not achieve its main goals," Chernomyrdin continued. "Not all refugees will come back to Kosovo, which will remain in some form under Yugoslav jurisdiction, and many billions of dollars will be spent rebuilding the country from the ruins." [5]

Many Republican lawmakers also charged that the U.S.-led bombing campaign only made things worse for the Kosovars. "You have to ask why are so many killed in Kosovo," said Sen. James M. Inhofe, R-Okla. "I have come to the conclusion that it is because of the bombing. . . . I am wondering how many of the Kosovar Albanians are dead today who would be alive if we had not gone in there and bombed." [6]

Other Republican lawmakers complained about the cost of the military involvement, which the Defense Department estimated would be about $5.8 billion through September, and called for a negotiated settlement with Milosevic. [7]

Still others emphasize that the conditions leading to the refugee crisis predated NATO's intervention. "The ethnic cleansing and the ground war of the Serbian forces against the Kosovars began a year ago," says

Fredriksson. "Although it intensified with the bombing by NATO, it was not something that Milosevic pulled out of his back pocket that surprised everyone."

Some critics of the bombing campaign do, however, credit the military for its role in alleviating the refugees' plight. "In this crisis, the humanitarian dimension has been very intertwined with military solutions from the very beginning," says Cohen. "The air-strike campaign did not help

French investigators sift through dirt at a mass grave in Isbica, Kosovo, on June 29. It is one of several graves used to indict Yugoslav President Slobodan Milosevic for war crimes.

any of the internally displaced people inside Kosovo or stop any of the refugee flows, cleansing or atrocities. But the NATO forces were extraordinarily effective in their humanitarian role because the U.N. agencies were overwhelmed and turned to them in desperation. The outflows [of refugees] were so extreme that only they were able to make what could have been a tremendous humanitarian disaster into something manageable."

Controversy over the use of U.S. military forces in helping refugees continues. According to a recent poll, nearly

half the public — 48 percent — opposed sending U.S. ground troops into Kosovo as part of the peacekeeping force to clear mines, help rebuild Kosovo's roads, buildings and other infrastructure and make it safe for the refugees to return. [8]

Should the United States make it easier for refugees to settle permanently in this country?

The sudden exodus of refugees from Kosovo threatened to destabilize neighboring countries, especially Macedonia, where ethnic Albanians constitute a strong and discontented minority. The arrival of hundreds of thousands more ethnic Albanians, government officials feared, could tip the balance and lead to civil unrest there as well. When the Macedonian government threatened to permanently close its border with Kosovo to stop the refugee flow, NATO countries, including the United States, agreed to accept 135,000 camp residents in an emergency evacuation.

On April 21, Vice President Al Gore announced plans for the United States to resettle 20,000 Kosovars until they could safely return to their homeland. To underscore the temporary nature of the evacuation, the Clinton administration initially proposed resettling the refugees at the U.S. military base at Guantanamo, Cuba. But when only a handful of Kosovars agreed to go to the prisonlike facility, the administration decided to house them in the United States.

The first contingent of 453 refugees arrived May 6 at Fort Dix, N.J., where they were processed by Immi-

Inside a Kosovo Refugee Camp

The CQ Researcher's Mary H. Cooper and other journalists accompanied American Red Cross Acting President Steve Bullock to Macedonia in April when he delivered 30 tons of supplies to Kosovo and toured the refugee camp at Brazda and other aid facilities. Since her visit, the population of the camp has shrunk to about 10,000, as Kosovars began streaming back home.

Brazda, Macedonia — Nuhi Rexhepi's transformation into a refugee began at about 11 p.m. on April 2, when Serb police knocked on his door in Ferijaz, a town in southern Kosovo. "They told me, 'If you don't leave, you're dead,'" he recalls. "They told me I could go wherever I wanted but that I had to leave my house. So my wife and I left with no food or even a change of clothes. They burned our house and everything in it. Now we just want to go back to our land, even though we don't have anything now."

Rexhepi was one of scores of ethnic Albanians who stood in line in late May at a Red Cross processing center for refugees in Tetovo, Macedonia. Stripped of their documents by Serb police before crossing the border, they were escorted in caravans of red buses to this predominantly Albanian town. There they received a "green card" from the Macedonian Ministry of the Interior enabling them to apply for food and other assistance.

Many Kosovars evaded the official bureaucratic process in order to avoid placement in one of the country's teeming refugee camps. Instead, they took advantage of the hospitality offered by Macedonia's minority Albanians, who welcomed them into their homes.

But for Rexhepi and many of his companions, the next stop on their journey was Brazda, the largest of Macedonia's refugee camps. Located on a wide, treeless plain at the foot of the mountains that mark the border with Kosovo, the camp is essentially a tent city that was hastily built by NATO troops and then handed over to the U.N. High Commissioner for Refugees (UNHCR), which manages it with the Red Cross and other relief organizations.

Snow covers the mountaintops, but by midday the camp is sweltering, especially inside the tents, where some 26,000 residents are housed in a space designed to accommodate 12,000. Overcrowding has made living conditions, crude at best, almost intolerable. There are not enough portable toilets, food lines are endless and laundry facilities are limited to a hose and a few buckets. The double fence that surrounds the camp serves as a clothesline.

The different relief organizations running the Brazda camp have divided the work to better cope with the overcrowding. The German Red Cross mans the field hospital, Oxfam provides water purification and the International Committee of the Red Cross runs the tracing service that helps camp residents find lost family members.

Sebahate Sahiti, a young housewife, ended up at Brazda with her husband and 11-month-old son. She wants to leave as soon as possible.

"There is just bread, cheese and canned meat to eat here, and the food is making the baby sick," she says. She and her family want to join her brother in Switzerland as soon as possible. "The camp is terrible," she says. "We don't have bathrooms, and we don't feel safe here."

Macedonians talk with an ethnic Albanian friend in the Brazda camp.

Mary H. Cooper

gration and Naturalization Service (INS) officials before being transferred to host communities around the country. As of June 29, 90,298 Kosovars had been evacuated to countries outside the region, including 8,817 to the United States.

The American public has opened its arms to the Kosovars. Relief agencies have been deluged with donations of food, clothing and financial support for the newly arrived refugees, as well as offers to sponsor families as they move from Fort Dix to communities in 27 states. [9]

"There has been an outpouring of support, warmth and even love that is very moving," says Lowman of Refugees International. "Our phone lines and those of other refugee agencies here have been jammed with people calling up wanting to adopt a kid, offer a spare house to families or help out in some other way."

But some critics charge that the resettlement program makes it less likely that the refugees will ever return to

Kosovo. "The general quality of life here is clearly much higher," says Daniel A. Stein, executive director of the Federation for American Immigration Reform, a Washington organization that favors stricter limits on immigration to the United States. "If they're here any length of time at all, they'll get a job, get an apartment and establish roots. So the prospects that they will go home are minimal. The president may want to guarantee their right to return with the NATO operation, but under U.S. asylum law, he can't force them to go back. He can't guarantee to the rest of us that they'll go back." (*See story, p. 278.*)

In Stein's view, the United States simply cannot continue to absorb the growing number of people who want to move here. "Do we want to grow to a half-billion people through immigration and refugee resettlement?" he asks, citing Census Bureau projections that the U.S. population could exceed 500 million by 2050. [10] "We now have the most rapidly growing population numbers in the industrialized world."

Many refugee advocates abhor such reasoning as callous disregard of human suffering by citizens of one of the world's richest countries. "I challenge any one of those folks who view themselves as guarantors of the American way of life by keeping people out to go through what these refugees have gone through," says Fredriksson of the U.S. Committee for Refugees. "Then let's see if they still say these folks are coming here because they just want a better life. It's an outrageous argument."

But advocates of tighter immigration limits are not alone in questioning the wisdom of resettling refugees far from their homelands. By agreeing to resettle refugees, writes author David Rieff, "NATO is doing exactly what it least wants to do. It is accepting the role of guardian of the refugees and, to an increasing degree, contributing to ethnic cleansing."

For all the expressions of compassion for the new arrivals at Fort Dix, Rieff writes, the United States and its allies are faced with a troublesome

Ethnic Albanian refugees line up for their daily rations in the camp at Brazda, outside Skopje, Macedonia, in April. About 26,000 refugees were crammed into the camp, planned for 12,000.

dilemma. "To allow the refugees to continue to rot in camps is unacceptable. But to resettle refugees in the United States, or Canada, or Switzerland, or Britain, however decent or practical a gesture, is to convert the refugees into exiles. These Kosovars are joining well-established immigrant communities; they are going to stay in the West, as most of us would if we were in their shoes; many were trying to get there before the crisis." [11]

Indeed, UNHCR, the world's leading refugee advocacy organization, has long held that refugees should be sheltered as close to home as possible to facilitate their return once it

is safe for them to go. "We have always been very cautious and very skeptical about resettlement in third countries," says Moumtzis. "So when the Kosovars started leaving, our initial reaction was to keep the people within the area."

But Macedonia's reluctance to accept more refugees forced the agency to support the emergency evacuation of Kosovars not only to Europe but to countries far from the Balkans, including the United States, Canada and Australia. "We had never done this before," Moumtzis says, "and we feared that we were creating a precedent in international law for a country to say it can't take refugees and leave it to the rest of the world to care for them. But also we did realize that this was a quite unique situation."

Other refugee advocates support the evacuation of refugees from Macedonia as the only way to make room for Kosovars who were unable to leave Kosovo. "Our feeling was that the group that we had to be most concerned about were the Kosovars still inside Kosovo," says Lowman. "It seemed to us terribly important to keep the borders open so that those who wanted to leave and those the Serbs would permit to leave could, in fact, leave. So we were very strongly in favor of the resettlement program."

Can refugee flows be prevented by outside governments or agencies before they occur?

In addition to encouraging refugees to stay near their countries of origin, UNHCR also supports efforts to help internally displaced people remain in their own country and not become refugees in the first place. Under its "preventive action" strategy, adopted as refugee flows mounted in the early 1990s, the agency closely monitors tense situations before they cause people to flee, trying to defuse problems with diplomacy and conflict resolution and providing economic and social assistance where necessary. [12]

But preventing refugee flows through diplomacy has proved difficult. International efforts to mediate the civil war between the Tutsi and Hutu in Rwanda produced a power-sharing agreement signed by both sides at Arusha, Tanzania, in August 1993. But the Arusha accord quickly fell apart, sparking massive genocide and the flight of hundreds of thousands of refugees from the country in 1994.

"Of course, it's always hard to point to the dog that didn't bark or the refugee flow that didn't happen," says Newland of the Carnegie Endowment. "But I'm really hard-pressed to identify a situation where I can say that because of early international action a crisis didn't deteriorate into a refugee flow."

Some experts say preventive action through diplomacy can be effective if the political will exists to carry it out. "It certainly is feasible, but we go through crisis upon crisis, and there never seems to be sufficient attention when tensions are building up," says Brookings' Cohen, pointing to Kosovo as the most recent example. "[Secretary of State] Madeleine Albright said we were not going to let Bosnia repeat itself in Kosovo,

and then we didn't do anything. It was very clear for many months that there was not the political will in the West to do anything, despite their being appalled that Milosevic was beginning to expel the Albanians. So there was a period when we could have changed the course of what happened diplomatically, but [only] with the willingness to use force."

Moumtzis agrees that UNHCR is powerless to make preventive action work on its own. "We often feel powerless and extremely frustrated because we can see problems building,

Rwandan refugees who fled to Zaire in 1994 wait to be taken back to their homes after they were expelled from Zaire.

and though we scream and tell everybody, it seems that no one is listening," he says. "We know that if there is an early reaction, we can save lives.

"Also, the cost is so much less," he continues. "Most likely, we're getting into the billions of dollars once the camps are winterized, demining operations are completed and Kosovo is rebuilt, not to mention the cost of supporting KFOR," Moumtzis says. "So why not intervene in these situations earlier?"

Some experts remain unconvinced about the feasibility of preventive action. "People talk a lot about ad-

dressing the root causes of refugee flows, but what can you do?" asks Lowman. "I guess that means making people be more decent to one another. But just how you go about doing that I don't know."

Even if diplomacy fails to defuse a crisis, there are other ways to reduce refugee flows, such as setting up relief operations inside the country in crisis. In Somalia, for example, UNHCR set up feeding areas to slow the flow of refugees into Kenya. But helping internally displaced people stay in their country by providing food and other types of assistance is not always possible. Indeed, Lowman says, it can easily backfire in situations where displaced people are targeted by hostile forces, as in Kosovo.

"Sometimes you want to do just the opposite, and that was the situation we faced in Macedonia," he says. "We didn't want to stop the flow; our priority was to keep the border open and make sure that the refugees' right to first asylum [under international law] was respected."

Another approach to reducing refugee flows involves creating "safe havens" inside the borders of a country in conflict that shelter displaced people. Safe havens generally enjoy military protection by outside peacekeeping forces. But they have had only limited success. During the 1992-95 war in Bosnia, for example, the U.N. peacekeeping force was woefully inadequate, and thousands of people were slaughtered by Serbian forces at Srebrenica, one of six safe havens, as the peacekeepers looked on helplessly.

"You can't make something a safe haven by calling it a safe haven," says

Rubin of the Council on Foreign Relations. "You have to actually make it safe."

The safe haven set up in northern Iraq after the 1991 Persian Gulf War, by contrast, has been more successful in protecting the region's Kurdish minority from hostile government forces.

"The safe havens in Bosnia were islands in a hostile area," Rubin says. "In contrast, the Kurdish areas are not [completely] surrounded by an Iraqi-occupied area, so it's much more defensible. Also, the United States continued enforcing a no-fly zone in the area and supplied enough military support to ensure its defense."

UNHCR also runs "open release centers" in Sri Lanka, where a civil war between the government and the rebel Liberation Tigers of Tamil Eelam has ravaged the country for the past 16 years.

"This kind of assistance provides in-country protection by helping internally displaced people so that they don't become refugees," says Cohen. "At the same time, they're free to come and go from these centers to get food, protection or shelter."

But safe havens are not UNHCR's method of choice for preventing refugee flows. "Our experience with Bosnia was that safe havens are not a good idea," says Moumtzis. "UNHCR was not in favor of them there simply because it was impossible to defend them. The civilian population was misled and given the impression that if they went there they would be safe, which they were not at all."

Even if military forces provide adequate protection, safe havens are only a stopgap measure at best, Moumtzis says. "The best solution is to have a lasting political settlement agreed to by all sides, so that they can work together from the beginning with a peacekeeping force and work over the long run on a plan of reintegration and coexistence." ∎

BACKGROUND

Setting Limits

R efugees have long sought protection in the United States. Decades before U.S. law defined refugees as a separate class of migrants, they comprised a large portion of new arrivals to this country. People from Germany, Ireland and the United Kingdom, for example, accounted for the bulk of immigrants from 1840 to 1860. They were fleeing war and famine resulting from Ireland's crop failures and political revolutions across Europe as much as they were seeking better economic conditions.

Similarly, many Chinese immigrants, who accounted for a third of all immigrants in the 1860s, were fleeing famine in Canton. As long as there were enough farmland and industrial jobs to absorb newcomers, there was no attempt to limit their numbers, whatever reasons they had for emigrating. [13]

Ironically, the newcomers' arrival and settlement in the United States led to the increasing mistreatment of Native Americans. Throughout American history, U.S. settlers, backed by the military, drove millions of Indians from their homelands, forcing most of the survivors into internal exile on reservations carved out of remote, marginal lands. The impact of this U.S. version of "ethnic cleansing" is all too apparent to this day. Conditions in much of Indian country are abysmal, and Native Americans are among the poorest Americans. [14]

Discrimination soon colored official policy toward new refugees and other immigrants in the United States. In 1850, in reaction to the influx of large numbers of Chinese workers at a time of worsening economic condi-

tions, California enacted the first state law limiting all forms of immigration.

Congress followed suit in 1882 with the first federal immigration law. The Immigration Act barred entry to criminals, the mentally handicapped and others considered unable to support themselves. The law also put the federal government in charge of regulating immigration.

A mix of racism and competition for jobs also prompted Congress to impose a series of laws aimed at limiting the influx of foreign labor. The first so-called Chinese exclusion law, also passed in 1882, sharply limited the number of Chinese immigrants allowed into the United States. It remained on the books until 1943.

Other laws expanded the list of excludable immigrants to include epileptics and anarchists, for example, required special inspectors to screen incoming immigrants and ordered deportation of all those who entered the country illegally. The 1891 Immigration Act also created the Office of Immigration. When the 1906 Naturalization Act framed the basic rules for naturalization, the office became the Immigration and Naturalization Service.

The 1880s ushered in a shift in immigration patterns. Not only was there a sharp increase in the number of new arrivals to the United States, but there was also a shift in their origins, from Northwestern Europe to Southeastern Europe. Responding to popular bias against the rapid influx of new arrivals, Congress set the first of a series of numerical limits on immigrants with the 1921 Quota Act.

Economic depression and the rise of fascism drew many European refugees to the United States during the 1930s. The flow of refugees increased after Hitler's invasion of Austria in 1938. But the Quota Act barred the vast majority of these refugees from immigrating to the United States.

In the aftermath of World War II, the United States and its allies violated one of the fundamental rights of refugees when they forced hundreds of thousands of ethnic Germans back to their homes in Soviet-occupied territory, where many faced certain death.

The forced repatriation was sparked by the arrival of some 10 million ethnic Germans in the Western-occupied zones between 1946 and 1951. Not classified as "displaced persons," they were ineligible for protection in the Allied-run refugee camps. Ignored by the Allies because of their complicity in Hitler's war crimes and resented by the local German population for their demands on the war-torn economy, the repatriated Germans had few sympathizers, and their fate went largely unchronicled. [15]

Postwar Policies

It was during the postwar period, when communist governments allied with the Soviet Union strengthened their control of much of Central and Eastern Europe, that U.S. immigration law first addressed the issues of refugees and asylum-seekers and the INS began processing refugees as a separate class of immigrants.

To deal with the large numbers of Europeans fleeing communism, President Harry S Truman issued a presidential directive on Dec. 22, 1945, allowing the admission of 40,000 refugees outside the immigration laws. In 1948, Congress passed the Displaced Persons Act granting preferential treatment of refugees from

areas affected by war. A special Displaced Persons Commission oversaw the admission of more than 390,000 refugees into the United States before it was disbanded in 1952.

Escalation of the Cold War prompted Congress to take further steps to protect refugees, whose

Cuban refugees in the Florida Straits in August 1994 prepare for pickup by U.S. Coast Guardsmen.

rights were spelled out in the 1951 U.N. Convention Relating to the Status of Refugees. The treaty defines a refugee as a person who, "owing to a well-founded fear of being persecuted for reasons of race, religion, nationality, membership of a particular social group or political opinion, is outside the country of his nation-

ality and is unwilling to avail himself of the protection of that country; or who, not having a nationality and being outside the country of his former habitual residence as a result of such events, is unable or, owing to such fear, is unwilling to return to it." The United States is a signatory to the convention, as well as to a 1967 protocol to the convention prohibiting the forced repatriation of refugees to their countries of origin.

The 1953 Refugee Relief Act inaugurated a new policy of issuing special visas, exempt from the quota system still in place for other immigrants, to European refugees and "escapees" from communist countries. But the law fell short of defining a sweeping policy for dealing with refugees, leaving it to the president and Congress to favor certain groups, usually in support of the anti-communist sentiment that dominated U.S. foreign policy during the Cold War (1945-1990).

Initially, the U.S. attorney general used his authority to "parole" groups of refugees into the country. Unlike formal immigration, parolees are admitted only temporarily for humanitarian reasons and must leave the country when the conditions for which they were paroled cease to exist. Later, Congress would pass special legislation exempting parolees from national quotas imposed under immigration law and granting them permanent resident status.

In 1956, for example, 32,000 refugees fleeing the communist revolution in Hungary were paroled into

Chronology

1950s-1970s
The rights of refugees are recognized in the wake of World War II.

July 28, 1951
The United Nations General Assembly adopts the Convention Relating to the Status of Refugees. The U.N. High Commissioner for Refugees (UNHCR) is created to oversee aid to refugees until they can safely return to their homelands or find asylum in other countries.

November 1966
The Cuban Refugee Act grants Cubans asylum in the United States without requiring proof of refugee status.

Jan. 31, 1967
A protocol to the 1951 convention prohibits "refoulement," or the forced repatriation of refugees to their countries of origin.

1971
The UNHCR deals with its first large-scale refugee emergency when 10 million Bengalis flee from East Pakistan to India.

1975
The first "boat people" sail from Vietnam. The exodus of refugees will continue for 17 years, the longest sustained flight in the postwar period.

1979
Afghan refugees begin to flee in large numbers to Pakistan and Iran.

1980s
The United States adopts a separate policy on refugees.

1980
The Refugee Act sets policies for refugees outside the existing immigrant-preference system and codifies the definition of refugees as used in the 1951 U.N. convention. The law also limits the number of refugees to be admitted to the United States each year.

——— • ———

1990s
Outbreaks of ethnic conflicts result in widespread refugee flows.

1990
The Immigration Act creates a "temporary protected status" program to provide special protection in the United States for aliens fleeing war or other catastrophes.

September 1991
A military coup prompts tens of thousands of Haitians to flee the impoverished island nation in mostly unseaworthy boats bound for Florida. After initially ordering the Coast Guard to take the refugees to the U.S. naval base at Guantanamo Bay for screening, President George Bush orders all Haitians interdicted at sea forcibly returned to Haiti.

1992-95
Civil wars in Bosnia-Herzegovina and Croatia create the largest refugee crisis in Europe since World War II.

October 1993
Eighteen American soldiers are killed in Somalia while on a mission that includes providing food for millions of starving Somalis displaced from their homes by a civil war.

1994
Hutu and Tutsi tribesmen flee Rwanda during the civil war and genocide that kills at least a half-million people. President Clinton ends the forced repatriation of Haitians.

1996
In clamping down on illegal immigration, Congress approves the summary exclusion of all undocumented aliens, including those requesting asylum.

March 24, 1999
After Yugoslav leader Slobodan Milosevic rejects a NATO plan to end his yearlong persecution of ethnic Albanians in Kosovo, the alliance launches a bombing attack against Serbian targets.

May 6, 1999
The first 453 Kosovar refugees — of a planned 20,000 — arrive at Fort Dix, N.J., for temporary resettlement in the United States.

June 2, 1999
NATO halts bombing after Milosevic agrees to withdraw his forces from Kosovo.

the United States. Two years later, Congress granted them permanent resident status. Similarly, after Fidel Castro took power in Cuba in 1959, President Dwight D. Eisenhower declared that all Cuban refugees were welcome in the United States.

After an initial parole period, Congress passed a special law granting Cuban refugees permanent resident status. The 1966 Cuban Refugee Act granted Cubans asylum in the United States without requiring proof of refugee status.

Apart from these exceptions, refugees were still subject to quotas until the 1965 Immigration and Nationality Act Amendments replaced the quota system based on national origin with numerical limits and a preference system. The amendments gave priority to refugees and other "conditional" entrants, to family members of citizens or permanent residents and to immigrants with skills in demand in the United States.

With the removal of national quotas, refugees increasingly came from Asia, especially Laos, Cambodia and Vietnam. A surge in refugees from Central America also occurred during the 1980s as a result of civil wars in the region.

The widening of the Vietnam War in the early 1970s overwhelmed the ad hoc system of dealing with refugees. The sudden surge in refugee arrivals from Indochina forced the INS to establish temporary offices and hire new agents and bolstered calls for a general review of refugee policy in the United States.

Congress responded with the 1980 Refugee Act, which separated refugees from the immigrant preference system and codified the definition of refugees as defined by the 1951 U.N. convention. The law set a limit on the number of refugees to be admitted into the United States each year. That limit, set initially at 50,000, was to be revised annually by the presi-

dent and Congress. The law also established a formal procedure for the attorney general to confer resident status on refugees who had entered the country as parolees.

Also in 1980, however, U.S. refugee policy faced its greatest crisis to date when Castro allowed a flood of Cubans to leave for the United States. More than 100,000 Cubans arrived in South Florida in five months during the Mariel "boatlift." Because the 1966 law granted blanket asylum to Cubans, President Jimmy Carter could do little but provide disaster assistance to help the Miami city government cope with the new arrivals. ■

CURRENT SITUATION

U.S. Policies Evolve

Civil wars and ethnic conflicts that erupted after the Cold War ended in the early 1990s vastly inflated the number of refugees worldwide. The conflicts also affected policies toward refugees, including those seeking asylum in the United States and other industrialized countries.

The 1990s have seen several changes in U.S. refugee policy in response to charges that it favored refugees from Soviet-bloc countries, East Asia and the Middle East over those from Latin America and the Caribbean. The 1990 Immigration Act, for example, created a "temporary protected status" program to protect aliens fleeing war or other catastrophes.

The law specifically designated temporary status for nationals of El Salvador, whose asylum claims had

been systematically rejected despite their claims of fear of persecution by the country's military junta. In 1992 the INS improved conditions for asylum-seekers by allowing them to be released from detention while their claims are pending.

President George Bush faced the first major refugee crisis of the decade in September 1991, when a military coup in Haiti prompted tens of thousands of Haitians to flee the impoverished island nation, mostly in unseaworthy boats bound for Florida. Coast Guard cutters intercepted refugees at sea and took them to the U.S. naval base at Guantanamo Bay for screening. The facility was soon overrun, however, by more than 12,000 refugees, and in May 1992 Bush ordered the Coast Guard to forcibly return to Haiti all Haitians interdicted at sea.

During the presidential campaign of that year, candidate Bill Clinton promised to reverse Bush's controversial order if elected. But when it was reported that some 200,000 Haitians were poised to flee to the United States shortly before he took office, Clinton announced that he would temporarily continue the forced-return policy.

Refugee advocates charged that the policy violated the international ban on forced repatriation and perpetuated the longstanding political and racial bias in U.S. refugee policy. At the same time that black Haitian refugees from a military dictatorship were refused asylum, they argued, white or mixed-race Cuban refugees from Castro's communist regime were readily admitted. However, in 1993 the U.S. Supreme Court upheld the president's authority to repatriate Haitian refugees. It was not until 1994 that Clinton ended the policy. [16]

As ethnic turmoil has grown in many regions of the world, and with it the number of asylum-seekers, the United

At Issue:

Should U.S. troops participate in the peacekeeping mission in Kosovo?

USA TODAY EDITORIAL BOARD

FROM "WHY U.S. MUST CONTRIBUTE," JUNE 14, 1999.
COPYRIGHT 1999 *USA TODAY*. REPRINTED WITH PERMISSION.

*t*he first of 7,000 American peacekeepers crossed into Kosovo . . . to the cheers of ethnic Albanians. But at home, not everyone is as happy.

Polls show that the same public that supported NATO's air war — in which more than 70 percent of the forces were American — is ambivalent about committing 15 percent of the 48,000-troop NATO peacekeeping force. Not coincidentally, some Republicans in the House have drafted a measure that would, after September, cut off military funds for the operation.

Whether viewed as the product of isolationist sentiment or political opportunism, the measure is irresponsible.

On a human level, it breaks faith with the deported Kosovars, whom weeks of bombing were intended to help. On a policy level, it undercuts U.S. leadership in NATO.

The Republicans' premise is that protecting the Kosovars is not worth the risk to U.S. troops. But while those risks are real — snipers, land mines, rogue militants — they also are manageable. In the Bosnia operation, which prompted similar concerns, not a single U.S. soldier has died in four years of peacekeeping. The Kosovo force will be heavily armed and under NATO command.

Secondly, the 7,000-soldier commitment is modest — less than a third of the total U.S. troops sent to Bosnia after the Dayton Accords. Thirdly, there's reason to expect that the administration will in time draw down even those numbers. That, again, was the pattern in Bosnia, where fewer than 6,000 U.S. troops are still on duty.

The best argument against peacekeeping is one the Pentagon has made in general terms — that extensive commitment to nonfighting missions could leave the military overextended should a crisis arise.

In the past decade, the military has conducted three times the number of significant deployments it conducted during 40 years of superpower standoff.

With up to 10,000 troops policing Iraq's no-fly zones and 35,000 guarding a Korean truce that's almost 50 years old, the commitments do raise the question of how much police work the Pentagon can manage.

But that threat is not immediate, and outside the Balkans, the USA's 500 peacekeepers in Haiti and 900 policing the Sinai Desert under the Israel-Egypt Camp David Accords add up to a modest burden.

SEN. JAMES M. INHOFE, R-OKLA.
Chairman of the Senate Armed Services Subcommittee on Readiness.

FROM "U.S. TROOPS ALREADY OVEREXTENDED," *USA TODAY*, JUNE 14, 1999. REPRINTED WITH PERMISSION.

*s*topping a war we should never have started is good policy. Placing U.S. troops in an indefinite peacekeeping mission in Kosovo, where there is no vital American national security interest, is not.

The European powers can and should take the prime responsibility for this mission. Our underfunded and overextended U.S. military has a more important job to do. It must get itself ready to meet America's minimum expectations for national defense: to be fully capable to defend our vital security interests on two regional fronts almost simultaneously.

Anyone who thinks we can adequately meet this challenge today and take on a costly open-ended operation in Kosovo, on top of those we already have in places such as Bosnia, Iraq and Haiti is kidding himself. Our military is in the midst of the most serious readiness crisis since the "hollow force" days of the late 1970s. The past six years of inadequate budgets coupled with unprecedented numbers of non-vital contingency deployments have put us at almost half the force strength we had during the Persian Gulf War.

How many Americans realize this? How many supporters of the Kosovo peacekeeping operation will back the kind of defense budgets that it will necessitate?

The limited Kosovo air campaign has put severe additional strains on our already-overstretched personnel and equipment. An unlimited and costly Kosovo ground operation threatens to do more of the same, degrading our military at a time when other more serious threats are looming in places such as Iraq and North Korea.

American leadership in the world is not a function of how many military interventions we undertake within the auspices of NATO or the United Nations. It is more a function of how prudent and justified those missions are in terms of our ability always to be prepared adequately to defend America's vital security interests.

Kosovo is not in America's vital security interest. It is in Europe's. We paid for the air war. Europe should carry the peacekeeping load. The U.S. military should return to its proper mission — defending America.

States and other industrial countries have placed greater emphasis on keeping refugees close to their countries of origin to facilitate repatriation and minimize the need to grant them asylum.

When the Balkan wars of the early 1990s uprooted residents of Croatia and Bosnia-Herzegovina, for example, Congress appropriated funds to help refugees in the area and approved non-binding resolutions calling for the United Nations to use "all measures necessary" to provide them with humanitarian relief.

But the policy was only partly successful. The early 1990s saw a steep increase in the number of aliens arriving at U.S. ports of entry without proper documentation, at one point more than 1,000 a month at New York City's John F. Kennedy International Airport alone. [17]

In response, Congress passed restrictions on illegal immigration in 1996 (as part of the omnibus fiscal 1997 spending bill) that included the summary exclusion of all undocumented aliens, including those requesting asylum.

Inequities Cited

Critics charge that the backlash against illegal immigration has penalized refugees. "The last 10 years have seen dramatic changes in our refugee policy," said Rep. Christopher H. Smith, R-N.J, chairman of the House International Relations International Operations and Human Rights Subcommittee. "For the first time in United States history, we have undertaken the mass, forcible return of people who have managed to escape from bloodthirsty regimes such as those in Haiti, Cuba, China and Vietnam. These actions of the United States, in turn, have served as an example and an excuse to other

countries which have repatriated people by the thousands and tens of thousands to places like Rwanda, Burundi, Afghanistan and Burma." [18]

Critics also point to persistent inequities in refugee policy, such as the recent Supreme Court decision allowing the deportation of a Guatemalan refugee because he admitted to committing vandalism during political protests in his home country, while former Salvadoran generals allegedly involved in the murder of thousands of their countrymen enjoy resident status in Florida. [19]

Claims of refugee status based on gender-based persecution also are controversial. A growing number of women from Middle Eastern and African countries have applied for asylum in the United States citing fear of persecution on the basis of religious or cultural practices, such as female genital alteration. [20]

In June, a federal immigration panel refused to grant asylum to a woman who made a similar appeal after fleeing a violent spouse. The Board of Immigration Appeals ruled that Rodi Alvarado Peña, who had suffered violent abuse by her husband in Guatemala, did not qualify for asylum because her fear of persecution was directed to a private citizen, not a government or government agent. [21]

Refugee advocates call on the administration to amend U.S. refugee policy to reflect the realities of the post-Cold War world. "We have a refugee program, but I would argue that we don't really have a refugee policy," says the Carnegie Endowment's Newland, noting that about half of the approximately 80,000 refugees resettled in the United States each year continue to come from former Cold War adversaries such as the former Soviet Union, Vietnam and Cuba. "Our refugee program is still very rooted in the Cold War. There hasn't been an articulation of principles to guide our refugee program that would tell you what it is trying to

accomplish and how we should configure our diplomatic efforts and our military presence — our carrots and sticks — to encourage other countries to conform to those principles." ∎

OUTLOOK

Kosovar Repatriation

As NATO's bombing campaign neared its end in early June, refugee advocates worried that Macedonia, eager to shed the burden of caring for some 250,000 Kosovars, would encourage or even force the refugees to return before it was safe. Retreating Serb forces laid land mines on roads, booby-trapped building entryways and poisoned wells in a last-ditch offensive against the surviving Albanians of Kosovo.

"I fully expect that they will be compelled to return, against the principles of the refugee convention," Newland says. "We must insist that the return be voluntary until we get to the point where it can be truly said that throughout Kosovo circumstances have changed fundamentally and for the long term. There has to be a serious effort to guarantee the long-term livelihood of the population, which means that basic infrastructure in Kosovo has to be restored."

But so far the Macedonian government has not had to prod the refugees to leave. Even before the first contingents of NATO's peacekeeping forces crossed into Kosovo, refugees defied all warnings and began streaming into the province to reclaim what was left of their communities and, in some cases, to avenge their losses on retreating Serbs by looting and burning their property, or worse.

By late June, more than half the

Kosovo refugees had returned, easing the pressure on Macedonia and other countries. On June 28, UNHCR began actively helping to repatriate the Kosovars by providing them with tents, blankets and other temporary shelter materials while they rebuilt their homes.

Refugee advocates worry that the apparent easing of the refugee crisis in the Balkans will diminish public interest in the millions of refugees who continue to suffer in other parts of the world.

"Right now there is a crisis in West Africa that nobody reads about, and we are trying to make sure that there is funding for those refugees as well," says Moumtzis of UNHCR. "But the funding provided by governments for various relief operations around the world has been shrinking in the past couple of years. There is less and less concern about foreign aid, and there is a certain donor fatigue, especially for refugee situations in Africa.

"But we are trying to capitalize on the high publicity of the Kosovo crisis, and we're hoping that it will have a positive impact on our ability to raise money for less popular refugee programs as well." ∎

Notes

[1] See Kenneth Roth, "Kosovars Aren't the Only Refugees," *The Wall Street Journal,* June 8, 1999.

[2] Quoted in Helen Dewar, "GOP Critics Accuse Clinton of 'Humanitarian Disaster' in Kosovo," *The Washington Post,* June 11, 1999.

[3] Kim R. Holmes, "No U.S. Ground War in Kosovo," *The Heritage Foundation Backgrounder,* April 22, 1999.

[4] From a televised address to the nation on June 11, 1999.

[5] Viktor Chernomyrdin, "'Impossible to Talk Peace with Bombs Falling,'" *The Washington Post,* May 27, 1999.

[6] Inhofe addressed the Senate on May 3, 1999.

FOR MORE INFORMATION

American Red Cross, 431 18th St. N.W., Washington, D.C. 20006; (202) 639-3520; www.redcross.org. One of the world's largest humanitarian organizations, the Red Cross aids domestic and foreign disaster victims and refugees by raising money, providing services and distributing supplies; it has raised more than $30 million for the Kosovo refugees. It often works with other members of the Red Cross Movement.

Federation for American Immigration Reform, 1666 Connecticut Ave. N.W., Suite 400, Washington, D.C. 20009; (202) 328-7004; www.fairus.org. FAIR seeks to reduce the number of immigrants admitted to the United States, including refugees seeking asylum.

United Nations High Commissioner for Refugees, 1775 K St. N.W., Suite 300, Washington, D.C. 20006; (202) 296-5191; www.unhcr.ch. Headquartered in Geneva, Switzerland, the UNHCR works with governments and voluntary organizations to protect and assist refugees worldwide.

U.S. Committee for Refugees, 1717 Massachusetts Ave. N.W., Suite 200, Washington, D.C. 20036; (202) 347-3507; www.refugees.org. The committee monitors the world refugee situation and informs the public about refugee issues.

[7] See Mary S. Dalrymple, "GOP Members Go Own Way on Kosovo," *CQ Weekly,* May 15, 1999, p. 1165.

[8] Richard Morin, "Americans Are Split on War Role," *The Washington Post,* June 7, 1999.

[9] See Rick Hampson, "Refugees Find USA Hard to Believe — It's So Kind," *USA Today,* June 1, 1999.

[10] U.S. Bureau of the Census, *Current Population Reports,* Series P25-1130, "Population Projections of the United States by Age, Sex, Race, and Hispanic Origin: 1995 to 2050".

[11] David Rieff, "Lost Kosovo: Scenes from a War Gone Wrong," *The New Republic,* May 31, 1999, p.

[12] For background, see David Masci, "Assisting Refugees," *The CQ Researcher,* Feb. 7, 1997, pp. 97-120.

[13] Unless otherwise noted, historical background in this section is based on Immigration and Naturalization Service, "An Immigrant Nation: United States Regulation of Immigration, 1798-1991," June 18, 1991.

[14] For background, see Mary H. Cooper, "Native Americans," *The CQ Researcher,*

May 8, 1992, pp. 385-408.

[15] For a description of refugee flows after World War II, see Gil Loescher and John A. Scanlan, *Calculated Kindness: Refugees and America's Half-Open Door, 1945-Present* (1986).

[16] See Vanita Gowda, "Winning the Peace: How Will America Help Rebuild Lives of 500,000 Kosovars?" *CQ Weekly,* April 17, pp. 907-908.

[17] U.S. Committee for Refugees, "U.S. Refugee Policy" Where We've Been, Where We're Going," www.refugees.org.

[18] Smith spoke at an April 7, 1999, hearing of the House International Relations International Operations and Human Rights Subcommittee.

[19] Carolyn Patty Blum, "Asylum for the Abusers," *The Washington Post,* June 14, 1999.

[20] For background, see Mary H. Cooper, "Women and Human Rights," *The CQ Researcher,* April 30, 1999, pp. 353-376.

[21] See Fredric N. Tulsky, "Abused Woman Is Denied Asylum," *The Washington Post,* June 20, 1999.

Bibliography

Selected Sources Used

Books

Bernstein, Ann, and Myron Weiner, eds., *Migration and Refugee Policies: An Overview*, Pinter, 1999.

This collection of essays by refugee policy experts examines the development of an international protocol for dealing with refugees as well as different countries' interpretations of those principles.

Loescher, Gil, and John A. Scanlan, *Calculated Kindness: Refugees and America's Half-Open Door 1945-Present*, The Free Press, 1986.

The authors trace U.S. refugee policy through passage of the 1980 Refugee Act and the last years of the Cold War, when U.S. anti-communist foreign policy was a major determinant of refugee admissions to the United States.

Malcolm, Noel, *Kosovo: A Short History*, New York University Press, 1998.

A British historian and journalist who has written extensively about the Balkans, including a similar history of Bosnia, provides a widely acclaimed overview of Kosovo's longstanding cultural divisions.

Trier, Jean, *United Nations High Commissioner for Refugees*, New Discovery Books, 1994.

This brief history of the leading international agency dealing with refugees presents the various ingredients in relief programs, including peacekeeping forces, coordination of humanitarian operations and repatriation programs through the early 1990s.

Articles

"Exporting Misery," *The Economist*, April 17, 1999, pp. 23-27.

The increase in refugees in the 1990s has created an anti-refugee backlash in industrialized countries and an operational problem for humanitarian organizations that increasingly are forced to conduct relief operations in areas of conflict.

Havel, Václav, "Kosovo and the End of the Nation-State," *The New York Review of Books*, June 10, 1999, pp. 4-6.

The president of the Czech Republic argues that NATO's decision to defy Yugoslavia's claim of sovereignty and conduct a bombing campaign to stop its persecution of Kosovo's ethnic Albanians is only the most recent indication of the international community's "recognition that human beings are more important than the state."

Sontag, Susan, "Why Are We In Kosovo?" *The New York Times Magazine*, May 2, 1999, pp. 52-55.

The author rejects charges that the U.S. decision to bomb Serbia to save Kosovar refugees while ignoring similar refugee crises in Africa amounts to racism. "If several African states had cared enough about the genocide of the Tutsis in Rwanda (nearly a million people!) to intervene militarily, would we have asked what right they had when they had done nothing on behalf of the Kurds or the Tibetans?"

Wilkinson, Ray, "A Decisive Year," *Refugees Magazine*, No. 114, 1999.

The author examines the events that transformed Yugoslavia, once considered the most progressive country in the communist bloc and a founding member of the nonaligned movement, into a leading generator of refugees in the 1990s.

Reports and Studies

Layne, Christopher, "Blunder in the Balkans: The Clinton Administration's Bungled War Against Serbia," *Policy Analysis*, Cato Institute, May 20, 1999.

The U.S.-led bombing campaign against Serbia succeeded mostly in worsening the plight of Kosovo's refugees, the author writes, by providing an excuse to accelerate their expulsion and massacre.

Newland, Kathleen, "U.S. Refugee Policy: Dilemmas and Directions," Carnegie Endowment for International Peace, 1995.

Refugee policy in the United States is inconsistent and contradictory, the author argues, reflecting the persistent confusion about U.S. foreign policy goals in the post-Cold War era.

United Nations High Commissioner for Refugees, "The State of the World's Refugees," 1997.

Caring for the world's burgeoning refugee population is becoming ever more difficult, in large part because humanitarian organizations increasingly are forced to work in zones of active conflict, such as Bosnia, Rwanda and Afghanistan.

U.S. Department of State, "Erasing History: Ethnic Cleansing in Kosovo," May 1999.

This report documents the campaign mounted by Yugoslav President Slobodan Milosevic to eliminate the ethnic Albanian population of Kosovo, which led to the exodus of more than 800,000 refugees.

Index

Index

Index

Index

Index

Credits